I CELEBRATE MYSELF ~

Allen Ginsberg and Peter Orlovsky at Aquatic Park, San Francisco, 1955 ~

BILL MORGAN

I CELEBRATE MYSELF ~

THE SOMEWHAT PRIVATE LIFE OF

ALLEN GINSBERG

Viking

VIKING

Published by the Penguin Group

Penguin Group (USA) Inc., 375 Hudson Street, New York, New York 10014, U.S.A. • Penguin Group (Canada), 90 Eglinton Avenue East, Suite 700, Toronto, Ontario, Canada M4P 2Y3 (a division of Pearson Penguin Canada Inc.) • Penguin Books Ltd, 80 Strand, London WC2R 0RL, England • Penguin Ireland, 25 St Stephen's Green, Dublin 2, Ireland (a division of Penguin Books Ltd) • Penguin Books Australia Ltd, 250 Camberwell Road, Camberwell, Victoria 3124, Australia (a division of Pearson Australia Group Pty Ltd) • Penguin Books India Pvt Ltd, 11 Community Centre, Panchsheel Park, New Delhi—110 017, India • Penguin Group (NZ), Cnr Airborne and Rosedale Roads, Albany, Auckland 1310, New Zealand (a division of Pearson New Zealand Ltd) • Penguin Books (South Africa) (Pty) Ltd, 24 Sturdee Avenue, Rosebank, Johannesburg 2196, South Africa

Penguin Books Ltd, Registered Offices: 80 Strand, London WC2R 0RL, England

First published in 2006 by Viking Penguin, a member of Penguin Group (USA) Inc.

10   9   8   7   6   5   4   3   2   1

Grateful acknowledgment is made to the Allen Ginsberg Trust for permission to reprint selections from Allen Ginsberg's writings and reproduce his photographs.

"Poison Oak" by Joanne Kyber is reprinted by permission of the author.

LIBRARY OF CONGRESS CATALOGING-IN-PUBLICATION DATA
Morgan, Bill, 1949–
    I celebrate myself : the somewhat private life of Allen Ginsberg / Bill Morgan.
        p.   cm.
    Includes bibliographical references and index.
    ISBN 0-670-03796-6
    1. Ginsberg, Allen, 1926–1997.   2. Poets, American—20th century—Biography.   3. Beat generation—Biography.   I. Title.
    PS3513.I74Z748   2006
    811'.54—dc22
    [B]   2006050045

Printed in the United States of America
Designed by Katy Riegel • Set in Dante

~

I CELEBRATE myself,

And what I assume you shall assume,

For every atom belonging to me, as good belongs to you.

—WALT WHITMAN

from

Leaves of Grass

~

~

TO LAWRENCE FERLINGHETTI

for greeting Allen at the beginning of a great career

CONTENTS ~

FOREWORD ～

I N N EW Y ORK C I TY , the first spring trees that blossom on the streets are the callery pears. To most people their fragrant petals herald the arrival of warmer days and signal the end of winter, but for the past nine springs their sweet bouquet has reminded three friends, Bob Rosenthal, Peter Hale, and myself, of the sudden death of the man we worked with, Allen Ginsberg. We haven't failed to remark on it once in those nine years. We note the early or late blooming of the flowers in comparison to the day in April 1997 when Allen died and left his world of triumph and suffering behind. It coincided with the moment the pear blossoms reached their peak. As we walked out onto the street after the deathbed vigil, their pleasant aroma was so invigorating and their ivory radiance so cheerful that it made a sharp contrast to our sadness. Our grief was shared by thousands of friends and fans in the days and months that followed, but each April fifth we've said to one another, "Well, the pear trees are late this year," remembering the day and date so vividly.

～

When Allen Ginsberg died, the country lost not only one of her most renowned poets, but also one of her greatest citizens, so great, in fact, that he could easily be called a citizen of the world. Political borders meant little to him and did not limit his influence. People constantly complain that we have no heroes anymore, at least no heroes in the traditional sense. We have, for instance, plenty of politicians pretending to be heroes. Some dress as combat pilots to strike a hero's pose, but everyone knows they're not. The news media identify the victims of great tragedies and illnesses as heroes, good people in the wrong place at the wrong time. Multimillionaire athletes are called heroes by their admirers, but what heroic virtues do they exemplify? At the same time, traditional heroes are only of interest if they can be toppled from their pedestals and exposed as hypocrites. It is said that Thomas Jefferson fathered children by his slaves, Martin Luther King was unfaithful to his wife, and Abraham Lincoln was gay. Have we missed the point that Jefferson wrote the words "that all men are created equal," which led to the end of slavery in America, or that King's appeals to nonviolently resist segregation led to an Equal Rights Amendment? The true liberties that we enjoy today were not easily won by these heroes, but were the results of lifelong struggles.

Upon closer examination, the unlikely character of Allen Ginsberg deserves to be considered one of the best examples of the true American hero, a sentence that might upset Ginsberg's admirers and detractors alike. Perhaps it would have upset Allen himself, although his beliefs and ideals exemplify all of the qualities that are outlined in the Declaration of Independence and the Bill of Rights. His patriotism was not blind obedience to the institution of the United States government—in fact a predominant theme in his poetry was a desire for liberty from all state control—yet his love for freedom and equality was unparalleled and uncompromising. Most politicians give lip service to the country's founding principles, but Ginsberg put himself on the line time after time to fight for those freedoms and was called un-American and subversive for doing so. People have been quick to forget that dissent is not un-American, but the very cornerstone upon which the country was founded. As a result Allen became a spokesman for a generation that was beginning to question the "my country right or wrong" attitude of the military-industrial complex at midcentury. More than effecting a political change, however, his work as a champion of free speech led to a cultural change that swept the entire world and continues to this day. All the equal rights movements of the fifties and sixties, from civil rights to gay rights to women's rights to sexual liberation, can be traced to earlier free speech movements.

Ginsberg's greatness as displayed through his poetry lay most of all in his manner of confronting life. He had a genius for living, a genius for examining himself wholly and expressing himself candidly. He loved life, even though he was fascinated and at times nearly obsessed with death, and he encouraged individuals to follow their own paths wherever they led. Allen influenced and changed the lives of countless people through his writing. He turned people on to poetry, he introduced them to spirituality, he showed them that activism could achieve results on both grass roots and global levels. His words are a unique part of our heritage as Americans and so is the story of the man who spoke them.

~

In the late seventies after finishing a comprehensive bibliography on the work of the San Francisco poet Lawrence Ferlinghetti, I moved to New York and started to compile a similar one on Allen Ginsberg's work. I was looking forward to working on a Ginsberg bibliography, even though it would take nearly fifteen years to complete. I considered it a bibliographic challenge since no other living poet seemed to be as prolific as he was. Geography was a happy coincidence in my choice of subjects as well, for Ginsberg lived just around the corner, in fact our kitchen windows overlooked each other. It would be convenient to comb through his archive for elusive publications, or so I thought. The initial problem was that his archive was not only enormous, it was also far from organized. His apartment was crammed with documents and the mountain of paper spilled over into hundreds of boxes stored in the vault at Columbia University's Butler Library. I suggested, and Allen readily agreed, that while I was examining his files, I would organize them so that he and researchers could find things when they needed them.

As I worked on the bibliography I began making notes for a biography. My role as archivist was never important enough to be anything more than a footnote so there's no reason to pretend that this is "my life with Ginsberg," but in addition to putting his papers in order, two things I did had major effects on him. It was through my efforts that Allen's archive was sold to Stanford, which gave him enough money to buy an apartment when he became sick. I was also the person who nagged him repeatedly during the early 1980s to sit down and re-examine his early photographs I had found scattered among his papers at Columbia. As a result he renewed his interest in picture taking for the rest of his life. Over the years one thing or another always kept me from sitting down to write the biography, even though I continued to keep notes and read all I could find about the poet and his life. With his death came the realization that the time had come to put it all together at last.

As I wrote, I was surprised to discover that Ginsberg's story turned out to be a love story, or at least a search for love. Recurrent themes are his unfulfilled desire to be loved by others and his search for a love of self, which I think he did come close to achieving in the end. His self-love was not wholly narcissistic. Theoretically Allen was able to trace his ability to love directly back to Walt Whitman, hence I chose the title and epigram for this book from Whitman's great autobiographical poem. Whitman's lesson to Allen was that it is possible to forgive another and love another only after you forgive and love yourself. That was the underlying reason why he felt that Whitman was so important to the American psyche. Whitman had accepted himself and from that flowed an acceptance of all things. Allen believed that Walt Whitman was the first American poet to take action in recognizing his individuality, forgiving and accepting *him self,* and automatically extending that recognition and acceptance to all other selves. In so doing he defined what he believed true democracy was, a condition of equality and respect for all individuals within a community. Allen followed Whitman's creed when he spoke of his love of comrades as being the basis of democracy, and later Buddhism helped Allen extend that love to "all sentient beings." He also felt that the key to this was self-acceptance, without which there could be no acceptance of others.

There is a distinction between a literary biography and a biography of a literary figure, and this is the latter. Trying to tell someone what a poem means is a waste of time, so I have tried to describe what was happening in Ginsberg's personal life that directly influenced particular poems or writing style. For that reason the titles of the poems Ginsberg was writing at any time appear in the margins next to the events unfolding in his daily life. Reference is made to the page number in *Collected Poems: 1947–1997,* enlarged edition, HarperCollins, 2006 *(CP)* and *First Blues,* Full Court Press, 1975 *(FB).* This is not the story of "The Life and Times" of Allen Ginsberg either, because he had a greater impact on his times than his times had on him. He was destined to lead a social revolution even if he hadn't planned it that way. A good deal of what happened culturally in the sixties and seventies derived from what Ginsberg did and wrote in the forties and fifties.

As a boy I enjoyed reading Reinhard Luthin's book *The Real Abraham Lincoln,* in which Luthin draws all his information for the biography from primary documents by Lincoln himself. I've tried to do much the same by quoting extensively from Ginsberg's own letters, journals, and poetry. I'm lucky to have had unlimited access to his archives and sometimes am egotistical enough to believe that I'm the only person to ever have read everything Allen ever wrote. I've found him to be extremely accurate and honest when he described contemporary events, and I have relied on those entries much more than on later interviews and memories.

Another factor that shaped the biography was length. My favorite quotation is not by Allen Ginsberg but by Blaise Pascal and goes something like, "If I had more time I would have written you a shorter letter." I've spent a lot of time writing a shorter book. A three-volume definitive compendium to Ginsberg's world would have been much easier. Fewer choices would have to be made, fewer events left out, fewer friends unmentioned. Working with Allen for two decades, I came to realize that nearly everyone I met had at least one Ginsberg story to tell. Whether it was a college student who drove him from an airport for a reading, or someone who stopped to chat with him on a street corner, or a cabdriver who took him uptown to meditate, each has a story of how Allen took the time for him or her.

Allen's address book at the time of his death contained over three thousand names, and I'm certain that each of those people had at least one memorable encounter with him. Ed Sanders in his wonderful 250-page narrative poem called *The Poetry and Life of Allen Ginsberg* addresses a future scholar with the lines, "Hey o bright scribe of 2002, / want to write a 50,000-page / bio of a bard?" Sanders wasn't exaggerating with his estimate of the necessary page count, but no publisher in the world would publish a biography the size of the *Encyclopædia Britannica*. In all honesty not many readers would have the time to devote to such an undertaking either.

I've focused my attention on the essential Allen Ginsberg and have found that his private life, much more than his public life, keeps the story moving. For the last thirty years of his career barnstorming from one poetry reading to the next, there was too much scheduled travel to even list all his appearances. Later in life he became a public figure whose busy schedule dictated his movements around the globe, so his tale is better told by what went on between those appearances.

Ginsberg was a man whose parents helped shape his future by accident instead of grand design. To know Allen it is well to see him not only as a poet, but as a son and brother first, then as a classmate and friend, and finally as a poet and teacher. Once more it seems appropriate to steal a line from Whitman, "this is no book, who touches this touches a man."

I CELEBRATE MYSELF ~

INTRODUCTION ∿

ONE EVENING, while out buying the *New York Times*, Allen Ginsberg stopped to talk to a friend on the street while Peter Orlovsky went into a store. As they were chatting a bizarre scene began to unfold on the sidewalk a few feet away. A woman, either drunk or on bad drugs, was stretched out on the pavement, one arm being yanked by her boyfriend, who was shouting, "Come on, you god damn bitch, get the fuck up!" The woman was ignoring him but with her free hand she was reaching toward a ferocious-looking dog, almost, but not quite, within her reach. The dog's owner was struggling to hold the canine back with the leash and yelled, "Keep your hand away, he'll bite." Instead of pulling back from the sharp fangs of the beast, the woman began calling to it with a raspy voice, "Here doggie, doggie." The animal snarled and strained at the leash, trying to snap at the woman, who continued calling drunkenly to it. Meanwhile, the woman's partner was struggling to get the woman onto her feet, so frustrated that he was on the verge of punching her. All this made the dog strain harder on the leash to the point where his owner could barely control him. By now everyone was screaming and there was nasty violence in the air. At that moment, while others on the sidewalk were beginning to move away to avoid the obvious conflict that was about to erupt, Allen walked over to the woman and held out a bag of cookies. "Would you like a Fig Newton?" he asked calmly. In an instant the tension of the situation disappeared as everyone stared at this new lunatic. The dog owner was able to yank the beast away and walked off down the street. The drunken woman looked in bewilderment at Ginsberg, who continued, "Oh, I haven't introduced myself, my name is Allen and this is my friend David," gesturing toward the man he had been talking to. By that time the woman's friend had dragged her to her feet, muttered something about Allen being crazy, and the two staggered away arm in arm. "Well," Allen said to his friend, "would *you* like a cookie?" Peter came out of the newsstand with the paper and the incident was all but forgotten, but once again Allen had proven himself a fearless and spontaneous peacemaker.

This story is one example of what made Ginsberg extraordinary. In this instance he was compassionate, resourceful, and merciful. So unusual was his courage that Norman Mailer more than once called Ginsberg "the bravest man in America." When Allen saw that something needed to be done to prevent violence, he did it without consideration of his own safety. He was always willing to be a mediator and to look for the common ground between opposing parties. He wasn't born that way. It took him years to realize that he could achieve more by compromise than by conflict.

Another incredible trait that nearly everyone who ever spoke to Allen Ginsberg recognized and commented on was his ability to focus his undivided attention on their conversation. He listened so intently that he made the person aware that he was truly sympathetic and understanding, even if he did not agree with what they were saying. This ability to pay attention gave him the chance to use tact and diplomacy to handle awkward situations. Lawrence Ferlinghetti felt that Allen wasn't merely listening to someone when they spoke, but that he was siphoning off their mind to use later. His was a rare talent, unequaled by all but the most curious of geniuses.

In spite of his reputation as an egomaniac, Ginsberg was sometimes a victim of low self-esteem and craved the recognition and approval of others, especially people he considered wiser, more talented, and more powerful. Many of his character traits were picked up through the examples of others, especially once he began to study Tibetan Buddhism. His insatiable desire for fame and celebrity did not diminish as he grew older, but he learned how to handle it better. Even at the end of his life, he sought validation from others. The last letter that he ever wrote was a few days before his death. His doctors had just notified him that he was terminally ill, and after calling his closest friends to tell them the terrible news, he wrote a letter to President Clinton. It was only a short note but it was heartbreaking to read. "I have untreatable liver cancer and have 2–5 months to live. If you have some sort of award or medal for service in art or poetry, please send one along unless it's politically inadvisable or inexpedient. I don't want to bait the right wing for you. Maybe Gingrich might or might not mind. But don't take chances please, you've enough on hand. Best wishes and good luck to you and Ms. Hillary and daughter."

Even at the end, after a life that many others would envy for his spectacular achievements, Allen was longing for acceptance and recognition. Allen's secretary felt that the letter was a tongue-in-cheek joke, but Allen was adamant that the letter be typed and sent out. It was possibly the dementia of an ill man, but it was no joke. Allen died only a few days after the letter was sent, and no answer ever came back.

1895–1926 ～

BEFORE THE BEGINNING: PARENTS

ALLEN GINSBERG'S FATHER, Louis Ginsberg, was born on October 1, 1895, the first son of Russian émigrés Pincus and Rebecca Schectman Ginsberg. As the years went by, four other children joined the family, Abraham (Abe), Rose, Clara, and Hannah (Honey). At the suggestion of his strong-minded wife, Rebecca, who was "the power behind the throne" according to Louis, Pincus started his own laundry business in Newark, New Jersey. After customers dropped off their dirty clothes at his shop, Pincus would bundle them and take them to a large industrial laundry, then press and deliver the clean garments back to the customers. Even though Pincus depended on a horse-drawn wagon for his deliveries, he had no knowledge of horses. As a result he put himself in the hands of a *landsman*, a man he knew from his own village in Russia, to act on his behalf in horse-buying matters. As it turned out, the *landsman* was in league with the horse trader, who conspired to sell Pincus one broken-down horse after another. When Pincus finally caught on he bought a good horse on his own, paying too much, but at least it served him well for years. His son Louis cared for the horse and helped around the shop, but he developed no interest in following Pincus into the business. Later Pincus lost interest in the laundry and bought a tobacco shop.

In spite of his forays into capitalist ventures, both Pincus and Rebecca were avid socialists. They were both active members of Newark's Minsker Branch of the Arbeter Ring, a progressive Yiddish labor and cultural organization, more commonly known as the Workmen's Circle. In Russia, the czar

Ginsberg's paternal grandparents, Pincus and Rebecca Ginsberg ~

had bloodily suppressed the workers' efforts to form trade unions, but in America the immigrant workers were determined to push through the political reforms necessary to make unions a strong voice in government. At the turn of the century sweatshop owners routinely forced poor immigrants to work for low wages in horrible conditions. In 1911 the Triangle Shirtwaist factory fire in Manhattan resulted in the deaths of 146 foreign-born working girls who had been locked into their shop so they couldn't take breaks. That tragedy not only helped give impetus to the labor movement but made a tremendous impression on sixteen-year-old Louis Ginsberg. He followed in his parents' footsteps and paid a good deal more attention to Socialist Party politics than he did to the neighborhood synagogue. The family might have been Jewish culturally, but Louis was best described as agnostic.

Louis was lucky enough to attend Newark's Barringer High School from 1912 to 1914. Barringer was proud of its academic history—it was the third-oldest high school in the country—and there Louis was to receive an excellent education. The mansard-roofed school sat on a hill overlooking beautiful gardens in a perfectly romantic setting. While at Barringer in 1912, Louis met and began dating Naomi Levy, the daughter of Mendel and Judith Livergant, whose family name had been Americanized at Ellis Island.

Naomi Livergant was born in 1896, a year after Louis, in Nevel, a town north of Vitebsk in the Pale of Russia. The family emigrated in 1904, and like many Jewish immigrants first lived in the enormous ghetto of Manhattan's Lower East Side. They rented rooms near the shops on busy Orchard Street, where Mendel opened an ice cream and candy store. In addition to Naomi, there were three other children, Elanor, Max, and Sam. Before long her family moved to Newark, where she also attended Barringer High School and fell in love with Louis. Much like the Ginsbergs, the Levys were interested in liberal politics and social change, but instead of being socialists like the Ginsbergs and many other earlier Russian émigrés, the Levys were devoted communists. Naomi and her family supported socialism as it was beginning to be practiced by the communists in the new Soviet Union. Louis was increasingly worried about the new government's lack of democracy and felt that the Russian people needed more freedom of expression than their one-party system would allow. Their different leftist views fueled many heated discussions between the Ginsberg and Levy families. Fortunately Louis and Naomi loved the give and take of these spirited political debates and it stimulated their romance. Louis was happy that Naomi had her own opinions and voiced them freely. She was active in the local Communist Party cell, which he accepted, but in the years ahead her support of Stalin would create a wider rift between them.

While in high school, Louis took a class on the poetry of John Milton from a dedicated teacher named Margaret Coult, who assigned him to write a poem in imitation of Milton's *L'Allegro*. The resulting poem won the praise of his teacher, and with her encouragement, Louis began to write poetry on his own. His first publication was a poem for the Barringer High School yearbook. Naomi was proud of Louis and flattered when he wrote love poems to her. She was Louis' first girlfriend and the two made a striking couple. He was tall, with thick wavy hair and dark-rimmed glasses that made him look dignified and scholarly. Although not especially athletic he loved to play tennis and taught Naomi the game. She was slender, dark-haired, round-faced, and earnest. Louis was attracted to Naomi not only because of her quick sense of humor and beguiling good looks, but also because she was every bit his match intellectually. She was charming, fun-loving, and exuded a natural sexuality that was unusual for the times. While she was vivacious and perky, talkative and exciting to be with, Louis was dapper and well groomed, more reserved and proper, as befit a future schoolteacher.

Due to his poor eyesight, Louis was excused from active military service during World War I. While the war went on in Europe, Louis attended Rutgers University on a scholarship and graduated in 1918. From there he landed a teaching job in Woodbine, a small town in southern New Jersey.

That year Naomi's mother died in the great influenza epidemic that was to kill more than twenty million people. It was in Woodbine that Naomi Levy married Louis Ginsberg the following year, but soon the couple moved back to Newark to be closer to their families. After studying for two years at Newark Normal School, Naomi taught disadvantaged children in Woodbine and then at a Newark grammar school. Louis joined the English Department faculty of Central High School in Paterson, where he stayed for the next forty years.

The same year as her marriage to Louis and her mother's death, Naomi suffered her first nervous breakdown. She recovered quickly but it gave Louis' parents cause for concern. Louis, however, felt it was an isolated event and was confident that it would not reoccur. He was head-over-heels in love, so his parents' reservations made little difference to him. He had no way of knowing that his future wife would suffer from mental illness throughout her life. After that first breakdown she never returned to teaching, but for the time being, things were going well and promised a happy future. On June 2, 1921, their first son was born, whom they named Eugene Brooks Ginsberg, after Louis' labor hero, Eugene V. Debs.

For nine years Louis rode the streetcars to and from Paterson, where he taught English to a fresh new class of youngsters every fall. In the evenings he sat at his small wooden desk and after he finished grading school papers he wrote poetry. In 1920 he published a short rhymed poem, "Roots," which began, "The other day, when I looked at a tree, / I thought, 'How deep can its dark roots be?' " Even though it was in the style of another poet, Edna St. Vincent Millay, it helped establish him as an up-and-coming writer. He joined the Poetry Society of America and attended as many literary functions in New York City as he had time for. He and Naomi became familiar with the Greenwich Village poetry circles peopled by the likes of Marianne Moore, Maxwell Bodenheim, Edward Arlington Robinson, and Elinor Wylie. Unfortunately, since Louis was living and teaching in New Jersey and had a growing family to support, he couldn't devote enough time to become anything more than an acquaintance of the Village bohemians. Louis routinely sent his poems to one magazine after another and slowly made a minor name for himself. His list of credits grew to include the *New York Times,* the *New Yorker,* and *Poetry.* When Louis Untermeyer chose Ginsberg's poem "Fog" as a counterpoint to Carl Sandburg's poem "Fog" for his anthology, *Modern American and British Poetry,* Louis was as happy as he would ever be in his life. Untermeyer wrote to Louis, "You have the lyric touch. You know how to make words sing something as well as say something." When Louis'

Collected Poems were published in 1992, his son, Eugene Brooks, wrote: "Most of his verse was songlike and rhymed, they were mostly quatrains with alternate lines rhyming or rhyming couplets celebrating nature, spring, love and twilight. One major theme is the transformation of natural objects into other glorious flame-like constructs; another stress is on pantheism: God is Beauty which infuses all nature and people. A third theme sounds a more somber note as the poet visits the poverty side of metropolitan Newark or New York City." Throughout the 1920s and 1930s Louis sent out his rhymed verse that celebrated life to a host of publishers and received many more rejection letters than acceptances, but it never stopped him from trying. In the end he wasn't able to find a publisher willing to finance an entire book of his poetry, so he borrowed money and subsidized his own books, *The Attic of the Past* (1920) and *The Everlasting Minute* (1937). The Ginsberg apartment was filled with boxes of books waiting for buyers and readers.

1926 ~

THE NEWSPAPERS IN JUNE 1926 were filled with descriptions of the adventures of Richard Byrd and Floyd Bennett, who made the first airplane flights over the North Pole in May. They were followed a few days later by Amundsen, Ellsworth, and Nobile, who flew over it in a dirigible. Babe Ruth hit two home runs to lead the Yankees in a victory over the Red Sox and people enjoyed listening to radio programs like *The Singing Groundhog* in the evening. The American Neurological Association was having its annual convention in Atlantic City where Dr. T. H. Weisenberg explained in his address that "nervousness is an attribute of genius." He suggested that the more highly civilized humans became, the more nervous we would find ourselves. On June 2, Columbia University's president Nicholas Murray Butler gave a commencement speech in which he said, "It has been my ambition to have it said there has been brought together [at Columbia] a group of scholars, trained investigators, scientists, teachers and personalities without comparison in the civilized world. Gentlemen, that has been done." Butler little suspected that one of Columbia's greatest alumni was about to be born that night in New Jersey.

On June 2, 1926, the same day that Eugene Brooks Ginsberg was celebrating his fifth birthday, his mother, Naomi, went into labor in the maternity ward of Newark's Beth Israel Hospital. There, at 2:00 A.M. on June 3, she gave birth to Irwin Allen Ginsberg, her second son. Irwin Allen's Hebrew name was Israel Abraham, but he would be called, simply, Allen. He was a happy baby, the apple of his mother's eye, and he took after her in many ways. Naomi smothered Allen with love from the day she took him home to their little apartment at 163 Quitman Street in Newark. Allen grew to be a sensitive boy, bright and gregarious like Naomi, happy despite the family's problems. He showed early signs of becoming somewhat eccentric himself. He was extremely intelligent, something noticed by his playmates, who eventually dubbed him "The Professor." He wanted desperately to be popular, but was not, and being a bit of an egghead made him lonely in school. He spent much of his time reading or playing with his older brother and cousins. His humble lower-middle-class background gave no hint of the international celebrity he would come to enjoy over the next seventy years of life.

BOYHOOD: FAIR STREET

IN 1930, after a decade of commuting to teach, Louis moved his family
to 83 Fair Street in Paterson. Louis later described this first of many Paterson
addresses as a "sad rooming house on dingy Fair Street," but for the time being it was a cheerful home. Eugene had happy memories of his father writing poems while sitting in a tiny alcove off the living room under the glare of
a gooseneck lamp. Allen's memories of this dark apartment were generally
not as pleasant. He remembered Naomi starting a fire in the wastebasket,
which quickly spread, necessitating a visit from the fire department. It was a
basket she had woven in an occupational therapy class on one of her increasingly frequent visits to rest homes and sanitariums. Allen may have misre-
membered the incident, because his father later wrote that a four-year-old
Allen had set the wastebasket ablaze, or perhaps there were other trips to the
house by the firemen. Maybe Allen remembered it because he was blamed
for something Naomi did. No one will ever know. He was certainly a typical
boy and got into his share of minor trouble on his own. One day, for example, he cut all the pictures out of his brother's astronomy books, too young
to realize that books were expensive. He also remembered wetting his bed
habitually and once was punished for peeing behind his Aunt Rose's piano
on a visit to her house. He couldn't remember exactly how old he was, but
he recalled that he was too scared to go down the dark hallway alone to her
bathroom. When he was taken to school on his first day he screamed and
cried the entire way. It was all pretty much average childhood behavior, but

Mendel Livergant, Eugene, Allen, Naomi, and Louis Ginsberg, ca. 1936 ~

unfortunately the most vivid memories from childhood are usually the most traumatic.

After the birth of their second son, the relationship between Louis and Naomi gradually unraveled. Subtle differences in their political views grew into heated domestic arguments that Eugene remembered would often end in insults like "bourgeois lackey" and "stinking Red." What had originally been diagnosed as Naomi's minor schizophrenia became more and more acute as the years passed. By 1932 she had been diagnosed with paranoid schizophrenia, at the time called "dementia praecox." The family's tranquillity was interrupted by her increasingly frequent emotional outbursts and even an occasional suicide attempt. Naomi suffered from hyperesthesia (an abnormally heightened sensitivity of the senses). For a while she couldn't tolerate sunlight and was ultrasensitive to sound, touch, and pain. During severe attacks she kept herself in darkened rooms for long periods of time. She began to withdraw from reality and exhibited increasingly unnatural behavior and intellectual disturbances. She had always been an advocate of nudism and vegetarianism, but she began to take these interests to extremes. She seldom wore a dress around the house and Allen became quite familiar with his mother's anatomy. He was particularly upset when he saw her wearing only a bloody menstrual pad while doing her chores.

Later, while talking to psychiatrists, Allen mentioned seeing her wearing "a G-string (Kotex belt), fat, and with long breasts," blood on her knees. It certainly appears that if Naomi didn't make sexual advances to her young son, she came pretty close to it, but Allen was too innocent to understand exactly what was going on. He became accustomed to Naomi's odd, erratic, unpredictable behavior and lacked a reference point to see what was so unusual in his mother's actions.

During the 1930s, she was in and out of treatment in the Bloomingdale Asylum and Greystone State,[1] which Allen later invoked in his most famous poem, *Howl*. Even though that poem was addressed to Carl Solomon, many of its references are to his mother and her experiences with insanity during the 1930s. Her unusual behavior was imprinted upon the boy so that he grew up seeing craziness as another side of life, an illness no different from other ailments. In his boyhood diaries he wrote about going to the movies to see *Oh Doctor,* in which Edward Everett Horton plays a lovable hypochondriac. "The latter would set a good example for my mother as she is pretty bad today. Her sickness is only mental, however, and she has no chance of dying." That was a casual reference to Naomi's frequent hysterical declarations that she was about to die, which terrified her son. Louis tried to shield Allen from her madness and never discussed Naomi's suicide attempts for fear of frightening him, but the little boy sensed what was going on at home more than his father cared to know. It was easier for Louis to pretend that Allen was too young to notice, but it affected the boy profoundly. Decades later Allen's stepmother summed it up succinctly by saying that "Allen saw things he should never have seen."

His mother's illness put a severe strain on Louis and on the family finances. As soon as they were married, Naomi and Louis had bought new furniture for their home expecting to pay it off over time. Louis was also in debt from subsidizing his own book of poetry after failing to find a commercial outlet for it. As a high school English teacher, he made a modest salary, but it wasn't enough to pay their debts, raise two children, and cover his wife's psychiatric treatments as well. After a few stays in private sanitariums, the bills piled up and Naomi had to move to state-supported hospitals where the quality of care was not as high. Financial difficulties made it necessary for Louis to teach summer school and take other jobs to earn extra cash, keeping him away from home even more. With Naomi in and out of hospitals, the boys ended up spending a good deal of time with neighbors and

---

[1] Greystone State: Greystone Park Psychiatric Hospital in Morris Plains, New Jersey.

Louis' relatives in Newark. By 1933, in an effort to economize, they moved out of the Fair Street apartment and for a time lived with the Field family on Carbon Street, across the Passaic River from downtown Paterson. After a few months Louis found an affordable white frame house with a small yard at 155 Haledon Avenue.

1933-37 ~

THE 1930S BROUGHT ECONOMIC HARDSHIP to everyone in America, and the Ginsbergs were no exception. As the Great Depression dragged on, fears of another world war increased as Hitler and Mussolini gained power in Europe. Paterson's days as a leading manufacturing center were over, and it was clear that the city was becoming one of the poorest in the country. Any hopes the family might have had of getting out of debt were dashed when the school district cut teachers' salaries by one-third in an austerity move. Eugene wrote that "despite this, Louis went on with the joy of teaching 'heedless' students and writing poetry." Every now and then he gave poetry readings to small audiences and his short verses appeared in local newspapers like the *Paterson Morning Call* and the *Paterson Evening News*. As a teacher, Louis was well known in town and the shopkeepers began to call him "Paterson's Principal Poet." He sent poems to literary magazines hoping for publication and each day on his way home from work, he'd check his mailbox to see if there might be an acceptance letter among the form rejections.

His two growing sons were sensitive and intelligent. Each had homework, after-school activities, and hobbies, which sometimes turned into great adventures. Eugene's interests were more scientific than Allen's. Astronomy and chemistry were his favorite pastimes. His giant chemistry set contained some very dangerous elements, such as sodium, which one day burst into flame completely by accident. Louis carried the burning material out into the yard and once again the firemen visited the Ginsberg house. At the time Allen was enrolled in PS 17 on the hill nearby. Despite the large, sunny classrooms and an unlimited supply of books, the school was terrifying to him. He remembered the place as cheerless, symbolized by the shadowy basement toilets, which were made even darker by huge slate partitions. One of his most vivid memories was of going to that bathroom and not being able to unbutton his own trouser fly. In those days, zippers were not as common as buttons, and he was embarrassed when all the other boys laughed at him and teasingly offered to take his pants down for him. Later Allen felt that this humiliation remained vivid to him because it aroused an infantile homosexuality. In class he often caused further embarrassment by soiling his pants for fear of that dark bathroom. Even at his early age he had masochist dreams about exhibitionism and experienced a juvenile sexuality based on urine and feces.

Like most children Allen was embarrassed by what were common youthful mistakes. Once when he took his father's letters to be mailed he put the stamps on the wrong side of the envelope and the clerk laughed at him so heartily that he never forgot it. Nathan, a local tailor, left an indelible impression on him, and it is quite possible that Nathan was the inspiration for his poem *The Shrouded Stranger*, his personal interpretation of the boogie man. In general, Allen's health was good, but when he was seven, he had a sudden attack of appendicitis. His father rushed him to a doctor to see what the problem was and both Louis and a nurse had to hold Allen down while the doctor put his finger up the boy's rectum to examine his swollen appendix. Allen screamed in pain from the penetration and remembered nothing more until he awakened from the anesthesia following the operation. A family cousin, Dr. Max Danzis, one of the founding physicians at Newark's Beth Israel Medical Center, had performed the appendectomy, but it hadn't gone smoothly and left him with an ugly scar. Years later he would recall that this surgery represented a betrayal on the part of his father, which he saw as an unacknowledged punishment. Being treated in the hospital must have made the small boy identify with his mother, who had already spent a good deal of time in mental hospitals by then. His groggy haze upon coming around from the ether was the first drug experience that Allen was able to remember.

Even though his lasting memories of childhood were painful ones, there were plenty of happy times around his home on upper Haledon Avenue, too. Allen's relatives remembered Allen as being basically a gleeful boy, not at all depressed or sad. His brother had the impression that Allen was "cherubic and seemed to go from place to place cheerfully. I don't remember any real grief, outward show of grief as distinguished from the inner grief that he must have felt about Naomi. I was totally grief stricken and Allen I think was a cheerful kid." On winter mornings Louis, Naomi, and the boys enjoyed family breakfasts in the kitchen near the hot iron stove that burned both wood and coal. In the evenings the family sat around the radio and listened to the serials that were a staple of life in the 1930s. Allen's favorite was *The Shadow*, and he daydreamed about living a more exciting life in which he would have adventures like his hero, Lamont Cranston. His parents enjoyed classical music and Allen learned to love opera. Mozart and Rosa Ponselle were among their favorites. He joined the *New York Post*'s record club and listened faithfully to the symphony broadcasts on WNYC and WQXR all through grammar and high school. Even though he took violin and piano lessons when he was nine, he was never enthusiastic about practicing. Once, in anger, he hit his mother in the chest during an argument about his lessons.

In school he made friends with a few of the boys, but was generally shy and even afraid of some of the students. On one occasion, to impress his friends, Allen stole tiles from his neighbor's roof. In psychotherapy years later, Allen recalled that when the neighbor, Dr. Mahler, came to the back door to complain, his parents would not defend Allen against the man's anger. One of his earliest friends, a boy named Morton, confided in Allen that sometimes he wanted to rush up to girls in school and grab hold of them. When he asked Allen if he didn't have the same feelings Allen told him flatly, "I don't feel that way, no." He began to feel like he was missing something important. "Well you wait when you're older," Morton said. Secretly, Allen had a crush on Earl, one of the other boys in his gang, but he never confided that to anyone.

On another occasion, Morton, Allen, and two other boys snuck into the bathroom of Morton's house where one of the boys put his lips to Morton's penis, but then complained that it didn't taste good. As an adult, Allen said that none of the boys were self-conscious or ashamed about this, even though they knew it was forbidden. He felt they were too young to have any social shame and weren't aware how much this would be frowned on by their parents. Obviously they all felt guilty enough to run when Morton's mother told them to get out of the bathroom and go play. Allen was also curious about bodily functions and unspoken private secrets, as when he questioned Morton about what he did with his snot. Then one day in a vacant lot near his house, Allen saw a gang of boys pull down Morton's pants. He was afraid to go to his friend's defense, for which Morton scolded him later, but Allen didn't want to risk suffering the same torture. Secretly, Allen said he enjoyed seeing the bigger boys humiliating Morton and baring his ass. Later, on his own porch during a spring downpour, Allen slipped his pants down, baring himself for a few minutes, a childish kind of exhibitionism that went undetected due to the porch railing. Years later, as an adult, he analyzed himself thus: "Perhaps my whole character is exhibitionistic and evidenced by fantasy and action on porch." He continued to dream of being spanked by gangs of boys for years. Fifty years later Allen often startled people by remarking that he was sorry that an older man hadn't taken sexual advantage of him during his childhood. No one ever knew whether he was serious or merely fantasizing about his unfulfilled youthful longings.

Naomi was still very much a part of family life during Allen's grammar-school years, although their time together was punctuated by longer stays in mental hospitals. In her absence other family members would care for Allen and Gene and often the boys would go to stay with their cousins in Newark. The last full summer the boys spent with Naomi and Louis together as a family was in 1936, when Allen was ten years old. They rented an old cottage near Woodstock, New York, along a rocky stream with a swimming hole. Naomi's father stayed with them and on the weekends Louis came out from Paterson where he was teaching summer school. During other summers when Naomi was not in the hospital they spent a few weeks at a Yiddish communist camp near Beacon, New York, that she liked. In the hills they escaped their problems, playing in the fresh air and enjoying concerts, dances, and lectures each night. Camp Nitgedayget was intended for workers and intellectuals; business owners and bosses were not welcome. Most of Naomi's later summers were spent in mental facilities, and Louis would send the boys to live with relatives at a family cottage in Belmar, along the Jersey shore. Louis' mother, sisters, and their families were all there, so there were plenty of children for Allen to play with. Allen's Aunt Rose prepared giant traditional meals even though the kids complained that they didn't like Jewish food, preferring hamburgers and hot dogs, of course. All in all it was a happy time for Allen with his large extended family.

Naomi's behavior eventually became so paranoid and capricious that her fellow Communist Party members eased her out of the local party cell. They did not wish to risk trouble by advocating nudism or vegetarianism, which had become her primary social concerns. She became a political liability and disrupted party functions. Convinced that the members were out to get her, which in a benign way they were, Naomi stopped attending the party meetings. More important, Naomi's madness was destroying her marriage with Louis, and Allen found himself torn between his affection for his mother and that for his father. As he grew older he was able to see the paranoia behind much of his mother's illogical fears and identify and sympathize with her sense of persecution at the hands of Louis and his mother. Rebecca Ginsberg, whom the children called Buba, had never really liked Naomi and was unsympathetic to her bouts with madness. She wished that Louis had never met Naomi, let alone married her. Driven by her insane paranoia, Naomi imagined all sorts of plots in which Buba was out to kill her or to turn her over to the secret police, and she clung tenaciously to these suspicions. Allen listened to his father's side of the arguments, too, and realized that he had an equally valid point. Naomi demanded most of Louis' attention, and it wasn't possible for him to devote all his time to her with two young boys to raise, debts to pay, and a job to hold down. Allen wished that he could be on both their sides and was greatly conflicted over his loyalties to his parents. Straddling this emotional fence made him feel that he was schizophrenic, too.

Several times when Naomi was at her most vulnerable, Louis asked Allen to stay home from school to watch her. By the time he was a teenager Allen found himself in the position of taking care of his own mother. As Naomi grew more and more suspicious of everyone associated with Louis and Buba, even her oldest son, Eugene, appeared to be an enemy. She trusted only her pet, little Allen, and she was bitter and resentful when her mother-in-law took over some of the responsibilities of the household. She feared that she was losing Allen to this evil spirit as well.

During the thirties, Allen witnessed his share of brutality on the streets of Paterson. He frequented a swimming hole behind the silk factory near the Passaic Falls, and it was there that he saw an older boy threaten to throw a skinny young kid off the dam onto the rocks thirty feet below. Allen remembered that he felt both fear and sexual arousal as he silently watched the scene unfold. Fortunately no one was hurt, but Allen's inaction made him identify with the Dr. Jekyll and Mr. Hyde character he had seen in the movies. He felt he was living two sides of a nightmare in Paterson, both inside and outside the home. Since he accepted much of his mother's psychosis as normal behavior, he didn't always see her world as demented, and he grew accustomed to unusual actions. He even found some of her outlandish behavior charming. Psychologically it helped protect him emotionally from the more frightening aspects of her illness. He learned to expect the unexpected and to think quickly in stressful situations. Louis and, to a lesser extent, Eugene were older and more capable of separating themselves emotionally from her illness, but Allen grew up a part of it.

Allen was curious about everything. He collected stamps and minerals and was interested in the microscope and in subjects like astronomy. While his father immersed himself in his work at school and a social life outside the home, Allen escaped to the solitary pleasures of the movies and books. Then in 1937, someone gave him a diary for his eleventh birthday. It was a little pocket diary with a lock and key, but it presented him with his first opportunity to record his private thoughts. It was the earliest of the more than five hundred journals he would fill during his lifetime. At first he kept a record of his daily activities, and then, with growing regularity, he began to record his thoughts, dreams, and fears. His earliest entries were all about his family life, and they document his fondness for his mother, father, and brother and relate his frustrations with them as well.

Allen enjoyed keeping a diary for several reasons, but interestingly enough, one reason was his deep conviction that he would become famous one day. He tried to document his life so that "if some future historian or biographer wants to know what the genius thought and did in his tender years, here it is." He also wrote that he had "a fair degree of confidence in myself." He attributed this to his being either a genius, an egocentric, or a schizophrenic, and he hastened to add that it was probably the first two.

As young as he was, Allen had already become a student of his own dreams, which he wrote down with increasing detail over the next sixty years. He described one dream in which he was chased by a monster. As he ran to safety on his porch where his mother was mopping, his feet became sticky and slowed his escape from danger. Some of his dreams were far grimmer. His father's death was a frequent nightmare accompanied by Allen's rehearsed display of sorrow, coldly calculated to impress his friends. Other dreams were more typical for a little boy, with horrible creatures menacing him from the fire escape until his father came to his rescue.

Eugene was typical of most big brothers, and Allen looked up to him and envied his maturity. Sometimes he felt that Eugene had a "big head," but most of the time they got along well. As a child it was Allen's habit to sleep in bed with either Louis or Eugene. In his diary he recorded his annoyance with Eugene's routine before going to bed. Each night he drank a certain amount of water, blew his nose a certain number of times, and then put the water glass next to the bed in a certain way. If Allen disturbed him, he would have to get up and repeat the whole process again before he could get to sleep. Despite minor annoyances like that, Allen loved to cuddle in bed with both his brother and father, and for years when he slept with Eugene, he clung to him even when Eugene pushed him away. As he grew older this snuggling took on a masturbatory aspect, but Allen was certain that neither

Eugene nor Louis ever realized it. When Naomi was away in the hospital for long periods of time, Eugene moved into her bedroom by himself, much to Allen's regret. He was so lonely that he would often crawl into bed with Louis as a substitute. He even had childish fantasies of sexual contacts with both Louis and Eugene. When he was twenty-five he wrote that he knew a lot about incest mainly due to these bedtime embraces "in fantasy and partial fact."

Puberty was a mysterious time for Allen, as it is for most children. As an adult he bluntly speculated that the secret at the core of his homosexuality was his unfulfilled desire to have "my father fuck me." Numerous times as an adult he lamented the fact that no older, wiser man had ever taken sexual advantage of him. In his teen years when Allen slept in the same bed with either Louis or Eugene, he usually had erections when he pressed close to either one of them. Allen said he woke during the night once and discovered his own wet semen on Eugene's underwear, but he couldn't really remember whether it was an actual memory or a dream masquerading as memory. Most of the time Eugene wouldn't let Allen touch him and pushed him away when he snuggled too closely, but Louis was willing to be more affectionate, possibly thinking that he was substituting for Allen's missing mother. Fondly, he called Allen his "little kissing bug."

Ginsberg's extended family made every effort to give Allen a sense of security and expressed continued concern about the effects on him of Naomi's mental breakdowns. Later Allen would say that he had learned about some kind of Gnostic miracle by taking care of his mother when she was mad. "I was too young to resist the realization that the world was hopeless, and therefore wide open to poetic imagination," he recalled. Louis did his best to hold the family together, but it was difficult to replace the love of a mother when she was confined in institutions for long periods of time. It was also a time when political crises outside the home started to encroach on family life. The Spanish Civil War had begun, and there was a good deal of hope for a socialist victory until the fascist forces of General Francisco Franco suppressed them. In 1937 the crash of the *Hindenburg* zeppelin in nearby Lakewood brought large-scale tragedy right to their own backyard, and the rise of the Nazi Party in Germany caused fear and anxiety in the Jewish community of Paterson. Louis was extremely interested in these events and the family conversations would often become heated as everyone debated the political implications of each new development.

1937–40 ～

IN 1937 THE FAMILY HAD to tighten its belt once more, so they moved down the hill to an even cheaper apartment on the second floor of 72 Haledon Avenue. Their financial problems were only partly due to Naomi's medical bills. This was the year that Louis subsidized Liveright Publishing Corporation to the tune of two thousand dollars for the printing of his second book of poetry, *The Everlasting Minute*, which contained some of his best poems yet. Once again he dedicated the book to Naomi, but by 1937 he was beginning to realize that her mental illness would never be cured. His financial hopes rode on his appointment as the head of the English Department at Central High School, but another teacher was selected over him.

These were some of Naomi's darkest days, and Eugene, five years older than Allen, was lucky to escape to college during this time. Her schizophrenia was growing worse each year and Allen was repeatedly kept home from school to watch over her. In June 1937 Eugene graduated from high school with plans to go on to law school and Louis threw a big party for him at their apartment. The morning after the party, Naomi locked herself in the bathroom and tried to commit suicide by slashing her wrists. Louis had to break the glass door to get to her and then rushed her to the hospital, while Allen watched in silence. That summer, as she recovered, he was sent to the beach to stay with Louis' relatives. It was the worst summer of his short life for several reasons. In addition to missing his mother, he contracted a skin disease known as impetigo, developed a sty below his eye, and caught poison ivy. The weather at the shore was terrible that year, too, but at least that gave

Naomi, Allen, and Louis Ginsberg at the New York World's Fair, 1940 ~

him a good excuse to go to the movies every day. *The Life of Emile Zola* and *Saratoga* with Jean Harlow were two of the big hits he enjoyed. Escaping into the world created by the cinema was Allen's chief pleasure during the Depression, and sometimes he watched several films a day.

When school was out each summer, Allen's aunts and uncles loaded their cars with relatives and tied their baggage to the roofs and running boards for the trip down to Belmar on the New Jersey coast. Allen spent nearly every summer vacation there until the outbreak of World War II. He played with his cousins Claire and Joel Gaidemak, wandered around the Playland amusement park, and rode the drive-em-yourself scooters for a few pennies. He loved the electric sparks, the mirrored ceilings, and the thrill of crashing safely into the other bumper cars. The kids spent their time playing in the sand on the beach, making sandcastles and climbing over the rocks on the breakwaters. Sometimes in an empty lot near their house on Sixteenth Avenue, they played Jungle Camp, a game that Allen had invented based on the adventures of Tarzan. He developed the script from the movies he inhaled one after another. By then, Eugene was old enough to find summer jobs while he was at the shore. He ran the Ferris wheel and the carousel to earn college tuition money. The big treat for everyone was to go a few miles up the beach from Belmar to Asbury Park with its larger amusement parks and arcades. Allen's favorite place was a giant movie palace in Asbury Park named the Mayfair Theater, built to resemble a Renaissance cathedral. There in 1936, Allen sat mesmerized by Paul Muni's Academy Award–winning performance in *The Life of Louis Pasteur*. Nelson Eddy was not only Allen's favorite movie star, but in his diary he designated him as "My Hero." On September 1, 1939, Allen remembered biking all the way from Belmar to the Mayfair Theater to tell his girlfriend—a niece, Allen said, of Hollywood mogul Louis B. Mayer—the news that Hitler's storm troopers had invaded Poland.

Occasionally the adults would whisper about their fears that Allen was "not quite right" in the head because of Naomi's history. They were especially sensitive to any of his actions that might appear to be a bit strange. One day, for no apparent reason, Allen lay down in the street gutter with his hands clasped behind his head, while talking to his cousin Joel. Eccentricities like that made word spread through the family that Allen was beginning to act in weird ways, "meshugeh," his grandmother would say with her strong Yiddish accent.

When classes began in the fall of 1937, Allen transferred to a new school in Paterson. He had grown to love his old one and had a difficult time adjusting to what he considered a horrible new school with "sadistic Dutchmen, fights with mad mean dirty Negroes and abusive morons." The kids there teased him and called him Ginsbug, Ginsbun, and Jewbun. One day a bully picked a fight with him in the grammar-school yard, and even though Allen was able to push him to the ground for a standoff, he ran home in tears to his mother. This was the single occasion that he could remember where she was able to give him love and affection when he needed it.

Allen was so unsettled by his new school that he began to neglect his studies. In class he daydreamed and secretly read unrelated books at his desk as a means of escape. He missed his arithmetic classes so often that his teacher had to send a note home to his father. For a while he lived in his own dream world in which he was a popular, witty, and brave leader. Despite his problems with many of the boys, he did make a few friends in his new school. In fact, even Black Joey, the boy he had fought in the schoolyard, eventually became a good friend. Another buddy, Danny Feitlowitz, spent long hours with Allen discussing the great questions of youth, debating problems like, "What is life?" and "How big is the universe?" Allen suggested that at the end of the universe was a rubber wall a billion miles thick, but when questioned about what was beyond that wall, he was at a loss. On the weekends he and Danny would walk to the Fabian Theater in downtown Paterson past a row of scary hedges along Broadway that they were both afraid of. Like most children, they were curious about sex. Once, walking a girl home from school, Allen, imitating the wolf in Little Red Riding Hood, said to her, "My what a big bust you have." Much to his surprise, she slapped him and chased him down the street. Later he was certain that this was yet another of the great Freudian traumas that turned him against girls, "sort of a silly denouement of decades of homosexuality, a scene that really bugged me out." He was ashamed of his naïveté because even though he was a boy he never wanted to appear immature. Perhaps because he was scholastically intelligent beyond his years, he didn't realize that emotionally he was callow.

As 1937 turned into 1938, Allen's mother remained in Greystone Park Psychiatric Hospital. Eugene was in college and Allen was shuttling back and forth between his home in Paterson and various relatives' houses in Newark. He was devoted to his two great passions, movies and books, but slowly he was beginning to take more of an interest in world events. When Germany absorbed Austria and a part of Czechoslovakia called the Sudeten, it became more evident that war was inevitable. The Fascist victory in Spain was another cause for concern for this young Jeffersonian Democrat, as Allen labeled himself. Still, to a preteen boy these struggles seemed very far away, and although he had a knowledge of what was going on in Europe on a political level, he was not experienced enough to imagine the human suffering that came with war. It was all a fascinating game, and his daily life in New Jersey continued pretty much the same. Then, one of his earliest heroes, Clarence Darrow, considered the greatest lawyer of the era, died at the age of eighty. Allen, who respected Darrow as a champion on the side of truth, resolved to follow in his footsteps as a lawyer.

In May 1938 Allen described himself in great detail in his diary. Physically he wrote that he was the smallest boy in his class and that boredom hung around him "like a shadow." After his initial problems adjusting to his new school, he had settled down and was once again a good student, earning high marks in all of his courses. He was so intelligent that his classmates considered him a genius and called him the class philosopher. The same year he volunteered to work on the school paper, the *Criterion*, as well as the yearbook staff, but his real passion was the debate team. It helped him develop a skill that he felt would be useful when he became a lawyer. He also had a flair for dramatics and was well liked enough to be elected president of both the Talent Club and the Debating Society. His taste in music leaned toward the classical (especially Beethoven, Tchaikovsky, Chopin, Schubert, and Wagner). Mixed in with that was an appreciation for a little bit of swing music exemplified by Johnny Messner's popular "Alexander the Swoose," which Allen particularly liked. At one point he even tried his hand at writing a piano concerto but abandoned that idea after the first twenty-five bars. Rounding out his list of interests were politics, history, and literature. He even cited in his diary the two things he hated most, "dull teachers and Republicans."

By the late 1930s Louis and Naomi's relationship was nearing an end. Her insanity had meant lengthy institutionalizations and whenever Naomi was released to be with Louis it was a continual domestic battle. Their quarrels were so violent that they usually hastened her return to the madhouse. It was around that time that Louis began to look for love and companionship with other women. One night when the telephone rang at 3:00 A.M., Allen's father answered it and fainted onto the kitchen floor. It turned out that the husband of a woman Louis had been seeing had found out about the affair and the wife had called to warn him. Allen and Gene didn't know what had happened until later, when they found a torn-up love letter in the wastebasket. Allen said that he lost trust in Louis after that and he never spoke to him about his secret love life.

In the summer of 1939, Allen graduated from grammar school and began to look forward to high school. He inscribed his own yearbook, perhaps half jokingly, "To the handsomest, most popular boy in the class. In my estimation you are the most bestist boy in the world. Sincerely, yourself." In the same yearbook Allen listed Edgar Allan Poe as his favorite author and *Dr. Doolittle* as his favorite book. He declared that his motto was: "Do what you want to do when you want to," and shocked his father by telling him that he had decided to become a teacher. Only to himself did he confide that he secretly "wanted to go into the great world of men and affairs and dreamed of being a senator or representative or an ambassador." It was the same summer he went to see *The Wizard of Oz* at the Mayfair Theater several times and the year that Yeats died, a singular loss to his father.

When he returned from the shore at the end of vacation, he entered Central High School. He did well in English, algebra, and civics and managed to squeak past in Latin. In the spring 1940 amateur talent show he displayed his acting ability in two sketches, "Department Store" and "Ask Dad, He Knows." He even performed a solo dance he called "Ballet Loose," which showed off his hidden gift for dancing. It was a spoof in which Allen dressed in a tutu and bumped his ass at the football players. He remembered clearly that one of his classmates, Basil Battalia, even kissed him in the excitement of the evening's performance. He was thirteen, and he admitted that he wasn't aware of any sexual urges then, but still he was sensitive to love and affection.

High school proved to be an improvement over grammar school, but Allen's real problems were at home. Allen's favorite aunt, Louis' sister Rose, was only forty when she became ill in the summer of 1940. In September she passed away from Libman-Sacks endocarditis, a complication of disseminated lupus erythematosus. Because of her illness, the family did not go to the house in Belmar that year. For a few weeks Allen stayed with his parents in a small bungalow in Arverne, a seashore resort on Rockaway Peninsula in Queens. Naomi was sullen and gloomy most of the time. As her appearance grew worse, so did her paranoia. When his cousin Joel visited them for a week, she wasn't happy to see him because she considered him a spy for grandma Buba. One night Joel remembered being woken up by Naomi's hysterical screams as she raced naked through the cottage with Louis following her, trying to calm her down. Even though it was a common occurrence in the Ginsberg household, it was upsetting to an outsider.

During their stay in Arverne, Allen's parents took him to see the World's Fair in Flushing Meadow Park. The fair was the talk of the town, with American companies introducing many new products that would help to define the following decades: television, air-conditioning, diesel trains, Lucite, nylon, and color film among them. The exhibits predicted a utopian future of consumerism with America's industries leading the way. Unfortunately the timing of the fair coincided with the outbreak of the war in Europe and even the motto for the fair had to be changed from "Building the World of Tomorrow" to "For Peace and Freedom." By the time the Ginsbergs visited the fair, the Soviet pavilion, which was one of the things they wanted to see most, had been closed due to Russia's alliance with Nazi Germany. As fourteen-year-old Allen and his mother posed for photos in front of one of the fair's colossal statues, they had no way of knowing that this would be one of their last family outings. Later that year Naomi "was seized by a fit of frenzied insistent accusation and yelled at me that I was a spy," Allen recorded. She then demanded that Allen help her escape and he was forced to take her on a mad horrible bus trip to Lakewood. There he had to leave her in paranoiac fear with her shoe in her hand, surrounded by police in a drugstore. He said that at that exact moment, he watched his own mother go beyond conceivable human horror into living death. From then on, Naomi considered Allen to be another one of her enemies, and she was beyond his ability to reach her. All this he was to capture in painful detail in his greatest poem, *Kaddish: For Naomi Ginsberg.*

1940-43 ～

BY 1940 LOUIS was three thousand dollars in debt and the violent quarrels with Naomi over money intensified. Once again the family had to move, this time to an apartment building at 288 Graham Avenue on the east side of town.

In September, Allen entered his sophomore year at Central High, a time vividly described in his diary, which he was writing to "satisfy my egotism," he candidly explained. He also wrote in his journal simply because he enjoyed writing. From birth he had been surrounded by poetry and literature and he was unquestionably influenced by the fact that his father was a poet. He didn't see his own writing as art at the time, merely something that recorded his thoughts and opinions. His first published articles appeared in the Easter 1941 issue of the *Central High School Spectator*. Allen wrote a humorous essay he called "On Homework in General" and conducted an interview with Canada Lee[2] titled "'Native Son' Makes Good!" By his own admission these were only average school newspaper articles that did not hint at the great poetic voice he would develop later.

In June he volunteered to write a column about high school events for the *Paterson Evening News*, which was so well received that the editor offered him two dollars per week to continue the column in the fall. In high school he became more involved in extracurricular activities and joined the student

---

[2] Canada Lee (1907–52): Movie actor and sometime boxer, most famous for his appearance in Hitchcock's film *Lifeboat* in 1944.

government board of publications, in addition to his continued participation in the dramatic and debating clubs. His literary interest led him to join the staff of the school paper, the *Tattler,* where he was appointed layout editor. That fall he also lost his bid for student government office when he ran unsuccessfully for class treasurer, relying on his father's popularity to win him votes instead of hard campaigning. What spare time he did have was spent at the movies, where he saw films like *The Grapes of Wrath, Of Mice and Men, The Great Dictator,* and *Fantasia.* He followed sports in the newspaper, but he weighed only ninety-five pounds and was considered fragile, although he was beginning to mature.

In the fall of 1941, Allen transferred from Central to Eastside High School for his junior and senior years. For some reason he had been placed at Central by mistake and the school administrators corrected their error after his sophomore year. This time the shift in schools was not accompanied by problems, and he adapted quickly. He continually improved as a student and excelled in many subjects, taking French, chemistry, and history and continuing his studies in English literature and Latin. His favorite teacher in his new school was three-hundred-pound Mrs. Durbin, who was the first to introduce him to Walt Whitman's poetry. In addition to Whitman, she persuaded Allen to look at some of Hart Crane's poems, which were not highly regarded by the academic community at the time. Allen's earliest poems were conventional metered verse written at Mrs. Durbin's suggestion.

What he couldn't verbalize or commit to paper was that his sexual thoughts were about some of the boys in his class instead of the girls. He had the first of many crushes on athletic boys, but never confided these feelings to anyone. One day he inscribed "Paula Loves Allen" on the cover of one of his notebooks and drew a little heart with an arrow through it. The secret was that it wasn't Paula, but Paul he was interested in. Paul Roth was a boy a year older than Allen, but until Paul went away to Columbia University they were very close. Allen vowed to follow him if he could. Curiously, Allen wrote in his own notebook that the object of his desire loved him, but not the other way around. That would have been news to Paul and seemed like wishful thinking on Allen's part. Allen never told Paul of his feelings until years later.

The Japanese attack on Pearl Harbor on December 7, 1941, was a turning point for America and a moment that defined Allen's generation of boys who were about to become men. Along with the rest of the country, Allen was shocked when he heard the news and even said that he looked out his New Jersey window expecting to see Japanese planes on the horizon. He blamed the war on all the shortsighted politicians in Washington who hadn't heeded Woodrow Wilson's call to join a League of Nations. Allen felt that such an organization might have been able to mediate the situation. Now it was too late and America was swept into another world war. Allen predicted that the death toll would reach four million on both sides before it was over and that the war would be an unparalleled catastrophe for all mankind. In fact, the Holocaust alone would account for a loss of more than six million people and more than that would die in battle.

At the start of the war, Allen's brother was in law school, but he was called up at once. He joined the Air Force and by 1942 he had been shipped out to London. At the same time, Naomi succumbed once and for all to her paranoia about Louis and his mother and except for a few brief visits, never lived with Louis again. When she was released from a hospital in 1943 she moved across the Hudson River to New York to stay with relatives of her own.

In Paterson in the fall of 1942, sixteen-year-old Allen Ginsberg campaigned strongly for Irving Abramson, the Democratic candidate for the House of Representatives. He ran errands and stuffed envelopes for the party and at his own initiative wrote passionate letters to the editors of the local newspapers and to Republican congressman Gordon Canfield, Abramson's opponent. Canfield had been a staunch isolationist before the war broke out and opposed any direct involvement in Europe's problems. Allen believed that isolationism was a mistake that America was about to pay dearly for. He felt it was time to fight fascism and "free humanity" once and for all. He was supportive of the Allied efforts to win the war against the Axis powers and hoped that the fight would be over quickly. To win re-election, Canfield ran a smear campaign against Abramson. He called him a "Red" since he was supported by most of the local socialists, including the editor of the *Passaic Valley Examiner*, Hyman Zimel, an old friend of Allen's father. A few years later, it was Zimel who would ask Allen to interview the New Jersey poet William Carlos Williams for his newspaper. Abramson lost the election and Allen wrote a personal letter asking Canfield to reconsider his position. He was furious when he received a form letter in reply. It was the first election in which Allen took an active role with disappointing results.

After school Allen spent his time writing mock radio programs complete with dialogue and station breaks and long poems about the war with titles like "To a Dead Soldier" and "To the Marshal Petain." He also wrote dozens of reviews, one comparing Eric Coate's *London Again Suite* to Gershwin's *Rhapsody in Blue*. In the evenings he helped collect clothing for the Russian war relief or earned extra money by baby-sitting. He did whatever he could for the war effort and joined the Civilian Defense, where he walked rounds each night in his neighborhood. Personally he worried a good deal about how the war might affect him and was upset when Congress amended a bill to allow for eighteen-year-olds to be drafted; the minimum age had previously been twenty. When President Roosevelt denounced Congress as inefficient, Allen applauded. His letters to Eugene reveal the deep political interests that they shared. He grew to love sparring with his brother and father over politics, just as his mother and father had debated communist and socialist ideologies during earlier, happier times. In those early 1940s, Allen, like many liberal Americans, still believed that Stalin's politics were "progressive and healthy nationalism." America was "all right," too, he said, and shouldn't be criticized at this point in her history either; improvements could always be addressed later.

1943 ~

ALLEN REALLY DIDN'T have any romantic life while he was in high school. He rarely went on dates with girls, but instead had a series of one-sided infatuations with boys in his school. During his senior year his love was directed toward Paul Roth in absentia. Paul was as popular as he was handsome, with a winning smile and muscular physique. Allen loved him from afar, well aware that his feelings would not have been appreciated or reciprocated, even though Paul liked Allen and affectionately called him "Shoulders." They corresponded as friends and Paul encouraged Allen to apply to Columbia, inviting him to visit the campus on various occasions. In April 1943, Allen went to see Paul at college and brought him a copy of Elias Lieberman's *Poems for Enjoyment*. Like Allen, Paul was interested in literature. He had heard Lieberman speak on campus and appreciated what he had to say about poetry. On the ride to visit Paul, Allen knelt on the deck of the ferry as it crossed the Hudson River and prayed that he'd be accepted to Columbia. If he did get in, he made a vow to God that he would somehow do something to benefit mankind forever.

On May 14, 1943, William Hance, Dean of Columbia College, addressed a letter to Allen. "It is a pleasure to inform you that at a meeting of the committee on scholarships of Columbia College held recently, you were awarded financial assistance at the rate of $100 each session." With his family's help and part-time jobs (Allen was working at the Paterson Public Library at the time), he could afford to go to Columbia. As soon as he heard the good news Paul Roth wrote to Allen, "I'll have you again as a

Ginsberg at Columbia, 1940s ~

schoolmate." When Allen replied to Paul's note he commented favorably on what he called Paul's "erotic" handwriting. Paul's next letter to Allen was typed and he pointedly went out of his way to tell Allen that he was dating several women. Allen didn't mention the erotic handwriting again.

Before he graduated from high school, Allen's first published poem appeared in the *Senior Mirror*. It was selected as the class poem and began, "We leave the youthful pennants and the books . . ." Several of his classmates mentioned his poetry and his writing talents when they inscribed his yearbook. His genius was also an often-noted characteristic.

On June 24, 1943, three weeks after Allen's seventeenth birthday, he graduated from Eastside High School with respectable although not outstanding marks. He placed above average in English, foreign languages, and social studies, and was average in science and physical education. He even managed to end with a ninety in algebra, which was not his easiest subject. Although he wasn't certain about a career, he wagered that he would probably do government or legal work; maybe he'd even go into labor law. His second choice might be a private law practice where he could apply his debating skills.

As he traveled to Columbia to register on July 1, he thought about his past and future. In some ways he was relieved to be leaving everything behind, especially the craziness of his mother. Years later Ginsberg began to realize how much he had lost by distancing himself from her. He wrote that he lost the ability to become close to "later friendly girls." He felt that he denied most of his feelings toward women out of a fear born at the loss of his mother. Her absences created such a deep void that he never wanted to risk reliving it. "Old feelings you didn't know were there and were ashamed of, like loving your mother and realizing that you and she were one and that you'd separated from her because you couldn't stand the fear of being one with her. And realizing that all women and your mother are one—for myself, at least—I cut myself off from all women because I was afraid I'd discover my mother in them, or that I'd have the same problems with them that I had with her."

For Ginsberg a good education was the only way out of the drab and at times disappointing existence he endured in Paterson. Barely seventeen, Allen was younger than most of the other freshmen entering Columbia in the summer of 1943. He registered for a history course with Jacques Barzun and signed up for economics with Louis Hacker. During his sophomore year he would switch his major to English literature, but for now he was considering a law career. Allen was a dynamic and spirited talker and with his experience on his high school debating team he was soon representing Columbia at intercollegiate debates. He also helped organize a student committee for Roosevelt's re-election, but following that flurry of activity his interest in politics began to wane and his literary interests took over. Ginsberg became one of the editors of the respected *Jester Review,* the school's literary and humor magazine, and was later elected president of Philolexian, Columbia's literary and dramatic society.

Even in high school Ginsberg, the class philosopher, had been formulating his own personal theories. He believed that man was a superior animal, due to his self-awareness and self-knowledge. That self-consciousness included a realization of a purpose and meaning to life, whether it was positive, negative, or neutral, as well as the ability to use natural force to achieve fulfillment of that meaning. He openly acknowledged that he, himself, didn't know what that purpose was yet, but he suspected that a general objective might be to find freedom from intellectual and physical limitations, to perfect the human machine, both in mind and body. Allen saw history as a river of development flowing steadily toward the ultimate goal of human perfection. He felt that man's physical freedom had already been achieved to some extent through scientific developments that freed people from manual work, but he was less certain about intellectual freedom. On the whole, he believed that the intellectual growth of mankind had progressed, albeit at a slower pace, since the birth of civilization. He embraced the theoretical ideal of communism in his belief that democracy was only one stop in the evolution of humanity toward complete self-conscious efforts aimed at the good of all of mankind.

Although Allen was more intelligent than many of the other freshmen in his class, he seemed much younger emotionally. He liked people and was naturally gregarious, but he pictured himself as a loner and a misfit and for a while he felt out of his environment as he often did whenever he entered a new school. At Columbia, because of the war effort, the navy had taken over many of the dorms on campus to train future officers under the V-12 program. The college tried to provide rooms for its own students wherever it could find them. During his first term Allen was assigned to a three-room suite a few blocks from the campus on the top floor of the Union Theological Seminary. There he was given two roommates, Jerry Rausch and Arthur Lazarus, the latter also a prelaw student. He made friends with them quickly, and during his first semester he threw himself into his studies. He took a full load of English, French, math, and humanities courses and did well, earning As and Bs in all his classes except physical education and hygiene, which he narrowly passed with a C-plus.

Initially Ginsberg's circle of friends consisted entirely of fellow Columbia students, like John Kingsland, whom Allen once described as "an overdeveloped and worldly-wise sybarite." One of Allen's friends thought Kingsland was "kind of a queen" and without a doubt bisexual. Besides Kingsland he made friends with William Lancaster, "a socialist of sorts, a neurotic"; Walter Adams, whom Allen described as being a "literary anarchist" as well as the son of a famous poet, Kathrin Traverin Adams; Jack Turvey; Grover Smith, "a Miniver Cheevy medievalist" who was translating Sir Thomas More's Utopia directly from the Latin; Ted Hoffman, "a hunchbacked poet"; and other sensitive boys, mostly from high society families who had breeding and class. Allen loved the sophisticated atmosphere he found among these new friends at Columbia. These were intelligent, upper-class boys; many were as smart as or even smarter than he was himself, quite a change from Paterson. Allen gravitated toward a group of students who were extremely sociable and among other things were beginning to experiment with sexuality in its myriad forms. Sex was the most interesting, mysterious, and exciting thing that Ginsberg discovered at college. In Paterson he felt he was the only boy in the world who had sexual thoughts about other boys, but here he met people who were more honest about their homosexual nature, even if it wasn't openly condoned. Allen himself was much too timid to act upon his feelings, but he made friends with many who were more adventurous and confident in their sexuality. His written record of his dreams reveals his repressed desire to have gay sex with many of the boys he met at Columbia, but he feared being exposed publicly as queer. During his second term that fall he fell to a C in math but otherwise remained overall a very good student.

When Ginsberg's roommates left for the Christmas holiday at the end of his second term, he found himself nearly alone in his wing of the seminary dorm. Echoing down the corridor from another student's room came Brahms's Trio no. 1. Always assertive when it came to meeting new people, he followed the music to a closed door. Characteristically, he entered the student's room uninvited with the excuse of asking what the title of the recording was. "My name's Allen Ginsberg, do you mind if I listen?" he asked the handsome boy with uncombed blond hair who looked to be a year or two older. "I'm Lucien Carr," was the reply, "and since you're in, you might as well sit down." Carr initially thought Ginsberg was a "shy little Jewish boy" with just enough chutzpah to walk into his room without knocking. Lucien was outgoing himself and enjoyed socializing with interesting people, and immediately he took Allen under his wing.

As was often the case with Ginsberg, he was attracted first of all by Lucien's good looks. He romanticized that Lucien was "gifted by the earth with all the goodness of her form, physical and spiritual." To Allen, who thought of himself as neither a romantic nor a visionary, Lucien was both. Allen saw himself as a Jew with natural traits of introspection and eclecticism, but he felt he was without grace. He believed he was ugly, or plain at best, but blessed with talent as a creator and initiator of art. However, art was a meager compensation for what Allen desired. He knew he continually overreached himself for love, but he could not help himself. Love to Allen was an opiate, and since Paul Roth had already left for the war, Lucien became his first serious college "crush."

Allen went out of his way to build a friendship with Lucien, and it was a friendship Allen kept until the day he died. One thing they shared from the beginning was a love of music. Carr knew a good deal more about the subject than Allen, so he appointed himself to fill in the gaps in Allen's appreciation of classical music and jazz. Since college was in recess for several weeks and neither of them planned to spend much time at home, they had time to indulge themselves and Lucien took Allen with him on his rounds of the city's jazz bars. In the course of their revelries, Allen began to meet Lucien's friends, a circle of interesting characters who would come to define Allen's life and change the course of American literature a decade later as members of the Beat Generation.

During the summer of 1943, Lucien Carr was living with his mother, Marion Carr, in her apartment on East Fifty-seventh Street, when he applied to Columbia. By that time, Carr had completed a series of sessions with a Chicago psychotherapist after a suicide attempt. This troubled Carr's mother so much that she never wanted to talk about her son's treatments and asked him to burn the doctor's discharge papers to hide the fact that it had ever happened. Lucien's college application was filed too late for the summer semester, but by fall he was admitted to Columbia and he moved to the room at the Union Theological Seminary where he met Ginsberg.

At nineteen, Lucien Carr was far more experienced and worldly than Allen. He had been born into a wealthy St. Louis family, but by 1943 his parents were divorced. His mother doted on him and indulged his every wish, while his father had little to do with him. Lucien was considered brilliant, bold, and rebellious by those who knew him. As a teenager, he developed a drinking habit and once drunk, he became pugnacious. Lucien arrived in New York from St. Louis in a roundabout way after having been expelled from schools in Chicago and New England. He was already a heavy drinker, and most of his problems with the authorities had come when he was quite drunk. At some point Carr had become the object of sexual obsession for his St. Louis Boy Scout troop leader, David Kammerer, born in 1911 and fourteen years Lucien's senior. Kammerer was the son of socially prominent parents in Clayton, Missouri, a suburb of St. Louis. David's father was a well-known consulting engineer who was proud when his son graduated from Washington University in 1933. In 1938 Kammerer received his master's degree and went on to teach English and physical education for the school where he met Lucien. Although weak-chinned, Kammerer was considered good looking, with a handsome Roman nose and short, thick red hair. He had a shy smile that Allen said seemed to mask a dark, not-very-well-kept secret. Kammerer was so infatuated with the good-looking Carr boy that when Lucien left St. Louis to attend school out of state, David followed him, first to Maine, then to Chicago, and finally to New York. In Manhattan, Kammerer took a menial job as the super for a building in the Village in exchange for his rent. In order to earn extra money to spend on Lucien, Kammerer occasionally even prostituted himself. Carr, who was basically straight and was interested in women sexually, was flattered by the older man's attentions. Nonetheless, he didn't want to end up in bed with him. After a lifetime of getting everything he ever wanted from his mother, he knew how to take advantage of the older man. While playing this game he told his friends that he found Kammerer's sexual innuendos and advances repulsive. In spite of the tension that caused, the two were close friends and frequent drinking partners, and when drunk their personalities clashed violently. Carr became mean-spirited, ready to fight anyone at the drop of a hat, while Kammerer became even more pathetically demanding of Carr's full attention. It wasn't a healthy mix and it was obvious to their friends that they were on a collision course.

On Saturday, December 18, a week before Christmas, Lucien decided to introduce Allen to another of his friends in the Village and go out drinking. Allen, who had never been drunk before, looked forward to getting inebriated. He planned it all out in advance so he could get the most from the experience. He said as much in a letter he wrote to his brother when he told him how he was looking forward to getting drunk, comparing it to one of their chemistry experiments. He recorded in his journal that he drank several glasses of Taylor's New York State Port wine and then waited for the effects of the alcohol as it went to his head. He observed how he lost control of each of his mental functions one by one. He was fascinated with the experience of trying anything for the first time, and this was only one of countless experiments he conducted on his own mind during his life. In the same letter to Eugene he mentioned a similar plan to go to a Japanese restaurant with a Japanese student and then compare that meal to Chinese foods. That December evening Carr and Ginsberg took the subway to the Village to pick up Kammerer, whom Ginsberg had already met in the Lion's Den, a student café on the Columbia campus where Kammerer had been working part-time as a waiter. Allen had found him striking in his white uniform, particularly because of his unctuous smile and shocking red hair. Ginsberg was uncomfortable with the homosexual innuendos in David's conversation, as when he looked at Allen and pointedly said, "I'm thirsty," and licked his lips in a licentious manner. Allen was too embarrassed to do anything but smile meekly. Although being free to acknowledge his homosexuality was what he desired more than anything else, Allen was confused about how to respond.

That evening they walked around the corner to introduce Ginsberg to yet another St. Louis friend, William Seward Burroughs II. He was twelve years older than Allen and, like Carr, had grown up in a privileged family and received a good education in the best schools. Burroughs was named after his grandfather, the founder of the Burroughs adding machine company, but he was not wealthy by any means. Both of William's parents worked to supplement the income they derived from the Burroughs company. They lived comfortably but not extravagantly and sent William a monthly stipend either from a trust fund or directly from their own pocket until 1959. Burroughs always resented the fact that people thought he was the heir to a fabulous fortune, when he only received what he considered a modest allowance of $150 to $200. Occasionally he took odd jobs to stave off boredom and provide a little extra cash, working for short periods as an exterminator, as a bartender in a Times Square dive, and once even as a low-level operative for the Shorten Detective Agency.

The night that Allen met him, Burroughs was living in an apartment at 69 Bedford Street, while pursuing male partners of his own. He and Kammerer had a good deal in common when it came to sex, alcohol, and drugs. They both liked to frequent the seedier joints in the Village, talking, eating, and drinking late into the night with good-looking, sexy young men. Years earlier, to impress one potential lover, Burroughs had cut off part of his own finger with a pair of shears and mailed it to him. As with Van Gogh's ear, the gift did not lead to romance, and in the end Burroughs was forced to seek psychological counseling. William had a droll sense of humor and a deadpan way of presenting the most outrageous comments, so everyone was always eager to hear what he would say next. The quartet of Allen, William, Lucien, and David spent hours hanging out together around the local bars like Chumley's, an old speakeasy that was down Bedford Street from Burroughs's place. Their lively conversations ran the gamut from philosophy and art to drugs and sex. Allen was impressed with Burroughs's wide command of literature and the broad scope of his general knowledge, but they were all inspired talkers once they got started. Allen, with his penchant for debating, was in his element. Semantics were a special interest of Burroughs, who frequently referred to Alfred Korzybski's[3] book on the subject, *Science and Sanity.* Everything William said to Allen seemed wise, as when he told him that art was only a three-letter word that could mean anything you wanted it to mean, a word that was defined by the user. Lucien and Allen had been arguing about whether a walking stick carved on the moon was art or not and when they asked Burroughs for his opinion he rejoined, "It is too starved an argument for my sword."[4] In doing so he was the first person that Allen had ever heard quote Shakespeare in a sensible way.

On that first night they met, a tipsy Allen rode the subway back to the

---

[3] Alfred Korzybski (1879–1950): Writer and theoretical expert on general semantics.

[4] The quotation is paraphrased from *Troilus and Cressida,* where Troilus says: "I cannot fight upon this argument; It is too starved a subject for my sword."

dorm with Carr and Kammerer. Lucien immediately fell asleep, but Allen and David stayed up into the wee hours talking mostly about their favorite topic, Lucien Carr. Kammerer stayed overnight, examining the books on Allen's shelves as they continued their conversation about Carr and then moved on to other topics like Thomas Mann (who was teaching at Columbia during the war) and their analysis of the German mind. Over the course of the next few months the two new friends shared many long evenings talking about books, smoking cigarettes, and comparing notes on Lucien, who enchanted Allen nearly as much as David. Together, Carr, Burroughs, and Kammerer made quite a raucous group. Once while drinking at Burroughs's place, Carr broke off a piece of his beer glass with his teeth. Kammerer tried to keep up with the antics and followed suit, which prompted Burroughs to go into the kitchen and return with a tray full of razor blades and lightbulbs as hors d'oeuvres. They constantly tried to top one another with outrageous behavior, one of their many traits that Allen found fascinating.

After the Christmas break Allen was reassigned to a dorm room on campus in Hastings Hall, but on any given night he might be found with his new friends in one of their rooms or at the West End Bar. Ginsberg sampled his first marijuana on one of his visits to Burroughs in the Village. As with his first experience with alcohol, he was curious scientifically about the effect tea (as they called marijuana then) would have on his mind. Allen was also interested in the social aspect of smoking it in communion with Carr, Burroughs, and Kammerer. As they all sat on the bed, puffing away, they became giddy. Kammerer made goofy faces in the mirror, while Burroughs became even more inscrutably Sphinxlike. It was a rare treat, though, for in those days alcohol was still the main catalyst for their nightly rendezvous, usually beer, but sometimes whiskey or whatever liquor they could afford. When drunk, Carr and Kammerer became animated and rowdy, Burroughs quiet, Allen silly. Late at night they'd find themselves sitting on stoops or lying in doorways after the bars closed, talking until daybreak.

Patiently, Burroughs explained all the workings of his intelligence to Allen, who was attracted by Burroughs's Old World, aristocratic nature. William had been in Europe before the war, during the era described so well by Christopher Isherwood in books like *Prater Violet* and *I Am a Camera*. He knew the Europe of Bertolt Brecht and George Grosz, "the glorious artistic time of the Weimar Republic in which, despite, or perhaps because of, the obvious cruelty of the police state that was emerging, it was clear to more liberated minds how true, free, tolerant, a bohemian culture might be. Burroughs had lived in that aura and brought that over to New York," Allen later said.

To seventeen-year-old Ginsberg his new friends seemed like exciting, sophisticated and worldly wise people. In the scheme of things Kammerer was
both wonderful and perverse. Allen was titillated by the sexual overtones of
their relationship because he had the same cravings for the handsome Lucien, but Allen was afraid to acknowledge them, except by veiled innuendo.
At the time he was confused by the erotic thoughts and fantasies he felt toward men. The world he grew up in considered homosexuality immoral, abnormal, a form of insanity in itself, and he wondered if this wasn't an
indication that he was as crazy as his mother. Nonetheless, Allen couldn't
help but feel sexually aroused by the young men surrounding him.

Ginsberg liked Carr because he felt comfortable with him, and Lucien
seemed willing to put up with many of Allen's self-indulgences. Sometimes
Allen could be overly dramatic, as when he wrote on the cover of his notebook "Out of the cracked and bleeding heart, Triumphantly I fashion—Art!"
At other times he might be hypersensitive and extremely moody, but none of
it seemed to bother Lucien. Allen even made it a point to learn Carr's vocabulary of sexual and scatological terms, which he carefully recorded in his
journal along with definitions of each one. He discussed Havelock Ellis's
books on sexuality and skirted the issue of homosexuality when he talked to
Lucien, for he was far too shy to acknowledge his interest. Like many college
students he liked sophomoric sexual humor and wrote down the lines of
many off-color songs and stories that were sung around the dorm. All of
them dealt with sex of a heterosexual variety, but several could be read in different ways with double meanings. One was taught to him by Lucien Carr:
"Violate me/In violent times/The vilest way that you know./Ruin me/Rav-
age me/Utterly savage me/On me no mercy bestow." This mildly masochist
song was closer to Allen's fantasies than he would care to admit and revealed
his secret desire to have an older, wiser, more confident man take charge of
his sexual education.

1944 ~

WITH THE START OF CLASSES again after the break, Allen found that his new friends were occupying more of his time than his studies were. He managed to maintain an A average in English that term, but he dropped to a C in chemistry and French. One course that he took with Lucien turned out to be his favorite. It was a discussion of the "Great Books" and was taught by Lionel Trilling, one of Columbia's superior minds. Both Allen and Lucien remembered that Ed Gold was the only other student in the whole class who was even slightly interested in the course. All the soldiers and sailors filling the rest of the seats were in school just long enough to become officers. They had their minds on the war and the part they were going to play in it and cared little about the great books. As a result Trilling had unlimited time to devote to the three boys, since it seemed that no one else bothered to listen to what he was teaching.

One night earlier in the fall, before he met Allen, Lucien had been introduced to a lively, sexy woman at the West End Bar, a favorite dive for students "slumming it" near the campus. According to Allen, the people who liked the West End were attracted by the mix of campus bohemians, intellectual maniacs, whores, fags, and drunkards who hung around the bar. The woman that Lucien met that night was Edie Parker, a perky Barnard student. Some of her friends called her "Bird Note" because she was chipper and had a birdlike face. Edie was the daughter of a well-heeled family from Grosse Point, Michigan. Her mother owned a small chain of shoe stores. Once Allen knew Lucien he also met Edie at the West End, too, where they had

Lucien Carr and Celine Young,
Summer 1943 ~

many heated discussions about the labor movement and politics over glasses of beer.

It was Edie who introduced Lucien to one of her classmates, Celine Young, another striking beauty from Barnard. Lucien began dating the sexy blonde, blue-eyed girl a few months into the fall term. Through Edie and Celine, Lucien also met yet another woman, Joan Vollmer Adams, who was sharing her apartment with Edie. Originally Edie lived with her grandmother not far from campus. When Joan put an ad in the paper for a roommate, Edie saw it as a chance to move away from her protective grandmother. She kept in touch with the old woman and her beloved dog, Woof It, but she, like Joan, was a bit wild and needed her independence. Adams was intelligent, attractive in some ways, but not nearly as pretty as Celine and Edie. She had impulsively married Paul Adams, who was away serving in the army, and Joan was raising their newborn daughter, Julie, on her own. She had already filed for a divorce by the time she met Edie. Self-destructive in many ways, Joan was always isolated and had become irrationally obsessed with her own complicated theory of universal radioactivity. Like Edie, Joan had an eye for handsome boys and had been living with a sixteen-year-old Columbia student named John Kingsland whom Allen knew from school. When Kingsland's parents discovered what was going on, they threatened to make trouble for

Joan if their son did not move back into the dorms, so Joan needed to find other roommates to share her expenses, which was how she met Edie. Before long, their apartment on the top floor of a six-story yellow brick building at 421 West 118th Street became the unofficial home of the nascent Beat Generation. Edie and Joan hit it off from the start and shared a love for interesting people and intelligent conversation. As outgoing as they both were, it wasn't surprising that their apartment was a hub of activity and a rendezvous point for all their friends.

Edie had been dating Henri Cru, a student at Horace Mann prep school in the Bronx, when she fell in love with his classmate and best friend, Jack Kerouac. Henri was glad to be rid of her so he could "play the field," and Jack was happy to have someone he could feel comfortable with because she balanced his natural shyness with her outgoing and playful manner. By late 1943, Kerouac was spending a good deal of his time at Edie and Joan's apartment, so in early 1944 when Burroughs wanted to learn the pros and cons of joining the Maritime Service, Carr brought him up to Edie's to meet Kerouac, who had already shipped out a few times and knew the ropes.

Jack Kerouac, four years older than Allen, was a native of Lowell, Massachusetts, who had won an academic scholarship to Columbia that included spending a year at the Horace Mann School in preparation for college. After breaking his leg in a football game, Kerouac had quit the team and before long had dropped out of school as well. He had come to New York in order to be a writer like Thomas Wolfe and he felt he didn't need a college degree for that. What he did need were interesting friends who would inspire him to write great stories, and in Joan and Edie's apartment he met some very interesting friends indeed. It was only a matter of a few days after Kerouac met Burroughs that Lucien showed up with Ginsberg to become part of their growing group.

Until his dying day, Allen vividly remembered climbing the stairs to the apartment where he met Kerouac for the first time. He was at once attracted to Jack's physical beauty, his maturity, and his ambition to become a writer. Jack was a tremendously handsome figure to whom women and men alike were instantly drawn. Being a football star and a budding writer to boot made Jack all the more irresistible to Allen, who had never met anyone who boasted of himself as a writer the way Jack did and who had supposedly written a million words already to back it up. Kerouac was eating breakfast in his T-shirt and chino pants when Allen met him. He looked sharp to Allen's eyes, with a dark complexion and princely face highlighted by a straight nose and beautiful dark eyes. Once again, even though surrounded by available women, Allen developed a crush on another man. He was intimidated at first when he met the older, more relaxed Kerouac, and with all the courage he could muster and for some unknown reason he paraphrased Shakespeare by saying, "Discretion is the better part of valor." It was the day on which Ginsberg was to move out of his room in the Union Theological Seminary and he wasn't shy about asking Kerouac to help him carry his stuff over to his new room, ten blocks away. Jack was surprised by Allen's nerve, yet he agreed. As Allen collected his valise, books, and clothes and locked the arched wooden door to his old room, he said, "Goodbye door." Then when they reached the stairway he turned and said, "Goodbye corridor, goodbye step number one, goodbye step number two" and so on all the way down the stairs. Naturally, Jack asked him what was he doing, to which Allen replied that he might never see that place again, "or if I do see it in the same body it will be twenty-five years later and it will be like walking back into an ancient classical dream." Jack mentioned that he frequently said goodbye to places when he left them, too. "We're only here for this hour or two and constantly saying goodbye," Jack said. That was their first moment of rapport and it made them realize that they were truly kindred spirits. Quickly over the next few weeks they became the best of friends.

Joan and Edie seemed to know just about everyone and Allen's circle of friends quickly grew. He was delighted to meet these young, intelligent bohemians, who read books, listened to opera and jazz, and talked knowingly about Wordsworth, Rimbaud, and drugs. Among his new friends, Allen may have been a "versatile, erudite, strongly intelligent person and respected for the solidity and variety of [his] politico-artistic accomplishments," as he immodestly put it. Although physically attracted to men, Allen tried to love women and went on dates to the opera or to concerts at Carnegie Hall. Still, he had to confess to his diary that his sexual interest in women was forced.

He envied what he considered the "healthy" relationship that Kerouac and Edie enjoyed. They seemed to be sexually compatible and loved to lie in bed together on quiet afternoons sharing their favorite snack of cold asparagus with mayonnaise and ripe olives. By World War II standards, the household was more liberated and heterosexual relations were freer than was generally accepted in the rest of the country. Homosexuality, although intriguing to the group, was still not out in the open except within a group of people who were recognized as "flaming queens." On West 118th Street the homosexual aspect of relationships was kept below the surface and brought out only during an occasional drunken flirtation. There was something seductive about the decadence of the household, whose libertine, bohemian atmosphere was both charming and appealing to Allen.

On campus he continued to be relatively hard-working and temperate, at least when compared to his new friends off-campus. In 1944 he became an editor for the *Columbia Review* and continued to work on the *Columbia Jester* as well. His idea about being a labor lawyer faded, however, when either Lucien Carr or Jack Kerouac (Allen later repeated differing versions of the story) pointed out his inability to put himself in the shoes of the working man. "What do you know about either labor or law?" one of them asked him. It was a gibberish abstraction in his mind, they said—"Better go and be a poet, you're too sensitive."

The hours spent in the apartment were filled with intellectual discussions about the secrets hidden in their own natures. They also experimented with whatever drugs they could find. They became obsessed with finding absinthe to drink, after they read about it in the works of several French authors, but it proved impossible to find. Absinthe is a green liqueur with a high alcohol content and a bitter licorice flavor that comes from wormwood mixed with a few other herbs. Finally Kerouac discovered some straight wormwood extract in a drugstore and they all drank a concoction of it mixed in Coca-Cola. Never had any of them felt so nauseated before; they vomited for hours. Even during Jack's most alcoholic period, Allen would never see him that physically sick again.

On June 3, the day that Ginsberg turned eighteen, he was required to take a preinduction physical for the army under the government's new draft laws. He was apprehensive about going to the war, but not because he was morally opposed to it, in fact he was strongly against Hitler. There were too many other things he wanted to do first with his life. On the bus to the induction center all the other boys began chanting "No 4-Fs allowed on this bus!" and cracking jokes about faggots. "Watch out for the doctor at table 17 when he makes you spread your cheeks," they laughingly warned each other. The problem of revealing his own homosexuality was one of Allen's worries with the physical exam. He didn't know if he should lie or tell the truth. During that first year away from home he was finding himself more sexually attracted to men like Carr, Kerouac, and even Kammerer. He still hadn't acted on his homosexual feelings, except in ways that could be interpreted as platonic or cuddly, but to his closest friends it was obvious that he wasn't interested in women nearly as much as in men. The army draft made him look a little more closely at his true feelings, because although declaring himself to be gay would eliminate him from active service, it would also officially brand him for the rest of his life. He knew that if he took that dramatic step it would be irreversible. Allen considered himself lucky when he flunked his eye exam so the need to declare his sexual preference was postponed. Because of his eyesight, if he was called up at all he would only qualify for "light service" duty. Later, upon the recommendation of his own doctor, Allen admitted to being gay and was classified as 4-F, "unfit for military service."

Back at school with his draft issue resolved, Allen seemed to live in a world of solitary introspection and spent a good deal of his time in self-examination. He felt that he, and in fact nearly everyone creative, was masochistic. "We love to be hurt and we love to have our unhealing wounds opened and reopened again; we sit staring in the mirror of art, fascinated by our own deformities," he wrote. He considered himself to be deformed by his homosexuality and was fascinated with himself because of it. He wondered what had made him that way and whether he could ever change himself. He was aware that his queerness would upset his family, especially his father, who would be repulsed by the very mention of it, so he kept his secret from them for as long as he could.

Along with plenty of self-analysis, Allen also scrutinized his friends' personalities and interactions, examining Lucien Carr carefully. Lucien was able to carry on sexual relationships with beautiful women while at the same time circulating in the homosexual subculture of the Burroughs/Kammerer group. He admitted that he liked to commit outrageous acts because his life and all the people he knew bored him. Allen theorized that many of Carr's social problems were caused by his repression of a true homosexual nature. He wished that Lucien would become more open in his feelings. Of course Allen was in no position to speak because he wasn't open about his own homosexual longings. Still he was critical of his friend and called Lucien a creative writer who didn't write, a man with wonderful ideas but no follow-through. When it came to putting his ideas on paper, Carr either destroyed the results or more often, didn't attempt to write them down at all. He said that since he was a perfectionist, whatever he created was not worthy because it was not perfect. As a result, in spite of talking passionately about art, he did nothing except criticize others. Allen wrote that Lucien assumed all the trappings of the bohemian, such as "red shirts, wild songs, drink, women, queer shoes, loud talk, arrogance, and infantilism," but was unable to create true art himself. "His ego demands intellectual recognition," wrote Ginsberg. One thing that they agreed on was that the real oppressor of art was modern bourgeois culture. They were both dissatisfied with all contemporary forms of poetry and each wanted to find a new style that would use a visionary vocabulary to discuss art and beauty. They hoped to formulate a "New Vision" that would govern their lives and art and in fact that's what they called their new philosophy. Carr found inspiration in his hero, Rimbaud, and passed on what little he knew about the French poet to Allen. All of this was completely outside their assigned course work at Columbia. Even though they were taking classes with some of the best teachers the school had to offer, they found that it wasn't enough. They weren't challenged by many of their teachers, although English teachers like Lionel Trilling and Raymond Weaver were better than the others. Allen was certainly pleased when Trilling invited him to his house for tea and conversation, but he left feeling that Trilling was too orthodox in his literary views. They even studied under the Scottish author David Daiches and the brilliant Mark Van Doren, but they were learning more from their lives outside the school than they would learn in the classroom.

By July both Lucien and Allen had moved into rooms at the Warren Hall Residence Club for eight dollars a week. It was a cheap place where Kerouac had once worked as a switchboard operator to earn spending money. There they had more freedom than in the dorms, and Allen took some summer courses hoping to speed up his graduation. By early August Allen was in more of a melancholy mood than usual and found himself composing a suicide note. It was only an intellectual, melodramatic exercise and didn't coincide with an actual suicide attempt, but it reveals how broken in spirit he was becoming by that time. He wrote it from the depths of self-pity he felt due to his unrequited and undeclared love for Carr and Kerouac. The note was written following a series of dreams he had in which he participated in sex with his father. Those dreams bothered him enough to make him seriously question his sanity. As he continued to play the amateur psychologist, he decided that the dreams revealed that he had been denied stability, economic, emotional, and familial, and love, emotional as well as physical, by his family. At the same time he noted that he had experienced two true loves, one in Paterson, probably referring to Paul Roth, and one in New York, probably a reference to Lucien, or maybe by this time Kerouac was more on his mind. "Mine was the life without childhood, the adolescence without love, the loneliness of the perverted genius," he wrote with his usual flair for the dramatic. "I have suffered more than all of you. If people knew me, I should have to commit suicide!" He felt that because he denied himself love he was either a martyr or a masochist. To keep himself alive, he consciously tried to experience everything as it was happening, reveling in both the immediate

joy and the anguish of life. One day while walking down the street near Warren Hall, he stopped and stared intensely at his surroundings realizing that it
was a stage on which he was meant to perform. He tried to memorize its
every detail, to be fully conscious, completely sensitive to the present while
it was the present, the living, the portentous, the sorrowful, all that would
soon become the forgotten past. It was one of his first moments of pure
awareness of experience.

Carr's disgust with Kammerer intensified as David's obsession grew ever
stronger. Even though Lucien's romance with Celine was blossoming, Kammerer would sneak into Carr's room in Warren Hall from the fire escape and
sit in the dark watching the handsome boy sleep. Lucien continued to lead
him on, either wittingly or unwittingly—opinions seem to differ on the subject. Allen tended to believe that Lucien secretly enjoyed David's attentions
and played coy with him on purpose. Lucien's solution to the Kammerer
problem was to escape via freighter on a mission to resupply the troops in
France following the D-Day invasion. He and Kerouac had nearly signed
on to a ship in Brooklyn before other mariners warned them that her first
mate had a nasty disposition. At the last minute they decided to wait for the
next ship.

A few days later Carr and Kammerer were seen drinking together at the
West End Bar until it closed at four in the morning. Then the two drunks
stumbled a few blocks down the hill to Riverside Park to sit on the riverbank
where they continued talking and drinking. As reported in the newspapers,
Kammerer once more pressed Carr for a blow job and drunkenly threatened
to hurt Celine. This time Carr was drunk enough and fed up enough to resort to violence. Pulling his Boy Scout knife from his pocket, he viciously
stabbed his old troop leader in the heart until he was dead. With a dead body
on his hands he panicked, and after he weighed it down with rocks he
dumped it into the Hudson River. Later Carr told his girlfriend that he could
not remember much of what had happened; his mind had gone blank. Allen
believed that Kammerer had become more aggressive and frightened Lucien
enough to cause him to draw his knife.

By the first light of dawn, with blood on his hands, Carr found his way
to Burroughs's apartment, but the only advice William could offer him was
to suggest he secure a good lawyer. Carr began to sober up as he rode the
subway back up to 118th Street where he found Kerouac. Jack helped him
get rid of the evidence, the murder weapon and Kammerer's bloody eye-
glasses. Then, for some unexplained reason, they went to the movies in Times
Square and had lunch. It was late in the afternoon before Carr decided that

he would have to face up to it and go to his mother for help, both legal and financial. Marion Carr was stunned, but had the presence of mind to hire a
good lawyer, who advised Carr to confess and throw himself on the mercy
of the court.

At first the police didn't believe Carr's story, since Kammerer's body had
not been found, but a day later, on August 16, when his body floated to the
surface, Lucien was arrested along with his "accomplices," Kerouac and Burroughs. Lucien was released on bail pending trial, as was Burroughs, who
was charged as a material witness and bailed out by his family for twenty-five
hundred dollars. Kerouac didn't fare as well. He was also held as a material
witness, but his father was so ashamed and disappointed in him that he refused to put up the five hundred dollars set for his bail. Jack and Edie had
been considering marriage, so they decided that if they got married immediately she would be able to get emergency money from her trust fund. The
police cooperated by escorting Kerouac from his cell to the Municipal Building, where Jack and Edie were married. Then she was able to get the bail
money and he was released. Lucien, only nineteen years old at the time, was
indicted on August 24, for the second-degree murder of thirty-three-year-old
Kammerer.

Before his bail was set, Carr was held in the city jail, where Allen and Celine brought him a copy of Gogol's *Dead Souls* to read. By coincidence, Kerouac had asked Edie to bring him a copy of the same book. At that moment
their own lives seemed to have the character of a Russian novel and for the
next few years they devoured books by Gogol, Dostoyevsky, and Tolstoi. *The
Idiot* by Dostoyevsky was to be Allen's personal favorite, with Prince
Myshkin, a sensitive, morally perfect misfit, as its title character.

Ginsberg was not arrested, since he hadn't known anything about the
murder until after Carr's arrest. When all the lurid facts of the murder were
revealed in the newspaper, Allen's father drove into the city to try to talk
some sense into his son. Allen had been asleep for nearly twenty-four hours
trying to escape from the terrible depression he felt, and he could barely
keep awake during his father's visit. The next day Allen wrote to him about
what he couldn't talk about in person. He described how Carr and Kerouac
had ridden around in cabs the day after the murder and discussed the ramifi-
cations—emotional, moral, and artistic. Everyone on campus was aware of
the friendship between Ginsberg, Carr, Burroughs, Kerouac, Kammerer,
and the rest, so Allen went to his professors, Lionel Trilling and Mark Van
Doren, for advice and counsel. On the Columbia campus a murder like this
naturally caused quite a lot of gossip, but through the efforts of the college

administration it was kept as quiet as possible in the press. The incident was portrayed as an honor slaying. The newspapers painted a picture of David as a child molester who had tried to touch a nice innocent student and had gotten his comeuppance. Carr's lawyer convinced the court that Carr had given Kammerer exactly what he deserved. Appearing before a judge on September 16, Carr pleaded guilty to first-degree manslaughter and the DA entered a plea for clemency on his behalf. On October 6, Carr was sentenced in General Sessions to an indefinite term in the Elmira Reformatory, where he was to serve a total of two years. Judge George L. Donnellan, in imposing the sentence, said he felt there was a better chance for the rehabilitation of the young boy by sending him to a reformatory rather than to Sing Sing, where he would live among hardened criminals. On October 9, Lucien was taken to Elmira with the hope that with good behavior he might be freed in as little as eighteen months, instead of serving fifteen years in prison.

Since there were no eyewitnesses and the knife that Carr and Kerouac threw down the storm drain in Morningside Park could not be found, a conviction for murder was not possible, even with Lucien's own confession. Although Allen was devoted to Lucien, he wrote about the sentencing to his brother and commented that it was "what I call getting away with murder!" Burroughs didn't agree with Allen's assessment and said that Lucien had no alternative under the circumstances except to stab Kammerer. A few weeks later Carr wrote to Ginsberg that his biggest crime was his betrayal of Celine and said that he realized now that he was truly in love with her. That was the last direct contact Allen had with Lucien for the next two years, since he was not permitted to directly communicate with his friends except through letters addressed to his mother.

The crime was all but swept under the carpet at Columbia, but it could not be forgotten by those directly involved. It was a catalyst for a complete change in their way of seeing and reacting to the world. No one could understand exactly what had gone wrong with their "New Vision" theories, which should have made everyone more tolerant of people like Kammerer. They all found the case fascinating in a salacious and demonic way. Each of them wrote about the incident and each began to formulate a new philosophy for himself. Ginsberg tried to capture his emotions in his poetry and journals. "I feel as if I am at a dead end and so I am finished," began one poem at that time. Kerouac retold the story in his books, and he and Burroughs collaborated on a fictionalized version of the murder called "And the Hippos Were Boiled in Their Tanks." Carr was the only person reluctant to discuss the incident in its aftermath. It could be argued that with all of Carr's intellectual talents, he could have become an important writer himself had it not been for this horrible incident. He certainly was moving toward a creative life; he was highly interested in art and literature, as Ginsberg's notebooks attest. After his release from the reformatory, he went to work for the United Press, rising to the level of bureau chief before he retired, but never publishing any creative work of his own.

Allen's world changed dramatically with the killing. He noted that when he walked into the West End Bar where there had always been a half dozen carousers to greet him, he found no one he knew, only strangers. For the longest time he could not get the song "You Always Hurt the One You Love" out of his head. Melancholy and lonely, he walked to the subway stop and sat on the bench that he and Kammerer had recently shared. When the train rolled past Allen shouted above the roar, "Kammerer, Kammerer, where are you? Dead? So soon?" and he wept. It was only then that he said he realized that Kammerer was truly, irretrievably, dead. When Allen and Edie went to pack up Kammerer's old room they found that someone had gotten there first and painted over all the penciled lovelorn inscriptions to Lucien that David had written on the plaster above his bed. "The snows of yesteryear seem to have been covered by equally white paint," Ginsberg wrote. Allen had been reading *Great Expectations* and *Wuthering Heights* for class and the melancholy tone of those books overflowed into his life.

Now that Allen realized he was not cut out to be a lawyer he began to feel that a creative life was his destiny. He asked himself if he wanted to follow convention, get a good job, support a wife and family, write poetry in his spare time, live and bury himself "among the million sands of faceless mediocrities," only to die unfulfilled. Or did he want to follow his creative desires and renounce all those responsibilities? Because his father had treated poetry as an avocation, Allen had never thought of it as anything but a hobby. He wasn't certain what he should do, but he sensed he wanted to break free of the societal bonds that restrained him, shake off his inhibitions and dependencies, and become free and jubilant to "soar above the rabble." He felt it was most important to be true to one's own self and "take his beating at the hands of God, if such a beating was to come," instead of at the hands of people he considered inferior. "If you must suffer, suffer nobly. Love, laugh through your tears, or cry, create and perhaps, perish," he wrote in his journal.

On September 1, after rereading much of Emily Dickinson's poetry, Allen composed another suicide note, more bitter in tone than the one from early August. He wanted to leave his books and desires to his father, his contempt and forgiveness to his mother, his affection to his brother, and "to all my friends I present my rue and disgust." He was emotionally drained by the events of the previous few weeks and had reached one of the low points of his life. Two weeks later, he remembered that he hadn't mentioned his soul, so he revised his mock will, bequeathing his disembodied spirit to oblivion. The note was obviously composed by a lonely eighteen-year-old whose closest friends had been dispersed by a tragic murder. He felt his old group would never reassemble and he was bereft with grief.

Ginsberg was a member of at least three different groups of friends at the time. The first and most important to him were the people he considered to be madman saints and artists, people like Carr, Kammerer, and Kerouac. He also included John Kingsland in that category and characterized him as having "a marvelous, irresponsible sense of humor." Kingsland would make a wonderful character for a novel, Allen thought, if he ever decided to write one. His second circle of acquaintances were those he called "sensitive youths, or young intellectuals." He placed classmates Walter Adams, Ted Hoffman, and Grover Smith into that category. The third circle included political scientists, the "historical crowd" around Columbia. Fritz Stern and William Wort Lancaster, Jr., whom Allen called a neurotic and a "socialist of sorts," were in that category. Lancaster, the son of a millionaire lawyer and chairman of the Directors of Foreign Policy Association, became Allen's roommate the following term. He also included his earlier roommate, Arthur Lazarus, in the third group. Only as an afterthought did Allen add the names of a few women to his list. He included Celine Young on his list of friends only after Lucien went to jail. Allen thought she needed a male friend who would not try to seduce her, as Kerouac had. Harriet Brodey was also added to his short list of female friends, described crudely by Allen as an eighteen-year-old with overdeveloped breastworks. Allen took Harriet out occasionally but reserved the bulk of his time for his male friends. Another woman's name cropped up in his journals a few times, that of a twenty-four-year-old poetess Allen had originally met in a bar. Later he introduced her to his father and speculated that their relationship might develop into something more than Platonic. He used his father's love of puns for the first and last time in his journal when he added that it would be "play" for her and "tonic" for Louis. Secretly he envied men like his father and brother who loved women and deep in his heart felt that his homosexual infatuations were decadent and corrupt.

That same summer, Allen's mother moved into her own apartment on West Eighteenth Street in Chelsea. She was once again out of the sanitar-

ium, but by 1944 she and Louis had permanently split up. For a while Naomi
had tried to live in the Bronx with her sister, Elanor Frohman, and later with
a cousin, Edie, on Rochambeau Avenue, but her eccentric behavior was too
much for either of them to deal with for very long. To support herself,
Naomi had found a job in Manhattan as the receptionist for Dr. Leon Luria,
a medical examiner with the National Maritime Union. She even dated her
boss for a time and slept on the leather couch in his office when she didn't
feel like going back to the Bronx at night. When she found an apartment
around the corner from union headquarters, Allen and Eugene helped her
move her few possessions and visited her occasionally. Her paranoid fear that
Louis and his mother were agents in a secret government plot to assassinate
her continued and as a result Louis could not come near her. At times
Naomi, whom Allen affectionately referred to as Nay, fantasized about becoming the Messiah and saving the world's less fortunate. Sometimes, cruelly, Allen would try to snap her back to reality by reminding her that she
was a failure and "a fat, middle-aged, neurotic housewife" to boot. Often
he didn't know what to say to her, and since she felt that Eugene was in on
the conspiracy against her, Allen was left to solve most of her problems
alone.

In the immediate aftermath of the Carr/Kammerer affair, Allen began
to write more poetry. In September he wrote "Elegy on Cemetery Rose-
bush," "Monologue on Deathbed," and "Jupiter Symphony." They were
largely influenced by his knowledge of the earlier romantic poets who hid
their meaning beneath layers of complicated structures and impenetrable
vocabulary. During this period he was also determined to use self-analysis to
examine his own sexuality. He even gave up masturbation for a while since
he believed it limited his heterosexual drive and social versatility.

His college classwork suffered due to his angst and lethargy over the
Kammerer tragedy and he took incompletes for two of his summer courses
that year. Since his tuition was $190, he considered it profligate to take
courses and not complete them. He felt guilty to be wasting his father's hard-
earned money and he resolved to do better that fall. By October, Allen had
made the decision to write a novel based on the Carr/Kammerer affair for
his English composition class. The case was so ripe with detail and significance that he believed it would make a brilliant, albeit dark, novel. After he
discussed his plans with Professor Steeves, his faculty advisor, Steeves
promptly reported him to the Columbia administration. On November 13,
Associate Dean Nicholas McKnight sent Allen an official letter stating, "A
matter of College policy is involved here, and I think I must ask you not to

choose this project. I would be glad to talk with you about the matter if you wish." McKnight had looked over the few pages that Allen had submitted to Steeves and deemed it "smutty," going so far as to label Kerouac a "lout." Allen gave up the project without much resistance and did other work, earning an A for his efforts, but it was not to be the end of Allen's problems with Columbia's administration.

1945 ～

ON JANUARY 2, Dean McKnight called Louis Ginsberg into his office at the college to have a talk with him about his son's future. The dean reported that although Allen's deportment seemed satisfactory and he was even showing some enthusiasm about working for the campus newspaper, something about him still seemed unsavory. Perhaps it was a homosexual temperament that lay beneath the surface that McKnight sensed and objected to, but that went unspecified at his meeting with Allen's father. Instead they focused on the fact that Allen didn't shave regularly as the other boys did and sometimes he sported a stubble that could almost be seen as a beard, unacceptable by 1940s Ivy League standards. He wore secondhand clothes that were often so wrinkled and dirty that he appeared to be a character from one of the Dostoyevsky novels that he so avidly enjoyed reading. Louis agreed with the dean, who felt that Allen had fallen in with a bad crowd. Since his studies were suffering the dean warned that unless something changed, he might not graduate from Columbia.

Dostoyevsky was only the tip of Allen's encyclopedic reading at that time. He noted in his journal that Burroughs had explained to him that every book should be read for a particular purpose. If he wanted to know about alcoholic withdrawal he should read Charles Jackson's *The Lost Weekend*, and the topic of homophobia leading to murder was obvious if you read Richard Brooks's *The Brick Foxhole*. Whether reading *The Castle* by Kafka, *Opium* by Cocteau, or *Dead Souls* by Gogol, they should be read for a reason. One book might teach about hypnosis, another about Egyptian grammar. At the time

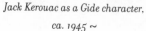

Jack Kerouac as a Gide character,
ca. 1945 ~

William Burroughs ~

Allen and his friends were also under the spell of André Gide's writings, which his father thought contributed to Allen's notion that even the abnormal was normal. After Louis left the dean he walked over to Lionel Trilling's office and asked him to help straighten Allen out, as he knew that Allen respected Trilling above all his other teachers.

By that time Allen's real mentor had become William Burroughs and not Lionel Trilling. After a short stay with his family in St. Louis following the Kammerer affair, Burroughs had returned to rent a damp, furnished room above Riordan's Bar on West Sixtieth Street. Burroughs could see that Allen was a natural writer and encouraged him to continue. Surprisingly, William was not writing anything to speak of at the time. The difference between the two was that Allen could fill one notebook after another with commentary, but after twenty pages Burroughs felt he had nothing more to say. He thought of himself more as an observer of life than a chronicler. Kerouac was also back in New York after a brief stay with Edie's family in Michigan, so he, Allen, and William resumed their discussions about the meaning of "supreme reality," a discussion they had begun before the murder. Using Rimbaud as their guide, they believed that a new reality could be discovered by examining their own confessions. Their ultimate goal was to be able to capture in writing the uninhibited nature of private speech. Burroughs, as their master, explained the difference between the semantic meaning of words and the things themselves, as he had learned by studying Korzybski. Burroughs also introduced them to the writings of Oswald Spengler[5] and his theory that civilization is cyclical and that America is in the declining period of her cycle. Over time this was incorporated into their own philosophy, which they continued to modify and refer to as the "New Vision." All these philosophical issues made Allen question his reasons for wanting to be an artist. Was artistry "the release of the pent up soul in self expression?" or was it merely the "exposition of thoughts?" he wondered. Why bother to write down thoughts and make them permanent anyway? Allen's conclusion was that "the ego is the true cause of permanent art, not the drive to self expression." He came to believe that it was an artist's desire for society's recognition and approbation that drove a person to create. Looking back on Ginsberg's entire career, this becomes a very interesting statement.

Allen seemed to need the encouragement and praise of his friends more than most other people. Perhaps it was because he was younger than many of his classmates at Columbia that he lacked confidence in his own ideas, or maybe it was a continuation of the feeling of abandonment by both his mother and father. It wasn't surprising then that, as Allen grew to manhood, he began a subconscious search for guiding figures, mentors, who would fill the gap created by his missing parents. Over the next fifty years Allen became devoted to many people he chose as his mentors. He was not the type of person who grew to love someone slowly, he loved instantly, wholeheartedly, and unconditionally. Once he made the commitment to love someone, he never wavered in his loyalty. He would support those people steadfastly, even if they became disenchanted with him. All the people he picked were remarkable people. They were all male, they all had distinctive attributes, and they all, to varying degrees, were able to return Allen's love and devotion. Lucien Carr, William Burroughs, Jack Kerouac, Lionel Trilling, Neal Cassady, Peter Orlovsky, Chögyam Trungpa Rinpoche, and Gehlek Rinpoche were a few of the people who helped him fill the void created by Naomi's insanity.

That fall, Hal Chase, a young, good-looking Columbia student from Denver, moved into the apartment on West 118th Street and took Lucien

---

[5] Oswald Spengler (1880–1936): German historian and philosopher whose most important work was *The Decline of the West.*

Carr's place in the group. He was nearly as handsome as Lucien and Allen fell in love with him at first sight. Life around the apartment slowly returned to normal and Allen continued to spend more of his time with his friends than he did in class. He continued to get his education on the streets and in the dives around Greenwich Village and Times Square. One day Allen ran into the eccentric writer Maxwell Bodenheim[6] and had a brief conversation with him, which he carefully transcribed in his journals. Ever the collector, he saved some of Bodenheim's pipe tobacco as a souvenir of their meeting. He recognized Bodenheim's minor fame as a writer and social commentator, but truly wasn't all that interested in his work. Later he heard rumors that Naomi had had an affair with Bodenheim during her bohemian days with Louis, but that was never corroborated.

Allen's friends, mostly older and all more experienced, were interested in experimenting with a variety of drugs. Allen was just as methodical about recording every drug he sampled as he had been about writing down the effects of alcohol the first time he got drunk. At one point he made a list of all of the drugs he had heard about and checked them off as he tried them. Marijuana was readily available in the jazz joints they frequented, but some of the other drugs proved harder to find safely. Burroughs was able to get some prescriptions for morphine, an extract of opium commonly used as a sedative, and gave Allen a half-grain dose that lasted about six hours. He stretched out on the couch in Burroughs's room, feeling relaxed, quietly waiting for the stupor that brought him clear, brilliant thoughts. On another occasion he took two No Doz tablets and discovered that it gave him more energy for writing and it helped bring some of his subliminal thoughts to the surface. He felt that it was an inferior drug for absorbing new ideas, though. Benzedrine, he discovered, made him amiable, but it caused depression. Another experiment with phenobarbital relaxed him and gave him much the same effects as the morphine, whereas codeine also relaxed him but gave him more sexual stimulation. Pantopon[7] gave him vivid dreams with vibrant images; in fact his first hallucinatory vision came in Joan's apartment while he was on Pantopon. Out of the blue he began to hear celestial music, which appeared to originate from an imaginary family phonograph. Allen checked other drugs off his list, including Delaudid[8] and Nembutal.[9]

---

[6] Maxwell Bodenheim (1893–1954): Poet and novelist, well known in Greenwich Village for living a bohemian life.

[7] Pantopon: A mixture of the hydrochlorides of the opium alkaloids.

[8] Delaudid: A morphine-like drug used to relieve pain.

[9] Nembutal: Trademark used for the sodium salt of pentobarbital.

Before long only laudanum,[10] cocaine, and heroin were unchecked. Yet even though he was extraordinarily eager to take every type of mind-altering drug he could find, he wasn't interested in taking them repeatedly. He avoided sustained use of any one drug, perhaps because he empirically knew that if he took the same drug too often he would run the risk of addiction. It was a pattern for Allen's drug use for most of his life. Curiosity led him to wonder what a particular drug would do to or for him and he would compare his reactions to those of Rimbaud or other writers who conducted similar experiments. Once he had an experience and had derived whatever he could from a drug he didn't try to recreate it again and again. He didn't understand why anyone would want to do that; for him it would become boring.

In March, still in his cataloging mode, Allen made a list of what he believed to be the five basic virtues: consciousness, stoicism, charity, love, and action. He felt he possessed only two of those virtues: consciousness and love. His list of five vices were: complacence and madness; sniveling, base Prometheanism and Satanism; niggardliness; neurotic antipathy; and quietism. Allen admitted to all of the vices except complacence and antipathy. All this was incorporated into the "New Vision," which Allen used as the basis for a long poem called *The Last Voyage*. "The new vision lies in a highly conscious comprehension of universal motives and in a realistic acceptance of an unromantic universe of flat meaninglessness," he wrote. Rimbaud had gone through a similar process, "refusing to pursue art as an unconscious devotee. He preferred to live in the realities accepting them as inevitable. Art for art's sake is a delusion. Only the dilettante is the exemplar of realism."

In addition to guiding Allen's reading program, William Burroughs had begun to psychoanalyze both Allen and Jack Kerouac for an hour each day in the room above Riordan's Bar. Burroughs was completely untrained for such a task and a few years later a professional psychologist blamed many of Allen's problems on William's amateur therapy. But at the time analysis was something of interest to both his "patients" and Burroughs seemed up to the challenge. It was a matter of Allen's lying on a couch and free-associating about himself, something that appealed to the rather self-centered young man who was beginning to question his own sanity. He knew that society had rules and standards with which he didn't agree and he was beginning to

---

[10] Laudanum: A tincture of opium used to relieve pain. It was widely used in the Victorian era by many poets such as Poe, Lord Byron, and Shelley.

think that either he was crazy or society was wrong. Kerouac used his sessions on the couch to exercise his remarkable memory by recalling obscure facts from his childhood. After one such session, when William accurately predicted that if Jack clung too tightly to his mother's apron strings he'd find his destiny closed around her, Jack went to Allen's dorm room to discuss it further. Kerouac had not left Columbia on the best of terms, so he had been deemed "an unwholesome influence" and banned from the campus. The dorm rules also prohibited any student from entertaining unannounced overnight guests, so they were breaking several campus rules when Jack arrived in Allen's room around midnight. Allen was putting the final touches on his most ambitious piece of juvenilia, *The Last Voyage*, his poem modeled on Rimbaud's *Le Bateau Ivre* and Baudelaire's *Le Voyage*. He had composed it in iambic quatrains somewhat imitative of his father's poetries. Now that it was completed, Allen was not satisfied and considered it a stupid poem for nearly all its fifteen pages of rhymed couplets. That night he and Jack talked about the poem, about their analysis with Burroughs, and about life and art in general. By the time they finished it was too late for Jack to return to his mother's house in Ozone Park, so he decided to sleep, chastely, in bed beside Allen.

For the previous week Allen had been feuding with the dormitory's maid, who never seemed to bother cleaning his room. He felt that she was not only lazy, but probably anti-Semitic to boot, so he resolved that if she wouldn't wash his windows voluntarily, he'd force her to do it. With his finger he scrawled "Fuck the Jews!" on the dirty windowpane. Below that he added "Butler has no balls!" a reference to the long-time president of Columbia, Nicholas Murray Butler, and added a hasty sketch of a skull and crossbones and a penis for good measure. It was all childish graffiti, he later contended, to prevent her from bypassing his windows again. His roommate at the time, William Lancaster, was in on the plot and agreed that it was an ingenious (and funny) approach to the cleaning problem. Of course they were being naïve, because instead of cleaning the mess the charwoman ran to the dean to report the obscenities. The dean also failed to see the humor in it and passed it on to the director of student-faculty relations, Dean Ralph Furey, to investigate. Furey happened to be one of Kerouac's ex-football coaches, so when he opened the unlocked door, he recognized the man in bed with Allen as Kerouac. Both boys were sleeping innocently enough, albeit in the same bed, but when Jack opened his eyes and saw his former coach, he jumped out of bed in his skivvies and ran into Lancaster's room to hide under the sheets. Allen was scolded and told to clean the window at once. When Allen went out, he found a bill for $2.75 for his unauthorized overnight guest and a note asking him to report to the dean within the hour. The dean immediately assumed the boys were "fooling around," but in those days Allen was too shy and timid to do anything but dream of blow jobs. He had never had sex with anyone, man or woman. He hadn't even confided in anyone that he was homosexual yet, so he was puzzled when the dean commented, "Mr. Ginsberg I hope you realize the *enormity* of what you've done." Allen definitely did not see the enormity of what he'd done, but aware of the dean's rage, he said he did and apologized, which seemed to be the best tactic at the time. Unfortunately the college suspended Allen that very day, March 17, and the dean dispatched a letter to Louis in the afternoon mail mentioning two infractions that were so serious that they could not be spelled out in his letter. Officially he cited "obscene writings on his window, and giving overnight housing to a person who is not a member of the College and whose presence on the campus is unwelcome."

Lancaster came to Allen's defense, since he'd been there all night and knew that nothing had happened between Jack and Allen. Louis appealed the college's decision to suspend Allen by asking Lionel Trilling to intervene, which his teacher did with only limited success. His suspension was lifted a year later and Allen was allowed to return to school with a letter from a psychiatrist who certified that Allen had been successfully treated for his problems. The result of his expulsion was that Allen felt he was surrounded by madmen in the Columbia administration. During his suspension, on Burroughs's recommendation, Allen read Céline's *Journey to the End of the Night*, in which the hero finds himself in the middle of a World War I battlefield. Céline's character realized immediately that everyone around him was completely mad and decided to flee as fast as he could. That text seemed parallel to Allen's current situation. Allen's father took it worse than anyone. He had spent the past twenty-five years worrying about Naomi's mental illness and now Allen seemed to be following her path to self-destruction and possible madness.

Many years later Diana Trilling reported the affair as if "Fuck the Jews" was the only thing Allen had scrawled on the window. Citing those words she determined that Allen was anti-Semitic and possessed a raging hatred for himself. The window incident became such an often-repeated part of Beat lore that Allen had to explicate it many times in the future and felt that his

Hal Chase, Jack Kerouac, Allen Ginsberg, and William Burroughs in
Morningside Heights, 1945 ~

critics were misreading the graffiti's significance since they didn't know the whole context of what had happened. He dwelt on the story so much that twenty years after the fact he was still identifying his cleaning lady as a "real grumpy old freak who read Westbrook Pegler and took *Daily News* editorials for Bible."

Following the Kammerer murder, the group who hung out at Joan's apartment had temporarily dispersed, and she moved to a new apartment in a building a few blocks south on West 115th Street. Her daughter, Julie, two years old at the time, wasn't doing very well emotionally. She had developed a nervous habit of biting and sucking her arm, and Joan was so involved in an amphetamine habit that she wasn't much of a mother for her. Kerouac and his new wife, Edie Parker Kerouac, returned to New York and moved in with Joan again, as did Hal Chase. The old circle of friends gradually re-assembled in the Cragsmoor building apartment, with the exception of Carr, who had begun to serve his sentence in the reformatory. With nowhere else to go after being expelled, Allen moved into Joan's apartment to share a room with Chase.

Before long a seminal discussion that Allen later referred to as "The Night of the Wolfeans" took place in his new apartment. In an all-night discourse, fueled by Benzedrine, two opposing viewpoints about writing, sex, and the future of America were debated. Kerouac and Chase took a position close to that of Thomas Wolfe,[11] or at least they shared an appreciation of Wolfe's ideas. On the opposite side, Burroughs and Ginsberg were designated as non-Wolfeans, or more to the point, Baudelaireans. Jack and Hal shared the belief that Wolfe exhibited the true optimism of the American spirit. They looked inward to America for inspiration, whereas William and Allen always seemed to be looking outward to Europe for their role models. Unspoken was that the split was also between the heterosexuals and the homosexuals, which created some underlying tension between the friends. William, and to a lesser extent Allen, wanted nothing more than to corrupt Jack and Hal, who acted so much like pure, innocent all-American boys. There was an undercurrent of anti-Semitism in the arguments that Allen didn't like either, but the discussion helped crystallize the differences between the two camps. During the course of the all-night debate, Allen had his second drug-induced hallucination caused by the Benzedrine they had taken when he saw the curtains fluttering in the otherwise still room. He alone was aware of what was invisible to the others.

A few weeks after his suspension, out of financial necessity, Allen applied for papers to work in the Merchant Marine as a "Helper Shipfitter." Ship work paid well during the war and it also afforded travel while allowing free time to write. Without classes Allen had plenty of time to hang out with his friends in what he referred to as "the lumpen world" around Times Square. He gravitated toward the seediest bars in the worst neighborhoods where he could find interesting characters, score drugs, and indulge in a little homosexual voyeurism. By 1945 Burroughs had already introduced the group to a petty thief, male prostitute, and minor drug dealer he knew by the name of Herbert Huncke. Huncke had lived in New York since 1940, after escaping a middle-class background in Chicago to indulge in the low life of Manhattan. Basically he was a hustler and when he saw this group of well-educated, middle-class boys looking for a little adventure amid the sleaze of Times Square, he latched on to them and decided that it would be profitable to become their guide and connection. His base of operations included most of the all-night cafeterias in the blocks immediately surrounding Times Square, as well as every dive bar and gin joint in the area. The Angle Bar, so named because it was a large L-shaped room with doors open-

---

[11] Thomas Wolfe (1900–38): Novelist whose books, such as *You Can't Go Home Again* and *Look Homeward, Angel*, told sweeping sagas about a new generation of Americans in the 1930s.

ing onto both Eighth Avenue and West Forty-third Street, was one of his favorites. The reason he preferred it was simple enough. If he sat at the back of
the bar and someone entered that he didn't especially want to see, he could
easily slip out the side door. Huncke seemed to know everyone worth knowing on the street, from criminals to policemen. In fact, in 1945 Professor Alfred Kinsey was canvassing people in the Angle Bar as research for his
pioneering study of American sexual practices. He recognized Huncke as
someone who could secure interesting subjects for his study, and he offered
Huncke a few dollars to bring him people willing to talk anonymously about
their sex lives. Huncke was more than willing to oblige. He brought Ginsberg, Burroughs, and Kerouac to Kinsey for study and their interviews were
integrated into his monumental study, *Sexual Behavior in the Human Male*,
published in 1948. Allen's responses undoubtedly were the most uninteresting of the group, since he was still a virgin.

Huncke was most valuable to the group as their connection to an entire
smorgasbord of drugs. He himself knew about, had tried, or was willing to
try any narcotic. He also knew how to score nearly any drug without getting
caught, something that was impossible for the uptown college boys. Ginsberg first met Huncke when Herbert and Burroughs were negotiating for
some Syrettes[12] of morphine. Initially Huncke didn't trust Burroughs—he
thought he looked like a narcotics officer—but then he said he realized that
William looked too much like a cop to be a cop.

Sometime during that year, Allen scored marijuana for the first time in
his life from a sailor hanging out around 105th Street. He remembered that
it was relatively unregulated there; the sailor had his family with him, and
Allen bought a cigar box full of grass for twenty dollars. Proudly he brought
the box back to Burroughs and Kerouac, his first chance to provide pot for
the gang. His later recollections about when he first smoked marijuana and
when he first got high are not consistent. At one point he mentioned that
shortly after meeting Burroughs and Kammerer, they all smoked grass and
felt the giddy effects together, which would have been in early 1944. On another occasion he said that he got his first grass from Puerto Rican mariners
on board a ship in New Orleans, which wasn't until January 1946. "I had already had Benzedrine, I had already had morphine and heroin before I had
grass," he said. On another occasion he said that the first time he felt the effects of marijuana was with his Columbia roommate Walter Adams. He de-

---

[12] Syrettes: A trademark for a collapsible tube filled with medicine, intended to be attached to a hypodermic needle.

scribed driving around the city high and stopping at an old-fashioned ice cream parlor where Allen had a giant black-and-white ice cream sundae. He remembered all the vivid details, the plate glass window, the sky, the entire experience, as one of the resplendent events of his life. Such are the inconsistencies of memory.

Life around Joan's apartment never ceased to entertain Allen. Adams shared not only Burroughs's serious interest in drugs, but also his disdain for politics and politicians. She was the first person that Allen said he ever met who openly made fun of a president. On April 12, as Truman was sworn in following Roosevelt's death, they listened to his inauguration speech together over the radio. "His tone of voice and prose is like a haberdasher's, what kind of a president is that?" Joan asked. It was catty, but it also impressed Allen because he had always assumed that the president must be smarter and wiser than everyone else. Especially during the war, government officials were not commonly questioned or held up to ridicule, and it made him a little more aware of some of their rhetoric and hypocrisy.

By spring as he continued to float aimlessly about without the structure of classes, Ginsberg had become depressed. In May he wrote in his diary, "Curiosity is the only thing that keeps me from suicide." While Allen was sharing rooms with one person or another, he dreamed of having an apartment of his own where his friends "could come, be fed, if they were hungry, and stay over if they had nowhere to go. A lot of good young artists are footloose at night and need some social center. Otherwise they will go around, as we once did, knocking on doors of acquaintances, waking them up in the middle of the night, rousing neighbors, and be in an unfriendly atmosphere which they have helped create. My ideal was a 'pad' or apartment where people I liked were welcome anytime and under any circumstances." It took him a few years, but that was exactly the type of apartment Allen created for himself.

In April he began training at the MSTS Welding School in the Brooklyn Navy Yard where he earned a spot welder's certificate and hoped to find a job in the shipyards. Then late in July, still suspended from Columbia, he formally enlisted in the Maritime Service in order to make enough money to finish college whenever they agreed to take him back. He arrived at the Sheepshead Bay training station in Brooklyn on Monday, July 30, a week before Hiroshima. By now he had sprouted to five feet eleven inches and weighed 130 pounds; he found himself one of a group of boys there whom he called "overgrown or warped adolescents." He mentioned that he was able to absorb the change to life in the service with an uncommon equanimity and dispassionate benevolence. The training station was governed by what he considered "a great deal of stupidity." The petty officers were all "fat-assed Marine sergeants" who gave confused and contradictory orders. The first thing Allen did at the base was to follow Burroughs's maxim, "Find out the layout and get the regulations down pat." He quickly figured out how to escape duties and punishments alike. He discovered that most of the procedures in the Maritime Service were mindless routines. They had no real purpose other than to maintain discipline through constant busywork. Since Allen didn't take the regimentation personally he found it refreshing and ended up enjoying himself. There was a beach on the base where he swam and lazed about in the sun on weekends, and the only thing he seemed to miss was music. He earned a reputation for being a "brain" when someone caught him reading Hart Crane, but he tried to cover it up by reading Batman comic books after that. Otherwise he was one of the boys, talking about Joan Adams as if she were his "broad," and cursing the "niggers" when he wanted to seem like a regular guy. In fact he quickly got into the habit of swearing about everything. His work consisted of buffing floors, washing latrines, and KP duty. On base he wore dungarees but on leave he wore navy whites or dress blues, which made him realize that he was really a serviceman.

In August, Allen received word that Burroughs was going to join him at the Sheepshead Bay training center and he began looking forward to their reunion. Before William arrived, Allen came down with a cold and reported to sick bay where the doctor laughed at him and told him he was goldbricking. Later when he vomited in a bathroom that was out of bounds he got into trouble, but it convinced them that he had pneumonia and bronchitis. That put him in the base hospital for a few lazy weeks. He took advantage of his convalescence by reading several books, including *War and Peace* and still more Rimbaud. One of the reasons he loved Rimbaud so much was that he felt Rimbaud was young and flexible enough to change his ideas to reflect his experiences. Rimbaud's writings taught Allen that Western civilization offered no hope for personal salvation and no vital activity either. When Rimbaud came to his conclusion that art was merely an escape, he abandoned poetry altogether and went to Africa. Allen wasn't ready to give up on art yet, but he thought it was a stroke of genius for Rimbaud to see that art was a tool and a salvation for battered souls. In sick bay he had lots of time to read, write long letters to his

Ginsberg (next to top row, third from left) at Sheepshead Bay, August 8, 1945 ~

friends, and work on his poetry, which he had been ignoring. He was ashamed that he had been writing obscure verse, wasting his time trying to formulate a "New Vision" that had little to do with poetry but was more philosophically or psychologically based. Early in September when Allen was released from the hospital, he was disappointed to discover that Burroughs hadn't lasted more than two days at the training center and was already gone.

Surprisingly, there is no contemporaneous mention in Allen's writings about the dropping of the atom bombs on Japan or the end of the war, both of which occurred while he was in training at Sheepshead Bay. In retrospect, so much has been written about how the atom bomb was the major catalyst that helped create the Beat Generation and change the course of American literature that it seems incredible that Allen didn't remark on it in either his journals or his letters of the period. There is no point in reading too much into this lacuna except to mention that it exists. Certainly the dropping of the bomb did change almost everything completely and forever, but what Allen thought about it precisely at that time remains unknown. Other biographers have noted that the end of the war was probably the reason that Burroughs didn't stay at Sheepshead Bay, but for Allen, his enlistment had been for employment opportunities, nothing more. With his Maritime Service training complete Ginsberg was qualified for duty on commercial freighters. His first posting was as messman aboard the four-hundred-foot slow transport ship the *Crossing Hitch*, which sailed from November 17 to 22 to ports up and down the coast.

1946 ~

AFTER CHRISTMAS, Allen worked from December 27 through January 15, 1946, as messman aboard the 523-foot tanker SS *Groveton*, a new ship with a quiet, romantic-looking young captain, bound for the port of New Orleans. Allen spent his spare time on board finishing a long poem he called *Ode to Decadence* and sent one of the first copies of it to Lionel Trilling, with whom he had been trying to remain in friendly contact. For the first time in his poetry, he began to use the jive talk that he had learned from the hepcats around Times Square, but Trilling thought its use was inappropriate in a formal poem. Three days out of New York on the *Groveton*, Allen became terribly seasick and experienced one of the most agonizing depressions he had ever known. When the ship docked in Norfolk, he was glad to set foot on land again before resuming the trip to Baltimore, and Newport News, and finally New Orleans. When he returned to New York he applied for the permit he needed to be a wardrobe checker in a nightclub, but he wasn't particular. Any type of temporary job would do as long as it paid the bills.

It was around this time that he decided to discreetly confide in Kerouac about his homosexuality, because the secret had been tearing him apart. Jack was spending the night in Allen's room at Joan's, this time Jack in the bed alone while Allen slept on a pallet on the floor. Lying awake, Allen said to Jack, "You know, I love you, and I want to sleep with you, and I really like men." Allen recalled that Jack moaned something like, "Oooooh, no . . ." and rolled over to sleep. There was no invitation for Allen to make any advances, but Allen was pleased that there was no rejection either. His declaration helped get things out in the open and cleared the air a bit, even if his passion remained unrequited. Allen later summed up his sexual history with Kerouac by saying that within a year or so, he blew Jack a few times and then once years after that a drunken Jack blew him, but there was never to be a great sexual union between them. Allen would have to look elsewhere for that.

When questioned later Allen dismissed the idea that he had "come out of the closet." He said, "It wasn't [a] closet; it didn't have that much style about it. It was just a whole change, growing up out of high school and puberty and closed-in-ness. It was just timidity and fear of rejection." Still, he wasn't ready to proclaim to society that he was queer. He was only brave enough to tell a few close friends, like Jack, who he hoped wouldn't reject him.

After a series of minor jobs, Allen shipped out again from June 8 through July 21. This time he worked in the saloon messhall aboard a collier named the SS *Jagger Seam*, carrying coal between Norfolk, New York, and Boston for the pleasantly named Mystic Steamship Company. Even though he had risked telling Kerouac about his homosexual longings, he wasn't brave enough to act on his "unnatural" urges yet. At a Revere Beach sideshow near Boston he ran into an old drunkard who mocked him about being a faggot. It was only a brief encounter, but it made Allen feel emasculated, and in an odd masochistic way he enjoyed that feeling, too.

During the voyage of the *Jagger Seam* Allen had been working on some new poetry. He wrote about thirty pages of hexametric verse, on the surface his best work to date, he believed, but he considered the result, *Death in Violence*, a "white elephant." It was merely pretty writing that said little of any real importance. Clearly he was having trouble finding his own voice, both in poetry and in life. With low spirits he wrote to Lionel Trilling on June 27, "In a way of speaking, I am closing my accounts with poetry." He planned to give up writing before he reached his breaking point and went crazy. He had read Trilling's *Matthew Arnold* while on board the ship but had found it much too bourgeois for his taste, preferring instead Stendhal's *Rouge et Noir* and Yeats's *The Vision*. Upon his return to New York he worked for a short time at Bickford's cafeteria in Times Square, busing tables and cleaning the floors. When he sat at the formica tables on his breaks, he daydreamed about making love to women, who by dream's end always seemed to transform into men.

Allen saw a good deal of John Kingsland during this period. Kingsland had been through analysis by that time and was making no effort "to be good and has gotten stouter and queerer and more indulged in appearance,

more desperate of mind," Allen wrote. When Allen first met him in 1944, he
wore a mask of social elegance and grace and reminded Allen of an Evelyn
Waugh character, but now his conversation had become more direct in his
homosexual allusions and was coarse, in Allen's opinion. There was no coolness left in him, no savoir faire, but in its place "demonism, slavery and disgust." Allen felt it was the result of the knowledge of self, and meeting the
self on its own terms. Allen was not turned off by Kingsland's outward,
more open, "queerness," but he knew it wasn't for him.

During the summer, Ginsberg petitioned Columbia for reinstatement.
On July 10, Dean McKnight wrote back, "I must ask you, as I did in March
1945 to take steps to provide me with the professional opinion of a competent psychiatrist as to your readiness to resume work in the College." Within
a few weeks, Dr. Hans Wassing sent an official letter to the dean: "There is
no doubt in my mind that he is sufficiently stable emotionally and sufficient
advanced intellectually to be equal to any disciplines required of him and in
addition be a credit to the school which he attends." Besides stating that he
was able to work hard, Dr. Wassing also assured Dean McKnight that "he
takes good care of his personal appearance and shows adequate attention to
the various necessary amenities of social intercourse." His conclusion was
that Allen was "pretty much as sound as they come." The lack of any technical medical language in the letter is probably due to the fact that Dr. Wassing
had suggested that Allen write the letter himself, which he did, and then the
doctor signed it. With the help of the friendly dean Harry Carman, who personally shepherded Allen's paperwork through the system, Ginsberg was
readmitted to Columbia that fall.

Life for the people in and around Joan's apartment began to change that
autumn. Just before his readmission to college, Allen learned that Carr had
been released on probation from Elmira. Lucien made it a point to stay away
from his old friends for a while and tried to keep a low profile as long as there
was any danger that his probation might be revoked. Allen longed to see him,
but Lucien avoided all contact. At the same time William Burroughs and his
oldest friend, Kells Elvin, were making plans to move to Texas and buy a farm
together as a business venture. William had developed a drug habit, and the
Texas project provided an opportunity for him to kick, so Allen was relieved.
Joan stayed in New York and kept in touch with Allen more than William did,
but she was suffering through her own serious amphetamine addiction.
Allen's biggest regret was that William wasn't around to continue the psychiatric therapy sessions with him, even if it had been only an amateur attempt.

By the beginning of September, Allen had finished a long introduction to his poem *Death in Violence*, taking Benzedrine again to give him some inspiration, but he had not written any new poems for several months. He was cheered when William wrote that he was clean and finally off the habit. He had quit mainly because Kells wanted to associate exclusively with energetic people, and William was forced to admit that junk seriously hampered his ability to be dynamic.

Things in Paterson were better, too. Allen's father's salary had been restored to its prewar level, and he had settled into a new apartment at 324 Hamilton Avenue. In 1947 he began to see Edith Cohen, a woman younger than him with two teenage children of her own, Harold and Sheila. A mutual friend had suggested that Edith might like Louis, and one day he showed up at her door to meet her with a copy of *The Rubaiyat of Omar Khayyam* tucked under his arm. Edith, who had separated from her husband, worked as a bookkeeper. On March 25, 1950, after a lengthy courtship, she was able to marry Louis after both of their divorces became final. For the first time Louis could settle down to a peaceful and emotionally rewarding family life. He continued to write poetry and publish occasionally, but the worrisome days with Naomi were over.

Allen frequently visited his father and once while he was there he wrote a review of William Carlos Williams's *Paterson, Book I*, for the local *Passaic Valley Examiner*. Allen had volunteered to do it so that he could interview Williams. He had never met Dr. Williams and hoped to ask him a few questions that might help him get over the writer's block he was currently suffering, but the interview never materialized. Moreover, Allen was embarrassed when the review was published because it had been changed by an overzealous editor who made it appear quite juvenile. Allen accepted it as a lesson to beware of editors in the future.

Allen was thinking about getting away from poetry and thought he might try writing a novel again. This time he would use himself, Jack, and William as the main characters and not worry about what Columbia thought about it. His plot outline called for each of the three characters to slowly morph into the personality of one of the other characters, but he did nothing more than make a brief outline of the complicated idea. During the summer he began to receive rejection notes from magazines like *Poetry* and *Partisan Review* for the poems he had mailed out earlier. His poems were so convoluted that he found he had to write long analytical introductions to explain them, and the more he looked at them the more he could see that they were pretentious. While he visited Paterson that summer he passed his time at a local bar, Sandy's, listening to jazz quartets and frequently went to the movies just as he had as a boy. To mark time until his classes began he even wrote diatribes against his old teachers. He likened his own poetry to Professor Steeves's work and made reference to "the dry udders of his pedantry." Allen had daydreams in which he lost the ability to write poetry altogether and pursued a business career. In his dreams he became rich yet was haunted by creative sterility. He drew the conclusion that he had tried to do too much and had therefore become confused about what style he should use in his poetry. What little he did write, he felt was not up to his abilities, and he tried to imagine what Burroughs would say about it. He called his own writing "self piteous or pretentiously hyperbolical." He wrote, "Until I am a man I shall never write good poetry, poetry which is tough in mind, poetry of which I approve: is spontaneous (should be) rejoicing in beauty, sensuality, sensation."

In order to get back on track and plunge into his academic studies, Allen rented a room with an Irish family, the O'Connors, on the Upper West Side, where he stayed from October 1946 until July 1947. During that time he applied himself to his courses, determined to finish his degree. He knew how important it was to his father, and he wanted to complete his formal education for himself, too, since he had already invested so much time in it. His English and history classes went well, but he dropped Arabic. In his opinion Arabic was the only challenging course he was taking that term, but it demanded too much of his time to do it well. He took weekend trips to Boston and Paterson to help keep his spirits up, but he was generally depressed by college life. Allen, Joan, and William (when he was in town) spent time together discussing topics that ranged from ancient Mayan and Egyptian magic to telepathy, all of which he found more rewarding than his stale academic studies.

Allen's psychological health wasn't improving and he knew that if he was going to make any progress, he would have to take some positive action. He felt he had unwisely used his psychoanalysis with William to escape from making decisions. Later Allen would write "he [Burroughs] tried unsuccessfully to psychoanalyze me, it was a mistaken psychoanalysis but it was an interesting experience, I spoke to him an hour a day for at least a year and we learned a lot." Allen and William explored most of his emotions and one day Allen had burst into tears saying, "Nobody loves me!" Burroughs had turned out to be a delicate and generous teacher in many ways, but even Allen began to have his doubts about Burroughs's abilities in some areas. He had to agree with Joan when she told Allen that William probably couldn't analyze his or anyone's sex problems because he was too uneasy and embarrassed about his own.

By late November Allen had become more depressed than ever. Now that he was back in school everything important seemed to be going badly. He had all but stopped writing poetry and his reading was desultory, with no real purpose. He found he had no energy and was fatigued all the time. As a result he had begun sleeping much more than he needed to and when he was awake he was irritable, lonely, and bored. At one point he wrote what he considered a "sloppy" paper on Korzybski for one of his classes. That paper gave him the idea to expand it and combine the ideas of Korzybski, Spengler, Freud, and Abram Kardiner to form another new philosophy, but it was all becoming overwhelming. His independent experiments with Benzedrine had made him more curious about imagery and hallucinations and he started reading about the process of thought in clinical psychology books he borrowed from the library.

Finally, that fall at the age of twenty, Allen had his first sexual experience. He picked up a thin blond man from Chicago at the Hotel Astor Bar in Times Square, then known as a homosexual hangout, and took him back to his rooming house. There, without much foreplay, the man fucked Allen in the ass. Forty years later Allen remembered, "I smelled the brown excrement staining his cock, I tried to get up from bed to go to the toilet a minute, but he held me down and kept plunging at me, serious and said, 'No I don't want to stop, I like it dirty like this.'" Allen thought that the comment was so remarkable that he repeated it in his writings several times. His new acquaintance may have been named Robert Lovett—Allen could never quite remember for certain. The next morning Allen left a dollar for him and went off to class expecting Lovett to be there when he returned in the evening, but he was heartbroken to find him gone. It was only a few days later that the truth dawned on Allen that Lovett was a hustler when he saw him in another queer bar picking up an older man.

In November Joan Adams suffered a complete breakdown due to her Benzedrine habit and was dragged off to Bellevue's psychiatric ward. Her father came down from upstate New York to take custody of his granddaughter, Julie, and the apartment was closed. Allen wrote to Burroughs on his farm in Texas to tell him the sad news, and William immediately rushed to New York to get Joan out of the hospital. Once released, they stayed together in a Times Square hotel for a short time and it was there that William probably made Joan pregnant in an uncharacteristic heterosexual tryst in celebration of her freedom. Burroughs had begun working a farm near New Waverly in east Texas and the couple decided to retrieve Julie and return to the farm together. One afternoon before they left Allen went with them to the Museum of Natural History to see an exhibit of Mayan Codices, which was a mutual interest. By that time, Allen was over Lovett and had a crush on a student by the name of Heaze. Burroughs jokingly said, "Why, you can't even get a Heaz-ard on," at which Joan giggled and added that it was because Allen was much too delicate. During the visit Allen and William also shared heroin several nights in a row, and Allen was lucky not to develop a habit before William left. William stopped to visit his family in St. Louis on his way back to Texas, and Joan and her daughter took the train to meet him at the farm, not yet aware that she was pregnant.

On November 30, Allen bought some Pantopon and shot half a grain, then lay down on his bed to read Baudelaire's "Spleen" and Yeats's "The Gyres." It was Allen's opinion that one could understand Baudelaire only if one had similar experiences with drugs and the same compulsion to take them. Since Burroughs seemed committed to his Texas farm idea and wouldn't be back in New York for some time, Allen decided to seek professional psychoanalysis. He went to see Lionel Trilling to ask him for a recommendation, since Allen relied on him quite a bit for advice. Trilling agreed that psychoanalysis was a good idea, but he didn't have any practical suggestions for any particular doctors and certainly didn't have any idea how Allen could pay for the consultations either. During their meeting, they talked about writing, and Trilling recommended that Allen eliminate the component of self-pity from his poetry. He sympathized with some of Allen's problems, but generally he thought the younger man was too self-indulgent and told him that it was about time for him to grow up. Allen didn't appreciate that advice and thought about writing a short story which would tell "Trilling types" to "go rob a bank, get off your ass and go out and do something." Allen felt that Trilling's scolding showed that Trilling was a hypocrite and that Trilling displayed conflicting ideas of humanistic social forms with his conduct toward him.

Thanksgiving that year was a lonely time for Allen. He had tried to get in touch with Carr, but Lucien was intent upon keeping his distance and didn't answer Allen's repeated notes. Kerouac, whose father had died earlier that year, was still living in Ozone Park, Queens, but he wouldn't come to the city to see him over the holiday either, and Allen wasn't welcome in Jack's house because his mother had taken a strong dislike to him the moment she first laid eyes on him. She felt that he was a bad influence on her son in much the same way that Louis felt Allen's friends were corrupting him. The fact that he was a Jew didn't help, as her feelings toward Jews were not Christian.

On December 3, Allen went to a psychiatric clinic and begged to be given analysis. He was told to come back after Christmas, since he couldn't afford to pay for private sessions, and he was forced to wait until they could fit him in. One night in a bar, his Columbia friend James Fitzpatrick declared his homosexuality in front of everyone. Allen admired him for announcing it so publicly, but even with Fitz as an example it was something that Allen was incapable of doing. He continued to use Pantopon until he realized he was starting to crave it. At that point he knew he was in serious danger of becoming hooked, like many of his friends, and he knew that psychologically he couldn't afford to do that. He had been using it to relieve the anxiety of boredom and loneliness, but he was finding it less helpful for visual imagery than he had at first. Instead, it was inducing a false sense of achievement. After each shot, his vanity was instantly satisfied and he was relaxed and less compulsive. His first dose had come under Burroughs's watchful eye in his apartment over Riordan's Bar. That night Allen had ridden home on the subway smugly, as if he were "bearing a sacred cup among the crowd," he wrote. Now he decided to exercise his remarkable powers of restraint and self-control by vowing to limit Pantopon use to not more than twice a week in the future. He made a chart for himself and followed it until he broke the habit. To Allen it was all mental discipline and no different from his decision to limit his masturbation. Several times in his life, Allen sensed when he was on the verge of picking up a drug habit and had the self-restraint to stop before he became hopelessly addicted. Not all of his friends could do the same. Later, in a draft of the preface to *Junky*, Burroughs stated, "You become a narcotics addict because you do not have strong motivations in any other direction. Junk wins by default. I tried it as a matter of curiosity. I drifted along taking shots when I could score. I ended up hooked." Possibly it was easier for Allen to avoid addiction because he had so many other things that he wanted to do. He was driven by ambition and curiosity, even when he was in a deep depression. To keep track of his drug use Allen wrote it all down in his journal. On December 12, for example, he took opium and noted that the effects were "more dull than before," but "strangely satisfactory," and he wondered whether he should increase the dosage. Since he allowed himself to take opium no more than once a week, he noted that his next dose would be on December 19. It was all somewhat scientific.

Allen's self-control didn't mean that he abstained from drugs, but it did mean that he would do everything humanly possible to avoid getting hooked. He recorded that he took Benzedrine on December 8 for the single purpose of writing a paper for class. He was pleased with the results and the Benny gave him zest enough to finish the assignment before the deadline. The next day he suffered a letdown from the aftereffects of the drug and started to think that writing things like college papers and critiques of his own poetry was a waste of time; his time would be better spent on writing the poetry itself. With Burroughs away, Allen hung out more often with Herbert Huncke, and one night in early December Herbert took him over to West End Avenue to meet a friend of his, Vickie Russell. Vickie, whose real name was Priscilla Armiger, was like Huncke in that she was also rebelling against her middle-class upbringing. She was a beautiful, six-foot-tall red-head, two years older than Allen, who was so striking that she turned heads when she walked down the street. She was experienced with amphetamines and taught the group such practical matters as how to use over-the-counter inhalers to get high. To pay for her addiction she became a call girl and a petty thief. Allen and Vickie got along well, but Allen's sexual interest in women couldn't be aroused, and he mused, "Too bad I'm not ripe for her." He saw her frequently but she was elusive and had a habit of dropping out of sight for long periods only to resurface later.

A week before Christmas Allen was able to contact Lucien, and they met for a couple of drinks. Allen had been waiting for two years to tell him that he was queer, and he wasted little time before telling Carr his secret. "So that's the set up!" he remembered Lucien saying. Unlike Kerouac, who didn't want to talk about it, Lucien was willing to discuss Allen's homosexuality as much as Allen liked. It almost sounded romantic the way Lucien talked about it in his morbid bohemian way, but Allen sensed that Lucien was not as experienced as Allen had assumed after hanging out with Kammerer. "I suppose the conversation was a sort of memorial landmark, after all these years," Allen wrote.

1 9 4 7 ～

ALLEN DIDN'T HAVE ANY PLANS for New Year's Eve and found himself alone. He decided to drop in to see Vickie, but she had gone out to the movies with Jack, Lucien, and Celine, so he wandered over to visit some other friends, Norman Schnall and Bridget O'Reilly. They blasted some marijuana and Allen sat in Bridget's orgone accumulator[13] without any noticeable effect. Schnall had some bongo drums and practice pads and as they smoked the grass they began to beat out rhythms, exchanging syncopated messages back and forth. Allen had his third visionary experience when the drumbeats seemed to give way to a secret sexual connection between Bridget and Allen. He even thought that they had both had orgasms, but in the bathroom he discovered he hadn't ejaculated, even though the sensations were as strong as if he had. He was puzzled why it had been directed at Bridget instead of Norman, because of his queerness. They played telepathically until six in the morning, Allen noticing that in the dim light Bridget began to look more and more like Lucien to him.

By January 9, Joan was settled on the New Waverly farm and sent fifty dollars to Allen for the purpose of buying Huncke a one-way ticket to Texas.

---

[13] Orgone accumulator: Wilhelm Reich (1897–1957) claimed to have discovered a universal cosmic and biological energy. He called this energy orgone and believed that a box built with organic material on the outside and metal on the inside could collect and accumulate orgone from the atmosphere. He further claimed that exposure to orgone, particularly through sitting in the accumulator, promoted health and vitality and was even an effective treatment for cancer. The FDA charged him with fraud, and a discredited Reich died in prison in 1957.

She knew better than to send the money directly to Huncke, who'd have no hesitation about using the cash for dope, so she trusted Allen to get him on the bus safely. They believed Huncke might like living on the farm, and he could help them grow a bumper crop of pot, figuring that if you smoked it you'd know how to grow it. For that reason they asked him to bring along a jar of marijuana seeds from the city. Allen did his best, but Herbert ended up getting so high before he left that he forgot to buy the pot seeds. Allen was doing more than his share of drugs, too, in spite of himself. A few days before Huncke's departure Allen tried mixing pot and junk together for a second time in a week. It was beginning to get risky and might have led to a real addiction if something else hadn't happened to distract him.

In late 1946, a young, good-looking man, just as handsome as Jack Kerouac, stepped off the bus in New York with his sixteen-year-old wife. His name was Neal Cassady. He had heard so much about the city from his Denver buddy Hal Chase that he came to see it firsthand and meet Chase's friends for himself. He was even thinking about going to college in New York, although academic studies were never his strong suit. Kerouac and Ginsberg had heard so much about Cassady from Chase that they felt they almost knew him. Neal had grown up on the wrong side of the tracks in Denver, and he knew the ins and outs of the street almost as well as Huncke. He was sharp, witty, gregarious, and lived for excitement and sexual conquests. He claimed he needed sex every day to live, sometimes several times a day, and it didn't matter where he found it. His wife, LuAnne Henderson, was highly sexed herself, so they were a perfect match. They may have been sex addicts before the phrase was coined. Directly off the bus they walked to Times Square and giddily took in all the bright lights and frenzied activity in the heart of the city. After eating their first meal at Hector's Cafeteria they went uptown to meet Chase and his friends seventy blocks north at the West End Bar. The moment Ginsberg saw Cassady, he fell in love again, only this time it would be reciprocated, at least to the extent that Neal was capable of loving any one person.

Neal and LuAnne stayed in Bob Malkin's apartment[14] on Lexington Avenue in Harlem for the first few days. Neal found a job parking cars in a lot, while LuAnne worked in a bakery. With their combined wages they found they could afford a cheap place of their own, so they moved to Mrs. Cohen's rooming house in Bayonne, New Jersey, but their stay was brief. After LuAnne and Neal had a knock-down drag-out fight in early January, LuAnne re-

---

[14] Bob Malkin was the cousin of a friend, Allan Temko.

Neal Cassady ~

turned to Denver and Neal decided to stay in New York with his new friends, Jack and Allen. A few days after LuAnne's departure, Allen reveled in a wild sexual weekend with Neal. As usual his euphoria was short-lived, and by Tuesday he was in the depths of despair again. After a weekend of debauchery, Allen realized what he was missing through his abstinence from physical love. He sat in his room for two days waiting for Neal to return to his bed and believed he would enter hell if Neal failed to show up. Already he began to dream of a new kind of life with Neal as his partner, and he wanted to suggest to him that they live together for a season, long or short as it might be. Allen was driven most of all by sexual desire and was encouraged by Neal's openness to him as a lover. He felt that he might be able to barter his intellectual knowledge for sex. He would offer Neal his learning and his cosmopolitan guidance as the "older" man, even though Allen was only twenty at the time and Neal was four months older than he was. Still, Neal seemed younger to Allen. As he waited alone for Neal he began to consider suicide as one of his options if Neal rejected his offer. Waiting gave Allen the opportunity to wallow in self-pity. Now that he had been able to experience the joy of sex with Neal, he couldn't imagine returning to the world of celibacy or heterosexuality. His spirit was enervated by the sheer thought of it. He found it difficult to honestly commit his feelings to paper in his journal, almost as if someone were reading over his shoulder who would discover his private inner demons.

During that winter Allen took a class on psychodynamics from the noted psychoanalyst Dr. Abram Kardiner. Dr. Kardiner ran a free clinic in

1 9 4 7　　　　　　　　　　　　　　　　　　　83

New York using his advanced psychology students as therapists, and Allen tried to enroll in it as a patient. He was turned down because, as Allen tried to explain. "I would have been too complicated, and my defensiveness subtle, for the unprepared control analysts." Kardiner suggested he find a more experienced analyst with some auxiliary psychiatric training or a psychoanalytic sanitarium for treatment. If all else failed, Allen's backup plan was to enter Reichian analysis. He had the address of Wilhelm Reich and wrote to him after being turned down at Kardiner's clinic. Burroughs had been independently exploring Reichian theories for years and was a proponent of his orgone therapy, which was both popular and controversial at the time. Burroughs himself had been psychoanalyzed by Doctor Ernst Federn,[15] who had once been a student of Freud, so through William, Allen felt that he had a direct transmission from the source of psychoanalysis. When he explained it all to Neal, he sobbed and told him about his conferences with Trilling, his phone calls to Dr. Kardiner, and the physical sickness he suffered after being refused treatment.

Neal saw Allen frequently for a while, although not nearly as much as Allen would have liked. Throughout February he and Neal smoked big marijuana bombers together and listened to jazz records. The pot helped them enter a world composed entirely of rhythms. With grass Allen could visualize a whole orchestra working together and experienced an orgasmic, spontaneous kick. They listened to a lot of Lester Young, Illinois Jacquet (Allen especially liked Jacquet's recording *Jazz at the Philharmonic*), Gene Krupa, Dizzy Gillespie, and Count Basie.

When classes began again in February, Allen applied himself to his studies with unprecedented vigor and set his sights on graduation. He signed up for four different English courses and did well in all of them. His strategy was to discipline himself, both in his school work and in his emotional entanglement with Neal. He knew that it would relieve his despair if he tried to move slowly. Allen was intelligent enough to recognize that Neal was a consummate swindler who took advantage of the people around him, yet at the same time he felt that Neal would be considerate of Allen's "special" needs. He was confident that Neal would do no wrong toward him and trusted him from the very start.

Apart from sex the thing about Neal that most intrigued Allen was his boast that he was capable of being aware of sixteen levels of thought at the same time. He said that he could concentrate and jump from level to level

---

[15] Ernst Federn (b. 1914): An Austrian-born pioneer of psychoanalysis.

at will. That impressed Allen, who tried it himself and could only identify four simultaneous thought levels at one time. It was easy for Allen to accept that his own thoughts were shallow, but he wasn't sure he believed in the existence of as many as sixteen increasingly deep and buried levels of awareness. He did believe that people like Neal and Jack truly experienced things more profoundly in a way he couldn't. Other people might think that Neal was a con man straight and simple, but Allen saw something much more in him.

Of course, it didn't take Allen long to fall head over heels in love with Neal. Since this was the first time that actual sex played a role in any of his relationships, it strengthened his feelings toward Neal all the more. While waiting for Neal, Allen passed his time by listing all the possible combinations of sexual positions that he wanted to try with him. "Try him laying me again, try breast to breast position, try 69 again coming both at once, try sitting on his chest and making him blow me, try laying his mouth, French kissing, etc., make him give me a trip around the world, try browning him (this requires real passion), also a good massage, laying his anus, laying him backward, thighs, kneeling and blowing, both ways, wrestling, whipping? Have I guts? Trip around world, complete, winding up with blow job. No, I want some real hip sex, what is it?" Before long Allen sensed that Neal was getting bored with him sexually and he gave up trying to make it with him every time they got together. He wrote in his journal, "Certainly my sexual advances are not pleasing? or are they?" He had no confidence in himself but hoped for the best.

Neal could never stay in one place for long. On March 4, he caught the six-thirty bus back to Denver. Allen went with him to the bus station and after saying goodbye walked the sixty blocks home. He didn't cry but he did feel melancholy, so he stopped to see Vickie at her apartment and they ended up having oral sex. Allen was surprised by how much he enjoyed it. For a while he felt that he had gained a peace and calmness through his affair with Cassady. It was an unusual feeling. He was even glad on some level to see Neal leave, but knew that he would need and miss him as the days passed by. He also realized that he wanted more than the few emotional crumbs that Neal had thrown his way; he wanted a real one-to-one relationship.

A Further Proposal,
CP, p. 757

A Lover's Garden,
CP, p. 758

It was also quite typical of Allen's relationships with his friends that he tried to see their side of every issue. Perhaps it came from his debating experience, but he knew both sides in an argument usually had a point. With that in mind he reconsidered the intense discussions of the "Night of the Wolfeans." It had been only an intellectual feud, which culminated when he sided with William and Joan, but he was loath to abandon the emotional side championed by Jack and Hal. Sometimes his ability to see all viewpoints meant that he did not feel confident voicing his own opinion. As he thought about it more carefully, he noted that if he followed his emotions and acted automatically, he became afraid of nearly everything. That's how he had gotten into trouble at school, by letting himself become so eccentric and disordered that it evolved into melancholic and suicidal thoughts. On the other hand, when he followed his intellect alone and weighed his actions before committing to them, he ended up shallow, mechanical, and sterile. Although he was now twenty he still sounded like a kid as he wrote, "I am really the lowest of the low, really, no one is as useless and unlovable as myself."

Following Neal's departure, Allen redoubled his efforts to enroll in some sort of psychoanalysis. He wrote to Dr. Wilhelm Reich, then in Forest Hills, New York, on March 11. "I lead an extensive and diverse social life and have a good number of close friends, both 'bourgeois' and 'hip,' that is, I have found myself drifting into intercourse with the periphery of criminal circles in NY. I have used narcotics pretty extensively, but not to the point of addiction to any; and by now I have stopped the use of them completely. My main psychic difficulty, as far as I know, is the usual oedipal entanglement. I have been homosexual for as long as I can remember, and have had a limited number of homosexual affairs, both temporary and protracted. They have been unsatisfactory to me, and I have always approached love affairs with a sort of self contradictory, conscious masochism. I have had a few experiences with women which were unsatisfactory from the start since my motivation was more curiosity than interest, and I have been pretty consistently impotent when with a woman. I have had long periods of depression, guilt feelings— disguised mostly as a sort of Kafkian sordidness of sense of self, melancholy and the whole gamut I suppose."

Allen had been hoping to get into some type of formal psychoanalysis for years, but with only a fifteen-dollar-a-week allowance from his father and his part-time jobs, he wasn't able to afford professional therapy. He had been grateful for what Burroughs had been able to do for him, but he realized that "the inevitable and unfortunate effect was that it left me washed up on the shore of my neuroses with a number of my defenses broken, but centrally unchanged, with nothing to replace the lost armor." Before long one of Dr. Reich's assistants wrote back to him recommending three doctors in the area who might agree to provide affordable orgone therapy. Within a few weeks

Allen had an appointment in Newark with Dr. A. Allan Cott, who outlined a course of therapy for him. He saw the doctor a few times but his treatments were stopped because he refused to give up smoking marijuana as the doctor requested. Dr. Cott made notes that Allen was "too mental, lonely and personally sadistic" to bother dealing with.

As spring wore on Allen continued to attend classes and relaxed by listening to as much jazz as he could. He loved Billie Holiday, Lenny Tristano, Dinah Washington, and a group named the Three Bips and a Bop. On one of his forays to the Village bars he bumped into W. H. Auden and talked with him about poetry. The two seemed to have little in common, much to Allen's disappointment. Auden disliked many of Allen's literary heroes, like Louis-Ferdinand Céline and Saint-John Perse, so they wound up in a silly superficial conversation about subways, the weather, and Mozart. Allen found the older, more worldly Auden aloof, but in contrast thought his companion, Chester Kallman, was a kindred spirit. Chester was rather outspoken and regaled Allen with some wild stories about making it with sailors and other "rough trade." Kallman's open homosexual flair and "fairy talk" titillated Allen, who wished he wasn't so shy and could be brave enough to say what was on his mind as Chester did.

Love Letter, *CP*, p. 759 Ginsberg successfully completed his spring term at Columbia with As and Bs and decided to take a much-needed break from New York for the summer. Since his departure in March, Neal had been exchanging love letters with Allen. Allen's letters were filled with open references to his sexual cravings and pent-up passions, while Neal's were quite a bit more vague. Neal had the ability to string Allen along while at the same time making the point that he was not interested in any long-term homosexual affairs. That didn't prevent the two of them from talking about spending the summer together, though. Allen had won the George Edward Woodberry Prize from Columbia for his poem *Death in Violence*, which included a cash payment of $150. He decided to use the award money to visit William and Joan in Texas and from there go on to see Neal in Denver. Neal had never met Burroughs but had certainly heard a lot about him from the New York group, so he was curious to meet him. Letters flew back and forth from New York to Denver, plotting the logistics of Allen's trip. It was agreed that Allen would go to Texas and stay with Burroughs on his farm, where Neal would hook up with them later in the summer. Then he and Neal would return to Denver together.

Allen took the long trip to New Waverly, Texas, by himself. He found

William, Herbert, Joan, and her four-year-old daughter, Julie, sitting on an isolated piece of land twelve miles outside the tiny rural town in the middle of nowhere. It was not exactly a Norman Rockwell version of a family farm, nor were the residents your typical farmers. William had bought the ninety-seven-acre tract after his earlier venture in the Rio Grande Valley with Kells Elvin had failed. William and Kells had hooked up to buy a ten-acre citrus grove a year or so earlier. With additional money from William's parents, they bought fifty acres of cotton land and tried to run the place as gentlemen farmers. They knew nothing at all about farming and hired local laborers to do all the manual work. Such things as crop selection and government subsidies were all new to them, and William quickly realized that he'd never make his fortune in agriculture legitimately.

At the end of 1946 Burroughs purchased the New Waverly farm deep in the pine woods of the marshy east Texas bayou with the idea of planting a cover crop of tomatoes or beans in order to hide his real cash crop, which would be either opium poppies or marijuana. Those were the varieties of produce that William could relate to, and he knew that in New York City he could sell whatever he grew for a huge profit. He settled on marijuana and probably didn't bother with a cover crop at all, since the farm was so remote. That was why they had asked Huncke to bring the marijuana seeds along with him. Even though he forgot to bring them, Herbert was able to find a source for them in Houston, where they went every week to buy drugs and replenish their liquor supply. By the time Allen arrived the seeds had already been planted and small plants were growing. All they had to do was sit back, not attract attention to the farm, and wait for the harvest. It was a good thing that they didn't have to tend to the cultivation of the plants very much, because they were all in pretty bad shape at the time. Burroughs was deep into a morphine habit and spent most of his time sitting on the porch. He was using Pantopon, which was being supplied to him through the mail by his New York connection, Bill Garver. Joan was awake twenty-four hours a day as she was using even more Benzedrine than she had before her hospitalization in Bellevue. By summertime she was seven months pregnant, and only Huncke seemed to be concerned about the effects that all the drugs might have on the baby. She busied herself by reading the newspaper religiously every day, taking special interest in articles about odd items like skin diseases and unexplained explosions.

The farm that Allen found waiting for him was not much more than a ramshackle cabin with a cistern for water and a few dilapidated outbuildings. It was so far from the neighbors that they hardly noticed William's frequent gunshots, for he liked to practice firing weapons of every kind. One of the things he liked most about his farm was that he had the freedom to carry and shoot firearms on his own property. Huncke was in better spirits than he had been for years. He thought the farm was a tropical paradise and didn't even mind the king-size scorpions, chiggers, and large rats that overran the house. William loved to shoot the bigger rats whenever he could and for a while considered buying a ferret to help keep them away.

Allen had never lived on a farm before, and this one was more exotic than most. Besides the scorpions, there were plenty of armadillos, moss-draped trees, and beat Texans. He worked a little in the fields under the hot sun, but spent most of his time sitting on the porch talking and listening to records on Burroughs's old secondhand Victrola; he even tried to learn to drive their Jeep. It was June and already the weather was beginning to heat up, with the summer promising to be unbearable to everyone except those born and raised in the Texas heat and humidity. A letter from Denver awaited Allen when he arrived in New Waverly. Undependable as always, Neal had made other plans and wasn't going to come to Texas after all. He didn't explain it to Allen, but he wanted to stay in Denver to pursue a new relationship with Carolyn Robinson, a graduate student at the University of Denver, while he continued to see his wife, LuAnne. There were a few other women he was juggling, too, so his sexual schedule was full. Still, he encouraged Allen to come instead to Denver to see him if he wanted to.

So, like a lovesick puppy, Allen left the farm in July for Denver hoping to convince Neal to return in August in time to help with the marijuana harvest. He talked to Huncke about building a large bed big enough for him and Neal to share, and Herbert assured him he'd take care of it before they returned. After spending the last of his prize money on the Denver bus ticket, Allen was disappointed to find that the job Neal had promised him had fallen through. Neal had no money to help support Allen and no apartment of his own for Allen to stay in, so Allen arrived in the strange city, penniless and without even a floor to sleep on. He wrote to a New York friend, Paul Bertram, "Now I am in Denver, broke, hungry, unemployed, depressed." Through Neal he met Helen and Ruth Gullion, two nurses who took pity on him and fed him. They invited him to stay with them and some of their other friends mothered him for several weeks while he looked for a job. He found one as a night porter, vacuuming carpets for the May Company department store. With his first paycheck he rented a basement room on Grant Street and hoped he'd be able to see more of Neal now that he had some privacy. There was little time for Allen in Neal's hectic schedule, though, running from woman to woman as he was, and Allen became more depressed. Jazz was the only diversion he had that summer. He listened to all his old favorites from Illinois Jacquet to Coleman Hawkins over and over again on the May Company record players. "Listen to the jazz for what they are," he wrote Bertram, "the life-force and profundity of personality as distinct from formal exposition of personality and old cultural forms." Working alone at night as he did gave him the chance to spend hours listening to all of the records in the store's music department, and it was there that he discovered Bartok for the first time. He also upgraded his wardrobe by pilfering a few items of clothing and a pair of new shoes from the store.

Neal was pleased to introduce Allen to Carolyn and they hit it off at once. Carolyn was an accomplished artist, and her portraits of Neal and Allen from that summer captured the youthfulness of the two twenty-one-year-olds. Because Neal was also busy with other women and with his wife, LuAnne, sometimes Allen and Carolyn had long talks of their own and they grew to be good friends. She felt Allen was sensitive and respectful of the feelings of others. Allen thought that Carolyn was very straitlaced and conservative in comparison to the other people in Neal's circle of friends, and he was surprised when she had sex with Neal in her tiny room at the Colburn Hotel while Allen was there. On July 28, Allen recorded in his journal that he had overheard the bedroom whisperings of Neal and Carolyn, saying, "I love you, I love you," as they made love for the first time. It broke his heart. "Such terrible nights. Denver Doldrums," he wrote.

On the heels of this disappointment, Allen received happier news from Texas. Joan had given birth to a baby boy, William S. Burroughs, Jr., on July 21. In the middle of the night she had knocked on William's door to tell him it was time to go to the hospital and they drove to nearby Conroe in the Jeep. It was an easy delivery. Both the mother and baby came through fine, and in true Texas pioneer fashion they were back on the farm the next day. Allen was happy for them and felt as if he had become an uncle, or maybe a big brother, as he considered William to be a father figure in many ways. Early in August Allen sat down and composed a long poem in honor of the birth, originally titling it *Birthday Ode*.

During his two-month trip to Denver Allen spent most of the time by himself, usually waiting for Neal, who was always busy elsewhere with one lover or another. It gave Allen time to closely examine his feelings, which he did on page after page of his journal. He recorded all of his dreams, too, in exquisite detail, and tried to analyze them as best he could. Logging his dreams was something that he had done sporadically before, but from this

point on he began to record them more consistently. Before long he quit
trying to interpret them and merely took pleasure in record-
In Society, *CP*, p. 11　　ing them. Later, in 1954, Allen wrote that "the most important thing about dreams is the existence in them of magical
emotions, to which waking consciousness is not ordinarily sentiment. Awe
of vast constructions; familiar eternal halls of buildings; sexual intensity in
rapport; deathly music; grief awakenings, perfected longings." Allen was in a
dream world when it came to his relationship with Neal, too. He was completely unrealistic and idealized his romance so much that his friends began
referring to him as "Allen in Wonderland." Even though Neal was screwing
women all the time, meeting and picking up new ones even while Allen was
with him that summer, Allen still believed that Neal would give up his heterosexual life in favor of him.

By July 30, Allen began to complain in his ever-lengthening journal passages that he was getting bored and weary of Denver. He read books like *The
Counterfeiters* by Gide while waiting for Neal, who never seemed to show up
on time. Allen no longer knew how to deal with the situation other than outright disgust, and he became jealous and hurt. Diagnosing his feelings, he
wrote, "Pain was not the word, nor grief, though grief, despite its connota-
tions is nearest. Melancholy is too languorous, heartache too banal a word."
From time to time it occurred to him that there was no way out of the mess,
and that it was all a fantasy that he and Neal would be united in any way, sexual or intellectual. He desired a relationship so much that he couldn't see
what seemed obvious to everyone else, that Neal was merely taking advantage of him.

In despair when Neal didn't come to see him, he began to think once
more about suicide, but this time he proposed to do it at the end of his
twenty-third year, two years away. "Just enough time for me to have accomplished the first great prose work, a small body of perfect poems, which
were of no use to me, and to have attempted some happy labor in the world,
and failed, and to have gone all the way thru analysis and come out the same
as before, only with different problems and different people about me." He
felt sorry for himself, yet couldn't bring himself to accept the obvious fact
that Neal loved women more than men and certainly would never be
monogamous with anyone. He pitied Neal, too, because Neal had been unfortunate enough to have fallen in with Carolyn, a woman who would never
be willing to share Neal with Allen. He was willing to share Neal with Carolyn and couldn't understand why she was so possessive. For his part Neal
wasn't about to tell Carolyn of the other women he was seeing, so he cer-

tainly wasn't going to tell her of the sexual nature of his relationship with Allen either. He even used Allen as his alibi for leaving her alone several times when he wanted to be with other women. On the infrequent occasions when Allen did see Neal, he began to give him ultimatums threatening to leave Denver if he didn't pay more attention to him. Of course, Neal could sense that Allen's threats were hollow. It was a pitiful scene as Allen cried steadily through several nights of loneliness while waiting for Neal. One night at the May Company, Allen's anxiety reached such a peak that he began to have delusions about hearing the telephone ring. His vacuum cleaner had such a high pitch that he repeatedly switched it off to listen for Neal's call, which never came. He was too paralyzed to vacuum and every few minutes he picked up the receiver to check to see if the phone was working. Neal wasn't entirely innocent in the affair either. Frequently he told Allen that he was indifferent to him sexually, only to string Allen along in other subtle ways, such as playfully winking at Allen when Carolyn's back was turned.

Late in July, Kerouac arrived in Denver on his way west to San Francisco where his old friend, Henri Cru, had a job waiting for him. Jack saw Allen occasionally, but Jack's Denver friends, Ed White, Allan Temko, and Hal Chase, were annoyed with Neal and didn't care much for Allen by that time either. To them Allen was a sad case, waiting in vain for Neal's attentions, and Neal had proved himself to be nothing but a juvenile delinquent in their eyes. Since Jack was staying at Ed White's house, he felt he owed his loyalty to Ed's friends, the sophisticated Denverites, more than to Neal and Allen. Allen's reluctance to leave his cellar apartment, lest he miss a call from Neal, also made it difficult for him to spend time with Jack during his ten-day stopover in Denver, so they barely saw each other.

"Remind Neal to ditch a few women," Allen wrote bitterly in his journal on August 5, just about the time that Jack was leaving town. Allen didn't hold a very high opinion of many of Neal's girlfriends. He believed that LuAnne was too vacuous for Neal and nearly as possessive as Carolyn. It upset Allen that Neal would prefer LuAnne's company to his, as a torn-up photograph of her found in Ginsberg's files would seem to confirm. It irritated Allen when she hung on Neal's every word when the men tried to have serious intellectual talks. Allen stuck to his own dream that Neal would realize they were destined to be a couple. He wanted to be with Neal, "even if it is necessary for us both to leave sexuality out," he wrote, probably trying to convince himself. The situation was complicated by the fact that occasionally Neal would let Allen blow him and lead him to believe they shared a unique relationship. Neal loved being in the dominant role so much that Allen believed Neal enjoyed breaking down his pride by making him kneel in front of him while he stood for the blow jobs. Allen hoped that if he let Neal dominate him (which he didn't really mind), Neal would grow to love him. He did want to be more aggressive sexually with Neal and "just get on top of him and fuck his mouth," but usually he was quite passive. The one time that Allen did act more forceful, Neal had to admit that it excited him, too.

He had so much free time during that summer that he wrote enough poems to make a series he called the *Denver Doldrums*. They were filled with allusions to nightingales, Eros, and death. Some of them were good, but even with these poems in hand, he complained that his writing was still incompetent. He worried that he was hampered by a lack of insight into what was truly going on in other people's minds, knowledge of which would be necessary if he wanted to write candidly. Certainly in Neal's case that seemed to be all too true.

Due to Allen's unrelenting pleas, Neal promised to go with him to Texas at the end of August. Neal still wanted to meet Burroughs, but he had trouble convincing Carolyn that it was a good idea for him to go with Allen. He told her that he felt guilty about ignoring Allen on his visit and told her that Allen was homosexual and in love with him. He said that the whole purpose of this trip would be to let Allen down gently without hurting his feelings. Without batting an eye, Neal denied that he had ever had sex with Allen, a story Carolyn was eager to believe. After a lifetime of living by his wits, Neal knew exactly how to phrase things.

On his last few days in Denver, Allen stayed with LuAnne, hoping to see Neal there. As he looked over the hundreds and hundreds of pages he had written, he realized that he had said nothing about Denver itself. Looking out of LuAnne's window, he observed, "Two bricklayers are setting the walls of a cellar in a dug out behind a neat doubly angled house of wood, grown over with ivy." Writing down what he saw in front of his eyes in carefully chosen words was only a prose exercise for him, it certainly wasn't poetry. Five years later he would convert this passage into one of the first poems written in a truly "Ginsberg" style entitled "The Bricklayer's Lunch Hour," but for now, it was only a fragment in his journal, waiting to mature along with the poet himself.

The Bricklayer's Lunch Hour, *CP*, p. 12

At two in the morning on Sunday, August 24, Allen and Neal hitched a ride out of Denver bound for New Waverly. Once again Allen was happy and he made a note about the vision he had at daybreak of papier-mâché mountains on the horizon and fields suffused with "cosmic physicality." At last he was on the road with Neal. "It's really begun," he wrote, cheerfully anticipating the romance he was certain would follow. It turned out to be a long, arduous trip, and they often had to wait for hours between rides. Once when stranded at a desolate crossroads in the cinder parking lot of a diner, Allen suggested that they exchange promises to love each other. "He loved me, a big hustler, we kneeled together on the road of Oklahoma in the middle of a four way cross of dirt roads, on an endless plain, at night fall. I hadn't imagined such a place or such an eternal vow: fidelity, union, seraphic insight, everything I could imagine. He accepted it all, a poor lost soul, looking for a father seraph." This vow was to be one of the pivotal moments in Allen's life. He would always remember their kneeling together and the pledge to help get each other into heaven as a sort of everlasting marriage ceremony. Suffice it to say that Neal didn't place as much importance on the occasion as Allen did. He might not have remembered it at all if Allen hadn't constantly reminded him. In 1952, Allen wrote about the pledge that "he wanted to make" with Neal, so quite possibly it wasn't even accepted at the time by Neal. Even later Allen remembered the poignant moment: "By hindsight I realize he was obviously just being nice to me, humoring me." Allen considered it symbolic of their eternal mental and physical union.

After traveling for two solid days on hot, dusty roads, they arrived in New Waverly at dawn. When they reached the farm, Allen was irritated to discover that Huncke had made no arrangements for him and Neal to sleep together as he had promised. Herbert gave up his room for them and was going to sleep outside on the porch, but there was no bed big enough for two people. Allen spent most of the first day trying to nail two cots together, but Neal refused to help. Since Allen had no skill working with his hands, everything he tried was for naught and the bed collapsed, throwing them both on the floor. That night lying with Neal, Allen whispered, "I love you," for the first time, only to realize how pathetic it sounded. His "I loove yoo" was even more pathetic than Carolyn's bedtime whispers that he had overheard in Denver. In his journal he noted, "When we got here, I expecting this happy holiday of God given sexuality, where was the royal couch?" The whole story about the fiasco of the bed was told and retold, not only by Allen but also by Huncke in his book *The Evening Sun Turned Crimson* and by Kerouac in *Visions of Cody*.

Neal hit it off with Joan and William instantly. He was amused by Burroughs, a pleasant surprise for Allen, since he half expected that Neal might not dig William's routines. So even though everyone got along well, Allen's hopes for a romantic honeymoon never materialized. He was too frightened by the likely prospect of total rejection to press Neal for any sexual favors. He was even too shy to kiss him in front of anyone else, which, also typical of Allen, he had been planning to do "unconsciously" for weeks. Allen felt as deprived of Neal's affection in Texas as he had in Denver in spite of the promises on the highway. Since things obviously weren't working out as planned, Allen abandoned his whole idea of traveling on with Neal to New York City to live together as lovers while he finished college.

Everyone by this time was flat broke and they had to spend a long frugal week waiting for Burroughs's September allowance to arrive. When it did Huncke was able to score drugs in Houston, while Allen was at the union hall signing up for work on a ship. It was easier than expected, and he was assigned to a boat carrying grain bound for Marseille. Huncke stayed in Houston that night while Neal drove Allen back to New Waverly to say goodbye to William and Joan. The next day they returned to Houston, found Herbert, and drove Allen out to the ship to sign on with the steward. In the evening, after visiting some jazz joints and getting high, they rented a single room at the Brazos Hotel for the three of them. At one time the Brazos, located near the train depot, had been the best hotel in town, but now, after decades of neglect, it was definitely on the wrong side of the tracks. Neal, high on Nembutal, took off alone in the Jeep and picked up a madwoman who fucked him to exhaustion. That irritated Allen, because Neal had promised to devote midnight to 6:00 A.M. exclusively to him and now he was exhausted and passed out cold until morning. Huncke was furious with both of them because he had found a boy he wanted to seduce but had no privacy in the tiny space. In the morning Allen was so angry that he kicked Neal's woman out and spent the whole day arguing with Neal. As a result he was so late getting back to his ship that he lost the job. They all returned to the farm barely speaking to one another and found William angry with them as well. He had been expecting them to bring ice for the icebox, which they had forgotten to buy, so now their whole supply of frozen food was spoiled. On September 6, for the final time, Neal drove the Jeep back to Houston and dropped Allen at the union hall to fend for himself.

Once he found another ship Allen wrote to tell his father that he was going to sea to earn enough money for psychoanalysis before he returned to Columbia for his degree. He even had the nerve to complain to his father that the fifteen dollars he had been sending him each week wasn't enough for his needs at school. "I am so disgusted with personal and financial and aesthetic problems that shipping out seemed the only way out," he wrote.

Then Allen told Louis to write to the college on his behalf requesting a leave of absence until the spring term. Dean McKnight granted his leave on September 19 and said that Allen could return to classes in February if he liked. His father's main worry was that Allen would never graduate from college, but Allen assured him that he had every intention of finishing his course work. In addition to his complaints about the lack of monetary support, Allen inconsiderately called Louis' poems "incidental lyrics." He told him that he didn't care much for his father's newest poems but granted that his earlier ones were "okay." He didn't mention to his father that the real problem at the bottom of his irritability was his shattered romance or that he was suffering from a broken heart. It would have been nearly impossible for him to tell his father that he was queer at that time, so it was better if Louis thought he was crazy. In the mid-1940s, there wasn't much difference, since even educated people believed that homosexuality was a mental illness. Allen believed that himself.

Allen signed on to another collier, the SS *John Blair,* of the Ponchelet Marine Corporation. He was hired as a utility man and was to set sail from Freeport, Texas, on September 12. To pass time the next few days, he read Henry James's *The Wings of the Dove,* which he had been carrying around. It was the story of a different kind of romantic entanglement, no less tragic than his own. While waiting to weigh anchor Allen resorted to looking for empty soda bottles in trash cans so he could get enough refund money for a meal. His ship docked once at Galveston before heading across the Atlantic on its voyage to Dakar, the capital of French Equatorial Africa, and he mailed his last letters from there. He knew that fifty days at sea on a ship filled with coal might not be pleasant, but it would bring him several hundred dollars, enough to pay his analyst, Dr. Cott, for a whole series of sessions.

After twenty days at sea, Allen stood on the deck of the rusting coal boat looking out at the ocean. He was in the doldrums, that lazy, sultry stretch of the Atlantic off the coast of West Africa, a calm tropical sea where violent hurricanes are born in the late summer. The doldrums was exactly the right word for what was going on inside Ginsberg, too. He was deep into one of his periods of listless inactivity and depression that frequently presaged an eruption of frenzied writing. He stood at the rail and contemplated suicide again. His mind raced with painful memories of the past and then looked ahead to his probable future of despair. He was only twenty-one, no more than a boy in terms of his experience, but he felt much older than the veteran crewmen below playing their never-ending card games. Before he jumped, he took a few minutes to watch the waves and dream about how he wished his life had turned out. In the distance he could begin to make out the lights of the port of Dakar, the freighter's African destination. If he hesitated much longer the other crew members would be on deck and his silent, romantic, suicide leap would be thwarted.

It was time for him to act, but he realized that he hadn't left a suicide note. What good would it be to kill himself if no one knew the reasons? He pulled his journal from his knapsack and began a note that took the form of a poem as he wrote, revised, and rewrote. He searched for the precise words to express the hopelessness that had brought him to this final desperate act of his life on a lonely voyage to Africa. It was essential to get the words right, to pass on his firsthand knowledge of how a "queer" didn't fit in anywhere in America. He had been longing for this escape to Africa, the mysterious, dark continent, where he had planned to jump ship and pick up mysterious, anonymous men to satisfy his wildest sexual desires. Now he realized that he was too timid, too shy, and too inhibited to ever approach anyone, to ever tell anyone his secret passions. Raw sex wasn't even the most important thing to him anymore. What he truly wanted was to be kissed tenderly and sweetly and held in the arms of a strong man who would love him and freely return his affection. He predicted that Africa was certain to be another in a long line of disappointments. He had planned to smoke opium, eat exotic food, invent a new life, and forget the past, the past that had made him spend two months sitting in a Denver basement waiting for his lover, Neal Cassady, to slip away from his wife and girlfriends long enough to visit him for a bit of impersonal sex, then leave him again for days at a time. Now he looked at the churning water in the wake of the propeller and picked up his pen. "By God, I am not going to be a meek nut anymore, I'm going to be crazy with a vengeance, a horrible vengeance. We have a right to our feelings! We're evil, all evil." He then looked up from his writing and saw that the deck was filled with his shipmates preparing to dock. It was too late to jump. Slowly he closed his notebook, stood up, walked to the rail, and looked ahead at the port of Dakar with a new resolve to follow his heart's desires. What was life but suffering anyway? Much later Allen would write, "Born in this world, you've got to suffer."

Dakar Doldrums, CP, p. 760

In port Allen hired one of the African natives to do all the menial kitchen chores. Allen's job was to get up in the morning, peel potatoes, boil eggs, carry oatmeal and bacon from the lockers and iceboxes downstairs, and so forth, so with a "servant" all he had to do was keep the fire going in the coal stove. Then he had the rest of the day free to read and write. He wrote a short story he called "The Monster of Dakar," while his helper did all his work. Then he caught up on letters, the first one to Huncke telling him that "sex was nowhere in Dakar. I have a couple of local pimps rushing around looking for likely prospects for me." There was plenty of marijuana at a penny a stick, big newspaper-wrapped cigar-size bombers. Lots of adobe huts, grass shacks, beggars, and so forth, but Allen's dream had been of an orgy with native boys. He wanted to smoke opium at last, too, something he had never done. But number one on his list was to "buy a man and have a totally uninhibited ball for the first time in my life."

When they had shore leave the native boys rushed up to sell the sailors seedy ties, marijuana, the services of women, and crudely carved black wooden idols. Allen had to fire his native helper because some of the southern crew members objected to being served by a black man. On shore Allen was too shy to ask the natives about male prostitutes. He did find one boy on the docks who showed him around and immediately started begging for everything he had; comb, handkerchief, wallet, money, T-shirt, it didn't matter. At last Allen mustered up the courage to ask the boy to find him a male partner for sex. His native was slow to catch on but eventually understood and said he would find someone. Finding an opium den proved to be equally impossible, but on his last day in port, Allen's contact found a boy for him. He was a small boy who looked at Allen in bewilderment through ugly crossed eyes. The pitiful thing had a stunted, rachitic body and the too-large, bulbous head of an idiot. Dejected, Allen paid him off and returned to the ship unsatisfied in every way. Dakar was not a city of sin as he had expected and hoped for; it was nothing but coalfields and displaced natives who belonged back in the jungle. The only fruitful thing to come out of the voyage was that he had begun to write again, and by the time he reached New York he had enough poems for a collection he would call *Dakar Doldrums*.

During the fall Allen divided his time between a rented room at 356 W. Twenty-seventh Street and his father's house in Paterson. While on his African trip he had decided to give Neal an ultimatum. "My own submissions and flexibilities were after all subtle secret ways of persuasion and education and weaning. They were in the end to make you submit, and now the time has come. So at last must act with demand, ultimatum, force, possession and unity, and that I add with appeal and for understanding and sympathy." In the end, Neal wouldn't respond one way or another to this or any of Allen's demands, but Allen would never give up trying.

Then on November 14, Allen received a letter from Dr. Harry J. Worthing, the senior director of Pilgrim State, the hospital where his mother was being treated. The doctor told him that they had decided his mother's mental condition "is serious enough to warrant a prefrontal lobotomy." In order to perform the operation they needed the consent of Naomi's nearest relative, and since Louis and Naomi were divorced and Eugene wanted no part of the decision, it was left completely in Allen's hands. Reluctantly, he put his faith in the doctors and signed the papers authorizing the drastic step, hoping that it would help free her from her paranoid fears; but sadly, Naomi was never the same again. For the rest of his life Allen felt guilty about what he had done. On November 25, terribly depressed, he wrote only a single line in his diary, "Allen, don't die."

It was a terrible season that awaited Allen back in New York City. Neal had been in the city but left for the West again, which depressed Allen even more. For a while, until Neal began to send him somewhat encouraging letters, he nearly gave up hope of having his love returned. Shortly after the holidays he applied to the college for financial aid so that he could pay his tuition and have enough money left over for therapy. He found that he wasn't able to apply himself to his studies with his previous vigor. When he heard that his chances for a fellowship were slim, he wrote to those professors he respected the most, Trilling, Van Doren, and Steeves, asking for strong recommendations. Even after complaining of the paltry amount his father was able to send him, he knew that he could rely on him for the tuition money, but there wouldn't be enough for his psychoanalysis. He felt that if he didn't finish school that year, he never would. The only subjects that held any interest for him during the winter term were his studies of Cézanne and Matisse in a class taught by Meyer Shapiro. Allen didn't have much background in art appreciation, but he was fascinated by the "cosmic vibrations" he received from Cézanne's paintings. Even though he didn't complete his term paper for the course on time, he managed to pass the final exam and narrowly squeaked by. While working on the Cézanne paper, Allen liked to smoke enough grass to get high and then visit the museums to look at specific paintings. It was his first premeditated use of pot for aesthetic purposes and he felt it deepened his aesthetic perceptions. "I was somewhat disappointed later on when the counterculture developed the use of grass for party purposes rather than for study purposes. I always thought that was the wrong direction, that grass should be used for mindful attentiveness rather than for kicks. That's silly," he said.

1948 ~

ALLEN'S IMMEDIATE GOAL WAS to finish school and graduate. He knew that what he wanted to learn wasn't being taught in college and the sooner he got out the sooner he could do what he liked. Once more he came close to becoming hooked on Benzedrine and had to seek advice from Burroughs, who was trying to kick his own habit. As he came off the drug, he fell back into his old habit of sleeping most of the day and had another bout with depression. "O Neal I love you still and I wish you were here, yet you become more lost each day," he wrote on Valentine's Day, 1948.

At the end of February, Huncke was back on the scene in Times Square, homeless and beat as always. In Texas, the "farmers" hadn't known how to dry and cure the marijuana crop and it rotted, so the whole experiment had been a flop. Huncke, who was practically living on Bennies himself by this time, stayed with Allen. "The most depressing thing is to get up to go to school and wake him (Huncke) and see him lift up his head, staring blankly, dumb, biting his lips, for half an hour at a time," Allen wrote. "I feel ashamed and I think I should remain away from everyone because per chance I may infect people, pollute them with my corruption and leave them with a diseased soul as mine is diseased."

About the only thing that was any different was Allen's sex life. That winter he spent more time haunting the queer bars around the Village and Times Square and had become more confident when picking up men. He also drank more than before and made a lot of new friends at places like the San Remo café on Bleecker Street, more of a bar than a café. His circle of friends widened to include new bohemians like Alan Ansen and Bill Cannastra. As he overindulged in nefarious activities to escape his sorrow over the loss of Neal, he divided his time between school, drinking, queer dives, Pokerino parlors, and writing. The only thing that cheered him up that winter was reading the manuscript of Jack's recently completed novel, *The Town and the City*. In Allen's opinion it was a masterpiece, surpassing his wildest expectations.

Two Sonnets, *CP*, p. 13

Since he hadn't received a fellowship, Allen couldn't scrape together enough money for psychoanalysis, but with a part-time job he had enough to buy a lot of records and increased his knowledge of jazz. Word arrived from San Francisco that Neal had divorced LuAnne and married Carolyn on April 1. The news of the wedding so unnerved Allen that he went a little crazy one day and asked Kerouac to beat him up. Afterward he wrote to Jack, "I long for death more than ever, but am afraid to take my life. My soul does not want to take any action, exist or die. I can't find the way out by thought, even action is useless it seems. My action is always balked and unworthy." In an interview years later Allen recalled his psychic state at the time: "For various reasons it had seemed to me at one time or another that the best thing to do was to drop dead. Or not be afraid of death but go into death. Go into the nonhuman, go into the cosmic, so to speak; that God was death, and if I wanted to attain God I had to die. Which may still be true. So I thought that what I was put up to was therefore [to] break out of my body, if I wanted to attain complete consciousness."

That Neal was thousands of miles away in California with Carolyn didn't stop Allen from being obsessed with him. He was still madly in love and painfully aware that nothing would ever come of it. As his twenty-second birthday approached that June he had an epiphany about his awareness of reality, of the evil that exists in the world, of the peace of the self that is possible, and of the value and reality of art. Allen was proud of Jack's accomplishment in writing *The Town and the City* and reassured to know that he had the ability to produce such a great book. The one regret Allen had was that Jack had set the bar too high and Allen didn't think he'd ever be able to match it. He noted in his diary: "Whom I love most in the world, in this order: Neal, Eugene, Jack, Bill (I should die for these) then Lucien Joan Huncke Neal." Listing Neal twice was either a slip or a real indication of how important he was to Allen.

Writing to Lionel Trilling a day before his birthday, Allen summed up a lot of his feelings in a more coherent way. "I have decided that I really don't want to teach, and furthermore I'm sick and tired of Columbia," he told his

old professor. The only thing he liked about college was the leisure time it afforded him to study on his own. "I am beginning to feel sufficiently sure of
myself to think that it is enough merely to write." Encouraged by the fact
that Kerouac had finished his novel, Allen began to assemble poems for a
possible book of his own. "The only clear profit is my book, which except for
one final spasm of revisions is actually finished and probably publishable," he
added to Trilling. Allen's hopes had been encouraged by John Crowe Ran-
som, the editor of the *Kenyon Review,* who, after rejecting Allen's first group
of poems, *Denver Doldrums,* had voluntarily asked Allen to send him something more "compacted."

Very gingerly, Allen broached the subject of Kerouac's book with
Trilling. Since Jack had been banned from campus as a bad influence, there
was little reason to expect that anyone at Columbia would help him get his
novel published, but Allen wanted to give it a shot. He told Trilling that
Jack had been working on this book in one form or another since 1942 and
had finally finished it. He assured Trilling that it was "a great book, monumental, magnificent, profound, far far finer than anything I had imagined,
a literary work of enormous importance, etc." Allen worried that Trilling
wouldn't put any stock in his opinion, "no matter how earnestly and
gravely or gleefully I tell you there is a Great American Novel under our
noses."

During the summer Allen needed to finish only one more class in order
to have enough credits to graduate. Although the course was in Victorian literature he chose to concentrate all his efforts on his continuing study of
Cézanne. His were the first works of art in which Allen was aware of the
mind of a living, intelligent person behind them. Until then, Allen had
viewed artworks as objects of beauty, but the mental acumen of Cézanne
himself was transmitted through his paintings in a way Allen had never before experienced. For a while he stayed in Paterson with his father and com-
muted to class, but then he sublet an apartment on East 121st Street in the
heart of Italian Harlem, from a friend and theology student, Russell Durgin.
Although happy to have an apartment of his own again, he was still depressed by his life in general. To cheer himself up he threw large parties and
invited a multitude of new people from the San Remo scene. For the Fourth
of July, Allen gave a big three-day party to which he invited, among others,
Ed Stringham, a friend of his who worked for the *New Yorker.* Ed came with
Alan Harrington and brought along another intelligent would-be writer by
the name of John Clellon Holmes to meet Allen and his friend Kerouac. Ed
and John had heard a story that Jack had completed a novel that weighed

nearly forty pounds. Holmes was eager to meet the author of all those words and found him sitting in Allen's noisy apartment, amid the jazz and cigarette smoke. As a writer himself, Holmes discovered that he had a lot in common with Jack, and over the next few weeks they became the best of friends, but on the initial day Jack felt John "watched with his wild shrewd look." Allen was always glad to be the intermediary between people and loved nothing more than introducing everyone to everyone, a pleasure he never lost.

His routine that summer was to get up at the crack of dawn for his morning class, then work for a few hours as a clerk in the musty office of a nearly defunct journal of political economy. After lunch he would walk home through Harlem and buy whatever he needed from the markets on 125th Street. He had all but stopped writing again and seemed to be drifting aimlessly. For a while he quit using drugs and stopped visiting his friends. Surprisingly the one thing that he did do was to gather the courage to tell Louis that he was homosexual and that he was in love with Neal Cassady.

Louis was shocked and disappointed with the news. On July 19, Louis mailed Allen a two-word note, "Exorcise Neal," which made Allen feel more isolated than ever before in his life.

Do We Understand Each Other?, *CP*, p. 17

Allen wrote, "Nothing I had experienced in my life led me to expect what would happen to me in my loneliness. One day in the middle of the summer as I was walking down 125th Street, I suddenly stopped and stared around me in amazement. It was as if I had awakened from a long dream that I'd walked around in all my life. I threw over all my preoccupations with ideas and felt so free that I didn't know who I was or where I was. The whole appearance of the world changed in a minute when I realized what had happened, and I began to look at people walking past me. They all had incredible sleepy, bestial expressions on their faces, yet no different from what they usually looked like. I suddenly understood everything vague and troubled in my mind that had been caused by the expression of people around me. Everybody I saw had something wrong with them. The apparition of an evil, sick, unconscious wild city rose before me in visible semblance, and about the dead buildings in the barren air, the bodies of the soul that built the wonderland shuffled and stalked and lurched in attitudes of immemorial nightmare all around. When I saw people conversing around me, all their conversation, all their bodily movements, all their signs, the thoughts reflected on their faces were of fear of recognition and anguished fear that someone would take the initiative and discover their masks and

lies. Therefore every tone of voice, movement of the hand, carried a negative overtone: this in the world is called coyness and shyness and politeness,
or frigidity and hostility when the awareness becomes too overpowering. I
felt that I would be crucified if I alluded with any insistence to the divine nature of ourselves and the physical universe. Therefore I did not speak but
only stared in dumb silence."

Allen had been studying the poetry of William Blake
more or less on his own ever since his advisors at Columbia
told him that Blake was too far out of the mainstream to
be worthy of serious scholarship. Allen had been attracted
to the world Blake created in his poetry, but he couldn't crack the complicated code to reveal Blake's hidden secrets. He kept reading and rereading
Blake's poem "Ah Sun-flower! weary of time," over and over again in his
room without fully understanding what Blake was getting at. At one point
Allen masturbated as he read and as he orgasmed he experienced an audi-
tory hallucination. He knew that he was hearing the deep voice of
William Blake himself reciting the poem and for the first time he became
aware of the poem's significance. It wasn't that he imagined he heard
Blake's voice, he actually did hear Blake speak directly to him, as surely as
the saints heard the Virgin Mary speaking to them. As Allen stared out the
window, another poem by Blake, "The Sick Rose," came to
mind. When he gazed out across the rooftops of the city,
the entire universe was revealed to him. Allen was intensely alive and alert for those few minutes. He realized
that what he was seeing had been there all the time; it was
an aspect of the imagination that is eternal, extending beyond his life and
his former consciousness back as far as Blake and beyond. He saw not objects but the process of creation behind them. It was a sudden flash of
recognition in which the secret of all universal mysteries was unlocked.
He could almost say that he saw God at that moment. It was all there if
only he observed. The most astonishing aspect of his vision was that the
actual location of the guiding intelligence was within the objects of the
world themselves, not in some remote corner of the heavens. Others
might have said that he saw God here with us on earth. He realized that
the world as we see it is complete, there is nothing outside it. His heightened cosmic awareness lasted for a brief time, less than an
hour, and then was gone. The important thing for Allen
was that the enlightenment remained.

Over the next few days the awareness revisited him, and during the fol-

The Eye Altering Alters
All, *CP*, p. 15

On Reading William
Blake's "The Sick Rose,"
CP, p. 14

Vision 1948, *CP*, p. 16

lowing week he had a similar vision as he looked at people in the Columbia Bookstore. The bookstore remained the same as always—he saw nothing new in form, no angels, no smoke—but there was an additional palpable reality to the faces of the people, a supernatural existence that dwelled in all forms, both living and inanimate. It was akin to what has been ascribed to the presence of the Holy Ghost in orthodox religion. He thought about Blake's phrase of seeing eternity in a grain of sand and knew it was literally true. He was astounded to be able to see the souls of men and women in their faces, in their attitudes, and in their gestures, as if a mask had been removed. It was remarkable, he thought, that their souls were "hiding themselves from admitting their awareness of the all inclusive peaceful prescience," and restraining them from acting in accordance with the happy total community of mind and being. Although he couldn't find the right word to describe it, a consciousness or awareness or intelligence seemed to be inherent in all things.

A Very Dove, *CP*, p. 15

It is disappointing that Allen didn't immediately record his impressions in his journal, but later he made continual reference to this period of enlightenment. Even in his correspondence over the next six months, there is virtually no mention of the actual visions. Possibly he realized that people would take it as a sign of insanity and believe he was going crazy like his mother. After the visions Allen read all of *Songs of Experience* and studied Blake's concepts of good and evil. He also read Yeats's final poems and many of his symbolic plays, Eliot's *Four Quartets,* the work of St. John of the Cross, and other writers he thought might be helpful. Due to his recent studies he also wrote about the influence Cézanne had on his own way of thinking.

It was the following year, 1949, before Allen was finally able to write about his visions, "So, seeing a light, I thought it was God." By that time Allen's Reichian doctors had convinced him that they were hallucinations, a type of "breakthrough," but not genuine reality. Still Allen wanted to make the most of the illusions, if that's what they were, and he consciously decided to pursue other out-of-body experiences. That search led him to believe that he might be able to find a drug that would take him back to that point of hearing Blake and seeing eternity again. "So I abandoned making up systems and set about attempting to seek into myself for the springs of that energy, or life force, or reality, or supernaturality, that had been momentarily released." For more than a decade, those few days of clear visionary insight in the late summer of 1948 were to govern much of his intellectual time as he searched in vain for ways to recreate the complete awareness that he had felt at that moment.

"I found the visions, finally, frightening and fled to Paterson where I scared my father with wild talk; then I went back after a few days to N.Y. and took up my routine existence again; only this time gnawed inwardly with recollection of these experiences, which, because of their absolute and eternal nature I assumed as the keystone and reference point of all my thought—a North Star for life; much as Dante says, '*Incipit Vita Nuova*.' I thought much of Dante, Blake, and St. John of the Cross. I wrote several poems incorporating the ideas—purely intellectual skeletons— which remained of the solid flesh of visions." Louis was shocked by Allen's "visions," as were most of his friends. After settling into a quieter relationship with Edith, Louis was hoping to have a calmer domestic life, something that had eluded him through all the years with Naomi. But now he feared that Allen was teetering on the brink of insanity.

The Voice of Rock, *CP*, p. 18

Refrain, *CP*, p. 19

A Western Ballad, *CP*, p. 21

"I spent a week after this living on the edge of a cliff in eternity. It wasn't so easy after that. I would get glimmerings, hints of possibility, secret amazements at myself, at the world, at 'the nature of reality,' at some of the wisdom other people seemed to reflect, at poets of the past, even at Shelley. I reread Dante and wormed through some of Shakespeare, Plotinus, St. Augustine, Plato, anything that caught my fancy." It was at that moment of frenzied preoccupation with visions that Herbert chose to show up at Allen's door. He stayed for a while and stole several rare and valuable books of seventeenth- and eighteenth-century English poetry from Durgin's shelves. Allen was absorbed in his visionary studies, which seemed to lead nowhere but promised the key to that light which Allen had witnessed. Every author he looked at had his own light, his own method, and his own renunciations. By the time that Allen noticed that the bookshelves were barer than before, his radio, typewriter, winter clothes, and an oriental statuette were also missing. He realized that Huncke had been slowly robbing him to feed his heroin habit. The worst part was that the books weren't his; otherwise he might have been able to overlook it. Since they belonged to Durgin, some restitution would have to be made. Allen could not bring himself to confront Herbert, who came and went, taking things with him, until one day he disappeared entirely. When Durgin came back that fall they hung out around Times Square looking for Herbert, but an

The Trembling of the Veil, *CP*, p. 22

old acquaintance told them that he was in jail again, charged with marijuana possession. Allen could make only partial repayment to Durgin for
the books, which were worth several hundred dollars. In spite of the
thefts, Allen maintained his sympathy for Herbert and wished he could
help him in his sufferings.

Some good news for Louis did come out of the summer after all.
Allen managed to finish his final course and earned his BA in English.
Technically his commencement date was the following year, June 1, 1949,
but Louis was relieved that his son would receive his degree after six long
years. Following the completion of his course work, two of Allen's professors, Barzun and Van Doren, gave him letters of introduction to
Gilbert Seldes,[16] an influential writer who had pioneered the idea that
popular culture deserved serious attention from critics. Seldes talked to
Allen about the possibility of a job, and he invited Allen to work with him
on some radio scripts. One of Allen's ideas was to base a children's program on the Dr. Dolittle series. Allen had read all the Dr. Dolittle books
as a child, and in fact they were still among his favorites. He wanted to
give the program a St. Francis–like overtone instead of making it "cute,"
yet keep it simple enough for children to understand. The second script
was for a Jewish program called the "Eternal Light" about Samuel Greenberg, the man who inspired Hart Crane. Allen thought that radio script
work might lead him to television jobs where he could de-

A Meaningless
Institution, CP, p. 23

velop some ideas for short blank verse plays. Coinciding
with these new ventures into an actual career field was the
consummation of an old crush. Allen had finally worn
down Lucien's resistance and ended up in bed with him for the first and
only time in November 1948. After having dreamed of the moment for
nearly five years it was anticlimactic to Allen and didn't lead anywhere,
just like his new radio career.

On December 1, Allen signed a lease for an apartment of his own at
1401 York Avenue on the Upper East Side for $14.95 a month. Since the
apartment was being vacated by his friend, Walter Adams, he was able to
move in a little earlier. It was cheap enough that he didn't have to worry
about the rent, and Adams even left some furniture for him. Within a few
weeks Allen landed a full-time job as copy boy for the Press Association, part
of the AP wire service, and began working in their Rockefeller Center office

---

[16] Gilbert Seldes (1893–1970): Critic, novelist, editor, playwright, and screenwriter who was at one time
the editor of the *Dial*.

about a week before Christmas at eighty cents an hour. He worked five days a week from midnight until 8:00 A.M., which suited his lifestyle. He loved the late hours, which gave him time in the evenings to see friends before work. Generously, Lionel Trilling helped him with a letter of recommendation. The job was pleasant enough and Allen saw it as a good stepping-stone to a better position in journalism.

1949 ~

WITHIN A MONTH his feelings about his job had changed drastically. He wrote to Trilling and told him, "My job is terrible, leads nowhere. I sure made a compromise with society. The more I think of it the more I think I'm being tricked by a lot of BS to assume some phony responsibilities. Everybody in the outside world is morose, sad or silly, including me." When he took the job he thought he could do whatever they told him to do, like in the Maritime Service, but he had become so frustrated with it that he said he'd rather "pay attention to an old bum" than do what they wanted him to do. Allen had enough spare time while at the office to write poems and record his daydreams, so he tried to stick it out. In his January 1949 journal, he wrote down some ideas for potential stories, including one that turned out to be prophetic: "Psychological portrait of young me, spiritual man, caught for robbery by the police."

A Mad Gleam, CP, p. 24

Complaint of the Skeleton to Time, CP, p. 25

Over the holidays, Neal Cassady, LuAnne Henderson, and Al Hinkle came east to visit Kerouac in North Carolina and to help him move his mother's furniture back to New York. That took two trips in Neal's brand-new 1949 Hudson. While in the city they stayed with Allen in his new apartment on York. Naturally they took in all the New Year's Eve parties, had a few parties of their own, and even went to hear George Shearing at Birdland, the best jazz club in town. Their absolute freedom to travel didn't help Allen feel any better about his office job with AP, which had him tied down permanently. The gang spent a lot of their time sitting around the apartment

Herbert Huncke ～

talking as they smoked a huge quantity of marijuana that Burroughs had sent from New Orleans, and postponed leaving until later in the month. This irritated Burroughs, who was waiting for their arrival in New Orleans, because Al Hinkle's wife, Helen, was staying there at William's house expecting them to pick her up and take her back to California. Around January 19, Neal, LuAnne, Jack, and Al left to swing by New Orleans on their way to San Francisco.

An Eastern Ballad,
CP, p. 26

To free himself from the boredom of office routine, Allen applied for a teaching job at the Cooper Union, which would begin in the fall. Van Doren, with whom he had been auditing a course, sent in a recommendation, as did Trilling. Their willingness to help gives some idea of how much Allen's teachers liked him. In June he and Kerouac planned to take a Huckleberry Finn–type raft trip down the Mississippi to New Orleans to visit Burroughs themselves, or if no rafts were available they'd hitchhike along the river. In the meantime Kerouac was working on an early draft of *On the Road* while Ginsberg was working on a series of fifty- and sixty-line psalms.

Sweet Levinsky,
CP, p. 27

Psalm I, *CP*, p. 26

Psalm II, *CP*, p. 28

By February Huncke was out of jail and once again so down on his luck and so "beat," as he called his condition, that he trudged through the snow for several days until his feet were frozen, swollen, and bleeding. Even though he hadn't contacted Allen since he stole Durgin's books the year before, he threw himself on Allen's doorstep begging for pity and help. Allen had decided not to put up with Herbert again, but when he saw him he relented, with his usual charity and compassion. Huncke had come to his door looking like a ragged saint: "His feet were bloody, covered with blisters and raw spots, and dirty. He hadn't slept for several days, the last time in the 50th St. Greyhound Bus terminal. He hadn't eaten except for Benny, coffee and donuts. He had no money." Allen boiled a pot of hot water and washed his feet for him and Huncke slept for a day and a half. He stayed with Allen for several weeks without moving from his bed except to eat the hot bowls of soup that Allen prepared for him. Gradually Huncke began to talk about himself and spoke of his Merchant Marine days and the terrible skin condition that had turned his face so monstrous. After a while a new dark beauty was revealed to Allen in the haggard thirty-year-old man. Allen never discussed the previous thefts and came to appreciate having Herbert as a roommate, as it was nice to have someone to come home to and talk to after work. Herbert was quite genteel in his own way. His modest ambition was to have an apartment of his own someday, decorated with low furniture and couches to recline on in what he called "Chinese Moderne." He'd have soft, dim lighting, wear oriental robes, and burn incense. Allen wrote that he never expected to find himself "so comfortably established and happy in the want and weariness of this foul house." Allen had managed to find someone who was more disillusioned and irreversibly depressed than himself.

After All, What Else Is There to Say?, *CP*, p. 37

In early March, Vickie Russell, the beautiful redhead whom Allen had known for almost as long as he had known Huncke, came by to see how Herbert was doing and brought along her boyfriend, "Little Jack" Melody. Allen hadn't seen Vickie in some time, and he had only heard of Little Jack secondhand. Vickie was now hooked on heroin and Allen was disappointed to see her with such a bad habit. To him it meant that she was no longer open to her true feelings but was encased in a heroin shell. It was Vickie's nature to be either overaffectionate with people or overcritical, but she had a soft spot in her heart for Allen. Little Jack was a member of a low-level Long Island mob family, and although he claimed to be a musician he was connected in a minor way to all sorts of criminal activities. He was reputedly a safecracker, but actually he had been in prison for stealing a safe, not for cracking it. Allen was surprised when he first met him, for he had expected a large Italian gangster, not the little, half-bald, elfin figure he turned out to be. Vickie and Little Jack returned a few times over the next week, bringing little gifts with them—marijuana, a copy of the *Arabian Nights*, cakes, and other goodies. Allen welcomed them and even moved out of his bedroom for Vickie and Little Jack, sleeping on the couch or the floor if Huncke was already on the sofa himself.

Pot wafted freely through the apartment and when Allen had a day or two off, he made it a point to get as high as he could and go out exploring the streets till dawn. Someone gave Allen an opium pipe picked up in Chinatown, a souvenir he had always wanted, and he used it for smoking his share of the grass. Then in March, when Allen had a relapse of bronchitis, something that had been plaguing him for more than a year, Herbert was happy to nurse Allen for a change. Little Jack and Vickie came over to entertain him and brought him a phonograph and lots of jazz records, especially Billie Holiday singing "That Ole Devil Called Love," which Allen grew especially fond of.

The Shrouded Stranger, *CP*, p. 34

Stanzas: Written at Night in Radio City, *CP*, p. 35

Fie My Fum, *CP*, p. 31

Pull My Daisy, *CP*, p. 32

Bop Lyrics, *CP*, p. 50

On weekends when Kerouac came in from his mother's house in Queens, he and Allen would fool around composing ditties by alternating lines and ideas back and forth. They called the most successful of these "Pull My Daisy" or "Fie My Fum." One day, Kerouac brought some good news of his own about his first novel, *The Town and the City*. Alfred Kazin, a well-known literary critic, had given a copy of the manuscript to Harcourt Brace to look at, but had gotten no response. Later Allen set up a meeting between Kerouac and Mark Van Doren to talk about the book, and no sooner had Van Doren read parts of it than he enthusiastically called the editors at Harcourt Brace. Shortly thereafter, on April Fools' Day, they accepted Jack's book and gave him an advance of a thousand dollars. As soon as he heard the news, Allen wrote in his journal, "Come, sweet Death, with madness marked/and end the senseless revelry." Was he jealous or did he feel that life and success had passed him by? He was finding it difficult to do any serious writing of his own in the apartment because of Herbert, Vickie, Little Jack, and any number of other people who had a habit of dropping in. The bedlam was too great and a quiet break seemed to be in order.

Since Allen and Jack were planning their Mississippi River getaway for that summer, Little Jack offered to take over Allen's apartment and pay the rent until he returned. Allen was even toying with the idea of transferring to the AP office in New Orleans once he got there in June. In addition to paying the rent, Little Jack offered to repaint the place, put in a telephone, and give Allen enough money for his trip, so he and Vickie gradually began to move their things into the apartment before Allen even left. Ginsberg began to notice that more and more of the clothing and furniture that was coming into the house didn't look like it belonged to them. In order to support themselves and their habits, they had been breaking into cars and apartments and taking things of value, and now they were using Allen's place to store their loot. Allen even drove with them on one of their crime sprees, heisting suitcases from parked cars around Fiftieth Street and Fifth Avenue. Little Jack invited Allen to join them and lose his "burglar's cherry." He declined and stayed in the car, but he made no effort to stop them.

By mid-April they had already brought home such things as a carved wooden cabinet, two large chairs, and an entire cigarette machine, which Allen found standing in the middle of his kitchen one morning. They broke up the vending machine and disposed of all the parts one by one, but the furniture remained, and even though Allen was frightened about being caught, he was pleased that his apartment was looking so much nicer with all the additions. In the meantime a letter arrived from New Orleans saying that Burroughs had been arrested for possession. William wanted to warn Allen that the police might come looking for him, since so many of Allen's letters talking about various marijuana deals had been seized. Huncke assured Allen that if the police came by searching for drugs they wouldn't notice the stolen merchandise. Most of Allen's friends could see that he wasn't being realistic, but Allen remained naïve. Lucien warned Allen that all his notebooks might incriminate him even more, since he was now writing so openly not only about drug use, but about homosexual sex and grand larceny, too. He suggested that it might be wise for Allen to store all his papers elsewhere. As someone on parole, Lucien was also worried that the papers might tie him in with the criminal activity and he'd be sent back to jail. Allen saw his point and collected his journals and correspondence to take to his brother's apartment on the Upper West Side for safekeeping. He didn't want to take them home to Paterson for fear his father would read the details of his queer sex life. Louis had already tried to warn Allen about putting anything on paper that he might "have cause to regret."

The journals were being written in the name of art, because Allen was recording the details of his life in preparation for the day when he would write "a large autobiographical work of fiction." That night Allen wrote a two-page manifesto to the household demanding that the apartment be kept as clean as possible because of the New Orleans bust; that meant no drugs and no stolen property. In the evening the trio of thieves, Huncke, Melody, and Russell, returned from a caper carrying a stack of dirty books they had stolen from a Harlem police detective. Needless to say, Allen's manifesto fell on deaf ears.

By this time, Allen had sunk as low as he would ever go. He, himself, never understood why he had allowed his criminal friends to take over his apartment and use it as a warehouse. He said he wanted to be loyal to Huncke because he thought that Herbert was basically unlovable. Allen's own self-esteem was so low, at that point, that once again, he thought he must be mad. To top it all off, his homosexual nature would be exposed if the police did investigate, and that in itself was considered a crime and another indication of mental illness. There was no reason why Allen shouldn't think he was crazy at that point in his life; all of his friends certainly thought he had finally gone over the deep end. His visions of Blake had been suspiciously questioned and condemned all around. He knew that his father thought he was going insane, Louis' response to his recent confession about his homosexuality was proof of that. Allen certainly felt that he was crazy in the eyes of the world—not that he found that altogether bad, as there was a side of him that saw insanity as a romantic trait for a poet. But even though Allen knew that the thefts were morally wrong, he wasn't confident enough in himself to do anything about it—further proof to himself that he must be mentally unstable.

On Wednesday, April 20, Little Jack stole about ten thousand dollars worth of jewelry, clothing, and furs from the home of Henry Pieretti in Astoria, and in spite of Allen's proclamation, he carried half the plunder up to Allen's apartment and left the other half in the car. Since the car itself had been stolen in Washington a month earlier, he was anxious to get the rest of the stolen property out of the car. So the next morning he decided to drive out to his mother's house on Long Island and hide the goods there.

The next day, Little Jack and Vickie agreed to drop Allen and his "hot" manuscripts off at Eugene's apartment on his way back into the city, so after stashing Little Jack's own loot, they drove back through Bayside, Queens, along Francis Lewis Boulevard. Little Jack missed his turn onto Northern Boulevard and made an illegal turn at the next street, right in front of a patrolman. The patrolman, George McClancy, held up his hand and waved the car over, but Little Jack panicked, since the car was stolen. He stepped on the gas and raced down the block at sixty miles an hour, flipping the car over twice when he hit the curb as he tried to turn a sharp corner. Miraculously, no one was seriously hurt, and Allen and Vickie ran from the wrecked car into someone's house and out the back door. Little Jack was apprehended on the spot, but the others got away. Unfortunately, Allen's papers, all with his name and address, were strewn about the backseat. He wandered around Queens for an hour by himself and didn't even have enough money for the subway home, but somehow he managed to get back to the apartment just ahead of the police.

When Allen arrived, Herbert and Vickie were waiting, but they had made no effort to hide any of the stolen goods; there was too much to conceal. Before long, two detectives knocked on his door and took them all to jail. This was Allen's first offense, so luckily they were more lenient with him. When the police contacted Allen's father, he was frantic and heartbroken. Allen was surprised to learn that the police had already gotten in touch with his therapist, Dr. Cott, who for some unexplained reason told them that Allen was "probably an incurable heroin addict." Once again Louis turned to Lionel Trilling for help and between the two of them they were able to convince the authorities that what Allen needed most was professional psychological treatment, not prison. Ilo Orleans, the family attorney, argued on Ginsberg's behalf that it was a case of a troubled boy falling in with bad company. The newspapers found the case interesting and depicted Allen as a Columbia-educated writer, living with criminals and dope fiends in order to gain experience for a book. There were articles and pictures in all the New York papers for the next day or two.

Sometime Jailhouse Blues, *CP*, p. 38

In the end Russell received a suspended sentence and Melody was sent to Pilgrim State Hospital. Allen was released into the custody of his father under the condition that he be admitted to a mental hospital for psychiatric treatment. On the advice of counsel, Allen didn't attend his own hearing, at which Lionel and Diana Trilling, Mark Van Doren, Dean Carman, and an analyst all testified. Actually, Allen breathed a sigh of relief. At last he was in a position to receive the psychiatric counseling that he had wanted to get for years but couldn't afford. "I really believe or want to believe really that I am nuts, otherwise I'll never be sane," he wrote. He was eager to begin treatments and intended to cooperate with the doctors in any way necessary. "All my doors are open," he wrote as he awaited his admission into the New York State mental hospital.

Please Open the Window and Let Me In, *CP*, p. 39

He was scheduled to enter the hospital around his

twenty-third birthday at the beginning of June, "the year of the iron birthday, the gate of darkness," as he dramatically observed. "In the hospital I
hope to be cured." He gave some thought to how often in
the past he had considered suicide, but now the prospect of   Tonite all is well, *CP*,
being treated erased his worries. He knew he was not going   p. 40
to die, "I am going to live anew." For the first time in more
than a year he slept well and had peaceful dreams. "My devils are going to
be cast out," he jotted down hopefully. He was assigned to a Dr. Fagin, and
Allen professed that he had complete confidence in the hospital's system of
treatment.

At the last minute there was a hitch in the red tape at the hospital,
which delayed his admission, but it was only temporary. Allen spent his
days waiting in Paterson and marked time by writing in his journal. Some
of his short prose snippets were later to become poems like
"Tonite all is well," but for now they remained prose frag-   Fyodor, *CP*, p. 40
ments. Cézanne was very much on his mind, and he wrote a   Cézanne's Ports, *CP*, p. 61
paragraph that was to become "Cézanne's Ports," too.   I attempted to
While waiting he was able to put together his earlier poems   concentrate, *CP*, p. 41
for a book. Cheerfully, he pushed himself every day from
noon into the late hours of the night working on the collection. For the
time being he was in high spirits. Three or four times each week he walked
down to the movie theater, and every night he read until he fell asleep. During his stay at home he began to realize how much emotional pain he had
caused his father over the past few years and almost summoned the courage
to beg his forgiveness. He hoped he'd be able to do just that after the doctors worked their cure.

Louis was as relieved as Allen was to have his son under a therapist's care.
He wrote to Lionel Trilling to thank him for all the generous help and support he had given Allen over the years. "I tried to give Allen what compensa-
tions I could; however, I suppose his wounded childhood had secreted some
imbalance; or some trauma had precipitated some disorder deep in his psyche. Bad companions in the last few years had aggravated his attitudes,"
Louis wrote.

Coinciding with Allen's admission to the madhouse was his mother's
release from yet another mental hospital. She tried to live with her sister,
Elanor, in the Bronx again, but it didn't work out. When Allen mentioned to
his doctors that he might live with her once he was released, they advised
him not to, as they would aggravate each other's mental problems. At the
moment he couldn't do anything but sympathize with his mother's lonely

plight. He remembered that on the last occasion he had seen her, she had become agitated with both Eugene and Aunt Elanor. Allen had winked at her to show his solidarity with her, but she was unable to recognize his compassionate gesture and began interrogating him compulsively in a monotone until he, too, became weary of it all and gave up trying to break through to her.

On June 29, after a delay of more than a month, Allen entered the New York State Psychiatric Institute on West 168th Street. More than anything else in the world he wanted to solve his personal and emotional problems through rigorous analysis, and he was eager to do exactly what they told him to do. Unfortunately, his first impressions of the hospital and the staff were not very good, and he began to lose confidence in them right away. He felt that most of the attendants had no idea of the true nature of madness; to them insanity was basically absurd, eccentric behavior. To Allen, the doctors were all "thin, pale lipped, four-eyed, gawky, ungainly psychology majors with vapid, half embarrassed, polite smiles on their faces." He wondered how these people were going to help his immortal soul. On one of his first days there, Allen heard a patient in a straitjacket screaming hysterically as he was being dragged to a padded cell. He had "flipped out" in the shower room, shouting "You're all gonna die!" dragging each agonized word out like a dog's howl, screaming as long as his voice held out. Before long Allen realized that it wasn't going to be as easy as he had hoped. He tried his best to be optimistic and wrote tentatively to Trilling on July 3, "Psychotherapy daily, no psychoanalysis; but I expect this to be sufficient and helpful, or hope."

Shortly after admittance, Allen met a long-term patient by the name of Fromm. He had been given every kind of therapy known—insulin and electric shock therapy, psychotherapy, narcosynthesis, and hypnoanalysis—but he remained unresponsive. All he did was silently sit and stare at the floor, occasionally shouting to no one in particular. It was obvious that Fromm's courses of treatment hadn't helped him, even though they had been administered by the same "liberal-minded social experimenters" who were about to treat Allen. Allen wished that he could break through to Fromm but realized that he could do no better than the doctors, just as he could not break through to his own mother anymore. Allen was given a partly catatonic roommate on the fifth floor by the name of Louis, who had snot continually dripping from his nose. He was a lovable character, the ward's mascot, but Allen didn't want to be distracted by a roommate. When the space was available, he was given a private room, which he thoroughly enjoyed.

Carl Solomon ~

Quite by accident, Ginsberg also met another young man in the wards who would make a profound impression on him and dramatically affect his life. Allen considered Carl Solomon one of his most interesting fellow patients. The first thing that made Allen notice Carl was his greeting, made upon coming out of an insulin shock treatment. "Hello, I'm Kirilov," he said to Allen, referring to one of Dostoyevsky's characters in *The Possessed*. "I'm Myshkin," was Allen's literate reply, identifying himself with the title character of the same author's book *The Idiot*. Allen had run across another kindred spirit in the madhouse, and he spent most of his free time over the next eight months talking with him.

Carl was two years younger than Allen, but he was already a veteran of several mental wards, and he was pleased to show Allen the ropes. Together they decided that if the doctors thought they were crazy, they should act crazy, so they started banging on the piano and yelling madly just for the hell of it. The staff almost lost their composure, but the pair enjoyed acting as foolishly as they could. Over the following weeks Carl told Allen the story of his life, how he had been born in the Bronx, where his father had died when he was eleven. He was so intelligent that he skipped a few grades before graduating from high school at the age of fifteen. Like Allen, he had been in the Merchant Marine, and on one trip had jumped ship in Brittany and made his way to postwar Paris. There he met some of the surrealists, and being fluent in French he became interested in their writings.

Carl was the first person to introduce Allen to the writings of Jean Genet, the homosexual criminal and hipster whose huge apocalyptic novels were "about the greatest, greater than Céline, perhaps," Allen discovered.

Through Carl's French literary magazines Allen also read the work of Henri Michaux and yet another madman, Antonin Artaud. Solomon had seen Artaud wandering the streets of Paris. He told Allen that he was shocked to hear a barbaric, electrifying cry echoing down the street and, investigating, discovered it was coming from Artaud. Solomon told Allen that "it was the most profound single instant he ever had," before the doctors gave him insulin shock treatments. Carl's favorite book was Isou's *Nouvelle Poésie et une Nouvelle Musique*, which he was happy to share with Allen. In this book the originator of Lettrisme, Isidore Isou, laid out his idea of placing emphasis on the sound value of poetry, so that readers could be free to ignore the actual meaning of the words themselves.

After Carl returned from France he enrolled in courses at Brooklyn College. One story that stuck in Allen's mind was of Carl's attending a lecture by Wallace Markfield, who was speaking on the subject of the surrealist work of Stéphane Mallarmé. Halfway through the lecture, Solomon began slinging potato salad at Markfield, a perfectly Dada act in itself. Instead of seeing the wacky charm in it, people began to question Solomon's sanity. Meaningless outbursts like that continued and multiplied. He stole a peanut butter sandwich from the cafeteria and showed it to the school guard, who referred him to the school's psychiatrist, who in turn recommended he enter a psychiatric hospital for evaluation. Solomon agreed, but when he showed up at the hospital he demanded a lobotomy, then he demanded an electrocution, then he demanded all sorts of tortures and soon found himself strapped to a table and given a horrific series of insulin shock treatments. Carl had calmed down quite a bit from those first few days in the hospital, when he had threatened to smear the walls with his own shit if they didn't assign him a private room so that he could finish reading Djuna Barnes's *Nightwood* in peace. Allen loaned Solomon some of the writings of Kerouac and Burroughs that he had smuggled into the hospital, and they discussed their mutual love for Walt Whitman. The doctors thought it was a good idea for Allen to continue keeping a journal in the hospital, and he wrote down many of his discussions with Carl verbatim. Those became source material for his future poem *Howl*, which was subtitled *for Carl Solomon*. Looking back on it years later Allen wrote, "In most cases I generalized the original incident to a sort of surrealist burlesque, blew up or exaggerated the original seed, or cartooned highlights of anecdote to make swift semi-surrealist verse anecdotes." As a patient, Ginsberg also visited the hospital psychiatrist on a regular basis and at the doctor's request began a long memoir explaining his involvement in the Huncke caper, which he titled simply "The Fall."

Allen wasn't kept under lock and key all the time, since he was relatively sane and obviously didn't pose a threat to anyone. He just needed help. As early as the middle of July, he was permitted to leave on weekends provided someone signed him in and out and took responsibility for him. Over the next few months, the hospital became more lenient with him, and he spent Monday through Friday in the hospital and went home to Paterson each weekend. Since Holmes, Ansen, Cannastra, and Ed Stringham were spending the summer in Provincetown, the resort town at the tip of Cape Cod, Allen considered signing out for a few extra days and going there with the doctors' approval. Outgoing as always, Allen took an active role in his psychiatric treatment and enjoyed socializing with his fellow inmates. He and Carl enjoyed the dances held on the roof of the hospital where everyone dressed in odd, homemade formal wear. In therapy class Allen even tried his hand at painting, but he wasn't very talented. He used the opportunity to make a painting of his Harlem visions as well as a series of paintings of Christ on the cross, whose suffering he identified with.

Epigram on a Painting of Golgotha, *CP*, p. 41

Allen and Carl came to the realization that the medical profession made no attempt to treat patients' true abstract madness as long as their social behavior was acceptable. He wrote in his journal, "I am torn between putting aside my loyalty and love directed to the past (the underworld, the mythical symbols of tragedy, suffering and solitary grandeur) and the prosaic community of feeling which I might enter by affirming my own allegiance to those bourgeois stands which I had rejected. Yet what do I know of the reality of all these bridges and ideas which make up the visible and invisible world?" His doctors' incompetence made it easy for Allen to picture himself as the wise, sane patient and the world as a madhouse.

In Death, Cannot Reach What Is Most Near, *CP*, p. 42

Solomon, in particular, and the other residents in general, made a lasting impression on Allen. At one point Carl carried his irrational behavior too far when he gave one of the doctors a handful of marbles and told him to swallow them. He had crossed a line and was treated severely. Allen wrote to Kerouac, quoting Carl, "There are no intellectuals in a madhouse," and it became one of their favorite expressions. He was a bit jealous when he found that other patients saw more visions in a single day than he had in an entire year, but it reassured him that he wasn't as crazy as he had thought. He discovered patients with the most profound mental disorders imaginable, from severe amnesia to schizophrenia and every degree of insanity.

This Is About Death, *CP*, p. 43

In the beginning Allen was more than willing to go along with his doctors' recommendations because he knew there was a chance that they were right and he was wrong. If society believed that fairies (as Allen called himself) were crazy, then Allen knew he was crazy and wanted to be cured. In those days very few people were living an openly homosexual lifestyle for Allen to use as a role model. In fact many of the overtly homosexual people that Allen knew were flamboyant queens, and he felt that he had little in common with them. More and more he realized that he was turned on by straight men, like Carr, Cassady, and Kerouac, and this puzzled him. Aside from the insanity issue, homosexuals were also treated as criminals, since their actions were illegal. In some ways Allen didn't mind being an outlaw as much as he minded being crazy, but both roles appealed to the young man. They were images both romantic and dangerous and he dreamed of being both.

Hymn, *CP*, p. 44

While in the hospital Allen still suffered from depression from time to time. After some of his poems were rejected by a little magazine and Jack's mother called him a "jailbird" one day, he seemed to regress even in his doctor's opinion. He began to complain about his health, and a pattern developed. When he returned from his weekends outside, he would invariably report that he didn't feel well. One week it was nausea, another a toothache, later indigestion, but always something that went away after a day or two. He was happy to receive whatever sympathy the staff gave him.

By mid-November Allen had altered his ideas enough to write, "This is the one and only firmament; therefore it is the absolute world; there is no other world. The circle is complete; I am living in eternity. The ways of this world are the ways of Heaven. The work of this world is the work of Heaven. The love of this world is the love of Heaven. This is to say that I know less theory and idea of eternity than ever."

Metaphysics, *CP*, p. 41

His opinions about his psychiatric treatments didn't change for the better during his stay in the hospital. He saw his doctors only two or three times a week, and when he did they seemed to be inexperienced young men and women who didn't care about or understand his particular problems. He tried to be cooperative because he had placed a lot of hope in psychotherapy, but now he felt that the doctors were too square. When they refused to let him join in the mescaline experiments they were conducting with outpatients he was disappointed. They tried to get Allen to fit into society by exposing his true feelings and desires and then pointing out how wrong they were. They discounted the Harlem visions and his interest in them, which irritated him, since they were of paramount importance to his

worldview. During the eight months he was in the hospital
he was under the care of four different doctors, all of whom
he considered basically rigid in method and of absolutely no
help to him. By trying to believe that they had some secret total knowledge,
he did his best to keep an open mind about their methods. He hoped that by
conforming, which to the doctors meant getting a job, finding a girlfriend, and leading a traditional active life, a miracle
might still be worked. The doctors were making notes of
everything in their reports and the director of the hospital
thought that Allen would "probably go definitely schizophrenic someday."

Sunset, *CP*, p. 45

Ode to the Setting
Sun, *CP*, p. 46

Paterson, *CP*, p. 48

A Dream, *CP*, p. 52

On New Year's Eve, Allen was furloughed from the hospital for the holiday and went with his new friends Bill Cannastra, Alan Ansen, and Russell
Durgin to a few parties around town. At one, he ran into a woman named
Helen Parker, a friend of Ansen's whom Allen described as "an interesting
doll who dug painters and was smart as a whip, drinks, with a beautiful generous nature." From her place the group made the rounds to other friends
like John and Mary Snow's house before they finished the night at Cannastra's
loft where a wild, all-night party was in full swing. A month later Allen wrote
to Helen apologizing for not having talked to her much that night. He said
that he was looking for "a compatible woman," hinting that she might apply
for the job. He had been thinking about her "with warmth and affection" and
asked her to write to him as if he were an old friend. This was a case of Allen
following the doctor's orders precisely and starting a relationship with a
woman. He assured her that he would soon be out of the mental hospital and
living with his family in Paterson. Although the prospect of being with him
might not sound romantic to her, it was what he needed at the time, he candidly confessed in his letter. His new stepbrother, Harold, also suggested the
names of a few women whom Allen subsequently wrote to for blind dates,
and his stepsister, Sheila, invited Allen to her sixteenth birthday party on January 21, 1950. Allen sat at the party with Harold having a good time while
they made fun of the kids, but deep down Allen envied their happy family. He
wished that he could be young once again; he was twenty-three but he felt
much older.

1 9 5 0 ～

BY FEBRUARY 27, the hospital staff felt that they had done as much for Allen as they ever could and gave him a certificate stating that he wasn't mad, merely run-of-the-mill neurotic. He left feeling a little better about himself and was determined to follow his doctors' advice by making himself fit into society in every way, but he knew that the cure he had hoped for had not been effected.

Long Live the
Spiderweb, *CP*, p. 54

While in the hospital he had stopped using Benzedrine, and as a result, "I felt relatively sane at the time," he recalled. Upon his release he went to stay at his father's in Paterson with a firm resolution to mend his ways.

Allen tried to get a job working on the *Paterson Morning Call*, a Democratic newspaper, but they had no openings. Next he went to the offices of the *Evening News*, which was a Republican paper. They remembered Allen from his days as a high school student when he wrote vehement letters denouncing the Republican candidates, so they questioned him at some length about the problems of taking on an employee with views contradictory to the newspaper's. Then he tried the *Passaic Herald News*, a conservative newspaper, where he had no better luck than with the others.

An Imaginary Rose in a
Book, *CP*, p. 57

Crash, *CP*, p. 57

In the meantime, Robert Giroux, an editor for Harcourt, Brace and Company, to whom Allen had sent his collection of poems, *A Book of Doldrums*, had been trying to place some individual poems. Giroux liked Allen's poetry and had hoped that if he could get a few little magazines interested, there'd be enough public recognition to warrant putting out an entire book. By February he had become discouraged and wrote to Allen that he was giving up. "I think that your very personal idiom needs some channel of contact with the reading public before book publication is possible," he said. Allen decided that the best course of action was to continue trying to get poetry magazines interested on his own. He fell back on his old Columbia contacts and visited Van Doren, who recommended he try the *Partisan Review* again, and maybe *Poetry* magazine, too. So Allen started the long process of getting his poetry published. He also gave Van Doren a manuscript of his father's newest poetry and asked him to advise his father on who might be publishing traditional lyrics like his. Van Doren was gratified to see that Allen was out of the hospital and eager to apply himself to straightening out his life. As an outpatient Allen saw his doctor each Monday, Tuesday, and Thursday morning, nearly as often as he had in the hospital, so that left him with lots of free time for writing and chasing publishers. He had set a few literary goals for himself. He decided to try his hand at nonmetrical poetry for a change, and he was also determined to rework his long poem, *The Shroudy Stranger of the Night*, into prose. Allen wanted to "begin in veils and supernatural mystery opening the window as in a dream and slowly reveal the Shroudy Stranger as a human without completion, unable to communicate or love, who does not know himself as a man like others and imagines that he is a satanic or divine incarnation and is waiting for another world outside of human reality to reveal itself to him, like Blake's 'Little Girl Lost'. As the poem proceeds the Shroudy Stranger becomes more human and tragic as in my vision in the movies of Dr. Jekyll and Mr. Hyde until his face is revealed in the end of the poem, as an old beat out decayed bum of America." After that, maybe he would continue his memoir about the Huncke caper. He had plenty of ideas.

The Shrouded Stranger, *CP*, p. 55

Eventually he found a job as an office boy with the *New Jersey Labor Herald*, a newspaper that at least shared his values. Allen's political views were beginning to develop, no doubt inspired by his spirited debates with his father every night. Spengler had predicted that a giant social transformation was going to change America, and Allen agreed with that theory. His opinion was that America was not really the "world-spirit-power," but that Russia was stronger both morally and militarily at that moment in history. This was the era when Russia was investing its resources in scientific advancement and developing atomic weapons, and the general public was not yet aware of the abuses of Stalin's regime. "We will become a sort of greater Spain or Portugal," Allen predicted.

He wrote to Kerouac, "A turning point has been reached in that I am not going to have anymore homosexual affairs anymore: my will is free enough now to put this in writing as a final statement." He thought, or at least hoped, that eight months in a mental hospital had "cured" him of that disease. Each weekend he went on dates with a variety of women, but nothing worked out. He wrote, "I wish I could meet a really gone sweet girl who could love me, but I guess a really gone sweet girl is too much to expect."

The Terms in Which I Think of Reality, CP, p. 58

At the beginning of 1950, Neal Cassady returned to New York once again. At the same time that Carolyn was giving birth alone in San Francisco to their second daughter, Jami, Neal was seeing another woman in New York, Diana Hansen, who became pregnant around the same time. Allen visited Neal and Diana a few times and made friends with her, but he found Neal "a little pathetic and dizzy."

The Night-Apple, CP, p. 60

He had also been thinking less of God since his hospitalization and more about his responsibilities as a worker, a scholar, and a writer of poetry. He wanted to read more about the poetic process, the history of meter and epic poems, but as usual couldn't quite find enough time to do everything he wanted and hold down a job as well. In the mental ward he had begun to think that God didn't exist and was becoming less afraid of Divine Wrath as a consequence. He was hounded by the old longing for his own death, but to counterbalance that, his desire to live had become much stronger. Again he found himself in the doldrums and was determined to keep himself busy and not lose heart because of it.

The Blue Angel, CP, p. 62

Two Boys Went Into a Dream Diner, CP, p. 63

A breakthrough occurred during the summer, which seemed likely to change everything. He wrote to Kerouac on July 8 as his brother and confessor, "Lift up your heart, there is something new under the sun. I have started into a new season, choosing women as my theme. I love Helen Parker, and she loves me." Allen had spent the Fourth of July weekend in Provincetown with Helen at her cottage. Several of his friends from the San Remo bar summered on Cape Cod, and Allen had always wanted to do the same. When Helen invited him to come up to her house he seized the chance to get away, see his friends, and even share the company of a woman. It proved to be a wonderful weekend for Allen. The first night there he slept with Helen and finally lost his virginity with a woman. To Jack he wrote, "She is very great, every way—at last, a beautiful, intelligent woman who has been around and bears the scars of every type of knowledge and yet struggles with the serpent, knowing full well the loneliness of being left with the apple of knowledge and the snake only. We talk and talk, and then we screw, and I am all man and full of love, and then we smoke and talk some more, and sleep, and get up and eat, etc." He said that after that first night of sex he wandered around in "the most benign and courteous stupor of delight at the perfection of nature." For the moment he felt that he had discovered heaven and all his previous queerness "was a camp, unnecessary, morbid, so lacking in completion and sharing of love as to be almost as bad as impotence and celibacy." True to Allen's obsessive personality, he fantasized about sex and the pleasures to come with other women. He even convinced himself that he was a great lover, which by most reports he was not.

A Desolation, *CP*, p. 64

Helen Parker was older than Allen, and as they both acknowledged, much more experienced. She had nearly been engaged to John Dos Passos and had lunched with Hemingway in Cuba. She knew everyone from Jay Landesman, the editor of *Neurotica* magazine, to Stanley Gould, another of Allen's subterranean junkie friends at the San Remo. She had two red-haired boys, ages five and ten, and it didn't take Allen long to realize that he was not mature enough to be a father to them. Even in the first few days of the romance, he worried about the financial responsibilities and commitments of a marriage as something he would never be able to live up to. Since he was under a psychologist's care and working a day job, he wasn't able to stay in Provincetown for the summer as Helen had hoped, and within weeks the logistics of a long-distance relationship had become overwhelming and they began to drift apart.

With Neal in New York in July, Allen wanted to spend more time with him, even though he was beginning to find him meaner and more unpleasant than he had previously. Neal and Diana were already having problems with their relationship. She was five months pregnant with Neal's baby and wept continually, which Allen said helped make Neal "shuddery and nervous." He revealed a good deal about his own thoughts on the subject of women when he wrote, "He [Neal] never should have let her have a baby— they were doing ok till she began to try capturing him with authority and ritual, and the baby was or became a kind of trick, which he let pass ambiguously; now it's marriage, they were in Newark the other day (with

Holmes and Harrington[17]) to get a license. Now he is restive, lost his job, had a call from the Frisco railroad, and is going back west in a few days. He promises to write, he will save money, he will be back when he's laid off; but she, that foolish girl, is beginning to see that she is stuck with the fruit of her too-greedy lust for him; and in the long run I believe she's fucked herself up, and him too, somewhat, by disturbing the balance they had before. She knew what she was getting into, but it was not only serious love, it was a kind of soupy insistence born of jealousy and vanity, that made her assume she would succeed in 'fixing' him up." As soon as their wedding ceremony was over Neal headed west again to return to his job on the Southern Pacific railroad, leaving Diana in the east. For a little while he even tried to maintain relationships with wives and families on both coasts.

Carl Solomon had left the psychiatric hospital in mid-November, long before Allen had been released, and at a party he met Jay Landesman, a guest brought by John Holmes and Alan Harrington. Landesman was intrigued by Carl's experiences and asked him to write an article about shock treatments that Jay subsequently published as "Report from the Asylum" in his magazine Neurotica. When Allen heard about Carl's success, he tried to get Neal to write a piece on car theft, which he thought could appear in the same issue. As far as his own writing was concerned, Allen felt that he didn't have anything good enough to submit, but he did send in "Pull My Daisy," the playful collaboration he and Jack Kerouac had worked on. It was included in the spring issue of Landesman's magazine and was the first poem of Allen's to be published since his student days. Allen was still hard at work on his long poem, The Shroudy Stranger of the Night, which was slow to take shape and wasn't ready to show any editors yet.

While he was living in Paterson, Allen went into Manhattan to hear William Carlos Williams read his poetry at the Guggenheim Museum. He was impressed with what he heard and wrote several admiring letters to Dr. Williams, who lived near Paterson in Rutherford, New Jersey. Allen had wanted to meet him ever since 1946 when he reviewed Paterson, Book 1 for the Passaic Valley Examiner. Even though Williams lived so close to Paterson, Allen didn't know much about him, and he hoped that if he did an interview with him, he might be able to get the local newspaper to publish it. Williams knew of Louis Ginsberg's poetry and was sufficiently impressed by Allen's letters to agree to the interview. He was in the middle of writing Paterson, his

---

[17]Alan Harrington (1918?–97): Friend of Holmes and Kerouac, the author of The Immortalist, depicted as Hal Hingham in Kerouac's On the Road.

epic poem, and parts of Allen's letters to him eventually wound up in *Paterson, Book IV,* identified as being written by A.P., which stood for "A Poet." Since Allen was trying to make the language in his poems more concrete, he was interested in getting Williams's advice on the subject.

When Allen finally visited Bill and Flossie Williams in their home, he was struck by the old man's casual, friendly manner. Allen thought that his dictum "No ideas but in things" was pure genius and made a great deal of sense. As they parted after their first brief visit Dr. Williams stood at the door and shared with Allen some pragmatic wisdom. "There are a lot of bastards out there!" he told Allen. As soon as he got home Allen wrote another letter to him and sent him samples of his own poetry. Williams believed that Ginsberg had talent, but was worried that Allen's early devotion to fixed patterns of rhyme and meter would hamper his creativity. He warned him that "in this mode, perfection is basic" and suggested that he try to create poetry out of everyday speech, which would free Allen from the traditional forms he was then struggling with. Although it seemed like an easy suggestion to implement, it wasn't. Without a pattern or model to follow Allen felt lost. After several failed attempts, he decided to find some of his old prose fragments in his notebooks and rework them into shorter lines of poetry. He sent a few of them, including "The Bricklayer's Lunch Hour" to Williams, who immediately and enthusiastically replied, "You've got it!" This encouragement from the elder poet was all it took and Allen began digging in his old journals for poetic inspiration from that moment on. He didn't see Williams often, but he acknowledged that he made "an enormous moral impact, moral influence, an esthetic influence" on the young poet.

Now that he was looking at his poetry through Williams's eyes he began to realize that his *Shroudy Stranger* poem was one more white elephant. Like most of his poems up until then, *Stranger* was fantasy, not reality. From then on Williams's motto, "No ideas but in things," became Allen's adopted credo, too.

By the end of that summer, Helen had begun to wonder if Allen was on the verge of cracking up again. He had become increasingly possessive and demanding of her attentions, often acting more like one of her children than her lover. He told her he wanted to write a long erotic poem in which he would compare their intimate sex talk to death, which gave her the creeps. Allen accused Helen of being ambiguous in her actions and said that he lived in constant fear of her criticism. By the end of October their relationship was over, and after that he could only think of her with disgust.

Ode: My 24th Year,
CP, p. 67

"She is a veritable Huncke of selfishness and deadbeat has-
sles. I don't want a whore, I want a finished product of self
education who has turned to stillness," he bitterly wrote at
the end of their affair.

Another sudden death was to jolt Allen and his friends that October,
much as Kammerer's death had back in 1944. In the past year or two Bill
Cannastra had become an integral part of their group, the central figure of
a big party scene that everyone reveled in. Bill had a reputation for being a
tremendous drinker—he was what Ansen called "a charming self-
destructive drunk"—and his West Twenty-first Street loft in a drab warehouse district was littered with the empty bottles of countless binges. Carr,
Kerouac, Holmes, Solomon, Ansen, and many others typically began or
ended their nights at Cannastra's, drinking heavily. Allen speculated that
Bill drank to excess to cover the fact that he was secretly queer. Cannastra
was not just wild, but partied to the edge of madness. His dissipations
and exploits were near legendary, so much so that Holmes and Kerouac
couldn't help but write about him. At one of his parties, Cannastra
stripped naked and challenged Kerouac to do the same and race him
around the block. A more modest Kerouac left his briefs on and followed
him out the door. In *Howl* Ginsberg had Cannastra in mind when he wrote
the lines about the man who "cried all over the street, danced on broken
wineglasses barefoot smashed phonograph records of nostalgic European
1930s German jazz finished the whiskey and threw up groaning into the
bloody toilet."

On the afternoon of October 12, Cannastra and a few friends were riding the uptown IRT subway when it stopped at Bleecker Street. On impulse
Bill decided to climb out of the subway window and go back to the Bleecker
Street Tavern for one more drink. As the subway car began to move Cannastra became wedged in the window, and try as they might, his friends couldn't
pull him back inside the train in time. When the subway reached the end of
the platform, he was crushed between the train and the tunnel wall and his
mangled body was dragged out of the train. It was a gruesome way to die,
and many friends speculated on whether it might have been the result of a
death wish. Allen was fully convinced that it was a conscious suicide related
to his secret queerness and he wrote to Helen in Provincetown, "I think
henceforth, this event being a crystallization of all that people are beginning
to understand, at least of my generation, that we will be glad of the lesser
joys of life and deal with the void less attracted by it, be more serious perhaps, not so tolerant and loving of the chaotic element which is ultimately

death-dealing. We should at last know enough about it by
now, if we didn't before."

In Memoriam: William
Cannastra, 1922–1950,
CP, p. 65

Unfortunately, Allen was once again out of a job; he had
been fired from the labor newspaper in New Jersey for incompetence and his unemployment compensation had not
yet come through. Losing the job had been another blow to his pride, as he
realized that he couldn't hold down even what he considered a "pissyassed"
job. He signed on to work in a Paterson ribbon factory near River Street, but
he wasn't able to get the hang of tying together the tiny broken threads on
the looms and was fired within a few weeks. Allen blamed a couple of the
women there for not showing him the ropes, although he also admitted that
he was guilty of daydreaming on the job most of the time anyway. Manual
labor was never to be easy for Allen. His lack of physical coordination was
also the main reason he never learned to drive—"If I did I would have an accident within a month," he wrote. He did get something out of the factory
job, though, for he documented it in his early poem "How Come He Got
Canned at the Ribbon Factory," which he wrote from the
viewpoint of the working girls. With his therapy sessions
coming to an end, his doctors had advised him to give serious consideration to entering intensive psychoanalysis. Allen

How Come He Got
Canned at the Ribbon
Factory, *CP*, p. 68

was mentally prepared for it, but his problem was financial.
He simply could not afford long-term treatment without a job, and he tried
to find a cheap clinic where he could continue analysis.

Due to his questionable mental health, when Allen's name came up for
the military draft again in 1950 he was summarily excused on psychological
grounds. He was thankful for little blessings. Even though Allen believed
his analyst had inferior intelligence and was able to treat him only because
Allen cooperated, he did allow that some good came from it. He believed
that his psychiatrist had been able to break him of "schizoid paranoid belief
and queerness." His doctor was quite generous with Allen and continued to
treat him for free even after Allen's benefits ran out. Through analysis Allen
felt that he was getting to a deeper understanding of himself. He still
wanted to die, but his fear of the act of suicide and the pain that went with
it preserved him.

A few days after Cannastra's death, Joan Haverty, one of Bill's old girlfriends from Provincetown, moved into his loft and tried to continue his
party house tradition. Some of his friends thought she was trying to build a
shrine to Cannastra by doing so. On November 7, Kerouac met Joan on his
way to another house for a party and ten days later, in one of those odd,

Kerouac, Lucien Carr, Ginsberg ~

spur-of-the-moment impulses that occurred in Kerouac's life, he married Haverty. The wedding was occasion enough to hold yet one more boisterous party in the Cannastra loft. It began with the civil ceremony at 6:00 P.M. and went on all night. Lucien and Allen acted as Jack's best men in the judge's chamber and then they went back to the loft to greet several hundred revelers who awaited the newlyweds. At three in the morning as the bride slept, Lucien, Jack, and Allen put their heads together, kissed drunkenly, and sang "Eli Eli." This was the kind of camaraderie that Allen longed for and preferred over the company of women. Later in a letter, he rudely remarked that Joan was "a tall dumb dark-haired girl, just made for Jack." In the next sentence he clarified himself to say, "Not dumb, really, since she's 'sensitive' and troubled . . . full of a kind of self-effacing naiveté, makes dresses as vocation; but she can't compare with Jack in largeness of spirit and so I don't know what she can give him except stability of sex life, housekeeping and silent, probably sympathetic company while he's sitting around, and children."

Allen, proud of his imagined sexual prowess with Helen Parker, was now acting and talking almost like a Don Juan and casually began dating several other women. For a few days in late October he had even schemed to sleep with Joan Haverty and take over the loft, fantasizing that she'd also be willing to support him financially. Jack beat him to it and married her, but since it turned out that Joan didn't have any money after all, Allen claimed he was relieved. Allen believed Jack's marriage to Joan was mad since they barely knew each other. "But we all should have beautiful intelligent wise women for wives who will know us and vice versa. And let several families gather together, menfolk and womenfolk, childfolk following, for society," Allen pontificated. He desperately wanted to restore the old group spirit that had permeated Joan Adams and Edie Parker's apartments six years earlier.

The Archetype Poem, *CP*, p. 69

A Typical Affair, *CP*, p. 71

As the Christmas season drew near, Allen was able to land a temporary job working in the Paterson post office. He lived at home, earned some money, and had time to write. Williams had become the most important influence on his writing, and whenever he could he went out to Rutherford to see the old doctor and talk to him about poetics. On one of these visits Williams gave him Ezra Pound's address at St. Elizabeth's Hospital in Washington, D.C., where Pound was confined in lieu of prison after being accused of treason for conspiring with Mussolini during World War II. Allen wrote to Pound asking for help with his poetry, telling him that he had spent the last eight months in a madhouse, too. He included his poem "Ode to the Setting Sun" with the letter and asked Pound to comment on his system of measure. Allen didn't believe that Williams had any concrete system outside his ear alone, or at least not a system that Allen could identify. It was clear that Allen was looking for a formula or pattern he could follow. Williams's poetry "isn't gone, wild, weird, whatever romantic enough, . . . no bounce, no beat." Allen wanted to carry poetry further. He wanted to write a long narrative poem in a new meter that would sum up all metrical or measurical progress and apply it to a clear narrative line full of intense American imagery. He hoped such a poem might even be apocalyptic. He summed up his request to Pound by saying, "I just want to get an angle on where to look and work in next years," and asked if he could visit him sometime in Washington. Pound answered negatively, "Dear AG, None of you people have least concept of FATIGUE. I have said it all in print, i.e. all answers to yours. Cantos no use to people writing shorts. E.P." In a separate letter to Williams, Pound suggested that his old friend keep his nuts to himself. Allen was disappointed but not discouraged by Pound's rejection and he didn't give up trying to meet him.

1951 ~

ALLEN WAS STILL clinging to his older poem, *The Shroudy Stranger*, working and reworking the lines, but it appeared less likely that he would ever be satisfied with it. By March, he wrote, "Right now I am beginning to get immersed in a real study of metrical possibilities. More, it can be measured not by accents but, as the Greeks, by length of time it takes for syllables." Due to Williams's influence he was starting to see poetry as an extension of spoken language. During the first week of March, Allen had a breakthrough. He saw portions of a giant, thirteen-thousand-word letter that Cassady had written to Kerouac about his love affair with a woman named Joan Anderson. The letter was interspersed with lots of autobiographical details about Neal's childhood in Denver and was to become so important in beat lore that it is still referred to in the literature as "The Joan Letter." Neal wrote the letter over a period of several days between December 17 and 22, 1950, but Allen had to literally steal it from Jack's desk to read it. Jack sensed its importance and was afraid that Allen might lose it. It was written in a narrative style that profoundly altered both Kerouac's and Ginsberg's methods of writing and heralded a new form in American literature. Allen wrote, "I read it with great wonder, stopping and laughing out loud every few paragraphs, so much clarity and grace and vigor seemed to shine in the writing." It was composed with "speed and rush, without halt, all unified, one molten flow; no boring moments, everything significant and interesting, sometimes

A Poem on America, CP, p. 72

breathtaking in speed and brilliance." It was written exactly as Neal spoke, a monologue on paper, and it inspired Jack and Allen to think about their own writing in a different way. In their future written work they strove to capture the spontaneity of Neal's pure speech.

At that very moment, Jack was about to rewrite his novel *On the Road*, which he had been struggling with for three years. It was the perfect time for him to receive the Joan Letter, because it inspired him to be equally spontaneous with his own prose. In April Jack rewrote the entire book as one nonstop discourse. It was the breakthrough that he had been looking for. It took him three weeks to do it, typing rapidly on long sheets of paper he found in Cannastra's apartment. Those he taped together so that it made a scroll that could be easily fed into a typewriter. Kerouac was able to tap into Neal's verbal energy and capture it on paper, in the end producing a new American classic. It took Allen a little longer to adapt Neal's rhythm to his own poetry, but it gave him an indication about the direction he wanted to follow. Reading Jack's new version of *On the Road* only reinforced the example set by the Joan Letter in Allen's mind. Allen wrote to Neal in May telling him that Jack had finished *On the Road*. It was a tremendous achievement, but Allen thought it needed a stronger ending to be truly great. He asked Neal to write a letter for Jack foretelling his future life that might inspire Jack to write a better closing chapter.

As these letters were flying back and forth, Carolyn had become pregnant again and Jack told Allen that Neal "went back to the woman that wanted him most." By then Jack had already left Joan Haverty in order to return to his mother, and Joan was left alone and pregnant with what was to be Jack's only child, Jan Kerouac. Allen sympathized with Neal's new ex-wife, Diana Hansen, and had lunch with her several times. She was extremely upset and completely destitute so Allen suggested she consult his brother, Eugene, now a lawyer, for a legal opinion about what options she might have. Jack also used Eugene as his lawyer during his battle with Joan over child support payments, which he bitterly contested.

After Dead Souls,
CP, p. 73

His friends' marital problems did not dissuade Allen from still trying to make it with women. That summer he briefly dated a woman named Mardine who quickly left him to marry a man Allen referred to as "Weak Joe." Allen had also been seeing another woman during this same time named Dusty Moreland, whom he occasionally and unkindly referred to as

Ginsberg and Dusty Moreland ~

"Dustbin." Dusty was an attractive, dark-haired woman who had come to New York from Lusk, Wyoming, to pursue a career as a painter. She was considered promiscuous by the standards of the day and enjoyed sex nearly as much as she enjoyed drinking.

Each night in bars like Fugazzi's and the San Remo Allen was making new friends, including Peter Van Meter and Larry Rivers, both of whom Allen was attracted to. Although he was trying his best to be heterosexual, Allen's interests were still primarily male. He had managed to land a little work as a book reviewer for *Newsweek* but it didn't lead to anything steady and only provided an occasional dollar or two. Jack and Lucien had been talking about a trip to Mexico, but Jack had an attack of phlebitis in his leg and couldn't go. Since Allen had nothing better to do and had just received a tax refund of sixty-five dollars, he filled in for Jack at the last minute. Lucien's girlfriend, Liz Lehrman, was also planning to ride along but she dropped out, too, leaving only Allen and Lucien (and Lucien's dog) to drive to Mexico. They sped south as fast as they could, trying to squeeze in as much fun as was humanly possible in the two weeks before Lucien had to return to his job with UPI. The reason for going to Mexico in the first place was to attend the wedding of Russ Lafferty, one of Carr's coworkers at the wire service. They also wanted to visit William Burroughs and Joan Adams, who were now living in Mexico City with their two children, Julie and Billy.

Unfortunately, William was out of town when they arrived in late August, and they didn't get to see him, but that didn't hold them back. They had a wild drunken week with Joan, attending Mexico City bullfights and climbing to the top of the Pyramid of the Sun. The visit ended with a hair-raising drive at breakneck speed across the Sierra Madre mountains to the Pacific Coast. Lucien and Joan were both drunk and shared the wheel, while Allen and the two children hung on for dear life in the backseat. Later, Allen romanticized the drive by remembering it as "great kicks and torment of continual threat of death," but at the time he was terrified. On the way Lucien was arrested for drunk driving and compounded the situation when he "insulted Mexican national honor" with a few loose remarks made to the policeman who pulled him over. Later Allen declared that the most beautiful scenery on earth was the stretch of rolling plains between Guadalajara and Tepic that he glimpsed for the first time on that trip. It was to be memorable for darker reasons, too.

After their vacation carousing in Mexico, Lucien had to get back to work. He was in no position to lose his job, so he and Allen drove north and got as far as Houston, where the car broke down. Allen was unemployed and more flexible with his time than Lucien, so he stayed behind with the car to oversee the repairs. Leaving Allen in Texas on September 5, Lucien flew back to New York with plans to return the following weekend when the repairs were completed; then they'd both drive back in the car. Two days later, on September 7, Allen opened the paper in his hotel room and was shocked by a news story that said that Burroughs had accidentally shot and killed Joan the previous day in Mexico City. Accounts of the story differed, but it seemed that William had returned from his trip right after Lucien and Allen left and had gone about his business as usual. He owned a handgun, which he was demonstrating to a potential buyer, and for a reason that will never be known, Joan put a glass on her head and dared William to shoot it, à la William Tell. Even when drunk, his aim was usually extremely accurate, but not this time. He missed the glass completely and shot Joan in the middle of her forehead. She was pronounced dead a few hours later. The Mexican police arrested Burroughs, but he was able to hire a lawyer good enough to get him out on bail. A few months later, before going to trial, his lawyer advised him to skip town, so he fled to South America, avoiding a likely prison term. Joan was only twenty-seven at the time, but Allen noted that she looked twice that age when they last saw her: "Drugs and tequila had ruined her beauty before the bullet." For someone so young, Allen had already experienced more than his share of violent death.

Once back in Paterson, Allen's life resumed where he had left off. He went to visit Williams again and showed him his new poetry culled from the pages of his journals. It impressed Williams so much that he offered to write an introduction for a book of Allen's poems. During their conversations that fall he advised Allen to leave poems unfinished if he wanted to. He said it was better to have a fragment consisting of a few great lines than to pad a poem with mediocre ones. It reminded Allen of Cézanne, who sometimes left his paintings unfinished if he couldn't think of what to do with a blank corner of the canvas. One day Dr. Williams treated Allen to an expensive meal in downtown Paterson, at which they had a great time gossiping about Genet, Pound, Robert Lowell, and Marianne Moore. Then they walked around looking at the Passaic Falls and the swimming holes along the riverbank that figured so prominently in Williams's poems. When it was time to go home, Allen asked the sixty-eight-year-old doctor if he was afraid of death, to which he simply nodded and said, "Yes." Before Allen said goodbye, he gave Williams more poems to look at and Williams seemed to like those, too, calling later to say he'd help him get a book published "even though I'm on my last legs." It was flattering for Allen to hear that his poetry reminded Williams of Jean Genet's work. Through his example Allen learned to be generous with the younger poets he would meet in the future.

One day that same year, while sitting in the Pony Stable Inn, a seedy lesbian hangout in the Village, Allen struck up a conversation with a good-looking young man who had recently been released from an upstate prison. The young man, only twenty years old, was there with Armando Diaz, a sketch artist who made a living by doing caricatures of the customers. In the course of their conversation, Ginsberg learned that the young man was also a poet and in fact was carrying a large sheaf of poems around with him. Allen read a few of them and noted the name, Gregory Corso. Corso told Ginsberg an exciting story of how he had been jailed for taking part in a sophisticated stickup of a Household Finance office using walkie-talkies. The story was not true, but it was typical of Corso to fabricate romantic lies about himself. Corso had grown up on the streets of Greenwich Village and had gotten into one minor scrape after another with the law. Finally he had been arrested for stealing a suit he had wanted to wear to impress a girlfriend on a date. He felt that he would get more respect in prison if he told the other convicts a better story, so he had invented the Household Finance robbery scenario.

On the day they met, Corso got into a long conversation with Ginsberg about watching one of his neighbors disrobing in front of her window every night. As Corso described the apartment and the people, Allen couldn't believe the coincidence, because Gregory was describing his own current girlfriend, Dusty Moreland. Allen decided to play the story up big, so he told Corso that he was a magician. He said that if Corso wanted to meet this sexy woman, Allen could conjure her out of thin air. That evening, Corso had the surprise of his life when Allen did, in fact, introduce him to that very woman, and before long Gregory's fantasy of making love to her was a reality. Allen, not jealous in the least, hoped that this act of sexual generosity might lead to a closer friendship or maybe even something more with Corso. On another occasion he and Dusty went to a party at Lucien's where everyone was drunk. Lucien and Dusty ending up having oral sex and shouting at each other, "I'm as nasty as you are." Nonplussed, Allen took Dusty home and slept with her the same night. He was much more possessive and jealous when it came to his male friends.

Allen began spending a good deal of time with Corso. He explained his new writing technique to him by saying that he wrote as often as he could in his journal and then later pulled out the things that seemed to be complete poems. That was the process that had brought him success in Williams's eyes. Corso was skeptical of all the hard work that Allen's method seemed to involve. He relied more on inspiration and didn't write anything needlessly. He told Allen that when he wanted to write a poem, he sat down and wrote it. They talked at great length about their different approaches to writing and became fast friends in the process. One of the first things Allen did was to take Gregory to see his old professor, Mark Van Doren, who lived in the Village. He wanted to get Van Doren's opinion about Corso's poems, which Allen believed were good on the surface, but too raw and undisciplined. "He's still wet behind the ears," Allen wrote to Kerouac. In his journal he noted, "Corso's poetry doesn't make sense. All mostly bloody imagination." Corso wasn't the least interested in the dictum "No ideas but in things," when Allen tried to explain it to him. It was the first time that Allen could act like the experienced older writer with anyone, even though he still hadn't had any commercial success. Recently he had been sending his poems out liberally and had been rejected by *Poetry* in Chicago, the *Berkeley Review*, and dozens of other magazines. Even though he had Williams's promise of an introduction, he wasn't close to having his own book published yet.

By the fall, Allen decided to move back into New York City, hoping to find a room at the Mills Hotel on Bleecker Street or move in with Seymour Wyse,[18] a friend of his who worked for Jerry Newman[19] at Esoteric Records. Wyse had been tutoring Allen in modern music theory for the purpose of mastering meter, which Allen hoped would help his poetry. To earn his rent Allen got a part-time job coding questionnaires for a market research firm in the Empire State Building, Doherty Clifford Shenfield. Within a few weeks, by the end of September, he had moved on to do similar work at the National Opinion Research Center on lower Fifth Avenue. It paid enough to support himself modestly, which was all that he needed. Carl Solomon and his new wife, Olive, worked for the same company, as did John Clellon Holmes, so it was a friendly environment for Allen. He always fared better at jobs with people he knew. The work was boring, but he kept active by taking a class on the cinema two nights a week. It was the first time he ever thought of film as an art form.

With Allen's newfound financial stability he was able to afford his own apartment, on the top floor of an old building at 346 West Fifteenth Street, not far from his office. There he stayed for the next year and paid a modest weekly rent. He had a blue-painted garret in the attic with dormer windows that faced the enormous Port Authority warehouse to the north and the rooftops of the Village to the south. He wrote feverishly and imagined himself as a figure not unlike Melville's Bartleby, the scrivener, pitiably respectable and incurably forlorn. The best thing about Allen's job was that it afforded plenty of time for writing and hanging out in the Village in the evenings. Holmes, who by now Allen had known socially for a year or two, was trying to make it as a novelist. Like Kerouac, John based his books on his friends, and Allen was one of the characters in his first novel, titled, simply enough, *Go*. It was while Holmes was working at the National Opinion Research Center in late December that Scribner's accepted his book, prompting him to quit market research work immediately. Excited by the news, Allen wrote a telegram to Jack to tell him about Holmes's great success. Then after further reflection he wrote a longer second letter to tell Jack that

Walking home at night,
CP, p. 78

---

[18] Seymour Wyse (b. 1923): A jazz aficionado who was originally a classmate of Kerouac's at Horace Mann prep school.

[19] Jerry Newman (1920–70): Owner of a record shop and music label that had recorded jazz greats like Dizzy Gillespie.

Go stank. Both Allen and Jack came to believe that Holmes was poaching
on their own territory by telling stories about their lives in
his book. Allen got over his jealousy quickly, but Jack har-   Gregory Corso's Story,
bored a grudge against Holmes and his quick success much   *CP*, p. 75
longer.

   Almost every day Allen wrote something in his journal. One day, after
smoking a little pot, he made this note: "It is December, they are singing
Christmas carols in front of the department stores down the block on
14th St. I felt like Baudelaire in his damnation, and yet he had great youthful moments of staring into space looking into the 'middle distance'
contemplating his image in eternity, they were moments
of identity. It is solitude that produces these thoughts."   Marijuana Notation,
Allen was also depressed because Lucien, the last of his   *CP*, p. 74
single friends, was planning to get married in January.
Allen never thought he'd see Lucien get married; he always hoped that
somehow he would be able to break through and win his love, even
though Lucien loved women and had dozens of girlfriends. Miserable,
Allen climbed the stairs to his attic room one day and put his hands to his
head and cried, "Oh God how horrible." He had a knife that he and Lucien had brought back as a souvenir from Mexico and he considered using
it to commit suicide. When he mentioned it to Corso, Gregory wisely advised him to remove the temptation by getting rid of the
knife. Allen sat alone reflecting on the past seven years and   A Ghost May Come,
his crush on Lucien. "Lost passions, now this real world   *CP*, p. 79
now seemingly dispassionate and fearful with anxiety   I Have Increased
growing in." As he once had done in his Denver cellar   Power, *CP*, p. 76
                                                                  I learned a world
while waiting for Neal, he wrote about his unrequited love   from each, *CP*, p. 78
for Lucien. Many of these notebook entries from this pe-
riod were later turned into poems. Now he saw his life as vile, painful, and
racked by the pessimism that he felt was Lucien's legacy to him. On December 10, he wrote about fleeting time: "I waste time—whole days,
weeks, years have passed by. I walk around aimlessly not noticing things,
not experiencing anything new, emotionally or spiritually, just dreaming
or analyzing without result and with an aimless aim." Once again in
nearly unbearable misery, he managed to forestall suicide.

   On December 31, he wrote his final entry of the year   I made love to myself,
in his notebook: "Tonight I made love to myself in the   *CP*, p. 78
mirror kissing my own lips—saying, 'I love myself, I love

you more than anybody.' " The short prose was arranged later on the page
as a poem:

> I made love to myself
> in the mirror, kissing my own lips,
> saying, "I love myself,
> I love you more than anybody."

1952 ~

O N J A N U A R Y 4 , Lucien married Francesca "Cessa" von Hartz, the daughter of Ernest von Hartz, the national news editor for the *New York Times*. Cessa was bright, attractive, and intelligent, in fact, the previous summer she had written her first article for the *Times* about the Alexander Hamilton–Aaron Burr duel. Depressed, Allen wrote that Lucien looked like a toy doll with his neat mustache and plastered-down hair. He noted that Lucien wore a gray suit with a flower on his lapel and talked with all the old ladies, making them laugh. Fortunately, Allen made it through the ceremony without a major breakdown, but his emotions were on edge all day and he couldn't believe that the marriage was actually taking place. John Hollander, one of Allen's college literary rivals, also attended the wedding and while talking to Allen praised his new poems, which John said reminded him of Rilke's. He was quite enthusiastic about them. At that moment flattery from Hollander was what Allen needed most, and John told him that he had grabbed the "whole metrical problem by the balls, breaking out of it and talking like we really talk." This was the true debt that Allen owed to Williams, who had inspired him to pay attention to ordinary American speech rhythms.

Saddened by losing Carr to marriage, Allen made plans to ship out with the Merchant Marine on the next available boat. The maritime union had promoted him in class to yeoman, so now he had the opportunity to make good money and do paperwork on board instead of washing dishes. His immediate goal was to make one or two thousand dollars to pay for analysis, which would help him break out of his New York doldrums. His love life had

I came home from the
movies, *CP*, p. 81

I feel as if I am at a dead,
CP, p. 79

An Atypical Affair,
CP, p. 80

been rapidly deteriorating. In response to Carr's marriage, Allen had asked Dusty Moreland to marry him, but she had turned him down and had gone back to her home town in Wyoming for an extended visit. It didn't upset Allen, as he was merely trying to follow his doctor's advice in the pursuit of a heterosexual relationship. The immediate result of his forced heterosexuality was that he became more passive with the women he dated. "I just lay back and let people blow me," he said. In fact, at the time he proposed marriage to Dusty, he hadn't had intercourse with her in several months. In one letter to Kerouac, Allen confessed that he had seduced Corso, but immediately felt remorseful. As Allen told it, Gregory had gotten drunk and been beaten up in a bar fight one night. He escaped, bleeding, to Allen's apartment, and there Allen had tended his wounds, patted his head, and consoled him. Then, also typical of Allen, he gave Corso a blow job. For a brief moment, it had made Allen feel more worldly and experienced than Corso, but it soon became something that they both regretted. Corso in particular held it against Allen for the rest of his life. Gregory later lamented that at the very moment when he needed sympathy the most, Allen had taken advantage of him. For his part, Allen felt guilty about it, but there was nothing he felt he could do except try to make amends. Shortly thereafter Corso left town for the West Coast, where he worked for a short time as a cub reporter on a Los Angeles newspaper and fathered his first child.

In February Allen received a letter from William Carlos Williams that picked up his spirits. Williams wrote, "Wonderful! really you shall be the center of my new poem—of which I shall tell you: the extension of *Paterson*. For it I shall use your 'Metaphysics' as the head. How many of such poems as these do you own? You must have a book. I shall see that you get it. Don't throw anything away. These are it." Allen was taken off guard by Williams's enthusiasm. He had sent him what he considered to be little more than scraps picked out of his journals. He had rearranged them on the page to look more like poetry. They were exactly what Williams was interested in, snatches of actual language set down on paper. Whether they were complete thoughts or not, Williams could sense in them Allen's keen ear for language.

His 1949 journal entry that read, "This is the one and only firmament; therefore it is the absolute world. There is no other world. The circle is complete. I am living in Eternity. The ways of this world are the ways of

Heaven," became the 1952 poem that Williams referred to in his letter as "Metaphysics."

> This is the one and only
> firmament; therefore
> it is the absolute world.
> There is no other world.
> The circle is complete.
> I am living in Eternity.
> The ways of this world
> are the ways of Heaven.

Mocking the simplicity of it, Allen wrote to Jack boasting that he could write ten of those a day. He did find it an interesting new method—"All you got to do is look over your notebooks, that's where I got those poems, or lay down on a couch, and think of anything that comes into your head, especially the miseries, then arrange it [in] lines of 2, 3 or 4 words each, don't bother about sentences, in sections of 2, 3 or 4 lines each."

On the heels of this praise for his own poetry, Allen was also about to have some luck as a freelance literary agent, too. Since all his friends were writers and no one had been able to find a publisher for his books, Allen had decided that he might as well do it himself. Burroughs later gave Allen credit for his whole writing career by saying, "Without the incentive of that publication [his first book, *Junkie*], I might well have stopped writing altogether." Ginsberg began by trying to place *Junkie* for William, but soon began sending out Kerouac's books as well as his own poetry to publishers. The thing that Allen never got used to were the rejection slips he received for what he considered the brightest works of his generation. Jason Epstein at Doubleday told Allen that if *Junkie* were the story of the heroin habit of Winston Churchill it would be of interest, but as it was only about an ordinary junkie, there would be no audience for it. Louis Simpson at Bobbs-Merrill also warned Allen that *Junkie* was unpublishable. Even though several people had cautioned Allen that he would never be able to find a publisher to take on *Junk* (as *Junkie* was originally named), Allen had Carl Solomon as his secret weapon. After being released from the mental hospital again, Carl had gone to work for his uncle, A. A. Wyn, who owned Ace Books. It was Carl who offered a contract with a $250 advance to Kerouac for *On the Road* after Allen sent him the manuscript. Allen certainly hoped Jack would sign the contract.

"Yes, Jack, *On the Road* will be the First American Novel, by gum we going places," he wrote, urging Kerouac to sign. But Jack was insulted by the low offer. Allen also thought Wyn might take on a book of Alan Ansen's poetry, too, and sent him a selection. In the meantime Carl showed interest in publishing Burroughs's book and gave him a contract with an advance of one thousand dollars in April. Burroughs, Ginsberg, and Solomon were all equally thrilled when the contract was signed. Wyn even talked about doing another book by William, but as the first manuscript was passed around the Ace office they began to have second thoughts. One staff member, Mrs. Phinney, complained that the book was immoral and quit her job straightaway, but in spite of that reception, *Junkie* slowly made its way through Ace's prepublication process.

Dusty returned from Wyoming, bringing her mother with her, and they found a place of their own in the Village at 19 Barrow Street. Even though Allen still wanted to marry her to prove he wasn't homosexual and join all his friends in wedded bliss, he realized that he didn't have the "force or money" to do it, and only as an afterthought did he add "and we don't love each other." It seemed love was the last thing on his mind when it came to women and marriage. He and Dusty remained good friends, and although they hung out together all the time and occasionally slept in the same bed, they never made love again. Allen made note of the fact that he was getting tired of sex with women. In a few months he was going to be twenty-six years old, "which is almost 30," he calculated. He felt he was getting close to the age when he'd possess his greatest creative energy, but he was feeling more isolated all the time. Many of his friends were changing, maturing and moving on. Lucien and Cessa were drunk much of the time, throwing things at each other, "just like always," Allen wrote to Jack. Allen also bumped into Bill Garver, one of their old drug connections who eked out a living by stealing overcoats from customers in restaurants. Garver told Allen that a mutual friend, Phil White, had committed suicide in the Tombs, the street name for the city jail. White had been sentenced to do time in Rikers Island prison where some thugs he knew were waiting for him. Garver thought that White had hung himself to avoid being beaten by them, but Huncke later explained the whole story. White hadn't meant to kill himself. His plan was to fake a suicide attempt so that he would be sent to the prison psychiatric hospital. Unfortunately, the guards didn't reach him in time and he died.

While waiting for the Merchant Marine to call him, Allen spent a lot of time with a new group of people that he began calling the subterraneans.

They were cool and hip young aesthetes. Bill Keck, who lived in the East Village and built harpsichords in his loft, Anton Rosenberg, who ran a frame shop and art gallery in the Village, and Peter Van Meter[20] were good examples of the type. Allen thought that he might move in with Van Meter until he got a ship. During the month of February Allen went to the union hall every day and sat from ten to three waiting for his name to be called. Then in the evening he met friends such as Alan Ansen, Richard Howard,[21] John Hollander, Carl Solomon, and Lucien Carr in Village bars.

During this period, Solomon was not having an easy time working for his uncle's publishing house. Allen was putting pressure on him to publish not only Burroughs, but Kerouac, Ansen, and a book of his own poetry. Ginsberg even proposed that Wyn give contracts to Cassady and Huncke, who hadn't even thought of writing books yet. He saw publication as a way to make his friends' writings legitimate and to create a literary movement around them. Ginsberg wrote to Jack, "All things considered I have really come to believe that between us three [Kerouac, Burroughs, and Ginsberg] already we have the nucleus of a totally new historically important American creation." Kerouac was quick to point out that it was not a literary movement but a small circle of friends, but to Allen that was splitting hairs.

In truth, the entire Beat Generation phenomenon could be seen as a group of writers who had little in common stylistically, but who were united by their friendship with Allen Ginsberg. There are few similarities in the works of many of these writers, except a possible sharing of sensibilities, which defines their friendship more than it defines a common literary style. So devoted was he to making sure that Carl didn't back off in his attempts to publish their work that Allen gave up the idea of going to sea and stayed close to New York. Carl was still having trouble convincing his uncle that *Junk* was truly literature, while at the same time Allen was pushing hard to negotiate more book contracts for his friends with Ace. Caught in the middle, Carl was trying to be careful with the books he recommended. He called Allen in April to say that he thought the last nine pages of the second version of *On the Road* were incoherent and needed to be rewritten. Allen could see that Carl was in over his head at the office and afraid to make a giant financial mistake with his uncle's company. Since Allen believed that Jack

---

[20] Peter Van Meter: A friend originally from Chicago, depicted as Paddy Cordovan in Kerouac's *The Subterraneans*.
[21] Richard Howard (b. 1929): Columbia classmate, poet, translator, and editor.

was the greatest writer alive in America, he knew that *On the Road* had to be published. With that as his main objective he continued to press Solomon for publication and ignored how all the pressure might be affecting his friend's fragile mental condition.

In his spare time Allen typed up a collection of his own poems, which he titled *Empty Mirror*, and sent it off to Mark Van Doren for his valued opinion. To Allen, the phrase empty mirror meant a "mirror uncolored by rainbow of one's own imagination and desire." With all of their books up in the air at Ace, Allen had to sit and wait; it was nerve-wracking. Once more he began to think that his life's work was heading nowhere. He did not have enough confidence in his own writing to know if it was good or bad; for that he needed the reassurance of other people's criticism and opinions, like those of Van Doren or Williams.

On March 12, as William Carlos Williams was dressing to go to a party at Clayton Hoagland's house, Allen happened to drop in to see him. Hoagland was a neighbor of Williams's in Rutherford who was also a poet and worked for the *New York Herald Tribune*, where Allen had been writing an occasional book review. Dr. Williams asked Allen to go along with him to the party, and on the way he showed Allen a copy of his *Paterson, Book 4*, which included excerpts from Allen's letters to him. This kept Allen elated through an otherwise dull party. He felt as if all the people he talked to were afraid to be themselves and so they put on erudite fronts. In his opinion all their talk about the things that they were reading in the popular magazines about southwest Indians and Mayans was esoteric nonsense. Allen was curious about the secret inner thoughts of each person, finding out what made him tick. He was bored by idle chatter and small talk on such occasions. On the way home in the car, Williams surprised Allen by confiding in him that he worried that his own poetry had no form. Williams said that he tried to squeeze his lines into pictures on the printed page and he was never confident about the results. In some ways, Allen was encouraged by Williams's lack of self-confidence; it meant his own self-doubts were not altogether out of line.

In those days Allen felt lonely and depressed much of the time and had reservations about almost everything in his life. Dramatically, he composed another will at the end of March, leaving all his tangible property to Louis and Eugene and his poetry to Kerouac. "In all the time I've lived (25 years) no one has ever looked into my eyes and said, 'I love you' the way I wanted to hear it said. . . . Do I want something wrong? Am I looking for something impossible? Or should I say no one I've ever wanted to has said it; though I have looked into other's eyes and said those words and meant it, in silence as an eternal vow. Some have hinted that they love me—but I couldn't or didn't love them—certain creeps. Some I've said I love you to have said, on different occasions I love you to me, but not meaning complete submission and self-delivery and total physical and spiritual sacrament and devotion (of body and soul)." Now he thought back to the vow he wanted to take with Neal while on the road to visit Burroughs at his Texas farm and how it had been like a dream "that nobody shared with me, a childish, solipsistic fantasy." This wasn't one of the high points in Allen's life, and only a few days later he wrote in his journal, "Right now at this very mo-   A Crazy Spiritual, ment I wish to be dead."   *CP*, p. 83

Van Doren didn't respond at once to the manuscript of *Empty Mirror*, so Allen sent a copy of it to Kerouac, who took the time to write a long commentary. Allen was grateful and for the moment he felt that Jack's was the only opinion he would ever value. In spite of that, he sent a copy of his poems to William Carlos Williams asking for his comments and even considered sending a copy to Auden for his feedback as well. Even though Allen noted that he wrote to "put naked self down on paper, to put truth to personal fact," he was ashamed of being homosexual and skirted the issue in his writing. When Williams asked him if he liked men after reading between the lines of Allen's early poetry, Allen categorically denied it.

Jack was staying with Neal in San Francisco at the time he critiqued *Empty Mirror*, and he invited Allen to drop everything and come out, but Allen was determined to go through psychotherapy in New York City before going anywhere. That month he took time to sum up his life, "I am 25 years old, good looking in a personal way, dark, wear glasses, am called Allen Ginsberg. My relations with the outside world are limited—I am dependent on my brother, on government, on parents and on friends for spending money, even for food. I can work if I set my mind to it at uninteresting jobs, sometimes show signs of gregariousness and get along well, sometimes am perceptive, but have a tendency to talk a lot, too much about myself, pointing attention to myself—almost obsessionally recurring conversations with other people to my own weakness, strengths or sense of self; almost all my concern is with my self and its manifestations. I have no strong relation with my father; more with my brother on equal, though dependent footing. I have no secure relationship involving my whole character with another person, though I secretly admire and love several men and few women—who usually have position or are popular and successful sexually—and who reject me as a sexual lover but accept my friendship—which is a friendship more maintained by me than by them, though they do respond and are warm and really like me; but I do not enter into or share their lives. I share my life with no one, and wish to share my life with someone, man or woman; though I do not know what a relationship with woman will mean to me, I hope it is with a woman and try to bring that about."

Wild Orphan, *CP*, p. 86

By now Allen had all but given up on Dusty Moreland as a viable romantic partner. He went out a few times with Helen Elliott, an old friend of Jack and Lucien's, but once again he felt no real sexual interest. Dusty advised him not to get tied up with her because she felt that Helen was too aggressive and didn't see them as compatible. She didn't give him any suggestions on who might be suitable, though, so Allen was lost.

His subterranean friend Bill Keck had come across some peyote, which he shared with Allen, and that gave him a new substance to experiment with. He tried it several times before he had any reaction to it at all, but once he had taken a strong enough dose he described it as a combination of Benzedrine and marijuana. Under the influence of peyote he played Tito Puente[22] records on his hi-fi, listening to them while he saw great Technicolor visions flashing before his eyes, as he recalled in a later interview. Once in Paterson after he took a few of the unpleasant metallic-tasting chunks of peyote he came up with the perceptive line, "We're flowers to rocks." Then he stretched out on his father's sofa and thought about a recent encounter he had had with Dylan Thomas at the San Remo bar which hadn't amounted to anything. "Ah, Dylan Thomas, I would have liked to know you that night, wish I could have communicated who I was, my true feeling, and its importance to you. For I too am a lover of the soul. How disappointing to come away empty-handed with no recognition from this chance meeting."

At one of the many parties he attended, Allen ran into Dick Davalos, a handsome man whom Allen described as "a flashy piece of flesh, contemptible." During his on-again off-again relationship with Dusty over the previous year, Allen had seen a little of Davalos. But Allen was so confused about his own position as lover, queer or straight, that he almost always waited for the other person to make the first move. Davalos was Allen's ideal of beauty, with soft tender eyes and a beautiful low voice. At Davalos's instigation they made it a few times together, but there was too much talk about love from Dick, which always seemed to destroy the possibility of love for

---

[22] Ernest "Tito" Puente (1923–2000): Puerto Rican musician, the king of Latin music.

Allen. The real problem with Davalos, according to Allen, was that he was too selfish and too much of a fairy for Allen, who by now preferred someone who was, or at least appeared to be, straight.

By the summer, after several months of severe depression, Allen's friends were beginning to notice signs of his madness again. Lucien warned him not to drift off into an unreal world and wind up in an institution again, as if it was something he was purposefully trying to do. Allen wrote, "I do not want to change, to begin to grow again; my life is so dreary and gray for me, this unfulfilled longing for boys, the frustration of disappointment with Dusty. I am growing older and grayer of mind and heart, and I want love, and I have not in my lifetime yet found love, nor do I see it in my future."

Allen was painfully aware that his depression and loneliness were pushing him to the brink of insanity. When Kerouac invited him to rendezvous in Mexico he had to decline, saying he was "terrified of going off into the night again, toward death maybe, or oblivion beyond the pale tenderness of New York daily life." Following a daily routine and the hope of a psychiatric breakthrough were the only two things that kept him from going back to the madhouse. He couldn't afford to travel anyway, and he was still occupied with pushing *On the Road* through the tangle of editors at Ace. Seeing Kerouac's book published had become Allen's primary goal. To keep Jack happy, Allen had to reassure him that he would not charge him an agent's fee, but Allen was doing it purely for the love of the writing anyway, so that didn't bother him.

In May Allen decided he'd try to guest edit an issue of the magazine *New Story*, so that he could publish excerpts of Kerouac, Burroughs, Solomon, Huncke, himself, and maybe even include Harrington, Holmes, and Ansen. He had entered his own story, "The Monster of Dakar," into a contest sponsored by that magazine and hoped that either he or Kerouac would win the grand prize of a trip to Paris. Jack had recently written to him about the invention of what he called "sketches," quick short portraits done at one sitting without revision, and Allen wanted to see some of them, hoping that he could get them published. He even sent a rare Burroughs short story to the *American Mercury* for their consideration, but nothing came of any of these efforts. Even though he devoted a considerable amount of time and energy to agent work he wasn't able to convince a single publisher, other than Ace, to risk money on any of his friends' work.

Everyone was becoming discouraged from lack of publication and Allen felt that if he could help just one of them break through, all the rest would follow. Well-meaning as he was, his single-handed efforts were wearing him out and he wished he could return to his own solitary writing. As Ace Books moved ahead with their plans to publish *Junkie*, they were becoming even more cautious about the book and wanted to make substantial changes. First of all, they felt that it was too short in the current form and they thought that if it couldn't be lengthened, it would have to be bound with another book, back to back. They also wanted to include more details about Burroughs's own life and a disclaimer so that the public would not think that the views expressed in the book were the views of the publisher. They were also considering another Burroughs book, *Queer*, for publication, but they wanted to change the narrative of that from first person to third person. In the end they decided to wait until they had a reaction to *Junkie* before they moved ahead with *Queer*.

It seemed inevitable with all the pressure from his job and his uncle, not to mention Allen's lobbying for more books by his friends, that Carl would have another breakdown. Finally, his wife left him as a result of his crazy outbursts. He smashed all their glassware and carelessly flooded the floors of their apartment with dishwater. When he tried to stop traffic on Eighth Avenue near Fortieth Street by throwing shoes and briefcases at the passing cars, Carl was sent to Bellevue for observation. All of Allen's hopes with Ace Books were put on hold until Carl could return to work, and that seemed unlikely to happen in the near future.

At that moment a completely new version of *On the Road* (which would later be published posthumously as *Visions of Cody*) arrived from Kerouac. At the beginning of June Allen read it and wrote back to Jack, "I don't see how it will ever be published, it's so personal, it's so full of sex language, so full of our local mythological references, I don't know if it would make sense to any publisher." Despite his reservations about the possibility of publication, Allen had no doubt about the extraordinary literary quality of the book. "The language is great, the blowing is mostly great, the inventions have full-blow ecstatic style. Also it's the best that is written in America," Allen said. He was certain that no publisher would take it in its current form, and he even doubted that anyone would ever publish it. In short, it was beautiful, but not publishable. It was by far so different from any other writing of the day that Allen felt safe in calling it "a holy mess." It wouldn't make sense to anybody, "except someone who has blown Jack," Allen explained to Neal in a letter, but that didn't stop him from trying to find a publisher willing to take a risk on it.

One of Allen's strongest attributes was his tenacity, and once he got an idea in his head he held to it obstinately. One such idea was his obsession with seeking out Ezra Pound for advice. Once again he wrote to Pound in St. Elizabeth's Hospital, "What I have is a lot of raw material. I don't know anything about what William Carlos Williams would call measure. Maybe you could help me find a way to make an artistic production out of the 'heap of crap' he speaks of." Pound wrote back stating unequivocally that he was too exhausted to see any more strangers, but Allen felt that if only Pound would agree to see him, he might be able to answer some of Allen's questions about meter. He was determined to keep trying.

That June, Dusty Moreland moved back into Allen's apartment. Then, following the death of her cat, Dusty suffered a nervous breakdown. She treated it herself by going on a six-day drinking binge. Allen's father saw their cohabitation as a harbinger of new trouble for Allen, but Allen felt Louis was being irrational and ignored his warnings. What seemed to help Allen the most was being surrounded by friends, whether crazy or sane. Jack had returned home from his trip and he and Allen commiserated with each other over their lack of success in love. Neither of them could muster up much enthusiasm for romance. On July 20, Allen sadly wrote in his journal, "I never ride on the subway toward an interview for a new job without dreaming of suicide."

Due to the turmoil caused by Dusty's return to his apartment, Allen decided to find a small, cheap place by himself. He also decided to latch on to the first job that came his way and make the best of it, no matter how menial it was. He was so insecure that he suffered terribly every time he went out to find work, so it was best to get it over with. If he found a job, he was certain he'd fail at it anyway, but he had to work or rely on other people for support. Analysis was still an important consideration and he needed to earn enough to pay for that. He believed that only through analysis could he resolve his problematic sex life.

Along with his lack of confidence on the job, Allen had completely lost faith in his own poetry. When he sent some of his poems to the poet and editor Charles Henri Ford, he apologetically added, "I don't myself say these are either prose or poetry, they're Writings. And if it ain't poetry then that's the best you can do." Allen had befriended Philip Lamantia in New York and Philip had kindly referred Allen to the surrealist Ford. He had also given him Kenneth Rexroth's[23] address in San Francisco, in case he should ever be out

---

[23] Kenneth Rexroth (1905–82): Influential leftist poet, critic, and translator; considered a father figure for the San Francisco Renaissance.

that way. Lamantia was a sweet young poet from San Francisco, who, as a teenager, had been adopted by the surrealists. Although he was likeable as a person, Allen thought that Lamantia's writing was too focused on cabalistic themes. Deep down Allen felt Philip was not an ignu (a special honorary posthip intellectual term he and Kerouac had coined to apply to like-minded people).

Three thousand miles away in California, Neal could sense Allen's unhappiness and depression through his letters and thought that a trip to the West Coast might cheer him up, so he wrote inviting him out. For the time being Allen repeated his desire to stay put until he could straighten out his life, but he was pleased to be asked. To Jack he wrote that he disdained the world, but now, "I see I was all along really cowardly and craven and running away from life frightened."

During these years Allen tried as best he could to do what society expected of him. He made an effort to hold down a regular job, but he was a terrible employee and didn't seem to be suited for anything practical. He was always late, he was clumsy by nature, he was forever daydreaming on the job, and most of the work he could find was not interesting to him. He longed for adventure. Nothing had ever held his interest for long, except poetry and writing. His market research jobs certainly seemed tedious and useless. The only positive thing about these jobs was the regular paycheck.

In October Allen found just the apartment he was looking for and signed a one-year lease. It was a "sweet little pad" at 206 E. Seventh Street for $33.80 a month, and even though it wasn't in a very good neighborhood, it was fine for him. He was pleased to have three rooms on the third floor, and he could leave Dusty in his old apartment on West Fifteenth Street without feeling guilty. His new place quickly became a clubhouse for his ever-growing circle of colorful friends, and Allen was never happier than when they dropped in to see him. The move was the easiest way to get away from Dusty because, even though she wouldn't marry him, their lives were entangled in many ways. Surprisingly, Allen let her move all her clothes into his new apartment, and before long they were almost back to where they had been before.

Then, in the fall, Dusty vanished and Allen had no idea where she was or if she'd ever be back. He realized that his move hadn't cured his depression and he frequently caught himself sitting in his new kitchen staring blankly at the white table and blue linoleum floor for what seemed like hours. He realized that kicking his cigarette habit was the only positive thing he'd accomplished in the last few years. Dejected and with no clear idea of what might lie ahead for him, he wrote the the title "The Life Failure of Allen Ginsberg" on his notebook. He knew that it was quite probable that his future would be just as disappointing as his past. He imagined that he would live alone in one cheap apartment after another and depend on mechanical, low-paying jobs to sustain himself. His friends would become successful, marry and prosper, and leave him behind. "Quiet desperation, as Louis used to say, which is to say the subject matter is still Death, now in its creeping form," he concluded.

He saw other people, such as a Columbia classmate Louis Simpson, who was now a successful editor and professor at the New School, with a jealous envy that drove him mad. Although he was in an influential position, Simpson could find no artistic merit worth mentioning in the work of Ginsberg or Kerouac, and that alone was enough to prove his ignorance to Allen. All the same Simpson prospered in the literary world, while Allen and his friends couldn't even pay their meager rents. He was afraid to face Simpson, lest he insult him and reveal his envy. The success of John Clellon Holmes with his novel *Go* was difficult for Allen to swallow as well. He wondered why Holmes should get a twenty-thousand-dollar advance for a mediocre book when the very people that *Go* described couldn't get their own books published. When Holmes presented Allen with a roll of toilet paper as a housewarming gift for his new apartment, it was meant as a joke, but Allen found it insulting.

Allen started to think that personal kicks were taking up too much of his time when he should be producing real work. Marijuana was a case in point. He and Jack had recently agreed on the negative side effects that came from the extended use of grass. "It is absolutely poison for the mind after the 3rd year if taken at length. Because it simply leaves you your fucking daydreams. Daydreams are alright but if you put all your effort into daydreams you wind up a pathetic old eccentric without a strength to his name, a spot of reality to call his own. Fuck kicks. On account of marijuana use you can't communicate, reassure, chitchat, joke with, talk serious with, etc."

At least Kerouac was able to continue working industriously on his novels even if no publisher wanted them. Every night he would stay up late at his mother's kitchen table writing until dawn, producing book after book. On October 17, Kerouac sent yet another finished novel to Allen to try to agent. This time it was *Doctor Sax*, which Allen recognized instantly as "better than *On the Road* [actually *Visions of Cody*] and I think also it can be published. I believe with *On the Road* and *Sax*, you have hit a whole lode of originality of method of writing prose, method incidentally though like Joyce is your own original and make and style."

1953 ～

OCTAVIO PAZ WROTE: "Man is the only being who feels himself to be alone and the only one who is searching for the Other."[24] Despite the fact that Allen felt terribly lonely, he wasn't alone very often. His gregarious personality attracted a circle of friends who socialized and partied endlessly. He was always able to find someone to talk to in the Village bars he loved to frequent, but he longed for that one special person to love and to return his love. On New Year's Eve he remarked to Kerouac that he hadn't had sex for months, with the exception of a "colored cat" he picked up one night in one of the bars. That holiday night he and Jack were making the rounds from party to party and ended up listening to jazz in Jerry Newman's recording studio. At dawn they grabbed a cab back to Allen's place where Allen attempted a heart-to-heart talk with Jack. Allen had read yet another new book that Jack had finished called *Maggie Cassidy*, about Jack's boyhood romance with Mary Carney. Allen had hoped to discuss it with Kerouac, but in his inebriated condition it was useless. More and more these days Jack was either at home with his mother and inaccessible to Allen or in the city too drunk to have a meaningful conversation.

On Sunday, January 18, Allen went to visit his mother, institutionalized once again at Pilgrim State Hospital. He watched her small, frail form as she walked toward him down the short hallway to the waiting room. The flesh on her face was ashen and she had lost the cheerful, robust look that he re-

---

[24] Octavio Paz, *The Labyrinth of Solitude* (1950), ch. 1.

membered from his boyhood. Allen always thought that she would somehow outlive them all, but now he saw in her eyes the old age that presaged
her death. After suffering a series of strokes and sicknesses she was no longer
rosy and sweet, but looked deranged and frightened. She began crying the
minute she saw him and immediately asked him to leave. As the attendants
led her back to her room, Allen went into the men's room and sobbed uncontrollably. It had been Allen who had signed the release papers for her lobotomy back in 1947 and he could never forgive himself. He had hoped the
operation would soothe her troubled mind, but now he saw that it had only
given her new fears and horrors that she could no longer express. The doctors believed that it had reduced her mood swings, but she was still paranoid
and believed that they had "put wires in her head" that now they refused to
remove. At other times she complained that the doctors had put three big
sticks in her back and between the wires and the sticks they were controlling
her like a marionette. She imagined that Hitler and Mussolini were still out
to get her and other unnamed enemies threw poisoned bugs at her from
which she could never escape. They were all images common among mad
people who felt controlled by unknown forces and voices inside their heads,
but Allen felt that by authorizing the lobotomy he had surrendered her to
these secret controllers.

During his life, fame was the one quality that consistently attracted
Allen to other people. He was brilliant at networking with people in order to
meet and befriend celebrated men. Allen had first arranged to meet Wystan
Hugh Auden at Columbia in 1945 when the distinguished British poet had
come to read to the students. Allen had volunteered to ride back to Sheridan
Square with Auden on the subway, hoping that he'd invite him up to his
apartment and seduce him, but he hadn't. After having bumped into Auden
around town several times, Allen went to visit him in his new apartment on
St. Mark's Place and found him with Chester Kallman, Wystan's long-time
companion and another acquaintance of Allen's. Auden and Kallman were
obviously close, which made Allen envious of the companionship they
shared. On this particular afternoon they talked about poetry and books and
Allen proudly showed him the introduction that Williams had written for
Allen's book of poetry. Auden barely looked at the pages before dismissing it
and told him that he considered Williams an eccentric. Even though Wystan
was a recognized intellectual, Allen found Wystan closed-minded on several
topics and he and Allen had little in common. Allen certainly didn't care for
it when Auden dismissed Genet's talents, and Allen couldn't stomach Percy
Jones, one of Auden's favorites.

Without Carl Solomon there to lobby for Allen's suggestions, it came as no surprise when Ace Books turned down Kerouac's *Maggie Cassidy*. Jack had suggested that Allen offer it to them, but he was displeased when Allen suggested that he revise parts of it for the publisher. He was getting tired of people, even Allen, telling him how to write his own books. When Allen asked Jack to write a blurb for the cover of Burroughs's *Junkie*, Jack refused angrily. He was unwilling to be associated with a book about a drug addict and thought it might draw unwanted attention to him. One evening as Allen said good night to Jack at the Delancey Street subway stop he reminisced about all they'd been through together over the past decade. Sad and burdened by his loneliness, Allen felt more alone than ever before, and it began to dawn on him that his inescapable queerness was beneath every one of his erotic and emotional thoughts.

An Asphodel, CP, p. 96

By May he had lost another job in market research and found work with the Scott Meredith literary agency. Among their clients were mystery writer Mickey Spillane and the mysterious writer B. Traven, author of *The Treasure of the Sierra Madre*. Ginsberg was assigned to read the work of amateurs who paid a five-dollar fee to submit their work for Scott Meredith's consideration. Allen was sympathetic with most of the people who sent in their work, none of which would ever be published. Most of their stories were little more than sophomoric writing with stupid, inane plots. He was told that it was his job to let them down gently enough so that they would send another story and another five dollars. Viewing this as a literary con, he lasted only two weeks. He said he was fired because he couldn't spell and wasn't able to work quickly enough to earn his salary. He continued to make ends meet by typing legal documents for his brother, sometimes earning as much as thirty dollars a week.

My Alba, CP, p. 97

Junkie, Allen's one success as a literary agent, was finally published in May and Allen sent the first copy and a check for $270 to Burroughs, who was in South America. Unlike Kerouac, Burroughs told him to keep the thirty-dollar commission for himself. Half humorously he told William, "Reaction has been very good from junkies." Next Allen wanted to place *Maggie Cassidy* with a publisher, but Jack was on the road again and Allen couldn't get Jack's mother to let him have the manuscript. Mrs. Kerouac was convinced that Allen was a bad influence on her son and didn't trust him. In the meantime in San Francisco, Neal had fallen off a train and broken his ankle badly, putting him out of work and on crutches. For Neal it was the perfect time to do the reading that Allen had suggested. Ginsberg had been spending a lot of his own spare time studying Zen Buddhism and looking at Japanese and Chinese paintings in the museums and at the New York Public Library on Forty-second Street. He suggested a similar course of education for Neal. With Kerouac's guidance Allen was trying to learn all he could about the "sublimity and sophistication of the East." Because he had no context for what he read, most of the Buddhist writings seemed vague and nebulous to him. Being visual, the scroll paintings were more inspirational and accessible. Allen was intrigued by one painting in particular, *Sakyamuni Coming out of the Mountain*. It was a portrait of the Buddha with long, tearful eyebrows and big ears, showing him after his year of meditation retreat. Jack had introduced the concept of *satori*[25] to Allen, and the word *satori* in particular seemed to fit Allen's own earlier Harlem illuminations. Another appealing aspect of many of the Chinese poems he read was their common thread of old friends' being far away from one another. Some of the poems had originally been enclosed in actual letters between the ancient Chinese poets, and that was exactly how Allen and his friends were sharing their work with one another now.

Sakyamuni Coming Out from the Mountain, *CP*, p. 98

By the end of June, when Allen wrote to Neal Cassady again, he had started to revise his method of composition once more. The Joan Anderson letter had inspired him to create a new form for his poetry. In his *Empty Mirror* poems, Allen felt that he had perfected his method of stripping down rhetoric to the bare bones, so now he began to lengthen his lines using Neal's Joan Letter and Jack's most recent books as models. "The Green Automobile" was his first attempt to do just that. "Mainly I discover life so unsatisfactory that I am beginning to use my imagination to invent alternatives," he wrote. When he was with Jack that summer, he showed him a page of sketchy notations he'd made about the Statue of Liberty. Jack was impressed and asked Allen why he didn't type it up as it was. Allen said that he would have to rework it into a poem, but Jack dismissed that notion. He directed, "Just start writing from the middle of your mind and type it up." Allen sat down at the typewriter on the spot and wrote what was in his head at that very moment about the copper-green goddess of liberty waving from her pedestal. It was a funny poem, sloppy in form and never published, but it excited Jack, who encouraged him. "See, you can do it too," he said. Further instructions from Kerouac were to "capture the segment of time, everything that is happening

The Green Automobile, *CP*, p. 91

---

[25] *Satori*: Term used to denote the experience of awakening.

in front of you, there is your perfect poem." This was one more giant step toward Allen's discovering his own poetic voice and style. It was a form of spontaneous writing that was not "stream of consciousness" or "automatic writing" but aimed at writing what was on his mind by being aware of what he was thinking, as he was thinking it.

Since Neal was laid up on crutches, an idea began to take shape in Allen's mind. He'd take a long pilgrimage, hitchhiking leisurely across the country for several months, and wind up in California to stay with Neal and Carolyn. It would give him a fresh start on life, with a new job and a new career in San Francisco. In New York, the best he had been able to do was work as copyboy for the *World Telegram* at forty-five dollars a week. That money was enough to pay his rent, but Allen was ashamed and felt the position was beneath him. "For a man of my education and background it's equivalent to being an errand boy."

He also felt misunderstood by all his friends. Neal had accused Allen of siding with Diana Hansen against him, which upset Allen since he loved Neal above all others. He couldn't believe that Neal felt he could betray his trust. Allen was also convinced that Holmes's *Go* had painted a misleading picture of him and set the minds of his friends against him. Holmes had described Allen as a sad, schizophrenic boy, clinging to his mad Blakean visions. Allen declared that Holmes was nothing but an "empty-headed idiot" who gossiped too much. He speculated that a respite from most of his friends might do him some good.

Before he left for the West Coast Allen had a few things to wrap up. He was still acting as Kerouac's agent and had finally gotten a copy of the manuscript of *Maggie Cassidy* from Jack's mother. It was promptly rejected by A. A. Wyn. On July 13, he picked up the manuscript along with Wyn's official rejection letter and took the book to MCA for their consideration. Jack was becoming more critical of Allen's failures on his behalf. In the meantime Burroughs, Allen's only success, was quite pleased with the publication of *Junkie* and had been writing long letters to Allen from South America, where he searched for an elusive hallucinogenic vine called *yage*. Allen collected William's letters with the idea that they would make a great book and encouraged him to write more. Burroughs agreed, eager to keep in touch with Allen, secretly hoping to someday have a more intimate relationship with him. He continued to charm Allen with his outlandish short vignettes that they began to call "routines," and he included some with each letter.

That summer, while planning his trip, Allen wrote an essay about Kerouac's prose to attract a potential publisher. He also reworked his poem "The Green Automobile," trying to understand Neal's account of the vow Allen believed they had made on the Texas road. In the poem he wrote, "And now renew the solitary vow/we made each other take/in Texas, once:/I can't inscribe here." After reading Neal's version of the pledge as retold by Kerouac in *Visions of Cody*, Allen realized that he had remembered it as being more significant than Neal had. He tried to work it out in this poem. Allen told Neal that he intended to "idealize it and make a legend of love out of it, a purely imaginary thing which exists and existed only in my own mind which since it has a beauty of its own I intend to clarify by hindsight and make eternal. The point of this poem is to rewrite history, so to speak, make up a legend of my poor sad summer with you." "The Green Automobile," written in large part in New York in May 1953, was a poem about what Allen had hoped would have happened in Denver 1947, not what really happened.

When Burroughs arrived at the door of Allen's apartment around August 30, Allen realized that he hadn't seen him since his visit with Neal to the New Waverly farm. Over the intervening six years, they had both been through many changes. William asked to stay with Allen briefly until he made up his mind about what to do next. He ended up staying for three months. At first Allen wrote, "He is really exciting to talk to, more so for me than ever. His new loquaciousness is something I never had the advantage of. I am older now and the emotional relationship and conflict of will and mutual digging are very intense, continuous, exhausting and fertile." Allen couldn't wait to get home from work each afternoon and sit with William on the old rust-red sofa, talking about everything into the small hours of the night. He couldn't get enough of the inspired conversation. William was seriously in love with Allen and was driven by his long pent-up desire to be with him. Allen preferred to think of it as a marriage of two minds, but William wanted a physical union, as well as an intellectual one. He pressed Allen continually for sex until Allen was forced to say that he wasn't interested in William in that way. He didn't do it in a gentle way either, but blurted out that he "didn't want his ugly old cock" anywhere near him. That comment broke Burroughs's heart, and Allen regretted his insensitivity for the rest of his life. Later he wished he had been more generous toward William, but he was frightened of all William's talk about "schlupping" Allen, which he described as a physical takeover that would absorb not only Allen's whole body, but his soul as well. As the weeks rolled by on Seventh Street, William began to throw jealous tantrums whenever Allen spent time with anyone else, especially Dusty. The situation seemed hopeless. Allen could see that William's possessiveness was going to force Allen's absolute rejection of him unless he could get away. Burroughs repeatedly stated that he wanted to put his life entirely in Allen's hands, which was a disturbing prospect for Allen, who felt he couldn't take care of his own life. Allen wrote, "Even I never went that far."

Around Thanksgiving, Burroughs made plans to visit his parents in their new home in Florida. After that he was considering a relocation to Morocco, where he had heard one could live cheaply and enjoy both boys and drugs with little worry about the authorities. During the visit Allen and William spent most of their time either at the apartment or in bars with friends like Corso, Ansen, Kerouac, and the rest of the subterraneans. Everyone in the literary world seemed to be hanging out at the San Remo that fall. One evening Kerouac bumped into Gore Vidal at the bar and after they were quite drunk, Gore took Jack home for a queer tryst. Differing versions of the night were presented by Vidal in his book *Two Sisters* and by Kerouac in *The Subterraneans,* but the real story was that Jack was too drunk to do anything and slept it off in Vidal's bathtub. According to Allen, Kerouac never initiated gay sex and the only times that he responded to homosexual advances were when he was drunk.

In October Kerouac and Ginsberg had had a heated argument about Allen's agenting of Jack's books to MCA. To preserve their friendship, Allen saw that he should step out of the agent role with Jack and leave that to someone else. At Allen's suggestion, Alene Lee, a black girlfriend of Allen's who lived a few blocks away, began to type up the letters William had sent Allen from South America for the purpose of making a book. Her love affair with Kerouac and Corso earlier that summer had already become the underlying theme for Jack's short novel *The Subterraneans,* written in a matter of a few days that fall. Later in life Alene admitted that it had been Allen she was originally in love with, not Jack or Gregory. The Burroughs letters became *The Yage Letters,* published in 1963 under that title by City Lights Books. Only William's side of their correspondence survived, because Burroughs hadn't saved Allen's letters to him in South America as faithfully as Allen had saved Burroughs's.

Even though Allen and Jack quarreled about publishing matters, the pair toyed with the idea of going into partnership together to publish small editions of their own books and those of some of their friends. That idea grew out of their mutual frustration at their lack of success with mainstream publishers. Allen had complete confidence that they were creating an important new form of literature, and he couldn't understand why the leading editors in the country didn't see it as he did. Kerouac, Burroughs, Corso, Ansen, and Ginsberg were all waiting to be published, and even if they had to do it themselves, they would. Only a small investment of a few thousand dollars would be needed to get their books out, but unfortunately, neither he nor any of his friends had anything at all to invest in the venture. Self-publication appeared to be something they might have to resort to later if nothing else turned up.

At the end of November, when Burroughs left New York, Allen was genuinely relieved. He enjoyed having Burroughs around but the pressure William had put on him was too much to bear. Alan Ansen, who had never been out of New York before, made plans to meet Burroughs in Tangier to help him type and organize his next book, to be called *Naked Lunch*. Even at that early date Ansen believed that Burroughs was one of the great writers of the century, something that Allen thought was hyperbole, but nonetheless charming. With William gone, Allen could begin to plan for his long trip west. Several letters filled with suggestions for living arrangements, job possibilities, and classes were exchanged between Neal and Allen. It was Allen's wish to pursue his studies of Chinese art and culture more formally and perhaps to settle in California for the next few years. Late in November an encouraging letter arrived from Neal and Carolyn repeating their invitation for Allen to live with them as long as he wanted in San Jose. By the time he was ready to go Allen had saved nearly three hundred dollars for his trip, a portion of which he sent ahead to the Cassadys for safekeeping. Along with the money he mailed them his only copy of *The Yage Letters*, for them to read.

One of the last things Allen did in New York was write a goodbye letter to Lionel Trilling in which he enclosed a copy of "The Green Automobile." Allen had been spending a good deal of time revising the poem and he wondered if Trilling thought it was worth the effort. Bitter and discouraged by the New York publishers, he told Trilling that once he settled in California, he intended to self-publish his own and Kerouac's books. Malcolm Cowley[26] had called Jack "the most interesting unpublished writer in America" and the truth of that statement irritated Allen. He couldn't understand why a publisher wouldn't take on at least one of Jack's five unpublished novels. In his letter Allen took one final swipe at Trilling, who he felt hadn't done enough for him over the years. "I seem to remember an essay of yours saying 'let the poets come forth and make their demands' if they are real poets and the

---

[26] Malcolm Cowley (1898–1989): Editor, critic, and poet. In addition to Kerouac, Cowley edited the works of Faulkner and Hemingway.

country would rise up spontaneous and do something or other fine in 'response.' That's absolutely silly," Allen sniped.

Allen grew excited with anticipation as the day approached for the beginning of his glorious trip. He had charted a course down the East Coast to
Florida, on to Cuba, and then over to the Yucatán Peninsula and southern
Mexico, allowing him time to see ancient ruins, jungles, and mountain highways before he reached the Cassadys in San José. On a bitter cold Saturday
morning, December 19, after one last round of raucous parties, Allen set out
on the initial leg of his great adventure. He went as far as Washington, D.C.,
that first day. Here he decided to drop in unannounced to meet Pound at St.
Elizabeth's, but Pound wouldn't come to the visitors' room to see him. Allen
retained the same unquenchable thirst for fame that he had written about in
his diary at age twelve, and he speculated that by befriending famous people
he would have more opportunities himself. His friendship with William Carlos Williams had grown out of Allen's visits and had led directly to several
contacts in the literary world and to Williams's still-unpublished introduction for his *Empty Mirror* poems. Disappointed by Pound's refusal, Allen took
in the sights of Washington, especially the inimitable oriental paintings in
the Freer Collection. He carried a small backpack with him, which contained
a used Retina camera, and he asked someone to snap his picture on the Mall
with the Capitol Building in the background. It was the first of hundreds of
photos that Allen would take to document his trip.

Hitchhiking from Washington to Florida wasn't difficult in those days. It
was the Christmas season and people were friendly. Allen jumped out at Jack-
sonville where he spent the afternoon drinking rum with Adelbert Lewis
Marker,[27] a former boyfriend of Burroughs's. Allen was curious to hear the
circumstances surrounding Joan's death, which he hadn't been able to get
from William during his stay in New York. Since Marker had been in the
room in Mexico City at the time of the shooting he knew he'd get the real
story from him. But Marker, like everyone else, couldn't say whether it was
an accident, suicide, or murder. Allen found Marker less than handsome. "He
is so starved looking and rickety and pitifully purseymouthed and ugly and
with a disgusting birthmark below left ear and skin the texture of a badly
shaved hemophiliac," Allen wrote unmercifully. Marker was sweet to Allen,
though, and gave him twelve dollars out of his own pocket for his trip.

In Palm Beach, Allen's next stop, he visited Burroughs's parents, Mor-

---

[27] WSB calls him Allerton in *Queer*.

timer and Laura Lee, who had moved there from St. Louis in the spring of 1952. It was the first time he had met them and they got along well. Allen liked Mote, as Mortimer was called, and saw some of William's own mannerisms and character traits in the man. They put Allen up in a fancy hotel and had him over to the house for Christmas dinner. While they drove him around town sightseeing, they questioned Allen about their son. Allen told them that he thought William was destined to become a very good, if not a great, writer, which seemed to please them.

Allen also had a cousin he wanted to visit in Miami Beach, so he found a room for a dollar fifty and walked around looking at all the fashionable hotels along the beachfront. He even bumped into Alan Eager, a jazz friend from New York, at Miami Beach's version of Birdland. Late the next evening Allen caught a ride all the way to Key West on the back of a truck, only to be disappointed when he got there. His first impression was that the town was a backwater at the extreme tip of America. The best thing about Key West for Allen was that it was only a short ten-dollar boat trip across the Strait of Florida to Havana.

Allen had been looking forward to experiencing Cuba, where he had heard there were wild sex orgies everywhere. Instead he found the pre-Castro, prerevolution island pretty tame. He stayed for a few nights on the Havana waterfront in the cheap Carabanchel Hotel and wrote home that the town seemed dreary, rotting away in the heavy damp atmosphere. One night he got drunk in a small village about twenty miles out of the city and had to be helped home by an uninteresting man   Havana 1953, *CP*, p. 100 who had been buying him drinks at the bar. He found it all depressing and was eager to be on his way to Mexico. The high point of his trip to Cuba was his departure by air on New Year's Eve day. It was Allen's first airplane ride ever, which he duly noted in his journal. The view was marvelous; he could see the small islands and narrow roads and trails below and little cities that reminded him of "mushrooms in pockets and hollows of afternoon hills." Excited as he was, he snapped several pictures from his window seat on the short flight to the town of Mérida on Mexico's Yucatán Peninsula.

1954 ~

AS SOON AS Ginsberg set foot in Mexico his trip became magical. The adventure that had been disappointing now took on a life of its own and swept Allen along with it. Apart from giving Allen a much-needed break from New York City life and the demands of making a living, the primary goal of his trip was to visit the ancient Mayan ruins of Mexico. He had been reading all about the archeological sites, lost and overgrown for centuries, that had recently been discovered in the tropical jungles. He wanted to be inspired by them as Lord Byron had been inspired by the ruins of Rome and Athens. Allen pictured himself as the great white explorer, going into the steaming jungle on horseback to discover a lost civilization, finding Indian tribes that still worshipped forgotten blood-drinking gods. Only then would he continue to California, where he would impress his friends with tales of the "manly savage solitude of jungles." His trip was mapped out to take him across the Yucatán to Chiapas and Oaxaca, then on to Mexico City and Pátzcuaro, the beautiful area he had seen from the window of Lucien's speeding car two years earlier. He planned to do all that in about two months, for he had told Neal he would arrive in California by March.

At the airport in Mérida, two Indians offered to take him around the city in a horse carriage for a few pesos. On the way into town they happened to meet the mayor's brother, who invited Allen to the town's New Year ceremonies at City Hall, complete with free sandwiches and beer on a balcony overlooking the large central plaza. Allen got along well with the mayor's brother and accompanied him to a formal dinner party that night. It was a high-society champagne affair, and every man except Allen was dressed in a tuxedo. Allen looked like a German archeologist in his hiking boots and sports jacket, but he chatted with the other guests and enjoyed the food and music under the stars. On a whim, he began to tell people in his broken Spanish that he was Ezra Pound, someone most of them had never heard of anyway. Late that night after the formal celebrations were over, Allen wandered into the poorer section of town and listened to the local mambo music coming from the peasant dancehalls. He felt a resentment toward the rich industrialists who drank champagne, while the rest of Mexico starved.

The next day, Allen went inland to see the great ruins of Chichén Itzá. Friends had tipped him off that he could get a free room near the pyramids by saying that he was an archeology student. For a few pesos a day he got plentiful food from the locals and had full access to the ancient city. In the evening he took his hammock to the top of the tallest pyramid and fell asleep watching the stars. A single clap of his hands in the dark brought countless echoes, which underscored his loneliness. Sometimes he took codeine in order to relax and enhance his dreams. He ate his meals at the Mayaland Hotel and socialized with some of the archeologists and tourists who came to see the ruins, but at night he preferred the solitude of the tropical jungle with its chirruping insects, bats, and owls. He found some stone carvings of cocks and took dozens of pictures of them along with the skulls that had been unearthed.

With his money beginning to run low, he left for Valladolid, another ancient ruin deeper in the forest. A local showed him around the archeological site with its Mayan observatory tower and shared his dinner with Allen. He recommended that Allen visit Tizimín, a town about twenty miles away, where the oldest fiesta in Mexico was under way. It was a ten-hour trip on a miserably cramped train, filled with natives carrying sacks of food and hammocks and babies to the fiesta. Allen had to stand the entire way and was exhausted when he arrived at the already overcrowded town. The Indians had come on a pilgrimage specifically to see the four-hundred-year-old cathedral with its carved statues of the three Magi. The air in the cathedral was smoky from the thousands of candles burning and the floor was slippery with a thick impasto of wax drippings. The village priest, who hated the pagan aspect of the festival just as much as Allen did, took him home for the night, since there were no rooms available. In the morning he dropped Allen off at the station for the terrible ride back in what amounted to a boxcar outfitted with rough wooden benches for the 110 people packed into each car.

On his way back to Mérida, Allen stayed in Chichén Itzá overnight on January 12, where he checked into a cheap room down the street from the main square. He was glad to get a good night's sleep at last. For a few days he hung around Mérida relaxing and wrote letters home asking for money because he was already down to his last twenty-five dollars. His American dollars stretched a long way in Mexico but he needed more than he had to get to California. His Spanish was improving with constant practice, so he experienced fewer language problems, but he was still fuming after he wasted nine pesos on the wrong kind of hammock due to his miscommunication with a merchant. All along the way he asked everyone for the names of people that he could contact in Mexico. One night in Mérida he ran into a rich old Spanish man in a hotel bar who talked to him all evening about Paris and New York and reminded him of an old evil Lucien, "full of misery and rich and drunken disregard of life."

So far Allen's trip had been interesting and educational, but it fell short of his expectations. Problems abounded. The mosquitoes were awful and he contracted dysentery, which he looked on as a minor annoyance. His biggest problem was a shortage of money that kept him from fully exploring the country. One of the archeologists he met generously gave Allen an official pass to stay in the archeologists' camps at all of the Mexican ruins. It proved to be the most convenient way for Allen to travel cheaply and to meet interesting people who could teach him more about the Mayans. Allen was most captivated by the images he had seen in the Mayan Codices depicting monstrous figures and actions. One showed a series of drawings of a beast growing out of the loins of a squatting man, who was eventually consumed by that same monster. "I am on a kick with the Mayans," he wrote. "I imagine actual seasons of the soul; psychology, which was the basis of their society as the machine is of ours; developed by the priests and gone out of control after ages of bureaucratic centralization."

Although fascinated with everything about the ancient culture, Allen was beginning to hate Mexico, in large part because he was so often cheated out of his few pesos by the locals. One night before leaving Mérida he encountered two men at a bar who introduced him to someone Allen understood to be the local queer. "A 35-year-old child effeminate Mexican," and a type that Allen didn't dig. Due to his poor Spanish, Allen couldn't make it understood that he wasn't interested, and he had to offer him a few pesos to get rid of him.

From Mérida, Allen went to see the subtle geometry of the ruins of Uxmal, considered one of the most important of the ancient cities. After a few days he headed on to Palenque. He had read about the Mayan ruins there, which were being dug out of the jungle after nearly a thousand years. Palenque sat at the edge of one of the most inaccessible jungles in southern Mexico and was surrounded by impenetrable forests. Few roads existed and most travel was done by canoe along the rivers that flowed down from the mountains of Chiapas. Palenque truly was a lost city, and Allen marveled at the civilization that had built it. While living in the archeologists' camp he met Karena Shields, an American woman who had grown up on a giant *finca*[28] that once included the whole Palenque site. She had retired back to Chiapas after a career in the States as a minor actress. Her credits included a supporting role in the 1930s radio broadcasts of *Tarzan*. She was also an amateur archeologist and had written several books and articles about the Maya and her own experiences as a girl growing up in the jungle. She had an encyclopedic knowledge of the region, and Allen enjoyed listening to her stories about the natives. Although she was no longer wealthy, she was generous and hospitable and invited Allen to stay at her small *finca* farther into the jungle.

Allen, now extremely low on cash, decided to stay with Shields and wait for some money from home. One morning they took a Jeep from the Palenque ruins to a jungle path where Allen and Karena met another woman, a boy, and an old Indian retainer who were also going to the *finca*. They had four horses and a mule ready for the seven-hour ride into the dark forest, which abounded with orchids, plantain trees, screeching parrots, and howler monkeys. The journey itself seemed like something straight out of *Tarzan*. It was the first time that Allen had ever been on a horse and he did pretty well, riding along the muddy path and jumping over fallen trees and small streams. Occasionally they passed hills covered with stones, which a thousand years ago had been buildings on the outskirts of the vast city of Palenque. Shields knew every path in the jungle from her childhood and was exactly the kind of person Allen had hoped to find in Mexico. She knew the location of a lost tribe of Indians in Guatemala who had kept their Mayan traditions alive, and Allen believed that they might know how to

---

[28] Plantation.

Ginsberg at Palenque, 1954 ~

interpret the Mayan Codices. By coincidence, Karen's editor was Robert
Giroux, the same man who had been Kerouac's editor for *The Town and the
City*. It is too bad that Allen was never able to develop strong friendships
with women, for had Karena Shields been a man, she would certainly have
become one of Allen's mentors. But due to her sex, Allen couldn't quite
consider her one of his "ignus." To him she was just an interesting case,
generous but somewhat nutty and tiresome and far too hung up on the occult to suit him.

Karena's *finca* was located at the base of Don Juan Mountain, where all
the guests lived communally in a large open-sided thatch-roofed hut that had
a central fire for heating coffee and food. The hut and fire were tended by an
Indian woman, who helped Allen string his nine-foot hammock across the
room. About six native huts were situated in the brush behind the main
house, and the families living there worked on the plantation in a sort of
feudal system with Shields as the not-so-wealthy landowner. Allen, as a
guest, wasn't expected to work, but he could do so if he wanted to. Most of
the time, he chose to lie sideways in his hammock and read and write in his
journal.

By the end of January, Allen had comfortably settled on the plantation and revised his travel plans. He would wait there for his money from home and then go by horseback and *kayuko*, a dugout canoe, downriver to the nearest town. From there he could take a cheap plane up to San Cristóbal de las Casas to meet Franz Blum, a renowned archeologist. Allen envisioned Blum as a romantic figure, who was now in disgrace for being an alcoholic, but was still the most brilliant man in the area. Blum had lived with Sherwood Anderson and William Faulkner in New Orleans before going to explore the Mayan ruins. Karena Shields knew him well and promised to provide Allen with a letter of introduction.

For the moment Allen was content to live in the jungle with "the white goddess," as he began to affectionately call Shields. They swam in crystal-clear mountain pools and at night went to some Mayan ruins with a bottle of rum to watch the moon rise over the mountains. On some nights they'd go fishing with long spears to catch giant crawfish the size of lobsters, a regional delicacy. While swinging in his hammock in the afternoon breeze, he read the works of Catholic mystics. *The Cloud of Unknowing*, by an anonymous fourteenth-century English monk who struggled with the distinction between humanity and God, led Allen to serious spiritual contemplation and thought. What he liked most about the book was that it said a true contemplative didn't have to do anything, he was free to sit and think and not worry or feel guilty about such things as money or responsibilities. That was the life for Allen. The only thing he missed was male companionship, not necessarily sexual, but he had to admit that he missed that, too. Even though Allen was surrounded by the evidence of an ancient civilization in the New World, he found himself dreaming of the old cities of Europe. Mexico hadn't cured him of his longing to see Paris, London, Rome, and Venice, and only whetted his appetite for more extensive travel.

The warm tropical climate agreed with Allen, and he ended up staying with Karena much longer than he had expected. On February 18, he wrote to Lucien that he was beginning to get restless. He had sprouted a beard and let his hair grow longer and was now beginning to learn to play the drums. He had put together a primitive log drum set made from the trunk of the ceiba tree, used long ago by the Mayans as drums for long-distance communication. The smallest drum in his set was three and a half feet long, while the longest was a log at least seventeen feet long that he had suspended from some wooden supports with vines. They were loud enough to be heard all over the valley, and Allen liked to think that he was so talented that people came from miles around to hear him play. Allen boasted to Lucien that his rhythms were like the African drumming he had heard in Dakar, quite different from the local native Indian drumming that he found "awkward and inept." The Indians who listened began to call him Señor Jalisco, possibly a reference to the State of Jalisco, where mariachi music was said to have originated.

Allen explored the shallow river that ran through the forest not far from the house and discovered huge elephant ear plants on the banks. One plant had cordate, or heart-shaped leaves that inspired him to write a love song to Neal, "Green Valentine Blues." Allen ate tortillas and frijoles at every meal and after a while decided to work for an hour or two each day in the banana groves, cutting, pruning, and gathering the bunches. Allen liked it there so much that he wrote a long letter to Lucien suggesting that they buy a *finca* of their own and go into the cocoa business. It couldn't fail, Allen predicted. All they needed was the land and the plantation would practically take care of itself. It was reminiscent of Burroughs's failed farming schemes in Texas, but Allen was convinced that all they had to do was hire the right Mexicans for a few pesos to do the actual work and he and Lucien could sit back and rake in a steady profit for the rest of their lives. They would need only five to ten thousand dollars to buy the land to get started. Allen figured it all out in an organized and detailed way. The only thing he lacked was the money, and Lucien never volunteered to send the start-up cash.

Green Valentine
Blues, *CP*, p. 103

Allen wrote letters to Neal and Jack and said that he wasn't sure when he'd be able to leave, "maybe next week, maybe next month." It had been several weeks since Allen had heard from anyone back home, because the mail in that part of Mexico was undependable at best. The erratic mail service meant that Allen's letters home and letters to him weren't getting through. Earlier on his trip he had told people to write and send money to San Cristóbal or Mexico City but they knew nothing about his stay on Shields's *finca* in the jungle. Without money he couldn't move on to those places to collect the letters. The white goddess was happy to feed Allen, but she didn't have extra cash to lend him to move on. Since Burroughs hadn't heard from Allen in a while, he began to worry about him more than the others. Was Allen lost in the jungle? Was he in trouble or sick? The more William thought about it, the more he imagined all sorts of problems Allen might have gotten into. Burroughs wrote concerned letters to all Allen's friends and family and began to get everyone nervous.

On February 8, Allen saw a meteor as big as the star of Bethlehem illuminating the night sky. That same day, residents on the *finca* felt the tremble of an earthquake strong enough to make their hammocks sway. Later they found out that the tremors were centered near the mountain town of Yajalon and they began to hear reports that the whole town had been destroyed. People said that the earthquake had caused a volcano to erupt within a cavern in the mountains above the town. Volcanoes had been increasingly active in Mexico during the previous decade, and some of them had killed people and engulfed whole villages. Rumors were rampant. Some said that eight people had been killed, that the village church had been leveled and the priest crushed. Others said the entire town was destroyed and that lava was pouring out of the ground. With no reliable communication, it became a real cause for concern to everyone in the area. Although Yajalon was only twenty miles away over the mountain as the crow flies, it took two days to get to the town by mule through the winding valleys. People in neighboring towns wondered whether they should evacuate, and the few government officials in that remote region could provide no help or guidance.

Allen realized that he might be sitting on a potentially newsworthy story. Since the eruption of a volcano in the cornfield of Paracutin and its attendant press coverage a few years before, readers were interested in any natural disasters in Mexico's volcanic mountains. Normally Allen would have had little interest in such a catastrophe, but being so close to the source, he thought it might be an idea worth exploring. Since Lucien Carr was working for the United Press, he believed that if he scooped a story about a new volcano, he could earn enough money to pay for the rest of his trip to California. With that idea in mind he wrote to Lucien, outlining the few details that he knew for certain, and said that if the wire service wanted to pay him for the story, he could find out more.

For months following the initial earthquake, there were strong aftershocks, which sometimes approached the original quake in magnitude. Allen decided to use what little money he had left to mount an expedition into the mountains in search of the epicenter of the quake and to witness the true extent of the damage. On Friday, March 26, Allen left the *finca* for the small town of Salto de Agua, which had an airstrip. He hitched a ride in a tiny 1914 biplane to Yajalon, thus cutting a two-day mule trip down to fifteen minutes. Yajalon was a sleepy village where the seven thousand inhabitants, mostly descendants of the Mayan Indians, spoke a dialect called *Bachahon* instead of Spanish. The town itself stretched for about ten blocks along the main road. In the central plaza where the Indians came to sell coffee or maize harvested on the mountainsides, bougainvillea vines grew full of colorful flowers. Rising like a wall seventy-five hundred feet high on the south side of town was La Ventana Mountain and beyond that was Acavalna

Mountain, supposedly the center of the tremors. Acavalna in the ancient Tzeltal language meant "House of Night," but according to Allen, no one knew why it had been given that name. Treating Allen like a visiting geologist, a large group of men gathered to escort him up the mountain trail to a much smaller village closer to the center of the devastation. A ranchero loaned Allen a mule and he rode up the steep, twisting trail to the top of the mountain. Allen must have pictured himself as the brave pith-helmeted adventurer at the head of a safari in the movies or in the jungle games he loved as a child. The experience of leading such an expedition was a once-in-a-lifetime thrill, made all the more unusual because Allen didn't know what he was looking for. The local rumor was that an immense cavern in the heart of the mountain had collapsed. The cave itself was well known to the natives in the immediate area, but had never been explored by outsiders, so there was an air of mystery about its very existence.

On Sunday, March 28, as Allen's expedition passed through the tiny hamlets on the mountainside, more people joined him. The locals were frightened, because even though it seemed obvious that there was no erupting volcano, the strong tremors were still shaking their homes. Allen reached the village of Zapata on top of the mountain the first day and dined with the villagers on monkey and tepisquintla, a large rodent the size of a pig. He was surprised and somewhat disappointed that there was only minor damage to the buildings in the village, for they were mostly thatch shelters with no masonry structures to collapse and crumble. Allen had trouble communicating with the natives, since they spoke little Spanish, but through sign language and hand gestures they managed to tell him that they were worried most of all about the newspaper reports of possible volcanic activity.

Early the next morning Allen led a group of more than fifty men single file up into the mountains. Within a few hours they came to a giant cavern in the side of the mountain with an entrance the size of St. Patrick's Cathedral. The aftershocks had dislodged giant stalactites from the cave's ceiling, but there was no sign of any volcanic activity. Allen was proud to have cleared up the mystery of the mountain's name, too, since the enormous cave made "House of Night" an appropriate title. When Allen got back to Yajalon he was treated like a hero, saluted by the old men and followed around by the children. He drafted an official report in Spanish to say that there was no reason for concern since there was no volcanic activity. The document was signed by the mayor and sent to all the neighboring villages to reassure their residents that they were not in any danger.

Back in Salto de Agua, Allen telegraphed his full report to Lucien but received no reply. Lucien had failed to see anything newsworthy in Allen's story about a volcano that wasn't and an earthquake that hadn't destroyed anything, so he had left for a long vacation in Brazil. Allen's hopes for a financial rescue dissolved and he was out the ten dollars in expenses that his expedition had cost him. He was lucky to receive a check for twenty dollars from the *World Telegram* for back wages, which he used to pay off his debts and his Salto de Agua hotel bill, but he had nothing left.

Ginsberg returned to the tranquillity of Karena Shields's *finca* and for the next six weeks he did nothing but lie in his hammock and read and write. The isolation was not wasted, for Allen worked five to ten hours a day writing poems, among them *Siesta in Xbalba*, which he considered his best poetry to date. He struggled with the form of the poem for the next year, trying to give some equality to the stanzas, then altering each stanza to stress syllable, accent, and weight of lines. He was determined to discover a new form of measure that would break up the line and give a musical sensation to the poem. Later Allen wrote that he never loved this poem because it didn't have an emotional base, it didn't reveal his deepest feelings, and it was too focused on style and structure. Even if it was too cool and arty for his later taste, he was happy with his progress at the time. *Siesta* was composed in two parts. The first was written on the *finca* and tied all the Mayan lands he had visited into one unit; the second part came later and dealt with his departure from Mexico. The central theme of the poem was Xbalba,[29] both a real geographical area centered on Don Juan Mountain and Palenque and an imaginary area, the place of limbo or obscure hope, a sort of Mayan purgatory.

Siesta in Xbalba, part 1,
CP, p. 105

Due to the vagaries of the Mexican postal system Allen continued to be out of touch with everyone except Lucien, but he had left for Brazil without telling anyone that Allen was all right. Allen was completely unaware that people were terribly worried about him. Since he hadn't shown up in California in early March as expected, Burroughs had sent letters to everyone alarming them with his vivid imaginings of disasters that might have befallen poor Allen. On May 12, once he realized people thought he was lost in the jungle, he wired Burroughs, Kerouac, and Cassady saying that he was okay, only broke. He chalked up their panic to William's loneliness and morbid obsessions and it reminded him how happy he was to have William in far-off Tangier.

Shields was as poverty-stricken as Allen, so they tried with no success to

---

[29] Xbalba, commonly spelled Xibalba, was one of the three levels of existence for the Mayans, the other two being Earth and the Heavens.

pawn her old camera for travel money. Finally her royalty check from Harcourt arrived on May 13 and Allen was able to borrow enough money from her to leave. He took a train to Coatzacoalcos, then a bus to Vera Cruz and on to Mexico City. Allen was glad to be traveling again, for he had stayed much longer than he had intended and he wanted to see his old friends before sailing for Europe to visit the ruins of those civilizations.

For a few days Allen stayed in Mexico City at the Hotel Geneva, which had been recommended to him by Shields. It was a cheap place, filled with bedbugs, but adequate for his needs. It was close to Orizaba Street, where he had last seen Joan Burroughs a few days before her death two years earlier. Unfortunately, Bill Garver, their old drug connection from New York City, had left Orizaba for parts unknown. Allen had hoped to stay with him, since he couldn't afford to prolong his stay, even in the most modest of hotels. Allen had letters of introduction with him from Meyer Shapiro to the artists Rufino Tamayo, Miguel Covarrubias, and Mexican poet laureate Carlos Pellicer, and even hoped to find a little extra money waiting for him with general delivery at the post office.

After leaving Mexico City, Allen spent three days at the artist colony of San Miguel de Allende in the early part of June. There he read *The Horn*, John Clellon Holmes's second novel, which had recently been published. He also met a young painter and was relieved to find some sexual contact for the first time since he left New York six months earlier. By bus he rode to Guanajuato, where he saw the mummified corpses in the catacombs that were to provide inspiration for part two of *Siesta in Xbalba*. Then he went across the Sierra Madre Mountains from Durango to Mazatlán so that he could once again see the beautiful scenery he had remembered vividly from the hair-raising car ride with Lucien and Joan. After a day of sightseeing in Guaymas, he was back on the bus to Magdelena and then took a fifteen-hour ride all the way across the desert to Mexicali. Allen spent his last night in Mexico in a raunchy hotel overlooking the poorest barrio of Mexicali, with its tin shacks clinging to a hillside of garbage. The next day Allen bade farewell to Mexico and walked across the border into California where he hopped a Greyhound bound for Los Angeles.

An exhausted Ginsberg arrived at the home of his cousin, Max Levy, in Riverside several hours later. He was completely worn out from his long trip, but he looked healthier, leaner, and more tan than he ever had before. Max told him that his brother, Eugene, was planning to marry his girlfriend, Connie, later that year. Allen felt that she had "a great many potential wifely virtues," and wrote giving Eugene his blessing to go ahead and "get hitched." After resting for a week at his cousin's house, where he continued to work on *Siesta,* he was ready to move on. He was anxious to settle down more permanently and to see Neal again. He caught the express train straight to San Jose and by the middle of June he was knocking at the door of Neal and Carolyn's house on East Santa Clara Street. The minute he arrived, Neal got Allen high and lectured him all night about the whole Edgar Cayce[30] system that he and Carolyn had been studying. Allen was not converted but was encouraged that Neal "got religion" and therefore, he hoped, might become more open to other new ideas. Since they had been expecting his arrival for several months, Neal and Carolyn were happy and relieved to see Allen. His disappearance in Mexico had worried them nearly as much as it had Burroughs, so they were glad to find him safe and more robust than they had ever seen him. A happy reunion took place at their house and his only regret was that he had just missed seeing Kerouac by a few days.

Siesta in Xbalba, part 2, *CP*, p. 114

Allen found it easy to settle into the peaceful domestic life at the Cassadys'. Due to Neal's leg injury he was home most of the time. Allen enjoyed having the time to pursue his studies and read at the San Jose Public Library. As Neal studied Cayce's theories, Allen began his own investigation of Buddhism with the encouragement of Kerouac, who provided him with a list of books to read. Allen found Buddhist texts difficult to grasp at first and, not having a teacher to guide him, meditation practice was impossible. After the kids were put to bed each evening, Allen, Neal, and Carolyn would have spirited conversations about their beliefs that lasted into the early hours. During these quiet days Allen took the time to write out a statement of his beliefs, his credo, as it were. "1. The weight of the world is love. 2. The mind imagines all visions. 3. Man is as divine as his imagination. 4. We can create a world of divine love as much as we can imagine."

Song, *CP*, p. 119

By the end of June Allen had begun to weigh his options for the next few years. He wrote to his father and hinted that he might continue his education at Stanford or Berkeley and work toward a master's degree so that he could teach. Since he was staying with the Cassadys, he was being honest when he told Louis that he was eating well, saving money, and writing. Allen liked to help prepare meals and took pleasure in cooking what he considered gourmet New York dishes such as steak or latkes. Carolyn, a talented artist, excelled in

[30] Edgar Cayce (1877–1945): Popular American mystic and psychic healer who first came to Neal Cassady's attention when he found a copy of Gina Cerminara's book about Cayce titled *Many Mansions.*

portraiture and began one of Allen. "Carolyn and I dig and understand each other," Allen wrote in a letter. Neal had convinced her that Allen's infatuation with him was over and that they were now just platonic friends. Little did she realize that whenever Allen had the chance to be alone with Neal, he would climb into bed and blow him. In fact, shortly after Allen got to San Jose, he and Neal drove to San Francisco by themselves and got a room at the Geary Hotel for a tryst. After having such wild sex that first day, Allen was surprised that his sexual desire for Neal had begun to wane. Allen's disappointment stemmed from the fact that Neal was losing interest in the sexual part of their relationship. "The pain of losing love and naked body lusts drives me wild," Allen wrote, but he loved Neal even if it wasn't reciprocal. Neal went home to Carolyn the next day, while Allen stayed in the city to explore San Francisco for the first time.

One of the first people that Allen met in the city was Al Sublette, whom he described as "a Huncke with an income." Like Burroughs, Sublette was not wealthy, but he did have a small trust fund that paid enough to take care of his various habits. This he supplemented by minor dope dealing to friends. Sublette hung out in seedy places in North Beach like the Bell Hotel on lower Columbus, and on subsequent trips into the city, Allen usually stayed with him. He liked Sublette because Al lived his life as he wanted, with no concern about the opinions of others. Allen seemed to be the opposite and worried about everything. Every week or so he and Sublette got together to drink cheap Tokay wine, talk, and even sleep in the same bed.

Even though evidence and common sense pointed to the opposite, Allen tried to convince himself that Carolyn would not mind sharing Neal with him. On June 27 he mused, "Would it make any difference if I slept with Neal to Carolyn?" On some level he understood that although it might afford him a moment's gratification, it would end up permanently damaging his relationship with Carolyn. It was also apparent that his dream of winding up with Neal as his life's partner was never going to come true. He felt like a sick junkie hooked on Neal, demanding as much affection and attention from him as his wife received. Allen longed to have someone make a special sacrifice just for him, and on the other hand he hated himself for wanting Neal to give up his family for him. Neal was not exactly guiltless in this odd relationship, for he led Allen on and occasionally initiated sex play with him, which clouded their relationship. Neal was the consummate con man, and he seemed to enjoy juggling as many relationships at one time as he could get away with. "In a way he is really a bastard inviting and rejecting, making things so

Love Poem on Theme by Whitman, *CP*, p. 123

unclear, . . . on the other hand, his offers, his carnality at moments, his future acceptances, his plight of sexual starvation leads me to hope I am welcome," Allen recorded in his journal. Basically he wanted to hear Neal say
that he loved him. In a poem from this time he wrote, "Don't tell me the
truth, I want to be lied to—Besides I know it all." He wrote a masochistic
note about his desires: "I want to be your slave, suck your ass, suck your
cock, you fuck me, you master me, you humiliate me—humiliate me, I want
to be tied and whipped, spanked on the behind over knees, want to be made
to cry and beg and weep for love."

By July, Allen was ready to begin meeting the literary celebrities of San
Francisco. Although Kenneth Rexroth, to whom he had letters of introduction from both Williams and Lamantia, was out of town, Allen made contact
with Ruth Witt-Diamant at San Francisco State College, director of the well-
known Poetry Center there. She worked with poet Robert Duncan, but
Allen wasn't interested in Duncan or his poetry. He felt that he was too domineering and dictatorial. Allen visited Duncan's roundtable workshop once
and curtly wrote to his father, "admission 50 cents and not worth a nickel."
The only literary person besides Rexroth that he was interested in meeting
was Norman MacLeod,[31] who also taught at San Francisco State College. At
the time, Allen considered Kenneth Patchen to be "a creep." Patchen was a
proletarian poet of some stature who had recently moved to San Francisco
from the East Coast, but Allen was glad that he hadn't run into him. Still,
Allen was practical enough to realize that it was important to meet other
writers and form bonds with them, so he arranged a meeting one afternoon
with Duncan to discuss metrics, but nothing more than a courteous ac-
quaintanceship developed between them.

Although he considered the literary scene dull, Allen did like San Francisco. "All in all a very active cultured city the rival of New York for general
relaxation and progressive art life," he wrote. He felt that the North Beach
bars had more life than their counterparts in New York and he liked the
mixture of surrealist movie theaters, art galleries, jazz joints, and basement
lounges that filled the neighborhood. He also grew to understand why Kerouac liked to live with his mother. It was great for Allen to be able to
carouse in the city and then retreat to the peace and quiet of San Jose and
do his writing, far from distractions. It afforded him the best of both
worlds. Allen was bothered by Neal's devotion to the "mediumistic cult" of
Cayce worshipers and wondered at Neal's naïveté. "He kneels and prays

---

[31] Norman MacLeod (1906–85): Oregon-born poet, editor, and teacher.

with his children; the doctrine is screwy and absurd, almost on a *Readers Digest* level, but the seriousness of the search for uplift is real enough and respectable." At the time Allen was skeptical of Kerouac's spirituality, too, because he didn't understand Jack's hang-up with Buddhist doctrine. Allen didn't "get" the Buddhist message, and to him it seemed Jack was chasing a dream. It would take Allen more than a decade to understand what Buddhism was all about.

When Neal's personal injury case was settled with the railroad, he received a lump-sum award of sixteen thousand dollars, part of which he and Carolyn put down on a house in Los Gatos, a small town in the hills above San Jose. The idyllic life that Allen was enjoying couldn't go on forever, though. Allen needed to find a job and begin to support himself, so he applied to be a brakeman with the railroad like Neal, but there were no openings at the moment. A good thing, too, for Allen was not suited for the perils of a brakeman's life, and hopping on and off moving trains would have terrified him. He was aware of his fears and bolstered his own courage by saying, "Should I who have entered the Cave of Night be afeared of an engine?" Nonetheless, there was no job available. When the railroad did finally call him to come in, he failed the physical examination.

In back of the real,
CP, p. 121

When Rexroth returned to San Francisco in July, Allen went to visit him, and they wound up discussing world politics instead of poetry. He liked Kenneth but thought that he was merely a conservative posing as a revolutionary. Rexroth had already read and appreciated Burroughs's *Junkie*, so that in itself was enough to win Allen over. Kenneth was even able to convince Allen that Patchen's poetry was worth reading. "He ain't Pound," Allen wrote of Rexroth, but he appreciated him nonetheless for what he was, one of San Francisco's foremost literary figures.

By August Neal was already beginning to get on Allen's nerves. All he did was sit around and shuffle his deck of pornographic playing cards, or play chess, which he was becoming increasingly obsessed with, or talk about Cayce. None of that was of any interest to Allen. "I come 10,000 miles and he sits and plays chess with the neighbor and I babysit and goof," Allen wrote in disappointment. Neal's friends Al Hinkle and Dick Woods were his most frequent chess partners, and although Allen liked them, he missed the good old days with a freer and wilder Neal. Now the few times they had sex, Neal acted uninterested and bitter. Another worry that began to bother Allen was that Burroughs had written to ask Allen's permission to come to San Francisco. Allen felt it was Burroughs's way of smothering him

and trying to "schlupp" his soul again, and he was cold to the idea. His rejection of Burroughs with the line "I don't want your old cock" was haunting
him and made him feel twice as guilty. He knew he had to re-
ject William, as he wouldn't be able to live his own life with   On Burroughs' Work,
William around. Allen needed his own freedom and William   *CP*, p. 122
was much too needy and dependent.

While Allen brooded about the possibility of Burroughs's visit and
about Neal's remoteness, his relationship with Carolyn was crumbling, too.
When he first arrived they had gotten along pretty well, but since then a
coldness had slowly crept in. He guessed it stemmed from jealousy. He had
told her that she was long-suffering, which he knew she resented as well. By
August Allen and Carolyn were barely able to be civil to each other. Allen
had idealized his love for Neal to such a degree that he couldn't see reality
anymore, and he seemed destined to be disappointed. Somehow he continued to believe that Neal would someday recognize Allen as the true love of
his life and decide to be with him forever. On rare occasions Allen would admit to himself that he was chasing a sexual fantasy that would never satisfy
his needs. "This kind of love of mine is a sickness—must be cured, I can't
stand it—too painful the dreams and then the daily longing and dissatisfac-
tion so obsessive and sore in my belly and the obscene lonely nites I spend
grieving and dreaming and making love to shadows of bodies. Am I nuts?"
he obsessed in mid-August. Things were about to change in the Cassady
household, and not for the better.

On August 19, Carolyn, wanting to ask Neal a question, tapped lightly
on the closed door to Allen's bedroom where Neal and Allen had been for
quite a while. Without waiting for an answer, she walked into the room to
discover Allen, fully clothed on the bed, giving Neal a blowjob. Carolyn
was shocked and angry. She might have expected to find Neal in bed with
another woman, but not with Allen. Neal didn't respond to Carolyn's surprise, but instead walked out of the room, saying nothing and leaving
Allen to face her alone. Once she stopped crying, Allen apologized, but
deep down he said that he did not understand her reaction. Her anger took
over and she shouted, "You've always been in my way ever since Denver."
Allen found that for once he was speechless. In truth Allen felt that he was
the injured party and afterward claimed that he hadn't been trying to hide
anything from her. He saw Carolyn as irrational and jealously possessive.
He thought she was staging her life like something out of *House Beautiful*,
and Neal didn't fit into that picture at all. It was obvious that Allen had to
leave their home, but he had nowhere to go. He listed some of his options

in his notebook. They included getting a room in San Jose so that he could be close to Neal, moving in with the Hinkles next door, returning to New York, or finding a room alone in San Francisco. He hadn't wanted to live in San Francisco until he finished revising his *Siesta in Xbalba* poem because he knew he'd get swept up in the nightlife of the city and not apply himself to his work. Later, when Neal returned to the house, he tried to pacify Carolyn, but it was too much for even the smooth-talking Neal to patch up. He and Carolyn jointly agreed that Allen would have to move out of their house. Surprisingly Allen stayed there for a few more days (which Allen later referred to as "a two-day upheaval") before packing his bags and having Carolyn drive him to San Francisco herself. That fifty-mile ride was one of the longest of his life, and he remembered only snatches of what she said to him. Mostly she repeated things about his "trying to break up [her] marriage." Allen had no money at all, so Carolyn felt compelled to give him twenty dollars for a room, as she let him out of the car in North Beach. He was depressed and frightened and recalled painful memories of the day as an adolescent he had helped Naomi escape on the bus to Lakewood.

He knew deep in his heart that he should apologize to Carolyn, but he honestly didn't think that her feelings had anything to do with him. It was his belief that even this current turmoil wasn't the result of his intrusion on her marriage, and he managed to resent her, while still feeling guilty toward her. He couldn't help but feel sorry for Neal, since he was married to a shrew, yet on the other hand, he felt that he was, himself, a pervert interloper.

Once alone on the street, Allen didn't know exactly what to do. In addition to Carolyn's twenty-dollar bill Allen had another fourteen dollars in his pocket, but he had no job and no place to live. She had dropped him off in front of the Marconi Hotel, one of the fleabag hotels in North Beach that Sublette frequented. One of the two friendly dykes who ran the hotel showed him to room number three, which was beneath Sublette's room. Allen unpacked his bag and arranged his few possessions on top of the battered dresser. "Back alone in a hotel and once again the great battle for survival," he melodramatically wrote in his journal that evening. "How sweet to be finished with Neal. The pain of masochism and the absolute angel gone. The absolute angel comes and goes. Suicide again?" The Marconi was on Broadway, directly across the busy intersection from a tiny bookstore called City Lights. From his hotel, Allen could see not only the bookstore but Vesuvio's, a neighborhood bar he had discovered on earlier trips to North Beach.

Now with a place to stay, Allen needed to find a job before he ran out of money. He was bored with market research work and wanted to get a job on a newspaper as a stringer, so he lined up an interview at the *San Francisco Chronicle*. Within a few days, even though Carolyn forbade their meeting again, Neal came to visit Allen at the Marconi Hotel. Neal's actions helped confuse Allen even more. Not only did Neal openly masturbate while he was in Allen's room, but he also had sex with a strange man in another room at the hotel. Allen could see that Neal was seriously mixed up, just as Neal's Rorschach reading had warned—"prepsychotic sexually sadistic with deluded ideas of reality." Neal ended his first visit by propositioning some of the customers at a lesbian bar around the corner named 12 Adler Place.

For quite some time Allen had been trying to figure out his relationship with Neal, and he was coming to the conclusion that it had a strong master-slave element to it, with Neal and Allen occasionally reversing the masochistic-sadistic roles of dominant and submissive. Allen had once theorized that they could lose human self-limitation through their eternal bondage, but now he thought simply that Neal had a screw loose. Nothing else would explain the crazy things Neal did. Why would he have frantic sex with Allen one minute and then run out to a complete stranger the next? He seemed to fuck one and all at random, even screwing a seventy-year-old woman one day while they were in downtown San Jose.

Allen didn't get the *Chronicle* job and then tried a few other newspapers. When nothing came through he had to fall back on his experience in market research. Without much trouble, he lined up a job scheduled to begin September 13 with Towne-Oller, a large firm with an office in the financial district on Montgomery Street just a short walk down the hill from North Beach. Despite a good starting salary of fifty-five dollars a week, Allen felt constrained at the prospect of a full-time job after nine months of absolute freedom. During the few weeks before his job began, Allen spent much of his time with new friends like Al Sublette and Peter Du Peru. Allen described Du Peru as "a mad Zen ex-amnesia shock patient," a bit like a mixture of Carl Solomon and Herbert Huncke. Considered odd at the time for such nonconformity as not wearing socks, Du Peru was viewed by Allen as beat, sensitive and curious with a great mystic mind. Sublette and Allen walked all over the city hills together with Du Peru as a guide who pointed out the odd architectural curiosities of each building. Sublette presented a shabby and unkempt image himself, with no front teeth and always sporting several days of stubble. He was seen wearing a filthy trench coat no matter what the weather. One night Ginsberg, Sublette, and a weird egotistic poet named

Cosmo were arrested for vagrancy and ended up spending the night in jail. The police had stopped and searched the suspicious-looking trio as they sat in a North Beach coffeehouse. When they found foot powder in one of their bags, the cops assumed it was heroin. All three were released the next morning when the police discovered their mistake.

A few days after moving to the Marconi, Allen met Sheila Williams, a pretty twenty-two-year-old woman from Salt Lake City. She was an aspiring jazz singer, who wrote advertising copy for a department store by day and made the rounds of the club scene by night. She knew Dave Brubeck and other jazz musicians and sang whenever she could at local clubs. Allen liked her and she liked him. He found her pretty in a classy, chic way, and was impressed with her hip, cool demeanor. Allen wrote to Kerouac, "She has a wild mind, finer than any girl I met really, a real treasure, such a lovely face, so fine a pretty face." She already had a four-year-old son from an earlier marriage, but Allen welcomed the normalcy of their heterosexual relationship after his recent trouble with the Cassadys. Without psychotherapy he feared he might slip back into his old queer habits, and he idealized the prospect of a normal life. Allen felt that nothing could be more normal than to make love to a woman, work a steady job in marketing, and raise a child. The facts that Sheila knew the ins and outs of the drug scene, too, and liked his poetry were icing on the cake.

In the few weeks he had at liberty before starting his job, Allen revised many of the poems he had written in Mexico and San Jose. He had about fifty new poems in his notebook, but he hadn't had time to type them and he continued to work on the long poem, *Siesta in Xbalba*, which took most of his creative energy. He read Robert Duncan's poem *Salvages: An Evening Piece* in the fall 1953 issue of *City Lights* magazine and was struck by the similarity between it and some of Kerouac's compositions, so he invited Duncan over to his room at the Marconi to discuss poetics. He still thought Duncan's poetry was generally "crappy," but he realized that he was an important figure in the San Francisco poetry world and since he was also a friend of Ezra Pound's, Allen decided to keep an open mind. When Duncan arrived, Allen answered the door wearing only his underwear, which embarrassed the more modest Duncan. Robert tried to concentrate on anything other than Allen's seminudity and so looked at the papers Allen had taped to the wall, including a list Kerouac had made of his "Essentials of Spontaneous Prose." When Allen wrote to Jack, he told him how interested Duncan seemed in those. Later, when questioned about it, Duncan couldn't remember seeing the "Essentials" at all. He did remember that he was desperate to look at something besides Allen's drooping shorts. It was an excellent example of Allen's willingness to trust anyone who showed interest in things that were important to him. Allen was slow to appreciate Duncan's poetry and declared it was "no good because too aesthetically hung up all about his sensibility faced with the precise tone of his piddle—Light, etc., that's the subject matter." "No ideas but in things" still remained Allen's motto.

One day in early September a letter arrived from Burroughs outlining his plans to catch a boat from Gibraltar bound for San Francisco on September 7. Allen wasn't at all happy with the news. He had decided to try to settle down with Sheila and live his own kind of *House Beautiful* life. He knew that William would only screw things up. He was aware that Burroughs would make impossible, possessive demands on him that he wouldn't have the strength to escape. It was certain to end their friendship unless Allen gave in to William and allowed himself to be swept up in his life. Allen's only hope was to stall Burroughs's visit to San Francisco, so he wrote immediately to ask him to wait awhile. Besides his misgivings about William's visit, Neal's erratic behavior was becoming more alarming. Like a madman, he had been driving at breakneck speeds up and down the "Bloody Bayshore," as they called the freeway from San Francisco to San Jose. Behind the wheel, Neal drove recklessly, tossing beer cans out the window, smoking grass, and beating on the dashboard in time to the music from the blaring car radio. Allen surmised that Neal was suicidal, and he was quick to blame it on Carolyn for attempting to tame poor, wild Neal.

Adopting a "normal" lifestyle seemed to be the only way Allen could escape from the pressure to be wild himself. So Allen moved into Sheila's homey apartment on the side of Nob Hill, promising to split her seventy-five-dollar-a-month rent. As scheduled, he started work at Towne-Oller in mid-September, so he would have money before long. In a poem written at this time called "In Vesuvio's Waiting for Sheila," Allen described himself. "I am thoroughly beautiful, dark suit, dark eyes, no glasses, money in my wallet, checkbook abreast, [heading] toward an evening of fucking and jazz." After all his personal problems of the past few years, he finally had what everyone—family, doctors, and friends—had been advising he should have: a good job, a nice apartment, and a steady girlfriend. All the outward trappings were now in place, so it was a matter of making sure it all worked out as he conformed to the role of the working man. But therein lay the rub. None of it was what Allen wanted for himself, it was only a submission to the routine and responsibility expected by 1950s American society. Still, Allen was determined to give it a try, almost as a last resort.

His experiment with orthodoxy didn't last long. Sheila, in spite of her youth, was no stranger to drugs, and together they continued to search for new "kicks." On October 17, while high on peyote, Allen looked out of their open apartment window toward the Medical Building and the Sir Francis Drake Hotel a few blocks down the hill. In the foggy mist, he saw the lights of those buildings transform into the face of an evil monster. It reared its ferocious head and became "the robot skullface of Moloch." The "Moloch whose eyes are a thousand blind windows!" set his mind racing with images of the Old Testament God to whom children had been sacrificed. To Allen, Moloch was the personification (or deification) of the mechanical, insensitive, inhuman world he lived in and was ready to accept for "success." He described this image of a living tower from Golgotha in his journal and it was developed into "Strophes," the title he gave to the first draft of what was to become Ginsberg's most famous poem, Howl, for Carl Solomon. Writing the breakthrough poem was to be a slow process that took him more than a year, but the initial inspiration for the masterpiece came that October night.

Neal continued to visit Allen regularly on Pine Street and liked to sit on Sheila's white carpet while he cleaned the seeds and stems from the pot that he continually smoked. When high, he and Allen would dig the Sir Francis Drake view together or listen to jazz records while reading Proust aloud. Allen thought it was kind of Neal not to seduce Sheila, but monogamy was not one of Sheila's major concerns, and she made it with Al Sublette behind Allen's back. Sexual fidelity wasn't important to Allen either, but he was glad that Neal was showing some consideration for his feelings.

Allen fared so well at his new job that his company gave him a raise and began to talk about promoting him to their New York office. Although he appreciated the extra money, Allen wasn't ready to think about returning to New York quite yet. His writing was beginning to evolve faster since he'd left San Jose and he didn't want to devote all of his life to a marketing career. The chief benefit of office work was the unlimited supply of typewriters and copying equipment that he was able to use for his poetry. He carefully typed his poems so that he could make a small edition of his work on the office Ozalid machine[32] and planned to bind them in-house. Self-publication was about the only way he would be able to distribute his own poetry, he felt, since large commercial publishers couldn't afford to take any chances on young unknown poets like Ginsberg.

---

[32] Ozalid: A trademark process used to produce positive prints using an ammonia vapor process.

One of the best things about being with Sheila was that it had frightened Burroughs away. As long as he thought Allen was chasing women in San Francisco he was discouraged from making the trip. Allen knew it wasn't the thought of homosexual sex that he was afraid of, but rather William's wild, strange, and sometimes frightening temperament. He was still enthusiastic about helping to get Burroughs's books published, even if he was happy that William was staying in Tangier. He gave an early version of *Naked Lunch* to Rexroth for his opinion, hoping he would recommend it to New Directions. Kenneth liked Allen and found his poetry interesting, but he didn't always see the merits in his friends' writings. Jordan Belson, a filmmaker Allen had recently met, read both *Yage* and *Queer* and wanted to make a movie based on Burroughs's writings. After Allen gave him more of William's "routines" to look at, Belson decided they were not for him. Eventually he became a good friend of Allen's, too—in fact, it was Belson's peyote that elicited Allen's Sir Francis Drake Hotel visions.

Less than a month later, on November 9, Allen noted a major argument with Sheila in his notebook. "Silence in the house, end of another affair," Allen wrote. After he told her that he wasn't satisfied with their relationship, Sheila had gone to bed, leaving Allen to his thoughts. The day after his argument with Sheila, he had his first therapy session at a local psychiatric clinic for a dollar an hour. Since Allen was working again, he could afford to pay for psychotherapy and felt that he needed it now more than ever. He was assigned to Dr. Philip Hicks, a young psychiatrist starting his practice at the Langley Porter Clinic. They began meeting for one session every week. Allen wanted to work out his problems and discover why he couldn't be happy now that he had everything a sane person could hope for. Far from being content, he was becoming terribly depressed again. He sensed that he would hurt Sheila emotionally if he led her on and was not able to love her in the way she wanted. He felt he was only using her for companionship and heterosexual pleasure. Although he had told some of his friends that he enjoyed coming home to a "regular screw" each night, that kind of security wasn't satisfying for him and he didn't want to destroy her chances for happiness, since besides being lovers, they had become good friends. As he had done in New York to elude Dusty, Allen began to hatch a plan of escape from Sheila to a "secret nice pad on [a] side street run-down height of Nob Hill." Maybe he would wind up living a secret double life as many homosexual people did at the time. He hoped he could save some money, stop working, and do nothing but read, write, and pray to solitude.

Allen was so involved with his own emotional problems during these

years that he didn't spend much time thinking about politics. During this period of McCarthyism, Allen never mentioned McCarthy or his witch hunt
for communists in any of his journal entries or letters. He certainly did believe that the country was in the hands of incompetent people who were
"fucking us up in the rest of the world's Spenglerian schemes. We should be
feeding Asia not fighting her at this point," he wrote. He wished that control
of the nation could be turned over to traditional dissidents, like Thomas
Paine. That was the type of revolution Allen favored, not the overthrow of
the United States by the communists. In fact, he sympathized with the proletariat in the Iron Curtain countries because he felt that their leaders were
just as evil as the leaders in the West. There was too much to be resolved in
his personal life before he could begin to think much about world politics,
but as it turned out, the resolution of his personal philosophy helped to
change the world's politics.

On November 25, after seeing Al Sublette off on a Merchant Marine
voyage, Allen was inspired to ship out again. As yeoman or maybe even
purser on a boat, he could earn good money and make a clean break from
his life with Sheila at the same time. "I said to Sheila last night in the middle
of a hassle about why I don't love her really. I thought maybe because I loved
men too much, but do I do that any more like I used to?" A little later in his
notebook he exclaimed, "How I hate women, but can't stand not to be in
love."

With his relationship with Sheila in decline, Allen had started to wander
the streets at night. One evening he walked over the hill to Polk Gulch, an
area of old bars and seedy hotels frequented by bohemians, queers, and al-
coholics. The neighborhood was only a step above Skid Row and attracted
an artistic crowd, mainly because it was relatively cheap and safe. On the corner of Polk and Sutter stood a Foster's, one of a chain of cheap, all-night
cafeterias in the Bay Area, a popular hangout for artists and writers. For a
nickel you could nurse a cup of coffee all night and swap stories with friends
without being pressured to leave. Looking for Peter Du Peru, who sometimes hung out there, Allen asked one of the regulars if they knew where he
was. The regular turned out to be the talented painter Robert LaVigne. He
was a robust young man, about Allen's age and nearly as outgoing, but he
made no secret of his queerness. The two talked about painting, in particular Cézanne, whom they both admired. Allen shared some gossip about the
younger New York painters that he knew, like Larry Rivers, Willem de Kooning, and Franz Kline. They discovered that they had a lot in common and
met at Foster's for coffee several times over the next few weeks.

Nude with Onions, *Robert LaVigne's
painting of Peter Orlovsky* ~

One afternoon Allen mentioned that he'd like to see LaVigne's paintings. Since Allen was now making a decent living, he thought he could help
support a fellow artist by purchasing something. They walked up the street
to 1403 Gough, a fine old Victorian apartment building with lots of small
rooms where Robert had his studio. On the wall at the entrance to the studio
was a painting of the most beautiful boy Allen had ever seen. It was a large
five-by-five-foot canvas called "Nude with Onions." Allen was struck by the
intensity of the male nude, who seemed to be staring unabashedly at him
from the canvas. He felt his heart throb and fell in love with the model at that
precise moment. Allen quickly asked, "Who is that?" to which Robert
replied, "Oh, that's Peter, he's here, I'll get him." A moment later the young
man from the painting walked into the studio with Robert, who introduced
him to Allen as Peter Orlovsky. Peter was LaVigne's current model, roommate, and sometimes lover.

Peter Anton Orlovsky's story is a book in itself. He was born in Manhattan on July 8, 1933, to tragically poor White Russian immigrant parents,
Oleg and Kathrine (Kate). Peter was one of five children, all of whom had
mental illness of varying degrees. Nicholas was the oldest and the first of
the children to be subjected to shock treatments. Julius was the second oldest and severely retarded, followed by Peter, and finally the twins, Marie and
Lafcadio, both of whom were institutionalized sporadically. At one point
the family was so poor that they lived in a converted chicken coop on Long
Island. Peter's mother, Kate, had serious health problems of her own. As a

result of a botched mastoid operation years before Peter's birth, she was left deaf and suffered significant facial paralysis. His father, Oleg, who was often absent from the family, had run his own hand-painted necktie business but had been put out of work by cheaper imports. As a boy Peter had been placed in a series of institutions, because his parents were too ill and poor to provide for all the children. He escaped the slums by enrolling in the city's agricultural high school in Queens and grew to love farming and the outdoors. Unfortunately, he was forced to leave the program a few months short of graduation in order to help support his family. Later he managed to finish his education at a night school in Flushing, Queens.

Once out of high school, Peter had been inducted into the army on November 10, 1953. Since he had once worked as an orderly at Jewish Memorial Hospital in New York, Private Orlovsky was assigned to duty in San Francisco in the same capacity. Peter was well-built and muscular and worked without complaint, but he couldn't fit in to the regimented army life. He questioned things that other recruits took for granted, which made him stand out from the group. When he was off-duty, he liked to walk all over the hills of the beautiful city. One day he stopped at Foster's for a cup of coffee and Robert LaVigne came over to talk to the good-looking young man in uniform. He asked him to model for him and eventually talked him into bed as well. Peter always liked girls and had little interest in Robert (or any man) sexually, but Robert persisted and became Peter's first male lover. Peter said later, rather naïvely, "My oh my, what a big cock he had, but I was young and strong."

When his sergeant found out that Peter was having sex with a man, he sent him to see the base psychiatrist. It took the doctors a full day to examine Peter and decide that he wasn't army material. During the interview he told the doctors, "An Army with guns is an Army against love." That common-sense comment baffled the military doctor, who was used to dealing with "Yes, Sir" types. When he told the doctors that he had once seen all the trees on the street bowing to him, they officially classified him "schizophrenic reaction paranoid type." On July 12, 1954, after he had served eight months, the army gave him an honorable discharge and released him. Since he was discharged for medical reasons, he was eligible to receive a modest veteran's benefit check every month for the rest of his life.

Peter was a good model for LaVigne, who painted him both clothed and nude several times during the six months that they were together. Robert even tried to teach Peter to paint, but he was not a very disciplined student and lacked drawing talent. By the time Robert met Allen, he was beginning to think that his relationship with Peter was going nowhere. Robert was also interested in Allen, and that might have been part of his motivation for telling Allen that his relationship with Peter was nearing an end. "Ooh, don't mock me," Allen said to Robert when the painter offered to hook him up with Peter and told him that all Peter needed was sweet companionship. Here was someone willing to fix him up with an Adonis just when Allen had virtually given up on any hope of having a relationship with a man. Until now his one consuming sexual love affair had been with Cassady, and that hadn't worked out very well. Most of his other experiences were nothing more than one-night stands and several of those had been drunken indiscretions with his friends.

One night in December while drinking in Vesuvio's bar, Robert, acting the role of the Yiddish matchmaker, had a conversation with Peter to see if he was interested in Allen. Peter was hesitant, since he wasn't gay, but he was also frightened by the prospect of being left alone if Robert did make good on his plans to move to Mexico. Peter agreed to test their compatibility by spending an evening with Allen. It was quite an unusual situation, even for Allen. He went to Peter's room, took off his clothes, and lay down beside Peter on his mattress on the floor. When it came to sex, Allen wasn't experienced, and despite his desires he hadn't slept with many men. He wrote in his journal that he had never openly screwed a man "with complete giving and taking" until then. With Neal, Lucien, or Jack, all men who were basically heterosexual, he had always been aware that they were doing it as a favor to him. He didn't ask for much in return and always did all the work. Whenever anyone did anything to please him, he considered it a blessing from heaven. "When you blow someone like that, they come, it's great! And if they touch you once, it's enough to melt the heart," he wrote.

That first night, Peter was naked underneath his big Japanese robe. He opened the robe to put around both Allen and himself, pulling Allen to him face-to-face. Emboldened by that sign of affection, Allen screwed Peter in the ass, after which Peter began to cry. Allen immediately became apologetic and became frightened, yet at the same time "the domineering, sadism part of me was flattered and erotically aroused." Later, Allen reflected on that moment and said, "The reason he wept was that he realized how much he was giving me and how much I was demanding, asking and taking. I think he wept looking at himself in that position not knowing how he'd gotten there; not feeling it was wrong, but wondering at the strangeness of it," Allen said.

When Robert heard Peter sobbing in the next room, he went in to try to comfort Peter protectively. That angered Allen, making him so jealous that he rudely pushed Robert away. That was the genesis of a dispute that lasted nearly two years between Robert and Allen. "Peter was primarily heterosexual and always was. I guess that was another reason he was shocked—the heaviness of my sadistic possessiveness in screwing him."

So much was happening in Allen's life at the time that it is impossible from his journals and remembrances to clearly date when he first consummated his love for Peter. A short trip back to New York also took place at the time. The details given above were from Allen's own contemporary account, but so also was another version: "Embraced, real sweetness in my breast, too much, I'd almost cry, but it's such poor pitiful fleeting human life, what do I want anyway? Nature boy—to be loved in return. So followed a night of embraces, not sex. Then NYC, then I return." Whether Allen had sex before or after his trip back to the East Coast isn't that important, but it does serve to show that it is sometimes difficult to discern fact from fiction, even when it's recorded in a diary. It is possible that Allen even slept with Peter a second time before he flew back to New York on Tuesday, December 14, to attend Eugene's wedding that Saturday.

After the all-night flight from California, Allen crammed as much into the next five days in New York as he could. He wanted to see all his old friends, especially Carr, Solomon, Kingsland, and Kerouac, and hang out with them once more at the San Remo. Surprising himself, he wanted to see and fuck Dusty Moreland once again, he told Jack. His family barely recognized him. They hadn't seen him since he left for Mexico exactly one year earlier and now he was trimmer and healthier looking. He was also dressed in a handsome tweed suit for the wedding, which made him look even more mature. Against the wishes of both families, Eugene was marrying the woman he had been dating for the past few years. Connie was a beautiful, blonde Protestant minister's daughter. Her marrying into an immigrant Jewish family with a crazy mother gave everyone something to be upset about. But the wedding at Riverside Church came off smoothly and the marriage lasted for more than forty years.

Over Kansas, CP, p. 124

While back in New York Allen even found time to visit Louis Zukofsky[33] to discuss the older writer's use of precise language in his poetry. Their conversation inspired Allen to be more exacting in his word choice, but Zukofsky told Allen that at twenty-eight, he thought he was a little old to be thinking about changing his style. Zukofsky was also kind enough to give

[33] Louis Zukofsky (1904–78): Objectivist poet and friend of Ezra Pound and William Carlos Williams.

Allen a letter of introduction to another New York poet, Charles Reznikoff,[34] who was then living in California. It was a whirlwind trip, and as much as Allen wanted to stay and visit with his old friends again, he was equally eager to get back to San Francisco to see what would develop with LaVigne and Orlovsky.

When Allen returned to California, LaVigne told him that if he needed a place to stay he could have one of the rooms in the house, and he began to spend most of his time there, instead of with Sheila. For the next week or two there was a minor love triangle in the studio on Gough Street. Peter had not made up his mind whether he wanted to have a long-term relationship with Allen, and Robert had not decided whether he wanted to give Peter up to Allen and move to Mexico. At the time, only Allen was certain that he had met the person he wanted to stay with for the rest of his life. Those strong feelings put a great deal of pressure on the relationship that was beginning to develop with Peter and caused Peter to pull back from both Allen and Robert. Allen saw no similarity between his growing obsession with Peter and Burroughs's most recent obsession with him, but the intensity of emotions seemed to be an obstacle in both relationships. Peter felt trapped between Allen and Robert and began to wonder what he was doing. Sexually he was interested in girls anyway, so he was puzzled about why he was allowing himself to be screwed by men. Complicating things even more was Sheila, who wanted Allen back and came to Gough Street one night drunk and pelted Allen's window with bottles and rocks, shouting, "You can fuck me in the ass, if that's what it's all about!" Allen realized that he had to make up his mind and choose between Sheila and Peter, before he hurt them both.

Besides Allen's physical attraction to Peter, he also learned that they had a lot in common due to the mental problems in both their families. In fact, instead of craziness being a deterrent, it seemed like another reason to be together. Naomi's insanity had taught Allen to accept erratic behavior without question, and often enough he was inspired by the eccentricity of others. The fact that Peter and his siblings were a bit childlike mentally only increased Allen's interest. He felt that he could offer Peter a life that was intellectually stimulating, if Orlovsky would offer him physical love in exchange. To Allen it seemed like a fair trade, and it was reminiscent of his previous proposal to trade literary tutelage to Neal for sexual favors.

One more complication arose when LaVigne allowed Natalie Jackson,

---

[34] Charles Reznikoff (1894–1976): One of the best of the Objectivist poets and a contemporary of Allen's father.

another of his models, to move into the apartment. She was a tall, good-looking redhead, with a large sexual appetite of her own. Around the time that Allen met Peter, Allen had also introduced Natalie to Neal. Within a few days Neal had fallen in love with Natalie and while Allen was back east at Eugene's wedding, Neal was in Natalie's bed. It came as a complete surprise to Allen when he literally bumped into Neal in the kitchen at Gough Street after he returned from New York. While Allen had been away, Peter had gotten high for the first time in his life with Neal and Natalie. They all wound up in the same bed together for what was Peter's first group sex and quite probably one of Peter's first sexual encounters with a woman. The Gough Street studio began to resemble a lively fraternity house. Allen described a typical scene on one of the last pages of his 1954 journal: "Neal rushes in 9AM W.C. Fields—Oliver Hardy pulling on or off his pants, makes it with girl, laughs again, puts on her clothes, she his vest, they blast—and he and I agree on nostalgia of the front door, we've both gained so much tender youth kicks in last two weeks."

LaVigne had been attracted to Allen ever since he first met him in Foster's, so for some reason Allen believed that Robert might loosen his grip on Peter if Allen made it with Robert. Of course that proved to create new emotional complications. Robert and Allen attempted to have a three-way with Peter, but that didn't help straighten out anything either. Allen noted that he only wanted Peter, "Peter being guilty only digging me, tho all love Robert LaVigne for sad genius ignu self." There was quite a bit of high drama that played itself out over the last days of December. Peter was more confused than ever before in his life and had no idea what these two men expected from him. Allen couldn't stop himself from falling deeper and deeper in love with Peter, and it all melted into a sad, depressing scene of anger and guilt on every side.

After several misunderstandings, the three agreed to go their separate ways. Peter wanted to strike out on his own, Robert decided to head for Mexico, and Allen resigned himself to finding a hotel room until he could get a small apartment somewhere. In the meantime Allen tried to distract himself by reading the manuscript of Kerouac's *San Francisco Blues*. It was an excellent collection of short jazz rifflike poems, which Allen came to conclude was Jack's best writing yet. He first read it on the plane from New York, but now he reread it carefully several times, each time seeing more genius in every line.

Robert and Allen were not sensitive to Peter's needs, and they fought over him like two lions with a carcass. One night as they were bickering over

Peter in the kitchen, Peter told them they were both "nothing but a pain in the ass" and walked out. At last Allen realized that he was on the verge of scaring Peter off forever by the intensity of his emotional and physical needs. He moved into a cheap room at the Hotel Young directly across the street from Foster's cafeteria windows. If he sat in his room with the lights out, he could watch until he saw Peter go into Foster's and then pretend to bump into him accidentally. Agonizing hours passed while Allen waited to catch a glimpse of Peter, as he lived out his own version of *Of Human Bondage.* For his part, Peter was unsure how much he wanted to become tangled in Allen's web. Allen sat in his hotel room and wrote long confessional passages in his journal just as he had in Denver when he spent the summer waiting for Neal. He felt sorry for himself and was plagued by his two aphrodisiacs, guilt and desire.

On December 29 Allen stayed home from work nursing a bad cold. He had taken some penicillin and was lying fully dressed on his pallet in the hotel room when Sheila surprised him with a visit. She still liked Allen and hoped to get back together with him, not quite believing that he was trying to make it with a straight man. She had only known Allen for a few months so she thought Allen might grow out of his queerness and return to her. Unknown to Allen at first, Sheila had been having sex with Al Sublette while he was away. When he found out, he was pleased for both of them, and it removed some of his own guilt about their breakup.

1955 ∿

ALLEN'S JOURNAL ENTRY for New Year's Day, 1955, began, "The first time in life I feel evil: conscious loss of innocence, betrayal of Robert— I feel as if I blundered unthinkingly—seen thru his eyes, and Sheila's eyes (unfeeling lout she called me)—shame for situation and complicity shared with Peter—tho I supposed to know better—I not fitted to 'teach' him now thru having compromised myself by allowing he and I to screw. Enticing him before Robert had done with the season, too early painfully betraying Robert, without slowly seriously enough accustoming myself to know Peter, lengthy sweet honorable courtship, under Robert's eyes as he departs, so that when we do make love, it is only after knowledge and long longing and real love of each other—this was, Robert was right, too fast, accompanied by guilt and Robert's repudiation, over anxiously blindly my grabbing him, fucking (and in front of Robert) so that we two are set adrift prematurely hardly knowing if we do know or like each other, both doubting, he my motives, I his (was he being specially insensitive and recriminating to Robert?)— each of us not really knowing what we want from each other."

For several days Allen kept a minute-by-minute account of his long vigil in the hotel room. He was in agony and his misery grew the more Peter hesitated. His journal is crammed with the lame excuses he invented for going to see Peter, much like any schoolboy's crush on the prettiest girl in class. After three days of Allen's endless watching for Peter to appear, Sheila took pity on him and walked up to the Gough Street apartment herself to ask Peter to go talk to Allen. Mercifully, Peter went to see him, but no sooner had

he arrived than Allen begin pleading his love: "I missed you," he kept repeating. Peter didn't know what to say and Allen couldn't restrain himself so he
blurted out his need.

A few days later, Robert and Peter rented separate rooms in the Wentley
Hotel, the apartment building directly above Foster's. They needed a place
to stay until Robert left for Mexico. Allen was still across the street, endlessly
writing about a fantasy life with Peter in which he planned to have sex until
he collapsed from exhaustion. He wrote that he didn't mind if Peter made it
with girls as long as he would take pity on him every now and then and let
Allen make love to him. "For as I know I want to be tied to bed and screwed,
whipped, want to wrestle and blow and come in unison." Since Allen visualized their relationship as a trading of talents he promised to tutor Peter in
creative and literary matters and to share his insight into the mystical qualities of God. He felt it was an equal exchange of souls and bodies as well as
talents and purposes. It would be a happy union for Allen, if only Peter
would agree to satisfy Allen's erotic needs and teach him "emotional lovemaking kicks." Allen was determined to become Peter's willing student in
bed even though Peter had little experience to draw upon.

For another week and a half Allen stayed in his hotel room, with dimin-
ishing hopes that Peter would come to him willingly. During this period
Allen commissioned Robert to paint a nude portrait of Peter for $150. Even
though he couldn't afford it, he did want the painting. At the same time
Sheila continued to visit him and he actually slept with her more than he did
with Peter, even fucking her in the ass at least once because she wanted him
to enjoy himself as he did with men. Marianne Moore had once remarked to
Allen, "Self pity is bad, friend," referring to his poetry, but Allen saw it as an
appropriate comment now, for never had he felt sorrier for himself. Peter
hadn't come even once to Allen's room to visit of his own free will, but Allen
was determined and wouldn't give up.

Each day Allen got up and went to work at Towne-Oller, but he began to
realize that everything he did could be done just as well by the new business
machines that were coming on the market. They didn't need him to manu-
ally tally all the columns of data anymore, because a simple office machine
could do it faster and better. Although his boss wanted to give Allen a raise
to $350 a month and promote him to their New York office, Allen had no in-
clination to leave San Francisco at this moment in his life. When the time
came to phase out his job, Allen wanted to collect unemployment compensation and focus on the task of winning Peter.

Allen's therapy continued every week and he grew to like his analyst,

Dr. Hicks. One day during his therapy session, Allen told the doctor all about Peter. "You know, I'm very hesitant to get into a deep thing with Peter because where can it ever lead? Maybe I'll grow old and then Peter probably won't love me—just a transient relationship. Besides should I be heterosexual?" Doctor Hicks surprised him by saying, "Why don't you do what you want? What would *you* like to do?" Without much hesitation Allen answered, "Well, I really would just love to get my own apartment, stop working, live with Peter and write poems." It was a simple statement, but the doctor challenged him. "Why don't you do it?" he asked. Allen was dumbstruck by the suggestion. He questioned the doctor about what would happen when he got old or sick, but Hicks assured him that he was "a nice person and someone would always like him and care for him." It was a revelation to Allen that anyone, let alone a psychiatrist, would suggest that he just be himself without regard for the consequences. It was exactly the guidance he needed at the time, and he decided to follow this advice.

Before long Peter was spending a good deal of his time in North Beach looking for girls and trying to escape the suffocation he felt around Allen and Robert. On the surface Allen gave Peter his space, but this distance made Allen aware that he was a burden to Peter. He and Peter rarely made love, and when they did, Allen sensed that Peter was only doing it to accommodate him and never because he wanted to for his own pleasure.

At the end of January Allen moved into a cheap room in the Wentley himself, to save a little money and to be even closer to Peter. He began looking for his own apartment, and by February 3 he had found one at 1010 Montgomery Street in North Beach with two bedrooms separated by a hallway and a kitchen. If Peter would agree to move in with him, Allen thought it would be perfect and provide all the privacy Peter wanted.

These were confusing times for everyone. Even though Allen was waiting for Peter to decide whether to live with him, he continued to make love with Sheila as much as when he first met her. He even screwed Natalie once in January, much to the surprise of Robert, who by then was beginning to think that Allen was more than a little confused sexually. One evening, Peter and Allen stopped for coffee at a Foster's cafeteria in the financial district near Allen's office and talked all night about the possibility of living together. Allen, for his part, felt he was ready to commit himself to Peter, body and soul. Peter, a little more reserved, nonetheless wanted to try living with Allen, since Robert was still planning to leave town. They made a vow of commitment to each other, similar to the one that Allen had made with Neal on the road to Texas. Like that earlier oath, this vow was more meaningful to Allen than it was to Peter.

Peter was extremely unsuspecting and inexperienced, in fact most everyone who knew them at the time felt that Peter was a little slow-witted if not "downright daffy." Peter's psychological discharge from the army and his own family history certainly gave some indication that he might have been predisposed to mental problems. But when Allen looked deep into Peter's eyes, his romantic dreams grew and "there was a kind of celestial cold fire that crept over us and blazed up and illuminated the entire cafeteria and made it an eternal place."

Malest Cornifici Tuo
Catullo, *CP*, p. 131

The day when Peter moved his few possessions to 1010 Montgomery wasn't the joyous reunion that Allen had hoped for. "Peter was very moody, very sweet, tender, gentle and open. But every month or two months he'd go into a very dark, Russian, Dostoyevskian black mood and lock himself in his room and weep for days, and then he'd come out totally cheerful and friendly. I found after a while it was best not to interrupt him, not to hang round like a vulture, let him go through his own yoga." On February 25, Allen wrote in his journal, "Waking every morning objective calm desire to go to his bed but he will not have me do so."

Amid all this, Allen was still acting as a literary agent for his friends and had left several manuscripts for Kenneth Rexroth to read. He also loaned Kerouac's *Visions of Cody* and even Cassady's Joan Anderson Letter to Gerd Stern for his consideration. Stern was both an editor for Ace Books and the publicity manager for radio station KPFA where he edited a magazine called *Folio*. Somewhere in the Stern-Ginsberg exchanges the only copy of Cassady's long letter was lost, much to everyone's regret.

One day as Allen and Peter were walking around North Beach, they stopped into The Place, a local bar frequented by artists and writers, and bumped into Robert Duncan. He invited them to come to see his play *Faust Foutu*, then being staged at an artist's gallery and performance space called the Six Gallery. At the end of the performance, Duncan stripped off all his clothes to explain the principle of nakedness to his audience. Years later, when Allen copied Duncan by doing the same thing at a reading, people thought it so outrageously daring and original that it became one of the most often repeated stories about Ginsberg, but Duncan's example is virtually forgotten.

In February Peter received disturbing news from his family in New York. His little brother, fifteen-year-old Lafcadio, was causing his mother a lot of difficulty at home. Peter decided that it would be best if he went back to rescue Lafcadio before Kate put him away in a mental institution as she threatened. Peter wanted to bring him back to San Francisco where he could finish high school in peace. They toyed with the idea that Peter might enroll as a student at Mexico City College and Allen might go on to Europe by himself around September. Even though they both dreamed of elaborate long-range plans, most of their ideas required money. The thought of marketing tooth powder, women's hair preparations, and other perfumed products for the rest of his life was unbearable to Allen. His last project for his company had been to work on the statistics for the sale of toiletry items on the front counters of supermarket chains in sixteen cities and to correlate those statistics with advertising campaigns. He grew to hate his nine-to-five office life and couldn't wait to escape it.

By the end of February Neal and Natalie had all but taken over Allen's bed in the Montgomery Street apartment. Carolyn had discovered that Neal was having an affair and had kicked him out of the house again, so Allen generously took them in. At the time Allen was angry with nearly everyone and everything, from his senseless job to Peter, who shut himself up in his room for days at a time, acting depressed, gloomy, and withdrawn. Allen found that he couldn't even speak to him anymore, except about money or necessities. Even Allen came to realize that Peter's heart was not in their relationship, although Peter had agreed to go along with the arrangement and had tried to put up with Allen as best he could.

Since the previous fall Allen had begun to read Dwight Goddard's handbook, The Buddha's Golden Path, but he was finding it too diffuse to understand. Then he went to the library for Goddard's Buddhist Bible and Rhys David's Dialogues of Buddha, both at Kerouac's suggestion. Those were easier to approach, and he began to appreciate Buddhist spiritual exercises and D. T. Suzuki's books in particular. Allen's Buddhist studies continued slowly, but with no teacher, he had trouble understanding many of the texts that Kerouac had recommended, like the Surangama Sutra. He couldn't follow it and lacked the groundwork needed to master the principles outlined. He read for days on end in a comfy old armchair. His room was long and dark with a fireplace at one end and he had Turkish rugs covering the floor. On a table stood a secondhand, three-speed, Webcor Victrola that he used to play classical and jazz records. All afternoon long, Cassady and Hinkle sat by the sunny street window playing their never-ending games of chess.

Allen's favorite spot in the neighborhood became the tiny City Lights Bookstore, a few blocks down the street, which had been in business since 1953. He explored their poetry shelves, and since customers were encouraged to linger, he'd sit there for hours reading until they closed at midnight. It was also a great place to meet other literate people. Even though it was quite small, writers from all over San Francisco used it as a hangout. The owner, Lawrence Ferlinghetti, was a writer, editor, and poet himself and had a knack for selecting only the most interesting books. It had been his idea to specialize in inexpensive paperback editions instead of hardcovers, unique for a bookstore at the time. On City Lights' shelves Allen found all of the books published by Jargon Press and wrote to Jargon's publisher, Jonathan Williams, about publishing Kerouac and Burroughs. Allen was still having no success placing his friends' books, and he wondered if Jonathan could help him. By March Kerouac had decided to hire Sterling Lord, a professional literary agent, to represent him instead of Allen. Allen was secretly relieved and passed along several of his ideas to Lord. He was glad to be spared future business dealings with Jack. Being his friend was turning out to be difficult enough as time went by. Rexroth had informed Allen that the eminent critic Edmund Wilson would read Kerouac's manuscript and give his opinion of it for fifty dollars and Allen offered to pay the fee, if Lord wanted to send one of Jack's books to Wilson. Allen felt that Jack needed a break and that Wilson's recommendation might lead to a publishing opportunity. Lord didn't feel that paying someone to read Kerouac's books was necessary just yet.

By April 20, when Allen sat down to record his most recent failures in his diary, he apologized to himself for not writing more, but he felt that the journal had encouraged him to write more "egocentric slop" anyway. Lately, he said, he had been overindulging in alcohol and taking codeine too often to relieve the pain and boredom of his life. At long last Towne-Oller had given him his long-awaited pink slip, effective May 1, 1955, at which time the IBM mechanical brain would take over his duties. He was relieved to be rid of the daily routine of the office so he could concentrate exclusively on writing, but he was depressed that Peter had not grown to love him and he was beginning to believe he never would. He felt isolated from all his friends who did love him, like Jack and William. "Peter I can't talk to when I need comfort, he repelled by my need as I was repelled by Burroughs's attachment to me for support. Masturbation also an art in desolation learned." That spring a melancholy Ginsberg listened to a recording of Bach's Mass in B Minor repeatedly in his room, slowly working on his notebooks and manuscripts, fearing that he was experiencing the permanent death of his ability to love. Bach was the perfect background for his whole life, since the music was permeated by love and sadness.

Even though Sterling Lord was officially Jack's agent now, Allen was disappointed by Rexroth's response to the Kerouac books he had loaned him to read. Rexroth liked *Doctor Sax* and *Visions of Cody* well enough, but he decided not to recommend them to New Directions, as he felt they were good enough for a traditional publisher to take on. He said he would help publish them only if he believed they had no commercial market. Unfortunately, the traditional commercial publishers seemed to think the works were too avant-garde for them. Then Duncan read parts of *Visions of Cody* and quoted Katherine Mansfield, who said upon reading *Ulysses*, "This is obviously the wave of the future, I'm glad I'm dying of tuberculosis." Allen couldn't believe that poets like Richard Wilbur, Daniel Hoffman, and Louis Simpson had already been published and were becoming well established, while he and Kerouac couldn't get into print. Allen was in such a generally foul mood that he was even disappointed by Herman Hesse's novel *Siddhartha* (published by New Directions in 1951), which he read and declared was "nowhere particular." There seemed to be nothing positive on his literary horizon.

The bad news didn't end there. At the end of April, Eugene wrote to tell him that Carl Solomon was back in the mental hospital, this time Pilgrim State, the same hospital where Naomi was being treated. By that time Allen was so depressed that he planned to pack up and leave San Francisco with his thirty-dollar-a-week unemployment check and move to Los Angeles for a fresh start. "There's nobody here but Peter and Neal I like," he wrote. Once he began to receive his unemployment compensation he decided to stay put for a few more months and use the solitude to polish his own writing. "I've lost too much time as it is and will pass my free days at leisure as I really want to." By being frugal, he knew, his unemployment would be sufficient to see him through the next six months at least. The only splurge he made was to buy Peter a used black 1947 Chrysler Champion for forty dollars. The car resembled a hearse so much that they couldn't resist nicknaming it just that. With Peter behind the wheel of "The Hearse," they escaped from the city and explored the mountains and seacoast. "Since there is no human company," Allen said, "I'll turn to the forests."

To break up his loneliness he decided to fly down to L.A. for a week and meet his old Columbia friend John Kingsland, who was coming west for a vacation. Kingsland had become more openly homosexual since Allen had last seen him in New York, and once turned loose together in Los Angeles, they had quite a drunken bacchanal. Allen and John weren't interested in each other as sex partners, but they did make the rounds together trying to pick up men. Allen ended up in bed with Dick Davalos, whom he knew from New York. Davalos was now a Hollywood actor, most famous for his role as the "other" brother opposite James Dean in *East of Eden*. During his San Remo days in New York, Allen had thought of Dick as not much more than a narcissistic poseur. His opinion hadn't changed, but he did enjoy running around with him to all the fancy Hollywood restaurants and clubs. Back in Davalos's apartment, he and Allen both stripped naked and emptied a big bag of letters onto the floor so they could dance on his fan mail. Allen reported to Kerouac that Davalos was so self-absorbed that he masturbated onto Allen's body and wasn't interested in helping Allen climax. It was lucky that Allen was too drunk to be disappointed. Then, with a terrible hangover, he stopped to see his Riverside relatives before flying back to San Francisco. An equally hungover Kingsland returned to New York.

On Allen's twenty-ninth birthday, he noted that he was on the brink of absolute despair, and his only wish was that he could find the words to describe the acute mental state he was in. His life had become a monstrous nightmare filled with problems, accentuated by a nagging feeling of desolation. Money weighed constantly on his mind. He also suffered from writer's block again and he felt unable to compose anything worthwhile. He said that he had hoped to write a book to equal Mary Butts's memoir, *The Crystal Cabinet*, in which Allen would use modern verse to describe a dream from which he would "awaken to a sudden cautiousness."

Allen was at a sexual dead end with Peter and he had even begun to sleep with a young woman downstairs, a certain Miss Philips, whom he considered a pesky neurotic in spite of her professed love for him. In one of his letters to Jack he complained that even though he saw a lot of Neal, he did not seem to be all there anymore. Sometimes Allen would find Neal sitting in The Place in a trance, focusing every ounce of his attention on a chess game; nothing else would interest him. For that reason Allen begged Jack to come out to San Francisco and help Neal get out of his funk. Allen himself felt dragged down by his own miserable life and was having trouble pulling himself out of it, so he had no influence on Neal. Marijuana hadn't helped either; Allen had virtually given up using it because it only exaggerated his depression and anxiety. Lately it seemed that every time he took any drug he came to another horrible realization about his life. The drug experiences made every bad thing seem all too real. A visit from Kerouac might help Allen as much as it would Neal, so he tried to coax Jack out by telling him about the girl downstairs who snuck up to his room every morning to fuck him. There were plenty of others like her in San Francisco, he assured Jack. "Too bad I don't have the appetite [for women]," he wrote.

Allen's real desire was to leave San Francisco and explore Europe, but the obstacle to that was his usual lack of funds. "How the hell are we going to get up $$ to get to Europe, and when that $$'s gone what are we going to do? How can we live with no future abuilding? That's what's bothering me. Especially since no poetry I might possibly write will ever produce enough $$ to even think of that as solving any problems," he worried.

In June, Allen found a bit of human solace in the arms of John Allen Ryan, a painter who was also the bartender at The Place. Ryan reminded Allen of Lucien with his good looks, gambler's mustache, and wavy hair. Allen pictured him as another Rimbaud figure, and the companionship couldn't have come at a better time for him. One night while

Dream Record: June 8, 1955, *CP*, p. 132

in bed with Ryan, Allen awoke from a vivid dream and went to his desk to write it down. It became his poem "Dream Record."

One trait that Orlovsky and Ginsberg did have in common was a deep love and loyalty for their families. In July Peter hitchhiked to New York to pick up his younger brother, Lafcadio, and bring him back to San Francisco. Allen went with Peter as far as Reno, stopping off for a few days to explore the Yosemite Valley on the way. They bade farewell to each other on the edge of town, where Peter stuck out his thumb for the long twenty-seven-hundred mile trip east alone.

With Peter away, Allen was quick to forget the suffering he'd endured since he met Peter in December and he began to miss him terribly. Neal and Natalie had recently moved into their own apartment so Allen was left alone on Montgomery Street. He had no concrete plans other than talking to Mark Schorer, the noted author and literary critic, about becoming a teaching assistant at Berkeley. He was thinking about studying Greek or prosody in the

Blessed be the Muses, *CP*, p. 133

fall and working toward a master's degree, which might be beneficial if he ever had to get a real teaching job. At least that would be something he could tolerate more than life in the corporate world.

After a party at Rexroth's, Allen and Philip Lamantia spent the night in a cafeteria talking about Lamantia's own visions and his subsequent return to the Catholic Church. Allen was envious of Philip's mystical experiences, which reminded him of his Harlem epiphanies of nearly a decade earlier. He couldn't remember why he had suppressed them, since they had once been so vivid and central to his life. On another night he bumped into Sheila in The Place and was surprised to hear that she had already married; now she was Sheila Williams Boucher. Allen coveted her new life, yet he was glad to be free of the guilt of leaving her. Sheila's later life was not any easy one. She became heavily addicted to drugs, had a few more marriages and children, and died homeless on the street.

Allen made good use of the absolute solitude at home by working at his desk ten hours each day. Corso's first book, *The Vestal Lady on Brattle and Other Poems*, arrived in the mid-July mail, and it moved Allen to tears. Gregory had an innate genius for words and showed his marvelous delicacy for the language in the small book, which had been financed by his friends at Harvard. The book helped to inspire Allen to resume work on his unfinished collection of 1952–55 poetry. In August, thinking of all his old friends, he wrote a new line in his journal: "I saw the best mind angelheaded hipsters damned." It touched off a burst of writing in which he described a host of the people he had seen fall victim to the apathy of modern society. Allen worked on his poem for most of August, using a new style of long prose strophes as poetry. He acknowledged to his brother that the new form was "more or less Kerouac's rhythmic style of prose, elegy for the generation, etc." The form also owed a good deal to Cassady's Joan Letter form and incorporated Allen's interest in blues rhythms and lyrics. The blues style provided a varied yet syncopated meter, which allowed many internal variants and changes of meter in midstream, like the conversational flow of language that he liked in Williams. He sent a few of the new strophes to Kerouac and casually mentioned, "I enclosed first draft scribble notes of a poem I was writing, nearer in your style than anything."

On August 25, 1955, Allen sat at his typewriter on Montgomery Street alone and isolated and composed the original draft of what would become the first section of *Howl*, his most famous poem. To Jack, who had been suggesting exactly this type of spontaneous   Howl, part 1, *CP*, p. 134 flow, he wrote, "I realize how right you are, that was the first time I sat down to blow, it came out in your method, sounding like you, an imitation practically. How far advanced you are on this." After Allen had become famous he was often quoted as saying that he always considered *Howl* a private experimental work, not one that would ever be seen by anyone but his most intimate friends. It's obvious from his letters of the time that these later comments weren't exactly true. For one thing, he had already been showing his poetry to Lawrence Ferlinghetti. It was Ferlinghetti's idea to publish books of poetry as well as sell them, like the Parisian bookstores that he had frequented while studying for his doctorate at the Sorbonne. He began by printing up little booklets of poetry, which he sold at City Lights for seventy-five cents each. According to a letter to Kerouac dated August 30, 1955, just a few days after Allen wrote the first part of *Howl*, Lawrence was already considering it for publication. Ferlinghetti liked the shorter poems of Allen's that he had read and offered to publish a small collection of them with *Howl* featured as the title poem. The composition of *Howl* and Ferlinghetti's publication of the book were the two things that irreversibly changed Allen's life and ultimately pulled him out of his doldrums forever.

When Peter arrived back on Montgomery Street at three o'clock one morning with his brother Lafcadio, he threw his arms around Allen at the door. "Sad noble Peter, truly an angel and not my joke boy," Allen commented to himself. Peter had missed Allen nearly as much as Allen had missed Peter, and they cried with tears of joy to see each other. This was to be the first of many times that Peter would have to take care of one of the members of his family during the next forty years, even when he could barely take care of himself. Allen had immediately recognized Peter's large heart and generous nature, which had made him love him all the more. From the very beginning Allen was aware of Lafcadio's eccentricities, and he tried to get used to them. He reported that Lafcadio spent about six hours each day in the bathroom. Whenever Lafcadio spoke to anyone it was in the form of incessant blather about striking it rich and getting $200 million for inventing a rocket to the moon or some such crazy scheme. They were both aware that Lafcadio needed special attention and they were afraid that the police might pick him up off the street one day and send him to the madhouse. Even in the remedial classes Lafcadio was assigned he proved to be a poor student and before long he began cutting class. He planned to drop out of school altogether the minute he turned sixteen, something that his mother encouraged in her letters. Peter had to write to ask her to reverse her advice, because he wanted Lafcadio to stick to it and get his diploma. By claiming Lafcadio as a dependent, Peter was able to have a VA psychiatrist see his brother, which they hoped might help end his truancy. Every once in a while Allen took him along to see Dr. Hicks for his professional advice, too. Any tips that they could get were welcome, because it was like "having an overgrown problem child, crazy kicks, pathological," and they were both ill-equipped to raise any type of child, much less one with his special problems.

Allen registered for classes at the University of California beginning with the fall semester. He found a cheap cottage in the backyard of 1624 Milvia Street, not far from the Berkeley campus. Peter and Lafcadio planned to stay on at Montgomery Street for at least the rest of the year and Laf took over Allen's old room. Allen was free to return to the city every weekend or whenever he wanted to. Happily his last night at the Montgomery Street

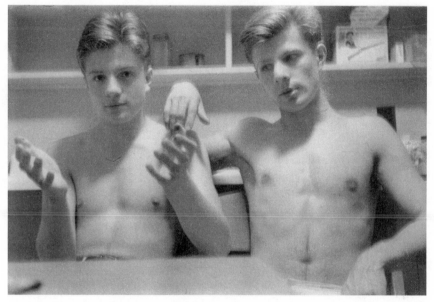

Lafcadio and Peter Orlovsky ~

apartment was spent in bed with Peter. Even though Allen knew by now that Peter wasn't sexually stimulated by him, Peter was able to get it up long enough to make love to Allen. While doing so Peter whispered, "I love you," which was enough to melt Allen's heart and rekindle his hope that deep down Peter did, or could, love him.

The Milvia Street cottage proved to be paradise for Allen. His one-room vine-covered shack was secluded and offered him complete privacy for only thirty-five dollars a month. It was close to public transportation and only a six-block walk to the university. He was so happy that on one of his first days there he had a vision in his yard and fell to his knees weeping in ecstasy. He loved everything about the house and wrote a wonderful poem to commemorate his move entitled "A Strange New Cottage in Berkeley." While he was waiting for the term to start he had time to write a good deal of poetry sitting at a large wooden table. When he became lonely it was easy for him to go into the city to see Peter or Neal. With all this and Ferlinghetti's promise to publish a book of his poetry, he was more content than he had been in a long time. At the university he made friends with Thomas Parkinson, a tall young English professor whom Allen described as an ex–San Francisco anarchist and a Yeats scholar. Parkinson arranged with Allen's advisor,

A Strange New Cottage in Berkeley, *CP*, p. 143

Four Haiku, *CP*, p. 145

A Supermarket in
California, *CP*, p. 144

James Caldwell, to allow him to work with Parkinson, examining Whitman's prosody. Over the next decade, the two became close friends and spent a good deal of time discussing the Bay Area cultural scene. College seemed like a good place for Allen to be in the fall of 1955. His newest poetry was being influenced by his study of Christopher Smart's "Rejoice in the Lamb," as well as his knowledge of Walt

Transcription of Organ
Music, *CP*, p. 148

Whitman's long-line style and his attempt to follow William Carlos Williams's advice. The academic world once again provided him with an anchor and a framework for his life.

In August Wally Hedrick, one of the artists who ran the Six Gallery, had asked Allen to help arrange a series of poetry readings for the fall, but Allen hadn't felt up to the task. He did toy with the idea that maybe he, Kerouac, and Cassady could read together one night, but Jack was out of town and Neal wasn't interested in a public reading. By mid-September, after talking it over with Rexroth, Allen decided he would volunteer to do a single event instead of a series. He had never given a public reading of his poetry before, and he felt it might prove interesting and help him see how the rhythms and meters worked when read aloud. Rexroth offered to introduce the speakers and recommended a few other local poets to ask. Allen also hoped that Jack would come up from Mexico in time to take part.

Until he spoke with Rexroth, Allen thought that there weren't many other poets worth listening to in San Francisco. He was about to discover a host of new poets with interesting work. One evening in late 1954 at Ruth Witt-Diamant's party for W. H. Auden, Allen met Michael McClure. McClure was six years younger than Allen and had arrived in San Francisco after growing up in Kansas and attending college in Arizona. There he had taken an interest in poetry and painting and was devoted to finding links between the two art forms. Both of the young men were standing like wallflowers in Witt-Diamant's living room, watching Auden circulate among the professorial types after his reading at the San Francisco Museum of Modern Art. Since neither of them knew anyone else, they struck up an intense conversation and soon discovered that they had much in common, especially their mutual interest in Blake. Allen was especially interested in McClure's childhood dreams of actually being Blake and wanted to see Michael's poetry as a result. They made plans to get together over tea with Michael's girlfriend, Joanna. Allen could see at once that McClure had found his own unique poetic voice, and he sensed the strength in his language. McClure said that he knew some other writers in town whom Allen would appreciate and from

that day on they became friends. Now, months later, Allen took Michael up
on the offer to learn more about some of the other local poets.

McClure and Ginsberg worked together on the lineup for the upcoming
Six Gallery reading, using Rexroth's suggestions as a starting point. Philip
Lamantia, a native San Franciscan whom Allen had known in New York City,
was a friend of Michael's, too. Since his recent visions, he felt none of his
own poetry was worth reading, but he volunteered to read the work of the
late John Hoffman, who had just died in Mexico. Also on Rexroth's list was a
young poet named Gary Snyder, who promised to read some interesting poems of his own displaying his calm Zen wisdom. Allen arranged to have dinner with Snyder and get to know him. He liked him immediately and was
also interested to hear about Philip Whalen, Gary's friend from Reed College. They made plans to get together with Whalen the following day and
he, too, was asked to read at the upcoming Six Gallery event.

On the same day in mid-September that Allen first met Gary, Kerouac
arrived in the Bay Area from Mexico. He headed straight for Allen's cottage
on Milvia Street and listened to records until Allen returned from his dinner
with Gary. Allen wanted Jack to read at the gallery, but Jack refused
adamantly, saying that he was too shy to perform like a court jester in front
of a large crowd. The two went into the city and got drunk with Peter, Neal,
and Natalie and then went to visit Rexroth, making a drunken nuisance of
themselves. One afternoon a few days later, Allen sat down and began composing a new poem using Jack's method of spontaneous composition. Usually he wrote in his notebook and then transferred poems to the typed page,
but this time he wrote directly onto five sheets of loose paper. Jack was getting ready to go into the city with him and kept urging Allen to hurry up and
finish. Allen wrote as quickly as he could while Jack tapped his toe impa-
tiently and finished the first and only version of "Sunflower Sutra" in less
than an hour. That week, Allen read his poetry for the first
time in public at the annual art festival being held near Fish-   Sunflower Sutra,
erman's Wharf. The crowd listened intently to him as he   *CP*, p. 146
read "A Supermarket in California," and they surprised Allen
with their laughter and applause. This experience bolstered his interest in
doing more public readings and made him realize that there were other people with similar feelings and interests out there, if he could only find a way
to reach them.

To pay the rent, Allen took on part-time work, correcting exams for a
professor of American literature and working as a busboy at Kip's, a student
hangout near campus. As usual, he was fired from Kip's for not working hard

enough to please the owner, but Allen saw it as the owner's problem for having high expectations of him.

The poetry reading given at the Six Gallery on the evening of October 7 was a defining moment in the history of modern American poetry. A handful of hip, young poets who didn't know each other very well got together to read their wildest work to a crowd of about a hundred people. That night saw the public birth of a new literary movement that would stun the academic world and help transform American society over the next two decades. Clues to a cultural revolution were evident in each poet's work. All of them presented poems on subjects not commonly thought of as fit topics for literature. Most people thought that American poetry was still frozen in the "I think that I shall never see/a poem as lovely as a tree" school of verse until the night of the Six Gallery reading. Some of the poets met at the City Lights Bookstore before the reading and squeezed into Ferlinghetti's Austin for the drive to the gallery on Fillmore Street. Ginsberg had sent out postcards announcing what he predicted would be a "charming event" complete with imaginary "dancing girls" to a mailing list of several hundred people. He felt he was putting his marketing background to good use at last. Allen was determined that this should not be the typical dry, staid, academic affair that poetry readings had tended to be during the forties and fifties. He wanted this night to be much more open, with each poet free to let loose and blow in the tradition of the great jazz musicians.

Although Jack Kerouac was in attendance, he couldn't be persuaded to read. Allen coaxed him with honest flattery, saying that his *Mexico City Blues* were among the greatest poems ever written, but Jack wouldn't read. Instead he managed to warm up the audience by passing around a few gallon jugs of red wine. Kenneth Rexroth, dressed formally, started the evening with a few remarks and acted as the master of ceremonies for the program. The first poet to be introduced was Philip Lamantia, followed by Michael McClure, Philip Whalen, Ginsberg, and finally Gary Snyder. After Lamantia read Hoffman's work, McClure read his prophetic poem "Death of a Hundred Whales," a warning to the planet of impending ecological catastrophe. Next Whalen added a bit of comic relief with his poems "Plus Ça Change" and "If You're So Smart, Why Ain't You Rich?" Snyder read his early masterpiece "A Berry Feast," which blends Native American imagery, an Asian sensitivity to language, and a homegrown anarchism.

By the time it came Allen's turn to read, he was slightly drunk on Kerouac's wine. He rose unsteadily and began reading his new poem, which he was no longer calling "Strophes," having decided on *Howl, for Carl Solomon* as the title. Allen had encouraged the other poets to read their wildest work, so he followed suit with *Howl* because he thought it was unconventional and honestly revealed his true opinions. As he read the long poem he gradually sobered up and his performance became more powerful. He was urged on by shouts of "Go, man" and "Yeah" from Kerouac who kept rhythm by tapping on a wine jug. Since it was only the second time Ginsberg had read in public and the first time that he had read any part of *Howl*, he had no expectations. At first he didn't have much confidence in the poem itself, so it was a surprise to him that it was so well received. The applause and cheers were deafening and he was elated. The following day Ferlinghetti supposedly sent him a telegram paraphrasing Emerson's letter to Whitman, "I greet you at the beginning of a great career—When do I get manuscript of *Howl*?"

Later, in 1964, Allen couldn't remember if Ferlinghetti had really sent a telegram or not. In some ways it seems unlikely, since even short telegrams were expensive, but Lawrence distinctly remembers sending it via Western Union. A twenty-year search of Ginsberg's archive has failed to turn up the telegram, but in sentiment, it certainly happened, if not in fact. It made such a great story that it has been repeated countless times, but Allen's spirited reading and the audience's reaction to it did prompt Ferlinghetti to press ahead more quickly with the publication of Ginsberg's book, just as they had been planning.

Even after his triumph at the Six Gallery and the renewed interest Ferlinghetti showed in publishing his book, Allen had misgivings about his future. He lay alone in bed, thinking that he was getting old, impotent, loveless, and unfriendly. Most of all he was sad because Peter did not love him. "My grief was at not loving myself," he wrote. "My mind is crazed by homosexuality."

Sather Gate
Illumination, *CP*, p. 150

The Six Gallery reading created an instant buzz in the San Francisco literary community. It wasn't the first poetry reading of that era, but it was the first time that new poets had come forward as a group with work that pointed to a possible revolution of political and social consciousness. It heralded the coalescence of the East and West Coast poets into a movement that would change the course of American poetry forever. On the heels of his success, Ruth Witt-Diamant asked Allen to read at the Poetry Center on November 20. She was the grand dame of San Francisco's literary elite and her invitation was a feather in anyone's cap. Dylan Thomas, T. S. Eliot, and William Carlos Williams had all read for her in the past, and Allen was honored to join their ranks. His new friend Philip Whalen came to the Poetry Center reading to listen and painter Ronnie Bladen and poet Helen Adam sat in the front row encouraging him. Held in one of the classrooms at San

Francisco State College, it turned out to be a sedate affair and not one of Allen's liveliest readings, but it gave him some much-needed practice.

The readings did nothing to solve Allen's financial problems. He still had to worry about supporting himself after his unemployment benefits ran out. Once again he would have to start looking for a job. Before the first term at Berkeley ended, he dropped out of graduate school, too. He was bored by the dryness of his bibliography course and he couldn't envision himself as a teacher, even if he were able to persevere and earn his master's. At the moment he felt his time was far too valuable to waste in school. His writing was improving by leaps and bounds and new ideas for poems were keeping him busy at his typewriter day and night. He needed all his energy to read and write. Finally, he was discovering how much better Walt Whitman was than Pound, Eliot, or Williams. Whitman was becoming his "great personal Colossus of American poetry," and he read everything Whitman ever wrote. In his journal Allen outlined his major poetic interests: "1) a spontaneous method of composition, 2) a long imaginative line, 3) using the immediate consciousness of the transcriber (or writer) as the subject of a poem."

Allen realized that something special had taken place among the writers who read at the Six Gallery, a kind of cross-fertilization, as when jazz musicians are suddenly turned on by each other and perform at the top of their form. Little of that wildness had been absorbed after Whitman into American poetry, Allen felt; poetry was "mealy-mouthed, meaningless, abstract, tight, controlled, tightassed, scared, academic, uninventive, attitudinized, afraid to show feeling," in short, "too 'Cool.'" That coolness happened to describe most of the hipsters who hung around the San Remo; they were intelligent but acted detached. Allen's new friends in San Francisco were hot, blazing with enthusiasms and ideas. They wore their emotions on their sleeves as Allen did, but up to now he had been too afraid to express them. He grew to believe that tight, formal, academic poetry was the result of a basic lack of technical understanding and not the mastery of it. He began to view poets who wrote in traditional forms as nothing more than trained dogs.

Through his encyclopedic reading of the poetry magazines at City Lights, Allen expanded his list of interesting writers to include not only Kerouac and Burroughs but McClure, Snyder, and Whalen. He also began to appreciate the work of the group made up of Robert Creeley, Charles Olson, Robert Duncan, and Paul Blackburn, who published their own books and put out two little magazines named *Origin* and *Black Mountain Review*. Their work had attitudes (hip, bop, free, imaginative, Zen, anarchist, sensual, modern, and sane) that Allen could relate to.

Late in the year, with his money running out, Allen had gotten on a rib-eating kick, because ribs were about the cheapest cuts of meat he could find. He ate veal ribs, beef ribs, lamb ribs, any kind of ribs as long as they were inexpensive. He cooked them with lots of garlic, basil, mustard, paprika, salt, and pepper and found that he could feed eight people for a dollar and a quarter. He loved to cook for his friends and enjoyed providing a communal table where they could sit around and talk. Beyond his belt-tightening measures, shipping out seemed to be the only way for him to survive. He decided to work in the Merchant Marine again for a few months and then live on that money as long as it would last.

If Allen hadn't already been exposed enough to tragedy with the deaths of Kammerer, Cannastra, and Joan Burroughs, another loss was in store for him. Neal and Natalie had been together for nearly a year when Neal convinced her to impersonate his estranged wife, Carolyn, so that they could withdraw twenty-five hundred dollars from Carolyn's bank account. Neal planned to bet the entire amount at the racetrack on a horse he considered a sure thing and double his money easily. The next day he would return the twenty-five hundred dollars to Carolyn's account and she would never be the wiser. Of course the plan went awry and Neal lost all of the money. Natalie, a fragile spirit to begin with, was emotionally distraught about her part in the crime and worried she would be arrested by the police. On November 30, for fear she'd do something drastic, Neal asked Kerouac to keep an eye on her while he went to work. When Neal returned, he discovered that Natalie had slashed her throat and jumped off the roof of the apartment building in panic when the police came to help her. Cassady and Kerouac didn't want to be implicated in her death and coldly denied knowing who she was. Allen blamed himself for ignoring her and wrote a poem for Natalie. He felt guilty for not inviting her to Berkeley, to his "rest house in my crazy lovely garden," over the Thanksgiving holiday.

By December Kerouac had become exasperated with everyone and left town following arguments with both Ginsberg and Rexroth. Allen closed the year in a negative state of mind. "My personal life's collapsed, I've got nothing to boast about to anyone, not myself, nor friends, nor accomplishment," he wrote in his notebook. All he had were heartaches and fantasies about lovers and jobs, not subjects worthy of great poetry.

1956 ~

AROUND NEW YEAR'S, John Allen Ryan, one of Allen's occasional lovers, asked Peter and Lafcadio to sublet his apartment on Bay Street. The lease on 1010 Montgomery was up and they were planning to move out to save a little money. Ryan wanted them to take care of his low-rent

America, *CP*, p. 154

apartment until he got back from Mexico later in the year. An earlier subletter had trashed the place and left it uninhabitable. Allen and Peter spent a week trying to clean the apartment, but the ceiling leaked and the walls dripped with moisture that made everything cold, damp, and moldy. Then Peter came down with a bad case of bronchitis at the same time the water heater broke. To top it all off, the landlord raised

Fragment 1956, *CP*, p. 157

the rent. Discouraged, Peter and Lafcadio looked for a more affordable place and found one in a project at 5 Turner Terrace on Potrero Hill, a few miles south of downtown.

While the Orlovskys were settling into their apartment, Allen went on a camping trip to the Pacific Northwest with two new friends, Gary Snyder and Philip Whalen. Kerouac had taken a similar trip with Gary a few months earlier, later described in detail in his 1958 novel *The Dharma Bums*. Allen had renewed his interest in learning about Asian philosophy after meeting Gary and Phil. They were more accomplished in their Buddhist practices than Kerouac and they understood that in order to learn meditation correctly a student needed a teacher. They had both immersed themselves in Asian culture and sought out teachers who had firsthand experience. To that end Snyder was getting ready to leave within a few months for Japan, where he was to study at a Buddhist monastery in Kyoto. Before leaving, he wanted to revisit the Northwest and do a few poetry readings there. He and Whalen had both been born and raised in that part of the country and had gone to Reed College in Portland, where they first met. They were still close to Lloyd Reynolds, their old English professor, and they planned to stop and see him on the trip. Allen had decided to go along with them and camp out along the way. That trip was to cement a lasting friendship among the three and rekindled Allen's interest in meditation practice.

By February 2, they had reached Seattle and checked out the sights on Yesler Way, the local Skid Row, which had originally been called Skid Road because logs were skidded into the water near the lumber mill there. Allen recorded everything they saw that day in his poem "Afternoon Seattle." He was on a roll poetically, having discovered a style of his own, and he sketched one scene after another in his journal, much as Kerouac had suggested. Each entry was a gem of a poem and by the time the trip was over he had enough new work to fill a book. They had all been invited to Seattle to give a reading at the University of Washington, which excited a lot of people there, except for "a few old ladies [who] walked out indignant," Allen wrote. Later he embellished his own story and said that five of them ran out screaming. Many people have a favorite store where they love to shop, and Allen found his in Seattle. One day the university professors took him to a giant St. Vincent de Paul thrift shop to look for used hiking clothes and camping equipment. Allen liked it so much that every time he returned to Seattle he went out of his way to go shopping there. On this first visit he bought "a black idiot wool cap and mackinaw" for the cool mountain temperatures.

Afternoon Seattle, CP, p. 158*

Tears, CP, p. 159*

It was a mild February and they hiked along the country roads close to the Canadian border, looking at the towering snow-capped mountains and talking to the cows along the way. They took a bus to Vancouver and gossiped with the fat Sikhs they found wearing black rain-soaked turbans and bumming in the fog. On the way back south they gave a poetry reading at Reed College on February 13 and from there went up to Baker Lodge in the Mt. Baker National Forest to see the jagged mountain peaks. Allen wrote that he wished he and Gary could get along better, which meant that Allen was developing a crush. Gary was straight and didn't respond favorably to Allen's sexual suggestions, which, from Allen's point of view, created a strain on their early relationship. In a letter to Gary written a little later, Allen said, "Sorry myself I needed you so on trip, I actually began by kind of loving you and pressured on the intimacy of the bliss of the red flower."

When they got back to the Bay Area on February 16, Allen discovered that Peter Du Peru, who had borrowed Allen's room while he traveled, had, for some unknown junkie reason, wrecked the place. In the meantime, Peter and Lafcadio had settled nicely into Turner Terrace in a remote part of town that Allen was unfamiliar with. He had a rough time finding Peter's dark cinder-block building at night on the hill above the slaughterhouses of Third Street. The bunkerlike houses had been hastily built during the war to serve as temporary quarters for the shipyard workers who were building a fleet at nearby Hunter's Point. Peter was glad to see Allen at his door and welcomed him warmly. Peter enjoyed a welcome-home blow job from Allen and then fucked him in the ass. Allen was sexually satisfied for the moment, after his celibacy during the Northwest trip. Their sexual reunion wasn't dampened by the fact that Peter had found a girlfriend, Sheila Plant, while Allen was away. A few days later Peter introduced her to Allen at a party in the old Berkeley cottage where Whalen was now living.

Completely out of money, Allen was lucky to get a job handling baggage at the Greyhound Bus Terminal at Fourth and Market for fifty dollars a week. Most nights he stayed in town with Peter or other friends, instead of going all the way home to the Berkeley cottage. After a month the monotony became too great for him, but he got one good poem out of the experience, "In the Baggage Room at Greyhound." Once more he felt he had lost his mind to Moloch, but managed to regain it quickly. Taking temporary jobs, like dishwashing and busing tables, he was able to make ends meet, but by the spring Allen was penniless and his depression returned. He fantasized, "What if my father heard that I committed suicide in my cottage in Berkeley? Charming romantic vision." He read a biography of another victim of suicide, Hart Crane, who had jumped from the deck of a ship, so poetic suicide was an option he might consider. Still, he was able to write hopefully, "There is no god and we do not have to be passing thru to god in order to receive approval and compassion from fellow humans—the light is our own, the light exists for everyone, the light of human mercy."

During the following month, Allen and Peter decided to give Lafcadio his first experience with peyote and to get him laid. They thought it might help him with his social problems more than anything else they could think of. Laf was about to turn sixteen and Peter baked him a big chocolate cake with fudge icing to celebrate. They were happy that Laf had improved to a C average in school and was not cutting his classes as frequently. It looked like he might graduate after all. Allen helped him with his homework and Peter

Scribble, *CP*, p. 160

In the Baggage Room at Greyhound, *CP*, p. 161

did his best to provide a structured, if unorthodox, home life. Things had gone well for Peter in Allen's absence and he wrote his mother, Kate, on March 21, "I've been feeling extremely good, so good that living doesn't seem like a big negative problem as it did before. There's a big blue eyed mystical looking 19-year-old girl here who likes me and I her, so the world's a little bit like heaven now. She goes to Cal. University English major, studying Thomas Hardy right now." Peter took a psychology course, too, and had become interested in dream interpretation. He found a good job driving for the American Ambulance Company on Bush Street, which paid him a nice salary. With his reasonable rent, Peter was managing to make ends meet. He was strong and handsome and looked so sharp in his hospital whites that Allen couldn't get him out of his mind.

Howl, in the form that Allen had read that night at the Six Gallery, was the first part of what became a much longer poem. Over the course of the next few months he expanded and revised the poem several times and added two more large sections to it. Ferlinghetti was making plans to print the book in England to keep the costs down, but Lawrence was afraid it might be held up in customs for obscenity reasons, "since I use cunts, cocks, balls, assholes, snatches and fucks and comes liberally scattered around in the prosody," Allen wrote to Eugene. He asked his lawyer/brother for his legal opinion about what potential problems might arise. Allen toyed with his options: "Should [I] cut out (which I don't want to do), chance it, or request book printed here, which City Lights is also willing to do?" The question of customs was especially important to Allen because he had asked Gary Snyder to look for a cheap printer in Japan to do books by Kerouac and Burroughs, which he was still thinking of publishing independently. So anything he could learn about the U.S. customs laws would help him when the time came for him to become their publisher. "Burroughs is getting fantastically dirty in his manuscript but it is high art, but he doesn't shilly-shally, in fact he's been writing pornography with a vengeance lately, and my own work is full of orgies," Allen informed Eugene.

So many people had missed the first reading at the Six Gallery that there was a great demand to do it again, so five months later, on March 18, 1956, it was restaged in Berkeley at the Town Hall Theater. By then *Howl* had been lengthened and revised into the form in which it appears in the City Lights edition of *Howl and Other Poems.* The Berkeley reading was more theatrical than the one at the Six Gallery had been. Rexroth was dressed in a Salvation Army cutaway tuxedo worn over a black turtleneck

Howl, part 2, CP, p. 139

sweater. Philip Lamantia, who was in Mexico living with the Cora Indians by that time, was the only one of the original poets who missed the second reading. The organizers were better prepared this time, and a professional-quality recording was made of the evening. Allen read his new, longer, and complete version of *Howl* with much more polish and added another new poem, called simply "America," that he had been working on since January. Once again Allen's work received an enthusiastic ovation and so much positive response that Ferlinghetti thought that other new poems like "America" should be added to his book.

As a result of the excitement caused by the reading, Allen was asked to help teach a class at San Francisco State College as part of a program run by Ruth Witt-Diamant. It was to be his first teaching experience, and Allen led the discussions about poetics with a class of about twenty students, half old ladies and half young hip kids, he said. The regular teacher did all the routine work of registration, preparing assignments, and grading. Allen told his schoolteacher father that his teaching technique would get him kicked out of any other place. "I bring in bums from North Beach and talk about marijuana and Whitman, precipitate great emotional outbreaks and howls of protest over irrational spontaneous behavior—but it does succeed in communicating some of the electricity and fire of poetry," he wrote to Louis. Allen's method was to personally involve his students in whatever they were writing. He criticized them if they turned in anything that sounded like "literature." The main thing he tried to do was to get them to express their secret lives in whatever form came out. One of the poems that they typed and mimeographed for the class to read as an example was his own *Howl*. Robert Creeley, who worked for the Poetry Center, typed it carefully and Marthe Rexroth ran it off on the school's mimeo machine. Once stapled together and handed out, it became Allen's first "book," and he proudly sent copies to his friends. "I practically take off my clothes in class myself to do it," he confessed. In May, before the end of the term, Allen became lethargic again and quit teaching, so the assigned instructor finished the class without Allen.

William Carlos Williams was one of the people who received a copy of that first mimeo edition of *Howl, for Carl Solomon*, and he liked it so much that he sat down and wrote an introduction for it. Then Fantasy, a record company in Berkeley, asked to tape Allen reading his poem and issued it as a long-playing album, using Allen's own words describing it as a jazz mass for a blurb. He was surprised by the interest in the poem and pleased when Rexroth told him that he and his friends were creating a renaissance of literary activity in the San Francisco area. Rexroth even invited Allen to his house to discuss the possibility of staging a jazz and poetry reading with a group of musicians he knew. Nothing came of the idea with Allen, but Rexroth and Ferlinghetti did a series of well-attended and much-publicized evenings of "Poetry and Jazz" at The Cellar in North Beach. One evening at Rexroth's weekly gathering, Allen got so drunk that he denounced Malcolm Cowley to his face for publishing "a commercial snot" like Donald Hall and neglecting a true genius like Jack Kerouac. Finally in January 1957 Viking put *On the Road* under contract. Allen was becoming more righteously indignant with each new success he had and he couldn't restrain himself from criticizing the literary establishment for ignoring the work of his friends. "You have no idea what a storm of lunatic-fringe activity I have stirred up," he proudly wrote to Louis. About that time, Richard Eberhart, a well-known critic, scholar, and poet, was invited by Witt-Diamant to read for the Poetry Center. While in town he heard a tape recording of Allen reading his poetry and became enthusiastic about it. He had first met Allen years earlier, right after Allen's release from the mental hospital, but Eberhart hadn't thought very highly of the poetry he was writing at that time. Now Allen's new work impressed him, and Allen gave him a copy of his mimeo collection.

While in San Francisco Eberhart invited Allen to go with him to Days College, about fifty miles north of town, to meet Karl Shapiro, a writer and friend of Eberhart who taught there. Allen had always thought highly of Shapiro and considered him a Jewish intellectual who made good, but he was disappointed when they met face-to-face. He complained that Shapiro was dull and acted more like an advertising executive than a poet. "Official literature, the foundations, the colleges, is run by people like him who have no interest in life except what they can get out of it through acceptable channels and all their work is one big psychic ass-licking operation. I mean dominated by a desire for respectability & acceptance rather than the bitter gaiety of their own souls," Allen wrote shortly after his visit.

More to Allen's liking was Robert Creeley, who had asked Allen to contribute an article on the poetry scene to the *Black Mountain Review.* That project grew into an entire issue of the magazine being devoted to the "San Francisco Renaissance," most of it edited by Allen. Aside from Ginsberg, the issue also featured Kerouac, Snyder, Whalen, and Burroughs. Other literary magazines asked for Allen's poetry, too, and he believed his group of friends was on the verge of publishing success. LaVigne was back in town from Mexico and mounted an exhibition of his paintings at The Place. He asked Allen to write an introduction for this show, which he printed in full on the exhibit's flyer. Allen began to find that he didn't have enough time to accomplish all he wanted to do. He had gotten into the habit of writing every day and with his newfound celebrity and continuing publicity he was finding it hard to sit down and write whenever he wanted without interruption. For several reasons it seemed like the right time to get away on board a Merchant Marine ship bound for Alaska.

Ferlinghetti had taken the time to consult with the American Civil Liberties Union about the legal problems that might result from the publication and importation of *Howl and Other Poems*. Financially unable to risk a court battle alone, Ferlinghetti wanted to be certain ahead of time that the ACLU would volunteer to defend Allen's book, and they formally promised legal aid if there was trouble. Without their support Lawrence probably would not have been able to go ahead with the publication. Allen wrote that he practically hoped it would come to a court battle. "I am almost ready to tackle the U.S. government out of sheer self delight. There is really a great stupid conspiracy of unconscious negative inertia to keep people from 'expressing' themselves." Allen was thinking about other banned books, such as Henry Miller's *Tropic of Cancer*, which he had recently discovered. The censorship of Miller's work made him aware that freedom of speech did not apply to creative writers in America.

In mid-May, when Kenneth Rexroth announced that Eberhart was planning to write an article on the San Francisco poetry scene, Allen had misgivings about how Eberhart would treat *Howl* in the article. Although flattered by Eberhart's praise for his poem, Allen didn't agree with his point-by-point analysis of it. Before Eberhart put anything in print Allen wanted to have his say. "You saw *Howl* as a negative howl of protest. The title notwithstanding, the poem itself is an act of sympathy, not rejection. I am expressing my true feelings, of sympathy and identification with the rejected, mystical, individual even 'mad'. I am saying that what is mad in America is the suppression of the expression of natural ecstasy, and when there is no social form for expression the person gets confused and thinks he really is mad and then does go off his rocker." Allen strongly disagreed with Eberhart, who had characterized his work as destructive and negative, because Allen felt the poem addressed the *realization* of love. He was also afraid that Eberhart would not see his technique clearly and would overlook his interest in the length of the poetic line and the form of the poem in general. Even though he admitted that it was experimental, he added that it was well built, "like a brick shithouse." Eberhart read Allen's comments with an open mind and agreed with much of what he said, modifying his opinions.

During the summer Allen was posted to the USNS *Sgt. Jack J. Pendelton* as a yeoman-storekeeper and assigned to restock outposts along the DEW (Distant Early Warning) Line. It meant spending the whole season in the Arctic, during which time he would earn $450 a month and be able to save enough to cover a trip to Europe. Whalen, who had taken over the lease on his Milvia Street cottage, ended up staying there for several years, but everyone else seemed to be leaving town. Snyder had already left for Japan after hosting one last unforgettable party at his Mill Valley cabin. Kerouac was leaving for the summer to work on Desolation Peak in northern Washington as a fire spotter, and Creeley had temporarily moved into Gary's cabin in Mill Valley.

As Allen's maritime service training at Fort Mason was beginning, he received two pieces of happy news. Eugene and Connie had a baby, whom they named after Allen, Alan Eugene Brooks. He was flattered by the honor and remarked that he wasn't aware that his brother loved him so much. Then he received the proofs for *Howl and Other Poems* from Ferlinghetti just as he was about to weigh anchor. Seeing his work set in type was a singular thrill. While his ship was stuck in dry dock for a few weeks, Allen was able to work on board each day and still enjoy life in San Francisco in the evenings. During that time, he also mailed his few remaining copies of the mimeo edition of *Howl* to T. S. Eliot, Ezra Pound, and William Faulkner, along with a funny letter to each. "Imagine, to T. S. Eliot," Allen wrote, amazing even himself with his chutzpah.

Just when Allen had so much to be happy about, he was struck by another tragedy. While holding in port, he received a devastating telegram from his father. His mother, Naomi, had died suddenly from a stroke on June 9 in Pilgrim State Hospital. The news sobered Allen. "My childhood is gone with my mother," he sadly wrote. In despair, he knelt and cried to heaven, "Life is a short flicker of love." There was no time or money for a big funeral and both Allen and his father agreed that it was unnecessary. Only a few people attended her burial near the mental hospital where she had spent her last tortured years. There weren't even enough men at the service for a *minyan* (ten adult males), so the traditional Jewish prayer for the dead, the *kaddish*, could not be recited.

Allen had tried to keep in touch with his mother as best he could, and they had been exchanging letters during her final months. He had sent her copies of his poems *Howl* and "Sunflower Sutra," but she didn't know what to say about them except, "It seemed to me your wording was a little too hard." She suggested he send them to Louis for his opinion since he was the poet in the family. Immediately before her stroke, she had written a final letter, which arrived after the news of her death. It was like a voice from beyond the grave giving Allen motherly advice that he'd remember forever, "I hope you are not taking any drugs as suggested by your poetry." Allen also thought about a letter she had written a few months earlier to Eugene in which she said, "God's informers come to my bed, and God himself I saw in the sky. The sunshine showed too, a key on the side of the window for me to get out. The yellow of the sunshine, also showed the key on the side of the window." These words would stay in Allen's mind, incubating until he called on them for his greatest poem, *Kaddish*.

A final surprise was in store for him from Naomi when he learned that she had left him and Eugene a thousand dollars each. For Allen it was a fortune, enough money to live on for a year while writing poetry. He could now afford to travel to Europe as he had hoped and maybe even go on to visit her native Russia, in her honor.

Late on the afternoon of June 15, sad at heart, Allen passed under the Golden Gate Bridge bound for Seattle before going on to the Arctic Circle. He stood on the fantail and watched San Francisco fade into the fog, and leaning against the railing near the flagpole, he shouted his poetry above the roaring sound of the sea. By June 19, the ship had reached Seattle, where Allen met a colorful character he nicknamed Tom Tagalong. Together they headed straight for Skid Row and managed to find some old men in a Turkish bath who were happy to give Allen a blow job. One even let Allen bugger him while Allen lay on a massage table. It wasn't romantic but it did satisfy his immediate sexual needs. He also got back to the thrift store he had found with Snyder and bought some more used clothes. The ship shuttled supplies between Oregon and Los Angeles for a few weeks and even stopped overnight in San Francisco on one of

Psalm III, *CP*, p. 163

the trips. Peter and Robert LaVigne came down to meet Allen at the dock and took him to a party at Witt-Diamant's, in honor of Oscar Williams. Rexroth was there and began to curse Allen the moment he saw him, convinced that Allen had somehow been involved in wild drunken orgies with his wife, Marthe, Creeley, and Kerouac in Allen's Berkeley cottage. Allen assured him that he was innocent, but it took Rexroth years to get over his hatred for Allen and his friends. Marthe Rexroth had run off with Creeley, but it had nothing to do with Allen and Jack. Kenneth was unforgiving and his personal hatred spilled over into disdain for beat writing. He was harsh in his criticism of them for the rest of his life.

Back on board ship, Allen spent his time reading religious works, including two biographies of St. Francis of Assisi and several books on the mystic saints, especially St. Teresa of Avila and St. John of the Cross. Before the trip was over he had also carefully studied half of the Old Testament, from Genesis through Chronicles. Near the end of July, the ship passed through the Bering Strait into the Arctic Ocean, but it was too foggy that day to see either coast. Allen had hoped to glimpse the shoreline of his mother's native Russia; disappointed, he threw a few coins into the water in her memory. Over the July 28 weekend, with the ship anchored off Icy Cape, Alaska, waiting for the weather to clear, Allen used the ship's mimeograph machine to print fifty-two copies of *Siesta in Xbalba*. At the next port of call, he mailed copies to his friends and sent a few others to important people who he hoped would discover and endorse his work, including celebrities like Charlie Chaplin and Marlon Brando. He also sent several copies to Michael McClure to sell for the benefit of his magazine, *Moby*. The Alaskan resupply trips lasted through the summer until the ice began to clog the channels in the early fall. The work was easy and Allen had a lot of free time. While on his stopover in San Francisco he was able to pick up the revised proofs of *Howl and Other Poems*, and he reviewed them carefully. He was disappointed to see that Ferlinghetti had cut out "Dream Record," his poem about seeing Joan Burroughs's ghost, and substituted "In the Baggage Room at Greyhound." He said that the Greyhound poem "stinks on ice," but otherwise he was pleased with the overall collection. On July 3 he mailed the proofs back to Ferlinghetti with his corrections. He resolved that if he ever had a second book, he would go at a slower pace and not be so eager to publish it before it was perfect. When he received the next set of proofs in the mail, he had second thoughts and felt it was better with Ferlinghetti's changes. Allen wrote to thank Lawrence for including "In the Baggage Room at Greyhound" this time. Allen was usually a poor judge of his own poetry, which he generally thought was egocentric and somewhat "sloppy jerry-built." He wondered if it was wise of City Lights to print a thousand copies of the book, and asked Ferlinghetti if he could really sell that many.

One morning while on board ship within the Arctic Circle, Allen woke up and wrote the words, *"Kaddish* or the *Sea Poem*, irregular lines each perfect. Now all is changed for me, as all is changed for thee, Naomi." He felt that he would have to write a poem for his mother sometime, and he also knew that it would be a mournful poem touching on his own frightening fixation on death. In the meantime, due mainly to bad weather and the slow pace on board ship, he had plenty of time to write letters. He wrote to Gregory Corso, who had arrived in San Francisco after Allen left, telling him to stay put until he got back in the fall. To Robert LaVigne he reported that he was surprised to find no "ice, snow, icebergs, aurora, whales, dolphins, seals, fish." Instead he found endless gray seas illumined by gray skies that never quite became night under the effects of the midnight sun.

Many Loves, *CP*, p. 164   Allen finished reading the Bible cover to cover before he returned to San Francisco, but he was as confused as ever about "the holy life to come." More than once he fell to his knees on the deck of the ship and asked God for crucifixion so that he could experience suffering as St. Francis and Christ had. He even resolved to "have no more to do with Peter as it is only futile anyway." For the moment Allen believed that Peter's sexual nature wasn't well matched to his own. He had been looking for the perfect homosexual union ever since he was a teenager, and the quest had taken on mystical proportions. One of the more obvious problems was that he seemed to only fall in love with heterosexual men, but being removed from the relationship while at sea, he thought he could change things when he returned.

In the weeks since June 3 when Allen had turned thirty, he had been evaluating his life, both past and future. Eight years earlier Allen had temporarily given up his primary sexual longings for the mystical divine longing generated by his Harlem visions. Now he thought about Matthew Brady's famous photograph of Walt Whitman, in which Allen detected a guarded look in poor old Whitman's eyes. Allen believed that sad look was caused by a self-imposed repression of his innate queerness. He fantasized about making a simple transference of his sexual love onto a spiritual level. Otherwise, he felt, the same thing would happen to him. Earlier he had come to the conclusion that there was no God, but now he was equally certain that the Lord did exist in some form, but for the moment he was unable to speculate about what that form might be.

By the time the boat docked in San Francisco in September, he had put aside a nest egg of nearly two thousand dollars for his long-awaited trip to see Europe and to visit Burroughs, too. Whalen was supporting himself by washing test tubes for the university's science department, and Allen moved into his former cottage with Philip for the next month while he made his plans. With some of his savings Allen thought he might now publish Burroughs's books himself; Alan Ansen had offered to chip in if he did. They would all discuss it in Morocco when he got there.

In the wake of Natalie's death, Neal had found a new girlfriend from Chicago, named Bette. Allen described her as a minor mobster, "a no. 1 girl in the rackets, bookies, gangsters, Mission Street, round eyes, mascara, slacks, cute little body, cool as cucumber, junkie, head, balls with spade chicks, blows Cowboy (trumpet) in alleys, thrice married, 28 years, cars and babies and husbands back in Chicago, digs his body."

Gregory Corso had waited patiently for Allen to get back to San Francisco and had made friends with some of the same West Coast writers and editors that Allen knew. He was anxious to fill Allen in on what had been happening in his absence. Ferlinghetti had offered to publish Corso as one of his Pocket Poets and Witt-Diamant had scheduled him for a reading at the Poetry Center. Randall Jarrell, the poetry consultant for the Library of Congress, had also been in town and had met Corso at one of Witt-Diamant's parties. Jarrell liked Corso's poetry and suggested he come to Washington, D.C., to record for the Library of Congress taped poetry program. Unfamiliar with Corso's wild behavior, the staid Jarrell had invited Gregory to stay at his home while in Washington. At another party, a drunken Ginsberg managed to offend Jarrell and his wife, while Corso remained in their good graces, a reversal of the typical patterns for both poets. Allen was so enthusiastic about Gregory's new poem, "Power," that he read it aloud to the Jarrells at the party. He believed that the poem showed Corso's real genius, and he compared it to his own *Howl*. He honestly believed that "Power" might even be the more important poem in the long run. Jarrell agreed with Allen's appraisal and a few days later invited Gregory to dinner without Allen. Gregory brought more of his own poetry with him and Jarrell offered to write an introduction to Corso's proposed City Lights book. Allen was glad that Gregory had his own sponsor now and the promise of a new book. Things were finally beginning to work out for the beats.

To Allen's dismay, he learned that Carolyn Kizer[35] had been contracted to write an article about the San Francisco poetry scene for the *Nation*. He thought it was absurd that the editor had asked her to write on something he felt she knew nothing about. Allen wrote a long, detailed letter telling her that if she was going to do it, she had to do it right. No "aesthetic bullshit about manners and form," he cautioned. He cited Kerouac as the most important writer for her to look at, but demanded that she include Snyder, Whalen, Corso, and McClure in her survey as well. In

---

[35] Carolyn Kizer (b. 1925): Editor and Pulitzer Prize–winning poet.

spite of his patronizing tone, Kizer wrote back courteously and Allen reversed his initial hostility due to her willingness to listen to his suggestions.

A new confidence had come with Allen's successful readings onstage and that, combined with his already large intellectual ego, made him appear overbearing at times. He and Duncan had "a slight ego war going on," he said, and Duncan's close friend, the poet Jack Spicer, had no use for Allen at all. But more often, instead of feeding on disputes, Allen tried to arbitrate problems and help people get along better. He knew that more could be accomplished by cooperation than by identifying too closely with the various literary camps. He always wanted to be inclusive and get everyone involved even if he didn't appreciate their poetry. In mid-September Kerouac decided to head back to Mexico, with Gregory and Allen planning to follow later. They had some reading commitments to fulfill and some unfinished business with City Lights to complete before they could get away. They all rode with Neal as far as Los Gatos, where Carolyn threw a farewell party for Jack. Allen had not completely given up on his dream of making it with Peter, but he had realized that Peter was not going to give up women for him. A tactic that seemed to work for both of them was to include women in their lovemaking. When they balled one woman, for example, Allen described in detail how she blew Peter while he screwed her from behind, then everyone changed around. "She shy at first but after awhile we all began goofing happily with our cocks and cunts and everybody woke up pleased." Allen was happy that in this way he and Peter could have a ménage à trois with various women and reach a new kind of Rimbaud-Verlaine love compact. It wasn't perfect from anyone's point of view, but for Allen, it was better than nothing.

Corso's and Ginsberg's reading at the Poetry Center was scheduled for October 21, and it would be Gregory's first public reading. Allen read his "Many Loves," which he called "a big queer poem" that he had written on his voyage to the Arctic, but the audience was disappointed, hoping probably to hear him read *Howl* and some of the other poems from the Six Gallery reading. Instead they heard lines like "Ass of a thousand lonely craps in gas stations ass of great painful secrecies of the years." It was shocking, especially by mid-1950s standards. Allen was harsh in his criticism of Gregory's reading that night, too. He said that Gregory had no steam in his delivery and wasn't as ecstatic as Allen would have preferred. Immediately following the reading, both Gregory and Allen were anxious to get on the road themselves,

hitchhiking south to Mexico to rendezvous with Jack. They
would all wait there for Lafcadio and Peter, who planned to
come down in a month or so, after Peter's current job ended.

Ready to Roll, *CP*, p. 167

Flush with money for the first time, Allen felt generous and was happy
to bankroll not only his own trip to Mexico but also the passage for his
friends. As long as the money lasted, he decided to give everyone, including
Kerouac, an allowance so they could "goof" on their own as much as they
liked with no strings attached. Corso was the only one unsure of when he
would sail for Europe. The first thing he wanted to do was take Jarrell up on
his offer to visit Washington, so he decided to go straight on to Randall's
house after a few weeks in Mexico City. It was all happening very suddenly
for Gregory, and Allen hoped that the academic establishment that Jarrell
represented would embrace Gregory's poetry as quickly. Corso had decided
to distance himself from the San Francisco bohemian group and try to make
it in Jarrell's highbrow literary world.

Earlier Gui de Angulo had promised to drive everyone south to Mexico
when the time came. She was an interesting woman, the daughter of Jaime
de Angulo, a maverick genius of Native American anthropology and linguis-
tics in California. Unfortunately, Gui hadn't recovered from hysterectomy
surgery by the time Allen and Gregory were ready to leave, and they began
hitching down the Coast Highway via Carmel. Allen's plan was to stop in Big
Sur and try to meet the reclusive author Henry Miller, whose uncensored
books he had long appreciated. They were slated to be in Los Angeles for a
reading to benefit *Coastlines* magazine on October 31 and stay with Allen's
relatives in Riverside, so they needed to be there on schedule. Rides were few
and far between, and they became stranded at a remote point south of
Carmel. As they walked along, Allen spotted the mailbox of Edward Weston, the great photographer. Since Allen was always interested in meeting
celebrities, he talked Gregory into walking up to the house. An old, old man
with shaking hands came to the door and courteously agreed to show them
some of his photos. Allen was amazed by his talent, and a photograph of a
dead pigeon on a rock at Point Lobos caught his attention in particular. As
they left, Weston stood on the porch in his bathrobe waving goodbye and
said, "I was once a young bohemian like you." Allen was charmed by his generosity to the two strangers and resolved to be equally generous with his
time with young fans in the future. It took the pair quite a while to get their
next ride, and they never did see Henry Miller, but they arrived in Los Angeles in time for the reading.

About seventy people had gathered in a private house to hear the reading. Allen was a little nervous when he learned that in addition to Stuart Perkoff[36] and Lawrence Lipton,[37] the writer Anaïs Nin was also expected to be in the audience. All seemed to be going well with the reading until a red-haired drunk began to heckle Gregory. Allen, by then a little tipsy, went to Corso's defense and screamed at the man, "Take off your clothes and be naked." Allen had been primed for this ever since he watched Duncan strip at the end of *Faust Foutu*, so the drunk played right into Allen's hands by challenging Allen to disrobe instead. Allen thought it would shock the heckler into silence, so he took off all his clothes to a mixed reaction from the rest of the audience. The drunk backed off, Allen dressed, and the reading continued. As Allen wrote to Creeley, "I disrobed, finally, been wanting to onstage for years." The story was repeated so often that its significance grew to gigantic proportions and the point that he was making became more symbolic, although originally it had merely been a quick improvisation to silence a drunk. To Allen the story came to mean that the poet had to be honest enough to reveal himself completely, nakedly. A legend grew that Ginsberg had disrobed at dozens of readings, but Allen frequently admitted that this was the one and only time he did it, although Orlovsky stripped onstage occasionally at future readings.

On November 1, while Allen was still in Los Angeles, the first copies of *Howl and Other Poems* arrived from the British printer, Villiers Press, without a hitch and were placed in the window of City Lights bookstore. It was the day Allen had waited for, and he was bursting with pride to have his own poetry between the covers of a real book. He was surprised that Ferlinghetti had the courage to print the thousand copies of the book, which sold for seventy-five cents each, and marveled at his publisher's bravado. Allen wasn't shy about promoting the book or distributing copies to reviewers and friends, but he didn't believe this book would ever find a wide readership. Poetry didn't sell in the mid-1950s unless it was by literary giants like Dylan Thomas or W. H. Auden, and Allen's book was far too personal to have a wide readership.

After Los Angeles, Allen and Gregory hitched directly to Mexicali where they found Peter and Lafcadio already waiting for them. They all rode the

---

[36] Stuart Perkoff (1930–74): Poet and artist, whose first book, *The Suicide Room*, had just been published by Jargon Books.
[37] Lawrence Lipton (1898–1975): Writer whose 1959 book, *The Holy Barbarians*, was one of the first serious works to focus on beat writers.

night bus across the desert as Corso fought with Lafcadio over who would sit by the window. In Guadalajara they went to see Denise Levertov, a poet they were beginning to appreciate. She lived in Mexico with her husband and children, a "pigtailed gap toothed busy crazy mother who mutually digs and knows William Carlos Williams and writes fine poems with ellipses and fine phrases too," Allen affectionately noted. She showed them around the markets in town and took them on a picnic to the edge of the vast canyon La Barranca to see its dreamlike landscape. She even allowed them to camp out on her floor that night.

They arrived in Mexico City to find Jack sleeping his afternoons away in his little monk's cell on the once posh Orizaba Street. Garver was living in the same building, but he had turned into an old and doddering junkie who sat alone in his room in pee-stained underwear. For the next two weeks they had wild and endless festivities, drunk and high so much of the time that even Allen was exhausted and eventually wrote, "I can't stand it anymore." One day he took them out to see the Pyramid of the Sun, and there they sat on the peak of the monument staring at the sky with the vast shining valley of Mexico below. Gregory traded his favorite Harvard belt for all the Aztec souvenirs that the little Indian boys were trying to sell to them, and they retreated from the sun into the network of cooler caves beneath the pyramids. On several occasions, they visited Organo Street, one of the red light districts of Mexico City. Peter got laid six times and came down with the clap, which he passed along to Allen before they knew he had it. Jack was more careful and used red rubbers, and although Allen made fun of him for it, he didn't get infected. In his journal Allen painted a word picture of their trip: "Walked late at night down grand streets all lit up full of tortilla and sweater stands and cheesy mex burlesque and comedian theatres, ate big steaks cheap at expensive restaurant, listened to Gregory recite incessantly, he was always spontaneously scribbling in big 10 cent notebook, Peter talked to children, Lafcadio dawdled behind us on the street, I met the fairies and had big orgies." He quickly revised the last phrase to say "little orgies," and then crossed even that out to say "not much of one really." Lafcadio wasn't comfortable traveling, for he worried about money constantly and fretted over the price of everything. Allen began to consider him a nuisance and wished he hadn't come along. With his guidebook in hand, Allen wanted to do all the tourist things regardless of the cost. They visited the floating gardens and went to the national ballet where they sat in the high upper balcony for thirty-four cents each. They even stopped to happily pose in the public garden for a souvenir portrait of the group.

Standing: Kerouac, Ginsberg, Peter Orlovsky;
kneeling: Corso and Lafcadio Orlovsky,
Mexico City, November 1956 ~

By the first of December, they had their fill of Mexico City and picked up a ride for $135 with a driver who took them all the way to New York. Corso stayed behind alone to wait for an airplane ticket to Washington and the Jarrells. Kerouac wanted to get back to his mother, and Allen and the Orlovsky brothers wanted to see their families after being away for so long. They drove nonstop for five days, drinking and taking Bennies across two countries.

On a cold, snowy December day, Kerouac, Ginsberg, and the Orlovskys were dropped off on a street corner in New York City with no warm clothing and no place to stay. They walked to the Greenwich Village apartment of the two Helens, as Helen Elliott and Helen Weaver were known to their friends. Helen Weaver was Kerouac's on-again, off-again girlfriend at that time, and when they stood in the snow in the courtyard calling up to her window, she kindly invited them to stay until they decided what to do next. After a day or two Kerouac returned to his mother's house on Long Island, but it took Allen and the Orlovskys a little longer to plan their next move. They agreed that after short family visits, Allen and Peter would go on to see Burroughs in Morocco. Then, if they were lucky and their money held out, they could tour Europe together. While in New York, Allen tried to visit e.e. cummings. "Came to your door, you were out, I sent you my book, *Howl*, did you get it, did you read it?" he wrote in a note. Cummings wrote back unenthusiastically that he didn't think they'd be able to get together. During his stay Allen took the bus to Rutherford, New Jersey, to see Williams again. By now his eyesight was failing and he couldn't read anymore, so Allen read some poems by Corso aloud to him, which Williams said he enjoyed. Williams praised Allen's new shorter poems, too, which he felt were even better than the long-line ones.

Allen was surprised to hear that Ferlinghetti had already ordered a second printing of fifteen hundred more copies of his book. It was encouraging news, but he didn't have any sense of what the potential market might be. "Can you sell another 1500 copies? I don't imagine you'll dispose of many in the Village," he wrote back to Lawrence. However, Allen did his best to help stimulate sales. He boldly walked into the office of the book review department at the *New York Times* and bearded them for a review. One of the reporters, Harvey Breit, took the time to interview Allen, and by the time he left Allen was convinced that they would review *Howl,* but they never did. Breit did mention Ginsberg's lifestyle in one of his columns, but the *Times* was not in the habit of reviewing tiny paperback poetry books from insignificant San Francisco publishers. Allen was persistent as he made the rounds. He visited the offices of New Directions, Grove Press, *Mademoiselle,* and a half dozen other publishers in Manhattan with a springboard binder under his arm, full of his and his friends' writing. It was often difficult for him but he didn't shy away from rejection; in fact, he continued to hammer away on behalf of his friends at potential publishers for the rest of his life. What Allen never could understand was the publishers' failure to see the genius in the works of Kerouac and Burroughs. He continued his efforts to get James Laughlin at New Directions to consider publishing both *On the Road* and *Naked Lunch* even without Rexroth's backing. He felt that the publisher of Pound, Miller, and Williams should recognize the merit of their work. Amazingly he had better luck with the editors at *Mademoiselle* magazine, who agreed to publish some work by Kerouac in their upcoming issue.

While in New York Allen stayed with John Kingsland for a few days, and Peter visited his mother on Long Island. To pass the time Allen made the rounds visiting all the old bars and caught up on who was doing what and what they were writing. He was particularly impressed with the new work of such emerging poets as Kenneth Koch, John Ashbery, and Frank O'Hara and wrote to Ferlinghetti right away to implore him to publish their work. He recognized these New York poets as a distinct group parallel to the San

Francisco renaissance writers. They, too, were influenced by Whitman and his use of the long line, but compared to Auden and other old-school New Yorkers, they were more independent and far more interesting to Allen.

By New Year's Eve, Gregory had worn out his welcome with the Jarrells in Washington and came to New York for the holiday. When he tried to go back to D.C. in early January, they gently asked him not to return. Ginsberg was becoming increasingly depressed from all the publishers' rejections, accusing them of "presumption and indifference." Corso was able to pick up Allen's spirits once he got to town, but Allen continued to enter into literary arguments with anyone who didn't share his view that the new group of poets was the greatest thing happening in literature. At one party, Allen found himself shouting at Bill Becker, a critic for the *Hudson Review*, "You're a shit, you always were a shit!" because Becker couldn't see their merits. His temper was a liability, it did not win him many friends or help get editors interested.

1957 ~

ON JANUARY 4, Allen invited Corso, Orlovsky, and Kerouac to New Jersey to meet William Carlos Williams. They took the bus and spent a few hours there, each reading something to Williams. Allen recalled that Williams "dug" Kerouac but admitted that he was too old to understand Jack's "Golden Heaven Buddhism," as he put it, yet he appreciated the beauty of his narrative. He was charmed by Gregory and his imaginative and inventive phrases like "swindleresque ink" and he talked to Peter about his family's interesting medical history. Allen wrote, "Then my father came in spurting big high school puns, I a Dostoyevsky embarrassed father and Mrs. W[illiams] unbent and had a long moony private confab with tipsy Jack in kitchen and brought out hard liquor and recollections of Creeley dancing in German beer gardens full of love lanterns." They ended up drunk and Allen's father drove them all home, raving and weeping.

Everyone except Lucien Carr was thrilled with Allen's success upon the publication of *Howl*. His complaint was that Allen had included his name in the dedication to the book. Instead of being flattered, as Allen had intended, Lucien was afraid it would draw unwanted attention to him, and he asked Allen to remove his name. Lucien had a career and a family to think about now and he didn't want to be remembered as the man who had given birth to the Beat Generation by stabbing David Kammerer. Allen immediately told Ferlinghetti to remove Lucien's name, and in all subsequent printings, it does not appear.

In early January Kerouac had some good news of his own to share with his friends. Viking had finally agreed to publish *On the Road* and had given him a contract and an advance. Now that there was a ray of hope, Allen began acting as if the poetry revolution had become a fait accompli. He felt there had been a lack of communication among the poets of the various schools, but with his undeniable talent for networking, he had poets talking to each other from coast to coast. For him, the communication problem was solved, as was the lack of publisher interest. "It just needed someone to run around yelling," he said. It was frustrating and tiring work but in the end he felt he had achieved good results. Years later, Allen's friend and Kerouac biographer, Barry Miles, would say that Kerouac's writings "may not have ever been published if it hadn't been for Allen." Once Allen proclaimed the success of the poetry revolution, he decided it was "time to go back to solitude again." Since he had been so active promoting poetry over the last six months, he hadn't found the time to write much, and he came to realize that he couldn't work unless he was more isolated from all the distractions—all the more reason why he should take off for Europe and escape his growing number of self-appointed activities.

Peter wanted to go along for his first trip to Europe, too, and was trying to make arrangements. He was the only functional person in his family and he needed to have several things settled before his departure. First, he helped Lafcadio find his own furnished room on Houston Street and get a job as a messenger. His next problem was his older brother Julius, who had been a mental patient in a state hospital in Central Islip for two years. No one had gone to visit him during that time and it appeared that he had stopped talking completely. Peter was planning to kidnap Julius from the hospital and set him up in his own apartment in the city, perhaps with the help of his sister, Marie. Peter's mother was only able to take care of herself at the moment and she was still living in the same homestead chicken coop, "stone deaf and ugly but a sensitive soul, frightened," Allen wrote to LaVigne. She couldn't take care of any of her adult children anymore.

While hatching these plans Peter and Allen took two girls to an art show on January 15, where they spotted the flamboyant artist Salvador Dali in the crowd. They rushed up to him and introduced Peter as a mad Russian and Allen as a mad poet, frightening Dali with their enthusiasm. Dali asked Allen if he knew of the great Spanish poet Federico García Lorca. That prompted Allen to take a step back and recite from memory lines from Lorca's *Ode to Walt Whitman*: "Not for a moment, Walt Whitman, lovely old man,/have I failed to see your beard full of butterflies." Duly impressed, Dali invited them to have lunch with him at the posh Russian Tea Room next to

Carnegie Hall. They were surprised by Dali's unexpected intellect and Allen added another notable to his ever-growing list of acquaintances.

Allen's itinerary was to include Russia for several reasons. All of his grandparents had come to America from Russia, and the current politics of the Soviet regime were of considerable interest to him, so he and Peter stopped at the Russian consulate to apply for visas for a side trip to Moscow. He had been reading a lot about Vladimir Mayakovsky, the great poet of the Russian Revolution, and he wanted to see the Soviet Union more than anywhere else in the world. Counterbalancing his interest in early twentieth-century Russian poetry was his newest interest, rock 'n' roll music. This "fad" was replacing his own generation's romance with jazz and bebop. In February he and Peter got tickets to hear Fats Domino and Little Richard in a concert at the giant Paramount Theater in Times Square. The crowd outside was fifteen thousand strong, all squeezing to get into the five-thousand-seat theater, and they eclipsed the earlier record turnouts for Frank Sinatra and Dean Martin and Jerry Lewis at the same theater. The continuous performances went on from 8:00 A.M. to one o'clock the next morning, each filled with the rhythms and excitement that the audience craved. Allen was amazed to find himself inside the auditorium as a witness to the crowd of screaming teenagers, all of whom were contributing to a minor riot. The fans were so carried away with the music that they stood on their seats and danced wildly in the aisles, a hint of what was to come in popular music during the next few decades. Allen had never seen anything like it and enjoyed every minute. The police rushed in to quiet the audience, but the pandemonium continued until the final song of the night. The next day newspaper interviews with psychiatrists compared the phenomenon to a medieval form of spontaneous lunacy, but the power of music to reach a whole generation of listeners was not lost on Allen.

In the middle of February Kerouac became the first of the group to leave for Tangier. Allen and Peter promised to follow within a few weeks, as soon as Peter could get his brother out of the madhouse. While waiting for their departure, Allen learned that there were problems with the copyright of *Howl*. As a result of filing snafus, Ferlinghetti was concerned that Allen might not own the copyright to the poem. Allen wasn't convinced that it was a serious problem and still did not consider the poem to be his best work anyway. "Though actually I guess no copyright is necessary and it's all just a bunch of bureaucratic papers so no point actually in doing anything, nobody has anything to steal except in paranoiac future lands," he modestly wrote back to Ferlinghetti.

Once the Orlovsky family was more or less settled and it was resolved that Julius would stay in the hospital, there was another departure delay caused by a tugboat strike. Allen and Peter would not be able to get a ship until March 10. Kerouac, who had been in Tangier for a month working with Burroughs on his book, was becoming impatient. Before leaving, Allen visited Paterson one last time for a tearful goodbye with his father. Allen didn't know how long it would be before he saw him again. They stood together under a street lamp waiting for his bus, crying as they hugged each other. There was a second sad goodbye at the dock as Lafcadio, Elise Cowen (an old girlfriend of Allen's), and Carol Heller (Peter's girlfriend) saw them off. As the freighter *Hrvatska* moved out into the harbor, the small group stood on the dock in a freezing rain and waved farewell. Allen watched the towers of Manhattan disappear behind him and looked at the gray rainy sea ahead, wondering what adventures Europe would bring.

Elise Cowen was only one of the many women who fell in love with Allen during his life. Always confused by those relationships, he was torn between wanting to be attracted to women, especially for the purpose of having children, and knowing that he was sexually drawn to men. Elise had met Allen in 1953 through her Barnard psychology teacher, Donald Cook, once a Columbia classmate of Allen's. Elise was an extremely intelligent and literate woman who Allen thought "was very deep." Although normally her friends characterized her as being her own person, once she met Allen she became obsessed with him and his ideas. Allen slept with her almost as soon as they met but shortly thereafter he had left for Mexico, San Francisco, and *Howl*. After Allen's return to New York, Elise renewed her obsession and began to change nearly everything about herself to be more like Allen. Elise's lesbian tendencies certainly didn't bother Allen, and soon Elise's girlfriend, Carol, along with Peter and Allen, were engaging in group sex. Carol loved sex with Peter but she wasn't fond of Allen because, in her opinion, Allen was intent on controlling Peter, body and soul. Allen liked Elise but did not worship her as she did him. Elise's close friend, the novelist Joyce Johnson, summed it up perfectly when she wrote, "Elise was a moment in Allen's life. In Elise's life, Allen was an eternity." He found it impossible to admit that any woman loved him, and decades later he still refused to acknowledge that Elise had been in love with him. The worst thing about Elise in Allen's mind was that she reminded him of his mother; for that he could never forgive her. Her hair even smelled of death, he once remarked in disgust, so he was glad to be leaving her behind.

From New York it was a nine-day voyage to Casablanca aboard the Yugoslav freighter. Allen and Peter had fairly comfortable accommodations for a modest passage of $185. Allen had plenty of time to read and write on the crossing. Reluctantly Peter let Allen blow him to relieve the monotony of the voyage. Sex caused several angry quarrels during the trip and on at least one occasion, Allen was left to pace the deck all night. He brooded about the fights they'd had over things that amounted to nothing and he wondered if he'd still love Peter if they didn't make love. Sex wasn't something that he wanted to give up voluntarily, but he could see that the original problems they had in San Francisco had never been resolved. They stopped for a day or two in Casablanca and visited the Arab quarter where they wandered through narrow alleys filled with exotic stalls and hooded women. On March 21, they left Casablanca by bus bound for Tangier to see Burroughs and Kerouac at last.

They found Jack comfortably ensconced in a room at the Villa Muniria, a small, cheap hotel a short walk from the *medina* and halfway up the hill from the port. Burroughs had a room on the ground floor off the poorly tended garden and Allen and Peter moved into another tiny room upstairs. By the time they arrived Jack had grown bored with Tangier and was eager to visit France before he returned home to his mother. Since his arrival he had spent a great deal of time working on Burroughs's most recent manuscript, later to be called *Naked Lunch,* a title in fact coined by Kerouac. For a week or so, the group enjoyed a friendly reunion, talking, frolicking on the beach, smoking marijuana, and eating *majoun* (a type of candy made with finely chopped kif, honey, and spices). Jack had already typed much of William's manuscript, but organizationally it was little more than a series of unconnected "routines" that had no unifying plot. The more Jack typed, the more he believed it was unpublishable. Allen was shocked to find that there was no story line to the book, but merely hundreds and hundreds of sheets of random typing. It had been Burroughs's habit to type quickly, yanking each page out of the typewriter as soon as it was finished and letting it fall to the floor, so all order was lost. Fueled by his heavy addiction, the individual routines flowed from his head easily enough, but together they did not form a coherent story and lacked any semblance of continuity. Allen, who had hoped to help William find a publisher for the book, was dismayed. In Tangier, Burroughs's aura of mystery was enhanced by his solitary nature. He sat alone in his room and wrote, leaving only long enough to meet his friends at the local café, or occasionally to go out on his own looking for Arab boys, easily available in the neighborhood. The locals began to call him the invisible man.

Burroughs had been apprehensive about meeting Peter, who he felt had stolen Allen from him. He was jealous from the beginning when he saw how young, strong, and handsome Peter was. He immediately concluded that Peter was inferior to them intellectually. Allen seemed to be the only one who didn't notice William's coldness toward Peter. Burroughs was aloof and distant at first, but as the weeks went by he became openly abusive toward Peter. Burroughs's superior, arrogant attitude didn't endear him to Peter's more timid and self-effacing character, and meeting Burroughs was a disappointment. He had been looking forward to making friends with Burroughs after listening to Allen's nonstop praise for the older man as the mentor and sage of their group. Now he was sorry to discover just how mean-spirited and petty he was.

While the personal tensions were beginning to smolder in Tangier, events of larger literary importance were taking place back in San Francisco. On March 27, 1957, Ferlinghetti wrote to tell Ginsberg that just as they had feared, U.S. Customs had seized five hundred copies of the second printing of *Howl and Other Poems* on their way from the British printer. Lawrence had notified the ACLU and was waiting for their promised help. The day after the seizure, Lawrence wrote to several influential people soliciting their support in the event that the case went to court. He also arranged for another twenty-five hundred copies to be printed in the United States so that in the future he could prevent the customs officials from acting as de facto censors. As soon as Allen heard about it he wrote back to Lawrence, "I suppose the publicity will be good." He suggested the course of action that Lawrence had already taken, namely to gather supportive letters from various literary authorities and send out a position statement about the poem to the press. Allen was more disgusted with the seizure than he was pleased by the possible notoriety he might achieve. "The world is such a bottomless hole of boredom and poverty and paranoiac politics and diseased rags here, *Howl* seems like a drop in the bucket-void and literary furor illusory." To Allen in Morocco the tempest in San Francisco seemed to be far away and had little to do with him or anything he cared about.

After a week or so in Tangier, Ginsberg and Orlovsky settled in for a long stay. Burroughs had shown them some of the cafés he frequented. Most of the European-style places favored by the expatriates in Tangier were along the Boulevard Pasteur, and the most well known was the Café de Paris. Allen much preferred the small Arab cafés around the Petit Socco within the *medina* for his afternoon mint tea. Sitting at an outdoor table, they were often approached by Arab boys offering shoe shines, lottery tickets, newspa-

pers, rubber sneakers, scarves, leather bags, and peanuts. In Tangier everything, even the boys, was available for a few pennies. Because it was an open
city and governed by several countries, it was divided into sectors. There was
an Arab quarter lying mostly inside the ancient walled city, a French quarter,
a Spanish quarter, and even British and American quarters outside the old
town. It was a wonderful place for Allen, who enjoyed investigating exotic
cultures and thoroughly exploring everywhere he visited, and he found the
Arab section especially intriguing. Its secret alleyways meandered to the
Kasbah, whose intricately carved doorways and dark cafés were always filled
with men smoking pipes of kif or tobacco and drinking mint tea. Young
boys played instruments and begged for handouts as the days passed lazily.
Peter liked to take long walks along the beach and look out across the Strait
of Gibraltar to Europe, but even at that time the harbor was too polluted for
safe swimming. Allen and Peter were allowed to cook in their room at the
Muniria, so living was cheap, and it was a daily culinary adventure to shop in
the open-air markets filled with merchants selling olives, raisins, freshly
slaughtered lamb, and seafood of every variety.

On April 5, the day Jack left for Marseille, Allen and Peter inherited his
twenty-dollar-a-month room at the villa. Light poured into the room
through French doors that opened onto a private red tile patio with a spectacular view of the harbor. On clear days they could see the brilliant azure
blue strait between the Pillars of Hercules, anchored by the wild mountains
of Africa on the south and the Rock of Gibraltar on the north. On gray days
Gibraltar seemed far off in the fog and mist and on cloudy days they
couldn't see it at all. Each time Allen looked at the coast of Spain, he daydreamed about the ancient castles he would see when their travels through
Europe began. Before that he had to figure out how to get Burroughs's manuscript into publishable form. Allen admired William's unique prose and
knew that it was intense, almost like poetry. So far about a hundred pages of
fast action routines had been roughed out by Jack, who had been calling it
William's "word hoard." Allen had always loved Burroughs's carelessly rib-
ald sense of humor, but here he felt that he had gone one step further than
Jack in his pure free association with strange, unrelated combinations of images. Allen grimly acknowledged to himself that no American publisher
would ever touch it. One of the most troubling routines included William's
fantasy about hanging victims getting hard-ons and having orgasms at the
very moment their spinal column was snapped. He described a scene in
which a beautiful young boy was hanged and all sorts of mad queens clustered at the gallows to rip off his clothes and fight over the spurting semen.

The ideas were more extreme than even de Sade, but Allen knew that William's intent was not to shock. He was merely relating the unconscious material he dredged out of his own psyche. When told about *Howl*'s seizure by the customs officials, William was more pragmatic than Allen. "That's nothing my dear, I'll have the distinction of being banned not only in [the] U.S. but also France." Except for his work on *Naked Lunch*, Allen's interest in literary matters evaporated during his stay in Morocco. He told Don Allen, an editor for Grove Press, that all the literary small talk in America had given him such anxiety that he could not think about it anymore and was enjoying his break.

Allen looked forward to meeting the writer Paul Bowles, who had been living in Tangier for years. Burroughs knew him slightly and Bowles's books about life in North Africa, *The Sheltering Sky* and others, were highly regarded. At the time of Allen's arrival, Bowles was away in Ceylon, but Paul's wife, Jane Bowles, was there and Allen went to see her. She was an accomplished writer in her own right and besides Burroughs, Jane became the only person in Tangier of any interest to Allen. In high praise, he compared her intelligence to that of Joan Burroughs and he appreciated her cool, shy manner, even her ability to speak Arabic. She liked *Howl* when he gave her a copy and they spent a long pleasant afternoon discussing books. She was extremely frank and straightforward and Allen liked her better the more he got to know her. Lately she hadn't been writing much, but she told him that she was now at work on a play.

Peter was having difficulty in the hot North African climate. He suffered from asthma and pleurisy and it would take him months to acclimate. They were also nearly broke, and Burroughs had to support them for a while. In return Allen and Peter helped with the cooking and cleaning. Their expenses weren't great, but they did need a few dollars every now and then, even in Tangier. After a protracted argument with the Veterans Administration over his disability pay, Peter was finally granted fifty dollars a month, so they had some small financial security. In addition to that, William Carlos Williams was able to get a two-hundred-dollar emergency grant for Allen from the American Academy of Arts and Letters, which satisfied their immediate needs. Each evening they relaxed by sitting in the Arab cafés, drinking glasses of tea and smoking kif. While Allen enjoyed watching the slinky little Arab boys dancing and wiggling their bodies to the tambourine beat, he did not approach any of them for sex even though they were available for a small token. William's manuscript kept Allen preoccupied and he wasn't accustomed to a culture that was open to homosexuality. Allen and Peter weren't making it very often either. In fact, Allen was virtually celibate except for occasional masturbation, he complained in a letter to Robert LaVigne.

Before long Alan Ansen, their old friend, arrived to help assemble Burroughs's manuscript, and it became a real community effort. They set up their own small editorial office in the Villa Muniria. Besides typing, both Ginsberg and Ansen edited and read pages out loud to each other as they went along. As a student Ansen had been forced out of Harvard under a cloud of homosexual scandal. He knew at least eight languages and was best described by Allen as "a large mad genius dilettante." Years earlier Ansen had been Auden's secretary, so he was able to give practical advice that helped with the editorial process. Ansen was not nearly as shy as Allen when it came to the Arab boys, and for fifty cents he enjoyed the delights of the flesh each day after lunch. Once he splurged on a boy for Burroughs as a present. Allen was hoping to enjoy the same before he left Morocco but he remained too timid. Peter, meanwhile, found himself at an even greater disadvantage. There were not many female prostitutes available in Arab countries and they were "three times more expensive and much less accommodating than the boy whores," Allen noted. Once, before Jack left, he and Peter brought two whores to their room for five minutes but they did little more than suck their breasts before the women pushed them away. Peter was becoming increasingly depressed as they stayed on in Tangier, not only from the shortage of women, but also from the rude treatment he was suffering at Burroughs's hands.

With very little success Allen tried to find some quiet time for himself so that he could write. He needed to distance himself from the frantic pace of the literary worlds of San Francisco and New York. For him the madcap rushing around was addictive, and he was glad to escape. Despite some positive results, the quest for fame was like a narcotic with him, and he doubted that the time and energy he devoted to becoming famous was worthwhile. "I guess solitary singing is the only way. Otherwise there is too much activity and delaying with things." He worried that he might have a split personality, one part gregarious and the other "much weirder but truer" to himself. He knew his best writing came from the weirder self, when he was cut off from all distractions. His short-term desire was to begin writing again as soon as the work on *Naked Lunch* was wrapped up. Kerouac had taken a small portion of the early manuscript with him to Paris and left it with Bernard Frechtman,[38] who believed that a daring French publisher like Gallimard or

---

[38] Bernard Frechtman: Translator and agent of French writer Jean Genet.

Olympia Press might be interested in publishing it. Olympia had a reputation for putting out offbeat or pornographic material. They took on books that no other legitimate publisher would touch, so there was a little hope for Burroughs on the commercial front. Frechtman never got around to taking it to any of the publishers, though, and the manuscript waited on his shelf for Allen's arrival in Paris. Since Jack had left Tangier, they had finished another hundred pages and shaped the book into a colorful mosaic of routines, dreams, scientific theories, and thought-control fantasies. The book now ended with a revelation of Burroughs's "Word Hoard."

By the beginning of May, they had nearly finished the typing and organizing of the *Naked Lunch* manuscript. Allen loved William's prose, the "pure free association of visual images, a sort of dangerous bullfight with the mind, whereby he places himself in acute psychic danger of uncovering some secret which will destroy him."

At that moment Paul Bowles returned from Ceylon and moved into a room in the Villa Muniria, too, so they had a hotel filled with writers. Allen had the chance to meet Paul and his traveling companion, Ahmed Yacoubi, an Arab painter whose pictures reminded him of the works of Paul Klee. Ahmed was a handsome, good-humored hipster who liked to hang out at the elegant Café de Paris and whistle at the passing girls. Although Bowles was shy and slow to make friends, Allen hoped that they would be able to form a close bond as he had already done with Jane. A few days after Paul's arrival, Jane suffered a slight stroke and Paul spent most of his time with her, so Allen didn't have the chance to get to know him. When Allen and Peter were finally invited to visit him in his room, they shared some Tanganyika marijuana and talked about Gertrude Stein. While listening to some of Bowles's recordings of Indian music, Allen realized that Paul was not as sinister as his books suggested. Instead, he seemed to lead a remarkably safe and comfortable life and was more conservative than Jane in most matters. Allen speculated that Bowles wished his life were a bit wilder but was reluctant to jeopardize his serenity.

Bowles introduced them to the curly-red-haired English painter Francis Bacon. Allen was familiar with Bacon's paintings at the Museum of Modern Art in New York; they depicted distortions of cadaverous people who resembled nothing so much as slabs of meat hanging in the windows of butcher shops. When he met Bacon, Allen remarked that he looked like a plump seventeen-year-old English schoolboy, even though he was in his late forties. More intriguing to Allen was the fact that Bacon liked to be whipped. He was also similar to Burroughs in that art wasn't the most important thing in his life; it was just something that he did when he had the time. He considered the art world's high regard for his work as chic bull-shit. His favorite pastime was gambling at Monte Carlo, where he always lost. If he managed to fail in his painting career, he told Allen, he could always fall back on being a cook. Bacon didn't like much of the abstract expressionist art that was currently in vogue, preferring instead the more realistic style of Willem de Kooning. It was Bacon's hope to discover a new way to paint a portrait. He described it as a psychic representation of the eyes, nose, and mouth, all of which would suddenly emerge from the canvas, as if by mistake. He was one of the few people who made Allen's stay in Tangier interesting, and as the town in general lost its appeal for Allen, he grew eager to leave.

Tension between William and Peter was continuing to mount and Allen didn't know how to handle the situation. Peter decided that his only way out was to escape to Spain with or without Allen, perhaps hiking solo. He made plans to go it alone, since Allen had promised to stick it out and complete the editing of William's book. Left alone while Allen was working, Peter had begun to take opium. He started to crave its big twenty-four-hour somnolent kick. In the evening he would feast on a chunk with warm tea and then read all night. Not even Peter with his growing appetite for drugs could handle Burroughs's homemade *majoun*, though. William knew the recipe and used the correct ingredients, chopped kif mixed with caraway seeds, cinnamon, honey, and nutmeg. Then he heated it until it was sticky, as he was supposed to, but instead of hardening like fudge, it stayed sticky. It was so strong that everyone who partook was seized with extreme paranoia. Though *majoun* was normally easy on the stomach, William's vile mixture gave them all nausea.

After months in Tangier Allen still found he had no time to write. He produced no poetry at all and only added an occasional entry to his journal. He did continue to read voraciously and finished the Koran, as well as several of Melville's books, including *Israel Potter* and *Typee*, the latter his favorite. Peter kept himself busy by reading Melville's "Bartleby" and by making pencil drawings of the harbor from the balcony of their room. Allen even curtailed his letter writing for a while, since many of the people he usually wrote to were with him. When John Wieners wrote to request something for his magazine, *Measure*, Allen had to admit that he hadn't finished anything of any value recently.

No matter how much Peter tried to get on Burroughs's good side, there was always something about him that annoyed William. Matters came to a head one evening when Burroughs ridiculed Allen for loving Peter. That enraged Allen so much that he lost his temper and slashed William's khaki shirt with a large hunting knife. Then Burroughs frightened everyone by insanely waving a machete overhead at Allen and Peter in retaliation. Later, Allen felt guilty for blowing up, but Peter had no history with William to fall back on and wanted to leave. He was willing to go anywhere he could find accommodating women instead of sitting in Tangier waiting for Burroughs to go crazy again. Finally Allen agreed with Peter that it was time to leave for Europe. Since he hadn't written one good word in Tangier, he hoped that his writer's block might disappear if he got on the road again. Their immediate plan was to sightsee through Spain and wind up in Venice where they had an open invitation from Ansen to stay with him. They waited a while longer in Tangier as Allen felt unwell and was recovering from undiagnosed liver or stomach problems. He was sure he would soon be fit enough to travel but as they were packing to leave, Peter came down with influenza and they had to stay in Tangier for a few more days.

While waiting for Peter to recover, Allen received another letter from San Francisco. Ferlinghetti's tactic of having copies of *Howl and Other Poems* printed in the United States had worked. The U.S. attorney in San Francisco had refused to institute condemnation proceedings against the book, knowing that they had a weak case, so the five hundred copies seized by customs were released. Then on the night of June 3, the situation with Allen's book took another dramatic turn. Two plainclothes detectives from the police department's juvenile division walked into City Lights and bought copies of *Howl* and a magazine called *Miscellaneous Man*. A little later they returned to make arrests. Shig Murao, the bookstore's manager, was the only person working that evening and he was taken into custody. A warrant was issued for Ferlinghetti and he turned himself in the next morning. Both men were charged with selling obscene literature, a more serious charge than the customs seizure had been.

This time there was no way around the arrest; Ferlinghetti would have to defend his publication of *Howl* in court. Allen wrote to ask Lawrence what he should do. Sitting in Tangier, he thought it was funny, but he sympathized with the financial and legal dilemma in which Lawrence now found himself. He told Lawrence to keep track of all the expenses so that he could try to raise the money to pay for any fines. At the time Lawrence and Shig were facing possible prison sentences and were less concerned about fines. It must have seemed insensitive to Lawrence when he received Allen's letter, "I wish I were there, we could really have a ball, and win out in the end inevitably."

Allen said that he never wanted to read *Howl* in public again, for he had come to the conclusion that it was an inferior poem. However, if it would help their case he said he would be willing to return to California to do it. If he returned for such a reading it might give the poem the "social protest" that Allen felt it lacked. In truth Allen was worried about returning to testify in the United States because he felt he had stated that he was a communist in his poem. "What would happen if I came back?" he asked Ferlinghetti nervously. Allen was relieved to hear that the ACLU attorneys thought his appearance would not help Lawrence's case, since the charges were against the publisher of the book and not the author. He would be quite content to sit it out overseas and wait for the trial and verdict with what seemed like only moderate interest.

While in Morocco, Allen had been toying with the idea of offering his next book of poetry to Knopf or another big New York City publisher. He hoped to break into a larger market than City Lights could provide. Now, with a trial pending, Allen decided to remain loyal and assured Ferlinghetti that he would stick with them through thick and thin and send City Lights his next book. "When I have a mss. I will send it to you to look at and publish if you can and want to; I won't go whoring around NY publishers I promise." Anyway, Allen wasn't certain that Lawrence would want to risk publishing his next book of poems. Burroughs had opened Allen's eyes to even more questionable areas of taste when it came to subject matter, and he planned to explore his own darker thoughts and dreams in his next poems. He couldn't begin to imagine where this would lead; perhaps he'd "write elegies to the asshole of some Istanbul hermaphrodite or odes to cocaine." Even if it meant that he would have no audience at all, he wanted to investigate that shadowy side of his imagination, the hidden thoughts that he felt were too horrible to reveal.

On June 11, Allen and Peter ferried across the strait on the two-hour trip from Tangier to Algeciras, Spain. Once out on the water they could more clearly see the Atlas Mountains that towered over the African coast east of the city. Dolphins swam ahead of the ferry to the continent, jumping out of the water in front of the boat a dozen times before they disappeared into the deep blue water. It seemed like a good omen. The steep rocky cliffs of Gibraltar loomed across the small harbor from the Spanish port where they wandered with their knapsacks toward the train station. There they bought passes that allowed them to take any train they wanted for a flat rate. Glad to be on their own again, Peter and Allen became tourists once more and traveled through southern Spain to Granada.

Nothing they had seen in Morocco prepared them for the elegant Moorish beauty of the Alhambra, perched high on a hill overlooking the city. Peter and Allen visited some gypsy spots, but Peter got sick on the cheap five-peso fish soup they bought. Fortunately, it was a minor upset stomach and didn't keep him down for long. For two days while he rested, Allen walked through the magnificent Arabic rooms at the Alhambra and delighted in the stimulation provided by the sensual architecture, which intermingled color, texture, sound, and smell. In a letter he described the overall effect as the "purest eyeball kick." He was well aware that Granada was where Lorca had learned to sing and he recited some of Lorca's poems from memory on the parapets of the city. Ansen had suggested that they explore Seville and visit the Cathedral de Sevilla, the largest Gothic cathedral in the world. It was extremely hot the day they arrived and they did their best to shelter themselves from the sun under the awnings. Peter enjoyed looking at the beautiful Spanish women, but he didn't know how to approach them. They spent two warm nights in Seville before moving on to Córdoba. The next day they toured the town and looked at its ninth-century mosque, the Mezquita, where Don Quixote had battled a terrible monster and where the poet Luis de Góngora y Argote was buried. William Carlos Williams was a fan of Góngora y Argote's florid, cluttered style, and Allen copied down a stanza from one of his poems onto a postcard to send back to him. Then he and Peter took the all-night train direct to Madrid.

As soon as they arrived in the capital they checked in with American Express, expecting to find mail waiting for them and hoping for a little cash. It hadn't taken long for things to go wrong back home. There was a disturbing letter from Peter's family reporting that his brother Nicky was considering signing a release to allow the doctors to perform a lobotomy on Julius. Peter was distressed and wrote back begging them not to sign any papers permitting such drastic and irreversible action. Allen's main purpose in coming to Madrid was to visit the Prado museum with its El Greco, Brueghel, and Bosch paintings. Instead he found Fra Angelico's *Annunciation* to be "exquisite and solid" and that one painting impressed him more than three rooms of El Grecos. He even tried smoking some pot before he visited the El Grecos again, but nothing helped him to better appreciate them. The pot only blurred things and the paintings disappointed him in the end. He was not disappointed with the Prado's Bosch masterpiece, *The Garden of Delights*, which he stared at for an hour, examining and ingesting the minute details. It was the first time Allen had ever had the opportunity to look carefully at every square inch of a Bosch painting.

Although food was cheap in Madrid, they found that the hotel rooms were not; still, by watching their pennies they were able to stay for several days after cashing Peter's VA check. In Madrid Peter developed a food allergy that gave him hideous blotches of hives and his ankles and knees swelled up so badly that they had to consult a doctor. He prescribed a strict diet of yogurt, fresh fruit, and zwieback, so for a few days they ate nothing but that while he recovered. When Allen brought him a salami sandwich as a special treat, it caused a relapse. Since he was sick, Peter stayed in their hotel room and Allen went by himself to the museums. Once a day for a whole week he dropped in to see the Fra Angelico, which he still found the most striking and captivating work of art he had ever seen. He bought postcards of the painting and sent them to all his friends.

By the end of the week Peter was beginning to feel well enough to go with Allen to a bullfight. However, neither of them cared for the blood and gore. Before moving on they took the train to nearby Toledo for a day and walked around the hills outside the city looking for the vantage point from which El Greco had painted his only landscape, *View of Toledo*, which Allen had seen so often in the Metropolitan Museum. They never found the exact spot because El Greco had used artistic license to change the arrangement of the buildings to fit his composition. For a little while they entertained the possibility of staying longer in Madrid, and Allen even interviewed for a job with a construction company, but realizing that the paperwork alone would take weeks, they moved on. Back on the road, they stopped in Barcelona on June 28 and managed to squeeze in most of the tourist sights on their two-day visit. Allen had been bitten by museum fever and wanted to see every art treasure in Europe, so they walked up the main promenade, La Rambla, exploring all the cathedrals and museums along the way. After climbing around Antonio Gaudi's half-finished church, La Sagrada Familia, they even took the funicular up Tibidabo to see the view from the top of the 1,745-foot mountain. Late that night they caught a train heading north for the French border. With a pocketful of marijuana and their shabby appearance, they were lucky not to be searched at the border and hopped on a modern electric French train for the short ride to Perpignan.

Paul Blackburn had told Allen that Perpignan was the center of the fruit-growing industry and that trucks bound for Marseille and Paris went out all night. That made it a great place from which to hitch a long-distance ride, but the easy ride Blackburn predicted didn't materialize. When they arrived at three in the morning, the truck stop café was closed for the night and there was no activity at all. They laid out their sleeping bags on a bench

under the trees and slept for a few hours until 5:00 A.M. when the produce
trucks began to roll past. Still, they had no luck catching a ride from truck
drivers or from the tiny European cars that couldn't hold two extra people
and their large knapsacks. After a while they got a short ride as far as Béziers,
a town that Allen remembered was mentioned by Ezra Pound as being a
haunt of the Provençal poets. There they were witness to a Dr. Mabuse–
style[39] funeral in the local church and once again became stranded trying to
hitch a ride out of the town. With their money now running dangerously
low, they decided that they couldn't dawdle in France and bought a cheap
ticket on a train scheduled to arrive in Montpellier at midnight. Everything
was closed when they got in, but they stumbled upon a bookstore where the
local French communists were meeting. Allen was reminded nostalgically of
his visits as a boy with Naomi to communist cell meetings in New Jersey.
Here in France he regarded these men as evil mentalists, but at least "they're
free to have open meetings, it was amazing to see like shift back in time to
US 1934 near River St. Paterson when reds were only innocent bupkis [sic:
bumpkins] I thought," he wrote to Kerouac. In the United States of 1957,
communists would envy that kind of freedom. At the train station they
bumped into a young traveler from Switzerland who was heading home after completing a six-month trek through the Alps. Allen was able to speak to
him in broken Spanish about his travels and stints of farm work along the
way, all while reading Nietzsche. Even though they couldn't communicate
very well, Allen instinctively knew that they were like-minded and he em-
pathized with the boy traveling completely alone. He helped Allen and Peter
load their bags on the next train to Marseille and kissed them goodbye. As
they clambered aboard, he gave them a small bag of grapes for their trip.
"That's how we should love each other," Allen thought. As the train pulled
out of the station, the boy disappeared into the fog. Once in Marseille they
immediately changed for the train to Venice to find Ansen, who had been
waiting patiently for their arrival.

Alan had a comfortable, book-filled apartment in the middle of Venice
near San Samuele. He, like Burroughs, had a modest fixed income that was
enough to pay his rent, so Allen and Peter were welcome to stay for free for
as long as they wanted to. Using Venice as his base, Allen planned to explore
the rest of Italy, especially Florence and Rome and their art treasures. Allen
and Peter visited all the museums and churches of Venice, discovering an-

---

[39] Dr. Mabuse: Title character of film director Fritz Lang's films about an insane man living in an asylum
in post–World War I Germany.

cient landmarks at every turn of the dark mysterious passageways. Although Allen didn't appreciate the Venetian artists as much as he did the Florentine painters of the High Renaissance, he grew to like the sad, troubled paintings of Titian, and the work of Giorgione, whom he compared in sentiment to Keats. Allen felt blessed to have the chance to live in Venice for a while and to wander around St. Mark's Square whenever he felt like it.

Shortly after Allen and Peter arrived, Ansen threw a small party and invited his friend, the wealthy art collector Peggy Guggenheim. She loved creative, gifted artists of every sort, but Allen and Peter were a little too rough around the edges for her. Much to her chagrin, they spent a lot of time talking about masturbation and smoked marijuana openly. It was so hot that they wiped their perspiration away with a big sweaty towel that they continually tossed back and forth to each other across the table, narrowly missing Guggenheim at one point. She was irritated when she left and ignored both Allen and Peter for some time after that. Later she insulted Allen further when she invited him to one of the surrealist parties at her palace, with the stipulation that Peter not come with him. Of course Allen refused to go without Peter and his feud with Guggenheim continued unabated. The story has always been told that Peggy was hit in the head by the sweaty towel, but Ansen testified that she was never physically struck, only aghast at their rude behavior. The following year Corso became quite friendly with Peggy through Ansen's introduction, only to have their friendship end after a crude remark from Gregory.

One of Guggenheim's own houseguests, Nikos Calas, an expert in surrealist art, secretly came to visit Ansen, Allen, and Peter one evening without Peggy's knowledge. He enjoyed Allen's poetry so much that he read parts of *Howl* later at one of her parties, much to everyone's delight, but he was unable to get Allen back into Peggy's good graces. He tried, unsuccessfully, to find a French translator for *Howl* and told Allen that he'd pass along a copy of it to his friend Andre Breton, which flattered Allen considerably.

Ansen, who seemed to fall in love with every sailor in port, was subject to bouts of depression much like Ginsberg's. After one of Ansen's boys ran off with the cash he had put aside for a gondola excursion, Peter tried to cheer him up by jumping fully clothed into the Grand Canal for a laugh. It helped pick up everyone's spirits for a little while. On another day they took a bus out to Padua to see the wonderful Giotto frescoes in the Scrovegni Chapel. Allen continued to have "museum fever" and on July 27 he and Peter left to see the treasures of Florence and Rome. They wanted to see more Fra Angelico and Giotto paintings and spent a long time in the Uffizi. The museum was filled with pictures of visions and glimpses into mystical events that seemed to speak directly to Allen. It was difficult to decide what masterpiece to concentrate on first; da Vinci, Botticelli, Giotto, and Angelico were all in abundance there. They ended the day by snapping happy pictures of each other in the sunlight on the Ponte Vecchio. Years later, Ansen gave credit to Allen for encouraging him to write verse that summer, which led to the publication of at least half a dozen books of poetry during the rest of his life.

When Allen and Peter arrived in Rome on August 1, they walked all over the huge city from the Coliseum to the Pantheon. The first day they visited St. Peter's Basilica in the morning and walked down the Tiber River in the afternoon to the Protestant cemetery where Shelley and Keats were buried. Allen wept over Keats's grave and then kissed Shelley's grave as he knelt to take a clover as a souvenir remembrance. Each day, like the indefatigable tourist that he was, Allen would get up and traipse all over the city taking pictures of Peter and himself in various ruins. On their fourth day in Rome, Allen went to the Vatican museums and became enraged when he discovered the fig leaves that had been added to cover the crotches of the nude Greek and Roman sculptures. It was maddening, especially after seeing the beautiful nakedness of Michelangelo's statue of David in Florence. On his final day in Rome, Allen visited Keats's house beside the Spanish Steps but didn't have the few pennies needed for admission to the room in which Keats had died of tuberculosis.

That afternoon they took the train as far as Assisi and hiked up the steep hill from the station to the basilica, where they wanted to see the impressive Giotto fresco cycles. With no money left for even the cheapest hotel, they slept on the grass in front of the great Basilica di San Francesco, the burial place of one of Allen's visionary heroes, St. Francis. During a sleepless night Allen was frightened by what he imagined were death clouds moving in front of the full moon. Trembling, he and Peter clung to each other in an ancient dark doorway as the nightmare subsided with the dawn. They arose to the bells ringing back and forth between the churches of St. Francis and St. Clare on opposite sides of the small town. While talking to one of the local priests Allen got into an argument with him about the fig leaves that he saw as desecrating the Vatican statues. He was still furious and held all priests accountable for what had been done generations earlier by a prudish pope. In Assisi he and a red-bearded Peter begged for food and queried priests about faith, in some ways acting more like St. Francis than the Franciscans did. Then they hiked a few miles out of town into the hills to the hermitage to which St. Francis had retreated for meditation. After walking back down the mountainside to the basilica they had enough energy left to argue once more with the priests, this time about using their lawn as a camping site, a violation of the rules. The next day, before they left Assisi, a kindly American priest took them around the Porziuncola, the first tiny chapel in which St. Francis had preached. Now the modest chapel was enclosed within the walls of the grandiose Santa Maria degli Angeli Church. They found it ironic that St. Francis, who had given up all his earthly wealth to preach the word of God, had been co-opted and enshrined in such an extravagant way. From Assisi they hitchhiked to Perugia, where they visited the Galleria Nazionale. They saw some good Perugino paintings before sneaking onto a train at dusk as stowaways all the way back to Venice.

By mid-August they were back in Ansen's apartment, where Allen settled down to more writing than he had been able to do all summer. They continued to socialize with Ansen's friends and Allen contributed to the household by cooking most of the meals. One evening Alan introduced them to Caresse Crosby, a literary expatriate who, along with her deceased husband, Harry Crosby, had founded the important Black Sun Press. Caresse was rather slow and halting due to her advanced age, but Allen sensed that she was generally good-natured, unlike his first impression of Peggy Guggenheim. They met Mary McCarthy through Ansen, too, and Allen read some parts of Burroughs's *Naked Lunch* manuscript to her. Although he expected McCarthy to be snobbish and shallow, much to his surprise she laughed heartily, especially during the Doctor Benway scenes.

No sooner were they back in Venice than Allen received a message from a reporter for *Time* magazine. The poetry renaissance in San Francisco was attracting national attention, especially because of the media interest in the upcoming trial of *Howl. Time* wanted to interview Allen, and they were willing to pay all his expenses to fly him to Rome for two days for the interview. In addition to the airfare they offered him $17.50 a day for his two days in Rome. At the time Allen was flat broke and knew that he could live comfortably on two dollars a day, so he accepted the offer and made reservations to go back to Rome to spend another two weeks exploring that part of Italy in greater depth.

On August 21, the day before his flight to Rome, Allen wrote to Ferlinghetti from Venice, "Not heard from you since July 17 letter, thought trial was due sometime round August 8 and so have been waiting on edge going down to American Express daily since the 13th hoping for news. Someone wrote me you had an extra good lawyer volunteer but beyond that haven't heard a thing." What had been transpiring in San Francisco was to become one of the most important events in his life, one that would help define his entire career.

Immediately after Ferlinghetti and Murao's arrest they had been released on bail posted by the ACLU. Their trial had been scheduled to begin August 8 in the old Hall of Justice on Portsmouth Square down the street from City Lights and it was to be presided over by Clayton Horn, a conservative judge. The random selection of Judge Horn, a born-again Christian, appeared to be a bad sign. The people's case was presented by Deputy District Attorney Ralph McIntosh. Ferlinghetti and Murao were represented at no cost by the ACLU lawyers Jake Ehrlich, Lawrence Speiser, and Albert Bendich. The charges against Murao were soon dropped because he had only sold the books in question and there was no proof that he knew what their contents had been. The magazine, *Miscellaneous Man*, was also removed from the case since it had not been published by City Lights.

There was tremendous critical support for *Howl* from almost every important literary person in San Francisco. Letters were received from Henry Rago, editor of *Poetry* magazine, Robert Duncan, Ruth Witt-Diamant, Thomas Parkinson, James Laughlin, Kenneth Patchen, Barney Rosset, Donald Allen (the last two being editors of *Evergreen Review*), and countless others. Nine expert witnesses testified on the poem's behalf, including Walter Van Tilburg Clark, Mark Schorer, and Kenneth Rexroth, who put aside his own personal dislike for Allen to come to *Howl's* defense. The prosecution lawyers admitted that they could not understand the poem themselves and were only able to muster the token support of a handful of people who were not experts in the literary field by any stretch of the imagination. The trial went on for several weeks, with frequent adjournments, before Judge Horn allowed himself two weeks to reach a decision. He even went to the trouble of reading *Ulysses* and all the court decisions related to its publication before he made his ruling. Finally, on October 3, Judge Horn issued a decision and agreed with the defense in saying that *Howl* was not obscene and therefore Ferlinghetti was not guilty, because the poem had "redeeming social value." It was a landmark decision and set a precedent that cleared the way for such banned books as D. H. Lawrence's *Lady Chatterley's Lover*, Vladimir Nabokov's *Lolita*, and even William Burroughs's *Naked Lunch*. The *Howl* case was hailed as an important judicial decision upholding the constitutional amendments protecting the freedoms of speech and a free press. It was one of the first rays of hope for the country after the repressive McCarthy era.

But in Venice that August, the trial meant little more to Allen than a free plane ticket to Rome. Perhaps he lacked interest partly because he still doubted that it was a good poem, so the outcome of the trial was not a major concern to him. Deep down he felt he had overgeneralized the images and it wasn't his best work. He wrote to poet Jack Hirschman at the time and said, "I [am] afraid the poem [*Howl*] almost too slight to support the enormous pile of bullshit piled over it, tho that's probably my own fault." On August 22 Allen flew to Rome and quickly gave the interview (which *Time* never ran). He conserved his money by sleeping in hostels and open fields and eating cheap pizzas and fresh fruit that he bought in the markets. As the trial dragged on in San Francisco, Allen joined the multitudes in Vatican Square to hear the pope say mass. Then he went south to Naples to see more of the country. Venice, Florence, Assisi, and Rome had been tourist destinations filled with Americans, so Allen thought that in Naples he would see real Italians at work and play. He even thought he might stay long enough to apply for a job shipping out from the port of Naples, since he was completely broke, and if not for Peter's fifty-dollar VA check each month, they would starve. He had tried to borrow money from his father so that they could go on to Greece, but Louis was no better off than he was and could only afford to send a little pocket money.

In Naples, Allen went to the museum, specifically to see the pornography salvaged from Pompeii, and climbed Mount Vesuvio in the afternoon. Then he walked through the ruins of Pompeii itself and saw the sunset from Herculaneum. The following day he took a ferry out to Capri and from there went on to Ischia, a jagged volcanic island a few miles out in the Tyrrhenian Sea, surrounded by the clearest blue water he had ever seen. Ischia was the summer residence of W. H. Auden, and since Allen knew him casually, he hoped to have a heart-to-heart talk with him about literature the way he had with William Carlos Williams. Their reunion turned out to be an unpleasant meeting. Allen got drunk at dinner and when Auden admitted he was only an old orthodox poet and didn't understand what the younger poets were rebelling against, Allen countered by insulting Auden, rudely calling him a "bad poet," which hurt Auden's feelings. The fame and notoriety of all the *Howl* publicity seemed to have gone straight to Allen's head and inflated his already large ego. When Auden stated that he couldn't stand Walt Whitman and didn't even consider his views democratic, that sealed the tone of their evening. Allen, who had been studying Whitman's *Democratic Vistas* carefully, now favored Whitman above all other American poets. He rejected Auden's critique and lambasted him. He was surprised at Auden's blindness to what he considered the "best statement I've seen anywhere on what [an]

American poet should be and do." Whitman felt that poetry should replace religion and that if American materialism wasn't infused with vigorous poetic spirituality, America would be on the way to becoming one of the "fabled damned of nations."

After this uninspiring encounter with Auden, Allen and Peter prepared to leave Venice. They wanted to visit Corso in Paris where Gregory had offered them the hospitality of his room for free. On the way Allen mapped out a stop in Vienna where there were seven important Brueghels, especially the large *Tower of Babel*. At the time Vienna was an inexpensive city and it didn't cost them much to stay over a day or two. Once settled in Paris they planned to remain through the fall and perhaps all winter as well. Allen's number-one complaint in Venice was the same as it had been elsewhere on his travels, lack of sex. He continued to be inhibited in situations that might have led to one-night stands at the very least. Ansen was the opposite. He was so gregarious and outgoing that sometimes he was attacked for making overt suggestions to men who were not interested in gay sex. Peter hadn't had much luck in Venice finding sex either. The Italian women he met were well protected by their men and the female American tourists were all looking for romances with Italian Casanovas. At any rate the women weren't interested in a bearded "beatnik" with no money. Both Allen and Peter hoped that sex might be a little freer and easier to come by in Paris.

Even from Europe, Allen was still trying to agent books for Burroughs and Kerouac. In spite of Ferlinghetti's legal predicament due to his publication of *Howl and Other Poems,* Allen pressured him to publish *Naked Lunch,* as well as a book of Jack's poetry. While trying to convince Lawrence to accept his friends' books, Allen confided in his publisher his own lack of confidence in his poetry. Ferlinghetti had asked Allen for permission to include one of his letters in a new magazine that City Lights was going to publish. Allen told Lawrence to go ahead and print the letter if he wanted to, noting "Besides I thought secretly you would anyway, while I was writing it—that's one of the problems I find now, vanity and self-consciousness—also the feeling I'll be suddenly stopped in my tracks by some frightening fiery Judgment— some pitiless eye in an objective alley full of real bones." He was afraid that before long someone would realize that he wasn't quite the writer that people had blown him up to be. He wasn't sure *Howl* was any good, even with all the kind comments from the literary critics during the trial. He felt that he would have to follow that poem with something greater, but he had no idea what that might be. The feeling that people were watching over his shoulder while he wrote had begun to stifle his creativity. He became inhibited by the awareness that at some future date everything he put to paper might be published. That was a serious problem for a writer like Allen, whose main goal was to record his own thoughts, unedited, exactly as they flashed through his mind. He wanted to "catch himself thinking" but didn't know how he could do that frankly and honestly if he was aware that others would inevitably be reading his thoughts once committed to paper.

Once in the Austrian capital Allen and Peter tried to do as much as they could in a short time. Since they had no neckties and were wearing jeans they were kicked out of the opera house where they had gone to see Mozart's *Don Juan*. On September 10 they left for Munich, stopping to see Hitler's concentration camp in Dachau along the way. Allen wanted to see the ash-strewn walks, now overgrown with fresh green grass, and view the rusted ovens of the crematorium where so many had perished only a decade earlier. The solitude in the camp overwhelmed him. They knew a girl in Munich who put them up for four days and drove them all over the city, but somewhat typically, Allen didn't note her name in his journal.

They arrived in Paris at midnight only to discover that Corso had fled to Amsterdam that same day to avoid a confrontation with some petty crooks to whom he had passed a bad check. Despite having nowhere to stay they were so excited to be in Paris that they walked around the streets all night taking in the sights and sounds of the city. Allen savored his first pernod at a café and they listened to the drum and jazz sax rhythms echoing back and forth across the basement of the cavernous Club St. Germain. George Whitman, an old friend of Ferlinghetti's and the owner of the Mistral Bookshop across the Seine from Notre Dame, was glad to put them up until they figured out what they were going to do next, so they stayed on cots in his bookstore for a few nights. One of Peggy Guggenheim's friends, the Dutch painter Guy Harloff, had recommended a cheap hotel for them to try at 9 Rue Git-le-Coeur not far from Whitman's shop, but there were no vacancies. They made reservations for the next available room, which wouldn't be ready for several weeks, and thought they might as well go over to Amsterdam to see Gregory in the meantime. They checked for mail at the American Express office, but there was no news from Ferlinghetti about the outcome of the court case. Instead there was a letter from Fantasy Records asking Allen to come back to make a recording of *Howl*, which Allen adamantly refused to do. He wrote, "I don't want to plan on coming to U.S. just to make another fucking recording of that fucking poem (which I'm positive was written two years ago in limbo by somebody else, not me, maybe Carl S.)."

Since no money awaited them in Paris, they couldn't afford to stay there for long. In Amsterdam at least they could sleep on Corso's floor for a few weeks until it was safe for Gregory to return to Paris. Once there they soon met lots of Dutch hipsters who knew all about writers like Artaud. Luckily they found cheap Indonesian restaurants that offered good nourishment and a wide variety of food, but the best thing they discovered in Amsterdam was the red light district. Prostitution was legal there and the custom was for the girls to sit in brightly lit windows almost like wax mannequins while they waited for customers to walk past. The whores were clean and quiet, and Peter was in ecstasy. If only he had money he could be sexually content for the rest of his life in Holland. Another advantage of Amsterdam was that everybody spoke English and there were plenty of hip bars to hang out in where they could talk with other writers. Some surrealist magazines there that had published Gregory's poetry also promised to review *Howl and Other Poems*, which pleased Allen. Once again he combed the museums

POEM Rocket, *CP*, p. 171   and studied the Rembrandts, Vermeers, and Van Goghs, while spending his evenings strolling along the canals and quiet streets lined with weeping willows.

On October 15 Gregory was finally willing to return to France and all three of them registered for one tiny furnished room at the nameless hotel on the Rue-Git-le-Coeur, not far from boulevards Saint Michel and Saint Germain. The hotel had the most modest accommodations imaginable, highlighted by a shared bath in the hallway and beds with mattresses that sagged to the floor. They had no heat, sporadic hot water, and the guests were forbidden to plug in any electrical appliances for fear they would blow a fuse. Still, it was very, very cheap by Parisian standards, thirty-five dollars a month, and when split among the three of them it was practically nothing. Allen discovered that he could boil eggs and potatoes on a little gas burner, so they wouldn't starve. Even the walls of the room were of the cheapest material, so thin that they couldn't talk after ten o'clock at night or the working couple who lived next door would complain. The hotel manager was an amiable old lady by the name of Madame Rachou who truly enjoyed the eccentric behavior of artists and writers, even to the welcome point of overlooking their frequent tardiness with the rent. She promised to give them an even cheaper room in a week or two with thicker walls. Madame was a strict disciplinarian when it came to the use of her electricity, though, and from time to time she would use her passkey to sneak into their room looking for secret radios that might be plugged into an outlet. The hotel became so popular with Allen's circle of friends in the years to come that it was dubbed "The Beat Hotel," and enjoyed quite a bit of literary fame in spite of itself.

The trio's return to Paris coincided with the news that Ferlinghetti had been acquitted and *Howl* had been ruled to not be obscene. Already five thousand copies were in print with another five thousand on order from the printer, and Lawrence sent Allen some royalty money along with clippings from the *San Francisco Chronicle* about the court's decision. Naturally, Allen was relieved and thankful that Lawrence had won the case. Once more he promised him he would not go "whoring around New York" to find another publisher, but would stick with City Lights.

Initially Allen did nothing but wander around the neighborhoods of Paris recording his impressions in his journal. He rode the elevator to the top of the Eiffel Tower one day and instead of being turned off by the touristy nature of it, he described it in wonderful detail as a beautiful dream machine in the sky. Once after staying out all night, he found himself at 7:00 A.M. in the middle of Les Halles, the butcher market district. He wrote a long poem about all the meat carts he saw filled with lungs and horns of naked goats, titling it "Apocalypse at Les Halles." He thanked God that poems were flowing from his pen again. He had been afraid that his writer's block had become permanent, but now that he was settled in one place, he had the time to concentrate on writing and once more became productive.

Squeal, *CP*, p. 173
Wrote This Last Night, *CP*, p. 174

Along with the good news about the trial came bad news from the Orlovsky family. Lafcadio had moved back into the chicken coop with his mother and was on the verge of going crazy. Kate was in bad shape herself, both physically and mentally, couldn't take care of her problematic son, and was thinking of having him committed to an institution. At any moment they thought they'd receive word that the cops had burst into the house, finding either Kate dead or Lafcadio raving mad. Kate had been forcing Lafcadio to go see his father, Oleg, asking him for support money, but Kate denied this adamantly and said she went to see Oleg by herself. Peter was beginning to feel that he'd have to return home to straighten out the situation if it didn't settle down soon on its own. Allen wrote to ask his brother Eugene to check up on the Orlovskys and see what was happening. Since Lafcadio never wrote they only heard Kate's version of the story, and it was difficult to get the full picture.

They prayed that Peter wouldn't have to return to New York, since he was beginning to enjoy Paris. He had met some girls and was content for the first time since they left the United States. Allen hadn't made it with any "female angels," as he called them, but thought that soon he might. He had met some young, eighteen- to twenty-four-year-old male cherubs whom he liked, but no girls yet. "Old angels are too down," he said, referring to their youth. Allen was still moderately interested in having sex with women, especially if it was in a threesome that included Peter or another nice-looking man.

Even though things were starting to go pretty well for them in Paris, Allen couldn't shake his old suicidal thoughts. In a depressed mood he wrote in his journal that he was getting old, nearing thirty-two, and continued to be spiritually unsatisfied: "I leaned out of the window and implored the sky to take my consciousness away. But jump? I couldn't—too sudden and brutal, even to think of, when high." When Allen did stick his head out the window he could see the bookstalls along the Seine and in ten minutes he could walk to the Louvre, both of them great diversions, so that thoughts of suicide were only momentary. The Boulevard St. Germain was around the corner, and it was lined with cafés where he liked to sit and write or talk to the existentialists and intellectuals who gathered there. Some of the more famous cafés were close to his hotel. Sartre himself lived above the Café Bonaparte and on the corner was the Café Deux Magots where he noted that the majority of tables were filled with "odd, respectable literary and theatrical types."

Death to Van Gogh's Ear!, *CP*, p. 175

Before long Allen got sick again, this time with a bad case of the Asian flu that kept him bedridden for ten days. He had several relapses before he truly began to feel better, and the damp, cold conditions in the hotel contributed to a new depression. Up until now Peter had usually been patient, but he was now using too much junk on a regular basis and repeatedly got mad at Allen's constant coughing. It kept them both awake all night and left Allen exhausted in the morning with a sore throat and lungs. Peter was getting worn out, too, from both the junk and the lack of sleep as well as his anxiety about his family. They barely managed to scrape by each day on an austere diet of oatmeal for breakfast and lentils for dinner.

While he was sick, Allen didn't feel much like writing. He began taking sleeping pills to get through the nights, and occasionally he'd take junk, too. In Paris, Corso had become a bit of a junkie, and with his help they scored some great heroin, much better than anything Allen had ever sampled with Burroughs or Garver in Mexico. The heroin was so pure that they sniffed it instead of shooting up with needles. A nasal hit was almost as satisfying as a mainline shot, but they found that it lasted longer and had stronger overall effects. Junk was cheap enough that they could indulge in it as often as they cared to, and they seemed to prefer spending their money on that rather than food. With Allen down with the flu they would have starved to death if

Corso in his room at the Beat Hotel ~

Gregory hadn't found a wealthy girlfriend who fed them. Then Peter's check arrived and they paid the rent and restocked their pantry.

During October and November, the newspapers were filled with headlines about the first artificial satellites shot into space by the Russians. *Sputnik I* was launched on October 4, the day Allen wrote "Poem Rocket," and *Sputnik II* followed on November 3. Everyone was talking about the Cold War battle for outer space between the Russians and the Americans. The satellites, although only about the size of a large beach ball, could be seen at night by the naked eye as they zipped around the earth every hour and a half. Everyone was trying to cash in on the Sputnik craze; television shows like *The Space Explorers* were rushed into production, comedians made jokes about Sputnik, and one company even made a potato product called Spudniks. In San Francisco, Herb Caen, the local gossip columnist, combined the word *Sputnik* with the Beat Generation moniker that had been applied to Allen and his fellow writers to create the term *beatniks*. The word caught on overnight and it was applied humorously and insultingly to anyone who did not accept middle-class conformity.

With Allen, Peter, and Gregory in France and Burroughs in Tangier, Kerouac was the only person left in New York that fall to speak for the Beat

Generation, and he was unofficially dubbed the "King of the Beatniks" by the press. This was a personal disaster for a shy man like Jack, who never fit the mold of what the media labeled "beatniks" anyway. In fact, few of the beat writers could be characterized in that way. Most people would have been surprised to know that Kerouac was politically conservative, religiously Roman Catholic, and had lived with his mother most of his life. He did sample a variety of drugs, like the beatnik stereotype, but he was partial to society's more acceptable drugs, alcohol and tobacco. Unfortunately, he was left alone in the beat limelight in New York, so much so that Allen wrote to give him advice. "I think play down the Beat Generation talk and let others do that, it's just an idea, don't let them maneuver you into getting too hung up on slogans however good, let Holmes write up all that, just as 'S.F. Renaissance' is true, but nothing to make an issue of (for us). You only get hung on publicity-NY-politics if you let them or be encouraged to beat BEAT drum— you have too much else to offer to be tied down to that and have to talk about that every time someone asks your opinion of weather—it'll only embarrass you (probably already has). Next time someone asks you say it was just a phrase you tossed off one fine day and it means something but not everything." It was good advice, but impossible for Jack to follow under the constant spotlight of media attention.

Earlier Allen had loaned Kerouac money for his European travel expenses and Jack had promised to pay some of it back soon. Peter had decided to return to New York, and they needed the cash for his ticket. He had to straighten things out with his family before any permanent damage was done. One of the positive side effects of the notoriety created by the trial of *Howl* and the media's focus on the beats was that Viking had decided to move forward quickly with the publication of Kerouac's *On the Road*, and it was released in September. On September 5, Gilbert Millstein, writing for the *New York Times*, gave the book a fabulous review that helped propel the book onto the best-seller lists. Finally, real money and fame would be coming to Jack. In the meantime Ferlinghetti sent Allen more copies of *Howl*, which he was able to sell to a few Parisian bookstores for food money.

As Allen slowly recovered from his bout with the flu during November, he sat weeping at a table in the Café Select, where Gide and Picasso had once hung out. He had decided to write a great formal elegy to his mother, something he had been thinking about for a year, ever since her death. He began by writing, "Farewell with long black shoe," a line eventually used in part IV of his masterpiece, *Kaddish*. A week or so later he composed what he called "Elegy for Mama." All the bottled emotions about his lost mother spilled out onto the paper. The passage of time was weighing heavily on him and he found himself obsessed with thoughts about death—not merely death as a torment, but rather death as the final achievement of life. It wasn't unusual for him to cry when he wrote in his notebooks, but this poem was more cathartic than any other had ever been. "I write best when I weep, I wrote a lot of that weeping anyway, and get idea for huge expandable form of such a poem, will finish later and make big elegy, perhaps less repetition in parts, but I gotta get a rhythm up to cry." As was his habit he put the unfinished poem aside to ripen.

Kaddish, part IV, *CP*, p. 234

He broke out of his depression for a while when good news arrived from Peter's long-silent father, Oleg Orlovsky. Oleg promised to send a small weekly sum of ten dollars to help with the family's immediate needs. Oleg even spoke in a dignified and fatherly way to Lafcadio and told him how important it was to try to get along peacefully with his mother. It didn't solve all the family's problems, but Peter was able to postpone his return to New York for a few months.

While living with Robert LaVigne in 1954 Peter had once tried his hand at painting but found he had no talent. Now with Allen's encouragement he tried writing poetry. Characteristically, Allen took most of the credit for himself, as when he wrote in November that Peter, "springing full grown from my brain also wrote a poem last week." It was just like Allen to push Peter to do something and then take credit for whatever the results were. Later, when Allen's photographs became famous, he always considered the pictures that Peter took to be products of his own talent instead of Peter's, even though it was obvious when the camera was in Peter's hands. As soon as it was written Allen sent Peter's first poem to John Wieners to publish in his magazine, *Measure*. Allen always wanted his friends to write, but sometimes he insisted that they write even if they didn't want to. Allen would frequently state that all his friends were great writers and some felt forced into that role against their will. Peter may have been such a case, for without Allen's continual prodding, it seems unlikely that he would ever have written any poetry at all. One of his poems is called "Right [*sic*] That Down, Allen Said," and the title reveals the forceful directive behind its creation. In January after Peter had written a second poem, Allen said, "I suspect he will be the next great wave to break out of San Francisco poetry. It'll upset Rexroth who may have thought I was in my queer dotage digging P.O.'s mind."

Burroughs was also a victim of Allen's pressure to write, but perhaps he represents the other side of the coin. When William began to send long letters to Allen from Mexico in 1951, he was thirty-seven years old. Up until that point he hadn't done much writing, but Allen had known William for seven years and was well aware of his fabulous storytelling ability. With Allen's encouragement, William wrote down his stories and enclosed them with his letters to Allen over the next few years. Faithfully, Allen saved them all and put them aside for later use. It was a testament to Allen's persistence that anything written by Burroughs was ever published at all, for during those early years Burroughs couldn't have cared less. His goal was only to stay in touch with Allen, whom he loved dearly. In the fall Allen gave a copy of Burroughs's manuscript *Naked Lunch* to Mason Hoffenberg.[40] Mason declared that it was the greatest book he had ever read and took it straight over to Maurice Girodias, the owner of Olympia Press. Hoffenberg assured Allen that Girodias would publish it without fail. Mason's enthusiasm for the book made Allen breathe a sigh of relief, and he assumed that everything would go smoothly. This time he was certain that, with Hoffenberg's blessing, the book would be published right away and in toto. Meanwhile, William sent Allen an additional thirty pages of manuscript and said that he was almost finished with another hundred pages, featuring a brand-new character, the Grand Inquisitor. That character was to help unify the whole book by filling in the gaps and giving it a more cohesive structure. Allen predicted that *Naked Lunch* would be in print by the spring. The terms Girodias set, however, were terrible, and William was to receive only six hundred dollars per printing, a fee so meager that Allen repeatedly apologized to Burroughs for it. From then on he wanted to turn all his future negotiations for William's books over to Sterling Lord, Jack's agent. He didn't want to be responsible any longer for disappointments, as when Ace Books had failed to publish *On the Road* five years earlier. Allen's primary goal was always to get the books published without regard for remuneration. However, Sterling declined the offer to represent Burroughs, saying that he needed to focus his attention on Kerouac's books, so Allen was forced to continue on Burroughs's behalf.

By December 2, junk had become the greatest diversion for Allen, Peter, and Gregory on the Rue Git-le-Coeur. Allen always tried to limit his use of junk to mental experiments, to see what types of visions it might produce. Peter and Gregory tended to take it for the pleasure of the high it brought, with little interest in experimentation or intellectual, visionary results. This caused them to develop habits that were difficult, if not impossible, to break. Junk also dulled their curiosity about everything else and

---

[40] Mason Hoffenberg was most famous for coauthoring with Terry Southern the porn classic *Candy*, first published by Olympia Press.

caused them to stay locked up in their rooms more than Allen thought was healthy. Usually alone now, Allen continued to go out and see all the Parisian sights. He went to the Louvre regularly and visited Baudelaire's grave in the Cimetière de Montparnasse where he left a copy of *Howl and Other Poems*. He loved being in a city steeped in literary history and filled with active writers like Breton and Tzara, whose books he was reading. Someday he hoped to meet all of the great French writers. His French was improving, to the point that he was now able to read Apollinaire's poetry in the original and get the feel for the sound of the words. At one of the used bookstalls along the Seine, Allen also found an old copy of Genet's *The Thief's Journal*, and he was reading that, too, hoping he'd get to meet the author someday.

Gregory had found a new girlfriend named Joy Ungerer. She was an artist's model and lustful enough to freely ball not only Gregory but Peter, too. Later, during the long, cold winter, even Allen wound up in bed with her. "She came, I didn't," he wrote to Kerouac. Allen preferred the company of the long-haired French boys with their dungareed girlfriends whom he encountered at a little family bar on Huchette. They were mostly young kids who were too poor to go into the jazz bars on the same block. They weren't writers or artists, but "they look like the true children of paradise of some golden 1890s age," Allen wistfully wrote. Usually they had no interest in Allen as a sex partner, but being with them was enough to keep him happy.

On December 19, President Eisenhower stopped over in Paris to meet with other NATO leaders. The Sputnik launches had given the Western alliance something to worry about and Ike's visit made Allen think a good deal more about America's position in world politics. He began to formulate a theory about the fall of America and the consequences of the decline of the West. He was by no means hoping for the fall of America, but he felt that he was already witnessing the beginnings of decay. Ike's trip made him think a little more about taking a trip to Moscow as he had dreamed of doing for so long. On the same day as the president's visit, Allen toured the famous Père Lachaise cemetery and sat and composed the first part of one of his best poems, "At Apollinaire's Grave." Just as he had with Baudelaire's grave, Allen left a copy of *Howl and Other Poems* on Apollinaire's headstone. In his new poem, Allen wrote, "I hope some wild kid monk lays his pamphlet on my grave for God to read me on cold winter nights in heaven."

At Apollinaire's Grave, parts 1–2, *CP*, p. 188–89

1 9 5 8 ～

BY JANUARY THE POLITICAL gulf between Ginsberg and Kerouac had widened and was threatening their friendship. Allen, now an expatriate in Europe, started to see United States policies from a different perspective than Jack did back in New York. Their debates became heated, and slowly even Allen had to admit that he and Jack were drifting apart. On January 4, after receiving a scathing letter from Jack, Allen wrote back, "Don't yell at me so drunk and wicked as in first aerogramme from Florida, it is actually very upsetting, I don't know how to answer, teach gentler."

Through his travels Allen was learning that the United States had been actively supporting too many dictators, and he feared that all America's past mistakes would come home to roost. The decline of America was coming earlier than anyone had predicted, and he prophesied that Spengler's ideas would soon come to fruition, just as he, Burroughs, and Kerouac had agreed more than ten years earlier. Allen started to think that his old socialistic ideas were not pipe dreams, but might be the wave of the future. The sheer number of people in Asia meant that Russia and China would inevitably become prodigious as nations, probably followed by Africa, too, and the importance of Western civilization would fade. "Now the bitter American reality encounters the Oriental century to come," he said.

Around this time Allen decided to write what he called a "monstrous and golden political or historical poem about the fall of America." He asked Jack, "If poetry can be made of ashcans, why not newspaper headlines and politics?" Once more he tried to counsel Jack to ignore all the bad press he was getting: "[It] doesn't pay to care what people are saying; important thing about all the publicity is that we've had chance to sow our dreams in market and lots of souls will read and see without doubt."

Politically, Kerouac and Allen had opposite viewpoints entirely. Jack felt that by tending to your own personal business and keeping out of the affairs of the state, you were free to write whatever you liked. There was a certain discretion about that theory that Allen admired. But when Jack was interviewed by Ben Hecht on television and was asked about John Foster Dulles and Dwight Eisenhower, Kerouac told him, "Our country is in good hands." That statement upset Allen, who couldn't understand anyone intelligent saying that the country was in good hands. Politics weren't the only thing they disagreed on either. Jack was disappointed that Allen wasn't following his spontaneous method of writing more closely. Allen found that he needed to constantly revise his work, and he couldn't settle down to writing free expression the way Jack did. Secretly Allen worried that he only wrote well anymore when he was on junk, a "shuddery dream," he realized.

Reluctantly, Allen, who was literally starving in Paris, had to remind Jack that he still owed him some money. Allen was now penniless except for fifteen dollars his father had sent him as a Christmas gift. He needed a little cash just in case Burroughs decided to join them in Paris. Peter's plans were to leave on January 1 for New York, but since he was also broke he had to wait until his VA check arrived later in the month. Everyone in Peter's family was waiting for him to arrive to rescue them from disaster. Allen had a hunch that Burroughs wasn't planning to come until Peter left, and in fact William arrived on January 17, the same day that Peter left for his ship. Luckily, Peter had convinced the U.S. consul that he was truly destitute and needed to get home to take care of a family crisis, so they agreed to lend him the emergency fare for passage on the *Mauretania*. Once more Allen and Peter parted without knowing if they would ever get back together again. Peter feared that Allen was drowning him in his sordid Parisian life, so he welcomed the separation. Allen hoped that they would get back together at some future time even if Peter wasn't certain it would be a good thing. They kissed awkwardly and waved farewell to each other at the station.

A few weeks earlier, Gregory had set off on his own from Paris for Germany. Ever since they had come back from Amsterdam, he had been sleeping on Allen's hotel room floor, and he, too, was completely broke. To make money he took a job peddling encyclopedias to the U.S. servicemen stationed in Germany, but he lasted less than a day. While in Germany he met

some poets who were interested in working with him on an anthology of
new American poetry, so Corso decided to stay there for a while.

Burroughs's arrival in Paris just after Peter's departure was a blessing for
everyone. Burroughs would not mistreat Peter and Allen could devote as
much time to William as he wanted to without guilt or jealousy intervening.
The day after Peter's boat sailed, Allen wrote him a long letter to let him
know how much Burroughs had changed since they last saw him in Tangier
four months earlier. Initially, Allen was afraid that Burroughs had come to
Paris to claim him now that Peter had left. To help calm his fears Allen got
high on marijuana. Usually grass did not soothe Allen during periods of anxiety, and this was no exception. He swore off pot entirely after that depressing experience. Soon Gregory returned filled with ideas for his German
anthology. Allen was relieved to have Gregory nearby and hoped that Corso
might act as a buffer to protect him from sorrow at the hands of "Satanic
William," as he called him. Late one night Burroughs sat down at a table
with Allen and they resolved everything. Allen told him about his fear that
William would try to take over his whole life and that he felt it might destroy
their friendship. William reassured him that things had changed. Since their
August visit, when admittedly things hadn't ended well, Burroughs had been
trying to self-analyze and had come to the conclusion that there was "a
benevolent sentient (feeling) center to the whole Creation." He said he
wasn't in Paris to claim Allen, but rather to see an analyst and clear up all his
psychoanalytic blocks. All of this was welcome news to Allen. The result of
the conversation was that William changed from a devil to an angel right before Allen's eyes.

William said that he realized that Allen loved him, but did not want to
express physical love for him. That was fine with the new Burroughs, but after having said all that, Allen went to bed with William anyway, in an act of
what he called friendship and sympathy. He thought that it helped to open
their relationship and from then on, sex would not have to be a factor in their
friendship. William convinced him that he had given up the idea of having
Allen as a permanent intimate lover and hinted that it was possible they
might both end up with women. Convoluted as all those revelations
sounded, Allen was convinced that everyone was saved at last. For him the
whole nightmare was cleared up by their one conversation. Allen was certain
that when Peter and William met again, there would be no more anxiety between them. Allen wrote that William had changed so much that he was no
longer even interested in torturing Allen's cat, which in Allen's mind was
proof of a remarkable about-face in attitude.

Without Peter, Allen didn't even have the small VA stipend to count on each month, so he was absolutely broke by the time Kerouac returned his $225 loan. When it arrived Allen was able to repay Burroughs what he had been borrowing from him and had plenty left over. For a while he supported Gregory, too, until Corso moved to Venice to live with Ansen, where he continued to collect material for the German anthology *Junge Amerikanische Lyrik.*

On January 28, Allen wrote that he had been to bed with William a few more times even though he felt it wasn't necessary at that point. There was now a great intimacy and relaxation between them, and Allen predicted that the result of having sex now would be that they would stop having sex together in the future. It didn't make sense but Allen seemed to believe what he was saying. Burroughs instructed Allen in his personal meditation techniques, and being more experienced with drugs, he was able to help Allen conquer his negative feelings about grass. Burroughs told Allen that the problem wasn't with the properties of the grass, but with Allen's own unwillingness to acknowledge the paranoid perceptions he experienced while stoned. Instead of trying to shut them out he should be accepting them at face value. The next time Allen got high he once more began to have the usual masochistic sexual fantasies. First he dreamed of having sex with Peter, which then turned into the more terrible notion of having sex with William. Finally, he thought of being screwed by his brother and then by his father, which was his worst hallucination. At that point Allen realized the truth of Burroughs's advice. He recognized that the masochistic dream of having sex with his father had always been with him but up until now it had been too ugly for him to acknowledge. After being made conscious of it, he could accept it as a dream and felt he was liberated from the fear once and for all.

Around Christmastime, 1957, Allen's advisor from Berkeley, Thomas Parkinson, had dropped in to visit him in Paris. Parkinson had recently moved to London and invited Allen to visit, so on the first of February Allen took the Calais train to the ferry for Dover. It was his first visit to England, and as he crossed the Channel in the fog, he daydreamed about the land of William Blake. Once in London Allen made the rounds, visiting people and places. He was disappointed when he met the writer Christopher Logue, since he had expected him to be a great man. Logue was sick in bed at the time and read Allen a few poems, which Allen felt were insipid. It was a letdown to find that he wrote so badly. Next he stopped in Worcester to visit Gael Turnbull, another poet Allen had always looked forward to meeting. He felt out of place in Turnbull's cozy house and uncomfortable with his low-key

English mannerisms. The Turnbulls took Allen on a short tour of Shakespeare's Stratford before he pushed on to Oxford University. There he gave a reading to a small group of about twenty enthusiastic students. Since he hadn't read in quite a while he was a little hesitant, but once he began speaking it felt great to be in front of an audience again. He wept as he read *Howl*, and then recited some Creeley, Whalen, and Levertov poems to the students. Triumphant afterward, he walked along a quiet stream near the college towers and listened to the bells ringing peacefully as they had for hundreds of years.

Not wanting Allen to miss anything, the Parkinsons drove him to Stonehenge to take a look at the ancient circle of stones and stopped at Salisbury on the way back to see the great cathedral on the lawn. They walked the same paths as Henry James and D. H. Lawrence, and Allen reveled in the literary history surrounding him. Allen stuck to his practice of recommending his friends' works when he looked up Stephen Spender, the great writer and editor. Allen gave him some excerpts from the *Naked Lunch* manuscript, hoping that he might print a small part of it in his magazine, *Encounter*. He also left a whole set of City Lights books and a few Jargon Press books with Spender to review and hoped for the best. Seymour Wyse was also in London at the time and dropped in for a visit. Wyse, who had introduced Allen to a lot of jazz, reminded Allen about how the jazz greats had adapted ordinary street speech to music, as in the classic "Salt Peanuts." Then Allen explained to him how *Howl* had been influenced by Illinois Jacquet's solo "I Can't Get Started," which Wyse had first played for him on a record called *Jazz at the Philharmonic*. They were happy to see each other again and Wyse extended an open invitation for Allen and Peter to stay with him if they ever came back to London together.

Parkinson asked Allen to make a short, five-minute recording that he could use on a BBC broadcast he was preparing about American poetry. The director of the program was Donald Carne-Ross, a conservative translator and classical scholar, so they were both somewhat surprised that he was receptive to the suggestion. When the people at the BBC heard Allen read, they dropped everything they were doing and asked him to record *Howl* and "Supermarket in California" in their entirety to be broadcast all over England as a separate program. Allen was flattered and began his reading of the half-hour-long poem slowly. He gave a great sorrowful rendition, building up the intensity of the poem until he almost broke down in tears at the end. He imagined that he was not speaking to England, but reading directly to Blake himself, and that thought inspired him to do his absolute best. There was even mention that they'd pay him one hundred dollars for the broadcast, which would certainly come in handy. It occurred to Allen that young people in England, like their counterparts in America, had been waiting for poets like the beats to come along, since the writers of the previous generation were too afraid to expose their inner thoughts publicly. Right after the BBC reading, Allen got drunk with the program manager and stopped in to see Simon Watson Taylor, a well-known editor and translator. Watson Taylor had met Allen a few months earlier at the Beat Hotel on one of his frequent trips to Paris, and the two had hit it off well. Simon took him on a wild Vespa motor scooter ride all over town, and they ended up back at Simon's house, where, in spite of Allen's desire to sleep with him, they found they were too drunk to do anything.

In a London bookshop Allen found a new edition of Mayakovsky's poetry containing his fantastic poem "Sergeiu Eseninu (To Sergei Esenin)." After he finished reading it, he sent it to Peter in New York. Since Peter's family had their roots in Russia, too, he knew that he would find it interesting. Quite by accident Peter had landed a job at the same psychiatric hospital where Allen had been treated in 1949–50 following the Huncke affair. As a former patient, Allen felt strange writing a letter of recommendation in support of Peter's job application there, but he did it. He wished they were together to share such experiences as seeing the Elgin Marbles at the British Museum for the first time, and he missed Peter tremendously. For Allen, being with Peter seemed like the only antidote to his unending loneliness. As usual, Allen wanted to see everything, do everything, and meet everyone. One day he climbed to the top of the dome of St. Paul's Cathedral and looked out over London's shops and factories, observing the river clogged with coal barges passing under the old bridges of the Thames. There were holes visible in the city where the bombs of World War II had fallen, and he could hear a steady din from construction hammers rebuilding the city. Allen paused and recorded the scene colorfully in his notebook.

The newest issue of *Black Mountain Review*, which contained a review of *Howl and Other Poems* by Michael Rumaker, arrived while Allen was in London. Even though it was a negative review, Allen thought Rumaker had at least taken the poems seriously. He believed Rumaker was wrong and had missed a lot about the actual structure of the poetry, but his feelings were not hurt. Because he was not attached to *Howl*, he didn't take the criticism of it to heart. However, he did fantasize about meeting Rumaker someday and correcting his mistaken ideas about the poem.

When he returned to the Rue Git-Le-Coeur in mid-February, he found Burroughs alone in his hotel room, gloomy, inactive, and junk sick on a paregoric habit. Allen tried drinking paregoric a few times, too, for kicks, since it could be purchased cheaply in any French drugstore to relieve diarrhea, but he didn't like it. It was a tincture of opium and the effects reminded Allen of the black opium they had tried in Tangier. As soon as he could persuade William, he took him to a doctor for a prescription for apomorphine to help him kick his habit. Allen automatically assumed everything would be all right again with William under the care of a doctor. In Paris he also found another concerned note waiting from Ferlinghetti, filled with worries that Allen would leave City Lights for a larger New York publisher like Viking or Grove Press. He replied to Lawrence to assure him that he was not considering a switch and told him that he wasn't ready to have another book published anyway. His last poetry had felt forced, as if he were trying too hard to be a prophet. As a result his recent work was too self-conscious and was not good enough to publish. Ginsberg also felt that his next book had to be better than *Howl* or he would lose faith in himself. He was still certain that *Howl* did not represent his best work.

Europe! Europe!, CP,
p. 179

The positive side of William's apomorphine cure was that he and Allen began to spend more time together in the cafés and bars meeting young writers and artists and generally just hanging out. Burroughs's habit had kept him focused inward, so that he never left his room or did anything he didn't absolutely have to do. Allen was surprised that William had become so open and friendly since breaking his habit, and they had also stopped having sex by that point. All sex for Allen at this time was not rewarding, although he still longed for it. Occasionally he had sex with Joy, but before long he began to frequent a few gay bars trying to pick up the young Arab men who hung out there. One night he got drunk and took one of them home with him. As Allen got undressed and fell onto the bed, the boy took off his pants as if to join him but instead put on Allen's pants and proceeded to rob him. Allen was far too drunk to protect himself and in fact generously offered the boy a few of his shirts that he didn't need anymore. The young man also wanted to steal Allen's new wool turtleneck sweater that he had just purchased in England, but Allen begged him to leave it and the thief acquiesced. Even though he pocketed all of Allen's money, Allen didn't feel angry the next day, just hungover. Burroughs, more practical in these matters, told Allen that it was his own damned fault and that he should have known better. Allen was merely disappointed that there had been no lovemaking before the robbery. Carol, Elise Cowen's friend from New York and once Peter's girlfriend, dropped in to see Allen around that time. They exchanged gossip and she told him that Elise had gone to San Francisco, gotten pregnant, had an abortion, and now had another boyfriend. Both Carol and Allen worried about what would happen to her, for she was addicted to amphetamines and seemed to be spiraling downward.

Then Allen received a second offer from Fantasy Records. Since Allen wouldn't go to San Francisco to record *Howl*, they had lined up a recording studio in Paris for him to use. It was to be a difficult reading for Allen, and although he made several takes, he wasn't at all satisfied with the results. He found that he couldn't muster the emotion necessary to give a great reading on demand. It also bothered him that the contract said he couldn't record *Howl* again for five years; it was all too businesslike for his taste. He felt self-conscious in front of the microphone and then and there resolved not to get into that kind of agreement again. It was like writing, for he had discovered that he couldn't write on demand either, he had to be free to do it if and when he wanted.

People were expecting Allen to write something to top *Howl* now, and as a result he wasn't writing anything. As he saw it, it might be a hidden blessing in a way, because it kept him from becoming a "pro" and left him wild and free when he did uncork and blow. Since he couldn't predict when he would be in the mood to perform, he couldn't very well schedule readings, so he resolved to give only mad accidental readings in the future. As he considered the advantages and disadvantages of reading in public for money, Allen made a decision not to read for pay at any kind of organized event in the future. Since even the most famous poets like Dylan Thomas or W. H. Auden couldn't survive on their poetry royalties alone, Allen knew this decision meant he'd always be poor.

The Lion for Real, *CP*, p. 182

By mid-March Allen was beginning to stagnate in Paris. Most of the writing that he had done since returning from England was unsatisfactory, and he called it all "meandering." When Burroughs was not alone writing his new novel about dope pushing or out seeing his analyst, he was getting high on hash now. Allen hardly touched drugs anymore and had stopped chipping with heroin altogether, so he and William had little in common at the moment. Allen felt lucky that he had used heroin so often without developing a habit, given what he saw happening to others with addictions. After Peter left, Paris had not been as much fun as he had hoped. For all its historical and artistic beauty, it now seemed dead and spiritless to him. He had half expected to fall in with strangers singing together in the cafés, but instead had found the growing fear about war in Algeria oppressive. There was a strong police presence on every corner of his quarter.

Corso returned from Venice at the end of March, and he and Allen spent one whole night walking around the city talking. Near the Hotel de Ville they ran into a battalion of armed troops with Jeeps and black vans preparing to spread out around the city. Each day brought new rumors of bloodshed and tension between the police and the Arabs in the neighborhood. The situation grew more ominous and more hopeless every day. Corso rented his own small room at the hotel and settled in to write with renewed vigor. Everyone congregated in Allen's room to socialize until he kicked them all out, even asking Burroughs to take his typewriter back down to his own room to work. With some temporary peace and quiet, Allen was able to work on a new poem he had been writing called "The Names." He planned it to be a continuation of the long-line form he had mastered in *Howl*. It focused on the concrete details of the lives of many of the people he had known and loved best, from Cassady to Cannastra.

The Names, *CP*, p. 184

Creatively Allen was debating whether he should write some political poems to urge both America and Russia to stop their warmongering. He believed that anyone who claimed that he was entirely right and the other side entirely wrong was insincere. Any attempt to force citizens to agree with one side or another or propagandize a particular opinion was an invasion by the collective ego of a country. All sides in most disputes were equally wrong, he believed. He was beginning to realize that he was famous back home and that now his arguments might carry some weight politically. Even in his absence from America the volume of his fan mail increased, and he suddenly felt as if he had real power. Later, he would come to realize that fame was not a blessing but something illusory. The only thing that should have mattered to him was his talent for wild writing, he thought. The fame and notoriety his writing brought began to invade his personality like a cancer. As the celebrated author of *Howl*, Allen felt he was in danger of developing an alternate self that wasn't genuinely him. That "other" self had caused him to be too eager to please and pressured him to try to follow up *Howl* with something even greater.

That spring Allen still hoped that Olympia would accept *Naked Lunch*. After Hoffenberg's strong recommendation some of the editors wanted to take it on, but they couldn't convince Girodias, the owner. He felt it wasn't smutty enough to sell very well as quality pornography. In an attempt to show how well it would be received, William read excerpts from it on April 13 at a reading organized by the Mistral Bookshop. Allen and Gregory read, too, and this time it was Gregory who took off all his clothes, much to the delight of the small audience. They had a great time goofing around and without any expectations or pressure, Allen read well.

A month later, on May 6, Allen and Gregory went to England to read together at Oxford. There they stayed with Dom Moraes,[41] an Indian poet. They were bored by the other poets who read with them that day and were restless to get away from their sponsors, the Henry Vaughn Society. While waiting onstage for his turn to read, Allen passed a note to Gregory, which said, "Food is not enuf of a bribe to sit thru another nite of this." Their part of the reading was livened up when the audience began denouncing Corso as a fascist for reading his poem "Bomb," in which he said he loved the lonely old atom bomb. One antibomb radical threw a shoe at him and shouted, "Do you know what it's like to die by an H-bomb?" From the podium Gregory called them all creeps, but Allen saw it as an opportunity to enlighten them and patiently got up and explained the poem. When they wouldn't listen to his calm explanation either, Allen resorted to calling them "a bunch of stupid assholes" and both poets stomped out of the hall.

Later on their tour they met Edith Sitwell,[42] who took them to lunch at her genteel lady's club. They had imagined she would be stodgy and conservative and were surprised to find her so friendly. Sitwell stood six feet tall and appeared even taller in her turban, which reminded them of Queen Elizabeth I; she even dressed the part in a velvet and brocade cape, dripping with tons of jewelry. She adored Blake and Whitman, much to Allen's delight, and another of her favorites was Shelley, which pleased Gregory. They talked for several hours and in parting Allen asked, "May we own you?" Sitwell extended her hand with her palm upraised in a hip mystic gesture.

Auden was also in residence at Oxford that spring, and Allen called him up, in part to apologize for his rude behavior on Ischia the previous summer. Auden barely remembered the incident, and Allen found him more charming and amiable than when he was surrounded by his acolytes in Italy. Wystan took them to tea and then walked them around the college, pointing out all the places he remembered from his days as a schoolboy. Playfully, Gregory asked him, "Are birds spies?" to which Auden replied, "No, I don't think so, who would they report to?" and Allen said, "The trees." They went away with a much fonder impression of the aging poet.

In England, Allen and Gregory found themselves stranded again when

---

[41] Dom Moraes (1938–2004): The youngest writer in Great Britain ever to win the Hawthornden Prize (1958).

[42] Edith Sitwell (1887–1964): British poet and critic as well as a member of the aristocracy.

their funds ran out, and they had to wait a few weeks before they could scrape together enough money to get back to Paris. They borrowed whatever they could from friends and tightened their belts. At last Gregory sold a poem to *Isis* magazine for a hundred dollars, and they were able to leave, right after Allen made a pilgrimage to visit Blake's grave in Bunhill Fields.

Worn out and tired from the trip to England, they arrived back in Paris the last week of May. There Allen found dozens of letters waiting for him to answer. He was depressed by the volume of his fan mail and said in one reply "I wanna write poems not letters." One of the letters was from Ron Loewinsohn, a young California poet, who brought him up to date on news about Neal Cassady. Allen hadn't heard from Neal in quite a while and was dismayed to learn that he had been arrested in San Francisco on April 8 after giving a few sticks of marijuana to plainclothes detectives. Later, Neal was sentenced to a term of five years to life. The atmosphere in San Francisco had changed, Loewinsohn said. The Place had been raided and Connie Sublette, Al Sublette's wife, had been strangled to death on a North Beach street. The letter convinced Allen that San Francisco wasn't the same anymore, and it broke his heart to think about Neal in jail.

To cheer Allen up, Corso gave him a copy of Vachel Lindsay's *Collected Poems*. Allen knew Lindsay's poetry from his father's reading it to him in the thirties and forties, but he read the poetry now with a new interest. The book inspired him to sit down and write two poems, "To Lindsay" and "Message," in the shorter-line style of Lindsay. Saddened by the unhappy news from California, he returned to Père Lachaise cemetery and sat for an hour at Apollinaire's grave making more notes, which he used to finish his poem, "At Apollinaire's Grave."

To Lindsay, *CP*, p. 191

Message, *CP*, p. 191

At Apollinaire's Grave, part 3, *CP*, p. 190

By this time Allen's sex life had become nonexistent. Since he had been in Gregory's company the whole time in England, there had been no opportunity to look for sex, and he had been careful not to approach Gregory about it, given what had happened before. Once back in Paris, he slept with a male acquaintance but afterward found that he couldn't look him in the face the next time he saw him. A few nights later Allen got drunk with some other male friends at the hotel and stripped nude, hoping for a little action. They were turned off by the very idea and after the incident began to avoid him whenever they saw him. Joy was about the only one willing to sleep with Allen, but he wasn't interested in her anymore unless another man was involved.

Allen's depression came back with a vengeance, and he wished he were back in New York so he could begin to see a psychiatrist again. It was the same old story and he was beginning to bore even himself. In his notebooks he made a one-line note: "Mental cancer—homosexuality." On his thirty-second birthday he received a few welcome dollars from Herschel Silverman, a poetry-writing candy store owner from Bayonne, New Jersey, who had befriended some of the beats. Allen took the money and had a few drinks at the bar of a ritzy hotel on the Champs Élysées. The splurge cheered him momentarily, but without Peter's companionship, he grew more homesick each day. Soon he felt that it was time to return to America. He wrote to Peter and told him that if Peter could find an apartment for the two of them, he'd come home and stick around until all the problems with Lafcadio and Julius had been ironed out. After that Allen hoped they would both be free to go to India with Burroughs and Corso, who were talking about going there as soon as they could afford it.

Once Allen made the decision to leave France, his spirits picked up and he became more active again. Now he wanted to see and do everything that he had put off. On the street one day he bumped into Tristan Tzara, the Dadaist whose manifestos Allen had been reading. Tzara's Dada jokes were exactly like Zen koans, Allen felt. They were riddles that freed the mind, and Allen appreciated them even more after meeting Tzara. The following day he went with Corso and Burroughs to a big party at translator Jean-Jacques Lebel's apartment and met several of his old genius heroes, including Marcel Duchamp, Man Ray, and Benjamin Peret. With the Dadaists as their audience, the beats were at their impish best. Gregory found a pair of scissors and cut Duchamp's tie in half. They kissed Duchamp and then made him kiss Burroughs, which he reluctantly did as a joke. The more they drank, the wilder and crazier they acted, ending up crawling around on the floor grabbing and kissing   To Aunt Rose, *CP*, p. 192
Duchamp's pant legs.

A new character cropped up at about the same time that Allen decided to leave Paris: Jacques Stern, a strange, twenty-five-year-old Frenchman, who was crippled by polio. He was a member of the wealthy Rothschild family and had once been a serious student of anthropology at Harvard. He was hard to miss because he had his chauffeur carry him around in his arms. Stern had devoured *Howl*, *On the Road*, and *Junkie*, and he was fascinated with Burroughs in particular, since they shared a strong interest in drugs. Stern had the advantage of being rich enough to supply narcotics for everyone. He and William sat and talked about junk, brainwashing experiments, and anthropology for hours on end, usually in Allen's room. Allen happily cooked big pots of ham and white bean soup to feed everyone. He wasn't able to get much work done, but each day he made it a point to write something. The writing seemed to mount up, even when he had the feeling that he wasn't accomplishing anything. The group also became acquainted with one of Stern's friends, Harry Phipps, a descendant of Marshall Field, the Chicago department store magnate. Phipps was a year younger than Stern. He gave the poets his expensive hand-me-down suits and invited them to parties in his luxurious home on the Île St. Louis. Phipps's parties were so elegant that he provided his guests with cocaine in little enamel boxes. It was an interesting time for Ginsberg, Corso, and Burroughs, who lived like paupers at the Beat Hotel and then went to elegant parties with wealthy socialites and famous artists in a limousine.

Unexpectedly they ran into Art Buchwald, a popular syndicated columnist, at one of the parties. He decided he'd jump on the beat bandwagon and did a silly interview with Allen and Corso. He wanted to be sympathetic but they were drunk and acted nutty, so he reported it in his newspaper column. Millions of people read about their intoxicated pranks, another lesson for Allen about the power of the media to project an image. Buchwald was kind enough to introduce them to director John Huston, who had just come back to Paris from Africa, where he was filming *The Roots of Heaven*. Burroughs tried to interest him in making a movie about a sick junkie looking for a drugstore in Tangier on the Ramadan holiday, all seen from Burroughs's unique perspective. Gregory asked Huston for a bit part in a movie, too, but neither request was granted.

In July, the novelist and literary historian Michel Mohrt arranged for Ginsberg and Burroughs to meet Louis-Ferdinand Céline at his home in a rather run-down part of Paris. They didn't have any business to conduct with him, but Allen as always was eager to meet his champions and receive their blessings if he could. Although Burroughs said that Céline had no idea who they were or what they wanted, Allen stubbornly disagreed and said that Burroughs and Céline hit it off like two cousins. Allen made mental notes about the afternoon that he used later in his poem "Ignu." "You really don't get to know a country unless you've seen it in jail," Céline told them, a line that Burroughs admired quite a bit. The following week they met Henri Michaux, another of Allen's French writer/heroes. He began to wish that he were staying longer, since things were finally beginning to happen. Allen's last party in Paris was thrown by John Huston on a riverboat on the Seine. They drank with the actor Errol Flynn and the producer Darryl Zanuck and once again acted so obnoxiously that they were asked to leave.

By a happy coincidence Allen's father sent him money for his boat

ticket at the same time that a royalty check arrived from City Lights, so for
once he had plenty of cash. On Thursday, July 17, he boarded a steamship
scheduled to dock in New York on July 23. As the ship steamed into New
York Harbor, Allen watched the skyline pass from the deck.
It was stunning, "like all the spires and architecture and   American Change, *CP,*
cathedrals of Europe all put together on one shelf and more   p. 194
massive height—you get a sense of eternity looking at Manhattan from a boat arriving—the buildings look as if they were manufacturing cosmic jazz," he rhapsodized. Allen was glad to be back home, where
his top priority was to pick up the pieces of his relationship with Peter
Orlovsky.

His first disappointment was that Peter wasn't there to meet him at the
dock. Later, Peter explained that he was there that day but couldn't find
Allen in the crowd of passengers. The next day they did get together and had
a much-longed-for reunion. Elise Cowen, who still worshipped Allen, was
back in town and loaned him the key to her apartment at Eighty-seventh
Street and First Avenue for a few weeks while Allen looked for his own place.
Peter was working the night shift at the mental hospital in Washington
Heights and was sharing a room with his father on the Upper West Side.
Near midnight on the day after Allen got back he woke up in bed with a
strange feeling and realized he was having a kidney stone attack. Since he
was alone, he called his doctor, who told him he'd give him a prescription for
the pain, so Allen sped down in a taxi to pick up twelve Demerol tablets from
an all-night pharmacy. It alleviated his misery as well as provided a few extra
days of Demerol highs for Allen, Peter, and Kerouac. After the kidney stone
passed he was able to relax and visit his father in Paterson and his brother on
Long Island. Then he stopped to see Lucien Carr at his apartment in the city.
All in all he felt glad to be back among his friends at last.

Even though many things seemed the same on the surface, everything
was magnified by the recent notoriety of the Beat Generation. Lucien was
unsuccessfully trying to stop drinking and Kerouac was drinking more than
ever, quite successfully. Jack complained to Allen that even though the movie
rights for *On the Road* had been sold for twenty-five thousand dollars, the
"shysters" wouldn't pay up. In Allen's absence Jack had been besieged by the
press for interviews. Every reporter scavenged for something sensational
about beatnik life, but they had little or no interest in Jack's writing. Jack's
mother held Allen solely responsible for all the negative comments the press
made against her son. At one point, she wrote a letter to Allen telling him
not to bother her son anymore, saying that Allen was an "evil influence."

Jack said it didn't matter, but Allen knew his mother's opinion was of paramount concern to Jack. For a while Jack tried to stay out of the limelight by hiding in his mother's house in Northport, Long Island, evading the reporters and avoiding the temptations in the city that led to his alcoholic binges. With his mother's hatred for Allen, it was unlikely that Allen would see much of Jack for a while.

By chance, the Kerouacs had bought a house a few blocks from where Peter's mother lived in Northport, and from time to time Allen and Peter dropped by to try to get Jack to come out. Jack's mother liked Peter nearly as much as she hated Allen, her animosity stemming mainly from the fact that Allen was Jewish. One time Peter went up to their door to get Jack while Allen hid in the bushes, but Jack wouldn't come out. "What good would it do?" he asked. So Allen went away crushed that their lives, once so close, had now drifted so far apart. He tried to put all the blame on Kerouac's mother, feeling that her madness was rubbing off on Jack, but finally when Jack told him that he had become a Republican, it seemed to convince Allen that Jack was nuts, too.

Since Allen's main reason for returning to New York was to hook up with Peter again, they had some long talks about their plans. It was agreed that they'd share an apartment in town for a year or so and Peter would leave Oleg to shift for himself. It was fine with Allen if Lafcadio wanted to move in with them again, but since he was doing okay in Northport, it seemed best for him to stay there for the time being. In San Francisco, Peter and Allen had behaved like strict parents, and Lafcadio knew he was better off reporting only to his mother. Laf was acting so oddly that Allen thought he'd probably wind up back in the mental hospital soon anyway, with or without them. He was still talking incessantly about spaceships and a rocket from Mars, which he said signaled to him one night and caused him to run into the woods naked to meet it. He said that the Martians had selected him because he was the most perfect human specimen on earth and they wanted to rescue him from doom on the planet. Lafcadio had also taken up painting and was creating wonderfully crazy and imaginative pictures. Allen bought one for ten dollars, which convinced Lafcadio that he could become a famous painter. Peter's brother Julius was doing well enough in the mental hospital to be released on weekends now, so things finally seemed more stable in the Orlovsky household.

Finding employment and an apartment were Allen's next priorities. He figured that he'd get a part-time job washing dishes to tide him over or go back to doing market research for the Gallup Poll company if he had to.

Even though he was somewhat well known, he didn't want to make money in the "literary entertainment world money scene" until he knew what was going on. As a result of all the publicity surrounding the *Howl* trial, Allen's fame as a poet had spread from coast to coast. He was in steady demand to give public readings around the country, which could have netted him a nice income. Still determined not to profit from his readings, though, he vowed not to accept money for them. If he chose to read for money, then subconsciously he would write only what he knew people wanted to hear. It was a form of pandering that he needed to avoid in order to create.

In general he felt that all the publicity surrounding the beats had stifled their creativity, even if fame had brought the promise of monetary rewards. Allen wasn't tired of the beat label as such, as Kerouac was, but he did think that the people who wrote commentary and criticism on the beats as a group had evil intentions or were just plain ignorant. Allen wanted to remind people that the beats were making a literary contribution and that he was not attempting to forge a "creepy sociological experiment." He was also distressed by all that he had heard about the San Francisco scene and the police crackdown on people like Neal. Perhaps he had been naïve in believing that the literary breakthrough there might help to liberalize the area. At least he realized that the law would be watching him more closely now that he was a famous "beatnik," and he intended to keep as clean as possible and pick only the fights he wanted to be involved with. Continuing his own psychoanalysis was a priority, too, as soon as he could afford it. He was ready for more changes, since his homosexual issues had obviously not been resolved through his earlier analysis.

After a few weeks of searching, Allen and Peter found a nice four-room apartment at 170 East Second Street on the Lower East Side, a few blocks south of where he had lived in 1953. The apartment overlooked a Jewish bakery that had a big illuminated clock in its front window, which served as his house clock. Their rent was sixty dollars a month, which Peter said he'd be happy to pay until Allen could find a job. Peter even painted the apartment a brilliant white. The place came equipped with a Siamese cat that they decided to keep, since Allen had owned cats in Paris and was accustomed to having one around. Each room in the apartment had a separate door, which was good for privacy when either of them wanted it. Allen also liked the location because it was only a few blocks from Orchard Street, where his mother had lived as a young girl newly arrived from Russia. The neighborhood's ethnic richness reminded him of her in many ways.

Their new apartment was also near the Five Spot, a legendary jazz bar they liked, and as soon as the owners heard that Allen was back in the neighborhood they invited him to give a reading. In keeping with his recent pledge, Allen declined a formal engagement. Even though he was dead broke he wanted to figure out how to discreetly combine poetry with money before committing himself to anything. At the moment he felt that he shouldn't mix the two. The Five Spot's owners often let him sneak in without paying the cover charge, though. When Thelonious Monk performed for a few weeks, Allen listened to him almost every night after Peter left for work. On one night Allen handed Monk a copy of *Howl and Other Poems*, then a week later asked him what he thought. Monk said he was almost finished with it but Allen continued to press him: "Well, what do you think?" "It makes sense," was Monk's funny, spur-of-the-moment answer, which delighted Allen so much that he repeated it countless times. On yet another night after the musicians had finished their set, Allen got up onstage drunk and read Corso's "Bomb" to the few remaining customers. At one of the tables Allen frequently found a tiny man, who he learned was Harry Smith, attentively listening to the jazz. Allen knew of Harry's groundbreaking work as a folk music anthologist and experimental filmmaker, and the two hit it off instantly. Here was another quirky genius whom Allen added to his ever-growing list of uncommon friends.

In Allen's absence Peter had been seeing a lot of Iris Brody, a wonderful painter of mystical landscapes whom Allen liked as well. Sheila Williams, Allen's old girlfriend from San Francisco, also passed through town after leaving her husband. She was strung out on something, so they let her crash on their floor. It was a very brief reunion, but Allen was glad to see her and wished the best for her. At the end of the summer a small FM radio station asked Allen to appear on a talk show as a spokesman for the Beat Generation. Allen didn't want to represent anything, but said he'd come on to talk about poetry as a poet. Then he turned up tipsy and acted crazy on the radio, shocking more conservative ears when he extolled the virtues of marijuana.

Now that Allen was back in town, old friends kept popping up. LaVigne wrote from the West Coast to ask if he could live with Allen while he tried to break into the New York art world. Although Allen loved LaVigne, he knew that he would be asking for trouble if Robert lived with him and Peter for more than a few weeks. Instead, he offered to help him get settled in his own studio in the neighborhood. Even though Allen needed solitude for his writing, the number of visitors at his place continued to grow. Sheila and her new boyfriend stayed longer than expected, and then another Sheila from

San Francisco, Sheila Plant, who had once made it with both Peter and Lafcadio before being hospitalized herself, came for an extended visit. A year after this visit to New York, Plant overdosed on pills, leaving behind a note: "I
am disillusioned but have found the beauty of love and am returning to the
womb."

With the constant parade of friends and acquaintances stopping by to
see Allen and hang out at all hours of the day and night, he couldn't get anything done. His time was already being stretched too thin and he had only
just returned. He felt guilty for resenting it, but the endless party was affecting his ability to concentrate on poetry, and what he needed more than anything else now was time to himself. He couldn't see any escape from it,
though, because he wanted to be with Peter and Peter needed to be in New
York near his family. Allen's next idea was to move out of his
bedroom and into a more private, isolated side room where   'Back on Times Square,
he could live as if it were a separate apartment. That af-   Dreaming of Times
forded some privacy, and when he wanted to socialize he   Square,' *CP*, p. 196
could come out to the larger apartment.

Still acting as an agent, Allen had gone to see James Laughlin at New Directions to talk to him about publishing his friends Gary Snyder and Phil
Whalen. Zealously, Allen also recommended Corso to Laughlin, since Gregory was not happy with City Lights. Laughlin listened carefully to Allen's
suggestions and went on to publish several books by Corso, Snyder, and
Whalen. He hoped that someday he could publish Allen's poetry as well, but
Allen was to remain faithful to City Lights, just as he had promised.

After years of yearning for a glimpse of God, Allen had all his expectations undercut by, of all things, the dentist. His dental work had been on
hold while he was in Europe, so once back home he went to Dr. Halper for
some routine work. Halper was Allen's cousin, as well as the family dentist.
He administered laughing gas before each procedure, and while Allen was
coming out of the anesthesia, he envisioned a dream cartoon universe in
the recovery room. He took out his notebook and wrote down his impressions on the spot. While under the effect of the gas, he experienced a cosmic awareness that he had not known since his Blake visions in East
Harlem. He realized it would have been forgotten if he hadn't written it
down during the instant it transpired. One thing he tried to do was capture
in words the precise impressions he had at the disappearance of consciousness. After the procedure, he sat on a park bench in front of the dentist's office and wrote that he saw the "Trackless Transit Corporation" bus go past;
it all made perfect sense to him.

Since his dentist was one of the family and liked Allen, he cooperated with Allen's controlled experiments, knocking him in and out of consciousness a few times on each subsequent visit so that Allen could write about it. It also convinced Allen that Kerouac, Snyder, and the rest of the Buddhists were in fact right, that all existence depends on being conscious of a void that doesn't exist. "So consciousness is sort of unbelievable like a science fiction world," Allen thought. He saw that the anesthesia acted much like intensive meditation, and the universe was like laughing gas, a big joke that wasn't real, in fact the whole fabric of existence seemed to be illusion. "Now I'm Buddhist," Allen wrote in September. His new ambition was to try to attain the same kind of enlightenment through meditation that he achieved through the dentist's nitrous oxide. "Contemplation, here I come," he said. The gas proved the easier method for him, and by the end of November Allen had taken laughing gas five times. Each time he found the most interesting parts to be the moment of departing consciousness and the instant of returning to consciousness. During those moments he caught a quick glimpse at the nature of consciousness itself, rather than at the objects that we are usually cognizant of.

Laughing Gas, *CP*, p. 197

Allen spent much of his time that fall working on a new anthology for City Lights. He had promised Ferlinghetti that he would compile a collection of what he considered the classic writing of the period. As the work began to pile up he wasn't quite sure why or how he had gotten himself into such an undertaking. He wrote to each of his friends asking for work and tried to shepherd the anthology through the selection process, but it required writing and rewriting and reminding everyone, which took up a tremendous amount of his time. Late in the year he decided to wrap up the project and then retire from that type of tedious literary exercise forever. It was easy for him to get bogged down editing other people's work and being a literary organizer, and it didn't leave him time to think and to write for himself.

Funny Death, *CP*, p. 208

On September 29, he and Kerouac went on an all-night binge with the painter Franz Kline. It was impossible for Allen to keep up with their unlimited capacity for liquor and he became very sick. At the time Jack was seeing a lot of Dodie Mueller, an artist who lived a few blocks from Allen and Peter, so he was in the city almost every weekend. Jack grumbled about being seen with Allen so much, since he was becoming more outspokenly homosexual. He worried about what his "public" would think until Allen called him a goof and reminded him that on numerous occasions Jack had drunkenly challenged Allen with lines like, "C'mon, I'll fuck you." "Screw

public relations, let's be kind and truthful, who else dare?" Allen scolded. Another night after drinking too much with Larry Rivers at the Cedar Bar, a popular artists' bar in the Village, Allen wound up naked in bed with Frank O'Hara, another poet. Too drunk to even get erections, they both nuzzled each other and talked about poetry, before they fell asleep in an alcoholic haze. Allen hung out with some of the abstract expressionist painters that fall, but he found that they had   My Sad Self, *CP*, p. 209
their own tight-knit circle already established and with the
exception of Frank O'Hara, they were strictly a macho painters' club. One weekend he was invited to Easthampton to stay with Rivers, but he didn't feel he belonged in their group.

In late October Allen gave his first public reading since his return from Europe. A cousin's boyfriend had asked him to read at Muhlenberg College, and Allen agreed to do so, only because it was family. He refused the modest fifty-dollar fee they offered and instead made the school promise to buy more poetry books for its library. He was determined to keep his pledge to not accept money for his readings, deciding instead he would either donate the fees to a worthy cause or appear for free. Allen read for a solid two hours, sweating and straining so much that he had to take off his shirt, not to demonstrate nakedness this time, but to cool off. He read from his own work as well as Corso's "Bomb" and Whalen's "Tantric Sermon" to a more-than-enthusiastic audience. Although the reading was a public success with the students, the professor got into trouble for hosting a "beatnik" night, and the reading created a scandal on the campus.

Now that Allen was becoming notorious in the literary world, Columbia College decided to sue him for three hundred dollars' back tuition. Allen asked one of his former professors, Jacques Barzun, to try to help have the debt set aside, but the college was adamant and wanted its money. "They really are evil," Allen said. He had already promised to go to Chicago on December 6 to read at a benefit for the *Chicago Review*. One of the editors, Irving Rosenthal, had asked him to help support their publication of Burroughs's and Kerouac's work. They had offered him $150 for the reading, so this time Allen decided that it wouldn't break his resolution if he took that money and used it to pay back Columbia. Allen liked Rosenthal, even if he did describe him as "a little runty, think push-cart raggedy, bearded myopic fellow, with thin sensitive tender voice, and watering eyes, like he'll burst into tears." Rosenthal had fallen in love with the work of the beat writers and planned to publish the most daring work of Kerouac, Ginsberg, and Burroughs in the *Review* and let the censors be damned.

By now the beats had become a hot item, and everyone wanted to host beat events. On November 9, Brandeis University sponsored a forum at Hunter College under the title "Is There a Beat Generation?" and invited Kerouac to speak on a panel along with the writers Kingsley Amis and Ashley Montagu and the journalist James Wechsler of the *New York Post*. Jack's natural shyness didn't help him when he was called upon to speak in public, and as a result he drank even more than usual before any scheduled event. By the time his turn came, he was completely drunk, and after presenting his talk on the origins of the beats, he read his poem "To Harpo Marx" and then tried to drag Allen up onstage to read more poetry. Allen thought it was a brilliant night for Jack, highlighted by his "big golden speech." Afterward they were mobbed by adoring fans, like Hollywood celebrities, and had to escape into a taxi. According to Allen, the press exaggerated and sensationalized the drunken writer's bad manners. He thought that Jack was heroic in his openness, compared to the others around him. The Hunter College English Club immediately invited Allen to come back to read alone on November 27. So with little notice, Allen read to an audience of well over a hundred, mixing his own work with Corso's, Creeley's, and a half page of some Kerouac prose that centered on masturbation. Allen always loved to shock his audience if he could. He turned out to be a big hit, and the college girls followed him home asking him to read more to them. The advisor for the English Club was not enchanted and resigned his position in protest of Allen's "type of performance."

Ignu, *CP*, p. 211

Because of his hectic public life, Allen redoubled his efforts to make his apartment more conducive to work. He brought in some furniture from his father's house in Paterson and set up a nice desk in the spare room. He was pleased when the apartment began to look good for the first time, and he hung up a huge reproduction of Brueghel's painting *Children's Games,* which shows youngsters getting into various forms of mischief.

Buoyed by public enthusiasm for his poetry, Allen turned back to the unfinished poem about his mother that he had begun in Paris. His intention wasn't merely to write one more poem; he planned to write a masterpiece about the one thing that mattered most to him, his memory of his mother. He was still haunted by the knowledge that he himself had signed the medical papers permitting her lobotomy. He needed to write a eulogy for his mother to ease his pain and guilt and to describe to the world her importance to him. It was to be an autobiographical account that told of the time when he was twelve and had taken her on the bus to Lakewood to escape from Louis, and the disastrous consequences of that trip. Allen realized it was a *kaddish* for her. He wanted it "to open the clouds through an ecstatic rhythmic buildup." Since there hadn't been enough Jewish men available at her burial, the *kaddish* had never been recited for her. He wanted this poem to make up for that affront and titled it *Kaddish for Naomi Ginsberg*. With this composition he wanted to reach the wild heights of prophecy, to see the world completely exposed, as he had been striving to do in his work for the past decade. Since Williams found poetic measure in the observation of normal American speech, Allen would look for measure in abnormally excited speech, such as the wailing and crying over his mother's death and similar moments of extreme emotional stress. To structure the poem, he thought he could find archetypal fixed rhythms that worked poetically. He had tried it in part III of *Howl*, and *Kaddish* was to carry it further.

Allen found the key to the poem in the notes his mother had written to him and to Eugene before she died. After a few false starts he discovered the rhythm that he wanted. "What I look for is the moment of supreme emotional stress and openness when the earth opens up and I see all the beings in it moving all at once, which moment dictates its rare powerful archetype rhythm. I have to get the rhythm first and then develop it like a photograph." One evening in November he combined a little morphine with methamphetamine at a friend's apartment. It acted as a catalyst for the release of his subconscious feelings. He walked home knowing it was time to write his poem for Naomi. He found the tempo he needed and stayed with it in his new writing room for forty hours solid, working from Saturday at 6:00 A.M. until Sunday at 10:00 P.M. He didn't stop typing except to go to the bathroom or eat a hard-boiled egg or drink a cup of coffee that Peter would quietly slip into the room to give him. He cried continually as he wrote and felt that a tenderness would shine through those tears. He thought of the tears in the final scene of Chaplin's movie *City Lights*, when the little tramp is recognized by the woman whose blindness was cured through his sacrifice. Allen worked in a trancelike state, taking Dexedrine and caffeine to keep his energy up. He didn't sleep until he was satisfied with the whole section. Then he collapsed into bed for an entire day. He wasn't completely finished. He spent another month on it, during which he expanded it and reworked it in spots, but the bulk of the long poem was finished in that one marathon weekend. Unlike *Howl*, which he was never completely satisfied with and whose greatness he doubted, *Kaddish* was nearly perfect and he knew it. The poem was what he had been waiting and hoping to write for his whole life. Finally, at age thirty-two, he had created something that he could be proud of.

Kaddish, part I, *CP*, p. 217

As he was relaxing after writing *Kaddish*, hoping to enjoy a little peace and quiet, Irving Rosenthal wired him from Chicago. The University of Chicago had forbidden him to publish the winter issue of the *Chicago Review*, which was to have included thirty-five pages of Burroughs's *Naked Lunch*, Kerouac's entire "Sebastian Midnite," and about thirty pages by Edward Dahlberg. Unfortunately, the *Chicago Review* was not Rosenthal's personal magazine, even though he had acted as if he had complete authority. The university funded the publication, and when the college administration heard that his next issue was to contain what they considered obscene material, they decided to prohibit publication under their auspices. In reaction to that, Rosenthal decided to resign and start his own magazine, which Kerouac would dub *Big Table*. Irving wisely saw that he would never win the university's approval for the works he wanted to publish, so doing it himself seemed to be the next best course. That meant there would be absolutely no financial support for *Big Table*, so Rosenthal needed to raise money wherever he could. Now Allen's poetry reading had become crucial for raising the printing money and getting publicity that might bring in additional funds to help launch Rosenthal's fledgling magazine. But since Allen couldn't be paid at all, he would have no stipend to use to help erase his Columbia debt.

Since Allen's departure from New York a few years earlier, the center of the bohemian scene had changed abruptly from the San Remo to the Cedar Bar on University Place and Louis' Tavern on Sheridan Square. One of the bartenders at the San Remo had beaten up one of the regulars and that caused the mass exodus to more friendly spots. Allen shifted his nightly routine and spent more time at the Cedar. There his circle widened to include Philip Guston, Fielding Dawson, Ed Marshall, Kenneth Koch, Paul Blackburn, Joel Oppenheimer, and various Black Mountain[43] types. On the night that Charles Olson visited the Cedar from Gloucester, Allen unfortunately missed him. That night, November 18, instead of being at the bar as usual, Allen had gone to Broadway to see *West Side Story*.

By that time Ginsberg was so popular that he was in great demand. He was scheduled to read at Yale on November 24, Hunter College on November 27, NYU on December 19, and the *Big Table* reading in Chicago at year's end. In addition, he wanted to do a benefit for Julian Beck and Judith Malina's Living Theater sometime in December. It was the beginning of an all-

---

[43] Black Mountain: Experimental college founded in 1933 in a small North Carolina town that attracted artists and writers who revolutionized the arts and sciences.

consuming reading schedule that would go on nearly uninterrupted for the next forty years.

The Yale reading was an unexpected hit. Nearly three hundred people tried to push their way into the small seminar room at Phelps Hall where the reading was originally scheduled to take place. Those left outside put up such a fuss that the venue was moved to the larger Harkness Hall nearby. Allen's audience was a mixture of Yale literature students and people from the New Haven community who wanted to experience the beat phenomenon firsthand. The only advertising that had been done was small mimeographed flyers tacked to the college bulletin boards, so it was extraordinary that such a large crowd assembled. Allen was in high spirits and, much to his listeners' delight, read at his best from not only his own work but that of Creeley, Corso, and Kerouac. He found that his theatrical experience from high school drama productions helped put him more at ease onstage before so many people, and he began to enjoy playing to the audience. He put more vocal emphasis on each poem than he had done in previous readings, overstating and crooning ecstatically such poems as "Sunflower Sutra," and the crowd responded with equal enthusiasm. Like any good performer, he recognized what worked well with the audience and what didn't. He read for their pleasure and found that trying out new material unfamiliar to them was "like opening up a grab bag of goodies."

Battleship Newsreel, *CP,* p. 214

A few weeks later, on December 19, Allen read at NYU with Denise Levertov. Although they had gotten along well on his visit in Mexico with Gregory and Peter, Levertov was annoyed that the press had begun to link her with the beats when, in fact, she had little in common with them. Allen regretted that she was upset by the beat label, but was also somewhat amused that she was so irritated. The reading went well in spite of this annoyance and they had another large turnout.

In the meantime, Gregory had written from Europe, where he was stranded, broke, and starving. Someone, possibly Allen, got the bright idea to put an ad in the *Village Voice,* requesting donations to help him get back to New York. Surprisingly, Steve Allen, the host of television's *Tonight Show,* and a few others sent in nearly a hundred dollars. Gregory was furious and complained about the lack of dignity in the public charity drive. Yet he accepted the money and returned before the end of the year, moving right in with Allen and Peter. They welcomed him there, since he was fun to be around, at least for the short term, while he decorated their walls with drawings and postcards of the great art treasures of Europe. Shortly after his arrival, Gregory read with Allen at the Seven Arts Coffee Gallery near Times Square and netted a few dollars, which, unlike Allen, Gregory gladly accepted. The beats already had their imitators and a half dozen other so-called beatnik poets also read that night. Those poets took delight in screaming their nonsense verse as loudly and as drunkenly as possible. Fielding Dawson was in the audience and pointed out to Allen that these were the monsters that he had created, like Dr. Frankenstein. "I refuse responsibility," Allen declared. The reading went on all night and besides the "creeps" there were a few good poets that Allen did like, but hadn't heard read before, such as Leroi Jones, Ed Marshall, Frank O'Hara, and Ray Bremser.

1959 ~

By January 10, Allen had written five large sections of *Kaddish*, with a centerpiece of strophic narrative interspersed with chants and hymns. It was better and wilder than *Howl*, and he felt it was close to Bach in construction. His own poetry was occupying so much of his time now that he decided to put the whole City Lights anthology on hold indefinitely. "The Goofbook," as he had been planning to call it, seemed relatively unimportant when weighed against his achievement in his latest poem. He never went back to the project, but Ferlinghetti put together a similar collection for publication and called it *The Beatitude Anthology*. Allen was also able to renegotiate the royalties for *Howl and Other Poems* with City Lights. Now that it had sold twenty thousand copies, he asked for a higher percentage from Lawrence, who agreed to give him 12 percent in the future, higher than any other City Lights author would ever earn. At the same time Allen asked that the next printing be made with all the "dirty" words in *Howl* reinstated instead of using an asterisk in their place. "It's legal isn't it?" he asked his publisher. Lawrence agreed, and beginning with the next printing, all the words were included and no further legal problems ensued.

Allen had been on the verge of seeking a regular job when he asked Ferlinghetti for the extra royalty money. Since returning from Paris, he had been living on Peter's wages and that money was stretched even thinner by Corso's return. Peter's younger sister, Marie, had also moved into the apartment while she was studying to be a nurse at Coit Memorial Babies' Hospital in Newark. Marie had also been in a mental hospital, but she was working hard to get out of the cycle of welfare and institutionalization that had plagued Peter's whole family.

At that moment, monetary relief came to Allen from an unexpected source. The photographer Robert Frank, a friend of Kerouac's, had been able to get financial backing for a black-and-white film he wanted to make with the beats. Frank was a plain man, without pretension, and one of the world's greatest photographers. His movie script was to be based on one of Kerouac's plays and was later titled *Pull My Daisy*. The best part of the project was that he needed everyone to work as actors, for which they would each be paid eighteen dollars a day for at least five days during the shooting. For Allen and Peter that was a great deal of money, and for Allen in particular, it meant that he could continue to write poetry and postpone washing dishes for a while.

The movie was shot in New York in the loft of Alfred Leslie. It roughly told the story of a bishop's visit to Neal and Carolyn Cassady. The painter, Larry Rivers, played Neal's part and Allen, Peter, and Gregory played them-selves as mischievous poets. When Allen wrote to tell Carolyn and Neal about the project, he wasn't able to think of the name of the woman who played Carolyn. "A good looking actress is acting as you Carolyn," he wrote. The actress was Delphine Seyrig, very much on the scene in the New York art world, but as a woman, not on Allen's radar screen.

This was similar to other situations concerning women in Allen's life. Years earlier in Mexico City Allen had been given the address of Frida Kahlo. He referred to her in several letters as the widow of Diego Rivera, but never by her own name, and in fact, he never bothered to visit her. Had she been a man, he would have gone out of his way to rendezvous with someone of her fame and stature. When identifying people in snapshots Allen frequently glossed over the women in the picture, either not remembering their names or identifying them as so-and-so's wife or girlfriend, "lady painter," and so on. It was a peculiar lacuna, possibly stemming from the boy's-club mental-ity of the 1950s, where women, like children, were to be seen and not heard. Allen had a few strong female friendships in later years with poets Diane di Prima and Anne Waldman, but it was almost as if he had to force himself to remember to include women in his normal routines. They did not play a large role in his life, with the monumental exception of his mother. Allen was not uncaring, or in any way misogynistic, but he had a blind spot for women and the female perspective.

January 1959 turned out to be a busy month for Allen. Al Aronowitz, a reporter for the *New York Post*, was working on a twelve-part series about the Beat Generation that was scheduled to come out in March. The series was

both sympathetic and interesting, and such positive coverage was highly unusual in those days. Aronowitz had interviewed Allen and relied on him for
many of the contacts he was using to write the series. Allen was only too
happy to help to ensure that it would be honest and well-balanced and not
sensationalized as most other "beat" reportage had been. All the attendant
publicity from the *Post* series added fuel to the "beat" craze and put additional demands on Ginsberg's time for more interviews. That same month
he agreed to write an introduction for Ron Loewinsohn's first book of poems, *Watermelons*. Loewinsohn was a twenty-one-year-old poet Allen had
gotten to know in California, and since Allen liked his work he encouraged
him, much as Williams had done for him. Kerouac continued to isolate himself at his mother's house, writing peacefully, but he was often in New York
visiting his girlfriend, Dodie. While in the city he tended to get drunk too
quickly and to engage in belligerent arguments with friends and strangers
alike. There was too much commotion for him in the Village bars, but he
couldn't resist.

Peter still strived to resolve his family's difficulties and was spending a lot
of his time in Northport with his mother and Lafcadio. Julius was being destroyed by the brutality of many years of institutionalization and had sunk
into complete isolation. Peter and Allen didn't know how to save him and
knew it would require their full-time attention if they were ever even able to
secure his release. They played amateur psychiatrists and Allen toyed with the
bizarre idea of having sex with Julius in the hospital, to snap him out of his
catatonic state. Burroughs wisely advised against it and Allen let the matter
drop. Peter discovered Julius in the bathroom eating his own feces from his
fingernails and was aghast. To bring him home would be an incredible challenge for them and with the requirements of his own all-night job, Peter
wasn't certain he could handle this responsibility, so for now, Julius stayed put.

Ferlinghetti was beginning to pressure Allen to send him his next book
of poems. He wanted to publish it in May before the summer when sales
normally slowed down. Allen wasn't able to work with a deadline hanging
over him, and he agreed to send it only if all the poems were finished and
polished by then. He reminded Lawrence of his resolve never to work on a
tight deadline; it wasn't in his nature and never would be. Publishing created one more pressure that he did not want and it didn't help him write
better poetry. In the meantime he liked the idea of trying poems out by
reading them in public, a process that, he discovered, helped to exaggerate a
poem's strengths and defects alike. A poem might look good on paper, but
when it was read aloud, any problems hidden in the lines were revealed. It

was a lesson Allen made good use of for the rest of his life. In response to Ferlinghetti's entreaties, he urged him again to publish books by Whalen and Snyder that were waiting and ready to go. Allen considered them two of the truly great poets of his generation and even offered to pay for the initial printing of their books. But Ferlinghetti replied that he simply wasn't moved by their work.

LaVigne had written to Allen, confiding in him that he had stopped painting. He was growing increasingly alarmed about his artistic block. Allen replied, "It's not up to you whether you paint or not, the gift and energy comes from outside. When you have something to do you will do it. It has nothing to do with our conscious choice. Like, the more I shut people out and make peace in house to work, the more I worry about 'work' the less I do, I wind up sleeping in midafternoon. The more I run around get drunk fuck up waste time and lose touch with my writing, the more I wind up putting down on paper. It's amazing. It's not under our control. I spent years since *Howl*, worrying whether I'd be able to make higher than that, finally have with huge poem about my mother, but that was not the subject I planned on, or foresaw, nor was it written in a way I thought likely, someone gave me a Benny pill one day and I came home and wrote for 20 hours and shat it all out at once."

Late in January, Allen, Peter, and Gregory flew to Chicago to help Irving Rosenthal in his efforts to raise funding for the launch of *Big Table*. Their appearance there was not much different from the other readings that they had been giving over the past few months, but the publicity surrounding it was enormous. They read at several different fund-raisers and even though Peter didn't read well and Gregory was drunk most of the time, they were an unqualified hit. *Time* magazine reported on the Chicago readings, dismissing Allen, Peter, and Gregory as dirty, unkempt beatniks with nothing interesting to say. The article failed to mention their poetry except to quote a few lines out of context to support the reporter's opinion that they had neither manners nor morals. They came away from this experience more famous as young rebels, but less understood as poets. If they said crazy things to have fun during otherwise boring interviews, the media reported their comments as if they were insane. Allen was learning the hard way that he had to be careful with reporters to get his point across reliably and to avoid the pitfalls of the media's bias. It also made him begin to wonder: If this was how reporters distorted the news about poetry readings, what did they do with political issues? By the time he got home, there were reporters everywhere, endlessly asking the same questions. The poets were amazed at this strange development and came to realize that no one wanted to know about their poetry, but everyone was interested in their lifestyle. The more they were interviewed, the more invitations they received to appear on radio and television to talk about "beatnikism." Allen wrote back to *Time*, "Your account of our incarnation in Chicago was cheap kicks for you who have sold your pens for money and have no fate left but idiot mockery of the muse that must work in poverty in an America already doomed by materialism."

One Thursday night in early February, Allen arrived at Columbia University's McMillin Theater for a reading. He   Mescaline, *CP*, p. 236 had been disappointed by Columbia's official reluctance to embrace, or even acknowledge, the Beat Generation. Since the whole group owed its birth to the people and events around Columbia in the mid-1940s it seemed only fitting that the university would support them, but instead Columbia had been most intractable and, as Allen put it, "devoted to a sort of vested ignorance." He had also discovered that they wouldn't even buy his book for the university library. Allen would have expected that his own alma mater, as well as that of Kerouac, Holmes, and Ferlinghetti, would be interested in their success. That evening he was looking forward to reading at his old college and wanted to perform at his best. He brought Corso and Orlovsky with him and hoped that Kerouac would also join them onstage, but Jack was already too drunk by the time they left for the auditorium. They had not been officially invited by Columbia per se, but by an independent student club, the John Dewey Society, who wanted to hear the notorious and infamous beats. Fourteen hundred people packed the hall to listen to them, with another five hundred left outside. It was the largest group to gather for a poetry reading in the school's history, surpassing even T. S. Eliot, who had read on that very stage. Allen performed well, but broke down in tears as he read *Kaddish* when he realized that his father was in the audience listening to it for the first time. Peter read his poems better than he had in Chicago and Corso had a good set as well. During the question-and-answer period, Allen took the opportunity to take some jabs at Columbia for being stuck in the nineteenth century and not teaching modern poetry, and his partisan fans loved it all.

Lionel Trilling had decided not to attend the reading, but Allen thought his wife, Diana, who had been there with a few friends, had enjoyed herself. She even went so far as to tell Auden later that evening that the reading had been a "great success." In spite of her comment, she wrote a derisive piece about it for *Partisan Review*, entitled "The Other Night At Columbia: A Report from the Academy." She misinterpreted Allen's poem "The Lion for

Real," assuming that Allen's dedication of the poem to her husband signified that this was a "faggy" love poem to Lionel. In fact the poem was not about Lionel at all, but about Allen's Blake visions, which he had dedicated to Lionel as an ironic gesture in response to Trilling's dismissal of Allen's vision of the lion (or God) a decade earlier. What Allen regarded as a triumphant night of poetry was seen by Diana as nothing more than the antics of bad boys performing in front of an auditorium of young fans she was certain "would smell bad."

Allen was surprised when he read what he called her "rather self-smug and bitchy" article. He was disappointed and more than a little hurt by the fact that his old teacher and mentor, Lionel, hadn't bothered to attend himself. Allen was proud of his newfound fame and would have been delighted to have his professor know that he had finally made good. Lionel had been like a father to him during his Columbia years and had helped him repeatedly with advice and support.

Allen had always liked Trilling and had never openly attacked him, but those critics who had been strongly influenced by Trilling, such as Norman Podhoretz, did not fare as well in Allen's eyes. He couldn't see why academic types didn't understand his expression of Whitman's democratic individual sensibility or the new form of prosody fitted to American speech patterns as championed by William Carlos Williams. More than anywhere else, Allen wanted to be recognized as a great poet in the sacred hallways of Columbia. Since he and Kerouac had been kicked out on a few occasions, he was hung up on forcing them to admit their mistake and making them recognize the importance of the new literature. Denouncing the English faculty as a pack of ignorant amateurs that evening was not the way to go about that, but Allen was young and brash.

Norman Podhoretz was a few years younger than Allen, a bright, albeit more conservative student, but just as interested in the course of literature. In 1946 when Podhoretz was only a freshman, he had submitted a poem to the Columbia literary magazine of which Allen was editor. Later, Podhoretz suggested that the poem was an imitation of Walt Whitman and that was the probable reason Allen accepted it for publication, but at the time he was happy to be included. In the following years Podhoretz grew to believe that T. S. Eliot was a more important figure in the development of modern poetry than Whitman, whereas Ginsberg reversed his own position of respect for Eliot and came to regard Whitman as the source from which modern poetry should spring. As time went by Podhoretz lost interest in writing poetry and became more influential as a literary critic, so as Ginsberg, Ker-

ouac, and the others began to make their mark in the world it was only natural that Podhoretz would comment on them. In articles such as "The
Know-Nothing Bohemians," which was published in *Partisan Review* in 1958,
Podhoretz began formulating his idea that the works of people like Jack Kerouac were too emotional and "hopped up" to make great literature. He
went on to say that the new bohemianism was "hostile to civilization; it wor-
ships primitivism, instinct, energy, 'blood.' To the extent that it has intellectual interests at all, they ran to mystical doctrines, irrationalist philosophies,
and left-wing Reichianism."

Since Allen knew Podhoretz personally, he couldn't let that criticism go
unchallenged, and he set out to correct him. He and Jack invited Podhoretz
to the Village and what followed was an evening of heated debate over the
merits of their work. Any attack on the writing of Kerouac was a personal
affront to Allen, and he was insulted by it more than Jack was himself. Allen
told Norman in no uncertain terms that Norman was the "know-nothing,"
and not Allen's beat friends. His arguments failed to win Podhoretz over and
thus began a feud that lasted for the rest of Allen's life. Having a corporeal
adversary like Podhoretz was helpful to Ginsberg because he always wrote
best when he had a particular listener in mind. When he wrote a poem he
thought about what it would sound like to Kerouac or Burroughs. Now
when he addressed anything to "the academy," he wrote as if Podhoretz
were listening.

Peter decided to leave his job at the hospital and missed work for several
nights so that they would fire him and he could collect unemployment for
the next few months. From then on, Allen and Peter scraped by in poverty
without having regular jobs, but happier in spite of it. All the beat writers
were in great demand. Allen read to a large audience at Brooklyn College on
March 4 and went with Leroi Jones, Corso, Orlovsky, and Ray Bremser to
Washington on a short reading tour of Howard University and George
Washington University. While Allen was in the capital, Randall Jarrell
arranged for him to record his poetry for the Library of Congress just as
Corso had a few years earlier. Weeks later, while visiting Cambridge to read
for the Harvard Poetry Forum, Allen spent an entire evening at Jarrell's
house debating poetry. Allen wasn't nearly as impressed with Jarrell as Corso
had been, and stated as much. He thought Randall was badly informed
about literary matters and was frozen in the past, his mind completely
closed to new poetic ideas.

Before long Allen began to tire from all the traveling, and he resolved to
quit reading for a while after he finished his upcoming tour of California.

Like many actors, he had been having stomach problems, and each morning before a reading he nervously vomited. Despite what he had told LaVigne about the work taking care of itself, being on the road took too much time and energy away from his first priority, writing. On April 22, he took his first trip by jet, flying from New York to San Francisco. The experience reminded him of a movie of topographical geography he had once seen in school. In California he stayed with Phil Whalen and ate in cheap Chinatown restaurants to conserve what little money he had. His reason for being there was ostensibly to read at both the San Francisco Poetry Center and the University of California at Berkeley. But his ulterior motive was to investigate what he might do to get Neal out of jail, where he had been for nearly a year since April 16, 1958. He debated whether using the money they were offering to pay him for the readings to hire a lawyer to review Neal's case was in keeping with his promise to not profit by his readings. One day he took the Novato bus to visit Neal in San Quentin, and there they talked about how he had been given such a harsh sentence for the possession of a few joints of marijuana. Neal was bitter and obsessed with the unfairness of it all. Allen brought Neal a secondhand typewriter, which Jack had financed for fifty dollars. Over the next few weeks, Allen visited Neal three or four more times and began to plan a legal strategy to secure his release.

Gavin Arthur,[44] a well-known San Francisco mystic, was teaching a comparative religion course at San Quentin, and one week Gavin asked Allen to take over his class. Allen read excerpts from *Kaddish*, and the hardened inmates became enthusiastic about his rendition of the "Caw caw caw" section near the end. He was proud when Neal told him later that all the cons were saying, "Man that really wails, Caw Caw!" Gavin made a detailed horoscope for Allen, but Allen didn't know what to make of it and was not interested in that form of the occult. However, he was captivated by the fact that Gavin said he had slept with Edward Carpenter,[45] who had slept with Walt Whitman. There seemed to be a direct lineage of spirits there, which fascinated Allen. Later, after his release from jail, Neal had sex with Gavin and thus brought the sexual link full circle from Whitman to Ginsberg.

Allen tried to keep in touch with Jack, but Kerouac's heavy drinking, combined with his rejection of being "The King of the Beatniks," was driving him to be abusive of many of his friends and of Allen in particular. Jack

---

[44] Gavin Arthur (1901–72): Astrologer and spiritual counselor, grandson of President Chester Arthur.
[45] Edward Carpenter (1844–1929): English writer and poet, author of *Towards Democracy*.

saw Allen as the cause of many of his problems, since Allen always promoted his friends as a group. Allen didn't like the term *beatnik* either, preferring instead "Beat Generation" if there had to be a name. But he did not object to being lumped together with Kerouac, Burroughs, Corso, and Ferlinghetti no matter what they were called. He understood the advantages of being part of a literary circle where each person supported and promoted the work of the others. Jack was the opposite and wanted to be known and respected as a serious writer on his own merit. Even though it had been Allen who had tirelessly carried Jack's manuscripts from publisher to publisher in the early days, he identified Allen as part of a New York Jewish intellectual publishing conspiracy set against him. Due to the efforts of a professional literary agent, Sterling Lord, *On the Road* had finally been accepted by Viking, but the earlier failures were not due to Allen's lack of trying. A strong case could be made that without the notoriety achieved through the trial of *Howl*, *On the Road* would not have been published by Viking when it was or gotten the attention or sales it received, nor would many other books by "beat" writers have ever seen the light of day.

When Allen saw a copy of the David Dempsey review panning Kerouac's fifth book, *Doctor Sax,* in the May 3, 1959, *New York Times,* he was furious at the lack of appreciation for the work of the person he considered the greatest writer in America. Dempsey had written that not only was *Doctor Sax* bad Kerouac, "It is a bad book." "I am writing this letter to warn readers that *Dr. Sax* is a work of Genius which will be lost to them if they accept Mr. Dempsey's shallow reading," Allen wrote to the editor in response.

Jack continued to regard Allen as the villain who had ruined his life by championing the Beat Generation, and when drunk, he would cruelly lambaste Allen on the telephone. Allen, always patient with his friend, was hurt but didn't abandon him. On May 12, the day after Allen had written a long letter to the *New York Times* in defense of Kerouac's books, Jack called and was more uncouth than ever. Allen concluded that if he didn't respond, Jack would wind up more paranoiac than he already was. After listening to some venomous Jew-baiting remarks Jack repeated of his mother's, Allen shouted, "Why don't you shove some shit up your mother's cunt?" The shock seemed to work. Although Jack's abuse did not end, it lessened temporarily and gave Allen a strategy for dealing with him in the future.

That spring Allen gave his first reading in North Beach, but he didn't feel well and read *Kaddish* badly. Jack Spicer, "the stinker," as Allen referred to him, hissed from the fourth row and walked out, which made Allen more nervous and helped contribute to an overall dull performance. The next day at the Poetry Center he rebounded, found his groove, and read the "caw caw" section of *Kaddish* with a deep, holy voice. Stephen Spender witnessed that reading and said he initially objected to the use of such highly personal material in a poem, but afterward found that he couldn't get the words out of his mind. He told Thomas Parkinson that it inspired him to begin writing poetry again after a long dry spell of several years, and his new work began to include personal material taken from his own life. Spender offered to print *Kaddish* in his magazine *Encounter*, but Allen said he was sorry, for he had already promised it to Rosenthal's *Big Table*.

With a $450 windfall that Allen received for a collaboration he and Kerouac had done for *Holiday* magazine, he was able to extend his visit in California. It gave him enough money to stay and enjoy himself for a month or two longer. Maybe he and Peter could even find a drive-away car to take back east and see the Grand Canyon and Death Valley along the way. Like Kerouac, Allen never had a driver's license of his own, but Peter loved to drive and it might be an opportunity for the two of them to take a pleasant, relaxing trip, in contrast to the frenetic, cross-country journeys Allen had taken with Neal a decade earlier.

As Allen lingered in California that spring, an unexpected diversion came his way, which accidentally would help create the youth counterculture that was to change the world in the years to come. Around May 18, Allen went down to the Palo Alto Medical Research Foundation, part of Stanford's Mental Research Institute, to volunteer as a subject in a research experiment for Dr. Joe Adams. Dr. Adams was working with Dr. Charles Savage and Dr. Harold Abramson, two CIA consultants who specialized in "mind-control" drugs. The scientists needed human guinea pigs to sample LSD-25, a drug they were experimenting with. The drug had been described by Aldous Huxley[46] in his book *Heaven and Hell*, and since it was an obscure drug, Allen wanted to take advantage of this rare opportunity to sample it. This was to be a phenomenal, life-altering experience for him. Allen lay back in the laboratory and listened to music after he took the prescribed dosage and waited for the LSD-25 to take effect. As part of the experiment, he had selected some random items to observe while he was high. He had a Tibetan colored string "ghost trap" and a recording of Gertrude Stein reading her own work, as well as some Richard Wagner records. Immediately he went into "a variation of a trance state," similar to

---

[46] Aldous Huxley (1894–1963): Author of many novels, including *Brave New World*, and numerous books on the drug experience.

the high of laughing gas. At first he imagined that he was in a fantastic Coleridge world of Kubla Khan's pleasure dome. His consciousness seemed to be transcendent under the power of the drug, and he began to feel in touch with the very origins of the universe. He saw a clear and coherent vision of the spirit common to everything. He was aware that it was really a glimpse of God. He also had several beautiful visual images of Hindu-type gods dancing on themselves. LSD seemed to produce mystical experiences in nearly everyone who tried it. "It's a very safe drug," he told his father, "you ought to contact someone at Rutgers who's doing experiments with it and try it." The hallucinations could be best described as a comic movie, he said. As Allen mused on the effects of LSD, he became certain that it was better than peyote or mescaline and even better than his previous favorite, laughing gas. He encouraged Peter to volunteer a few days later, which he did, with equally astonishing results.

Immediately, Allen signed up to take another dose of LSD. This time he knew better how to prepare, so he made a list of some of the items he wanted to examine while under its influence. He thought photos of freaks might be interesting, maybe an ant farm, reproductions of paintings by Van Gogh, Cézanne, Rembrandt, Klee, Picasso, and Braque, some drums to beat, and Bach, Tchaikovsky, Schoenberg, and Charlie Parker records to play along with some traditional Indian, Japanese, and Tibetan music. Allen began dreaming of taking the experiment out of the laboratory to the seashore where he could observe the ocean waves. After the second successful "trip," Allen decided that LSD was the real thing. He caught another glimpse of the same billion-eyed God that he had seen the first time. With LSD the mind-control scientists had finally invented a useful   Lysergic Acid, *CP*, p. 239
drug, one that could "destroy" the world in a positive way, he said.

By late spring Allen's life in San Francisco had become as hectic as it had been in New York. On May 23, all the local poets assembled at Garibaldi Hall to give a benefit reading to resuscitate John Wieners's magazine, *Measure*. Besides Ginsberg and Wieners, McClure, Meltzer, Whalen, James Broughton,[47] Duncan, and even Spicer took part. They gave a tremendous performance for the four hundred people in attendance, each of whom donated a dollar, more than enough to support the next issue of *Measure*. From Allen's point of view, the most rewarding thing was that all the various

---

[47] James Broughton (1913–99): Poet, playwright, and filmmaker who spent most of his life in California exploring the theme of sexual freedom.

literary factions had united and put aside their own petty disputes, at least for that one evening. Following the reading at a house party in Berkeley, Allen tried to patch up bad feelings by giving Spicer a blow job in full view of the other guests. Spicer was so drunk that he couldn't respond, but the attempt shocked many of the people there, even if it didn't alter Spicer's poor opinion of Ginsberg's poetry. After several more free readings around town, Allen declared that he was finished with reading in public for a few years. The strain of these emotional performances had made him sick, and it had ruined his digestion.

The Beat Generation gave the press plenty of fodder for ridicule, but Allen never let them get away with anything without a fight. He wrote to *Time* magazine once again, warning them not to edit or cut his letter if they printed it. "You betrayed your word last time over telephone," he wrote. "Your present task tarnishes you with dishonor." They chose not to print his letter at all, but continued to focus their attention on outrageous beatnik behavior.

One evening before he left San Francisco he went to hear Robert Duncan read his long poem *Opening of the Field* at the Intersection Coffee House, a corner storefront in North Beach. That night the audience was full of Duncan's friends, mixed with a smattering of new faces. "It is across great scars of wrong I reach toward the song of kindred men and strike again the naked string old Whitman sang from," Robert recited, as Allen sat on the floor listening to his tremulous voice cadenced to his heartbeat. Duncan expressed his inner disjointed pattern of thought just as he had experienced it in his mind before transferring it to paper with all its discontinuities, correspondences, and rapturous wanderings. Allen felt that Duncan had finally expressed his being completely and he was in awe of his continuous prescience. From that moment on, Allen had a much greater respect for Duncan's work.

On one of his last visits to see Neal in San Quentin, Allen took a short side trip to San Rafael to see Dr. Hicks, the psychiatrist who only a few years earlier had advised him to follow his own inclinations and live the life of a poet if he wanted to. It seemed like such a long time ago to Allen, who had already grown nostalgic for the people and places of his not-so-distant past. Now Neal was in jail, Jack was estranged and secluded with his mother, and his relationship with Peter continued to be unresolved. He rode back through Berkeley looking for his old cottage on Milvia Street, and although it was still standing, it was vacant, dilapidated, and slated for demolition. The backyard with the red hydrangeas was overgrown and wild, but the apricot tree that Jack had camped under in his sleeping bag was still there. The house next door where he had heard strange organ music coming from the basement was already reduced to rubble, yet the smells of his tiny cottage were the same. The huge table where he wrote his poetry had been taken away, even though he once believed that giants could never lift it. He wrote a description of the current state of the cottage in his notebook: "I revisit with old heart, as my heart was old/When I sat here before laughing and contemplating my own doom."

He postponed his departure for another week and stayed with Whalen while he fulfilled his commitment to record one more album for Fantasy records. Against his better judgment, Allen had agreed to make the recording, but couldn't decide how to approach it. He had already sent his advance money to Burroughs, who needed another session with the doctor to kick his current addiction. Allen also persevered in his collection of reference letters in support of Neal's parole application. He wrote to everyone he knew with any influence at all, including Don Allen, Ruth Witt-Diamant, Parkinson, Ferlinghetti, and Laughlin, and asked them to send letters on Neal's behalf to the Division of Adult Parole at San Quentin. The warden seemed to be reluctant to recommend Neal's parole, although he had been a model prisoner. Articles like Aronowitz's series in the New York Post had painted a picture of Neal as "a beatnik, a prime example of the species," and that was now a dirty word around the country. Jake Ehrlich, the lawyer who had successfully defended City Lights in the Howl trial, told Allen there was nothing else he could do, but Allen continued to petition the parole board and tried to convince them that Neal was a socially acceptable litterateur, and not a vulgar beatnik creep.

Neal was up for parole in October, and even if Allen didn't have much hope that he could get out on his first attempt, he wanted to give it his best shot. In some ways Allen felt guilty about Neal and thought that he and Kerouac had turned the spotlight on Cassady by writing about him. All that attention had brought about his subsequent entrapment and stiff sentence. Almost everyone that Allen contacted followed through with letters of support, including James Laughlin, who said that New Directions would even consider publishing Neal's autobiography. Laughlin also encouraged Allen to get Corso to send New Directions his next book of poetry if City Lights didn't want it. Allen couldn't believe that Ferlinghetti wasn't in accord with him over the quality and importance of Corso's poetry, but he was glad to know that Laughlin was receptive. Each poem of Gregory's was unique and filled with a rare genius. Allen and Peter's last few days in San Francisco were spent in a seedy hotel on Broadway where Allen attended to the many details of Neal's parole application and Peter spent his time typing up a few of the poems he had been writing at Allen's insistence. He had finally convinced Allen that his erratic spellings were an important part of his work, so he typed them in the same eccentric, phonetic way that he had originally written them. Allen sensed that his whimsical style was part of "the beauty of his soul. I was always trying to clean them up," he said regretfully.

At the beginning of July it was time for them to head back to New York. They hitched a ride with Robert Creeley, who was going as far as the poet Ed Dorn's place in New Mexico, south at first via the rugged coastal highway through Big Sur. Robert and Allen discovered they had a lot in common and talked spiritedly for most of the trip. Creeley was on his way to work as a tutor on a *finca* in Guatemala, and he planned to drive straight through Mexico to get there. While crossing the Mojave Desert Allen slept in the backseat as Peter and Robert shared the driving. Then they all bathed in the bluish-green water of the Colorado River before they reached the Grand Canyon. There Allen for the first time looked out over that spectacular landscape and saw the rain streaking down on the vast canyon's opposite rim, one of the most beautiful sights he had ever seen. In Albuquerque, Peter picked up a car for someone who wanted to have it delivered back east, and they set out again, slowly, vacationing and enjoying the sights along the way. They took Route 85 north along the east slope of the Rockies as far as Mt. Rushmore and the Black Hills and then turned east through the Midwest, stopping to explore the tiny towns along the way. When they got to Camden, New Jersey, Allen made his first of many pilgrimages to Walt Whitman's house on Mickle Boulevard and saw the poet's old gray hat and eyeglass case resting near his bed as if he would return some day. The famous lilac bush in his backyard was nearly dead, overgrown by a giant ailanthus tree that was sprouting from its center.

On the way back into the city the first week of August, they stopped to see Allen's father and stepmother in Paterson. Allen had celebrated his thirty-third birthday that summer and was feeling like an old man. As he revisited several of his childhood homes for nostalgia's sake, he felt lonelier than ever before. Many of the buildings and places he knew as a boy had been torn down and the neighborhoods were even more dilapidated than they had been in his youth. He sat on the sandstone porch of the Haledon Avenue apartment and remembered how happy he had once been playing there on sunny afternoons in 1933. He also had the chance to talk to his father about his intended publication of *Kaddish*. He wanted Louis' blessing because he knew that his father was sensitive to some of the things he wrote about so openly. In point of fact, his father thought that a line in the poem about the "beard around the vagina" was too vulgar to print, but Allen defended it, saying that it was probably a common experience with children who see their mothers naked. He offered to remove the phrase if Louis insisted but felt that it was nothing to be ashamed of. "It looks from the outside, objectively, probably much less shocking than it appears to you," he said. Louis didn't insist and the line remained in the poem. Poetically, Louis didn't care for the "Caw caw" section either, but after having read it in public several times, Allen knew that it was critically important and in fact it was the climax to the musical construction of the poem. The two themes of "Caw caw," which represented realistic bleakness-pain-materialism, and the "Lord Lord" section, which represented mystical aspiration, merged in the last line into one cry. Allen reassured Louis that when read aloud, it sounded all right.

Back in the city in the apartment on East Second Street, things returned to normal. Although he managed to stick to his resolve about not giving many public readings, Allen's life as spokesman for the Beat Generation remained exciting and exhausting. He couldn't bear to leave any letter unanswered, and his mailbox was always filled with correspondence from friend and foe alike. He answered them all, or at least tried to, and spent a lot of his time explaining to people that he didn't have time to answer. He wrote letter after letter justifying his policy about not earning money from poetry readings, and he continued to expand on that philosophy with each new note. He wrote to Miles Payne, the editor of Light Year magazine, to say, "I have long ago taken a vow of poverty and have not taken money for reading," but later he refined his wording when he wrote to Richard Eberhart, "I have no vow of poverty, I have a vow of penury—i.e. live cheap and buy clothes at Salvation Army and not get things complicated with too many possessions, this is strictly a personal convenience and not a public stance." He was becoming aware, however, that although he didn't need to be wealthy, he didn't want to be destitute either. He wanted to have enough money to do the work that he deemed important and to help those friends who were in need. Since being poor was not his goal, penury seemed to be the word that best explained what he strove for, but the dictionary's definition of penury is extreme poverty, and that wasn't exactly what he meant either. He formulated two personal rules for those occasions when he did read. The first rule was to never read the same poem more than a half dozen times, to avoid a hackneyed recitation. The second rule was to never accept money (except for expenses), lest his readings become business and subject to influence or pressure by the patron. If a college or organization was paying for his reading, it might justifiably feel that it had the right to tell him what to read or not read. It boiled down to a form of censorship, and Allen felt that censorship was yet another way of controlling a person's mind.

Since he had spent so much time formulating his stand on public readings, Allen decided to codify many of his other beliefs in writing. He noted that he always wanted to speak his mind freely and honestly on all occasions. He lamented that for every thousand people he was able to reach at a reading, a million had already been brainwashed by what they had read in *Time* magazine. He knew that because he spoke to people candidly as individuals instead of taking crafty public stances, he continually left himself open to all sorts of ridicule. He wanted to maintain his empathy with those he considered fellow god-seekers and experimental thinkers. He defended his homosexuality as his own nature and therefore a fit subject for poetry, even though gay liberation was a decade away. One's sexuality shouldn't be suppressed or dealt with as a dirty joke regardless of what form it took, and Allen would not tolerate the hypocrisy of denial. God gave him his Karma to "endure and deal with openly not hide in secrecy with and apologize for." He swore that he would not leap naked into the waters as Hart Crane had, an act of suicide he interpreted as forsaking his public struggles. Narcotics for Allen had always been a catalyst, they opened his mind to self-examination and made concepts like eternity more accessible. "It is a study, not a debauchery," he said of his own drug use. As he spent more time considering his past, he began to assign more symbolic meanings to events that had originally seemed little more than fleeting moments. Taking off his clothes at the Los Angeles poetry reading was distilled until it became a display of the holy virtue of naked truth. His vow on the road with Neal Cassady grew into an eternal promise to all his friends to be loyal and maintain the flame of their purity. And the definition of the word *beat* ceased to mean beaten down and tired, but became symbolically beatific.

By September Allen had convinced two of his friends, Ted Wilentz and Leroi Jones, to go into partnership on a joint publishing venture. Wilentz was the co-owner of the Eighth Street Bookshop in the Village, and he had already established his own Corinth Press with a small distribution system along with some capital for new projects. Jones was a poet and coeditor of two important avant-garde poetry magazines, *Yugen* and *Floating Bear*. He had no funds whatsoever but had an assortment of books by his fellow poets waiting to be published. It seemed like a perfect match to Allen, and Wilentz and Jones agreed to issue attractive yet inexpensive paperback editions of heretofore unpublished writings under the joint name of Totem/Corinth. Together they went on to publish dozens of extraordinary books over the following years.

Now that Allen had decided not to schedule any more readings he was free to think about travel again. Things with Peter's family looked as if they would never be resolved, and Allen's desire to break from the various distractions of daily routine was growing. He thought that this was the right time to go to India to continue his spiritual quest, especially since Corso and even Burroughs were considering going along. In the meantime Allen was busy reading Plutarch, taking mescaline, and trying to put the finishing touches on his next book, *Kaddish and Other Poems*, for Ferlinghetti. Working in solitude was a pleasant change for Allen. He enjoyed listening to Wagner while on mescaline, which made the music seem both sexy and paranoiac to him.

I Beg You Come Back & Be Cheerful, *CP*, p. 243

That fall Allen went to the YMHA on Ninety-second Street and sat in the audience with Marianne Moore and other distinguished writers to hear T. S. Eliot read. Eliot looked older and fatter than Allen thought he'd be, but his voice transfixed his listeners. For a long time after the reading, Allen remembered being mesmerized by "Preludes" and by "Little Gidding" (from *Four Quartets*). A week later Allen was inspired by Eliot's example and broke his resolve by appearing in a reading at the Gaslight Café. At 3:00 A.M. Allen walked home in a light rain thinking about young Shelley's insight as he faced death alone. He was overcome with the certainty that he was passing through his own life toward an ever-menacing death, the inevitable end of it all. It occurred to him that he was only one of many who had passed the same way before. A few days later as he sat in a doctor's waiting room, brooding about death and reading an article in *Look* magazine on Kennedy's bid for the presidency, he remarked, "He has a hole in his back thru which Death will enter." It was a strange prophecy, which four years later tragically became true. He couldn't shake his intense obsession with death, and some days later, he noted in his journal, "Death is like flying an airplane, it's scary or frightening at first but once you're up there and flying it feels normal."

It was around that time that Herbert Huncke was released from prison after a four-and-a-half-year sentence. Allen helped him get a room on the top floor of his own building on East Second Street and Herbert began taking his meals with Allen. One of Allen's most endearing qualities was his commitment to remain steadfast and faithful to his friends, no matter what they might have done to him in the past. At one point Burroughs cynically commented on Huncke, "If you do him a favor, he'll never forgive you," and Allen had done him countless favors. At Allen's urging Herbert had begun writing short stories about the interesting characters he had known and was able to sell one to *Escapade* magazine for one hundred dollars. In Allen's mind that indicated that Herbert should start work at once on his own book and he practically forced Herbert to become an author. Soon friends from the West Coast arrived and the house was filled once more with people. Allen and Elsa Dorfman (a new friend of his who had started working for Grove Press that June) helped Whalen and McClure set up a reading tour around New York City in November. When McClure came down with bronchitis, the penicillin given to relieve it caused a severe allergic reaction, so Allen filled in for him. He performed out of generosity in spite of his wish not to give readings, for he didn't want McClure to lose the little money the readings brought in. Allen read from his own poetry as well as Creeley's at several different venues around town, including Queens College and Fordham University.

When Ferlinghetti asked Allen to help him edit an issue of *City Lights Quarterly*, Allen was flattered but hesitated because of the additional work it would mean. He was already overextended in what he called "the literature business." All he wanted to do was quit and be unknown and primitive again. He was still handling most of Burroughs's work as an informal agent and was also advising Irving Rosenthal and Paul Carroll about contributors for new issues of *Big Table*. He was helping Barney Rosset and Don Allen to select articles for their new magazine, *Evergreen Review*, too, with a conceited fear that the magazine would go downhill without his help. He even squeezed in time to solicit work for Jones's *Yugen*. All the office work tired him out and before long he complained that when he sat at his desk he felt like a secretary instead of a poet. Avon Books invited him to edit one of Jack's books, in spite of the fact that they rejected most of his suggestions. Allen didn't want them to censor any of the words, which they felt was necessary for a mass market paperback. Even Don Allen, who was under contract to do a beat anthology for Grove Press, asked Allen for his help. Eventually that book became the seminal *Anthology of American Poetry 1945–1960*, perhaps the most important of all the "beat" anthologies. In addition, Allen advised Max Gartenberg, Thomas Parkinson, Seymour Krim, and Alex Trocchi, all of whom were assembling various anthologies of contemporary poetry. Even though he constantly complained about wasting his time on those projects, Allen couldn't restrain himself from suggesting specific poets and poems. To top it off, he became upset if the editor didn't follow his suggestions, unleashing a chain of letters and discussions. All of his editorial collaborations and the ensuing controversies consumed his time and contributed to his own problems with writer's block. Kerouac felt much the same way as Allen, but he was able to retreat behind his mother's closed door and didn't get nearly as involved in editorial work. Surrounded by all his friends all of the time, Allen was in a more vulnerable position and saw no way out. He couldn't bring himself to say no to anyone.

Just in the nick of time, the opportunity arose to escape to South America. In November Allen was invited by Fernando Alegria to attend an international poetry conference in Chile to be held the following January. Alegria was a Chilean professor of literature living in California who had translated *Howl* into Spanish for a bootlegged edition. Ferlinghetti was also invited to discuss the new spirit in American poetry. Both Allen and Lawrence suspected that they had been invited because Alegria felt guilty about not paying any money to publish *Howl*, but they never knew for sure. Allen attempted to use that guilt to secure free passage for Peter, but the sponsors in Chile ignored his repeated requests. He wrote to them, "I am living with someone, married you might say, to poet Peter Orlovsky." He didn't push the issue further when he discovered that Peter didn't have his passport anyway. They had forgotten that when the government had advanced Peter the emergency money to return home from Europe, they had kept his passport until the loan was repaid. When Allen received his next City Lights royalty check, he paid off the loan and retrieved Peter's passport. That check proved to be quite a windfall, an "immense check beyond wildest nightmares," as Allen phrased it. He was able to pay back the $60 he owed to friend Bob Merims, $50 to Al Leslie, the $203.11 tuition that he still owed Columbia, $17 to his dentist, and $5 to his doctor, in addition to the State Department's travel loan for Peter.

Marie Orlovsky continued to live in their spare room and one night was terribly frightened when Kerouac drunkenly burst in on her. The next morning when Ginsberg admonished Kerouac for his behavior, Jack said, "Ginsberg, you're a hairy loss!" Allen made note of every word that Kerouac uttered and this comment was a gem; it was certainly never dull when Jack was in his cups. On another night in early December, Kerouac, Lew Welch, and Albert Saijo pulled up in front of the apartment after having driven straight across the continent from San Francisco in Welch's Jeep. They presented Allen with a wooden cross stolen from an Arizona roadside memorial along Route 66, and it was ceremoniously nailed to the wall of the bedroom.

They only stayed in town for a few days before Jack returned to his mother's house and Welch and Saijo headed west again, but each day they spent there was wilder than the one before. Ginsberg began to look forward to his trip to Chile and a nice, quiet escape.

A few days before New Year's, Lafcadio finally came into the city to live with them. He didn't want to leave Northport, despite the continual arguments with his mother, but he was on the verge of being institutionalized again and Peter wanted to keep him out of the hospital as long as he could. They tried to entertain him with old Charlie Chaplin and Harold Lloyd movies and Peter kept a watchful eye over him. Peter was happy with Lafcadio being there, as he had been feeling guilty about not taking care of him over the past year and a half. Laf seemed to be suffering a kind of Jekyll and Hyde paranoia, with a different personality taking over his mind at least once every day. It was frightening to see him slip in and out of his own body as new characters took over, Allen admitted. Occasionally there was even a witty side to his newest personality. Once, when he was possessed by something, he said, "Jack Kerouac lost a dime and found a penny and now he's a millionaire." On another occasion, in answer to a Buddhist koan, "What color is wind?" Laf intelligently answered, "The color of wind would come close to the color of water." Allen was beguiled by these creative tricks of his mind. After seeing his mother go through that same kind of split personality, he wasn't as frightened as others might have been, and Lafcadio's condition became just another interesting side of human consciousness to Allen.

Over the holidays, Allen went home to Paterson to say goodbye to his family. There he caught a cold and spent four days on their couch wrapped in blankets. While nursing his fever he read Gershom Sholem's book *Major Trends in Jewish Mysticism,* which had been recommended to him. He had long been interested in the Kabbalah, the Zohar, and the Gnostics but had never found the right book about them. As he rested on the sofa in the dark house he listened to Handel's *Messiah* late into the night and drifted out of his body and into the music, something he considered a new form of Jewish Yoga.

Psalm IV, *CP*, p. 246

1960 ~

ON NEW YEAR'S EVE, Jack Kerouac came into the city to attend the holiday parties and met up with Allen, who was currently being visited by John Wieners. Allen described Wieners as "a pure flower," although at the time he had become totally silent and was beginning to exhibit bizarre behavior. John wore sandals in the snowy January streets, which even Allen considered peculiar. When Jack shouted directly at him to recite a poem, John would not respond at all. Jack was drunk, of course, and Allen found Wieners's nonreaction a charming rebuff, "like the Chinese good luck god." They all watched the first sunrise of the year from the roof before Allen cooked a big batch of chicken soup to welcome in the new decade. They toasted the sad light of the old decade, "old decayed," they said, playing with the words, as they speculated on what the sixties might bring.

Financial good fortune again greeted Allen just as he was about to sink into the depths of abject poverty. This time the godsend took the shape of a Longview Foundation award for three hundred dollars in appreciation of his overall achievements in poetry. Besides paying the rent with that money Allen bought a large stock of mescaline and a phonograph on which he could play his records. He and Peter both began growing beards for the first time. Allen's came out black, of course, but they were surprised when blond Peter's beard grew in red.

While Elise Cowen was helping Allen retype his final version of *Kaddish*, she questioned Allen about his mother: "You haven't done with her, yet?" Elise was so much like his mother that it was one of the reasons Allen was frightened away from her. He couldn't understand why intellectual mad-women found him attractive, but they did. A final request to alter the poem came from Allen's father, who quietly asked him to take out the reference to his affair with the grocery man's wife, which Allen was happy to do.

Around noon on Thursday, January 14, as sleet fell outside, Allen leaned back in his seat on an airplane headed for Chile, where he planned to stay for the next two months. He also hoped to visit the lost Inca city of Macchu Pic-chu before returning. Allen had his first glimpse of the towering Andes from the plane window on the flight down. They were incredibly high and stretched endlessly south. He planned to explore them as much as he could during his short stay. The international literary conference he would attend was being held at the University of Concepción, but the only preparation that Allen wanted to do on the plane was to read the work of the great Chilean poet Pablo Neruda.

The conference lasted a week, one long, boring week for Allen. In fact, he found almost everyone there particularly unpoetic. The most interesting thing for him was watching the communists take over the literary discus-sions and turn them into political diatribes. The whole affair became a giant argument between writers interested in political affairs and those who thought politics had no place in art. The most vocal attendees stood up and made fiery speeches about the rights of workers and everybody called for revolutions of one sort or another, but it was all just so much bad theater to Allen. He delivered his address in a combination of broken Spanish, English, and French and then read some of Wieners's queerest poems along with Lamantia's "Narcotica" and Corso's "Bomb." He spoke about jazz, drugs, and souls all mixed together in what he thought was one wild, amusing speech. It went over pretty well with the crowd, so Allen thought he had done his part. Conversely, he was disappointed in his performance at the po-etry reading that evening with Ferlinghetti. Lawrence read his poems well, but Allen felt he lacked emotion during his own reading. Again the audience seemed to enjoy it, but Allen knew it was not the best he was capable of. He had hoped to "deliver the lamb to the communists," as he put it, but had fallen short of his goal. When the communist writers organized a side trip to Lota a few miles away, Allen and Lawrence went along to observe the coal miners there who worked eleven hours a day for a dime an hour. The mines were deep under the sea and the workers suffered unbelievable pain on ac-count of the bends caused by the tremendous air pressure.

The American poetry that Lawrence and Allen presented at the confer-ence made a strong impression on the Latin Americans, and the other attendees regarded this work as the wave of the future. In the short time he was there, Allen made friends with Luis Oyarzun, a rotund philosophy professor from the university. He was a botanist, naturalist, astronomer, and poet, and more important for Allen, he was homosexual. He introduced Allen to various queer friends, all of whom were interesting and fun to be with, but none of these introductions led to any sex for Allen. At least it was a revelation to discover that there was a secret, queer society in Chile. Allen was also delighted to meet the great Latin American poet Nicanor Parra at the conference. He discovered that Parra's fatal weakness was his passion for blonde Swedish girls. Through various anthologies Allen was familiar with Parra's intelligent and sincere poetry and found that Parra was highly interested in Mao Tse Tung and Chinese politics as well. Ferlinghetti had just published a book by Parra in translation so they spent a lot of time together swapping stories.

Allen didn't stay long in Concepción after the conference ended, and Ferlinghetti left to stop in La Paz on his way home. Allen now sported a dark beard, which brought him unwelcome attention, and several times children followed him down the streets shouting "Fidel!" Alone, he took a cheap third-class train out of the city to Temuco on January 27 and drank posole (a mixture of ground farina and water) with the natives as he once had in Mexico. In his knapsack he carried the final typescript of *Kaddish and Other Poems* and tried to complete his revisions for City Lights, one more unfinished project hanging over his head. His destination was the Isla de Chiloé where he planned to stay a week, eat fish, and work on the book. He hoped to find the Chilean equivalent of *yage*, the psychedelic vine drug that Burroughs had discovered ten years earlier on his own South American adventures. Allen was already growing lonely for Peter and tried to keep in touch with him via long letters, but the mail was slow and unreliable. At first the landscape along the way reminded him of California, but then the land began to break up into thousands of islands that extended to Tierra del Fuego at the southern tip of the continent.

When he stopped for a few days in a town called Valdivia, he came down with a bad case of diarrhea from too much of an awful cough medicine he was taking to cure the cold he had caught on New Year's. Necessity kept him from moving on until he felt better. Valdivia reminded him of what New Orleans must have been like in frontier days. Riverboats and barges filled the waterways where three or four wide rivers converged and every destination necessitated a cheap boat ride through the busy harbor.

By February 9, Allen had made it only as far as Calbuco, on the southern

tip of mainland Chile's isthmus. There he stayed with a tall, peculiar poet by
the name of Hugo Zambelli, who owned a fish-canning factory. Zambelli
had servants who cooked and cleaned and did Allen's laundry, so it was a
comfortable place to relax. Calbuco reminded Allen of a little Brueghel town
with its sailboats, rowboats, and enormous piles of seashells along the
beach. From a tall hill behind the house, Allen had a great panoramic view of
the archipelago to the south, so filled with islands big and small that you
couldn't tell where one ended and another began. He toyed with the idea of
taking a ship down through the narrow channels between the islands to the
southern tip of the continent, but decided to save his money and time for
other things. Zambelli was an interesting person who taught Allen how to
eat delicious sea urchins with yellow-orange interiors. The real delicacy in
the region was a parasitic crablike animal found living inside the sea urchins,
which Allen's host ate live, still wriggling, by the dozens. Allen had the opportunity to go out with the workers to the bays and open waters around
Calbuco where they bought fish from the local fishermen. There he saw his
first penguins in the wild. The penguins sped along underwater, right beside
the boat, eating little schools of sardines. Since Allen was having such a good
time he decided to extend his trip for an extra month. In his letters to Peter
he said that he'd even given up hope of finding any boys in Chile and had cut
way back on masturbation. Most enjoyable was his escape from the whole
beat scene, for in Calbuco the Beat Generation was completely unheard of.

Allen didn't venture any farther south, but stayed on with Zambelli for
nearly two weeks. Then he began to wander inland, crossing the Andes into
Argentina as far as San Carlos de Bariloche by February 24, before his return
to Santiago. The high mountains were among the most beautiful landscapes
he had ever seen. Since the mail was slow, his City Lights royalty check
seemed to have been hopelessly delayed or lost in transit. Once back in Santiago he settled down at Nicanor Parra's house to wait for his money to arrive. Parra was kind enough to set him up with a paid lecture at the
University of Chile so that he would have a little money for his expenses in
the meantime. Santiago was more genteel than the area he'd been traveling
through and he easily fell into the habit of taking his lunch at the Sao Paulo
Café, the poet's cafe, where he met many of the famous old Chilean litterateurs. They were all veterans of ancient Latin American literary wars, but
the one genius who stood out was Pablo de Rokha.[48] Allen was also thrilled

---

[48] Pablo de Rokha (1894–1968): Chilean poet and political activist.

to visit the remarkable poet Pablo Neruda, who was a professor at the university. He had spent years in exile away from his native Chile because of his communist sympathies. Allen learned that President Eisenhower was also coming to that part of South America and he reported that the town was crawling with lots of drunken FBI men. When Ike spoke at the American Colony, Allen was in the crowd and noted that the aging president seemed tired and confused.

Chilean politics were more interesting to Allen than Eisenhower. The communists were growing stronger all the time, but he felt they certainly had their work cut out for them. The peasants were all poor and hungry and the communists seemed to be the only party sympathetic to their plight. The other political parties were only interested in increasing their own fortunes, but that was where the real power was. Stuck in Santiago waiting for his check, Allen became bored and depressed. Even Parra was beginning to get on Allen's nerves by expounding his Marxist views and obsessing on Chinese politics. They argued about Parra's political preoccupations and Allen's drug fixations. At one point, driven to desperation by his new friend's proselytizing, Allen told Parra that he didn't care about the sufferings of the proletariat, which, for Allen, was a lie. At least his isolation in Santiago did afford Allen the time to sit down and finish the manuscript of *Kaddish*, and he sent it to Ferlinghetti on March 10. Two weeks later, after nearly a month of waiting and with only four dollars left in his pocket, Allen finally received his check from City Lights. It was a relief to be able to move on again.

Ferlinghetti's letter that accompanied the check warned Allen not to bother with La Paz as Lawrence had found it to be a "miserable, mud covered, dung hole of humanity." Regrettably Allen had already planned to spend a day or two in La Paz on his way to Lima. From there he'd proceed up the Ucyali River to Pucallpa, where, according to information from Burroughs, there was a *brujo*[49] who knew the correct way to prepare *yage*. As Lawrence had warned, La Paz was awful. Allen got off the plane there and was immediately struck down by a combination of the high altitude and bad food. He spent the first twenty-four hours in bed taking morphine tablets to deaden his throbbing headaches. For a dollar a day he took a room at the decaying Hotel Torino off the central Plaza Murillo, and he was brave enough to eat great juicy red pork stews from the market without disastrous effects. Once he recovered from his initial altitude sickness, Allen enjoyed his walks

---

[49] *Brujo*: A sorcerer or wizard, sometimes a "black magician."

through the town and his visits to the markets over the next week. He bought a lot of cheap tourist junk, like little silver pins in the shape of flies, spiders, and butterflies and some colorful shawls that local women used for carrying their babies. In an antique shop next door to the hotel, Allen found a few Chinese scrolls, which he thought might be valuable. For thirty dollars he bought one that he considered quite magical with some clouds disappearing behind a green cubist mountain landscape and shipped it back to New York. He wrote to a few of his friends to persuade them to send money to buy more old scrolls as an investment, but no one took him up on the idea. From La Paz he went on a few side trips and hiked along Lake Titicaca to visit the town of Sorata at the base of twenty-one-thousand-foot-high Mt. Illampu. Even though he had the courage to eat in the open markets, it didn't protect him from getting what he described as a "rare disease of the ass." He developed an unnamed and nonmalignant tumor, which cost him a whopping forty dollars for the doctor and the medicine to cure it. Even then it didn't go away completely. One thing was certain, it wasn't sex related, because he'd been completely celibate since arriving in South America. Almost forty years later it would seem that the harm this disease did to Allen's body, and the hepatitis that probably came with the doctor's needle used to cure it, contributed to his death.

Now that he was becoming fluent in Spanish again, Allen wrote to Ferlinghetti suggesting that City Lights publish a book of translations of South American poetry. As usual, along with the suggestion Allen included a long list of recommended poets to consider, from Rokha and Neruda to Cesar Vallejo and Nicolas Guillen (a Cuban poet). Allen saw a relationship between their works and those of the San Francisco Renaissance writers. He even went so far as to list possible translators for the proposed book. Even when Allen tried to get away from the literature business, he couldn't help himself when he read something that looked interesting.

In late April, Allen finally moved on to visit Macchu Picchu, the lost city of the Incas. When he saw it he was reminded of the ruins of Palenque in Mexico that had been covered for centuries by the rain forest. Here it was not the jungle but the rugged terrain that had kept the city hidden from outsiders since the Spanish conquest. He explored the ruins for almost a week and sat night and day on a promontory overlooking the ancient city with only the stars for company. There he spent a good deal of time thinking about the spirits of all the ancient inhabitants from a thousand years ago. As Allen kept vigil over the sleeping city through the night he fancied himself as the king of the dead.

When he arrived in the city of Lima, Allen found an unexpected surprise waiting for him at the post office. Elsa Dorfman, his friend at Grove Press, had taken a particular liking to him and had been sending him letter after letter. They had been accumulating at the post office during Allen's trip into the mountains. Dorfman was worried about Allen and imagined that she knew "what was good for him." She decided she would marry Allen and get him to settle down and raise a family once and for all. As he read her proposals, Allen was more than a little shocked. He liked Elsa, but certainly he hadn't led her to believe that he wanted to marry her. It was the presumption of the "what was good for him" comment that irritated him the most. He replied quickly to put an end to the nonsense at once. "One, I am not in love with you," he wrote, and two, he assured her that he was not depressed. He told her that he had been too busy traveling to write much. He cautioned her that if she persisted in this vein she would drive him away from New York City completely. He had already been through much the same thing with Elise Cowen, who had moved into his building to be closer to him. Elsa was more rational than Elise and dropped her suit immediately, and the two managed to remain close friends. Allen could always find love where he didn't want it, but he had difficulty finding it with those he was interested in.

In Lima Allen stayed at the Hotel Comercio for the next three weeks. He shopped around for local drugs and discovered an excellent source for ether. While sniffing some of it, he thought about Kerouac and imagined he heard a railroad station clock chiming out of the mysterious depths of time. His extensive notes were published as the poem "Aether." On May 31, Allen packed his knapsack once more and walked across the street from the hotel to the truck stop. Leaving Lima behind, he looked forward to what would prove to be the great adventure of his trip. He was heading into the interior jungle to the town of Pucallpa to find the hallucinogenic *yage* vine that grew wild in that region. Burroughs had been to Pucallpa in 1953 on his search for the elusive drug and had found it there; he had even brought some samples of it back to Allen in New York. So Allen was quite familiar with it and wanted to experience the effects for himself on site. He had been studying botanical manuals and asked some local botanists where he might locate the plant (called also *ayahuasca* or *Banisteriopsis caapi*) from which the drug was made. The process involved crushing and boiling the leaves and lower part of the plant's stem in water. Allen planned to find a local medicine man who could administer the drug to him in the traditional manner.

To an Old Poet in Peru, *CP*, p. 247

Aether, *CP*, p. 250

It was slow travel in the mountains and he stayed the first night at Cerro de Pasco, a dirty town with what he considered an ugly name. The town market was full of Indians selling handmade blankets with bright orange stripes. Once again Allen awoke in his room at the Hotel Central with a terrible headache from the lack of oxygen at fourteen thousand feet. It took him all day to reach the next town of any size, Huanuco, where he ate at a Chinese restaurant and saw, of all things, a Jerry Lewis movie, *The Delicate Delinquent*. He had to wait awhile for the next leg of his trip farther into the jungle and passed the time by writing some long-overdue letters home telling everyone about his experiments with the local herbs and witch doctors. Things moved slowly in that part of the world, the trucks and buses on the road traveled in only one direction on alternate days. He was anxious to get on with his trip and find the *brujo*, or *curandero*, who specialized in psychic cures using jungle plants. He told his brother that his plans were simply to study witch-doctoring at the source for a few weeks. He mentioned that he was even considering the possibility of taking a boat down the Ucyali River to Iquitos on the Amazon River and then continuing twenty-five hundred miles farther downriver all the way to the Atlantic.

Huanuco, like most of Peru, was inexpensive, and his room in the Hotel Argentino cost him only forty cents a night. Even though it was a grim little cell with a door that didn't close, it was good enough for Allen. His money was holding out longer than usual, since living was so cheap, and he had plenty left on which to travel further. Since he was isolated he had also been writing a lot in his journals. Solitude once again had afforded him the luxury of time for work, but his loneliness and the poverty of the countryside were depressing. He was lonely enough to begin masturbating again, "a true bearded freak in the universe, making love to myself," as he explained in his journal to no one in particular. In spite of everything he was glad to be taking a break from all the distractions of celebrity life. In Peru he was free to pursue an interest in whatever came along, botany or archeology or Indian pottery or *yage* visions. He didn't have to conform to anyone else's ideas of what was good for him, or what someone else felt he "should" do. On his thirty-fourth birthday, June 3, Allen caught a ride on the back of an old rickety truck loaded with sacks of sugar and covered with spiderwebs that took him flying through the night all the way to Pucallpa. On the ride he reflected again on Kerouac's having called him "a hairy loss." The phrase had been bothering him ever since Jack had uttered it, and Allen had to admit that once again Jack hit the nail on the head.

Once settled at the Hotel Peru in Pucallpa, Allen found a connection who scheduled his first appointment with the *curandero*, the witch doctor who would prepare the *yage* for him. Ramon, Allen's contact, took him to a *curandero* he knew who was renowned for his supernatural curing powers. He was called "the Maestro" and turned out to be a mild, simple man of about Allen's age. During his first session with the *yage* it took about an hour for the effects of the drug to slowly creep over him. During that hour Allen lay down and thought about what he expected to discover through *yage*. He hypothesized that he was trying to find something real about the universe, but then it dawned on him that he was already in a real universe and always had been. After about an hour he began to see, or feel, what he described as the "Great Being" approaching his mind like a big wet devouring vagina. The only way he could explain it was to call it a big black hole of God surrounded by all of creation. He made a drawing of this in his journal so he could remember it later, careful to note that it was a drawing of what he felt, not what he saw. The effects were pleasant and lasted for about two hours. Then the feeling of an alien presence took over his mind, "a combination of death, blindness and a nausea for life itself," as Allen put it. He felt sorry for the agony he'd caused Peter and his father, who were both aware of how close Allen had come to suicide. He also realized that they knew deep down that he would never choose death. At that moment Allen was frightened by the intensity of the emotions he experienced. He felt he had the power to die, but he was also afraid to die, scared to leave this present world of consciousness to enter a world of permanent spiritual consciousness. Despite the terrifying nature of these visions and emotions, Allen was left wanting more experiences with the drug after its effects wore off.

A few days later Allen attended an all-night *yage* session with about thirty other men and women in a small hut on the outskirts of town. The brew was prepared fresh as they waited and were presented with a full ceremony. The Maestro, dressed in a pair of old pants and shirt, barefoot, with a baseball cap, crooned over the solution for several minutes before he allowed Allen to drain the cup. Allen lay down on a mat expecting another pleasant vision, but as he began to get high, "the whole fucking Cosmos broke loose around me, I think the strongest and worst I've ever had," he wrote. His LSD experiences had been near perfection but didn't get Allen so horribly deep into his own mind. He felt that he was finally about to face death, but then he became nauseated from the drug and began to vomit. He hallucinated that he was surrounded by a circle of snakes and that he himself was a giant snake vomiting out the universe. After throwing up Allen went back and lay down on a mat again and Ramon came over and tenderly nursed him. The whole hut seemed to be alive with the spectral presences of the other participants, all undergoing transfigurations of one kind or another. It was as if they all had made contact with a single mysterious "thing" that was everyone's shared fate and sooner or later was going to kill everyone. Allen remained terrified as wave after wave of death fear washed over him. He realized that he might die, right then and there. After this experience Allen had to muster the courage to continue with the drug. He was beginning to fear that *yage* might lead to some real madness, or that his universe might become permanently changed. To protect himself from insanity he regarded his illusions as temporary and tried to remind himself that he would return to his normal consciousness after the effects of the drug wore off.

Allen's brain was working overtime and he filled notebook after notebook with observations. He wrote many letters trying to explain his newest visions to his friends back home and composed "Magic Psalm," a more experimental poem than anything he had written before. Now he felt he understood Burroughs when he talked about approaching the unknown frontier via his writing.

Magic Psalm, *CP*, p. 263

Allen hesitated before trying *yage* a third time, but the Maestro told him it would be okay. "I might die," Allen said, but the Maestro laughed and assured him that he would not. "This is really a ball," he wrote to Peter later, "I'm getting my money's worth of visions finally, enough to scare me finally." Going back again took a lot of nerve, but Allen wanted to learn all he could while he was there. This time he drank the concoction with about ten natives. As the drug took hold of him, Allen asked himself, "Why do I fear death, do I want to live forever?" This time he became conscious that the condition of life was suffering, too, a fundamental principle he would later rediscover through his Buddhist studies. He had his share of human problems, among which he counted a love of men, a fear of women, and his own childlessness. Those problems would remain if he lived to be a thousand years old. Strangely enough, Allen came away from this third trip with the conviction that he and Peter should try to have children. The drug was also beginning to give him some idea about what schizophrenia must be like for people like his mother, who lived in several different yet "real" universes at the same time, shifting back and forth painfully from one to another. It proved to him that a schizophrenic's experiences of multiple universes was no worse than living in the single universe he normally inhabited. He came to a major insight that "the purpose of

The Reply, *CP*, p. 265

life is death." So far the three sessions had brought him closer to "truth" than he'd been before, although he wasn't sure what that meant. He didn't hesitate a few days later when the time came to go back for a fourth dose. This drug activated the unconscious mind without putting the regular consciousness to sleep, so that he was both awake and dreaming at the same time. A neat trick, he thought.

One of the German professors in town told Allen of a native witch doctor in the remote jungle village of Iquitos who knew more of the secrets of ayahuasca. To find him Allen boarded a riverboat heading down the Ucyali. During the trip Allen dozed in his hammock thinking about what to do with his life, and at night he sat on deck gazing up at the Milky Way. The trip was interrupted occasionally by a few ports along the river, such as Contamena and Orrellana, where Allen got off and explored the markets. He kept busy by reading the New Testament once again. By June 21, the boat had entered the waters of the Amazon proper, a flat brown stream nearly as wide as a lake. That evening when he reached Iquitos he mailed a note to Elsa Dorfman apologizing for his harsh letter of a few weeks earlier. He still had no intention of marrying her, but that was no excuse for him to be as cruel and callous as he had been in his earlier reply. He also sent a letter to his father telling him that the one lasting resolution he had made after taking *yage* was to have children before it was too late. He knew that would boost his father's spirits.

Iquitos was the Peruvian river port at the western end of the Amazon, and it was there that Allen was to make contact with the *curandero*. He settled into a cheap hotel and dined in Chinese restaurants while he waited. Finally he located the *curandero*, Julio Maldonado, living in a cabin on the outskirts of town. Under his supervision Allen sampled his brew of ayahuasca four more times with results remarkably similar to what he had experienced in Pucallpa. From Iquitos he decided to fly back to Lima instead of taking the long boat trip down the Amazon so that he could then use the remainder of his prepaid round-trip air ticket back to New York. He stopped overnight in Panama but did little more than sample a drug called *soma*, which did nothing more than help him fall asleep on a park bench. He was awakened at dawn by the nearby military barracks' bugle and headed back to the airport.

By then he had been away for a little more than six months, and he was eager to get back to Peter in New York City, so he canceled his planned visit to Creeley in Guatemala. As a gift for Peter and his friends, he had gotten permission from the Peruvian government to bring home a gallon of ayahuasca for "scientific purposes," as the permit said. That meant that he could continue his experiments back home if he wanted.

Allen arrived home to find three hundred letters waiting for him on his desk. One of the more interesting ones was from Burroughs telling about his new method of cutting up prose and reshuffling it to expose the "secret message" hidden inside. Before long this process became well-known as his "cut-up" method. Initially Allen thought it sounded totally irrational, and he worried that it meant that Burroughs would not be able to communicate with anyone again through his writing. He wanted to think about the idea more before he drew any conclusions. In Allen's absence Peter had taken work as a messenger making deliveries on foot throughout the city. No sooner had Allen settled in than both he and Peter had to visit the doctor and be treated for the clap, which he probably picked up the very day he returned.

By now Allen's building was filled with even more of his friends. Bob Kaufman had moved into an apartment upstairs next door to Elise and Huncke, who were already renting in the same building. Carl Solomon was allowed out of the mental hospital every weekend, and he spent most of his time at Allen's, too. Carl was still angry with Allen for using his name so freely in *Howl*. His paranoid nature encouraged him to believe that Allen had stolen his identity and completely ruined his life by parading his mental problems in public. No longer was he just plain, ordinary Carl Solomon, but instead Carl Solomon the madman to whom *Howl* was addressed.

Soon after his return from South America, Allen became lethargic and depressed again. His break from depression had lasted little longer than his trip. A tattered copy of the *Tibetan Book of the Dead* was being circulated through the apartment building, and Allen read it with heightened interest, as it seemed to describe the identical sensations that the *yage* had given him.

The End, *CP*, p. 267

In the same large pile of mail was a letter from Gregory, who was in Europe, asking if he should come back to New York. After some thought Allen told him to stay put, that he and Peter would come over there. Allen needed to get away again before his depression became permanent. Once he had gotten a taste of anonymous freedom in South America, he wanted to remove himself completely from all the distractions so that he could think and read and write in peace. Gregory had been talking about visiting India over the past year and now the time seemed right for Allen, too. Burroughs probably wouldn't go along with them to India, since he was having too much fun sifting through his prose for items to cut up and randomly paste back together. Allen speculated that William had gone crazy from a lack of sex. As a joke, Allen and Peter cut up some of their own poems and rearranged them on the page and sent them to Burroughs with the note, "Just having a little fun mother." Burroughs was not amused; his cut-ups were serious attempts to get at the true meaning of words and not a parlor trick. His friends didn't understand that yet.

Peter's biggest concern was uncertainty about his family's ability to take care of themselves without him. He wasn't certain that he could leave them yet. One day he took Lafcadio to the state unemployment office to find out if there were any part-time jobs they might have for people with his special problems. If he could get him settled with a steady income, maybe they could get away. To break the monotony Robert and Mary Frank took Lafcadio to the theater to see the mime Marcel Marceau, which pleased the mostly silent Laf quite a bit. While Allen had been in South America, Peter had found a new eighteen-year-old girlfriend, Janine Pommy, an aspiring poet herself, who was waiting on tables at the Café Bizarre, one of the Village venues for poetry readings. Like Allen, she had grown up in nearby New Jersey and headed straight for New York City as soon as she was old enough to leave home. In fact, she had lost her virginity to Peter two years earlier on a weekend escape from high school, but Peter hadn't remembered that until she reminded him. Janine was young, beautiful, and so sexually open that she took compassion on Allen's needs, sharing Peter with him and sometimes taking part herself when Allen jumped into bed with the two of them. Before long she had become best friends with Herbert Huncke and was sharing the rent with Elise Cowen, who had   Man's glory, *CP*, p. 268 moved to a new apartment down the street from Allen.

Allen got word that Leroi Jones had been invited to visit Cuba later that year by the Fair Play for Cuba Committee, and Allen was hoping he could go along. He was eager to see Cuba and Russia and some of the other countries where the communists were in power so that he could witness first-hand how the revolution was working out. It was all to be part of his political education.

That September, Ted Wilentz threw one of his regular parties at his apartment over his Eighth Street Bookshop. John Wieners, who had been living with Irving Rosenthal, was invited, and Allen was pleased to find him looking more like an elegant alcoholic now than the "disheveled cockroach" of the previous year. Everyone was drunk, so when Wieners started to feel up Allen, Allen dragged him into the bathroom to have oral sex, but found that John was too drunk to orgasm. This prompted Allen to say to him, "Alright skeleton art thou not yet disillusioned with thy orgasmal corpse?" to which Wieners replied, "Long ago," and proceeded to take his teeth out, which reminded Allen of a death's head skull. They both laughed hysterically about their decaying bodies there on the bathroom floor. Allen was going to miss this kind of camaraderie in India, but it interfered with his real work as a poet and he was determined to get going. Later in the month when Fidel Castro made his historic visit to New York to address the UN, Allen went up to the Hotel Teresa in Harlem to see him at a reception. Allen respected that Castro had transferred from the posh Hotel Shelburne in Midtown to the working-class Teresa. Castro shook Allen's hand, for now he was famous enough to be recognized even by someone like Castro.

When Kerouac came into the city in October, Allen poured him some of the *yage* solution to sample. It didn't seem to have much effect on Jack, according to Allen, but that night was one of the rare occasions when Jack ended up in bed with Allen and Peter. Later they all watched the Kennedy/Nixon debates at Cessa Carr's house, and Allen wondered how Kerouac could ever favor Nixon. "Obviously Kennedy is more liberal and for more foreign wheat aid type and less tied up with phony military patriotic grandeur and less an FBI type, in intention. Not that it makes much difference America is sunk either way because it's just plain selfish. Both are phony and both are outright warmongers, the communists are right on that. Nixon and Kennedy combine all that's most obnoxious in America. But Nixon does take the cake," Allen wrote. He wanted to vote for the Socialist Party candidate, but fearing that Nixon might win by one vote, he cast his vote for Kennedy.

Around that time the trip to Cuba with Leroi Jones was postponed indefinitely, but something else came along that was destined to take up even more of Allen's time and energy. A conservative psychology professor at Harvard by the name of Timothy Leary had been experimenting with psilocybin (a synthetic form of the Mexican magic mushroom), which in Allen's experienced opinion was a useful visionary mind-opening drug. Dr. Leary and some others in the medical community were curious to find out if they could achieve positive results by giving hallucinogens like psilocybin to mentally ill patients. The problem was that when they gave the drugs to mentally ill patients to test, the subjects were not perceptive enough to describe the effects of the drug. It was Leary's idea to test the drug on artists and writers who were trained to verbally and visually communicate their observations. It would enable the researchers to find out what the effects were and to decide if they were worthwhile or not.

Leary had contacted Allen asking him to try psilocybin for the study and, naturally, this was exactly the kind of experiment Allen would enjoy. During the first week of December, Allen took Peter with him to Harvard, where they gave a special poetry reading for the psychoanalysts before they got high on the synthetic mushrooms. They finished the tests for the scientists and before anyone knew it, the Psychedelic Revolution was under way. Allen immediately realized that this drug was too wonderful to be kept secret by the scientists, and he convinced Leary to extend his experiments further afield. "We're starting a plot [Tim Leary and Allen] to get everyone in power in America high. I flipped my lid last week at Harvard and rushed out stark naked to telephone Jack and wake him up," Allen wrote. Under the influence of psilocybin, Allen began to realize that although he had been looking for a greater power outside himself, the fact was that the power, or God, was inside everyone already. It wasn't long before they had managed to turn on Charles Olson, Jack Kerouac (who didn't like it), Robert Lowell, and Barney Rosset of Grove Press to the wonders of psychedelics.

Allen had to write to Corso to postpone their rendezvous in Europe, which he had originally scheduled for early December. "I am in doldrums and don't know what I want to do—how to go to Sweden with Peter—and what to do with Lafcadio? And Peter has girlfriend who really likes him who would be sad if we left right now with fates unsettled—and this week Konstantin Simonov and Russian writers visited us, we took them [for a] walk on Brooklyn Bridge and showed them your educational alliance street—and they said come to Moscow and live with us free—we could go there from Sweden." Everyone was also flat broke once more and Allen was living on Peter's meager messenger paycheck. Even if they had been ready to leave, they couldn't have afforded to make the trip. Then out of the blue, an unknown benefactor, The Poets Foundation, sent Allen a check for one thousand dollars.

1961 ~

WITH HIS WINDFALL, Allen wanted to leave New York as soon as he could make arrangements, so he began packing up his books and manuscripts to move to his father's basement for safekeeping. If he stayed around any longer he felt as if he'd drown in "a sea of literary bullshit." Although he was biased after his use of psilocybin, Allen saw that a national political battle was brewing over the new "psychedelic" drugs. The drug laws in America were outdated, and Harry Anslinger, the first commissioner of the U.S. Bureau of Narcotics, was lobbying for new and tougher restrictions. The media coverage of drug issues seemed completely misguided, so Allen decided to connect all the myriad people who were good sources for drug information once and for all. While he continued his solicitations to publishers on behalf of his writer friends, he also circulated copies of the LaGuardia Report[50] and hoped he could find a publisher willing to reissue that, too. Many doctors, lawyers, and scholars were involved with the sociological, psychological, and legal aspects of drug use, and Allen was optimistic enough to think that this was the right moment to make positive changes in the American position on drugs.

Who Will Take Over the Universe?, CP, p. 273

---

[50] LaGuardia Report: Official report prepared for New York's mayor Fiorello LaGuardia by a blue-ribbon commission under the auspices of the New York Academy of Medicine during 1939–44, which in part stated, "Smoking marihuana does not lead to addiction . . . does not lead to morphine, heroin, or cocaine addiction."

Allen believed that the problem was less with the drug laws and more with the narcotics bureau that enforced those laws. In interviews he pointed out that the original laws governing the control of narcotics were created as a stamp tax so that the government would get its revenue from drug sales; that was why drugs were under the jurisdiction of the Treasury Department. As Anslinger became more powerful, he lobbied to have more drugs added to the list under his department's control. Allen felt that it all came to a head the moment Anslinger took control of drug addicts away from medical doctors and placed it in the hands of the police. Allen faulted the AMA for not defending the few doctors who had been trying to treat addicts. He even discovered that the Bureau of Narcotics had been setting doctors up for busts if they tried to help addicts get drugs legally. It was all outlined in scientific papers by many knowledgeable people, but the information rarely reached the popular press.

Allen was aware that since Anslinger controlled the bureau, he also controlled the "official" information being disseminated about drugs. Allen believed that it was the purview of medical professionals to provide that information and not of those who would profit by making the drug problem seem worse than it was. At one point Anslinger had even stated that marijuana was more vicious, destructive, and habit forming than heroin in spite of all the medical research to the contrary. That specific bit of propaganda allowed Anslinger to add grass to the growing list of dangerous substances. Allen concluded that the reason for the suppression of information was to increase the power of Anslinger and his Bureau of Narcotics. It was another case of a cancerous bureaucracy needing to grow, perhaps no different from what happened in every other government department. The more power Anslinger had, the more he wanted. If drugs were decriminalized and put under the control of the medical profession, then the whole black market in drugs would collapse overnight and the crime attendant on it would also disappear. There would be no need for either a narcotics bureau or a mafia and they'd all be out of jobs along with many in the judicial and penal systems. Anslinger and the mob were doing what they had to in order to protect their livelihoods. It was made easy because the government could pretend that it was nobly fighting a national drug menace, but it was really only expanding the number of criminals by automatically turning addicts into lawbreakers. Allen wanted to make it clear that government control of benevolent drugs like marijuana meant that the government controlled people's perceptions and states of awareness. He even seized an opportunity to discuss drug policy with Eleanor Roosevelt. The two sat down and talked cordially about the problems of a drug bureaucracy, but Allen knew that the meeting wasn't going to lead to any help from that quarter, since Mrs. Roosevelt couldn't imagine any positive reason for people wanting to use drugs in the first place.

Allen was bothered by the hypocrisy of singling out certain drugs for prohibition while alcohol and tobacco were treated with respect. He believed that the only way to avoid the further spread of heroin addiction was to cut off the black market supply of junk by making it legal and taking the profit out of it. No one would "push" it if there was no profit in it. Then doctors could work on the real problem of finding a cure.

When Leary came down from Harvard to stay at Allen's apartment, he gave samples of psilocybin to Jack Kerouac and Bob Kaufman. After taking it, Jack went out to the street with Leary to play football with a loaf of rye bread from the bakery. When Jack came back inside he told Allen, "Walking on water wasn't built in a day." Allen was so impressed with the truth behind the witty statement that he quoted it for the rest of his life, whenever he commented on any difficult project. In Allen's view, it was a charming glimpse into the heightened awareness caused by psilocybin, one that approximated classic mystical experience. Jack sat at the kitchen table and spoke of barracuda Buddhas and hinged penises late into the night. "So what are you up to, Dr. Leary, running around with this communist faggot Ginsberg and your bag of pills? Can your drugs absolve the mortal and venial sins which our beloved savior, Jesus Christ, the only Son of God, came down and sacrificed his life upon the cross to wash away?" Kerouac said. Taking a dose of Leary's psilocybin himself, Allen realized that he, himself, was the true Messiah, as was every person on earth. Leary continued to study the effects of the drug in a strictly scientific way and planned a seminar at Harvard the following year where students would take psilocybin and discuss its effects and its possible applications to logic, theology, and psychology. If Allen was around then, he wanted to take an active part.

Journal Night Thoughts,
CP, p. 275

By 1961 some of the larger New York publishers had set their sights on luring Allen away from City Lights. Knopf offered to do his next book for more money than he could ever earn from a small publisher. Allen had decided to remain loyal to Ferlinghetti, but he left the door open by telling Knopf to contact Ferlinghetti directly to negotiate for a hardcover edition of his work. City Lights only issued paperback books, so it was impossible to break into the library market, since libraries generally did not purchase paperbacks. Allen wrote to Ferlinghetti about Knopf's offer, but he straddled the fence and told Lawrence that he was indifferent to their plan. In some ways he liked the idea of staying with City Lights where he had what he called a "preferred amateur standing as far as the industry goes." For the time being he had enough money and he felt that sticking with City Lights gave him a kind of purity, with "one thin book issuing every few years." On the other hand, he didn't discount the fact that going to Knopf would be more lucrative and his work would reach many more people and "be read in White House by Mrs. Kennedy's social secretary." Years later John Kennedy, Jr., said that his mother had in fact read both *On the Road* and *Howl.* Even though *Kaddish and Other Poems* was just being released that February and was only his second book, Allen thought that it might be time to think about a hardback edition of his collected poems. He ceded the decision to Ferlinghetti, who had no intention of sharing Allen with another publisher unless he had to. By 1961 Allen's poetry was not only supporting the City Lights publishing business, but subsidizing the bookstore as well.

One night in February Allen took a mixture of methedrine, junk, and mushroom pills and sat at his desk from eight o'clock until noon the next day typing steadily. It was roughly the same combination of drugs he used when he had written *Kaddish.* This time he produced a more political poem that he titled *Television Was a Baby Crawling Toward That Deathchamber.* After completing it, he put it aside to consider more carefully at a later

Television Was a
Baby Crawling Toward
That Deathchamber,
CP, p. 280

date. His first thoughts were that it might be an even better poem than *Kaddish*, but it would be a year or two before he was ready to pull it out and rework it.

In February he was also invited to appear on the John Crosby television program where he gave what he called an eight-minute "lucid advertisement for pot." Since it was live, it aired before the FCC had a chance to censor it, and when they saw it they threatened to take legal action against the station. Allen was wise enough to see that pretaping a show with any political content was dangerous, since it invited censorship. Allen always enjoyed the spontaneity that a live show provided and always worked best live, so he was disappointed later when stations began to pretape most of their programs. Allen wrote that the FCC investigation of the Crosby show would never amount to anything anyway because within a few months there would be so much negative publicity about the narcotics bureau that "the drug brainwash will be reversed and the whole climate changed." He compared it to the repeal of Prohibition and said it would signify the death knell of the McCarthy Era. Allen suggested that the McCarthy witch hunts had nothing to do with communism, but were an assault on an individual's psychic freedom. His faith in the public's ability to force changes in the government became his customary response to major issues. If he saw even the slightest hint of a shift in public opinion on any issue, he was optimistic enough to believe that the problem was as good as solved. This optimism carried over into personal and domestic matters, too. If a friend had a drug problem and laid down his needle for a day, Allen was convinced that his problem was permanently solved. When Kerouac apologized to Allen for his abusive insults on one occasion, Allen was convinced that it would never happen again. If a demonstration drew a large crowd in opposition to the Vietnam War, then the war was all but over. It was an engaging quality in Allen's nature but also led his critics to view him as extremely naïve.

Ever since the publication of *On the Road* and its subsequent publicity, it seemed that Kerouac had been drinking heavily. Fame had arrived so suddenly for Jack that it was pushing him to self-destruction. In 1961 he returned from California where he had unsuccessfully tried to sober up at Ferlinghetti's cabin in Bixby Canyon, as described in painful detail in his book *Big Sur*. Jack continued to heap verbal abuse on Allen, perhaps due to his own disappointment with fame or perhaps because Allen was the most vocal proponent of the concept of a "Beat Generation." It was easy for them to argue, since their political views were counterpoint. In February on the telephone, Jack unleashed a vicious diatribe and screamed at Allen that Hitler was right, with Jack's mother in the background loudly agreeing. Allen wrote back to him, "Don't be paranoiac about imaginary Jews. Ginsberg; Podhoretz; 1/8 L. Carr; [Robert] Brustein; Gilbert Millstein; *Newsday*; Seymour Wyse; Holy Beat Gen. man, etc. The line-ups are too mixed to categorize your 'enemies' as Jewish. You could make similar line-ups of Catholics, Protestants." Allen acknowledged that the insults annoyed him, but he never gave up on a friend and he was willing to forgive Jack anything. Jack's alcoholism prevented Allen from having any normal dialogue with him anymore.

Although Kerouac suffered from liquor, Allen's other friends were addicted to a wide variety of drugs. Allen had spent the previous ten years experimenting with nearly every type of drug imaginable, and he was surrounded by people whose lives had been consumed by drugs. After his Blake visions in 1949, Allen had intentionally tried to recreate that same feeling via the drug experience. He hoped that through drugs he could unlock a new and unexplored part of his mind, and he tried, unsuccessfully, to replicate his earlier Harlem epiphany. To that end he had taken marijuana, heroin, laughing gas, opium, mushrooms, *majoun*, amphetamines, hash, and an array of hallucinogens. In the course of his experiments, he was careful never to get hooked on anything. He was lucky to be aware of his own limits. He took notes recording the effects of each drug, and to avoid dependency, he tried to allow enough time to pass before taking the same drug a second time. Although he did smoke marijuana for pleasure more frequently, he tried not to use addictive substances merely to "get high," for he knew that it could be a dangerous course. He had witnessed the terrible effects of addiction on close friends like Burroughs, Corso, Huncke, and more recently Peter Orlovsky. Peter was currently trying to kick a junk habit before they left for Europe and was sick for a week with withdrawal symptoms. With the worst of that week over, Allen was convinced that Peter would be fine once again. He thought that New York was the problem, since drugs were too readily available, especially in his household. Allen wrote to Gregory about "strangers taking baths in bathroom right now," and it was past time to get away.

Plans were soon made to settle Lafcadio at the *Catholic Worker* farm on Staten Island where he could get compassionate care and Peter wouldn't have to worry about him so much. Corso had grown tired of waiting for them in Athens and was now on his way to Paris, so they revised their travel plans to meet him there at the end of March before they all moved on to India. In his final weeks in New York, Allen generously gave the original draft of the manuscript of *Kaddish* to Julian Beck and Judith Malina to auction off for the benefit of the Living Theater. The company desperately needed money to pay off their debts and to go on tour. Many other artists contributed works for sale and they were able to raise seventeen thousand, enough to be on their way. Unknown to Allen at the time, his manuscript was bought by his friend Ted Wilentz, who donated it to NYU's Fales Library. It was the only manuscript Allen ever parted with, but for such a worthy cause he was happy to make an exception. He also by now had enough poetry for a third City Lights book, which he at first intended to call *Some Skin, a Body of Poems,* but would rename *Reality Sandwiches* before publication. In March he sent the manuscript for that book to Ferlinghetti with specific orders to hold it back for a year or two. He was planning to be out of the country for quite a while and wanted it to be published while he was away. Three days before their ship sailed, Allen made the familiar trip to Rutherford to spend the afternoon with William Carlos Williams. He wrote to Ferlinghetti that Williams had aged noticeably and was more decrepit than the last time Allen had seen him. All the same Williams had completed yet another book of poetry. It was to be the last time that Allen saw his eminent teacher and mentor alive.

At the last minute the plans for Lafcadio to stay on the farm fell through. Allen decided that Janine Pommy, Peter's girlfriend, could take care of him in their absence. Janine, Lafcadio, and Huncke wanted to stay on in the Second Street apartment until the end of March and then move to another apartment around the corner on East Sixth Street. Laf had been active since he moved in from their mother's house. He had been going to dance classes regularly, then stopped abruptly in order to take up painting with Bill Heine, who was also living with them for a while. Janine had lost thirty pounds from her addiction to methedrine and things were falling apart quickly around the house, but Allen didn't know what he could do about it except escape. Peter hoped that leaving his brother with Janine would benefit both of them. He had once again assumed the role of parent, and Lafcadio was dependent on him but also resented Peter for this dependence. He believed that life might be smoother without Peter's domination and overbearing threats.

Allen and Peter had booked passage on the SS *America* scheduled to leave March 23 with an arrival planned in Le Havre around April 1. Aside from their passage, they had made no definite plans. They sailed on a blustery day, with a wet snow falling as they stood at the rail waving their goodbyes. It was too cold to stay on deck for long, so they went to their cabin to read and write. Allen's thoughts centered on politics as he started the trip. Even if he had stayed in America and tried to organize public opinion on the issues of Cuba, China, Russia, and so on, he didn't believe it would have had any impact. The average American seemed to be eager to believe whatever political propaganda the government issued. His arguments with Jack seemed to exemplify that discouraging state of affairs. Allen viewed his job as poet as communicating with that "grand majority" and doing what he could to "dynamite the emotional rock bed of inertia and spiritual deadness" that hung over the country. He'd have to figure out a way to "enter people's souls and shake their emotions and wake their souls to the fact of God on earth." Only then would it be possible for the people to seize power over their own universes and end their dependence on external authority. "I hope America will still be there when we get back," he wrote in his journal as the ship sailed to Europe.

From LeHavre they took a train to Paris and got a room in the familiar old hotel on Rue Git-le-Coeur. Allen was puzzled when Brion Gysin told them that Burroughs had just left town, not wanting to stay to greet them. He couldn't imagine what he had said to upset William, but he was distracted by Corso's arrival in town on the same day. Gregory had finished writing *American Express*, his "weird Candide-like book" for Olympia Press. His publisher, Maurice Girodias, was planning to host a book party on April 24 at the Grand Severin restaurant, the chic place Girodias owned and into which he'd sunk all his publishing profits. Girodias was even hoping that the American Express company would sue him over the title of the book, for he thrived on such publicity, both good and bad, and he knew a lawsuit would boost sales considerably. No such legal problems materialized, and the sales were so sluggish that Corso's book never went into a second printing.

In spite of his determination to get away from literary business, that's exactly how Allen spent much of his time in Paris. He met with Nanda Pivano, who came to discuss Italian translations of his work. She had translated *On the Road* into Italian, as well as Hemingway's books, and she soon would become Allen's translator as well. Ted Wilentz forwarded bushels of Allen's mail, so he was kept busy answering all of that, too. In addition to his first-class mail, Allen also asked Wilentz to send him *I. F. Stone's Newsletter* and the *Fair Play for Cuba Newsletter,* so that he could keep up with current events.

One day Allen ran into Henri Michaux on the street, where they stood talking, when a tourist across the street held up her camera and started waving at them. Allen tried to pose for the picture with Michaux, but Michaux wanted to step out of the frame so that the woman could get Allen alone, assuming she recognized Ginsberg as the truly famous celebrity. They both laughed when the woman told them that she didn't want either one of them in her picture, but instead was trying to take a photograph of the building behind them. For Peter, Paris was fun. He was letting his hair grow longer and found a new girlfriend quickly, so he was adjusting. He even took a French course at the Alliance Française, but wasn't a good student. As time passed Allen's life became more relaxed in Paris and he became a regular at a table in the Deux Magots Café each afternoon. It didn't take Peter and Gregory long to find a good source of heroin either, and even Allen began   This Form of Life Needs shooting up occasionally.   Sex, *CP,* p. 292

In late April, the Bay of Pigs invasion splashed across the headlines. The United States had trained and backed a group of Cuban exiles in their attempt to overthrow the regime of Fidel Castro, but the poorly executed invasion was discovered and squashed. Allen was amazed that there were no mass demonstrations in America to protest the government's complicity. He saw their apathy as the final bankruptcy of the liberals. Naïvely he believed that the U.S. government would have to begin treating Cuba with diplomacy instead of aggression due to this fiasco. Before the invasion most people in the United States believed that the majority of the Cuban people hated and reviled Castro. Americans were surprised to learn that this was not the case and that a great percentage of the Cuban people supported Castro and his revolution. Allen felt vindicated because he had continually warned against the deliberate government manipulation of the press, and he was certain that people would now stop believing everything that U.S. politicians told them. America had no intention of recognizing Castro's communist dictatorship and tension continued to build.

At the end of April, Peter, Gregory, and Allen, along with jazz saxophonist Alan Eager, whom they had bumped into in Paris, went to the Cannes Film Festival on the Riviera. They were invited to be the guests of Shirley Clarke, the director of *The Connection*, a black-and-white film that was to be screened there. *The Connection* was a documentary about a group of addicts waiting for their drug connection. It was based on Jack Gelber's play of the same name and had been successfully produced onstage by the Living Theater. The members of the cast, who were for the most part addicts, stayed together as a group, and the poets roomed with them for a few weeks. Gregory had arrived in Cannes with his pockets full of heroin from Paris, but by May 5 they had used the last of it. Ginsberg remembered that he shared a needle with Eager in the train's bathroom and then went back to join the others sniffing and nodding all night long in their compartment.

Life with Clarke and her cast of characters off-screen was not much different from the scenes on-screen. Allen and Peter stayed in the basement of the house Clarke had rented, and Gregory stayed with his girlfriend in her room. He was always high and always arguing with her. Soon the girl was sorry she had come along with them and went back to Paris. Peter met a tall Jewish woman from England whom he spent time with, and they went to all the movies being shown without enjoying any of them. After Cannes, Allen, Peter, and Gregory went to stay with Jacques Stern, their wealthy Rothschild friend, who had a house in St. Tropez. They had run out of money again and were living on cheap salami and bread by that time. Overnight their diet changed to lobsters and champagne, courtesy of Stern. But this fortunate turn of events wasn't enough to satisfy Gregory, who made himself unwelcome by quarreling endlessly with Stern. They scrapped like children and called each other names like "you stinky cripple" (Stern being a victim of polio) and "you stupid loudmouth poet" (Corso being a loudmouth poet). While it lasted they enjoyed all the luxuries that Stern could offer, swimming at his beach club, riding around in his chauffeured limousine, and drinking unlimited quantities of expensive liquor. For some reason that opulence made Gregory even more unbearable than usual. To get rid of them, Stern was happy to give them all enough money for their boat fares to Tangier at the end of May. En route, they stopped in Marseille and took a side trip to

Aix-en-Provence so Allen could see Mount Sainte-Victoire, the subject of so many of Cézanne's landscapes. He was so excited to see it in person that he bought a postcard reproduction and compared each brushstroke in the painting with a geological epoch on the mountainside. Unfortunately, a new housing project had been built on the exact spot from which Cézanne had painted the mountain's steep south face.

On June 1, the trio arrived in Tangier harbor aboard the SS *Azemour*. Burroughs didn't bother to meet them at the dock even though they had sent him a telegram to confirm their arrival time. He was sitting in his room at the Hotel Mu-niria, oblivious to their docking. At immigration Corso was stopped by the Moroccans because his passport had expired, and they wouldn't let him enter the country. They locked him up on the ship, which was continuing to the capital, Casablanca, where his documents could be corrected. Allen didn't want to leave Gregory alone, so he went back on board and thirty hours later both Gregory and Allen arrived in Casablanca. Peter was left on the dock in Tangier to take care of their luggage and set up housekeeping while Allen ironed out Corso's bureaucratic paperwork. The American embassy was sympathetic and hurried down to the port to kindly rescue Gregory with a new passport. It took them a few days but eventually they caught a bus back to Tangier and returned to find a Burroughs indifferent to their adventure. Gysin had been right, William didn't care whether he saw them or not. The next month and a half were filled with incomprehensible petty jealousies and hor-rors, "actually a great weird scene," Allen wrote, putting his usual cheerful spin on things. Most of the unpleasantness was directed against Peter, whom Burroughs continued to dislike. He still thought Allen was wasting his time with someone who was so far beneath him intellectually, and William chose to show his disdain for Peter at every opportunity.

By now Burroughs was working on more advanced electrical cut-ups, made from snipping and reassembling audiotapes. He told Allen repeatedly that poetry and words were finished. He hadn't even bothered to read the specially inscribed copy of *Kaddish* Allen had sent him. Allen respected no one more than Kerouac and Burroughs in literary matters, and the fact that Burroughs believed poetry was dead, not even worth reading, gave Allen a jolt. He found it difficult to ignore Burroughs's stance and hoped to under-stand it over time. Instead of staying again at the Hotel Muniria where Bur-roughs was ensconced, they found even cheaper quarters down the street at the Hotel Armor for only twenty dollars a month. Allen and Peter shared a little tile room on the top floor, with a spectacular terrace and a

Sunset S.S. Azemour, *CP*, p. 295

view overlooking the tiled rooftops of the port and the bay beyond. Gregory had a tiny room downstairs that cost him only fourteen dollars a month, but he spent most of his time in Allen's room anyway. For the rest of June they lived in the Armor and tried to figure out what was wrong with Burroughs.

Every day William worked in his room and made cut-up collages from newspapers and photographs, juxtaposing pictures like President Kennedy stepping off airplanes onto Queen Elizabeth's forehead. Allen kept busy writing in his notebooks and answering prodigious amounts of correspondence, while Peter walked the streets of the *medina*, usually high, and did his best to avoid Burroughs. The political climate in Tangier had changed drastically since their last visit. Since gaining independence, Tangier was no longer an international free trading port ruled by the Western powers. It had become more tranquil and less European, with fewer interesting people living there. There was beginning to be a flow of young beatniks who passed through town as the counterculture discovered Tangier. They came mainly to smoke legal pot and swing with the Arab boys. Most of the locals, including Paul Bowles, were sorry to see the changes. Morocco was cheaper than Mexico and more interesting and exotic to Allen than Paris. He was happy to be there, but he could tell that the halcyon days were over. Bowles was around town more on this second visit, and he and Allen became fond of each other. Bowles's friend, painter Ahmed Yacoubi, found great bargains for them on used clothes and opium, and Allen grew to like him, too.

When Allen came to Tangier he was expecting to settle in for a long stay. On this trip he had his own work to do and wouldn't be tied down doing editorial work for William. He had promised Dave Haselwood, the owner of Auerhahn Press, that he would edit his journals from his 1960 South America trip for a book, tentatively titled *Journal of the Death Vine*. It would be a big project, for he had at least a dozen notebooks consisting of thousands of pages to type and edit. Peter was not having such a great time in Tangier, but somehow Allen didn't seem to notice. On June 20, after a month in Tangier, Peter wrote home, "I'd like to be off for Istanbul coming beginning of next month, off on my own, away from Allen and Gregory, who are getting me down, somehow to arrive in India where my hundred a month should be enough to live on. I've been depressed this past week."

In addition to his coldness toward Allen, Burroughs's newfound companions presented a significant obstacle to their old friendship. William was hung up on an "18-year-old spoiled brat English Lord who looks like a pale faced Rimbaud but is a smart creep," Allen wrote to Lucien Carr. The spoiled brat was Michael Portman, whose aristocratic family lent their name to London's Portman Square. No one was ever quite able to discern the relationship between Portman and Burroughs—possibly it was platonic, Allen thought—but it certainly was "some kinda awful relation with him." Portman seemed to bug everyone, including Ginsberg, unusual since he was generally unflappable when it came to all things Burroughs. Portman would never leave Burroughs's side and no one else, including Allen, was ever allowed to be alone with William. It appeared that the arrangement met with William's approval, since he did nothing to change it. Another, slightly more angelic British cherub, by the name of Ian Sommerville, was continually in tow helping to keep William isolated from his old friends. Allen found Sommerville more likable than Portman. He was a genius in mathematics and physics from Cambridge who talked nonstop about various electrical cut-up machines he planned to build. Their newest project was William's cut-up book, *Soft Machine,* which now Portman and Sommerville, not Allen, were helping to assemble and edit. When Bowles invited Allen to go with him to his house in Marrakech for a few weeks to soak up the native culture, Allen gladly accepted and was happy to get away from Burroughs and his entourage. Allen didn't invite Peter or Gregory along, which did nothing to raise Peter's spirits. Why Allen left Peter behind has never been made clear, but probably Bowles hadn't wanted a large party. Marrakech was inland, near the foothills of the Atlas Mountains, and more like Allen's vision of an authentic Moroccan town. Bowles's house had a flat roof where they sat on mats every evening and drank mint tea while listening to his portable radio. They both slept downstairs where there was little in the way of furniture, only a stove, rug, air mattresses, and a candle lamp. The two wiled away the time by smoking countless cigarettes and kif pipes and eating the local *majoun* while they watched the stars glimmer in the dark sky. There was a large, open-air market in the center of town almost the size of Times Square, where Allen bought a native basket and some shoes that proved impossible to break in. The square was always filled with Sudanese dancers, acrobats, fortune-tellers, and snake charmers, who were eager to perform for a few pennies from the shoppers who came to buy spices of every variety. Later Allen would remember that the most un-American lavatory he ever saw in his life was here in Dja M'alfna Square. It looked like a circular bomb cellar with Arab excrement smeared all over the floor and strokes of brown excremental fingerprints covering the walls like a Jackson Pollock painting. Having noted that, he hoped that the recent modernization initiatives in Marrakech would fail or these changes would kill the best aspects of their regional culture.

Arriving back from Marrakech on July 26, Allen found Peter sick with a mild case of jaundice, stubborn dysentery, and hepatitis to boot. Besides being fed up with Morocco, Peter was in such poor health that he felt as if he were trapped inside one of Bowles's novels himself. With Allen away, Peter had made the decision to move on alone to the Middle East as soon as he felt better. He needed to get away from Burroughs and his sycophants. Allen, who usually would have been much more focused on Peter, could think of no one but Burroughs at that moment. Perhaps they could meet later in Tel Aviv or even India, or maybe not at all. Time alone would tell.

After his return from Marrakech, Allen spent every afternoon at his favorite table in the Petit Socco with a glass of hot mint tea, while Peter spent his time sick in the hotel room or with a woman at the local whorehouse. Gregory was curled up in bed, nursing a cut finger and taking whatever drug he could find that day. As Allen waited for Peter to return from the prostitutes in the *medina*, he couldn't help thinking about "all the happy and past years we had lived together." He was afraid that their separation might become permanent, and if Peter disappeared Allen would be alone. The entries in Allen's journals seemed to ignore the fact that ever since the day he had met Peter there had been no assurance or unity at all between them, even though Allen waxed nostalgic about their past relationship. Peter had always been on the verge of leaving, but somehow Allen appeared to be blind to Peter's true feelings. He wanted to make allowances for Peter so that he wouldn't be alone, but beyond the obvious difference that Peter loved women and Allen loved men, he couldn't accept that they had little in common, except for an interest in drugs. And even on the subject of drugs, Allen's interest was truly experimental, while Peter's use was addictive.

In a few days Alan Ansen was expected to arrive from Venice, and Allen begged Peter to postpone his departure. He thought the whole matter of Burroughs might be cleared up when Ansen arrived, since he had a way with William, and probably if anyone could cut through the layers of bullshit, it was Ansen. William had "declared independence from all passions, affections, mayas, thoughts and language and was sitting around listening to the messages of static on transistor radios and staring at stroboscopes and making super collages of his own photographs of photographs," Allen wrote.

Orlovsky, Burroughs, Ansen, Corso, Bowles, Ginsberg, Tangier, July 1961 ~

He believed the cut-up philosophy and the smothering presence of Portman and Sommerville were at the root of the problems. Burroughs's work continued to be brilliant as always but his personality had become inhuman and that scared Allen. He could see that William was persecuting Peter, but he was puzzled about how jealousy could cause this behavior, especially because William was otherwise an emotional blank. Allen was trapped in a dilemma. He couldn't reject William, his earliest teacher, and he couldn't relinquish Peter for fear of losing his companionship. He theorized that perhaps the experience was all worthwhile because it would teach him that he was bound to lose Peter, William, poetry, and even himself in the end. He'd be a sadder, wiser man for it and then he could start life anew.

By the very end of July Peter felt healthy enough to leave and boarded the ferry for the crossing to Gibraltar. He was looking forward to traveling alone for a change, and it wasn't hard to leave since he was disgusted with everyone in Tangier. Peter explained his philosophy behind the breakup simply enough: He felt that there was a God in everyone that wanted us to come together in a happy bed of love. Allen, William, and Gregory, he believed, felt that the God of War was the god that always won out in the end, so all they thought about was death. They had all laughed at Peter when he voiced his ideas and called him an idealist while criticizing him for having a one-track mind about love. As he sailed from Gibraltar to Piraeus, the port of Athens, he was relieved and open for a new adventure. He knew that wherever he landed it had to be better than what he had just been through.

Allen spent his first two days without Peter on one long opium high. Timothy Leary had surprised them by arriving in Tangier as Peter was leaving. Leary, with Corso's help, had no trouble finding local sources for all the drugs they wanted, courtesy of Tim's expense account. Leary was staying in town only long enough to invite Burroughs to Harvard, before he flew off to speak at an LSD conference in Copenhagen. A few days later Allen wrote to Peter to express his regret over their quarrels; he felt that when they met again things would be better. At the dock Peter had said that it might be "years" before they saw each other again, and Allen said that he hoped it wouldn't be that long. "But if years alas, then years alas, I'll still cry to see your old eyes," he wrote sentimentally to Peter.

Even after Peter left, William was cold to Allen and Alan Ansen's presence did nothing to change that. Allen's letter went on to tell Peter that it was depressing to lose not only Peter, but Burroughs, too. He tried to convince Peter that he was willing to do anything to make their relationship work, even suggesting that he would have sex with women again, to support their sexual compatibility. Leary had agreed with Burroughs that poetry was an obsolete form of expression, and Allen was feeling more adrift than ever. Leary posited that the world was ready to move on to a new super-consciousness and words and ideas would be eliminated altogether. Allen realized that it was exactly that point that had hurt his pride with Burroughs. Since Allen depended upon his identity as a poet and knew his life work was to be a wordsmith, he could not envision living in a world without words.

After Leary and Ansen left Tangier, Allen asked William to see him alone, without Sommerville and Portman in the way. Burroughs agreed and for a few short hours they regained a little of the rapport they had had in the old days. William confided to Allen that he sensed Portman was much too dependent on him. Allen became convinced that William recognized the problem but was unable to act. William assured Allen that it wasn't an intentional conspiracy to keep him at arm's length. However, their discussion changed the situation little. At a party at Bowles's place, Burroughs and Portman gave a lot of *majoun* to a new kid by the name of

Mark Groetchen, a friend of Portman's. A neophyte to drug experiences, Mark freaked out and panicked, and Burroughs and Portman were too far gone to notice his plight. Even though Allen was high on opium he was able to care for Mark and guide him through his adverse reaction safely. William later admitted that he was in error, but Allen held Portman solely responsible. Allen could never bring himself to believe that William was to blame for any malicious acts.

When Burroughs and Corso flew to London on August 20, Allen was left as the last of the group in Tangier. He stayed for a few more days and then boarded the SS *Vulcania* for Athens, via Palermo and Naples, on the twenty-fourth. Just before he was to leave, Allen received a letter promising a windfall of several hundred dollars from *Show Business Illustrated* for an article about the Cannes Film Festival's premiere of *The Connection*. As his ship steamed into the Strait of Gibraltar, Allen watched the hillside, dotted with tiny white Arab houses, disappear behind him into the blue mist. He was once again floating alone, solitary, and hopeless with his beat-up knapsack beside him, ready to explore the Acropolis, inspect the Sphinx, and then fade into India by year's end. Once again his loneliness prompted him to remember Hart Crane's farewell leap off the ship and into the dark depths of the sea.

When Allen got to Greece, he was thrilled to find a letter from Peter waiting for him at the American Express office. Peter wrote from Cairo that he was planning to move on to Beirut soon and was generally doing well. Allen spent a few pleasant days exploring Athens and smoked some pot by himself on the Acropolis. That evening he walked around the old streets of the Plaka underneath the Parthenon feeling romantically wistful and nostalgic. The tables in the tavernas were all filled with couples and he was alone. The money from *Show Business* hadn't arrived yet, nor had the money Gregory promised to send him from London, so he was down to his last three dollars. When the check from the magazine finally arrived, Allen was able to pay his hotel bill and all the travel expenses. In celebration he splurged on sex with one of the street boys who hung around Ommonia Square looking for tourists. For the next month Allen leisurely explored Greece. He spent four days in Delphi walking through the shepherd valleys and idyllic landscape of Mt. Parnassus, before going on an arduous train trip to Olympia. He managed to see all the ruins along the way and returned through Athens once more to check his mail. He wrote to his father that he hadn't been very happy on this trip but had seen a lot. In addition to

Seabattle of Salamis Took Place off Perama, *CP*, p. 296

being lonely, Allen was attempting to give up smoking and was sick from the effects of nicotine withdrawal.

From Athens he took a ferry to Hydra and wandered around the tiny island for three days. Gregory had told him of a vision that had come to him on the far side of the island, but Allen's only vision was of a handsome young man who reminded him of Paul Roth, his high school heartthrob. Hydra was a relaxing stop with no car traffic. Donkeys walked along the island paths and it was unspoiled and wonderfully peaceful. From there he took the next boat to see the famous Mycenae ruins, and at the famous Lion's Gate he sat down to describe everything in his notebook. By the time he got back to Athens at the end of the month, Allen had lost contact with Peter again. He didn't know if he was in Turkey or Israel or Lebanon, and he wrote to him in care of General Delivery everywhere. At least since arriving in Greece he hadn't been suffering from a lack of sex. The beautiful boys he met were all queer, and it was a revelation for him to be in a place where homosexuality wasn't frowned upon. He even met Katsimbalis, the great storyteller Henry Miller had described in *The Colossus of Maroussi*. Allen found him as magnificent as Miller made him out to be.

Allen spent almost two full weeks on Crete and took buses to see most of the archeological sites. He took this opportunity to read *The Odyssey*, enjoying the fact that he was treading the same paths described in the epic poem. A fellow traveler gave him some great opium, which he used for inspiration while writing a long piece he called *Prose Contribution to Cuban Revolution*. Contrary to the title, it had little to do with Cuba and much more to do with Allen's personal philosophy of life. In it he recapped his life up until then and focused on the fact that he had learned to trust his own natural love feelings and stop trying to be a prophet/saint. Influenced by Burroughs, he even wondered whether words might be "oldhat dinosaur futile" and whether an expanded consciousness might not include a world without language or even a world without a world.

Finally, when he passed through Athens in mid-October, there was a letter for him from Peter in Beirut. He told Allen that he hadn't received his government check, and without funds he had been reduced to selling his own blood. Another note written later that Allen picked up at the same time stated that Peter was heading off to Damascus, Jerusalem, and Haifa. Although not as personal, still another letter that awaited him was more upsetting. The editors from *Show Business* wanted to censor his article by removing the word *shit*. Allen was diametrically opposed to any censorship, but he had already spent and given away most of the money they had paid him. If he didn't allow the cut, he would have to pay the money back somehow. It was a significant dilemma for Allen, but he decided that his integrity was more important than the money, and instructed them not to cut the offensive word from his article. He would have to wait for their final decision, but in the meantime, he thought he would have to find a way to earn several hundred dollars to pay them back. Months and months later, *Show Business Illustrated* decided not to publish the article and did not ask Allen to return the money, but in the meantime he believed himself to be deeply in debt.

After completing *The Odyssey*, Allen went on to read *The Iliad*, which he finished on his crossing to Israel aboard the SS *Athene*. Despite the temporary pleasures of the Greek boys, he was desolate and yearned for a reunion with Peter. Planning was difficult, since they were not in direct contact and had to rely on mail that always arrived weeks later. Simultaneously, in Damascus, Peter wrote in his journal about his own loneliness. It had been more than two months since he and Allen had split, and he had found it difficult to travel through strange parts of the world completely alone. Allen cried as his ship pulled into the port of Haifa, and he longed for Peter as much as he looked forward to seeing the ancient promised land where he was about to set foot for the first time.

For several months Allen had been corresponding with Gary Snyder, who was still in Japan studying Buddhism. They were planning to meet around New Year's in Bombay, where they would give a few readings together for travel money. Allen was determined to find Peter first and still make the scheduled rendezvous. Gary's letter changed their meeting place from Bombay to Ceylon. The welcome news was that they would not need to do any readings in India after all, which cheered Allen, since he wanted to continue his break from that for a while. After being off cigarettes for two weeks he started again. Quitting wasn't as easy as he expected, and this would be only one of his many efforts to stop smoking over the next thirty years.

In Israel Allen's top priority was to find Peter, so he hung around in Haifa near the American Express office, hoping to get word from him. He made a few side trips to see some of the biblical spots in Galilee, but most of the time he stayed with people he knew who were kind enough to offer him a bed. He avoided the Israeli literary   Galilee Shore, *CP*, p. 297 scene and stayed away from doing interviews and readings as well, preferring life as an anonymous traveler. Still, there were some painters and poets in Israel whom he wanted to meet. In Jerusalem he was lucky enough to visit philosopher Martin Buber, with whom he discussed drugs. Buber counseled Allen not to go seeking after visions, as he felt they were illusory and unimportant. Allen was disappointed that he wasn't allowed to visit Old Jerusalem or the Wailing Wall because they were on the Jordanian side of the border at that time. Politically, the Israelis he met seemed isolated from what was going on in the rest of the world, and he was surprised to find that the Arabs in Israel were not well treated. He saw the Arab/Israeli conflict as an insurmountable problem that could not be solved until people were willing to forget their differences and identities, which he thought neither the Jews nor the Arabs were capable of doing. He remarked that Israel was filled with millions of people exactly like his own family, and that wasn't necessarily a good thing. Their stubbornness and loyalty would not permit them to compromise. On November 8, he left Haifa for Tel Aviv to visit a doctor. He was treated for "clap up the asshole," as he described it in his journal, probably a souvenir from the hustlers in Athens.

Once he located Peter, he hoped they could go south to the Red Sea port of Elat and get seamen's jobs there to pay for their passage to India. He planned to stay with family friend Ethel Broide in Tel Aviv, and since she worked for Zim ship lines, he assumed she would be able to help them get jobs on a boat. Allen even located a few actual relatives while in Tel Aviv, and that made him feel more at home.

It wasn't until mid-November, after several weeks of waiting, that Allen and Peter were reunited. In a letter to Jane Bowles, Allen wrote that he was surprised that Peter and he had gotten back together at all, but he candidly confided to her that it was more out of habit than anything else. Even after combining their money they were nearly penniless, and Israel turned out to be the most expensive place they had yet been. Too late they realized that they had made a mistake in coming to a Jewish state. Once inside Israel, they couldn't leave, as none of the surrounding Arab countries allowed travelers to enter directly from Israel. That meant that they would have to sail or fly somewhere else first. Visas to India were almost impossible to get as well, since India did not maintain diplomatic relations with Israel. Everything had to be done through the British consul. And the Indian government did not permit entry to travelers without funds. Allen and Peter had to convince the Indian authorities that they had enough money to support themselves while in India. The government required travelers to have return tickets before it allowed them to enter the country. They stayed longer than they had anticipated in Ethel's apartment doing the necessary paperwork to get their travel affairs in order. They relaxed and took some of the opium Allen had bought, and from her top-floor balcony watched the orange-purple sunset. Israel had become a friendly prison for them. Allen wondered at Israeli nationalism and found that Israeli Jews spoke only of being Jewish. He found their self-focus maddening, and he compared it to a bunch of Texans constantly talking about Texas.

With little else to do, Allen wrote a number of letters and practically caught up with his giant pile of mail. He wasn't inspired to write anything more creative, but he had hopes that all that would change in India and he would enter a new fertile period. Peter received word from his sister, Marie, that both Peter's mother and Lafcadio had been taken to Central Islip State Hospital. Allen wrote to Eugene and asked him to look into it. They had feared that Lafcadio would wind up there sooner or later, but they were shocked to learn about his mother. "She isn't crazy," Allen wrote to his brother. She was deaf and very excitable, but they were certain that she shouldn't be committed to a mental hospital.

After pursuing myriad ideas for their escape from Israel, they decided to go to the port of Elat and catch a boat to West Africa. From there they could probably book passage on a boat to India. On the trip to Elat they stopped to float on the salty waters of the Dead Sea as all tourists must and visited Sodom after a long bus ride through the wilderness of Moses. After interminable delays they were able to leave Israel on December 28 bound for Mombasa. On the boat to Africa, Allen was more absorbed in reading than in the voyage. He had picked up several books on Hitler and his concentration camps, as well as another book on Buddhism. As they passed through the Gulf of Aqaba they saw the brown, cragged mountains on both sides of the gulf and a vast beach in Egypt. On January 3, the ship docked in Djibouti, where Rimbaud had landed a century earlier. There they spent the day in town wandering around the paved elevated market square, before returning to the ship for the rest of their trip. It was a slow boat, and it wasn't until January 9, 1962, that they approached Dar es Salaam. They were on the other side of the equator at last. From there they'd have to retrace their steps and head back north to Mombasa, Kenya's major seaport, to find a boat to India.

1 9 6 2 ∿

THE PAIR REACHED MOMBASA and finally left the ship on January 12, after a two-week voyage. Immediately they went to the steamship office to book passage on a boat to India, but found the next one available would not depart until February 6, and that one was to Bombay, not Ceylon. Allen wrote to Gary quickly to tell him that they'd catch up to him and his new wife, Joanne Kyger, somewhere in India during February, but it wouldn't be nearly as soon as they had hoped and it wouldn't be in Ceylon. There was nothing they could do but sit still and kill time hoping that a berth might open up on an earlier boat, but that was highly unlikely in the busy season.

Allen found Mombasa charming and, more important, inexpensive. Israel had drained their wallets, and at least in East Africa they were able to conserve what little money they had left. They checked into an Indian hotel equipped with the necessary mosquito netting and dined in cheap restaurants on local delicacies like curried prawns for only forty-five cents a dish. Meeting people was always easy for Allen, and he made friends with a man named Shontay who took them out to get high with his friends. Later the group went to hear native drumming and watch dancing on the outskirts of town. Since they had the better part of a month to kill, they decided to take a trip inland toward Nairobi to see some wild African animals and authentic native life.

A two-hundred-mile ride brought them to Nairobi, and along the way they saw lions and giraffes from the bus windows. After leaving their bags at the Vadrahmut Hotel, they went to the Kanu Party headquarters looking in vain for information about African poets. The bureaucrats ignored them because they looked unkempt and scruffy. Allen found Kenya a drag like Israel, except that everyone was hung up on race rather than religion. While in the Kanu office they saw a flyer inviting everyone to the wedding party of a local politician, Tom M'Boya. The notice wasn't intended as an open invitation, but they borrowed ties and went to the trustees' hall on Juwanjee Street anyway. For most of the night they had a good time talking to everyone there, but by 1:00 A.M. they were more than a little drunk and boisterous and were asked to leave, ostensibly for not having jackets.

The next afternoon they went to Nairobi Stadium for a gigantic Kanu Party rally to hear Jomo Kenyatta speak. There were thousands and thousands of people there—Allen later estimated twenty thousand and even later said thirty thousand. Peter and Allen seemed to be the only whites in the vast audience. The attendees listened as Kenyatta spoke about the importance of African nationalism in a voice that reminded Allen of the stereotyped black characters from the old Amos and Andy radio programs. Although Allen's wallet was stolen by someone in the crowd, overall it was a positive dream-like experience that he would never forget. Another day they took a bus to see Mt. Kilimanjaro, which was hidden in the mist that day. They did see Massai warriors drinking blood fresh from their cattle's necks. Allen liked the Massai and recognized them as naturally good-humored, poking each other in the ribs and making funny remarks. They were a far cry from the menacing Kenyan special police stationed everywhere in the city. The Massai were tall, ebony-skinned men with huge holes in their earlobes who wore dried-blood-colored robes. They carried spears wherever they went, and to Allen they represented the native life he had hoped to find in East Africa. Back in Nairobi they stayed in the poor Indian district and passed the time by watching Indian movies. Allen prepared for India by reading everything he could lay his hands on: sacred texts like the Ramayana and the Mahabharata, the Upanishads, and the Bhagavad Gita, books on Hinduism, the Buddha, Gandhi, and Indus Valley history, and even *Kim*, by Rudyard Kipling.

Now that he was back with Peter, Allen sat on his bed in Nairobi more confused than ever. His trip to India had been stalled, and after months of separation his wonderful reunion with Peter hadn't changed anything between them. Allen stared out the window at the dark African sky wondering what was going wrong with his life. He had been obsessed with having sex with Peter, but now that he was alone with him, he had lost any sexual attraction for him. Peter was playing with his boogers as Allen was writing all this in his journal, not a very romantic image, but his feelings stemmed from more than a physical disgust. Allen concluded that Burroughs had somehow managed to kill his ability to love; whatever it was that made him love people seemed gone. Also at this moment he thought he might have become an atheist. Without faith, he didn't know how to operate in the world. He felt that he was an accident of life, not part of a well-ordered grand scheme. His old depression returned with a vengeance, now fueled by these new questions and new doubts.

They packed their clothes and went back to Mombasa, to stay at the Hydro Hotel for one final week. They checked to be certain their boat would sail on schedule and Allen wrote to Gary to update their rendezvous plans. When their ship arrived in Bombay, Allen and Peter would take a train direct to Delhi and catch Gary and Joanne there around February 18 or 19. Bowles had warned Allen that Indian hotels were dirty and eating in cheap restaurants would be instant death, so Allen had been worried that their money might not last long if they had to upgrade to better accommodations. He was happy to find that the Indian hotels and restaurants in Africa were clean and the Indians who ran them reported the same of India. He included this news in his letter to Gary, telling him with relief that Bowles had been overcautious and they would be able to get along fine even in the least expensive places.

Allen's ability to live on a shoestring and his disdain for the comforts other tourists required enabled him to stretch his travel dollars to the maximum. He did come down with sicknesses like diarrhea, dysentery, and worms quite often, but these inconveniences didn't bother him much. When ill, he would take it easy and nurse himself back to health without worrying about it continually. It left him open to many experiences that the average traveler wouldn't have. On the fifty-dollar voyage to Bombay, they were assigned a space in the crowded hold of the SS *Amra*. Allen counted his blessings by saying that he was glad to be on the upper level of the hold near the hatches where they could get some fresh air. They had planned ahead and brought air mattresses to sleep on, and the food was at least palatable. They were surrounded by six hundred vomiting Indian families, all fleeing East Africa because of the country's upcoming independence, but to Allen this sort of travel was a once-in-a-lifetime thrill, not a voyage to dread. After a week and a half at sea the ship arrived in Bombay.

They docked within sight of the imposing Gate to India monument, the exact spot where the British formally withdrew from the Indian subcontinent in 1947 and gave their colony back to the Indian people. As they walked past the Taj Mahal Hotel, Allen was glad that Bowles had been wrong about the need to stay in more expensive quarters like this, where a room might cost as much as three dollars a day. They had arrived in Bombay with only one dollar left between them in their pockets, but fortunately there was a check from City Lights for the first royalties from *Kaddish and Other Poems* waiting at the American Express office. Allen cashed the check and went across the street to the huge train station to purchase third-class tickets to Delhi. They checked into a cheap hotel for the next two days before leaving on an all-night express train to Delhi.

They had done their homework well and knew how to get around. Instantly, they were thrust into the exotic and it was more exciting than Allen had dreamed possible. Even the air they breathed seemed different, infused with the smells of India herself. On that first train ride they began to sense the enormity of India with its hundreds of millions of people. Allen saw a man cut to bits when a train ran over him, but he also saw that death and human bodies were viewed differently here. At every turn there was something odd or interesting and new experiences and adventures awaited them. India was a world unto itself; the customs and rules of the West were nonexistent here. If he had spiritual and visionary questions and new doubts about faith, they would certainly be answered.

In Delhi they stayed at the Jain Rest House, a dormitory-style building near the Jain Temple in the middle of the old city that was set aside for pilgrims and travelers. They could stay there as long as they wanted and it was practically free, with cheap, simple food provided for the guests. They left messages for Gary and Joanne at American Express, hoping to intercept them before they left for Rishikesh.

Since leaving San Francisco years earlier, Gary Snyder had been studying Buddhism in a Japanese monastery. Fellow poet and friend Joanne Kyger joined Gary there, but since Japanese culture frowned upon couples living together, they decided to simplify things by getting married. They had both been students of Japanese language and culture together in San Francisco, and marriage seemed like a harmless way to share the joys of Japan. By 1962, they needed a vacation and visiting some of the holy sites in India sounded like a good idea. Since they had been in touch with Allen and knew of his travel plans, they decided to hook up with him and tour some of the sacred places together. While Allen and Peter had been stuck in Israel and East Africa, Gary and Joanne had covered a good deal of northern India, making whirlwind visits to places of pilgrimage. Now they were in Delhi for a few days, staying in a Hindi version of a YMCA, which, unknown to Allen and Peter, was only a few blocks away.

A friend from the BBC had given Allen a list of the most important musicians to hear while in India, including Ali Akbar Khan and Chatur Lal. On February 24, Allen looked up Chatur Lal, one of India's greatest tabla players, who invited him to a concert he was giving that night in honor of a thirty-two-year-old man who wished to take a vow of total silence. Shri Krishnaji was a disciple of Meher Baba, a sort of Hindu saint, who had told Krishnaji, "Thru silence the first meeting between man and the mystery of God is accomplished." Krishnaji intended to follow this advice literally and to stop speaking for the rest of his life. For one solid hour, the musicians serenaded him with improvisations, building the music to an amazing tempo and ending in a trancelike frenzy. Allen had never heard classical Indian music like this before and resolved to enjoy as much of it as he could during his trip.

The next day they finally located Gary and Joanne. Allen hadn't seen Gary in six years, and he noted that he looked a bit older, his baby face now gone. Now that he was married, he also seemed to have become more domestic. He spoke simply and directly, which Allen found appealing. After the two couples found each other, they decided to leave Delhi for the Himalayan foothills. Gary did most of the planning, since he had researched the places he wanted to see and people he wanted to meet. It was fun for Allen and Peter to be along for the ride. Joanne had little to say about where they went but was extremely interested in everything they saw and more than happy to be part of the party. From Allen's journals and letters, it is obvious that he focused his attention more on Gary than on Joanne. She was the person who helped make things happen smoothly each day and solved problems as they arose, but on this trip Allen saw her merely as Gary's wife and not as an equal or a writer of any importance. More than thirty years later Joanne wrote about this blind spot in a poem she called "Poison Oak for Allen": "Here I am reading about your trip to India again / with Gary Snyder and Peter Orlovsky. Period. / Who took cover picture of you three / with smart Himalayan mountain backdrop / The bear?"

Their daily routine was strictly one of religious tourists. They each carried guidebooks, which they consulted for every town they visited. They toured as many of the spots as was humanly possible and visited particular holy men and Buddhist and Hindu groups in the vicinity. Staying in cheap rest houses and retreats set aside for pilgrims, they moved quickly but missed

Snyder, Orlovsky, and Ginsberg snapped by Joanne Kyger ~

very little. They also sampled the local drugs whenever they could get them. Morphine was a favorite. It was cheap and they could buy it almost anywhere with no questions asked.

Allen wrote several letters before leaving Delhi, regaling his friends with descriptions of the sights and sounds of India. "India has everything Mexico has, poverty and dead dogs. It has hoods like Morocco and Moslems and shrouds and Indians like worse Bolivias and garbages like Peru and bazaars like Hong Kong's and billions of people like nowhere I seen." It was just what he had hoped to find, "crowded streets full of barbers and street shoe repairmen and bicycle rickshaws and Sikhs in turbans and big happy cows everywhere stealing cabbages from pushcarts."

Their first few weeks were spent in the springtime foothills beneath the backdrop of the high Himalayan mountains. Near Dharmasala they were fortunate to gain an audience with the Dalai Lama, who was in exile from Tibet. Snyder prostrated himself in a formal Buddhist manner befitting the lama's high rank, but Allen didn't have the experience to do it. Gary used his time wisely, questioning the Dalai Lama about breathing exercises and meditation practice. Allen's questions were less spiritual. He asked about peyote and mushroom use by the Tibetan monks; in the years to come, he regretted not taking better advantage of this private audience. Near Nanda Devi they stayed in an ashram, enjoying vegetarian meals and watching the mists rise from the valleys below the snow-capped peaks of the inner mountains on the Tibetan border. They met swamis and lamas in the mountains and Allen began to practice Yoga exercises in the mornings. After meeting Swami Shivananda and observing him murmur "om" every time an American woman came up with a question, Allen classified him as a charlatan of the mass-production international nirvana racket. Gary was wise enough to realize that the important thing about India was that even the fake holy men were, in fact, holy men, and there was something to be learned from each of them. That gave Allen something to ponder during the rest of his trip. The swami gave Allen a little book called *Raja Yoga for Americans* and then handed each one of them a present of five rupees. The next day, Allen returned to ask him where he could find a guru. The swami smiled and touched his heart and advised that the only guru was your own heart: "You'll know your guru when you see him because you'll love him, otherwise don't bother."

They stopped in Rishikesh on the way down from the mountains. The Kumbh Mela, a huge religious festival held every twelve years, was taking place there. Naked *sadhus* (ascetic holy men) had gathered from all over India to bathe in the Ganges as a purification ritual. Hundreds of nude holy men marched by in an endless procession, accompanied by elephants and musicians by the score. Allen had begun to wear traditional Indian Gandhi-style shirts and pants made of white handloom cloth. He tried to forgo meat with his meals, taking vitamin pills to supplement his new vegetarian diet. In a letter, he bragged to his father that he was beginning to look exactly like an Indian native and photos of the period prove him right. His hair was down to his shoulders and he blended in with the local population. The same wasn't true of Peter, though; his lighter hair and red beard, coupled with his muscular physique, made him stand out in the crowds.

It was great to have Gary with them for he was able to answer most of their questions about the Buddhist and Hindi rituals that they saw. He explained things lucidly in a way that Allen could understand and it made all the difference in their introduction to India. By March 19, they had circled back to Delhi, where Allen and Peter visited their first opium den. Allen had been looking forward to it for a long time, and finally they found someone who could take them there. At midnight they walked down a sordid Muslim alley in the oldest part of town to a mustached opium dealer. His job was to tend the flame in a bottle and spin the amber bubble of opium on the tips of iron needles over a pipe through which they smoked. Allen reclined on his left hip on a cozy burlap-covered shelf, his head resting on a brick, and drew in the smoke in the classic fashion. Smoking opium turned out to be the supreme junk delight for him. It was qualitatively better than any other method he had tried. The dreams that opium produced were exactly what Allen was looking for. He woke from the fine, gossamerlike dreams and wrote furiously and then smoked and dreamed again. These successive dreams grew over the evening and culminated about six hours later, when he was back in his hotel room. He experienced a new world, a new dimension of junk, smoother, sweeter, and dreamier, more relaxed, subtler, and stronger than heroin. "I thank the kindly gods who reserved that charming surprise for my middle age," he wrote.

A few days later they left Delhi to visit Jaipur and stayed in another ashram there while touring some of the famous ancient palaces. Allen took morphine a few times and lay on his charpoy to bask in the detachment that the drug afforded him. He felt as if he were standing outside his own life as it rolled along and he surveyed it from afar. He realized that he would soon be thirty-six years old and felt more mortal than ever as he imagined his future death. While he was high, he made a list of the various drugs he had tried and noted that for all his efforts, he had not yet been able to comprehend eternity. He listed his possessions as his knapsack, his literary fame, and all the attendant correspondence stored in his father's basement, nothing more. He mentioned that his sole desire was to be a saint. He couldn't understand why this single aspiration was important enough to him that he'd be willing to suffer for it, though.

Returning to Bombay where Gary and Joanne were to catch a ship back to Japan, they stopped to see the cave temples at Ellora. The several dozen Hindu temples cut out of the solid rock cliff and decorated with fantastic sculptures were the most impressive monuments they had seen yet. Allen only wished he knew more about the iconography of what he was seeing. A few years earlier in New York, he had met a wealthy Indian woman at Dorothy Norman's home. Her name was Pupul Jayakar, a disciple of Krishnamurti and a friend of Indira Gandhi. She directed the India Handloom Industries, a government-run business that sold Indian-made products worldwide. She and her daughter, Radhika, lived in a large house on Malabar Hill, the wealthiest neighborhood in Bombay. She had plenty of extra room and had offered to host Allen if he ever got to India. Her home was true luxury after living in ashrams and sleeping in third-class train compartments for the past months. She had servants who brought them trays of eggs in the morning and tea in the afternoon. Allen relaxed and enjoyed the chance to rest and catch up on his mail before he and Peter set out on the next leg of their journey. Before Gary's departure, he, Allen, and Peter gave a little reading in Bombay, but Joanne was not asked to participate. Before long, Gary and Joanne's boat sailed, leaving Allen and Peter behind for what they expected to be a long Indian retreat.

Allen could never specify what he was looking for in India, but he was glad to be away from the "beat" spotlight. He spent a good deal of time talking to Mrs. Jayakar about marketing Indian musical instruments and clothing through her son's store in New York. Allen believed that young Americans would love the Indian style of loose shirts and pajama pants they made, and he convinced her to promote exactly the type of clothing that became popular later in the 1960s and 1970s. On Malabar Hill, Allen and Peter explored the antique shops that sold Tibetan Buddhist paintings (*thangkas*) picturing various gods and devils. They were inexpensive by American standards and Allen wrote to his family and friends encouraging them to send money so that he could buy these great treasures as investments. He correctly deduced that the *thangkas* were available at that point in history because of the mass Tibetan exodus after the Chinese takeover and he knew their value would increase. He bought a few for himself, but none of his friends had any money to spare for these treasures.

They found one opium den in Bombay, but they were given some bad opium that made them sick and they didn't go back. They found plenty of *charas* (a cannabislike drug) and *bhang* (cannabis mixed with milk as a drink), which was used by the locals for religious purposes. Allen was exuberant about everything and wrote, "India is the greatest nation of earth and wild as it's rumored, everybody's turned on to the cosmos. Peter and I now Hindu worshippers of elephant headed god Ganesha." The press did manage to track Allen down for interviews even in India. It wasn't nearly as intense as New York, but there was still an interest in the beats they couldn't completely escape.

In April while at Jayakar's, Allen heard from Irving Rosenthal that Elise Cowen had jumped from her parents' apartment building window on the first of February. Allen was shocked by her suicide. He felt guilty for not being able to help her; in fact, he had rejected and ignored her more than he cared to remember. As with his mother, he had never been able to break through to her or understand her. He had kept a distance between himself and Elise and felt responsible for much of her depression. A few days after her death, Harry Phipps, one of the rich addicts they had known in Paris, was found dead of an amphetamine overdose in his New York hotel room.

Elise had also been a heavy amphetamine user, and Allen knew that if you took that drug regularly, you were bound to end up either dead or a thin-faced paranoiac nervous wreck. He was all the more frightened because amphetamines (speed) had become Peter's drug of choice by that time.

When Allen wrote to Corso asking him to come to India as he had planned, he mentioned that they had run into Gregory's old love, Hope Savage. She had appeared at their poetry reading talking hypnotically and nervously, not in her right mind. They took her for a meal and showed her around Bombay. She had become disoriented wandering around India alone and envisioned imaginary spy plots and intrigues at every turn. She had been in India much longer than Allen and Peter and had managed to pick up some of the Hindi language. Before they knew it she disappeared back into India as abruptly as she had materialized, without saying goodbye.

Allen also wanted to look up some of the Indian writers he knew. In New York he had met Kushwant Singh and in Bombay he visited him and was introduced to some new poets who were publishing a literary magazine. They had translated some of the material from a recent issue of *Big Table* into the local Marathi language. The poets took Allen and Peter on a long walking tour of the impoverished Bombay whorehouse district, where Peter took his pleasure for only two rupees, just a few pennies. Allen stayed out on the street talking to the transvestite eunuchs who squatted on the littered pavement, camping at passersby with their outlandishly made-up faces. Allen was delighted to see that the police sat at the corner peacefully surveying the scene instead of hassling everybody. Their job was to keep the peace and protect the whores, queers, and customers alike, but Allen didn't realize that they were accepting bribes and profiting by turning their heads.

On another evening they were invited by a friendly stockbroker to his house in the downtown bazaar district. He prepared *bhang* for them to drink and took them to visit a nearby temple to hear Sanskrit chanting and devotional hymns. Allen was fascinated that *bhang* was considered a respectable drug, one used by middle-class devotional cults. The stockbroker's wife had doll-like statues of the baby Krishna and spent hours dressing and playing with them. Everybody in India seemed to be a *sadhu* following his own path, and Allen felt that the Indians were more   Stotras to Kali Destroyer
sophisticated because they let everybody be as crazy as they   of Illusions, *CP*, p. 298
wanted to be.

Morphine was available cheaply without a prescription, and they took full advantage of the easy access to that and other types of drugs. By the beginning of May they had become regulars at an opium den, sometimes smoking as many as sixteen pipes apiece a day. This was way too much opium, in Allen's opinion, but it cost less than a dollar and was hard to resist. One evening while high, he and Peter argued about what actually did happen between them in Tangier. As much as Allen claimed he loved Peter, he certainly wasn't aware of how Burroughs had hurt his companion. It showed that William's views were more important to him than Peter's, something Allen was reluctant to admit. The more Allen looked back, the more he agreed with William's view that cut-ups were a useful method for examining the mind and breaking free of it and found the process similar to many forms of *saddhanas* (pious practices) recommended by Indian sages. He still would not admit that Burroughs was jealous of Peter, though. Peter spent most of his time with Radhika, Pupul Jayakar's daughter, and Allen began to feel lonely again.

On May 6 an article about Allen and Peter appeared in the *Illustrated Weekly of India*. The article called attention to their unconventional attire, pointing out that even for bohemians it was unusual. Then the reporter went on to focus on their goals: "Apparently both Orlovsky and Ginsberg are in search of something which they realize they cannot find in the West. What it is they themselves do not know." On that subject Allen would agree; he wasn't certain what he was looking for in India. For Allen it was first and foremost a good place to avoid the pressure he had put on himself in America. He tried to explain to the reporter that he was traveling to improve his education, not merely to escape life in America, which he admitted he usually found pleasant. He didn't consider himself an expatriate like Paul Bowles, even though he had been away for a long time already. He wrote to Kerouac that the "subjective result on me of India has thus been to start dropping all spiritual activity initiated since Blake voice days and all mental activities I can discard, and stop straining at heaven's door and all that mysticism and drugs and cut-ups and gurus and fears of hells and desire for god and as such." His hope was that before he left India, he'd find out what he had come for.

It took them fifty-two hours to cross the country by train from Bombay to Calcutta. Their plans were to move to the mountains to gain relief from the summer's heat and stay in some of the hill stations as the British colonials had done until cooler weather arrived. But bad news was waiting for Peter in Calcutta. The Veterans Administration bureaucracy informed him that in order to continue receiving his pension checks, he was required to take a sanity exam. If he were sane enough to travel around India, he might

be sane enough to hold down a regular job and therefore not need their assistance any longer. Peter had to stay in Calcutta to complete paperwork and
to make the necessary arrangements to take the test in India, hoping that he
would fail and thus ensure his continued disabled status.

Allen was intent on traveling more and decided to go on alone to Darjeeling near the Nepal/Sikkim border. The mountainous country was exot-
ically beautiful, and Allen saw several marvelous monasteries and passed
Tibetan refugee camps everywhere. He sat in the Ghoom monastery's ancient prayer hall for an hour listening to the monks chanting sutras. The
foggy weather gave him only brief glimpses of the higher peaks, but the
terrain was spectacular. After his passport and most of his money were
stolen in Darjeeling, he could only get a temporary three-day pass to visit
Gangtok in Sikkim. In that short time he was able to meet the head of the
Karma Kagyü order, Gyalwa Karmapa, and witness the Buddhist black
crown ceremony. Without a passport, he couldn't stay any longer, and because of his strained relationship with Peter, he was reluctant to tell him
that he had lost money, so he couldn't ask him to send more. By June 6,
when he got back to Darjeeling, he had begun to feel lonely and homesick
for Peter, and some of the old romantic stirrings returned. He visited another monastery, this one of the Buddhist Nyingmapa sect, and asked the
lama there for *wang* (initiation). Allen talked to him for an hour about his
various visionary experiences, but unfortunately the lama could not accept
him as a pupil, due to his own health problems; he suggested Allen return in
September. Allen explained to Peter that when initiated, you are given your
own mantra (a short verbal formula) and a text to recite while meditating.
It's like being on LSD, Allen explained, when your mind conjures up images
like the ones you see on the *thangkas*. The best advice the lama, Dudjom
Rinpoche, gave Allen was to be careful and not get hung up on visions,
whether beautiful or ugly. "If you see something horrible, don't cling to it.
If you see something beautiful, don't cling to that, either." In later years
Allen regretted he hadn't returned for more instruction that September, as
the lama had suggested.

The problems with the VA were not resolved by the time Allen returned
to Calcutta, and he could be of no help to Peter, as he was stricken with
bronchitis following the change in climate from the cool mountains to the
oppressive humidity near sea level. The streptomycin injections he was given
offered him some relief. Allen spent much of his recuperation writing extensively in his journals. Even though he had all his South American journals
with him and had promised to edit them for Dave Haselwood, he was unable

to muster up any enthusiasm for the project. The weather had become hot and muggy, but he and Peter took it as a challenge to see if they could survive in Calcutta through the most torrid months of the year. They had a room in the Amjadia Hotel, a Muslim-run hotel in one of the poorer neighborhoods of the city. It was centrally located, but it was so filthy that even Allen's Indian friends didn't want to visit him there. The common bathroom in the hall was remembered as a filthy nightmare by most of the people Allen knew, yet Peter and Allen didn't complain. It was not as bad as the Marrakech public restroom he had visited. Their whitewashed room on the top floor overlooked a small mosque down the side street and was among the cheapest in the city, but without Peter's VA check to rely on they were going broke. Conditions were made worse by the garbage piled up on the street during the hot weather. They hoped their shots would protect them from a threatened cholera epidemic. With all these problems, it's difficult to believe that they were enjoying themselves, but they were.

To P.O., *CP*, p. 301

On July 8, for Peter's twenty-ninth birthday, they splurged on dinner at a Chinese restaurant, ordering eggplant and prawns, fish and tomatoes, and pork noodle vegetable soup, all for about forty-four cents. They stopped in at a Chinese opium den for a few pipes and then took a long walk up Chitpur Avenue past the large Muslim mosque. Allen described their walk in such vivid detail in his journals that it is obvious that it was intended to be source material for future poems. The system he had developed, writing down prose snippets and later converting those fragments into poems, seemed to be working well for him. He recorded the minute particulars as they were observed, then the literary shaping could be done later.

Health continued to be a serious problem for Allen. Even though he wrote to his friends that everything was healthy and clean in India, he was suffering through a long litany of illnesses. First he had a slight cold, followed by bronchitis and a touch of fever. Then his arm became swollen, a sure sign of an allergic reaction to the shot of penicillin-streptomycin that the doctor had administered for the bronchitis. Then he had a slight kidney stone attack for which he was given an atropine injection. Then his arm swelled up even more after some tests for allergies. The results from his urine test indicated that he had elevated levels of phosphorus and calcium oxide. All this was followed by a sudden dysentery attack and chronic fatigue. As if all that was not enough, in mid-July he noticed a small bump near his rectum, which he feared might be a hernia. He asked Peter to look at it closer and after checking him out, Peter said, "Uh oh, you got worms."

The next day he went back to the doctor and got some pills, which killed the little white needle-thin parasites. He was moved to write a will then and there, leaving everything he had to Peter in the event of his death. Finally, near the end of July, he said he was feeling better again.

Allen's life didn't seem to be taking on any particular di-   Heat, *CP*, p. 302
rection. As he showed his "Aether" poem to a Bengali poet, Jyoti Datta, he realized how much of his energy he had put into the exploration of his mind through drugs. Now it all felt futile and sad. Hallucinogens had not given him what he was looking for, and he was close to the point of giving them up completely, as the nightmare visions were becoming too frightening and morbid to continue. He and Peter had been smoking a lot of opium, which now began to seem like a waste of time and money. All he had to show for his half year in India were a few rolls of photographs he'd taken of the beggars and cripples in his neighborhood, some of them quite beautiful, but all of them heartbreaking.

Even though they survived the worst of the summer's heat, they were now completely broke and couldn't afford to travel even if they wanted to. Their financial salvation hinged on Peter's VA checks, which they hoped would be reinstated soon. They hadn't received the results of his psychiatric tests yet, but they hoped the VA still considered him too crazy to work. Now that the monsoons had broken the heat wave, they wanted to be on their way again, exploring more of India. As it rained continually, the Calcutta streets became flooded ankle deep with water, and dead rats floated around the huge piles of garbage that were strewn everywhere. Since they intended to stay in India longer, they sent in their applications to extend their visas for another six months. Then they began to plan a move to Benares even if Peter's checks hadn't arrived. Benares was the one city in India that Allen wanted to experience, and if he had to cut his trip short due to lack of money, he didn't want to miss seeing it. Benares was the holiest city in India and had been continuously inhabited longer than any other place on earth.

While marking time in Calcutta in early August, Allen received word from home that his grandmother Buba had died. He was sorry that he hadn't been there to comfort Louis and wrote his father a long letter of sympathy. Their string of bad news was broken the same month when Peter got a call from the U.S. embassy telling him that his veteran's benefits had been approved and a check had arrived. At last they had enough money to pay their meager rent again. To celebrate they treated themselves to liver and heart soup. With the reinstatement of the monthly checks, the rush to

Benares was not as crucial, and they postponed their move for a while. Peter bought an Indian stringed instrument called a sarod with his first check and began to take lessons. By now, they both had hair to their shoulders and wore only Indian-style clothing. Allen liked the bright red and yellow pun-jabis (knee-length shirts made of khadi cloth) and pajama pants for the street. In a letter home Allen described how loony he and Peter looked, but said "everybody here also looks loony so we pass unnoticed more than if we were in slacks and U.S. hair."

Stuck in Calcutta, Allen finished checking the proofs of *Reality Sand-wiches* for City Lights and sent them back to Ferlinghetti. He wanted to include a poem he had begun to write shortly after *Howl* called "The Names" in which he was more specific in his identification

Fragment: The Names
II, *CP*, p. 269

of his friends and their roles in his life, but he thought he should ask each of them for permission to publish it before using their real names. Lucien Carr and Carolyn Cassady objected immediately to having the spotlight focused on them again, and Allen removed the poem from the book without hesitation. There was more than enough work for a good book, and he put it away for several more years.

They also stayed longer in Calcutta because Allen had made a new friend who was showing him another side of the city. Ashok Fakir, who Allen said was "a real great energetic *sadhu* teahead reminds me of Ted Joans with an M. A.," was the first holy man Allen had gotten to know well. Ashok was a thirty-seven-year-old man whom Allen considered one of his "ignus." He had long hair and wore saffron robes and fit the image Allen held of a holy man. All of Ginsberg's Indian friends knew Ashok was phony and hypocriti-cal, but on the other hand Allen remembered Gary's advice that "even the fake holy men are holy men." One day Ashok had appeared in Allen's room at the hotel unannounced and introduced himself. He had been a profes-sional magician, a movie actor, and a politician before he became unem-ployed and homeless. Fakir had selected Ramakrishna[51] as his guru and he carried Vivekenanda's[52] personal copy of a book called the *Raja-Yoga,* which Ashok claimed spoke to him aloud and taught him about Yoga. He said he slept on a park bench for two years listening to the teachings of Muslim fakirs and owls. Then a miracle happened while he was slumped on his park

---

[51] Sri Ramakrishna (1836–86): Indian spiritual leader.
[52] Swami Vivekananda (1863–1902): Disciple of Ramakrishna who founded a religious order in his honor.

bench; he saw Kali's feet pass by right before his eyes and he had been a holy man ever since. Fakir was the sort of intelligent con man Allen found fascinating, like Cassady, Huncke, Du Peru, and many others. He might take advantage of Allen, but he gave something that Allen needed.

Ashok knew all of the holy men in Calcutta, and he took Allen to the burning ghats to meet them. Every Tuesday and Saturday night, the holy men went to the stone steps along the Ganges where bodies are cremated and smoked ganja all night long. They lifted their small red clay chillum pipes to their lips, took mighty draughts of the smoke, and shouted, "Boom Boom Mahadev!" Some of the younger holy men acted as attendants, watching the burning bodies and helping push an arm or a head back onto the burning coals if it fell off. Fat grease bubbled out of the consumed bodies, a particular smell permeated the air, and it was believed to be good luck to inhale the smoke of the burning corpses. Allen considered it one of the most beautiful scenes he had ever witnessed.

He had been to the ghats several times before, but didn't have a local guru to guide him, so he was considered a tourist. It was a thrill for him to talk with the weird half-naked *sadhu*-saints sitting in the ashes of burned bodies smoking ganja. The holy men watched as the bodies burned and the smoke from the fires rolled over their heads as they meditated and occasionally danced to a blind man's drumbeat. Body after body would be brought to the ghats for cremation by families who, instead of being sad as in Western society, were joyous and sang merrily as they watched the body burn. Each family purchased their own pile of wood and the attendant directed them to a particular section on the steps where their pyre was lit and the body burned. Once the body was completely incinerated, the ashes were swept into the Ganges, which in Calcutta was known as the Hoogley River, and the ceremony was officially over. To Allen it seemed like a natural conclusion to life, and he loved the fact that sorrow could be erased by the process.

Everything about the ghats appealed to Allen, from the "tantric" meditation, the holy men, the burning bodies, and the free smoking of pot to his witnessing of the end of suffering and the joyous acceptance of death as a natural part of life. These were all things he had been looking for without knowing it. It was a revelation and he now understood that this was the reason he had come to India. Once introduced to the burning ghats, Allen returned every Tuesday and Saturday night as his stay in Calcutta stretched on.

Allen was surprised to learn that Ashok Fakir had been corresponding with Bertrand Russell, the noted British philosopher and pacifist. Ashok tried to persuade Russell to convert his antibomb sentiments into a crusade to end the threat of nuclear holocaust. At the end of one of his letters to Russell, Ashok handed the paper to Allen for a postscript. Allen added a paragraph in which he asked Russell how people could possibly go about organizing against organization. He could not resist asking Russell's opinion of Blake as well. Surprisingly, Russell responded with a three-page letter to Allen. As a young man Russell had also had a vision similar to Allen's Harlem experience when Russell himself had magically heard Blake's poem "Tiger Tiger" recited aloud. On that occasion Russell had been moved to nearly faint and broke down weeping uncontrollably. He told Allen that the "immediate overwhelming danger is that of nuclear annihilation." He went on to say that he felt all nuclear technology was faulty. "Radar cannot distinguish a goose from a Congressman. It is a problem in elementary mathematical statistics: nuclear war is a matter of statistical near certainty." Allen was grateful that the old philosopher had gone to the trouble to respond to him, but he was disturbed by what he said. He immediately wrote letters to all his friends asking for their opinion about the phrase "nuclear war is a matter of statistical near certainty." If that were true and mankind was doomed, there was no purpose in going on in the face of certain apocalypse. But Russell had added a caveat at the end: "unless we prevent it." Allen wrote to his father, who was always his greatest political confidant, to ask his opinion. "If I thought his figures and reasoning were really correct, I would be inclined to set out to do something," Allen said.

Russell's fears did make sense to Allen, and he was faced with a direct challenge to do something about the imminent danger the world was in. For weeks, nuclear annihilation became the number-one topic on Allen's mind. From India he could see things more clearly. He wondered why only the United States should be right and saved. He felt that the country didn't need to be defended, the world needed to be defended. Either we all would live or we all would die; individual nations didn't really matter. The more he thought about it, the more questions he had. He wondered what difference it made anyway; the universe didn't really need mankind at all to keep on turning. Probably it was not worth organizing for, because Allen believed that organizing brought about other negative things like centralization and power struggles. Organizing against an organization seemed to be a method for replacing one bad thing with another. He requested that Russell send him back precise statistical information that would prove destruction was a "near certainty." Allen had no desire to add to the public hysteria unless it could be proven to him beyond a doubt that the world was on the brink of total annihilation.

As he pondered this problem, he received a letter from Robert Creeley in late September asking him to participate in a poetry conference the following summer in Vancouver, Canada. Creeley, Charles Olson, Robert Duncan, Denise Levertov, and several other poets had promised to participate, and they offered to pay Allen's travel expenses, including an around-the-world ticket. That was a godsend for several reasons. It would give Allen almost another year to stay in India and after the conference he could visit his family in Paterson before he came back. With an open-ended ticket and unlimited stops, he could also visit Moscow at last, see Gary in Japan, look in on Ferlinghetti in San Francisco, and maybe even set foot in Australia, Hawaii, or Tashkent. His mind raced with the names of the places he could visit while circling the globe. Peter was willing to wait in India for Allen's return, where he could continue taking Indian music lessons. Since Peter now had a steady girlfriend, named Manjula, things would be fine with him.

With the promise of a big trip in the future, it was easy for Allen to make good use of the time he had left in Calcutta. He divided his attention between the two cremation spots in the city. One was the Kali ghat in the southern part of town on a small tributary of the Hoogley and the other was the Nimtallah ghat in the north, on the main river above the marvelous Howrah Bridge. The bridge was constructed like a giant toy Erector set and was the only bridge across the wide river for miles and miles. Allen and Peter walked across the engineering wonder many times and observed the flow of humanity back and forth, reminding Allen of a scene out of Chaucer.

At the Nimtallah burning ghat, Allen squatted with the rest of the holy men amid the ashes of the burned bodies. They gathered around piles of devotional flowers and burned incense as they passed chillum pipes from one *sadhu* to another. A few of the older ascetics sat cross-legged in meditation in little alcoves or temple structures for hours on end. Allen respected the idea that there was nothing to fear or to love about death, even though he had experienced both those emotions. It was an important lesson for him to learn. He had heard that inland there were other secret necrophiliac practices, and he wanted to know more about them, but he knew no one with connections to those cults. After living in Calcutta for four months, he was at last beginning to understand some of the religious practices and was reluctant to move on before the Durga-Kali Puja holiday, which would take place in October. It was defined by Allen in a letter as "the worship of the twenty armed avatar of Kali who killed the big bad buffalo demon," and he certainly didn't want to miss that celebration. Every Hindu helped make large papier mâché statues of the gods and set them up in big tents around town. Then they marched in the streets banging drums, gongs, and cymbals and sang and worshipped and drank *bhang* and smoked ganja. The Hindus sat on the pavement all over the city and chanted ragas about Kali, the goddess of destruction, who was often depicted with her necklace of human skulls. After the holiday the images were ceremonially tossed into the river. Calcutta was named after Kali and was the center of Kali worship, so it was by far the best place to observe this festival.

After the holiday was over, Hope Savage caught up with Allen and Peter again and stayed for a few weeks. She had received an expulsion order from the Indian government and Allen helped her write letters to the Home Ministry to contest it. It was unusual for a Western woman to travel alone in India, especially one with no money and no visible means of support. Everyone was suspicious of her and most Indians assumed she was a prostitute. Allen took her to visit one of the *sadhus* who lived in a hut under the Howrah Bridge and there they sat smoking and watching the world. They walked under the great bridge and listened to the cyclonic steel roar over their heads. The *sadhu* told Allen that it was "a great machinery," meaning, he supposed, the universe, not the bridge.

In October, Allen, along with the rest of the world, waited while the Cuban Missile Crisis was played out. President Kennedy had released a report that Soviet missile installations had been discovered in Cuba and he dispatched the navy to blockade the island until the missiles were removed. For several days the world hung on the verge of nuclear war, until October 28, when the two countries reached an agreement that averted disaster. Allen immediately saw the truce as meaning that the Cold War was over and that Bertrand Russell's prediction of a nuclear holocaust was incorrect. As soon as the news broke, Ginsberg, Ashok Fakir, and Shakti Chatterjee, a young poet and member of a beat-inspired group called the Hungry Generation, traveled to Tarapith, a small village about two hundred miles from Calcutta. It was the town where the naked drunken pot-smoking guru Bama Kape had lived during the nineteenth century. It was currently popular as a pilgrimage destination for tantric *sadhus* to study Yoga. They slept on the floor in the house of the temple priest for three days and ate food prepared for the holy men who sat in their red robes and smoked ganja morning to night. The Sanskrit root word for ganja meant knowledge, and Allen was quick to note that the main *saddhana* (study practice) of most of the holy men included smoking ganja. Besides smoking more grass than he ever had in his life, Allen visited the burning ghats of Tarapith and watched the cremation of more bodies, describing it in great detail in his journal. On this trip Allen also began to practice Pranayama Yoga himself. The complete course required several years, but the basic breathing exercises were easy to learn and similar to the method in which pot is inhaled. Allen was delighted with that discovery, but when he found that the full Yoga course required "no outlet of semen and strict diet control and complete solitude," he knew he would never stay the course.

After returning to Calcutta, Allen and Peter used what little money they had to take the train to Konarak and Puri, two towns a few hundred miles south along the Bay of Bengal. They did not want to miss the most famous of the Konarak Hindu temples decorated with erotic sculptures. They had a wonderful time exploring the temples and examining the sculptures up close, and Allen took roll after roll of pictures, trying to capture the uninhibited approach to sex displayed by the early Hindus. He couldn't help but compare Hindi attitudes to the Christian fig leaves that he felt had desecrated the statues in the Vatican. His trip to the Konarak temples was just like visiting an artistic Times Square porn shop, he explained.

Allen spent his free afternoons back in Calcutta hanging out with a group of young literary men. Sunil Ganguli, who had studied in the United States, Shankar Chatterjee, and Shakti Chatterjee met each day at a bohemian coffeehouse near Calcutta University and discussed literature. It turned out that Allen knew more about some Indian writers than they did. He was surprised to find that the Hindi, Bengali, and Marathi poets didn't know much about each other or their work and how divided the poets were by language, custom, and religion within their own country. He enjoyed the friendly camaraderie of the scholarly group but preferred the education he was getting with the holy men at the burning ghats. He was certain that Benares would be the culmination of his Indian education and began to look forward to getting there. On December 10, he bought his train ticket and made his last visit to the Nimtallah ghats via rickshaw as a splurge. There he sat with the ganja smokers for the final time and one familiar old *sadhu* put a red-and-black third eye on his forehead in homage to Kali Ma. Allen shared a box of milk-boiled sweets he had brought as an offering to the holy men in appreciation of their letting him take part in their world. The half moon rose over the busy city and the roar of trams drew his attention once again to the Howrah Bridge in the distance as the large flag of the Will's Gold Flake cigarette factory floated in the breeze.

While packing he began to feel the first familiar discomforts from a urinary tract infection. He knew he'd have to see a doctor as soon as he was settled in Benares. While on the train to Benares after taking a horse cart across the great bridge to the station, he described the mighty roar of the Howrah from the ghats and the images of all the Chaucerian pilgrims moving across the span lined with beggars, lepers, peddlers, fortune-tellers, and astrologers. He debated with himself whether perhaps he should have married Hope to save her from her troubles with the Indian government.

As well as being the oldest and holiest city in India, Benares was untouched by Western culture. For thousands of years people have been living and worshipping on the stone steps that lead down to the Ganges. It was no wonder that Allen found the city intriguing. On his first night, he wandered for hours and hours along the riverfront and visited the Manikarnika burning ghat at midnight under a full moon. Peter and Allen had found a place to stay a few miles away from the Ganges in the Cantonment, an area suburban by Indian standards, but much too far away from the action on the ghats. Within a few days they had found a cheap room for only nine dollars a month on the third floor right above the important Dasaswamedh ghat. Its windows overlooked not only the beggars lined up in the street below, but also some small temples and the river itself only a few hundred feet beyond. Their floor was bare stone and the room had the benefit of nine large French doors that opened onto the north, south, and west sides of the building. Their balcony was screened in by chicken wire for protection against thieving monkeys. The new apartment was about a mile up the river from the Manikarnika ghat, and Allen's daily routine included at least one walk to those ghats. Every day he sat on the stone ledges above the ash sand shelves that were filled with woodpiles and funeral pyres. From the river's edge he liked to watch the cows steal the yellow stalks of straw that were used as kindling for the fires. As it had been in Calcutta, his main occupation several nights each week was to smoke ganja with the holy men and watch the bodies burn.

To furnish their new apartment, Allen and Peter bought a few basic household supplies, like straw mats for the floor and clay pots for storing clean water. They installed a bright hundred-watt light bulb and dangled it in the center of the room so they could read at night. Peter put his statue of the red-bellied Ganesh in one of the alcoves above the door along with their transistor radio and a few other possessions. Then they bought a cook stove for a dollar so Allen could boil potatoes, and before long it began to feel like home. They treated the scene outside on the street below like a wonderful stage show that they watched from their balcony for hours on end. Roaming cows fought with the women selling vegetables, trying to steal spinach and radishes from their open baskets before they could be chased away. Their street was one of the main passageways to the bathing ghats and all morning long thousands of pious Hindus walked past on their way to purify themselves in the Ganges. Dozens of beggars sat in a long row along the side of the street, waiting for a friendly offering from the pilgrims. It was considered good luck to give a few pennies after bathing in the river. In no time at all, Allen and Peter became familiar with the beggars and adopted some of them as their favorites. Every now and then they gave a few extra coins to a black-haired old lady, whom they nicknamed Kali Ma. She sat across from their doorway each day and wrapped herself in a mattress every night, talking to herself like a rooster. Peter was even more generous than Allen and sometimes before he reached the corner of the block he'd given away all his money to the beggars.

Allen made friends with some of the naked *sadhus* who meditated in the little stone dens scattered about on the steps of the Manikarnika ghat. He smoked ganja with them and watched the tourists floating by in rowboats offshore, examining the unusual scene without knowing that one of the bearded holy men was actually an American poet from New Jersey. One of the *sadhus* who befriended Allen was named Shambhu Bharti Baba and when Allen brought his camera one day, Shambhu allowed him to take naked pictures of him, one of which later graced the cover of Allen's *Indian Journals*. After they had been in Benares for a few weeks the police summoned them to their station house to answer questions about their stay in India. It wasn't normal for tourists from America to live in dirty, squalid rooms and hang out with beggars and holy men on the ghats, so they thought they must be up to something. Allen and Peter answered all their questions and things seemed to be straightened out for the moment. Except for continuing bouts of diarrhea and various infections, things were going well for them and Allen seemed content.

At Christmastime they treated themselves to a trip to Agra to see the Taj Mahal. It was such a familiar tourist icon that Allen was ill-prepared for what he saw as the most beautiful building in the world. Its glorious white dome hung in perfect balance in the blue sky. They were able to stay for two nights inside the Taj Mahal itself because it happened to be the anniversary of the death of Shah Jahan's wife, for whom the Taj was built as a tomb. In those days, the tradition was for the Moslem caretakers to leave the doors open all night and invite friends to take part in a big Kawali contest (improvised Urdu poetry singing). Allen slept in his bedroll on the cold stone floor and listened to the poetry and chants that echoed inside the marble structure. He referred to it as the most perfect hotel in the universe, and it felt to him like being in a three-dimensional De Chirico painting. That single experience alone was worth his whole trip to India, he felt. With every letter he wrote home, he increased the hyperbole, naming the building "a giant Martian vibration eternity dome" and the greatest human creation on the planet. Smoking plenty of ganja with the Urdu poets increased the power of the experience, too. They spent a few weeks in the Agra area exploring the abandoned Mogul cities of Fathepur Sikri, Mathura, and finally Brindiban, the birthplace of Krishna. One of the old lady Bhakti (love-faith) saints in Brindiban, a member of a Bhakti Yoga cult there, told Allen to start practicing Bhakti and stop looking for a human guru. If he needed one, he should take Blake as his guru, she advised. She assured him that when the time came a guru would find him. Allen took her advice seriously and wrote, "Key of Blake I now think is acceptance of body, dismissal of all alternative universes and bliss in present love belly, rather than seeking spectral eternity."

He continued to receive his real education at the burning ghat, where he found no social hierarchy and everyone was treated equally (if they had the price of the wood for the funeral pyre). The cremation process functioned as a ritual to help the family of the deceased really see the corpse as the spent shell. When the body was reduced to ashes in front of their eyes, they saw the finality of death and the meaninglessness of the dead body. That body was like "a broken-down old sofa or pillow or meat doll." Allen found it an important, sublime lesson and tried to describe it to everyone he wrote to. Treating the corpse as a treasure, as was done in the West, led to all sorts of unconscious misunderstandings and fantasies about heaven and hell. Thinking of himself as a piece of meat sometimes came in handy to Allen in the years to come. It was a good way to lose one's ego, and a large ego was one of Allen's biggest traits.

1963 ～

BY THE FIRST WEEK of January Allen and Peter were back in Benares and had been visited by another government official. The CID (Central Intelligence Police) wanted to know exactly why they needed to extend their stay in India. The police made extensive notes and left only after interviewing many of their neighbors, which upset everyone.

Allen had still not met his obligation to edit his South American journals, promised more than a year earlier to Auerhahn Books. In fact, he hadn't even begun to transcribe them. It was becoming a millstone around his neck and he wasn't sure he'd ever be able to find the time to get back to the work. In the future he would be more careful about making commitments. Right now at least they had some money from Peter's VA check and a small advance from City Lights for his third book, *Reality Sandwiches*, which was to come out in June. Financially they were in better shape than usual. Vancouver's promised fourteen-hundred-dollar airplane ticket was the only thing he was anticipating in the near future. He was aware that he was stretching his own rule of not taking money for readings, since he was willing to accept their travel check. He rationalized this as the only way he could get back to the United States again to see his family, and he saw no other way to swing it. Peter disagreed with him strongly and felt he was breaking his vow.

Allen did keep his promise when he read and lectured for free at one of India's largest schools, the Benares Hindu University. He had been invited as a guest of a communist student group there, but they were shocked to hear Allen's poems peppered with four-letter words. The students were openly angry at Allen for what they considered his rude and insulting language. Later, when they found out that Allen was considered "kosher" by Moscow standards, they were mystified. Allen was upset that they had invited him to speak without knowing what his poetry was like and then had the nerve to criticize him for doing what he always did. His rudimentary practice of beginner's Yoga enabled him to calm himself. He told Ferlinghetti in a letter that since he'd been doing this, he had become more aware of his bad habit of projecting his own hate onto other people, which backed them into a corner. He wished he could practice Yoga more often, but it required a lot of time. He also wrote that he would have to stop smoking and even cut down on the excitement of letter writing in order to help quiet his nerves. He pledged to himself that he would try to control his temper and diminish the universal mass of hate by not spreading his own frustrations. It would prove a difficult vow to keep, but with the help of his *prahayama* (breathing) exercises, he was sure he could do it. Later, Allen commented that his ability to control his temper better was the best outcome of his Indian visit. This was reflected in his letters home to Louis. Instead of getting angry or throwing a tantrum at his father's political comments, he was able to remain calm. Instead of asserting his own viewpoint all the time, he attempted to understand Louis' point of view. "I wonder to what extent it is possible to totally neutralize emotional violence in environment by total impassivity neutrality indifference/unmoved awareness in self, i.e. not trying to force change on anybody," he wrote. As a personality, Allen was easily excited and was frequently angry when things didn't go his way. But he knew it was a hindrance to understanding and he learned valuable patience and control techniques through his experience in India.

In late January Allen and Peter both left Benares for three days to see the *sadhu mela*, where one hundred thousand holy men came to bathe in the Yamuna River at the point where it joins the Ganges near Allahabad. It was yet another impressive display of Indian faith. Returning from his latest pilgrimage, Allen received a message from the Indian government tourist bureau. An American photographer from *Esquire* wanted to do a story about Allen in Benares for the magazine. Allen couldn't see any harm in it, so for two days they visited all the local points of interest with the photographer, who took a thousand color photos of Allen bathing in the Ganges and smoking ganja with the *sadhus*. Later a reporter was scheduled to visit to write the

Ginsberg in India ~

text to accompany the photographs. Allen recommended that they send Kerouac to cover the story, but someone else was assigned. Probably due to the photographer's interest, a CID agent began to lurk about their building, talking to Allen's neighbors again and spreading weird rumors. Manjula became upset and complained to the local police, but that didn't stop the surveillance. One day Allen and Peter grabbed the agent and marched him off to the CID office, where they demanded an explanation from his superiors, but the authorities double-talked their way through the explanation and pronounced the inspector overzealous. The neighbors told Allen that it was the police's way of getting *baksheesh* (bribe money) from him, but Allen wasn't convinced that it was that simple. This surveillance could have occurred because of the attention that *Esquire* was drawing to them, or it might have been because Peter's Indian girlfriend often stayed overnight, or maybe it was because the communist students at the university had complained about Allen's obscene poetry. There were several days of uncertainty, and the timing couldn't have been worse. Since Allen's visa was due to expire on February 15, he needed a special dispensation to have it renewed for another six months. The next thing he knew the government rejected his application and stated that he should "leave India [at the] earliest possible time."

Describe: The Rain on
Dasaswamedh Ghat, CP,
p. 303

Allen wasn't ready to leave India and he certainly wasn't about to be forced out of the country without knowing exactly why. He had already made plans to visit cities in the south near Madras over the next few months and then fly to Vancouver for the poetry conference in the summer. Eventually he wanted to return to India where Peter would be waiting with Manjula. They decided to fight the expulsion order and get to the bottom of the bureaucratic red tape. It was useless to try to pursue the case in a provincial town like Benares, so Allen wrote to a few friends in Delhi, especially Pupul Jayakar, who had political connections. He took the train to visit the central CID office there in the early part of March. Fortunately, the American embassy, the *Times of India*, the old Gandhian groups, and the Congress for Cultural Freedom were all able to vouch for Allen, and he was allowed to remain until June. Peter's visa was extended until August, but basically the government wanted them out of the country after that and no further negotiations seemed likely. The CID saved face by saying that they hadn't understood that Allen was in India on "an intellectual level," and at last they were able to place him into the correct pigeonhole.

Allen learned later what had prompted the expulsion order. The students at the Hindu University where Allen spoke had felt that he had insulted the head of their English Department with his obscene reading and they had sent a copy of *Howl* to the CID with all the offending words underlined. They had also suggested that Allen might be a CIA agent. The CID couldn't imagine any other reason why two poets would want to remain so long in India, and further imagined that they must be Chinese-imperialist spies drinking whiskey with Indian girls in bad neighborhoods while distributing pamphlets to incite the populace. This experience reinforced Allen's most recent notion that he should do everything in his power to disarm conflicts instead of fanning the flames by confrontation, as he had at the Hindu University. He was fortunate to have friends like Pupul in the government who were able to intercede on his behalf so he didn't get into any serious trouble. In Delhi, Allen had gotten a close look at the enormous bureaucracy of India and could understand why the country was starving and could do nothing to reverse centuries-old social patterns.

On March 8, while still fighting with the secret police over their visa extensions, Allen and Peter took another risk by participating in the Delhi-

Peking Peace March. They walked for a day with the World Peace Brigade as it passed through Benares. The march was organized to pressure the governments of India and China to cease hostilities and stop their border war. Allen believed the marchers to be the only peacefully sane people around. Elsewhere in India people were digging trenches for defense works and stoning the windows of Chinese restaurants, provoked by loudspeakers blaring messages of hate and nationalist propaganda in favor of war with China. It all seemed out of harmony in a country filled with holy men at every turn.

News arrived from New Jersey that William Carlos Williams was dead. It was not a shock to Allen, who knew Dr. Williams had been in declining health for years, but he was sad that he would not have the chance to see him again. Sitting at Williams's kitchen table, talking about poetry, had been a formative experience for him. He walked quietly under the trees on the Hindu University campus to the home of a German instructor he knew to read the obituary in *Time* magazine.

Death News, *CP*, p. 305

In India Peter retreated into drugs even more than he had in New York. He smoked increasing amounts of opium in Calcutta and shot even more morphine once he got to Benares. He retained his interest in mastering the sarod and began taking Indian singing lessons, but he and Allen were discovering that they had little in common. It seemed that the pair had been on divergent paths ever since they had met. Peter made his own friends with some local musicians and they often came over and sat around on their mats, drinking tea and reading Peter's copies of *Playboy*. Allen kept to himself much of the time and busied himself by catching up with his unending flow of correspondence. Instead of sharing harder drugs with Peter, Allen preferred to go to the ghats to watch the burning corpses while he got high with the naked holy men on the much less harmful ganja. The pot helped put an end to much of his anxiety about death, the major preoccupation of his adult life, but it didn't bring him and Peter any closer together.

In the spring Peter decided to marry Manjula, so that she would be able to emigrate to the United States. It was to be a technical marriage for whatever period seemed respectable and after enough time had elapsed, they could be divorced and she could retain her American citizenship. Allen wrote to his brother asking him for his legal opinion of such a marriage and how Peter should proceed. Eugene discouraged the idea and told them that getting American citizenship wasn't as easy as it once had been, so Peter and Manjula abandoned that idea. Although they seemed to be going their separate ways, Peter continued to support Allen on his monthly VA checks, and Allen found himself completely out of reserve funds once again. The next hurdle for their visa renewal was a request by the government that Allen and Peter prove that they both had enough money to leave the country, when the time came. Allen wrote to Creeley asking him to hurry and send the round-trip airplane ticket for Vancouver. That would provide proof that he had the means to come and go as he pleased. Peter stalled his paperwork hoping that he could save enough money to prove he could afford to leave. He never succeeded, so an Indian friend of his signed a note promising to pay for his airfare home, in case of sickness or emergency.

In the meantime, Allen and Peter had noticed that one of the beggars on the street across from their building was extremely ill, and they had been watching the man waste away for more than a week. Allen described him in a letter as "a skeleton-like Buchenwald looking man stick long arms legs and ass brown pelvic-bony no meat, bleeding arm wounds, covered with flies and obviously dying. Still breathing tonight, I gave him milk." Several times they had given food to starving beggars only to find them dead a few days later. This time they decided to give special attention to this one man among the millions of the starving masses and nurse him back to health themselves. They found him lying in a fetal position in the gutter that hundreds of people used as a public toilet. Peter and Allen carried him to the Ganges, washed him, and fed him slowly. Then they hired an orphan boy to care for him and keep him clean. Peter knew the basics of care from his days as a hospital orderly, and he supervised. After a few days of this slow feeding they took him to a doctor, who said his illness was nothing but starvation, and slowly, with their help, the man regained his strength. It was a heartwarming effort, and for a few pennies, Allen and Peter were able to save one of the victims of India's streets. Allen realized that if he stayed on in India he would have to do something practical about the problem of hunger, but he also realized that the old man was only one in a nation of starving people.

Peter stayed behind to nurse the man while Allen traveled to the Buddhist sites in Bihar and Bodh Gaya. For hours Allen sat under Buddha's bo tree and talked to the funny *sadhu* who slept underneath it at night. While in Bodh Gaya, Allen discovered the Buddhist design of three fish that share a single head, which he would adopt as his personal logo. In Rajgir he visited the site of the first Buddhist theological councils and saw the hot springs and the earlier fifth-century B.C. walls of kind King Ashok's city before he moved

Buddhist fish logo as drawn
by Harry Smith ~

on to Nalanda, the site of the ancient university that influenced Tibetan
Buddhism so greatly. After that he went to Rajagriha and climbed up Vulture
Peak Gridhakuta where Buddha had lived with Ananda.
From there he went to Patna for a few more days of sight-

Vulture Peak: Grid-
hakuta Hill, *CP*, p. 3o6

seeing and visiting friends before returning to Benares in late

Patna-Benares Express,
CP, p. 3o8

April.

With Peter's constant care, the beggar had become
much stronger by then and was able to speak a little. His tongue had been
cut out by the Muslims during partition, but still he could be somewhat
understood. Miraculously, Allen and Peter sneaked him into a hospital,
where he regained much of his strength. A Hindu postal clerk who had
watched them curiously as they were taking care of the poor man was able
to get his family's address and wrote to them about his condition. On May
5 they received a letter from the family in the Punjab, a thousand miles
away, saying that he'd disappeared six months earlier and they had been
looking for him ever since. They thanked everyone for their help and sent
his brother to collect him and take him home to his elderly mother. This
entire experience gave Allen an education into the corruption of the health
and welfare system in India, where a few pennies a day could save a dying
man, but the bureaucracy was too large and inefficient to function at all.
Their money was nearly exhausted through this modest generosity, so they
were relieved when a gift of one hundred dollars arrived from Allen's translator Nanda Pivano. It was a sum large enough to feed several more starving beggars for months. Allen wrote that if he stayed in India he'd organize

a Schweitzer[53] brigade to help the street people. It was disheartening when one of the orange-robed *vedanta sadhus* connected with a conservative Hindu group on the same block accosted Allen and criticized him for helping. He felt that Allen had committed a sin by saving the man's life and interfering in things that did not concern him. Allen agreed with the man and told him that he couldn't help it and asked him to pray for him, but the man said, "Your sins are too big." At that moment Allen realized that he had in fact become responsible for this beggar, and without Allen he would die. He wouldn't have known how to handle the situation he had created through his act of mercy. Fortunately, the problem was solved by getting him into the hospital and discovering his family, who took him home and off Allen's hands.

Allen's return from Bodh Gaya coincided with a noticeable deterioration in his relationship with Peter. Peter had shaved his head while Allen was away and was unwelcoming and silent, determined to live apart as soon as he could find his own place. He moved to a cheaper room in an old cobblestone alley in Bengali Tola, a neighborhood closer to his sarod teacher. Peter began acting nearly as mute as his brother Julius and gave only short, curt answers to anything Allen asked. They quarreled severely one night while he was high on morphine and Peter told Allen in no uncertain terms that he was washed up. He felt that Allen was breaking his word about public readings and had sold out for the price of the airplane ticket to Vancouver. Allen agreed with him to some extent, but it forced their parting to be melancholic and strained. Allen was left alone in the bare whitewashed room above Dasaswamedh ghat with only the monkeys as company. He was reminded of the time he said farewell to the hallway at the Union Theological Seminary twenty years earlier, when he first met Lucien and Jack, and now felt that another chapter in his life was about to close.

At dawn on May 20 Allen awoke to the sound of the usual rickshaw bells in the street below and went to take his last bath in the Ganges. He was going to miss being able to run downstairs wearing only a loincloth to take a dip in the cool river whenever he was hot and sweating. Peter stopped by to take Allen to the train station and say goodbye and Allen wrote him a note as soon as he got to Calcutta, "That was a nice look you gave me at RR station. I always feel bad to part from you if we're cold to each other, and I feel happy

---

[53] Albert Schweitzer (1875–1965): French humanitarian who worked with the poor in Africa, earning the Nobel Peace Prize in 1952.

to be alone when I know there's still a little tender look between us left over in eternity." Allen's kidney had been acting up again, but he felt better as he rode the train to Calcutta where he hoped his airfare would be waiting. He was looking forward to his around-the-world travels and had a dozen different ideas about where he'd go first. The heat was returning to Benares and before long, travel in central India would be agony during the hot dusty summer. If the money for the ticket was there, he'd have time to stop in Cambodia, Burma, Vietnam, and Japan, but as the weeks dragged on in Calcutta, no money arrived.

Allen stayed with his friends there, saw a doctor about his kidney problems, and marked time. He had reservations for a flight scheduled to leave on Sunday, May 26, for Bangkok, but it was beginning to look as if the check might not arrive and he wouldn't have the money to go anywhere. On May 22, thinking about his departure, he wrote the poem "Last Night in Calcutta." Finally on May 24, the Vancouver check arrived in the nick of time and Allen spent the next day writing his final letters from India.

Last Night in Calcutta, *CP*, p. 309

On May 26, as planned, Allen left India and flew to Thailand. By now he was a seasoned traveler and knew what he wanted to do and how to do it even in the most exotic of places. He was happy to find that in Bangkok there were plenty of nineteen-year-old Chinese boys willing to go to his hotel room with him for a dollar or two. He had been all but celibate in India for the last year and a half, and he indulged himself a few times right away. Afterward the boys stuck to him like adhesive tape and he couldn't shake them. It was somewhat like Tangier in that respect, but the boys were more polite. While in Bangkok, he also broke his abstinence from meat. After nearly a year of vegetarianism, he gorged himself on duck and pork in the great Chinese restaurants he found there. Armed with his guidebook, he visited all the sights and then met a few artists and writers who showed him other parts of the city. Allen was sorry that he didn't have time to stay longer, but he was scheduled on a May 31 flight to Saigon early in the morning and there was plenty he wanted to see there.

He spent four days in the capital of South Vietnam, which was just beginning to experience the U.S. military buildup that would grow into the all-consuming Vietnam War. Allen dropped into the U.S. embassy and noted his conversation with a U.S. information officer for the State Department. He was told

Understand That This Is a Dream, *CP*, p. 311

that the "U.S. regards the civil war as an internal issue" and that "we will do everything possible to keep from being enmeshed in internal political infighting." Allen was not reassured by those comments and wrote that he had butterflies in his stomach the whole time he was in South Vietnam. He met several reporters from *Newsweek, Time,* and the *New York Times* through Neal Sheehan, a man he knew from the United Press. They briefed him on the actual inside story of the war. Allen described being in Saigon at the time as walking around "in a mescaline nightmare." The reporters volunteered to make arrangements for Allen to fly inland and see model hamlets and army battles, but Allen was frightened by it all. The newsmen were so bored waiting for something to happen that the day Allen left Saigon, they concocted a story that ran in the *New York Times* under the headline "Buddhists Find a Beatnik 'Spy.'" They reported that Allen, because of his unusual long-haired, bearded appearance, was mistaken for a spy by the local Buddhists who were in a struggle against the U.S.-backed government of South Vietnam. Of course none of it was true, but it made a colorful story. Since it was on permanent record in the *New York Times,* Allen spent his whole life denying the story.

After Vietnam, Allen was glad to get to peaceful Angkor Wat, an enormous area of temple ruins in Cambodia the size of a small city. He bicycled around the ruins and examined the sculptures and bas-reliefs, which had been overgrown by the jungle. On his final day in Cambodia, Allen wrote a long poem in his notebook called *Angkor Wat,* which sounded the
Angkor Wat, *CP,* p. 314 beginning of a new fertile period of poetry for him. The following day he was on an airplane bound for Japan to visit Gary Snyder. The first things Allen saw of Japan were tiny blue streetlights thirty thousand feet below him along the coastline, reminding him of a string of fireflies. He touched down at 11:00 P.M. and quickly discovered that, compared to India, Japan was expensive. Hotels in Tokyo cost five or ten dollars a night, so instead of spending money he didn't have, Allen gathered up some cardboard and slept in front of the railroad station. He caught the early morning train for the seven-hour ride to Kyoto.

As soon as he arrived he went straight to Gary and Joanne's house. To Allen, Japan was like a modern, glistening dreamworld. Everything was clean, the trains ran on time and were not crowded, even the dogs were well-fed, not bony and flea-bitten as were the strays in Calcutta. He was exhausted from his trip and spent his first twenty hours in bed sleeping and recuperating. No sooner had he gotten his strength back than he began writing letters. Gary was holding a stack of mail for him, and he answered most of it as quickly as he could. He found that he had to explain to everyone that the article from Saigon in the *Times* was all fabrication. Another clipping he saw had quoted Ferlinghetti as saying that Allen was the greatest living poet, and Allen wrote to ask him not to repeat that. He thought it was a big-hearted gesture on Lawrence's part, but since he was heading for Vancouver to see Duncan, Levertov, Creeley, and Olson, he didn't want to face poets he respected as the "greatest" anything. In fact, Allen wasn't even certain that he was a good poet anymore. His trip had left him feeling completely inadequate and out of touch.

Within a few days of his arrival, Allen immersed himself in Snyder's world of Japanese culture. One evening he took his first sitting meditation practice with Gary, spending two and a half hours cross-legged on the floor. His ankles began to hurt from the unusual position but he persisted, wanting to learn more about breathing from his belly. He noted the calm, quiet, silent atmosphere in the Buddhist meditation hall, where every bow and movement meant something. It was much simpler than the complicated Hindu methods he had tried to learn in India. The rules were to keep your back straight and balance by crossing your legs, focus on your breath, and when your mind wandered concentrate on your stomach-breathing. He was amazed that with someone to teach him correctly he learned more about sitting in a few days than he had in more than a year in India. He was able to enjoy himself as he hadn't in several years, due to all the aggravation of traveling on a tight budget. It felt good to be there, "Gary very soft and playful and Joanne cooks meals and irons laundry, no big Hindu anxieties, everything neat and nobody starving on streets," he wrote, without noticing that the women around him might be more than merely cooks and housekeepers.

Gary and Joanne were pleased to show Allen around, so they went on picnics to see rice fields and teahouses that reminded Allen of the misty, rainy landscapes of Japanese paintings. They had a rock garden in the yard and a mat room in their little house where Allen enjoyed sitting and daydreaming. In early July they took a four-hour train to the Sea of Japan with its pebble beaches and razor-sharp rocks. With snorkels and masks they swam around nude in the refreshing clear water. Once he went out at night alone to visit some of the queer bars in Kyoto and got drunk. He enjoyed looking at the sexy young people but found no willing partners. He realized that in India he had been badly depressed by all the poverty of his surroundings and here it felt good to have that weight lifted.

On his last evening in Kyoto, Allen found himself in bed with Joanne and "all of a sudden I dug Joanne since it was all right for me to feel what anyway I felt, I want a woman wife lady, I want life not death," he explained in a letter to Kerouac. A change had come over Allen in Japan. He found that his short stay catalyzed and precipitated everything that he had been absorbing in India. He felt as if he was being turned inside out. He decided that his search for visions and death, the classical decision to be or not to be, had been a colossal waste of time. What was going to happen would happen regardless. He also wrote that he had discovered a hidden longing for women, and he felt liberated at last when he realized that "all hearts were right if they were true."

On the express train to Tokyo Allen was overcome with emotion and broke down crying in what he described as an "exalted open state." He wrote poetry the whole trip, confident that something good always came from writing while he wept. He called the poem "The Change," because it was exactly the moment when he felt that everything that happened in his life from that point on would be different. "In my train seat I renounce my power, so that I do live I will die," he began. It was also to be the first important poem he wrote with a new conscious understanding of the importance of breath to the length of his line. He followed the traditional mantric-pranayamic-belly-breathing cycle and hoped his readers would experience the sense of self and identity in their own bodies through breathing and cast off the metaphysical confusion of mental worlds. If read aloud, the poem was designed to cause the reader to exercise that same breathing pattern. The second section, in fact, was one big long sigh, "OH."

The Change:
Kyoto–Tokyo Express,
CP, p. 332

Allen had slowly come to the belief that the keys to a person's life were already within each individual. Drugs could sometimes be used as catalysts to trigger self-realization, but self-realization was always there. Now he felt that all the chemically induced mental worlds he had explored in the past were vampire images that sucked inspiration and energy away from him and were not connected to his inner feelings at all. In his letters he began to advise his friends to stick with themselves, to bare their own feelings to the point of crying and not to be deluded into seeking the self through the mind mirrors of drugs. Junk might feel good, but the same good feeling was possible without it in your soul, he said, when the flesh body is allowed to weep and love. He advised John Wieners to "take care of yourself like a baby should be took care of. Others will too."

He spent a couple of quiet days in Tokyo digesting all that he had thought about on the Kyoto-Tokyo Express. One night he went to a dreary party with some expatriate Americans, and he spent an afternoon with Ruth Witt-Diamant, who was visiting from San Francisco. The closest he got to sex was being aroused in the public baths when a pretty girl washed him. Tokyo was only a short stopover on his way to the July 21 Vancouver Poetry Conference.

When Allen arrived back in the West he was in such a fragile emotional state that he said he ended up weeping and softly touching everyone he met for the next few months. He was quite a sight to see with his long dark hair and scraggly beard, his Indian garb and beads. He was surprised to discover how much he loved teaching the students at the conference. Although Allen's trip to India hadn't been very spiritual, as he acknowledged several times in his *Indian Journals,* he had encountered teachers and teachings that would influence him for the rest of his life. In Vancouver his spirits seemed to be lifted every time he sang the Hari Krishna mantra. No one had ever heard such chanting, and he began to practice it at every opportunity. Allen's definition of a mantra was a short magic prayer that was designed to have a holy effect on the person chanting it. He knew that certain mantras, when repeated in ritual, could indeed regulate a person's breathing in such a way as to cause a temporary physical change. The Vancouver Poetry Conference became one of the first times that mantras were chanted by a group of non-Hindus in North America.

Glad to be back in the West, Allen experienced newfound admiration and respect for the other poets at the conference. He reunited with Duncan and was delighted to meet Olson, whom he found to be a great and kind man. Even Levertov surprised him with her ability to open up when she read a long poem about her cunt. Allen preached his own version of free love to his students and wished Peter were with him to illustrate nakedness at readings. He encouraged everyone to go skinny-dipping in the surf. Drummond Hadley, a young poet just beginning to write, was at the conference and met Allen for the first time, impressing him with his uncontrived ability to instantly communicate directly and deeply. To Peter he wrote enthusiastically about the conference, "I'm telling you the cold war's over, Hurrah! All we got to do is really love each other."

After the Vancouver conference, Allen was still reluctant to commit to any more public poetry readings, and he asked his brother, Eugene, to cancel plans for a giant reading in New York with Kerouac and Corso. Allen said that he had nothing new to read and continued steadfast in his resolve not to read on demand for money. Even without scheduled readings, he was faced with a heavy workload before his eventual return to India. Following the conference, he drove to San Francisco with Phil Whalen and settled into Ferlinghetti's attic on Potrero Hill to work on the proofs of *Reality Sandwiches.* When Lucien Carr learned that Allen was back in the country, he hopped on the next plane with another friend, Lois Sorrells, and flew out to San Francisco to see him. They had quite a wild week, and Lawrence's wife, Kirby, had to ask them to leave in order to restore peace to her home. Lucien moved down the street to the house of an eccentric neighbor for the rest of the visit. Allen told Lucien that he had gotten what he wanted from the gurus in India, "namely my own face." Slowly Allen realized that there was no use in going back to India; the work he needed to do was in the West.

The enthusiastic reception that Allen found among the poets and students in Vancouver continued in San Francisco, and he basked in the admiration of his poetic peers. He wrote to Creeley, "All well here and soul of Vancouver continues uninterrupted. Whalen suddenly started jumping! galvanized! McClure radiant!" Things in America looked more interesting to him now. He even had the intermittent urge to make it with women.

As usual, Allen was down to his last dollar when he arrived in San Francisco, but once again some unexpected money came his way. His old friend Robert Frank, who had filmed him in *Pull My Daisy* a few years earlier, now wanted to film a movie version of *Kaddish*. He had financial backing from a wealthy patron and was able to offer Allen a nice hourly wage to work on the script for the film. The screenplay would require a few months of his attention and enable Allen to replenish his bank account. On September 9, Frank arrived in San Francisco to work with Allen on the movie. As it turned out, Frank wasn't able to raise enough money to complete the project, but Allen did get paid for the work he did, so he was happy and solvent again. The film that Robert made instead was finished in 1965 and was titled *Me and My Brother*, a personal look at the Orlovsky brothers.

Now temporarily settled in California, Allen made the rounds visiting his old friends. Neal Cassady was out of jail, divorced from Carolyn, and seemed much sadder. One of Allen's top priorities was to help Neal edit his autobiography, *The First Third*, for City Lights. By coincidence, Neal was living in the same house on Gough Street where Allen had first seen LaVigne's painting of Peter and fallen in love a decade earlier. Now the house was occupied by other friends, who gave Allen one of the empty rooms near the old kitchen stove where he and Peter had once sat getting to know each other. Neal had a room just down the hall with a new girlfriend, Anne Murphy. Dave Haselwood of Auerhahn Press was living upstairs. Allen was embarrassed because he hadn't begun to work on the South American journals for Haselwood as he had promised years ago, but he speculated that he might now have the time to attack it. Michael McClure was there, too, and introduced Allen to Charles Plymell, a twenty-eight-year-old poet from Kansas, who was living in yet another room in the house. Allen got to know him well and ended up in bed with Plymell and a few girls. He thought Plymell had a great sense of humor and liked the poetry magazine *Now* that he was editing. In bed with soulful Plymell, Allen commented that he was "again plunged bewildered into childish bliss." Tempted by the promise of a new romance, Allen decided to hang around for a while. His personal challenge was to keep himself balanced and have the solitude to write poetry. On the one hand he wanted to stay out of the public eye, but on the other hand, he enjoyed chanting Hari Krishna everywhere to growing audiences. He was thrilled to find that his listeners responded enthusiastically to his chants, so he was torn between the pleasures that fame brought him and the solitude he knew he needed. After Vancouver, Allen's private and public lives became one and the same. He was soon in the business of being Allen Ginsberg again, and in many ways this was the result of a conscious decision he made at that time. He was determined to break down the distinction between public and private demeanor and display the same frankness and inspiration in public that was usually reserved for private encounters. In public he found that many people display a more polite, formal manner than they do with close friends. He saw that as schizophrenic behavior and never wanted to project any kind of "act."

Peter, who was still in India, wrote to ask Allen to help him raise the money for his airfare home to the United States. Before Allen could reply, he received a second letter, on October 5, in which Peter outlined his new plan to travel overland through Pakistan and Turkey to Europe and then fly back from there. Allen missed Peter dearly and hoped that when they were reunited, things would work out better. He sent Peter what little money he had, along with an admonition to stop taking so many drugs. They were "no substitute for love," Allen said, vaguely reminiscent of Naomi's last message to him.

While Allen waited for Peter's return, he settled into his big carpeted room and set up a large round kitchen table as a desk. Then he rented a typewriter with the intention of getting down to serious work. Since Neal couldn't sit down long enough to write, Allen borrowed Ferlinghetti's tape recorder to record Cassady's oral memories. It took Neal a while, but slowly he developed a flow and began dictating. Even though Allen felt that Neal was wasting too much of his time at the horse races, he hoped they'd get the book done, eventually.

Even though Robert Frank had given Allen the assignment to make a working film script out of *Kaddish*, Allen didn't have the faintest idea how to go about it. He did like the idea of having complete artistic freedom on the project, however. He envisioned filming orgy scenes with men and women in his old Berkeley cottage, madhouse scenes and collages of old Chaplin-Hitler newsreels cutting in and out of scenes of his mother's hospital hysterias. Plotting it all out in detail became painful work for him. As a film, he felt it might turn out to be personally embarrassing, and he understood at last how Louis must have felt when Allen used their private family stories in *Kaddish*.

That fall Allen heard from Calcutta that six of the poets of the Hungry Generation had been arrested: Malay Roy Choudhury, Debi Ray, Samir Roy Choudhury, Saileswar Ghose, Subhas Ghose, and Pradip Choudhury. They were charged with conspiring to produce and distribute an obscene book, which was an anthology of their writings. Allen felt responsible, because of the example he had set, which had gotten these poets into trouble in their own country. He wrote letters to Indian officials and did what he could from afar. Malay spent time in jail, but the others were soon released. It reminded Allen that he and Peter could have gotten into much greater trouble with the secret police than they did had it not been for his political friends. News from Corso was also troubling. He had a serious drug habit by now, one that he would never truly be able to break. Allen wrote advising him to lay off the drugs and surprise himself by finding out how nice the universe was when you were straight. This was easy advice for Allen to give, but impossible for an addict to follow.

On October 30, Madame Nhu, the wife of South Vietnam's chief of the secret police, Ngo Dinh Nhu, was scheduled to be in San Francisco. She was widely considered to be the country's de facto first lady, every bit as bloodthirsty and ruthless as her husband. Allen made his own picket sign and for the first time went to a demonstration to protest the U.S.-backed regime in Vietnam. He constructed his sign in LaVigne's studio using a large sheet of cardboard and gold and silver paint. The placard read in part, "War is Black Magic, Satan Go Home," and he added a red, white, and blue drawing of the three Buddhist fish with one head symbol that he had discovered in India. Along with a small group of demonstrators, he picketed in front of the posh Palace Hotel where Mrs. Nhu was staying. Little notice was given to this protest by the media, but over the next decade, the demonstrations against the Vietnam War grew into a movement that eventually divided America for a generation.

The following month Allen felt it was time to get back to New York. His relationship with Charlie Plymell had fallen apart and Allen couldn't figure out exactly what had happened. Allen was interested in Charlie, but Charlie seemed to believe that Allen was trying to steal his girlfriend. He became jealous whenever the two were around each other, which Allen attributed to paranoia caused by Plymell's smoking too much grass. Neal was distracted and distant, too. He picked up a job recapping tires for a garage on Van Ness and could spend only an occasional hour or two each week on the *First Third* manuscript, so work had been progressing slowly. Allen gave a reading with McClure and Whalen as a benefit for Auerhahn Press, but otherwise he shied away from public readings. Additionally, after several years of travel, he was look-

Nov. 23, 1963: Alone, *CP*, p. 341

ing forward to seeing his family again. By the end of October, Peter had crossed the English Channel and would be getting back to New York City around the same time that Allen came home.

Peter's trip back from India had been a real adventure. In June he looked at the price of boats to Singapore, Hong Kong, and Japan, but the rates were so high that he had decided to go overland by train to pick up a cheap flight to New York from England. In September he left India for Tehran via bus and train and ended up giving away most of his money as bribes to border police along the way. From Tehran it took him days to get to the Turkish border, and then by train he headed for England, where he waited for his next VA check to pay for the final leg of his trip. Allen's flight got him back to New York a few days after Peter got home and the following afternoon Allen went to Peter's mother's house to see him for the first time in six months. They reunited tearfully. Peter was so happy to be back home that they never talked about their arguments and breakup in Benares. They seemed committed to staying together in spite of their basic differences.

1 9 6 4 ～

UNTIL ALLEN AND PETER could find a place of their own, they stayed with Ted Wilentz in the apartment over his Eighth Street Bookstore in the Village. It was a nice, central location and most of Allen's mail was being forwarded to the store anyway so it was convenient. Allen's first mission was to visit Kerouac. It had been more than two years since they had last seen each other, and many things had happened to them in the interim. Jack's mother still loathed Ginsberg, so Allen found himself hiding once more in the bushes outside Jack's house while Peter knocked on the door to invite him out. Mrs. Kerouac saw through their ruse and wouldn't even let Peter talk to Jack. It was obvious to them that Jack was lurking inside but didn't have the courage or the will to rebel against his mother's edict. Loyal as always, Allen wouldn't entertain the thought that maybe Jack just didn't want to see him.

Why Is God Love, Jack?, CP, p. 343
In Allen's mind, it had to be Jack's mother who kept them apart, so they rode the train back to the city without talking to Kerouac at all. Allen called from the city several times during the following weeks, but Mrs. Kerouac refused to take his messages and hung up on him each time he telephoned.

Around the Village that winter, Allen heard a lot about a young folk singer by the name of Bob Dylan. Allen had first listened to his records in San Francisco and played some of them for Peter as soon as he got back into the country. It wasn't only the music that impressed Allen, but Dylan's lyrics as well. He thought the song "Masters of War" was almost a cowboy version of Blake; in fact, Allen said he wept the first time he heard it. It was clear to him that "a torch had been passed to another generation" in music. One night shortly after they moved in, Wilentz threw a welcome home party for Allen and Peter and invited Al Aronowitz, the *New York Post* reporter who had written the long series sympathetic to the beats a few years earlier. Aronowitz brought Dylan along as his guest especially to meet Allen. The beat writers had made a big impression on Dylan while he was growing up in Minnesota, and he looked forward to meeting one of his literary heroes. Before the party, Dylan had received an award from the Emergency Civil Liberties Committee and during his acceptance speech had made it a point to say that his songs were not meant to be political. He declared independence from all political allegiances, which upset many on the committee, but the statement intrigued Allen. The two talked about poetry and politics, and about how poetry should be a reflection of the mind, independent of politics. Dylan also told Allen that Kerouac's *Mexico City Blues* had "tuned him into American poetry" in a way that nothing else had, and nothing could have made Allen happier. That night, they became fast friends, Allen later told an interviewer. "He invited me to go out with him and see how he worked, so we went to Princeton for a concert he gave there. There was a photographer there who took photos that he used on the back of his album, *Bringing It All Back Home.* It has a picture of me, without a beard, wearing a funny top hat." Dylan repaid that visit by going to one of Allen's infrequent readings at NYU. He stood unnoticed in the back, watching as Allen and Peter improvised some poems onstage and chanted Indian mantras.

In the middle of January, Peter found a four-room apartment for thirty-five dollars a month at 704 East Fifth Street, in a badly run-down, drug-dealer-infested neighborhood. The rooms were on the top floor of a walk-up that was in terrible condition, so Peter spent most of the next few weeks painting and fixing it up while Allen tended to his paperwork. The nicest thing about the space was the view of the towers of lower Manhattan from their windows. They furnished their new apartment with discarded furniture and rugs that they found on the street and Allen built his own desk using two sawhorses as supports for a large piece of plywood. At last when he hung the oriental scrolls he had brought back from India, it began to feel like home. For the first time they had their own telephone, OR3-3638, which seemed to never stop ringing, and for the next thirty years was Allen's link with the rest of the world.

Morning, *CP*, p. 345

Allen's long-range plans were to spend a year or so in New York getting caught up on various publishing projects, then visit Russia, the one important country he hadn't seen yet. His work as the unofficial agent for his growing circle of writer-friends continued, even though it seemed endless at times. Now he was searching for a publisher for Huncke's manuscript and needed to find outlets for the posthumous writings of Elise Cowen and Alden Van Buskirk as well. He had promised to write the introduction for a collection of Ray Bremser's poems, and Irving Rosenthal's semifictional memoir, *Sheeper*, was a book that Allen considered a modern underground classic. He wanted to do his best to place that book, too.

In Allen's opinion, Peter was doing just fine, even though he had been walking around the wintry city in nothing but a light summer jacket and sandals. Allen chalked it up to his hot Russian blood, no different from the Polar Bear Club members who took dips in the midwinter ocean. He couldn't see that it was a sign that something might be wrong. Allen and Robert Frank were still making progress on the *Kaddish* film project. They managed to complete nearly a hundred pages before Frank lost his backer and had to put the script aside. Unexpectedly, another film commission came Allen's way from producers George Foster and Bob Booker. They offered him a fortune, three thousand dollars, to write a short ten-minute film treatment for a big-budget Hollywood movie they were developing. That was more than enough money for Allen and Peter to live comfortably on for a whole year, so Allen put aside his aversion to writing on demand and accepted the commission. By now he knew the basics of scriptwriting from working with Frank, and in a short time he produced a treatment called "Don't Go Away Mad." In the end, that film, like Robert Frank's, never came to fruition, but a book entitled *Pardon Me, Sir, But Is My Eye Hurting Your Elbow?* containing Allen's piece was published and Allen received the fee.

By the mid-1960s, the Lower East Side had become the new Hollywood for underground filmmakers, who were finding that handheld movie cameras made their work affordable. Most of their creations were individual artworks produced on a shoestring outside the framework of polite society. The filmmakers were attracted to the cheap rents of the East Village, and before long Allen was appearing in more than his share of the new films. It was a thrilling period for avant-garde cinema, with excitement and parties and tragedies that paralleled the poetry renaissance of the 1950s. Filmmakers like Jonas Mekas, Harry Smith, Barbara Rubin, and Andy Warhol were creating little masterpieces in lofts all over the neighborhood and Allen came to know most of them. Although he acted in many of the movies, film appears to be the one art form that he never tried himself.

Right around the corner from Allen's new apartment was the Peace Eye Bookstore. It had already become the underground headquarters for a new generation of literate bohemians by the time Allen got back to New York. Younger people were hard at work transforming the introspective ideas of the writers of the 1950s into the political activism of the next generation. Peace Eye was run by Ed Sanders, a young classics scholar who had a flair for bringing people and ideas together. He used humor and imagination to re-shape politics from a dry, unexciting subject into energetic street theater. It was Ginsberg, always networking, who gave Sanders a copy of William Burroughs's outrageous routine "Roosevelt After Inauguration," which several editors had considered unpublishable. It was exactly the kind of thing that Sanders had been publishing in his own irreverent magazine, which he called *Fuck You, A Magazine of the Arts*. Without hesitation, Sanders published the piece as a chapbook under the Fuck You Press label, complete with a cover drawn by Ginsberg. The Peace Eye Bookstore became Allen's second office, and both Allen and Peter contributed work to Sanders's magazine as well as making countless suggestions for other poets, too.

That winter things were beginning to pulsate in New York City. From Lenny Bruce's arrest to the trial of the Living Theater group, everything seemed to be happening at the same time. In early 1964, artistic creativity seemed to be under attack from the conservative establishment, and the artists rallied to support one another. Each day brought a new, exciting event and Allen wanted to see and do it all. The government's reaction to the new artistic avant-garde was the same as it had been nearly a decade earlier in San Francisco when Ferlinghetti first published *Howl*. The city fathers made every effort to silence them and censor their works, and things were beginning to percolate at about the time when Allen arrived. On December 9, 1963, the New York License Department suspended operations at the Pocket Theater for allowing the Pocket Film Society to show questionable films without the state censor's seal of approval. A few days later, the same department closed down a showing of *The Flower Thief* by filmmaker Ron Rice. Then, on February 17, 1964, the authorities closed the Gramercy Arts Theater. Jack Smith's *Flaming Creatures*, a forty-five-minute film that pushed the boundaries of gay and transvestite flamboyance to the limits, was seized at the New Bowery Theater on March 3. Quickly, the court ruled the movie obscene, which cast a pall over the efforts of the whole underground film community.

On January 30, Allen wrote to New York City district attorney Robert Morgenthau, on behalf of the founders of the Living Theater, Julian Beck and Judith Malina. The government was preparing the legal case against them, and a grand jury had been convened to investigate. An eleven-count felony indictment had been issued for impeding federal officers as they tried to shut down the Living Theater for IRS violations. Allen hoped that he could intercede to prevent a lengthy and expensive court battle. It was the first time that he tried to apply the principles he had learned in India to preserve the dignity of his opponent. Typical of Allen, he didn't beat around the bush. He directly asked the DA if he had any legitimate grievances against the Living Theater or if all he wanted to do was silence their radical political activity. There was no stopping the wheels of justice in this particular case. In May the trial of Beck and Malina began, and by early June they had been found guilty and fined twenty-five hundred dollars.

So far the crackdown had been aimed solely at movies and plays that charged an admission, but then the city expanded its attack to include coffeehouses where poetry readings were being given without charge. On February 10, the Le Metro Café on Second Avenue received a summons charging it with operating without a cabaret license. Obviously, the city's new tactic was to force the coffeehouses out of business by treating them as nightclubs. The cafés were told that they now needed an expensive cabaret license in order to remain open. A coffeehouse couldn't afford the fee for the expensive license unless it began charging admission to the poetry readings or sold something more than ten-cent cups of coffee. The local poets, led by Allen and some others, decided to take a stand and fight it out with the city. To show support for the coffeehouses, Allen's father came in from Paterson and gave a benefit father-son reading with Allen to raise money for legal fees. It was the first time the two had ever read together, and they had a great time. Even though his father's poetry was old-fashioned by sixties standards, Allen was proud of him and appreciated his support for their cause. A group of poets led by Ed Sanders, Paul Blackburn, and Allen created a formal committee to politick against the closing of the coffeehouses via the cabaret license requirement. Activists like Diane di Prima and several other poets lent their support by staging a number of benefit readings at various venues all around town. Quickly, they expanded their mission to include support of the underground film theaters that were also under attack from the city. Quoting Allen's words to Ferlinghetti, all hell was breaking loose in New York. "I'm in middle of struggle with license dept. on poetry reading in coffeehouses, now Jonas Mekas been arrested twice, once for showing *Flaming Creatures* and once for showing Genet film." In spite of, or maybe because of, the threats from a repressive city administration, it was a great period to be living on the Lower East Side. The communal excitement of the artists and their creative spirit and freedom of expression were inspirational to Allen, who hadn't seen anything like it since his San Francisco poetry renaissance days. He spent lots of time with Sanders at the Peace Eye Bookstore preparing defense strategies against the new wave of censorship. They planned a major reading at NYU in April to pay for the coffeehouse lawyers, and the ACLU also volunteered to enter the fray in support of the coffeehouse poets. There was considerable hope that they would prevail.

Waking in New York,
part 1, *CP*, p. 347

Allen toyed with the idea of naming his new defense group the First American Church of Poetry, but instead settled on the Committee On Poetry, or COP for short. Several poets got together to form a reading committee to coordinate all the benefit readings and events for the cause, and a visiting committee that included Sanders, Jackson MacLow, Harold Dicker, and Paul Blackburn was put together to lobby support from city agencies. They stood on their First Amendment rights when they appealed to the lawmakers to permit them free readings of poetry on a noncommercial basis. Allen calmly asked the city to allow him the freedom to sit and talk with his fellow poets in public places without annoyance, as it was the very essence of his craft. The committee made the rounds, going directly to the mayor's office as well as to the cultural commissioner before stopping in to see their local congressman, Ed Koch, who was sympathetic to their cause. They methodically enlisted the support of every coffeehouse and theater owner and set up a plan of action. Henry Stern, the city council member-at-large, shared his honest insider's knowledge about the reasons behind the crackdowns. He said that the city was reacting to the "mess" made on MacDougal Street, when each weekend the area was flooded with thousands of kids going to all the coffee shops and clogging the streets, creating noise and havoc. That congestion and disruption was the original practical problem that had precipitated the government's crackdown, Stern said.

Allen became so involved in the struggle that he began to feel more like a politician than a poet. Nevertheless, he thrived on the debate and came up with dozens of ideas he wanted to implement to solve the problems. When Robert LaVigne came to town he stayed with Allen and Peter temporarily, but Allen found he was too busy with his committee work to spend much time with him. Stan Brakhage visited to show his *Dog Star Man* movies at underground film venues like the Charles Theater on Avenue B, and Allen spent more time with him since his films were related to the current COP struggle. Remarkably, on April 3, the poets won their case and the License Department agreed to stop issuing summonses to coffeehouses for hosting noncommercial art and poetry scenes. The key to this positive outcome was Allen's insistence that the poets appeal peacefully to Mayor Wagner, instead of acting with anger and threats as was their usual response to restriction and suppression.

Allen's private life was not going as well as his public work at the time. He wrote to Snyder in Japan, "Here in NY with Peter still no resolve the sex confusions and timidities but at least I know where I am." Kerouac, living quietly with his mother on Long Island, wasn't the least bit interested in the new bohemia being forged in Manhattan and remained incommunicado. Allen had only seen him once since he came back from India, but on May 11 Allen received a phone call from Jack in the middle of the night. Jack was drunk as usual and when he began to spout the same old accusations against Jews, Allen cut him off. Generally, Allen would have been more patient and extended the greatest degree of tolerance to his friend, but he was fed up with Jack's anti-Semitic remarks and his extremist views. The more political Allen became, the more conservative was Jack's reaction against him. This time Allen decided to scream back at him, which seemed to snap Kerouac out of his tirade for the moment.

Waking in New York, part 2, *CP*, p. 348

Allen was nearly forty now and realized that working with younger people on the coffeehouse case had given him new energy. He met Harry Fainlight hanging around the Peace Eye Bookshop. Harry was a young English poet whom Allen called a "Cambridge grad urinal queen." Allen thought Fainlight was a mixture of Hart Crane and Constantine Cavafy (the Greek/Egyptian poet) with a bit of the Lower East Side thrown in. They hung out together for a while talking about poetry, police, and politics. With the success of his Committee On Poetry in New York, Allen received requests from around the country to help fight censorship in other places. An art gallery in San Francisco had been closed by the police, poetry readings in Wichita were stopped, and even Allen's own poems were being censored again in new anthologies and translations. Allen was being drawn into the role of elder spokesman for the new avant-garde, and he was both flattered and distressed by the prospect. He wanted to help as much as he could, but he worried that he wouldn't be able to balance the political activism with his own writing.

After Yeats, *CP*, p. 351

As a spokesperson for a new media-oriented generation, Allen's bearded image began to appear regularly on the pages of magazines and newspapers around the country and his fame spread well beyond the narrow confines of the world of poetry. The high-fashion portrait photographer Richard Avedon took a series of pictures of Allen and Peter nude, one of which Robert

Frank even considered Avedon's best photo ever. That same photo appeared as a controversial subway advertisement for the new "underground" cultural magazine called *Evergreen Review,* published by Barney Rosset at Grove Press. The picture showed the two middle-aged men naked with their arms around each other, quite shocking in 1964 America. Allen literally became the poster child for the new subculture and attracted both praise and criticism by his high-profile exposure. The reactions to all this publicity were mixed. When John Hersey responded to a request from the National Institute of Arts and Letters to give five hundred dollars to Allen, he reluctantly agreed. "I'd be happier about saying this if the mail that brought the copy of his appeal hadn't also brought a copy of a very slick book by Avedon and James Baldwin with a grotesque picture of our needy poet in the nude." The Stonewall riots that ignited the gay liberation movement were a few years away and the country was not yet ready to see a photo of two bearded males hugging each other in the buff.

After the coffeehouse case was decided, Allen realized that there were other causes that could be supported by COP, and he decided to keep it going as an umbrella action group for future needy cases. The next battle to be fought by it was for the defense of the comedian Lenny Bruce. He had been arrested for allegedly making obscene comments during his nightclub act, and Allen wrote an open letter in support of Bruce's First Amendment rights. In mid-June when he mailed a COP petition in support of Lenny Bruce to attorney Richard Kuh of the DA's office, he included his own beard, which he had cut off as a protest. Allen said that snipping off his beard had been a spiritual bribe so that Kuh would look at the petition in a friendly way. It is hard to imagine the lawyer being pleased when he opened the envelope full of Allen's hair. Privately, Allen didn't respect Kuh, whom he described as a "40-year-old bachelor freak-out artist ex-liberal psychopath with a hang-up on 'The Law' like Javert in *Les Miserables.*" Allen's petition did little to help Lenny Bruce, whose troubles continued to mount every time he opened his mouth onstage.

In June, Neal Cassady arrived in town at the wheel of an old school bus carrying a wild and motley group of fifteen people all armed with movie cameras. The Merry Pranksters, as the LSD devotees called themselves, had driven across the country led and funded by the novelist Ken Kesey. Corso and LaVigne were already living in Allen's apartment at the time, and Neal and Ken could only stay in town a week. They were there trying to get a major movie producer to sign a contract for a film about Kesey's journeys. Jack even came to Allen's apartment one evening for a rare visit, and they all

Cassady at the wheel of Kesey's bus, June 1964 ~

ended up at a party given in a wealthy patron's home on the Upper East Side. Jack and Neal did not have much to say to each other that day. They had long since gone their separate ways and had little in common except their memories. Jack was interested in almost nothing except drinking, while Neal was dedicated to taking speed. Politically, Kerouac was a staunch supporter of Barry Goldwater, who was then running for president, and he saw no problem with the growing U.S. involvement in Vietnam. There were no arguments at the party, but it was not the happy reunion that Allen had expected. The only incident that Allen bothered to note in his journal was Jack's respectfully and correctly folding an American flag that someone had draped over the back of a sofa to be used as a blanket. That evening was to be the last time Jack saw Neal alive. After visiting the World's Fair in Flushing Meadows, the Merry Pranksters drove on to Millbrook, New York, where Timothy Leary, by now fired from Harvard, had established a commune to explore the limits of LSD and other psychedelic drugs less scientifically. Allen went along on that leg of their trip before returning to the city a few days later.

With his usual enthusiasm, Allen quit smoking again in early June. In a letter he wrote optimistically, "I quit smoking 45 hours ago and seem to have that habit licked," but his resolve lasted only a little longer than it took to write the letter. Since he was not accepting fees for his readings, Allen was having difficulty paying his bills and any extra money always went into COP to help various causes. He began to apply for whatever grants and emergency money he could get, but that process was getting to be time consuming and fruitless. When thieves broke into the apartment and stole his typewriter, he didn't even have the funds to replace it. Fortunately, his Italian translator, Nanda Pivano, and her husband, Ettore Sottsass, sent him a brand-new Olivetti to replace the purloined machine.

During the worst of the summer's heat, Peter's brother Julius was released from the Central Islip State Hospital after twelve years. He had been completely silent for most of that time, but once in their apartment for a few weeks, he began to talk. Not only did he speak, but he began to talk a blue streak. He had been as silent as Bartleby the Scrivener, but Allen attributed that to the medications, such as Thorazine, they had given him. Now, free of those drugs, he was like a big kid, full of questions. He wanted to know what an encephalograph was and who Kennedy was and what year it was. His curiosity was boundless. For a few weeks, this new domestic situation took up more of Allen's time than the recent coffee shop petitions had.

I Am a Victim of Telephone, *CP*, p. 352

Allen was happy to realize that he could still remain sexually close to Peter if he participated in group sex with Peter and at least one woman. Group sex seemed to be the best solution for Allen, since he loved straight men so much. Even if a young man was unwilling to get into bed with Allen alone, he might be willing to wind up naked with him if there were one or two women involved. Then during love play Allen could focus his attentions on the man instead of the woman. None of Allen's psychoanalysts in the future were ever able to determine why straight men appealed to him so much. The fact remained that he was usually more attracted to heterosexual men and by comparison seemed to have less interest in homosexual partners.

Today, *CP*, p. 353

One of their new underground filmmaker friends, nineteen-year-old Barbara Rubin, took part in some of these sexual free-for-alls. Rubin was more interested in Allen than Peter, though, which was unusual. As a Long Island teenager she had been shy and chubby and considered something of an oddball. Her parents, seeing her as a misfit, put her in the care of well-meaning psychoanalysts. Their strategy was to help her by changing her. She soon discovered that if she wanted out of their clutches, all she had to do was act the way they wanted her to. When the doctors released her with a supply of diet pills to help her lose weight, she soon discovered that she could get quite high by taking several of them at a time. With the recommendation of an uncle who was an art critic, Barbara got a job with Jonas Mekas at the Filmmaker's Cooperative, and by the time she met Allen she was making films of her own. Her first movie, *Christmas On Earth,* gained her an underground reputation and caused a scandal wherever it was shown due to its erotic content. Even before she met Allen she had already toured Europe with her film. She wore her hair short under a turban, dressed in odd scraps of clothing held together by safety pins, and adorned herself with tons of cheap Indian and costume jewelry.

Before long Rubin moved into Allen's apartment, aggressively took over the space, and began planning her life with Allen. She said she wanted to have twelve children by a dozen different famous men, and the first of these was to be Allen. The apartment became quite chaotic with five or six people living in three and a half rooms, exactly the nightmare Allen had hoped to avoid. Now, in addition to Peter's current girlfriend, a great beauty named Annie Buchanan, Allen had one of his own. He confided to Snyder at the time that he had learned the BIG heterosexual secret. All he had to do was lie back passively and let a woman make love to him from nipples to knees. After that stimulation he didn't have any trouble getting it up and screwing her. Since he always preferred men, he could not be the aggressor and instigate sex as he believed a man was supposed to do with a woman, but as long as the woman understood he needed a lot of foreplay to get him aroused, he was okay. Meanwhile there was plenty of group sex to preoccupy everyone in the house.

That August, Cardinal Spellman established a citywide antipornography committee with Mayor Wagner as chairman. Allen was concerned that this was a step backward and that ground would be lost in the struggle for free speech. He increased the number of benefit readings he gave and tried to get more people involved in actively fighting censorship. At each of those performances Allen started by chanting the Hari Krishna mantra for five or ten minutes, usually the first exposure most people in his audience had to mantras.

By October, Allen was convinced that there truly was a sexual revolution taking place. Not only in his own apartment, but all over the country there were groups forming to alter and enlarge the basic family unit and indulge in a freer, less inhibited approach to sex. Everybody was making it with everybody else, sometimes even in huge orgies, as Allen had been encouraging since Vancouver. The downside was that the more open people were about it, the more likely they were to earn the wrath of the conservatives.

In his own neighborhood, Allen found the Kerista group on Suffolk Street to be one of the most interesting of the new open societies. Kerista was a utopian free-love/pothead group that had been around since 1956, led by a charismatic, bearded Whitmanic figure named Brother Jud. Jud had seen visions himself and had been told by an angel that he should establish a paradise of love on the Lower East Side. One day, out of curiosity, Allen went there with Peter and Barbara, and found what he called "a happy Eden of young pot smokers mixed with some paranoid ex-amphetamine types." They all dreamed of retreating to an island where they could live naked and make it among themselves. Most of the members dressed in a postbeatnik fashion with long hair and basic black clothing and many were interested in hip things like Sartre and jazz.

One of the younger members, a sprightly girl named Rose Feliu, didn't know who Allen was, but he hit it off with her at once and invited her to his place. Rose sat on his lap and teased him about his beard as if he were an old uncle, and Allen dubbed her Rosebud, a name that stuck. Rosebud was even more intrigued by Barbara and her dynamism than she was by Allen, so the following day she dropped into the apartment to visit. Not much later, on October 16, the police raided Kerista and a dozen members were arrested on marijuana charges. Rosebud escaped and wound up barefoot at Allen's door asking for shelter. With her was a cute young man, also from the commune, named Stephen Bornstein, whom Allen liked immediately. Rosebud stayed with them, and even though Allen wound up in bed with her a few times, it was Stephen he was truly interested in, and he helped him move into a dilapidated apartment across the hall. In fact, one of the things that Allen liked most about Rosebud was that she was cute and attracted a lot of handsome young men to the house. He liked the whole idea of Kerista and saw in it signs of a coming change in sexual consciousness. The fact that they practiced ideas like free love instead of only talking about them was appealing to him. Through COP he helped the group find a lawyer to represent them.

Barbara and Rosebud became the best of friends and went on a secret mission together to transform society by uniting all the artists they could find. Barbara's unique talent was her ability to make introductions among people who would stimulate each other's creativity. They saw their network as a big spiderweb that they hoped would grow and influence people from every artistic discipline. Early on, Barbara recognized that musicians like the Beatles were the ones most capable of influencing the largest number of people, so rock stars became her heroes. One of her new friends was Angus MacLise, a musician and poet who was forming a band he called the Velvet Underground. Barbara and Rosebud sat for hours on end in the apartment of another band member, John Cale, listening to the new group rehearse. Rubin's plan was to introduce them to Andy Warhol, whom she knew through her role as an underground filmmaker. So one night she dragged him down to the Café Bizarre in the Village to hear the Velvet Underground perform. Warhol instantly fell in love with the group's sound and style and made the necessary introductions for them to become the house band at a Ukrainian dance hall on St. Mark's Place called The Dom. One evening, Barbara and Rosebud, desperate to dance, went into Le Metro Café and dragged Allen around the corner to The Dom. Ed Sanders, Tuli Kupferberg, a Warhol protégé named Gerry Malanga, and a whole entourage of poets followed and the place caught on quickly. Just as Barbara hoped, Warhol's Factory people mingled with the poets, and a new movement began in which music, art, and poetry were combined. Out of this union came rock venues like the Balloon Farm, later the Electric Circus, and suddenly the East Village became the New York center of the 1960s psychedelic rock 'n' roll scene.

One evening at the Café Metro with Bob Dylan, Allen complimented his music and told him he hadn't realized how accomplished he was with his lyrics, "good as a poet," Allen said. Dylan quickly replied that he was not a poet. "I don't believe in their terms," he told Allen, but the line between poetry and music was fading. A few months after Allen met Ed Sanders, Ed joined with Tuli Kupferberg and Ken Weaver to form a satiric rock group called the Fugs. They combined their talents as poets with a desire to play music in an irreverent manner that attracted interest from the younger generation. Allen spent his weekends at The Dom, now turned into a giant Beatles jukebox of sound, with huge happy crowds coming from all parts of the city to dance. He felt the new music was a breakthrough that was destined to change society once and for all and paraphrased Plato, who had said, "When the mode of the music changes the walls of the city shake."

Allen was so swept up in these developments that he no longer had time to sit and meditate or even write poetry. Since it seemed Allen could not escape his evolving public life to work on more mundane matters, he hired Marshall Clements to help him type his Indian journals. It was now his plan to offer those journals to Dave Haselwood in place of the long-postponed South American journals. The Indian notebooks seemed more pertinent to what was happening in 1964, especially after his revelations on the Kyoto-Tokyo train as recorded in "The Change." The work would have proceeded more quickly if his typist had been able to read his nearly illegible handwriting. The experimental trial of working with a secretary was successful, and Allen realized that with secretarial help he could put books together and have time left for other concerns.

As work on the *Indian Journals* progressed Allen was unofficially invited to Harvard to be a guest lecturer at Lowell House and give a reading there. On his way to Boston with Peter he wrote in his journal that he was no longer in love with Dick Davalos, or with Lance Henrickson (one of the men he had met on his second trip to Tangier), nor even with Rimbaud. Those infatuations were all behind him. Now his consciousness was being consumed by the Beatles. Allen spent the next three weeks in Cambridge and performed four readings in the Boston area. They were kicked out of Lowell House when Peter read his "Sex Experiment #1," which was nothing but a detailed description of Peter masturbating Allen. Later they redeemed themselves by giving a great reading on campus. The *Harvard Crimson* referred to their political-psychic act as a First Amendment battle for "more ample standards of behavior." The fact that Allen slept with several of their students on the trip no doubt made the Harvard administration a bit nervous. By now his readings always started with mantra chanting during which he accompanied himself on a harmonium they had brought back from India. Allen's reading at Brandeis was professionally recorded by Atlantic Records. It was one of the rare occasions on which he agreed to read the complete text of *Kaddish*, and Jerry Wexler, a producer for Atlantic, wanted to issue that poem as a complete seventy-minute album. When they got back home, they found that their apartment had once again been burgled by the neighborhood meth freaks. This time they lost all their paintings and wall scrolls from India as well as Allen's new Olivetti.

The invitations to appear on college campuses continued to pour in, and Allen urged Peter to go with him and read his poetry, too. They read at Columbia with the Umbra Group of black poets,[54] and that time it was Peter who surprised the crowd by stripping down to his undershorts. By now it was expected that the beats would shock their audiences, and people were disappointed if something outrageous didn't happen. In December, William Burroughs came to New York, his first visit in more than a decade. After a short trip to St. Louis to do a story for a magazine, he returned to stay in New York for the next nine months. When Allen went to visit him at the Chelsea

[54] Umbra Group: Black activist group of poets consisting of Albert Hynes, William and Charles Patterson, N. H. Pritchard, Ishmael Reed, and Roland Snellings that was active in the early 1960s.

Hotel he seemed gentle and showed no trace of the anger and obsession he had exhibited in Tangier. Peter was wary of him and chose not to go along with Allen. They didn't get to see much of each other because Allen was in the midst of making plans for his next foreign trip. He had been invited to judge a literary contest in Cuba, all expenses paid. Haydee Santamaria, the director of the Casa De Las Americas in Havana, was aware that Allen wanted to visit Cuba and had orchestrated the tour. Cuba was on the list of forbidden destinations for Americans, so Allen had to exert special efforts to have the State Department issue him the proper visas and permits. His lawyers were forced to threaten an injunction against the State Department in Washington to get his clearance papers. At the last minute, permission was granted on January 7, 1965. Allen went alone because there was no chance he could obtain either clearance or money for Peter to accompany him.

1965 ～

TWO LAST COMMITMENTS were to be met before Allen left for Cuba on January 15. On January 10, he and Ed Sanders led a second march in front of the Women's House of Detention in the Village in support of the legalization of marijuana. A few weeks earlier Sanders had formed a group called Lemar (LEgalize MARijuana) aimed at beginning a dialogue to legalize pot. Lemar's goal was to remove marijuana from the domain of the narcotics department since it was not a narcotic. The first demonstration had been staged in front of the Welfare Department at the Christodora Building on Avenue B, around the corner from Sanders's Peace Eye Bookstore. About a dozen people picketed the building, choosing it because it was the only government office in their neighborhood. It was an impromptu affair with no press coverage, and no photos were taken. The *Village Voice* heard about the picketing and wanted to run an article about legalizing marijuana so they asked the group to restage the demonstration for the press. Lemar took full advantage of the opportunity for publicity and on a cold, snowy winter's day, another small group gathered at the Women's House of Detention with placards that read "Pot is a Reality Kick" and "Pot is Fun."

Allen had also promised to appear at the obscenity trial of *Naked Lunch* in Boston. He flew there the following day to testify with Norman Mailer at the request of Ed de Grazia, the lawyer working on behalf of Burroughs's publisher. Grove Press had finally published the book in March 1962 yet it had been banned in Boston. The judge found the book obscene even though Mailer, Ginsberg, John Ciardi, and a host of college professors had testified to its outstanding literary value. The following year a higher court reversed that decision, making it one of the last censorship battles to be fought in the country during the 1960s.

Allen continued to lobby for the legalization of pot by appearing on the Barry Farber radio show and then did a television interview with Joan Konner the night before he left for Cuba. With these efforts behind him, he thought he would be able to relax and enjoy a peaceful vacation, far away from political headaches. He slumped back in his seat and spent most of the flight to Mexico City writing a long letter to Sanders outlining Lemar's position papers and petitions. Allen felt their suit had been short on facts and the signers to their petitions had not been influential enough to make an impact. In the future they needed greater professionalism, so Allen began making lists of contacts and resources to consult as soon as he returned. If it was within his power, he would have marijuana legalized before the end of the new year, he said.

The previous year of political skirmishes had exhausted Allen. He had been invited to stay with Margaret Randall, the editor of *El Corno Emplumado*, at her home in Mexico City, and he was looking forward to it, but as soon as he arrived, he collapsed in bed with the grip. He stayed there on his back for three days even though he wanted to revisit some of the haunts that he had frequented with William, Jack, Lucien, Garver, and poor dead Joan. Mexico City still had that beautiful funky smell of "Mex Tabac and detritus and tropic earth perfume" that he remembered and at night the same green lamps lit Alameda Park, but he couldn't enjoy it on this occasion. He felt as if he were living in another lifetime now, far removed from the old one, which had become a distant memory.

On January 18 Allen was feeling well enough to take the short flight to Cuba. He had set foot there only once before for a few hours back in 1953, long before Castro's revolution had changed everything. Cuba had become what he called a place of "Marxist Historical Revolutionary Futurity with Wagnerian Overtones." At last he would be able to see a socialist society firsthand, and he was looking forward to it with enthusiastic optimism. A limousine met him to drive him to the Hotel Havana Riviera, where he stowed his bag and walked out into the night air to begin exploring the city. He took a bus to La Rampa, the center of Havana's nightlife, and by coincidence bumped into three boys who had been trying to contact him at the hotel. They whisked him off to a nearly empty nightclub in Vedado to meet several more friends and share a bottle of rum. The boys complained to Allen about the government's crackdown on homosexuals and the random arrests of "beat" types on the streets. They were also disappointed in the right-wing communist literary dialecticians and explained to Allen that they could only talk freely about it because they were alone. They had even checked to make certain that Allen had not been followed. When they parted company, they asked Allen if he had the chance to meet Castro to tell him to end capital punishment. Allen was surprised to hear their tales of repression, not just of homosexuals but also of a literary nature, but he left them with an open mind, thinking that maybe he had managed to find the only disgruntled Cubans around. He wrote to Peter that so far "Cuba is both great and horrible, half police state half happy summer camp—mixed."

The next day, after a large breakfast in the hotel's baroque dining room, he was taken to meet his hosts, the official cultural heads of Cuba. He brought them records by Bob Dylan and Ray Charles, which they had never heard before, and Allen hoped they would broadcast them over Cuban radio.

It did not take Allen long to realize that being a guest involved a subtle form of brainwash. And whether it was at Harvard by the faculty, or in Cuba by the liberal communists, guest status demanded that he offend no one no matter how strongly he disagreed with them. After being wined and dined by the Cuban litterateurs, he was invited to lunch with an English translator of Cervantes. Then he spent the afternoon with Miguel Barnet, who explained the Yoruba-Bantu Santaria cults to him. The revolution seemed to be an obsession with everyone he met, just as hallucinogenic drugs were with him. The commonality was that neither one represented reality.

Allen had a dinner interview with a reporter from *Hoy*, a Spanish-language magazine. Since Allen had heard that Billie Holiday's records had been banned in Cuba for causing social disintegration, he talked about censorship. After supper, two of the boys he had met the night before, seventeen-year-olds named Manuel Ballagas and Jose Mario, came to bring him a translation they had made of *Kaddish*. The hotel manager stopped them and refused them access to Allen's room, so Allen had to meet them in the lobby. The manager informed Allen that visitors were not allowed in the hotel rooms as a matter of policy. This irritated Allen, who had already seen a steady stream of quasi-official editors and bureaucrats visiting other guest rooms all day long. Allen consulted Mario Guide, his International Cultural Exchange Program (ICEP) officer, who cleared the way for the boys to go up to Allen's room. There they were able to talk candidly all evening and discussed the persecution of homosexuals and the Cuban laws prohibiting marijuana use. It developed into a scene from Kafka, where Allen's public statements about pot and fairies got his visitors into McCarthyite trouble

later on. Allen later wrote to Leroi Jones and Marc Schleifer, staunch supporters of Castro's revolution, to tell them that they did not understand
what was really going on in Cuba. He remained sympathetic toward the
goals of the revolution, but he didn't think Jones and Schleifer knew how pu-
ritan, conformist, and pervasive the communist brainwashing was. It was the
same old Marxist anxiety about controlling people that he had seen before.

Most Cubans claimed that the lack of a free press was unimportant since
Cuba was so small and everybody knew everybody. If you had a complaint
you could go directly to Castro or take your grievance to the person in
charge. Allen saw that Marxism had replaced Catholicism as the dictator of
morality, and since the revolution had to succeed at any cost, most Cubans
were willing to go along with less freedom. For Allen, curtailing freedom of
speech was too great a price to pay for the revolutionary state.

For the next few days, Allen played tourist with the poet Nicanor Parra,
who was also in Havana. They visited Hemingway's house, a museum of
pre-Columbian artifacts, some old forts, and even an alligator farm. Each day
he had a full schedule planned for him by his hosts, and what little free time
he had left he spent with Tom Maschler, a British editor who was also a guest
of the Cuban government. Continuing to play literary agent, Allen convinced Maschler that he should publish his friends in England. In public fo-
rums Allen spoke about homosexuality until he realized that he might be
causing trouble for some of his hosts by focusing too much attention on
them. It was becoming evident that the only protection a person could have
was to know someone within the Cuban government bureaucracy. Only
then were you absolutely free to do as you pleased.

Near the end of the month Manuel Ballagas called to warn Allen that he
had been picked up by the police the night before. He and Allen had been followed and when they split up, Ballagas was taken in for questioning until five
in the morning. He was eventually charged with talking to foreigners and released to his mother's custody. From then on he was afraid to meet Allen
anywhere except at official Writer's Union functions. That night Allen lay in
bed masturbating to sexual fantasies about Fidel Castro and the dashing
young Che Guevara. He unwisely recorded all the minute particulars in his
notebook.

With each passing day Allen descended deeper into trouble by discussing unpopular issues. One government representative asked Allen to
confirm that he had said that Raúl Castro, Fidel's brother and the head of the
armed forces, was a fairy and that he wanted to sleep with him. Allen
couldn't remember the statement or where he might have made it. Everyone

seemed to be a spy in Cuba. He gave up all hope of ever scoring pot, since he was so carefully watched everywhere. Some of the boys Allen had been seen with were arrested and accused of hanging around acting in an effeminate way. After doing what he could to get them released, Allen decided to stop talking about homosexuality and drugs. He was concerned that it could lead to the closing of the Writer's Union, his official host. The fear of having the fantasies and dreams he had entered in his journal misinterpreted made him afraid to even continue keeping it. When asked for interviews Allen declined, stating that he was preoccupied with the arrests of his friends and didn't want to discuss politics anymore. Any critical remarks were considered antirevolutionary, so Allen knew it was best to say nothing if he hoped to defuse the situation. By February 3, his hosts began to cancel his university lectures. It was obvious that they couldn't afford to let Allen make any more public statements.

The bureaucrats gave Allen the runaround when he tried to find out if the boys had been released from prison yet. He was told not to worry about it: "What we need now is more cement—work and cement is our need, afterward will come other matters." Against his own better judgment Allen found himself walking around the city freely talking to young writers about homosexuality and the revolution. Radio propaganda reported how happy their famous beatnik guest was, but by then Allen felt completely isolated and wasn't certain who was a friend and who was a government spy. His analysis of the situation was that Castro's government was using sexual repression as a method of training obedience. Even though Castro had charisma and tremendous charm, he was also the absolute law and he was prepared to keep control even if it meant a military state buildup as in Russia or China. Allen couldn't see how any change would be possible as long as Castro was in power.

Intellectually, Allen knew that having sex with any Cuban would cause more trouble for the other person than it would for him, but he couldn't help himself. Since he found Manuel and another boy named Jose to be quite sexy, he hatched several different schemes to get them into bed. They liked Allen, too, but were fearful of being caught. Most of the time they were content to keep their pants on and walk around Havana visiting nightspots with the American poet. On February 16, Allen threw caution to the wind and had sex with Manuel in Jose's apartment. It was a relief to be intimate with someone after a month of abstinence, but they were soon to pay dearly for it.

Two days later Allen was awakened by a sudden knock on his hotel door. It was a representative from the ICEP accompanied by three soldiers in olive green uniforms, with his notice of deportation. "We've arranged for your departure this morning at 10:30 on a plane to Prague," he was told. Allen was confused and pleaded for more information, thinking perhaps there was a mistake. He asked to call Haydee Santamaria, one of his hosts, to verify the expulsion order, but the ICEP officer replied that everything would be explained later. For now he was to pack immediately and go with them to the airport. As the car sped along, Allen pulled out his finger cymbals and chanted the Hari Krishna mantra quietly to calm his nerves. He was frightened, not knowing if they were taking him to the airport or somewhere worse, and moreover he was frustrated because he sympathized with their revolution. His deportation would look bad for everyone. In any case, he wanted to know what he had done wrong. They informed him that the government felt he lacked respect for their laws and his private lifestyle did not support the goals of the revolution. Fortunately, they never examined Allen's notebooks, in which he had explicitly outlined everything he had said and done in Cuba, even to the extent of naming the people he had smoked dope with as well as describing his sexual activity with Manuel in detail.

When he realized that he was truly on his way to the airport and not going to jail for further interrogation, Allen sat back in his seat, somewhat relieved. Waiting on the runway was a silver jet with the word "Czechoslovakia" painted on the fuselage, and passengers were boarding already. Allen graciously shook hands with his captors, said goodbye, and got onto the plane. He turned at the top of the stairs before entering to wave to the soldiers and they waved back. On the plane he noticed a story in a Cuban newspaper that said, "In Cuba there is true liberty and revolution." The socialist and capitalist worlds were just the same, he thought, "a mountain of dogs."

When the plane landed in Gander, Newfoundland, for refueling that evening, Allen called to tell Peter what had happened and where he was headed. Silently he resolved to himself that he would be quiet in Czechoslovakia, grant no newspaper interviews, and deflect all attention away from him. Peter had some news of his own to relate. Their apartment on East Fifth Street, with no heat or hot water that winter, had been condemned by the city. Peter had moved all their possessions to another apartment five blocks away at 408 East Tenth Street.

On February 20, after sleeping most of the way on the long transatlantic flight, Allen arrived in Prague. His stay in Cuba was a disappointment caused by hysterical bureaucrats and their police state mentality. Here he hoped things would be different, and if they were, he planned to get a Russian visa and visit Moscow at his own expense as a private citizen. He was tired of his status as a state guest and the personal self-censorship that it required. In addition to the seventy-five-dollar fee that the Writer's Union had promised for his visit, he earned a little extra spending money by reading at the Viola Café on Prague's main square. As a guest of the government he was put up for two weeks in the luxurious nineteenth-century Ambassador Hotel in the center of the beautiful old blue-gray stone city. The same rule of no guests in the hotel rooms was in force here, but he had learned his lesson and did not complain. With his guidebook in hand he made the rounds of the museums and castles and began to write some new poems. He located Kafka's old apartment, the very place where he had written his masterpiece *The Trial*, and then visited his grave. He noted how much like Kafka's story the current communist police state was, yet managed to keep some faith in the ideals of socialism. He predicted to his father, "Now they are opening up, which means, technically, de-centralization of economic authority, and consequently political and artistic." Allen couldn't resist making broad statements about the future based on the tiny signs of change he perceived.

While in Prague Allen received a letter from Manuel. He told Allen that the newspapers had reported that Allen was expelled from Cuba for smoking pot. That was the first time Allen had heard that excuse for his deportation, and he flatly denied the report. Rumors were circulated that Allen had even brought the pot into the country from the decadent United States. At least Manuel was out of jail and Allen was hopeful that his Cuban friend would have no further trouble on his account.

In Prague Allen had a better time. Having learned a lesson in Cuba, he studiously kept his mouth shut in public. At the Univerzita Karlova, one of the oldest universities in Europe, he read to a crowd of three or four hundred students. For a rare treat he read *Howl* as well as some new poems he had worked on in Prague. Then, although he knew better, he began to write and speak more freely again. He'd heard that "sex relations with anyone male or female is legal over age of 18." He exaggerated when he boasted that he was so popular that he was making it with teenage kids in orgies and going to wild Turkish baths to pick up men whom he blew in the dark alleys of old Prague. He went shopping and bought a new pair of tennis shoes to wear on his trip to Russia and took long walks around the snowy city, ending up in cheap restaurants eating delicious meals. His depression and paranoia following his Cuban misadventure had   Message II, *CP*, p. 356
subsided and he was relieved that things weren't as bad be-   Big Beat, *CP*, p. 357
hind the European Iron Curtain.

When his officially sponsored trip to Prague ended without incident,

Allen felt invigorated and caught a second-class train to Moscow, where he arrived forty-eight hours later on March 20. As a tourist he was required to pay seventeen dollars a day in advance for a week's stay, so his time was limited by his budget. He regretted that he was in Russia without Peter, as they had always planned to go there together. However, he was certain they would be able to return together at some point in the future. Allen was able to use the royalties from his Czech translation sales to pay for the trip to Russia, and that arrangement was perfect since he couldn't bring that money back to the West with him anyway.

His contacts in Czechoslovakia warned Allen that if he thought communism was a disappointment in Prague, he'd find it worse in Russia. Publicly people were afraid to talk, but privately they had many complaints against the state. Allen had looked forward to finding the truth for himself and he had personal reasons to visit Russia as well. Both his parents' families had left Russia for America around the turn of the century, and he had the names and addresses of some of his relatives who still lived there. They could tell him what the political situation was like. He also had read the poetry of Andrei Voznesensky and Yevgeny Yevtushenko, whom he wanted to meet and get to know. Russian poetry was very much an oral tradition and he longed to hear them recite in their native language.

The day after his arrival in Moscow, a cousin of Allen's, Joe Levy, and his wife, Anne, met him at the hotel and took him to their apartment. That side of the family had stayed behind in Russia and had survived all the pogroms, war, and revolutions since Naomi had left over sixty years earlier. From them, Allen learned the true history of his mother for the first time. Naomi had been born in Nevel, a town near Vitebsk, and in fact all the family came from villages in that area. In 1904, when Naomi was eight years old, Russia went to war with Japan and her father was drafted. Naomi's mother was in delicate health and silent much of the time. She was not able to care for their four children by herself, so her father moved the whole family into a cousin's small two-room cabin in Vitebsk. Assorted relatives took care of the children while Mendel, Naomi's father, bribed his way aboard a ship to America. A year later he had saved enough to send for his family, and it was then that Allen's mother arrived in New York City. As Chopin played on the Levys' radio, they looked at photos of Allen's mother at age ten. They even had pictures of Allen and Eugene as children, sent to them by Naomi years before. They all sat with tears rolling down their cheeks, each with their own memories, enjoying their reunion.

Allen wanted to see and do everything while in Russia. He caught a train to Leningrad and headed straight for the Hermitage Museum to see its fabulous collection of Rembrandts. Once back in Moscow, he met Yevtushenko and the playwright Vasily Aksenov for drinks several times. One night Yevtushenko, quite drunk, recited his poems in his powerful voice, the muscles in his neck bulging as he spoke. Allen wanted to talk with him about sex and drugs, his favorite topics, but Yevgeny would not hear of it and told Allen that these topics demeaned him. He and Allen did not share the same interests outside of poetry and even though Allen considered him a "good fellow" he was a different type of "political soul." When Allen complained to Yevtushenko about his friends in Cuba being jailed overnight, Yevtushenko laughed and explained that in Russia he had known people to be in jail for twelve to twenty years, so one night didn't concern him. "That's child's play," he said. Allen explained that he was used to "making scandals without paying consequences," as with his censorship trials in America. "You live in paradise," was Yevtushenko's astute response.

By chance Allen was there to witness the crowds of people gathered in Red Square to welcome the cosmonauts back from space. Red Square was so vast and beautiful that Allen would never forget the dramatic scene, with the Kremlin's towers in the background and the flags waving in the breeze. Voznesensky was out of town, but Allen extended his stay long enough to meet him. The arrangements were made by the Writer's Union directors, Romanova and Luria, who secured him a one-week expense-paid visa extension, despite his discomfiture at being an official guest again. His hotel room was upgraded to one that looked out across the river at the Kremlin clock tower and the onion domes of St. Basil's Cathedral. Publicly, Allen was on his best behavior in the Soviet Union. He projected an agreeable demeanor and confined his criticism to ideological double-talk instead of flatly stating his views in his usual candid fashion. For the short time he was there he maintained a low profile and stayed out of trouble. He found politics in Moscow depressing and wrote to Leroi Jones again, saying, "You better think twice before you buy any paradises, or better, take an extended trip thru here and listen to all the story so you can judge. Not that it's so bad here, as a system it works, not that it's so good," Allen hedged.

By April 2, Voznesensky had returned to Moscow, and Allen spent most of the day with him; they read their poetry aloud to each other and went to the theater. Then Andrei took him to visit the poet Bella Akhmadulina, who had once been married to Yevtushenko. Allen described her in his journal as being attractive, "like super angelic redhead girl with big tits, and writes pretty." Later that evening he spent some time with cheerful Lilya Brik, Mayakovsky's old girlfriend, now an aged but intelligent advisor to all the poets.

On his last day in Moscow Allen visited another poet, Alexander Yessenin-Volpin, who had been exiled to a madhouse for complaining about Russian politics. Finally Allen had met someone with a completely free and independent mind who worked on the basis of emotional reactions, rather than writing what was socially acceptable. Of all the people Allen met in Russia, he liked Yessenin most of all. When Yevtushenko and Aksenov ran up to Allen at the train station to bid him farewell the next morning, they promised that they would visit him in America someday. Allen hadn't had an opportunity to meet many younger people in Russia or even to give a reading there, so he promised that he would return. As the train sped toward Warsaw, Allen sang mantras to himself and anyone else who would listen in the train compartment. He was content that things behind the Iron Curtain weren't quite as bad as his Cuban experiences had led him to believe. Unfortunately, that conclusion was to change radically in the next month.

In Warsaw, Allen enjoyed three weeks at the Hotel Europe. Nothing much was happening in town. Allen was treated as a guest of the Ministry of Culture during the first week and then paid for the other two weeks with his Polish translation royalties. The government even gave him some extra spending money and he met with Polish poets. He also ran into David Halberstam, the *New York Times* reporter whom he had last seen in Saigon. They visited tourist sights together and saw that much of the old city had been destroyed by the war.

Café in Warsaw, CP, p. 358

Allen wanted to see the Jewish Ghetto and went there with the Jewish editor of *Jazz* magazine (in which a translation of *Howl* had been published). Before the war the editor had lived in the Ghetto and escaped to become a journalist with the Russian army before the final destruction. The former Ghetto was now a vast green space surrounded by new government housing projects, with only a memorial to remind people of the extermination that had taken place there. The monument showed the Jews facing the invisible legions of annihilation, and its sadness brought Allen to tears. Whatever tragedies had happened on that spot were now erased, and a whole new town had been built that bore no witness to the suffering. Voznesensky happened to be passing through town on a reading tour so they got together for an evening; here they

The Moments Return, CP, p. 360

could talk poetry and politics a little more freely than in Moscow. Allen also visited the old city of Krakow, which seemed nearly untouched by the war; he stayed for a week. He was driven out to see Auschwitz and the same emotions he had felt in Warsaw welled up in his heart. It wasn't difficult to envision that had he or his family been in Europe during the war they might have been killed, too. He had his picture taken under the famous "Arbeit Macht Frei" (Work makes you free) wrought-iron gates before heading back to Prague through Wroclaw.

When Allen's train pulled into Prague on April 30, he left his bag at the station and walked over to his old hotel to register, but the Writer's Union could not cover the cost of his room again. He didn't have much money so he couldn't stay on his own for long. He wanted to see the May Day celebrations and say goodbye to some friends he'd made earlier. He had no sooner checked into a cheaper hotel than the writer Josef Skvorecky, one of his new friends, called to ask him if he would like to enter the King of May contest as the representative of the Technical School. Everyone agreed that it would be a funny joke. It was the first time that the traditional May festival had been allowed in Prague in twenty years, since the communist takeover in 1945. Since then it had been supplanted by the large May Day labor parades. The last few years, May Day had been marred by student unrest that ended in skirmishes with the police. This year the president had suggested that the old medieval student fiesta be reinstated, thinking that this gesture might help keep the peace. In earlier days it had been the students' tradition to elect a May Queen and May King (or Kral Majales) to rule over a bacchanal each May Day. Allen was honored to take part in the revival and agreed to be nominated for May King. It sounded like a small affair at the Technical School, and probably a lot of fun besides.

In the morning he got up early to watch the government-sponsored May Day parade in Wenceslas Square with a friend. Afterward it was warm enough to sit in an outdoor café drinking lemonade and eating frankfurters. Following lunch Allen napped until a playful band of students dressed in 1890s costumes complete with parasols and top hats knocked on his door and officially announced, "Mr. Ginsberg, we have the honor to beg your presence in a procession to the crowning of the King of May and to accept our support for your candidacy of Kral Majales and we humbly offer you crown and throne." They gave him a small golden paper crown and escorted him outside to a homemade float, a red-draped chair on the back of a truck. Allen quickly got into the spirit of the party and took out his finger cymbals and started chanting mantras and singing songs. Everyone was

Ginsberg in Prague, 1965 ~

happy, drinking beer and carrying on merrily as the crowd swelled and more joined in the procession. In the courtyard of the Technical School there were other floats with other candidates and Dixieland bands were playing. Slowly, they all paraded to the fairgrounds where a few thousand students assembled to vote and to party. It was a beautiful day and the streets in every direction were clogged with thousands and thousands of revelers. After Allen drunkenly chanted "Om Sri Maitreya" to the crowd, it took everyone by surprise when he was elected Kral Majales. The students were happy with their new monarch, but the government party leaders were not. At midnight they deposed Allen as King of May and put an actual student on the throne. Allen had already had a great day and didn't protest. His spirit and ego were buoyed by the public acclamation, and he decided that the Iron Curtain countries weren't so bad after all. Then and there he decided to extend his trip and visit Hungary and East Germany before returning to the West.

A few nights later as Allen strolled with a young couple, a stranger came around the corner toward them. He looked at Allen and shouted "Bouzerant!" (Fairy!) "Bouzerant!" and physically attacked Allen, knocking him to the pavement. Suddenly, almost too quickly, in fact, five policemen with billy clubs surrounded Allen and dragged him off to the police station. The man swore that Allen had been doing naked, obscene acts on the street and that Allen had attacked him. Allen could only imagine that this stranger was a police provocateur, hired to cause trouble for him. In the skirmish one of Allen's notebooks disappeared from his pocket. He didn't realize it at first, but the journal contained a few poems and descriptions of what he had been doing. It included an account of masturbating on the floor in his hotel bathroom with a broomstick up his ass, but other than that, he thought it was fairly benign. He had used initials instead of real names for people, a lesson learned from his Cuban misadventure.

The next night the police came back and told Allen that they had found his notebook, initially a relief to Allen, since he had not made copies of his new poems. They took him to the station house, where he was required to sign a statement of ownership to claim the notebook. Once his "confession" was signed, their faces went cold and they said, "We must inform you that we are turning your notebook over to the public prosecutor for closer examination because we suspect it contains illegal writings." They released Allen, but a few days later an agent brought him back to the station house and told him that "due to many complaints about your presence in Prague from parents and scientists and educators who disapprove of your sexual theories we are terminating your visa and you will leave Czechoslovakia today." They drove him back to his hotel to pack his belongings, and as in Cuba he was escorted to the airport under armed guard and put on a plane, this time bound for London. It was raining when the jet left the runway, and while it began to climb into the sky, Allen took out a new notebook and wrote "Kral Majales." "For I am the King of May . . ." and continued to write feverishly until the plane touched down in London.

Kral Majales, *CP*, p. 361

Allen was lucky to have friends in London who were glad to see him and hear the news of his travels. He stayed overnight at the apartment of his Finnish translator, Anselm Hollo, whom he had known for a few years, and read him the first draft of "Kral Majales." The next morning he went to the Savoy Hotel to see Bob Dylan. He and Dylan spent the next two days together, before Dylan's concert on May 9 at the Albert Hall. The auditorium was filled with thousands of screaming fans and Allen was given a seat of honor right in front, next to Barbara Rubin, who by chance happened to be in London to see Dylan, too. After the concert they all went to Dylan's room to party, and it was there that Allen met his idols, the Beatles. The Beatles loved Allen's poetry and were as happy to meet the poet as he was to meet them. Allen was tipsy and kept falling into their laps while raving

about William Blake, whom John Lennon pretended not to know. They did
know about marijuana, though, and discussed its virtues at
Guru, *CP*, p. 364   some length. Allen was envious as he watched Dylan and
the Beatles hailed by a new generation of long-haired English girls and boys.

London was wilder and more alive now than New York, and nothing
could have been a happier change from the gray stolidness of
Drowse Murmurs,   Eastern Europe. Nightly concerts and gallery openings were
CP, p. 365   everywhere and excitement buzzed through the town. A
Who Be Kind To,   week later Allen traveled to Newcastle to visit an old poet,
CP, p. 367   Basil Bunting, and the visit inspired him to write his poem
Studying the Signs,   "Studying the Signs." Clustered around Bunting in Newcas-
CP, p. 371   tle were many younger poets, like Tom Pickard, who were
creating a poetry renaissance of their own in England.

Allen stopped at the U.S. embassy to complete papers in a futile attempt
to get back his Prague notebooks. He was most sorry to lose the poem he
had written onstage as he was crowned May King; he remembered it as being pretty good. He knew that making too much of an issue might prompt
the Czech government to take action against friends and associates mentioned in Allen's journal and still living in Prague. Their persecution would
be much worse than the loss of the poems. A much better poem, "Kral Majales," came out of the affair anyway, thanks to his expulsion.

In London Allen settled in for a month's stay with Tom Maschler, the editor at Jonathan Cape whom he had recently met in Havana. Maschler lived
in Chalcot Crescent, a neighborhood that Allen compared in excitement
level to Queens, New York. They talked more about bringing out a volume
of his "Complete Poems 1948–1965," and Allen wrote to Ferlinghetti to set
that process in motion. He also went to Liverpool to give a reading and listen
to the new rock groups there. Liverpool was the home of the Beatles and
everything new and mad in electric music happened there first. When he returned to London he went to hear John Ashbery read at the embassy for the
USIS and they had a nice reunion, talking about Dylan and the documentary
movie about him, *Don't Look Back.*

At the suggestion of Ed Sanders, Allen moved in with Barry Miles, a
young writer Sanders knew who managed Better Books, a great literary
bookshop in London. Later that year Miles went out on his own and became
a co-owner of Indica Books. Cape Goliard gave a reception for Allen with all
the literati in attendance and before long his wild public life was in full swing
again and as frenetic as ever. This time Allen enjoyed all the excitement, and

he came to appreciate the fact that fame opened doors and allowed him experiences and introductions he would not have otherwise obtained. He
found, too, that he could now write whenever he had a spare moment, without having to sequester himself for long, isolated periods as he had when he
was younger. He was able to enjoy his celebrity status and get some quality
poems written, even if he only wrote a few lines a day.

Barbara Rubin stayed on in London for a while, too. Allen sensed that
she had matured in the six months since he had seen her last in New York.
She still harbored the dream of being an impresario, and it was she who
discovered that someone had canceled a concert at the Albert Hall at the
last minute, leaving it unused for the night of June 11. She and John Esan
hired the auditorium for the purpose of producing a giant poetry reading.
Ferlinghetti was coming to London, as was Voznesensky, so Barbara began
putting together an all-star lineup of poets. Allen was interviewed in all the
London papers and publicized the reading everywhere he went. When the
hall opened that evening, it quickly filled with six thousand people, an astonishing crowd for a poetry reading. Allen's old friend from India Pupul
Jayakar came and brought Indira Gandhi and they were seated in the front
row. Voznesensky said he was too shy to read and sat beside them. Seventeen poets read, including Corso, Harry Fainlight, Ferlinghetti, and Ginsberg. Allen read less well that night in part because of the wine he had
drunk, but also due to his chagrin at his short time slot and the large number of readers. In spite of all that, the audience enjoyed the night, which
was odd enough to be considered a "Happening" in those days. Several
days later Corso, Ferlinghetti, and Ginsberg gave a more traditional reading at the Architectural Institute. Voznesensky joined them that evening
and closed his set with a fantastic and powerful deep-voiced recitation of a
new poem devoted to the blood sacrifice of all artists of all countries, a
poem written in slow meters imitative of the tolling of the bells of the
Kremlin towers.

Allen read at Cambridge to several hundred students and spent a few
days studying Blake's original manuscripts in the Fitzwilliam Museum. By
then he was staying with Miles, who organized a thirty-ninth birthday
party for Allen. At the party Allen took off all his clothes and drunkenly
sang and danced with a hotel "Do Not Disturb" sign tied to his penis. John
Lennon and George Harrison came in around midnight but were alarmed
by Allen's antics and ran away laughing over whether their "reputations"
had been ruined. They were thankful that for once no photographers were
present.

When Corso returned to Paris, Allen went with him. Without stipends, he was broke again and spent a week sleeping on a cot in George Whitman's Librarie Mistral. Each morning he woke up in the bookstore, surrounded by shoppers browsing the shelves above his head. With his money running low, he had to finally say goodbye to Europe and fly back to New York on his still-valid Cuban round-trip ticket. When he passed through U.S. Customs at the airport, the guards pulled him aside and took him to a room where he was strip-searched for drugs. Even the lint from his pockets was examined for signs of marijuana, but they found nothing. On the inspector's desk he saw their orders: "Allen Ginsberg (reactivated) and Peter Orlovsky (continued)—These persons are reported to be engaged in smuggling narcotics," it read. He realized he had left one police state only to return to another.

During his journey behind the Iron Curtain, Allen was able to formalize his thoughts about the legalization of marijuana. His first conclusion was that more accurate scientific information and medical reports about pot smoking were mandatory. Second, the pro-pot movement needed the support of professional doctors and researchers who could give advice and support when called for. They also had to determine exactly what the official objections to pot legalization were, so that they could be addressed successfully. Only when all that was done would it be possible to draft legislation and pressure politicians into passing reforms. As a last resort, Allen thought there would eventually have to be massive demonstrations and acts of civil disobedience on a grand scale to achieve anything.

By the time he got home in July, Allen was completely worn out and glad to be back. In his absence Peter had been forced to find a new apartment, but dope fiends there had robbed Peter of his Indian harmonium and Allen of another typewriter. He had planned on making good use of that typewriter to respond to the charges made against him by an official Czech Socialist Party youth newspaper. They put forth their own account of what had happened in Prague. "They didn't report any accusations I hadn't already said myself publicly," Allen wrote. "I never made a secret of the fact that I smoke pot and fuck any youth that'll stand still for it, orgies etc. That's exactly the reason they elected me May King in the first place." He tried to make the best out of losing his notebook, saying that bootleg copies were probably already circulating and being read by amused litterateurs in party headquarters. Maybe it would become an underground Czech classic, he mused. He hoped someday to see it again, but it never appeared. Unfortunately, as tired as he was, Allen was only able to stay in New York long enough to catch up on some of his mail. He was due in Berkeley for a poetry conference that began on July 13.

There were two monumental poetry conferences in America during the 1960s and Allen took part in both of them. The first was the 1963 Vancouver conference that had brought him back from his self-imposed isolation in India. The second was in July 1965 at Berkeley. It was put together by Thomas Parkinson, Allen's old friend and professor at the University of California. Parkinson's 1961 book, *A Casebook on the Beat*, had effectively helped academia to understand that the Beat Generation writers weren't a bunch of know-nothings who couldn't spell. Parkinson assembled many of the Black Mountain poets, the San Francisco Renaissance poets, and a smattering of beat and New York poets for a week and a half of intensive study, lectures, and readings. Robert Duncan led the program with a lecture titled "Psyche-Myth and the Moment of Truth." In the days that followed, Jack Spicer, Gary Snyder, Charles Olson, Ed Dorn, and Robert Creeley addressed large audiences of what Allen described fondly as "raving barefoot apocalyptic teenagers." Allen himself read poetry for more than an hour under the title of "What's Happening on Earth." He was most impressed by Creeley reading his work syllable by syllable, which helped Allen to reach a new appreciation for Robert's poetry. Until then he hadn't quite been able to get it.

What was most important to the poets was the chance to get together for the first time since Vancouver and to meet some of the younger writers who were following in their footsteps. An exchange of energy between the generations took place at the conference. Ted Berrigan, Ed Sanders, Lenore Kandel, and Anne Waldman were among the new generation of writers who came to the conference and felt the transmission from the older poets. Waldman, who was a Bennington College student at the time, was so inspired by what she experienced that she took a vow then and there to create zones like the Berkeley experience and devote her life to poetry. Over the next three decades Allen would grow to appreciate Waldman's "open form poetry, collaborative work, and oratorical discipline" and see her as a peer, but for now she was a young student looking for her own path.

Allen stayed on in the Bay Area after the conference and took part in sit-ins to support the Berkeley students who had been expelled and arrested during Free Speech demonstrations. He chanted mantras through a microphone in front of the courthouse where their trial was to be held and promised to take part in the teach-in against the Vietnam War, planned for October 16.

Unexpectedly, Allen received a Guggenheim award, and with some of the money he bought a used Volkswagen minibus for two thousand dollars. Gary Snyder and Allen had been talking about taking a camping trip together to visit the Pacific Northwest again, as they had in 1956 before Snyder's departure for Japan. Allen bought the van, even though he didn't have a driver's license, because there was always someone around who did. At the last minute Peter decided not to go with them and stayed in Berkeley with "his girls." After the camper was provisioned with an icebox, stove, Coleman lamp, and writing desk, they drove north through the redwood forests toward Oregon with Gary at the wheel. The VW could do almost sixty-five miles an hour on the open road and Allen hoped it was sound enough to last for the next ten years, since he was already planning more trips. It was comfortable for two people but it wasn't quite large enough to sleep three. Since Gary's girlfriend, Martene Algiers, was with them, Allen was happy to spend his night in a sleeping bag on the ground outside. Each morning the travelers jointly read a chapter of the *100,000 Songs of Milarepa* (a twelfth-century Tibetan Buddhist saint, a poet of illusion and dreams). Pitching camp along the way, they passed through Crater Lake National Park, and Allen remarked that he had never before seen anything as godlike and beautiful. They also stopped to visit a friend of Gary's on a farm near Albany, Oregon, before they pushed on to Portland on August 20.

They stayed in town long enough to hear the Beatles perform at the Portland Coliseum on August 22. Midway through the concert John Lennon addressed the crowd: "We hear Allen Ginsberg is in the audience and we send him our greetings." Allen was delighted and hoped he could get backstage to see them, but they were whisked off to the airport immediately after the concert ended. A few days later, Allen wrote "Portland Coliseum," his memory poem of that evening, revealing his wish to be a rock star and reach ten thousand people at one time.

Portland Coliseum,
CP, p. 373

After hiking for two days in the Mt. Rainer vicinity, Allen and Gary proceeded to Seattle, where Allen visited again the secondhand shops on Skid Row that he had discovered a decade earlier. That evening they went to see the Beatles' movie *Help!* before moving north to the Mt. Baker National Forest where they spent eight days backpacking in the Northern Cascades. They slept in sleeping bags, cooked over wood fires, and enjoyed the fantastic mountain scenery. One morning Allen and Gary got up extra early and climbed with ropes, ice axes, and crampons over glacier crevasses to the top of Glacier Peak. From the summit they could see for fifty miles in every direction. Allen was completely exhausted by the time he reached the top of a long ridge of scree near the summit, but Gary was in much better shape and already sitting on the mountaintop. There they ate a picnic of smoked salmon and cheese and by 2:00 P.M. were on their way back down. "I finally found a climbing companion," Gary told Martene as Allen listened proudly. The next day was September 9, the ninth day of the ninth month, a Japanese folk holiday, Gary explained. "Anyone that doesn't make love today will have a year of bad luck." "Well, perhaps we could try each other," Allen said. Gary declined, saying, "That would be worse luck for me, than all the bad luck I'm going to get next year anyway."

They continued north to visit Warren Tallman, an editor and professor in Vancouver, before returning to San Francisco via the high desert and Reno. On the ride home, Allen practiced writing strophes in the style of Whitman and Saint-John Perse in his journals. He produced a poem called "Beginning of a Poem of These States," which detailed his trip back through Oroville, Omak, and Colville, while listen- ing to the AM radio play everything from Dylan to the Beach Boys. Back in San Francisco, Allen and Gary were not sur- prised to receive the news that Jack Spicer, whom they had seen at the Berke- ley conference, was dead. It seemed that he, like Kerouac, had been on a crusade for several years to drink himself to death.

Beginning of a Poem of
These States, *CP*, p. 377

In San Francisco, Allen stayed with Shig Murao, who had a small apart- ment on upper Grant, not far from City Lights and central to everything Allen needed. For decades it was Allen's home of choice when he came to town. On this visit Allen spent time with many of his old friends. He dropped in on Michael McClure and listened to a tape McClure had made of his Lion Graaahr poem. Allen and Michael went to the Fillmore together to hear more of the new San Francisco psychedelic music, such as Quicksilver Messenger Service and the Jefferson Airplane. Allen couldn't resist dancing as soon as he heard the new rhythms coming from the stage. Almost every day he saw Bob Kaufman hanging out on Grant Avenue or Neal Cassady, who seemed to be more cheerful now than Allen had seen him in years. Neal was in and out of town with his girlfriend, Anne Murphy, and various mem- bers of the Merry Prankster gang that convened at Ken Kesey's house in the La Honda hills south of the city. Though penniless, Neal was constantly high and slept in his old white Plymouth in Kesey's driveway. Ken's household could best be described as one continuous LSD vaudeville show. There was an incredible array of electronic equipment that could be used for taping, playing music, and making movies. To keep the scene going, Kesey had spent a small fortune out of his royalties for *One Flew Over the Cuckoo's Nest*.

At this time they were making final plans to get into their brightly painted bus named "Further" with Neal at the wheel, ride to the Yucatán, and disappear forever into the jungle.

Stephen Bornstein, the young man Allen had met through New York's Kerista group, happened to bump into Allen in San Francisco quite by accident and moved in with him at Shig's apartment. Bornstein wanted to apprentice himself to Robert LaVigne and learn as much as he could about art from a master. While staying with Allen, Stephen began working on a major project to illustrate *The Psychedelic Experience*, Timothy Leary's interpretation of *The Tibetan Book of the Dead*, which had just been published. He used long sheets of rice paper taped together to make a six-hundred-foot-long scroll that he filled with drawings of a myriad of interesting Tibetan deities. Peter and his silent brother Julius were in Berkeley, and along with Allen they all decided to rent an apartment together on Fell, right across the street from the panhandle of Golden Gate Park.

Allen's fame continued to grow by leaps and bounds. People knew he was a poet, but he also became a spokesman for the new generation of "hippies," as the media had begun to call the younger bohemians. Allen was frequently quoted in the press as a self-appointed advocate for marijuana and drug reform. And as the U.S. involvement in the war in Southeast Asia escalated, he became an outspoken critic of American foreign policy. It came as no surprise to him when he heard that the feds in New York had tried to get Huncke and another person to set him up for a pot bust. That was the easiest way for the government to deal with perceived troublemakers. If they couldn't catch them, they could frame them. Allen was livid when he found out that they were planning to hide drugs on him and wrote a letter to his congressman, protesting the plot. He was so vocal about their scheme that the narcotics bureau backed off, knowing by then that if he was set up, everyone would be aware of it. Allen did his best to remain squeaky clean at home; he never bought or held any type of drug himself and warned his visitors not to bring anything to his apartment. He did not stop smoking grass or dropping acid, but did it only with friends and people he knew he could trust. As Peter's drug use continued unabated, this became an additional area of friction between them.

On October 1, Allen got back into his VW camper with Peter, Julius, Stephen Bornstein, Neal, and Anne Murphy. They stopped to see Kesey in La Honda on their way to Carolyn Cassady's house in Los Gatos. Carolyn welcomed her old friends warmly and they enjoyed a mellow evening telling stories about the crazy adventures of Peter's brothers. Allen insisted on cooking a nice dinner with the groceries they'd brought and Peter cleaned the dishes, giving Carolyn a chance to enjoy her own guests. Then they retired to the camper parked in Carolyn's yard and in the morning set off for Ferlinghetti's cabin in Big Sur, planning to relax for a week.

Once safely situated in Ferlinghetti's remote Bixby Canyon hideaway, far from the drug police, Allen took LSD for the first time in more than four years. He had been scared away from it by "the cosmic creepy feelings" he always seemed to get, but this time there were no "reptilian ghosts," as he put it. Allen had memorized a Zen *dhairani* designed to forestall disasters and chanted it every time he felt anxious. This time it felt great to be high. He had no worries at all and spent several hours watching the ocean waves from Bixby Beach, which was sheltered under the bridge by the towering walls of the canyon. It was all sunshine and romantically beautiful, like something in Wordsworth or Blake. Allen wound up on his knees praying for the safety of President Johnson, who was undergoing gall bladder surgery that same day. LSD made Allen appreciate that more harsh words from him would send out bad vibrations into the atmosphere that might curse poor Johnson and further damage both their souls. In front of Allen, Peter danced naked before the giant green waves and the world seemed pleasant for a change.

Allen had promised to be back in Berkeley for the Vietnam Day Committee's huge teach-in on October 15, so it was a short idyll. Duncan read his "Uprising" poem, Ferlinghetti read "Where Is Vietnam?" and McClure read passages from "Poisoned Wheat." They all sat down together and composed manifestos in preparation for a peaceful protest march to Oakland's Army Induction Center. The motorcycle gang known as the Hells Angels threatened the peace marchers with violence if they crossed the city limits from Berkeley into Oakland. Allen and Snyder climbed on the back of the sound truck and chanted into microphones to help keep the crowd calm, but the march was turned back by the police before it reached the Oakland border.

The next day nearly seven thousand people gathered to march once more and this time, with Allen in the front line, they reached the Oakland city limits. As expected, they were confronted not by the police but by the Hells Angels dressed in leather and swastikas. The Angels tore down their "Peace in Vietnam" banner and were poised to attack the marchers themselves, when all the demonstrators calmly sat down as a defensive tactic. The police intervened and broke things up and the demonstrators returned to Berkeley to begin planning their next march to the induction center.

The leaders of the Vietnam Day Committee represented a cross section of the youth movement at the time. There were some hippies, some Marxists, some Progressive Labor, and some liberal types, but for the most part it was composed of ordinary people, more spiritual than political by nature. The new generation was united in the idea that a change of consciousness had to occur before anything progressive could happen in society. For the next march Allen issued a flyer, "Demonstration or Spectacle as Example, As Communication or How to Make a March/Spectacle," which outlined dozens of imaginative, funny, and peaceful ways to avert violence. He was surprised by the bitter reaction against the marches in the popular press and thought that if everyone could remain calm, it would illustrate that the prowar voices were more baldly hysterical than the antiwar ones.

It was a time of great activity and community spirit in San Francisco as all forms of protest were united for a brief period to become simply "The Movement." Robert LaVigne hosted a party at his studio, to which Ken Kesey came with all his Pranksters wearing outrageous multicolored costumes. Joan Baez and Bob Dylan were in town and stopped by the party as did Neal and the San Francisco poets. There seemed to be an endless supply of pot and DMT.[55] The DMT at the party was the first that Allen had ever smoked, and it gave him a little of the old laughing gas consciousness for a half hour or so. It provided more visual phenomena than other drugs he had tried, and it made everything, including people, appear like transient phantoms of colored waves. The more Allen thought about it, the more he realized that the only common thread in all his drug experiences was the impression of fleeting existence. He left the party that night vomiting red wine, but he was happy. Dylan promised to give him six hundred dollars for a portable Uher tape recorder after Allen had told him about his first attempts at writing poetry in the VW driving back from Vancouver with Gary. The Uher could run on batteries for ten hours and then be recharged by plugging it into a wall outlet, a state-of-the-art machine for 1965. Dylan also gave him an amplifier for Peter's electric guitar and an autoharp for McClure.

Carmel Valley, *CP*, p. 381   The committee for the next peace march needed donations, and Allen offered to give a reading with the Fugs as a fund-raiser. Allen increasingly saw that his primary role was to keep everyone calm and peaceful and to avert any violent disaster. By now he knew from experience that a calm-bellied "OM" out-breathed over a loudspeaker could create a tranquil atmosphere, in contrast to strident hate speeches that stirred violence. He tried to persuade Dylan to help,

---

[55] DMT: Dimethyltryptamine, the drug present in ayahuasca.

Dylan and Ginsberg, San Francisco
1965 ~

since he was in San Francisco, but the prospects of violence were too
great, and Dylan did not want to take part. Not everyone in the growing
antiwar movement was in agreement over how to proceed. Some thought
that impassioned confrontation would get more publicity and further the
peace movement, but to Allen that seemed like an absurd contradiction.
The next march was scheduled for November 20, and Allen worked nonstop to make it as peaceful as possible. He saw that violence might come
from the Hells Angels again if the police decided not to protect the
marchers from them, a tactic that seemed highly likely. To that end, Allen
participated in a panel with the Hells Angels' leadership at San Jose State
College on the topic of the antiwar demonstrations. During his comments
Allen did not debate or argue with the Angels, but inquired about their position and attempted to explain his own. He was surprised that most of the
thousand students there were hostile toward the peace marchers and supported the Angels' plans to disrupt the demonstration. When Allen, incredulous, asked if what they honestly wanted was a bloodbath, they all
shouted, "Yeah!" It would be a few years before the majority of young
people opposed the war. Later, Allen convinced Kesey, who knew many of
the Hells Angels, to host a meeting at his home to discuss the march further. It was a brave move, and when the Angels descended en masse on
Kesey's La Honda cabin, it looked like a foolish mistake. Incredibly, the
meeting evolved into a giant party where many of the Angels were turned
on to their first LSD. Eventually, they moderated their position and prom-

ised not to hassle the marchers. Allen turned all that into a poem called "First Party at Ken Kesey's with Hell's Angels," and gave credit to LSD for pulling the hatred from their hearts. The November 20 demonstrations went off without any disruption from the Hells Angels.

First Party at Ken Kesey's with Hell's Angels, *CP*, p. 382

Allen wrote to Louis about these events and admonished him that he was being as hostile as the Angels when he called Allen a "Pinko coward Commie draft dodger, etc." Allen's father already believed that the Vietnam War was a farce, but it would take Allen years to win his father over to his way of thinking on how to resolve the situation, as it would take the nation years to see the error of that war.

Allen wanted to stay in San Francisco long enough to see Dylan's concerts, and then spend a few more days with Ferlinghetti in Big Sur at his cabin, before starting a slow cross-country drive back to New York in the VW bus. His only plan was to travel with no plans, to take his time, to go where and when he wanted for the next few months. He could live cheaply in the van and travel with no commitments. On December 15, Allen, Peter, and Julius drove down to the cabin and spent a week walking in the woods and sitting on the beach staring out at the waves. Allen was able to relax and got high among the pine trees where he could watch the tiny wildflowers growing at the bottom of the canyon walls. He felt safe and enjoyed his solitude while he could. Allen used Dylan's Uher tape recorder for the first time, recording his mantras and chants and capturing the natural sounds of the ocean waves breaking on the beach. The tape recorder gave

Continuation of a Long Poem of These States, *CP*, p. 383

him a whole new approach to composition, making it much easier to sketch words and phrases and sounds wherever he was. It was also handy for recording his conversations and comments while experimenting with various drugs, like the morphine that a friendly doctor had given him recently. He cooked stews on Ferlinghetti's stove and read Kerouac's *Big Sur* for the second time. It was an amazing book, Kerouac's own firsthand description of his unsuccessful attempt to dry out in this same Big Sur cabin after a lifetime of alcoholism.

Stephen Bornstein was still in Bixby Canyon working on his scroll illustrating the *Tibetan Book of the Dead*. One morning he rolled it up and they all piled into the VW and set off south down the Pacific Coast Highway. They were in Los Angeles by the end of December, where they had planned to stay with artist Wally

These States: into L.A., *CP*, p. 384

Berman[56] on Crater Lane. A few days before New Year's, a mud slide in Topanga Canyon leveled his house and destroyed his entire lifetime of art- work, so the travelers stayed with Bob Branaman instead, another graphic artist, whose home was nearby. Later they found a place of their own in Canoga Park, on the other side of the hill.

A Methedrine Vision in Hollywood, *CP*, p. 388

---

[56] Wallace Berman (1926–76): Artist famous for mixed-media assemblages and editor of *Semina* maga- zine.

1 9 6 6 ～

RIDING AROUND STONED on the L.A. freeways on New Year's Eve in his private VW bus made Allen feel like he was an alien in a bizarre space-ship. To keep himself grounded he took the opportunity to visit his mother's family in Riverside a few times. Even though Allen resolved to relax, he could not turn down any invitation. One night he had supper with Christopher Isherwood and surprised himself by enjoying what he called "the fairy table gossip." Isherwood told him that he and Charles Laughton used to read Kerouac's prose aloud to each other for pleasure. Allen was thrilled to hear that and he couldn't wait to tell Jack. While in Riverside he received word that Ed Sanders was in trouble with the law. The police had raided his Peace Eye Bookstore on New Year's Day and confiscated all the inventory, charging him with publishing and selling pornography. They closed him down, and since he had nothing left to sell, he was broke. Allen mailed him the few hundred dollars that he had been offered for a reading at the University of California, Riverside, and earmarked it to pay Ed's overdue phone bill so that they could keep in touch about the legal developments as his case went to trial. John Fles, the editor of the little magazine *Trembling Lamb*, had organized a midnight benefit for Sanders on January 21 at the L.A. Cinema Theater, so Allen stayed long enough to do that reading. It was then that he decided that he should incorporate the Committee On Poetry as a permanent not-for-profit foundation in order to accept money and grants, which he could funnel to poets in need without the tax burden. "No use wasting the money offered floating around," he wrote to Ed. The creation of his foundation caused Allen to re-evaluate his vow of not reading poetry for money. From then on, if money was available for a reading, Allen accepted it and put the money directly into COP, where it was used for funding writers in distress.

In Los Angeles, Allen had been hanging out with people in the rock music business, including members of the Byrds, Al Grossman (Dylan's manager), and "a teenage rock king kid" named Phil Spector, who briefly toyed with the idea of managing Allen's career himself. Always interested in meeting his heroes, Allen visited Laura Huxley, Aldous Huxley's widow. She told Allen that on her husband's last day of life the discomfort was so great that he asked her for LSD, which eased the pain and put him in a peaceful state of consciousness as he died.

In addition to Peter, Julius, and Stephen Bornstein, Peter's girlfriend, Stella, came down from San Francisco to stay with them in Los Angeles for a while. By the time they were ready to move on, Stephen had found a new girlfriend and decided to stay behind in California. On February 1, the same day that LSD was outlawed in the United States, the motley group arrived in the town of Placitas, New Mexico, to visit Robert Creeley. The new law did not purge the drug from the scene, but it made anyone who bought or used it a criminal. It turned people who were law-abiding citizens into outlaws and a growing number of young alienated kids now felt more outcast than ever. Allen enjoyed his visit with Creeley, but he needed to get back on the road sooner than he wanted, for against his own resolve, he had made commitments to read in Kansas.

Charles Plymell had returned to his hometown of Wichita and booked a half dozen readings for Allen in Lincoln, Lawrence, and Topeka. As many as twenty-five hundred students showed up for the readings, and Allen continued to attract a great deal of media attention. After a February 18 reading in Lincoln, he drove back to Wichita to read at the university on February 21 under the auspices of the Philosophy Department because the English Department was afraid to host someone so controversial. *Life* magazine reporters and photographers followed Allen around for three days, and he was under police surveillance everywhere he went. In Wichita he was stopped by the vice squad and in Lincoln the police searched him for drugs after a reading. Periodically, patrolmen along the highways stopped their VW bus to search for drugs. In Indiana the state legislature threatened an investigation of the whole

Hiway Poesy: L.A.—Albuquerque—Texas—Wichita, *CP*, p. 390

Wichita Vortex Sutra, *CP*, p. 402

Chances "R," *CP*, p. 401

Kansas City to Saint Louis, *CP*, p. 421

university system after Peter read his "Sex Experiment" poem to the students in Bloomington. The John Birch Society was also screaming for action against them, but luckily they finished the tour without any arrests. As they drove, Allen worked on his huge poem *Wichita Vortex Sutra*, using the new tape recorder. After a long month of intensive readings and travel throughout the Midwest, Allen imagined himself back behind the Iron Curtain, with secret police at every poetry reading waiting to arrest him. He was at the center of all the Birchite hatred, repression, and fear mongering in the country, and he questioned who they were speaking for because it certainly wasn't the Americans he knew. In *Wichita Vortex Sutra* Allen openly declared the end of the Vietnam War and he expected that before long, American public opinion would follow his lead and demand an end to the war.

Auto Poesy: On the Lam from Bloomington, CP, p. 420

By the time he arrived in New York City, Allen felt he had worked on *Wichita Vortex Sutra* enough, and he sent a portion to Michael McClure to distribute. The poem was subsequently published in the underground press through a dozen newspapers around the country. With no time to rest, he headed to a reading at Buffalo University on March 10 with Herbert Huncke. Herbert read for hours and had everyone, including Allen, in tears listening to his sweet, melancholy stories.

Bayonne Entering NYC, CP, p. 427

Growing Old Again, CP, p. 431

Back in the city, Al Grossman called to tell Allen that Town Hall was free on April 5. Instead of having the house dark, the theater's manager was willing to give it to Allen for a benefit reading to enable the Leary Defense Fund to appeal Leary's March 11 conviction in Laredo, Texas. Leary had been sentenced to the maximum thirty years and fined thirty thousand dollars for being in possession of a small amount of pot. Although he had initially not wanted to get very involved with Leary's problems, Allen immediately began fighting the harsh punishment. He couldn't believe that the government would send such a prominent researcher, the author of more than fifty scholarly articles on the subject of drugs, to jail for such a long time for the possession of such a small amount of grass. The case was being appealed in higher courts, but Leary's legal fees were astronomical, part of the government's scheme to bankrupt anyone who opposed their outmoded drug laws.

Within a few hours Allen had lined up friends who supported the legalization of pot, such as Ed Sanders and Tuli Kupferberg, to perform at the charity function under the banner "The Politics and Ethics of Ecstasy." The evening was a success and within a month they opened the theater again for another Leary benefit. In the

Uptown, CP, p. 432

meantime, Leary was arrested once more on April 17 for drug possession at the Millbrook estate of his Castalia Foundation by G. Gordon Liddy, then a member of the Dutchess County Sheriff's Office. The authorities were doing their best to isolate Leary so that he would not be able to "corrupt" any more kids. Allen had tried not to get sucked into the Leary case since he didn't have all the facts, but he was more than willing to help by raising money for his defense. Allen could not resist entering this fray, and he was to work tirelessly on Leary's behalf through much of the 1960s.

In New York, Allen started work on the manuscript for his next book, *The Fall of America*. Allen wanted City Lights to do a better job with distribution this time. Many times in the past he had read at colleges where the bookstores were unable to provide copies of his books to sell, and he wanted City Lights to publish this new book in conjunction with Doubleday or Grove Press, someone with top-notch distribution. He wanted to attract the largest possible audience for *The Fall of America* because he felt that the political message behind the poems was crucial to the survival of the country and would help mobilize his readers to end the war in Vietnam. He had already received offers as high as ten thousand dollars from New York publishers for a hardcover edition of his collected poetry. Possibly he could figure out a way for City Lights to share in the profits from such an advance and his work would reach a wider readership. He offered to waive his portion of any advance to City Lights, but the idea was stalled and never progressed beyond the discussion stage.

In March Allen's new Russian friend Andrei Voznesensky had come to New York on a reading tour, and Allen wanted to repay him for the hospitality Andrei had tendered Allen in Moscow. He sent a list of three people that he felt Andrei simply had to meet on his initial American visit. The first was Jonas Mekas, the genius behind the Film Maker's Cooperative and the only person Allen felt could explain to Andrei the American underground cinema. The second was Ed Sanders, who was one of the few underground publishers to show true imagination and take real risks; plus he was turning the country on with his rock group, the Fugs. Finally, Allen wanted Andrei to meet Bob Dylan, the hero of thousands of young people and the real key to understanding American youth culture, in Allen's opinion. Ginsberg was able to take Voznesensky to a Fugs concert, but Allen was banned from most of Andrei's other official functions by his Soviet "handlers." Even though he saw him a few times, Allen couldn't get him alone long enough to turn him on to LSD, which was something he also wanted to do. Voznesensky remembered it a little differently. In one interview Andrei said that Allen visited him at the Chelsea Hotel and gave him something that Allen described as a little like LSD, but it was a new drug called STP.[57] Andrei swallowed the white pill but Allen left before the effects took hold and Voznesensky said he spent most of the day in a blackout. He was scheduled to read with Robert Lowell that evening and "for the first time in my life I forgot my lines," he said. Allen had hoped to change the course of Russian poetry by introducing psychedelics to the Russian people through Andrei, but after that incident Voznesensky said he was afraid of drugs and wanted nothing more to do with them.

Every reading that Allen gave drew even larger crowds than the one before. On a cloudy day in March he read at a Central Park peace rally to twenty thousand young demonstrators, one of the largest audiences of his career. He sang mantras and read part of his "First Manifesto to End the Bringdown," his prose essay on the virtues of marijuana.

The Old Village Before I Die, *CP*, p. 433

In May, Allen spent a week in Washington to lobby his congressmen and senators and to inform them about the narcotics bureau's attempts to entrap him. He spoke with clerks in the offices of Senators Robert Kennedy and Jacob Javits and hoped that he had made enough of a case to discourage the police from following through with their plans to frame him. On June 14, Allen was invited to speak about his own drug experiences before a special subcommittee of the U.S. Senate Committee on the Judiciary.

Consulting I Ching Smoking Pot Listening to the Fugs Sing Blake, *CP*, p. 434

Dressed in a seventy-dollar Brooks Brothers suit that he purchased especially for his testimony, he presented a clear, concise, well-researched report, outlining not only his own experiences with drugs, but also facts about the misinformation that was being spread by the government through the media.

Allen's old friends were mainly on his side through the drug controversy. Jack Kerouac, however, alone and suffering from alcoholism in Hyannis, Massachusetts, had no interest in the struggle to change American drug laws. He was continually pestered by young people who saw him as a spokesperson for their own disaffiliation, but Jack had never been political and his personal views were much more conservative than Allen's. Late at night, he continued to call Allen and other old friends and drunkenly blame

---

[57] STP (also called DOM or 4-methyl-2, 5-dimethoxyamphetamine) was first synthesized in 1964. The initials were said to stand for Serenity, Tranquillity, and Peace.

them for the sorry state of affairs in 1966. Usually his calls to Allen became abusive and ended with his calling Allen a "kike," or referring to Peter as "Allen's secretary" or "prat boy." In the end Jack's mother put a stop to his calls altogether because they were so expensive. Allen was weary of the abuse, but he never grew tired of Jack's writing. He reread *Desolation Angels* and was struck again by Jack's ability to give more detail in a few pages than Allen could in a million words. To Allen, Kerouac represented the writer's pinnacle of Herculean achievement. "I feel like a mean politician when I read a page of his," Allen commented.

Following his Senate testimony, Allen flew to San Francisco in mid-June to take part in an LSD conference organized by Dick Baker, later Baker Roshi, but at the last minute he was bounced from the program because he was deemed too controversial. Still, he had business to dis-cuss with Ferlinghetti and plenty to keep him busy. Not only Wings Lifted over the Grove Press but Random House had now made generous of- Black Pit, *CP*, p. 435 fers for a book of collected poems from Allen, and he hoped that he could convince City Lights to reach some kind of agreement with them. At one point Random House gave Allen an assistant to help him col-lect and edit his essays, and Allen enjoyed having clerical help, even if it was only for a brief time. He was able to ac- To the Body, *CP*, p. 439 complish twice as much with the help of a secretary.

Shortly after the Fourth of July, Allen and Lawrence took a ten-day holi-day together at Bixby Canyon. This time it was Lawrence's turn to take acid and experience the wavy canyon walls from a new, more tender perspective. The press of work never let up, even when Allen was isolated in Big Sur. He had mail to answer, manuscripts to revise, and proofs to correct. When he returned to Ferlinghetti's attic on Potrero Hill, he barely had time to look out the window at the sunny panorama. With all the legal entanglements caused by the cases against Leary and Sanders, plus his work to end censor-ship and reform drug laws, Allen was beginning to believe that he should have become a lawyer after all. He had just celebrated his fortieth birthday in June and found he was now spending almost no time writing poetry.

With no steady sexual companion, Allen's own urges led him to chase whatever boys would let him catch up with Iron Horse, *CP*, p. 440 them. In San Francisco he gave up in despair, after being re-jected for the umpteenth time in a week by boys half his age. He com-mented that they always woke up the next morning to see "this bearded monster nuzzling their breasts." Allen desired the thrills of a variety of sex-ual partners, but he also wanted a permanent relationship with a young

man. His relationship with Peter was complicated, the long-standing union
of a couple who stayed together from habit, convenience, and loyalty. Peter was using drugs more regularly, and Allen was abstain-

City Midnight Junk
Strains, *CP*, p. 465

ing more often in order to avoid being busted. They were
going in different directions more than ever, but Allen's loyalty and love never wavered.

Time was the one thing that Allen needed more of. He was not satisfied
with the poetry he was writing for his next book, *Planet News*. Some of the
work was good, but Allen considered many of the poems drivel. This represented his last six years of work, and he lamented that little of it was perfect
or even memorable. A plan had been fermenting in Allen's mind that might
provide him with the quiet, sheltered time he needed for his poetry. He envisioned the establishment of a poetry retreat somewhere in the country. Possibly the purchase of a farm in California or on the East Coast might provide
the perfect refuge for himself and for friends like Kerouac and Orlovsky. All of
them could escape from their various addictions, and Allen could enjoy the
peaceful life of a country squire. He would be able to write poetry all day
long if he wanted, and Peter could garden, raise animals, or follow other
wholesome country pursuits. Allen believed that if he were removed from the
city, where drugs were too readily available, Peter would win the battle
against his addiction. On a farm, he imagined that Jack could give up drinking, hide out from a relentless press, and get back to serious writing.
Throughout his life, Allen had seen many people destroyed by their drug
habits, but surprisingly, he never saw drugs as the inescapable addictions they
often became. Because he himself had been so careful never to get hooked on
anything, he believed that others could easily do the same without professional help. Selfishly, he also wanted to have Peter settled somewhere safe, so
he could return to India with Snyder and hike into the Himalayas to meet
more holy men.

During the time when Allen, Peter, and Julius had driven around the
Midwest in their VW, Robert Frank had flown out to Kansas and shot several
hours of film, which developed into his movie about Julius and Peter, *Me and
My Brother*. Once back in New York, Robert continued to work on the movie
script with the playwright Sam Shepard. At one point when Julius had run
away and disappeared, Robert had to use an actor, Joseph Chaikin, as a substitute for him, which added another layer of schizophrenic surrealism to his
movie. Julius turned up again just as Robert was finishing the film. Around
that time, doctors started Julius on a new type of chemical therapy, using vitamins to correct the adrenaline imbalance that was causing his sensory dis-

tortion and catatonic schizophrenia. They placed Julius under the care of the same Reichian doctor Allen had gone to eighteen years earlier. Allen and Peter tried out their own treatment ideas on Julius, too. Peter gave him Benzedrine to see if that would help, and then they introduced him to sex in a variety of forms in an attempt to snap him out of his catatonia.

In spite of all his experience to the contrary, Allen was always optimistic in his dealings with the press. He cooperated time and time again with reporters who he believed were sympathetic toward his poetry and politics, only to find out that they used whatever he said to ridicule his positions. He became more assertive and demanded to see proofs of the articles before giving final approval to quote his words. Since he had to do all this himself, it cut further into his time. But if he failed to do it, he was invariably quoted out of context. A case in point was Capitol Records, which had decided to record a documentary album on the topic of LSD. When they approached Allen to participate, they promised him they would lay all the information, both good and bad, out in the open. Allen believed them and agreed to participate. The end result was nothing more than antidrug propaganda, with no balance in the presentation. This infuriated Allen, and he was forced to spend time and energy arranging to have his voice removed from their recording.

Late in September Allen, Peter, Lafcadio, and Julius all piled into the VW camper and drove to Gloucester, Massachusetts, to see their old friend John Wieners. Panna Grady, a wealthy patroness of the arts who lived in the Dakota apartments in New York, accompanied them. While in Massachusetts, they decided to drop in on Kerouac, who was living with his mother in Hyannis a few hours away. They found Jack sitting in his backyard, but he didn't want to see them, and pretending to be his uncle Bill, he snuck inside the house. Soon Jack's mother came to the window and told them that she had called the police to chase the "bums" away. When Jack called Allen a few weeks later, he said that his mother had had a slight stroke and that she was nuts like Allen's mother so it was best to leave her alone. That strange encounter with "Uncle Bill" was the last time that Allen ever saw Jack alive.

Allen's other old friends were very much a part of his daily life, and they frequently needed his help. Huncke was in jail again, this time for stealing a sweater from Gimbel's department store. One night in late September, Allen was awakened by a call to bail Billy Burroughs, Jr., William's nineteen-year-old son, out of jail. He and his friends had been arrested for using speed at the Hotel Albert in the Village. He looked like William, Allen said, after he picked him up at the police department, and it appeared that he was following in his father's footsteps in more ways than one. On October 8 Billy was arrested again, this time with friends who had a variety of drugs and a few guns, too. Allen posted his bail and paid for the lawyer, who got the charges dropped in both cases, due to illegal search and seizure.

A Vow, *CP*, p. 468

The nation's antidrug hysteria continued to occupy Allen's attention throughout most of the sixties. On October 24, he gave a poetry reading in Paterson at the YMHA with his father. It was the first time Allen read with his father in his hometown and they enjoyed themselves thoroughly. Louis was proud of his son in spite of their political differences and the reading was a big success. In the course of the question-and-answer period at the end of the reading, Allen mentioned that he'd "smoked some pot at the falls that day," referring to the Great Falls of the Passaic River nearby. The next day, Allen was surprised to hear that the mayor of Paterson had sworn out a warrant for his arrest based on this impromptu comment. It was the first time that Allen had heard of anyone being arrested for merely saying that they had smoked pot, without actually being caught in the act. It was more than a nuisance, since Paterson was his hometown and he was concerned that when he next visited his father he might be picked up by the police. Even Louis, who was conservative when it came to drug use, thought it was one of the craziest things he'd ever heard.

Considering the large number of people Allen knew and hosted, it was almost impossible to keep his apartment drug-free. He continually warned Gregory that even though he was always welcome in his home, he had to refrain from bringing anything pharmaceutical with him, since he was being closely watched by the police. By this time another old friend, Maretta Greer, had come back to New York and was living with them and occasionally sharing Allen's bed. She had been recently released from a mental hospital and, with no place else to go, had turned up on his doorstep. After living in Asia for several years, she knew a lot more than Allen about Hinduism and was teaching him mudras (hand gestures) to go with the mantras she had taught him several years earlier in India.

Having Lafcadio, Julius, and Peter all now in the same house was not a peaceful domestic arrangement, and the brothers bickered constantly. Returning after a reading at Dartmouth, Peter got mad at Allen and drove off in the VW alone, leaving Allen stranded in the middle of New Hampshire with Lafcadio and Barbara Rubin. As soon as they got back home, Julius ran away and disappeared for nineteen days. Luckily, someone recognized him at the Port Authority bus station and brought him back to Allen's house. He was shaved

Autumn Gold: New England Fall, *CP*, p. 469

and clean, but would never say where he'd been. Philosophically, Allen surmised, "I guess he knows where he is."

Gary Snyder made one of his infrequent visits to New York City in November, and he and Allen spent a lot of time together. Allen left for a few
days to lecture in Boston at the Arlington Street Church, where, from the
same Unitarian pulpit from which Emerson had addressed the congregation,
Allen urged that spiritual leaders and educators recommend the use of LSD
for "everyone in sound health over age 14 at least once." He went on to suggest that the town fathers hold orgies on the Boston Common as an acceptable Whitmanic community sacrament. Allen couldn't resist shocking
people and tried to push the limits of propriety wherever he was. In the
process he continued to make headlines with some of these outlandish, candid comments.

With Maretta, Allen went to Leary's ashram at Millbrook
again and took an LSD trip with all the appropriate "mudras   Done, Finished with the
mantras mandirs mandalas and belly breathing." This time   Biggest Cock, *CP*, p. 474
he saw nothing but the beauty of Krishna everywhere, so fi-
nally he had conquered the old fears that always surfaced whenever he took
LSD. In a safe, protected environment, the experience was easier and more
relaxed. Back home, Allen was delighted to hear that A. C. Bhaktivedanta
Swami had rented a storefront on Second Avenue on the Lower East Side. He
and Peter had been chanting the Hari Krishna mantra at poetry readings
since their return from India and it was reassuring to have someone more
knowledgeable about Hinduism in the neighborhood. Allen was pleased to
say "The reinforcements had arrived." He went to visit Bhak-
tivedanta in December and they had a nice meeting, with   Holy Ghost on the Nod
                                                                  over the Body of Bliss,
Allen giving him suggestions for publishers for his books.   *CP*, p. 475

1 9 6 7 ~

Bayonne Turnpike to
Tuscarora, *CP*, p. 476

An Open Window on
Chicago, *CP*, p. 481

Returning North of
Vortex, *CP*, p. 484

GINSBERG RETURNED TO CALIFORNIA in January by car and
made more auto poesy with the tape recorder all the way. He had scheduled
several readings there, for more seemed to be happening in
San Francisco than in New York. Many of the benefit readings he gave were for spiritual groups ranging from Buddhist
organizations to Bhaktivedanta's International Krishna Consciousness movement. He was in constant demand to raise
funds and to introduce a younger generation to Eastern spiritual practices. Allen was enthusiastic and more than willing
to help various gurus publicize their missions in the West,
but he had yet to find his own guru or to discover his own spiritual path.

One of the landmark assemblies of the new counterculture took place
in Golden Gate Park on January 14. It was billed as a "Human Be-In," a gathering of the tribes of the younger generation. Part of the event was centered
on the acid experience, part on the new music coming out of San Francisco,
and part focused on the spirituality of the movement and its search for
meaning. Allen, as a sort of father figure to the hippie movement, helped to
plan the event and acted as a master of ceremonies onstage, along with Snyder, McClure, Ron Thelin, and the editors of the *San Francisco Oracle*. The
psychedelic posters plastered all over town brought tens of thousands of
young people to the park to hear poets, musicians, and spiritual leaders from
Suzuki Roshi to the Jefferson Airplane and Timothy Leary, in what became
the introductory event for the "Summer of Love" in San Francisco. Allen and

Gary circumambulated the gathering as a holy ritual to open the event. Allen closed the day by asking everyone to help clean up the park as they left, "kitchen yoga," he called it. Then he chanted "Om Sri Maitreya" as the sun set on the perfectly peaceful day. Lisa Law took a photograph of Allen dancing onstage in his flowing white Indian garb that was to become an icon of the period.

After the Be-In Allen took a short break from public life and traveled to Bixby Canyon for a retreat with Snyder. Without telephone or mail delivery, he was able to escape from everything for a brief moment. Gary continued to teach him all that he knew about Buddhist meditation practice and they set up an altar with images of Ganesha, an old *dameru*,[58] some sticks of incense, an oracle's ring, a bronze *dorje* (a thunderbolt), a bell, offerings of rice and tea, and some brass rings. Each morning Allen would sit for a while and meditate in front of the altar, but without real training he did not accomplish much, except to learn that sitting meditation was a discipline.

On February 11, after a reading at UC Davis, Allen, Snyder, and about fifty other hikers went on a circumambulation of Mt. Tamalpais, a mountain just north of San Francisco. They spent from 8:00 A.M. to 11:00 P.M. walking around the mountain, stopping from time to time to chant mantras and sutras along the way. Gary's peacefulness was a welcome contrast to Allen's usual travel companions, especially Peter with his nonstop frenzy, so often fueled by his amphetamine addiction. After the hike, Allen flew off to Toronto for a reading before he returned to New York City. It was the beginning of years of continual travel to and from readings, lectures, and appearances. It became increasingly difficult for him to find any empty blocks of time on his calendar, unless he scheduled a week or two of inactivity. In February alone he was slated to visit Chicago, Milwaukee, Detroit, East Lansing, Pontiac, St. Louis, and Princeton. All the money he earned went directly into COP, and many of the readings were benefits he gave for the causes he wanted to support.

For the next few months Allen kept busy flying from reading to reading. On April 15 he was invited to San Francisco for the Spring Mobilization against the war. Seventy thousand people marched through the streets and ended up filling Kezar Stadium in Golden Gate Park. The program there was dominated by uninteresting political rhetoric, and as the speeches droned on, the crowd dwindled to only a few thousand. No one on the podium

---

[58] *Dameru*: A two-sided, ritual hand drum.

spoke for the hippies who had made up the bulk of the audience. In mid-April Peter drove cross-country to San Francisco to pick up Allen and retrieve Julius who had once again disappeared, only to resurface in Napa. Together they all drove down to Santa Monica for a benefit reading with the Fugs. From there they took the VW to New Mexico to see Native American dances on the Pueblo Indian reservation; Larry Little Bird, a friend of McClure and Snyder, showed them around and took Allen to a Pueblo girls' initiation dance. He loved the instructions that were given to the girls to entice the men to make love to them once they became women. He also loved the countryside of New Mexico and began to dream again of buying some land for a poetry ashram. He continued on the road in May, appearing in the Pacific Northwest in Eugene, Corvallis, Portland, and Bellingham.

In the meantime, Barbara Rubin, who had also been living on and off with Allen, looked for a farm for Allen to buy in upstate New York. She had become interested in her Jewish heritage and explored the area around Sharon Springs, an old Yiddish resort in the rolling hills on the edge of the Mohawk Valley. During her tour of the countryside, she discovered what she believed to be the perfect spot for Allen, a seventy-acre farm on East Hill, outside Cherry Valley. It was a four-hour drive from New York City via the thruway, but only one hour from the Albany airport, so it was both secluded and close to a transportation center. She was convinced that the farm had a mystical aura, and that helped her persuade Allen that it was the right spot for him.

Ginsberg had long contemplated the purchase of a piece of property in an isolated location, and his pleasant experiences at Ferlinghetti's Bixby Canyon cabin encouraged him to move ahead with the idea. He had earned enough money on his nonstop reading tours to afford to buy a modest place, and he would probably be able to maintain the farm through fees from future readings. Allen, of course, was a city slicker, and had very little idea of what running a country property would entail. For him, it was enough that it be beautiful, quiet, and secluded. He assumed that mundane concerns like water, sewage lines, and electricity came automatically with any piece of property. Barbara was relentless in her determination to put Allen on the farm and used all her considerable powers of persuasion to convince him. In the end, no one ever knew whether Allen bought the farm of his own free will, or to appease Barbara. She loved Allen to the point of wanting to have his baby, and for a short time she saw life in the country as a snapshot of rural bliss, a great place to raise their family. Her intentions were pure, but Allen was not meant for the slow pace of family life in the country. He was not going to end up sitting on the front porch of a farmhouse, watching the children play in the yard. Peter thought the farm was a good idea, and remembered the happy times he had spent on his high school agricultural farm. Everyone had individual and unrealistic dreams of an idyllic life getting "back to nature."

On May 9, Allen wrote to the owner of the farm, a Mrs. LaSalle, who was living in Buffalo at the time. "The farm land that you own on East Hill is to my heart quiet, green pines at the state-land edge where there's still a stream in May with trees I don't know names of." He continued, "Your old farm is like a lonely Eden. . . . I feel strongly enough about the purity and goodness of the land itself that I think that if we humans can solve our complications, East Hill will show itself a good and healthy place to live." Before the sale was completed, they began camping on the land, and with the help of a neighbor, Ed Urich, started to clean out the silt from the bottom of the well. They planned to lay pipe to the house and install a pump, put in a gas heater, and generally fix up the property for year-round use, since it had not been inhabited for years. It took a bit of coaxing from Allen, but eventually Mrs. LaSalle agreed to sell him the farm.

Allen knew that he could not manage a farm by himself, so he asked his friend Gordon Ball and Gordon's girlfriend, Candy O'Brien, to help run the farm. Gordon was a handsome young filmmaker whom Allen had met through Jonas Mekas. He was somewhat interested in farming and had just returned from Mexico where he and some of the members of his commune had been jailed by the police for an unspecified crime, or maybe it was their long-haired hippie appearance. Gordon was also a friend of Barbara's, and having nothing else in mind, thought farming with Allen would be a good way to support himself while he continued to make movies. While living on the farm Gordon made a film titled *Farm Diary* in regular eight-millimeter and recorded many of the daily activities that constituted their lives there. It reveals Peter's enthusiasm for farm life, but also shows that he was not able to give up amphetamine use as Allen had hoped.

Allen didn't have much time to debate the pros and cons of buying a farm, as he had a million other things to do, from fulfilling his long list of reading obligations to making sure he met commitments for fund-raisers and benefits. He left no stone unturned in his quest to find financial support for a dozen different causes, even going so far as to write a letter to then CIA director Richard Helms,[59] asking him for ten million dollars for COP. Allen had read that the CIA was funding many right-wing organizations, and he thought that in all fairness they should fund a few liberal causes as well. "Otherwise one part of the citizenry has been unfairly defrauded of its prerequisites and dignities," he said in his letter. It came as no surprise to anyone when the CIA failed to send a large check to the Committee On Poetry.

Controversy continued to follow Allen wherever he went. He gave a reading at Portland (Oregon) State University in late May that caused a great disturbance in the Portland community. The student newspaper published a photo story about Allen before his reading in which they reprinted Richard Avedon's famous portrait of Allen and Peter in the nude. A scandal ensued; the newspaper editors were reprimanded and the whole issue seized. Allen wrote to the Portland newspapers calling the affair a tempest in a teapot and hoped that university administrators would act calmly and take no rash actions against the student newspaper. Then Ken Kesey and Neal Cassady picked Allen up in Portland in their magic school bus, Further, and drove him to Bellingham to teach classes for a few days at Western Washington University. Allen listened to Neal's nonstop babble and related it to "Joycean syntax in 20th Century English Prose." The following evening Ken, Neal, and Allen acted as masters of ceremony for the Jefferson Airplane, who played at the college gym. That would be the last time that Allen and Neal would ever see each other. With these and several other readings Allen was able to earn enough money to pay for the land in Cherry Valley without taking out a mortgage. He was getting tired of life on the road and looked forward to vacationing in Europe that summer.

When Allen got back to New York he attended Ed Sanders's victory party on June 27 at the Peace Eye Bookstore. Ed had finally been found not guilty on the obscenity charges. It was a hot summer night and the small store was packed with well-wishers. As the celebration was under way, the neighborhood kids began to throw Fourth of July firecrackers in through the open door of the shop. Courageously, Allen went out to the sidewalk and knelt on the pavement offering a peaceful mudra with his hands. The firecracker-throwing continued until one of the young thugs rushed up with a sharp hunting arrow, as if to stab Ginsberg in the neck. Allen kept his composure and spoke to the kids calmly, eventually winning them over with his mild-mannered heroism.

Allen's father was now retired and growing older. He had never been

---

[59] Richard Helms (1913–2002): CIA director from 1966 to 1973.

abroad, and since Allen had been asked to read at the Spoleto Festival in Italy that July, he decided to invite Louis with him to visit the great cities of Europe. Louis wanted to see the graves of Keats and Shelley in the little Protestant cemetery in Rome, and Allen thought they could even try to get an audience with the pope. Allen still wanted to meet Ezra Pound; he wrote to Pound and asked if he might be allowed "permission to come visit briefly at that time and pay my respects." Olga Rudge, Pound's companion in his later years, replied that Allen would be welcome to drop in when he was in Italy.

Because of his heavy reading schedule, Allen was making enough money to hire Alene Lee, an old girlfriend as well as the woman featured as Mardou Fox in Kerouac's novel *The Subterraneans*. Alene earned her living from secretarial work and the one thing Allen needed was a secretary. During that summer she typed his 1955–56 journals for a possible Grove Press book. It relieved Allen from some of the pressure, since he was inundated by paperwork and there were not enough hours in the day for him to manage it alone.

On the Fourth of July, Allen flew to Italy. Louis and his wife, Edith, planned to follow him a few weeks later and to meet him in London. On July 7, Allen went to hear *The Magic Flute* in the tiny red-velvet-seated Spoleto opera house and there he caught a glimpse of Ezra Pound in the audience. Before the opera began, Allen went down to introduce himself to the older poet. Allen took his hand as Pound graciously stood up and then stared at Allen for a long time, remaining perfectly silent. It was a wonderful moment for Allen as he at last met the old man, and Pound's silence did nothing to spoil their meeting. After Allen helped him sit back down, he returned to his own seat.

Two nights later, it was Allen's turn to read. The police in Spoleto seemed to be waiting for him, and they picked up copies of the Italian translation of his poem "Who Be Kind To" that were being passed out at the door and took them to the police station. There was no trouble at the reading, however, and his appearance went smoothly. Allen read a selection from his work including a small Spoleto mantra he had composed and the noted Italian poet Giuseppe Ungaretti translated. After his reading Allen walked over to have a beer in the little café across the plaza from the Duomo with fellow poets Octavio Paz and Desmond O'Grady. While Allen was standing by the bar waiting for his drink, a tall man in a business suit approached him and identified himself as a policeman. He ordered Allen to come with him. Allen's fear of the secret police, learned so well from Havana and Prague, welled up inside and he felt a wave of panic. He slipped back to his seat at the table and told Desmond that the police were there to arrest him. For the next three hours he was interrogated at the police station with Nanda Pivano and

Patrick Creagh there to help interpret. The police explained that any word that was in the Italian dictionary with the italicized word *obscena* written next to it was unfit for publication; Allen was subject to arrest if he uttered those words in public. Allen responded that the words themselves didn't matter and when read in context with the rest of the poem, they were not obscene at all. He told the police that his poetry was a message that expressed goodwill to peaceful men and not an obscenity.

After the police interview, the Spoleto organizers rushed him back to the festival to prove that he had not been imprisoned and to nip any rumors to the contrary. The paparazzi snapped even more pictures than usual and the story ran in all the Italian newspapers. By that time, Allen was beginning to find the whole scene invigorating and, unlike his experiences in Cuba and Prague, he enjoyed being at the center of another controversy. The festival organizers agreed to pick up the legal bills for Allen's defense, and the next night Spoleto's founder, Gian Carlo Menotti, went onstage and stated that he would support Allen and his work in front of the court. After initial assurances by the police that no action would be taken, they hinted that "a slight legal process would be instituted against the poem in Allen's absence," which went on for years. Allen began to smell a rat. It was not until five years later in 1972 that the case was finally decided in Allen's favor.

After the festival Allen flew to London and stayed with Panna Grady in her Hanover Terrace garden apartment near Regent's Park to await his father. A few nights later, he and seventy-nine-year-old Ungaretti teamed up again to read in London's Queen Elizabeth Hall. Allen read Blake's poetry, and this time Ungaretti read his own Italian translations of the same poems. It was all part of a larger poetry conference and was the primary reason for Allen's trip to England. Allen had met Ungaretti years earlier in New York and found him to be the liveliest of a distinguished older generation of Italian poets. At one of the parties they attended together, Panna sampled her first hashish brownies and imagined she was having a heart attack. Allen was able to calm her and reassure her that everything was fine and that she was experiencing the normal effects of the drug. A few days later he was invited to watch Mick Jagger, Paul McCartney, and John Lennon record "Dandelion," the trio of superstars performing together for the first time. Ginsberg stood in the control room, wearing a bright red satin shirt that Paul had painted for him, and pretended to conduct the music through the soundproof window as he watched the singers perform inside the studio. They were all dressed in paisley and velvet and looked like "Botticelli graces" to Allen. He was in ecstasy; in fact, being with these musicians was one of the high points of his life. Before the evening was over they were treating Allen like a "familiar holy phantom" and they all talked about their souls and spirits.

Later that month at the International Dialectics of Liberation Conference in London, American black activist Stokely Carmichael appeared and shouted angry admonishments at the audience. Allen did his best to calm the crowd by chanting the Prajnaparamita Sutra afterward. In England he also had time to check the proofs for a small book called *TV Baby Poems* to be published by Cape Goliard, and then went with Tom Maschler on a short trip to his house in the Black Mountains of Wales. Sitting on a hill in the Welsh countryside, Allen took LSD and composed a Wordsworthian English landscape poem, which he considered one of his best efforts. He wrote about the nature surrounding him, the lambs and cows and the fog drifting over the mountains. He had a peaceful trip with no recurrence of the earlier terrors and fears he had previously experienced with LSD, and he used that experience as proof that you could be creative and make something beautiful while high.

Wales Visitation, CP, p. 488

Early in August Allen heard from Irving Rosenthal and Barbara Rubin that Peter had a serious methedrine problem back home in New York. He had hallucinated that the apartment was on fire, called the fire department, and then proceeded to smash most of the windows and destroy much of the furniture. Allen phoned Peter as soon as he got the news, and although he still sounded shaky, Allen believed the worst was over. By telephone, he got the feeling that Peter was still in touch with reality, but he was completely at a loss about what he should do from Europe. Aside from his honest concern for Peter's own safety, Allen was worried about the security of his manuscripts and tapes, which were all in the apartment. He sent Irving a detailed list of the most important items and asked him to rescue them if Peter continued to act crazily. He was afraid that Peter would either destroy everything in a rage or be taken to Bellevue, leaving the apartment unguarded. He wrote directly to Peter asking him not to harm his manuscripts whatever else he might do. He reminded him that they had seen other people using meth and it always brought actions that were completely chaotic and irrational. He advised Peter to quit speed and all needle drugs fast and clean up before it brought them more heartache. He left it up to Peter to tell him if he wanted him to return home or if Peter wanted to join him in London. Barbara promised to take care of Julius if Peter wanted to go to England to be with Allen for a while. "Not much more I can do meanwhile best I sit out here and take care of Louis," Allen wrote to his brother, Eugene. He halfheartedly hinted that he could come back to take care of things once his father's trip

Edith, Allen, and Louis Ginsberg ~

was over. Then he sent some money to Peter to fix the windows and their moldings, which apparently he had damaged badly, but, of course, Peter spent that money buying more drugs. Before long the electricity and telephone were disconnected and Allen was even more out of touch than before.

When Louis and Edith arrived on August 15, Allen became too busy being a tour guide to think much about the situation back in New York. He and Louis gave a reading together at the Institute for Contemporary Arts, and his father came on so vibrant that one of the small publishers in London offered to publish his next book. Louis hadn't had a book of his own in more than thirty years and he was quite flattered by the offer. They all stayed in Panna's comfortable apartment and soaked in the charm of London. Louis, in particular, enjoyed the literary history that seemed to exist on every block. Their plans were to stay in Europe for three weeks and after London see Paris, Rome, and Venice. It turned out to be a nice trip for everyone. Allen enjoyed playing the tour guide and this gave him the perfect occasion to do just that. He took his parents to see the Tower of London and the British Museum, but his father caught a cold that landed him in bed for his last two days in London.

After England they moved on to Paris, sat in Hemingway's cafés under the summer trees, and went on a sightseeing cruise along the Seine. Allen had the pleasure of showing his own father some of the world that Louis had heretofore seen only in movies and photographs; he realized that part of his enjoyment was in having his father see how much his son knew about everything. In Paris they wanted something a little more comfortable than the Beat Hotel, so they stayed at a cozy hotel across from the church of St. Germain des Prés, near the statue of Diderot. Louis had always dreamed of traveling to these great cities on a grand tour. They strolled down to the Seine and browsed in the wooden bookstalls on the Left Bank, buying a few etchings of those same bookstalls as souvenirs. It was a pleasant part of the trip, and they enjoyed quiet days drinking coffee, visiting Napoleon's tomb, and exploring the Ile de la Cité.

From Paris they went to Rome for a week, staying at the Hotel D'Inghilterra on the Via Bocca di Leone. One evening they met Desmond O'Grady, who took them to a traditional wild goat supper and escorted them back to their hotel on a midnight carriage ride through the ancient Roman Forum. A little excitement was added to their trip when Allen went to the Spanish Steps in the middle of a sultry night to relax and cool off with some of the young homosexual men who gathered there. He hadn't slept with anyone since leaving New York, he complained in one letter, but it was okay and he didn't have any "sad longings." But on that particular night, if someone was available who liked him, he hadn't planned on turning them down. While he was sitting on the steps amid more than a dozen other long-haired men, a police van came along and scooped them all up. Allen tried to melt into the background, but they nabbed him, too, and took him to the police station for questioning. Although Allen was well known and over forty years old at the time, the police called his father and asked him to come down to the station to pick up his son. By the time Louis arrived, they had already released Allen, but it made a great story. No one had done anything wrong, but the police had been making a sweep to look for troublemakers and pot smokers and Allen was caught in the net along with the other hippies. He was pleased that Louis was called because Louis was able to see that Allen had been harassed merely for having long hair and not for just cause. Louis enjoyed telling the story of going to the jailhouse to spring his son.

All three of them were becoming exhausted from the rigors of the trip, and after more sightseeing at the Vatican, they made their final stop in Venice. Of all the cities they visited, this was the most charming, in Allen's opinion, and he enjoyed seeing Louis and Edith happy and enchanted by Europe. They met Ungaretti on the Piazetta San Marco in the moonlight and it was a spectacular way to end their vacation.

After he had seen his parents off, Allen went to stay with Nanda Pivano and her husband, Ettore Sottsass. He continued sightseeing in Milan and visited the Brera Palace, whose galleries were filled with paintings by Caravaggio and Raphael, and followed that with a walk around Milan's magnificent marble Duomo. Compared to Allen's normal Spartan accommodations while on the road, Nanda's giant apartment was quite luxurious. He was given his own key to a two-room guest suite and was free to come and go as he pleased. By this time Allen had convinced himself that things were back to normal with Peter in New York and wrote to ask him if he wanted to come over. "You wouldn't have to make it with me sexually if that's what's making you shy," he reassured Peter. He wrote to Louis and Edith telling them that Peter sounded fine again and that the house was in good order, so there was no need to worry. Neither was true, but Allen didn't know that at the time.

Pentagon Exorcism, CP, p. 491

In early October Allen wrote to Peter again and tried to define his sexual position as it concerned Peter. Allen thought that candor might help the situation and that if Peter was overdoing the methamphetamines because he physically hated having sex with Allen, a formal statement might help clear the air. "I'm happy making it with you alone as long as we make it. I just chase after boys as substitute when I get the idea that you don't want to be stuck with me and that I'm generally too old and repulsive to you now after so much familiarity. I mean I really got the idea the last year especially that you basically don't dig making it with me and so as not to lay my needs on you I diverted sex lovemaking to others and accepted the situation cheerfully rather than getting hung up on it and laying guilt on you or me. I don't in any case want to monopolize all your sex imagination and don't fantasize monogamy for you or me. If you've been at all avoiding lovemaking with me because you think I need or deserve younger various cats, well stop that thought and lets make it more again, I'd rather stick with you, if it were still pleasant to you. But basically, I think you've told me, that I'm getting physically too unappealing, which is no betrayal or fault of yours, that's nature. So I've not wanted to force myself on you lest I seem even more unappealing in the cold light of detached awareness. I have need for love touch and sex come but I'm not so nuts as to think that you or anyone has to find me sexy, so I've just been taking what comes to me without my having to force the situation by willpower." Ultimately, Allen was concerned about the effect that drugs were having on Peter, and he didn't know what frame of mind Peter was in. In conclusion he again worried that his manuscripts would disappear during one of Peter's rages, so he asked other people to check on him.

Allen stayed in Milan for a few days and worked with Pivano on some translations before leaving for a tour to Pisa, Siena, Florence, and some smaller readings in bookshops in Naples and Turin. Again Allen wrote to Olga Rudge, asking when he might visit Ezra Pound. "If he finds conversation value-less or difficult, I'll be happy to sit in silence, or sing mantras for an hour," Allen offered. By now he was familiar with the Buddhist act of *darshan*, when a disciple sat at the feet of the master, without speaking, learning by watching and merely being in the presence of his guru. He realized it was not a mystical exercise, but a practical way of "seeing and examining someone whose intelligence is unobstructed, whose breath is unobstructed, whose body is unobstructed, whose psycho-physical make-up is unobstructed or full of character. That isn't a rationalistic or mystical or mysterious matter—it's common sense." Allen hoped to do the same with Pound, although it wasn't exactly in Allen's nature to learn by quiet observation.

Olga agreed that Allen could visit them at their Rapallo retreat along the Ligurian Sea for lunch on September 23. Nanda drove him there for the day and again Pound sat perfectly silent throughout the meal. Pound's apartment was modestly furnished and overlooked the bay from the hillside. His room was filled with blue light reflected from the water. Olga chatted and asked questions, but Pound himself did not say a word, except at Olga's prompting when he asked Allen if he wanted to wash his hands before lunch. Otherwise he was almost dead silent, which reminded Allen somewhat of Julius in his catatonic state. At the end of the visit Allen sang the Hari Krishna mantra and the Prajnaparamita Sutra to him, which Nanda thought startled him. Olga said he must have enjoyed it or he would have left the room. Before leaving, Allen, Nanda, and Ettore took him out for a drive alone to a waterfront café a mile or so away in Portofino and sat for an hour over iced tea. The most he ever said was an occasional "no" to some of Allen's never-ending questions. He wanted to know if Pound had ever smoked pot, what he thought of Williams's poetry, or if he wanted more iced tea. Allen was convinced Pound was completely aware of everything that was going on, his silence to the contrary, because at lunch Olga asked him directly about the name of a book Pound had liked by author Paul Morand and he said in crisp, correct French, *Ouvert à la Nuit*. They took him back to Olga and concluded their visit.

A week or so later, Allen wrote to Olga thanking her for the luncheon and asking her if he might visit again when they were back in Venice in the fall. Allen was convinced that through perseverance he could get Pound to open up and talk. Olga replied and invited Allen to come to their house in Venice on October 22 around noon. With a month to kill in Italy before the visit, Allen was able to catch up on translation work and correspondence. One letter that he wrote was a warning to Ferlinghetti that because of America's involvement in Vietnam, Allen was refusing to pay the portion of his taxes that went to the military to finance the war. He had recently received a notice from the government indicating that the IRS would seize the $182.71 that Allen owed them, so he suspected that they might try to garner this directly from his City Lights royalties and he needed to give Lawrence a heads-up in case that did happen.

Allen went alone to Venice and found a quiet room with a little balcony in a *pension* around the corner from Pound's house on the Calle Querini. He arrived punctually for lunch as invited and brought along some records as a gift. He had the Beatles' *Sgt. Pepper's Lonely Hearts Club Band*, Dylan's *Blonde on Blonde*, and Donovan's *Sunshine Superman* that he wanted to share with Pound. They enjoyed some wine and then Allen smoked a joint at the table with his coffee, "without calling attention," he wrote. What Olga thought is not recorded. Pound said nothing throughout the luncheon and Allen looked him straight in the eye and asked directly, "Well, old man, how old are you?" Finally Pound spoke, "82 in several days." Allen played the records he had brought and then chanted for another hour before leaving without Ezra's uttering another word. Pound was going to be a tough nut to crack, but Allen was determined to get some words of wisdom from him, no matter how long it took.

For the next few weeks, Allen hung around Venice, trying to see as much of Pound as he could. One day they attended a concert of Vivaldi in a nearby church and a few times they ate lunch out when Olga didn't want to cook. Allen discovered that if he asked specific questions about references in the *Cantos,* Pound would offer brief answers. So Allen asked about the holy water font Pound mentioned that was supposed to be to the right of the entrance of St. Mark's, and Pound said that the location of the font had been changed since he wrote the poem. Olga told Allen that no one had invited Pound to read in the United States in years, and Allen said that he might be able to get the University of Buffalo to officially invite him. Pound discouraged it by saying that it was "too late." Even if an invitation had been extended, they probably would have been too worried about the possible political backlash to make the trip. Pound's answers were all too brief, but Allen found them infused with sage wisdom. He pieced together the snippets of the things Pound said into a short summary, "A mess . . . my writing, stupidity and ignorance all the way through . . . the intention was bad, anything I've done has been an accident, in spite of my spoiled intentions, the preoccupation with stupid and irrelevant matters." The weeks spent with him were boiled down to a few pithy phrases. On Pound's eighty-second birthday, October 30, Olga invited Allen to come over and he sang the Prajnaparamita Sutra to him by the fireplace. Pound sat quietly. He appeared to be sad and ate some birthday cake and sipped his champagne. The high point of these visits came when, near the end of Allen's stay, Pound said to him, "But my worst mistake was the stupid suburban anti-Semitic prejudice, all along that spoiled everything." That was the one sentence that stuck with Allen, for he felt that Pound was apologizing and by doing so had redeemed himself for all the evil things he had said about the Jews during his years of Fascist support. Except for the period in 1954 when he first met Peter in San Francisco, there was no other time that Allen documented so extensively in his journals than these few weeks with Pound.

Allen felt he had devoted as much time as he could to getting closer to Pound, and by November believed that his presence was becoming tiresome for Ezra and Olga. He stopped once in Verona to find some more of the locations mentioned in Pound's *Cantos*. Then he visited Nanda, who was in the hospital in Milan for gallbladder surgery. He boarded his flight to New York on November 15.

Elegy Che Guevara, *CP*, p. 492

When Allen arrived home, he found that Peter had left the city in the VW bus to drive Irving Rosenthal to San Francisco. Allen had lost his keys on the trip and had to climb in through a window from the neighbor's, only to discover that his electricity and telephone had been disconnected. By stringing an extension cord out the window to the neighbor's apartment he was able to hook up a single lightbulb. Unfortunately, Allen had been naïve enough to send the money for the electric, phone, and rent bills to Peter, instead of paying them himself. Peter had used all the money to buy more drugs. The neighbors were eager to report Peter's strange behavior and hoped that Allen would do something about it. Disheartened, Allen wrote to Peter asking him to take whatever drugs pleased him, except for meth. He said that he wanted to live with Peter but didn't want to live with meth: "Things are so chaotic outside the house I need calm in house."

But Allen's home was never to be calm. Within a few weeks, he had been pulled back into the vortex of the antiwar movement. During "Stop the Draft and End the War Week," December 5–8, Allen, along with the noted pediatrician and

War Profit Litany, *CP*, p. 494

activist Dr. Benjamin Spock and fellow writer Susan Sontag, was arrested for blocking the doors of the Whitehall Draft Board in lower Manhattan. Nearly two thousand demonstrators had symbolically tried to disrupt the induction of new recruits, but were stopped by an even larger number of police, who surrounded the draft offices like an army of occupation. Represented by the ACLU, those arrested were given an unconditional discharge by the court with no arrest appearing on their records. Allen took advantage of the court appearance to read his "Pentagon Exorcism" poem, in which he asked, "Who represents my body in Pentagon? Who spends my spirit's billions for war manufacture?"

1968 ～

AS THE NEW YEAR OPENED, on January 4, a severe verdict was
handed down in the trial of Leroi Jones. Jones had been arrested and beaten
by the police during the five-day Newark riots the previous summer, during
which twenty-eight people had died. The police charged that Jones had been
in illegal possession of two revolvers and had openly advocated rebellion.
Allen believed that the cops had planted the guns on Leroi in the same manner that they were trying to frame him on drug charges. He testified on
Leroi's behalf in court, pointing out that violence within America was escalating along with the war in Vietnam. The court found Jones guilty of the
charges and Essex County judge Leon W. Kapp gave him the maximum sentence, two and a half to three years in prison plus a fine, with no possibility
of probation. In spite of Allen's attempts to help, Leroi was angry with all
white people, including Allen, and he refused to return
Allen's calls. Leroi's secretary told Allen that Leroi had   Kiss Ass, *CP*, p. 501
replied "kiss my ass" when Allen tried to get through to him.
Other white friends were turned off by Jones's hostility, but Allen understood his anger and was not deterred from continuing to support him. To
Allen the political games of the sixties were turning into brutal nightmares.

In between all the political intrigues, Allen was working on manuscripts for both City Lights and Grove Press and was making slow
progress. He was trying to quit smoking once again and was suffering
through nicotine withdrawal. While Peter was in San Francisco, Allen suggested that he drive up into the Sierras and look at some land he was

considering purchasing as a West Coast retreat. In 1966 Richard Baker had told Don Walters (Swami Kriyananda), Gary Snyder, and Allen about this land, and since then they had been planning to buy it together. Negotiations were moving along and Allen suggested to Phil Whalen that he might want to live on his part of the property for a few years until Allen could officially retire to the mountains. Gary suggested that Lew Welch might want to build a small cabin there as well. However, Peter never got the message; he was already back in the VW heading for New York by the time the letter arrived in San Francisco.

In the meantime Allen was putting the finishing touches on an extensive reading tour that he was planning for February and March, designed mainly to earn ten thousand dollars in fees for COP. If he had that amount in the bank, he could afford not only the California acreage but also the Cherry Valley farm. He discovered that it took nearly as much energy to plan a thirty- or forty-stop reading tour as it did to do the readings themselves, even with the assistance of his agent Charles Rothschild.

Then, at five o'clock on the morning of February 10, the phone rang in Allen's apartment. "Have you heard the news?" came a voice from Denver. Allen said he'd been away and hadn't heard anything. "Neal Cassady is dead in Mexico!" Allen nearly went into shock. "Sir Spirit's now home in Spirit," he thought. Neal had actually died on February 4 in San Miguel de Allende, Mexico, reportedly of exposure after having fallen down along some railroad tracks at night, but Allen had been away on a reading tour. Allen believed that Neal had been worn out by his years of taking speed, but publicly he would say that Neal's "happy spirit had been released from his body into the air." Personally, he was grief stricken. He looked out at the faint blue light of dawn and remembered all their years of friendship when sex was the one bond that had held them together. He couldn't help but feel that Neal's death was truly the end of an era.

Allen was melancholy and wrote in his notebook, "I'll be glad to get out of the burden [of life] myself, it's a dream." He called Kerouac and Jack told him he felt "as if the bottom dropped out." Jack didn't want to accept the truth, and for the next year refused to believe it, saying that Neal was hiding out somewhere. Allen wrote in his journal that Neal's liver had been damaged by speed, but he made a Freudian slip and wrote "lover damaged by speed," which was even more accurate. With a heavy heart Allen wrote "Elegy for Neal Cassady," in which he prayed, "Tender Spirit, thank you for touching me with tender hands/When you were young, in a beautiful

body." Neal was cremated and the ashes were given to Car-   Elegy for Neal Cassady, *CP*, p. 495
olyn, so Allen made a pilgrimage on his next trip to San Fran-
cisco that summer to see them, writing his poem "On Neal's
Ashes" at that time.

Despite his grief, Allen had dozens of reading dates to honor, and soon
he was on the road himself, appearing at thirty colleges over the next forty
days and reminiscing about Neal at every stop. Before he left New York, he
gathered together a huge sheaf of documents relating to the Leroi Jones
case, which he submitted to *Playboy* as absolute proof of the unfair sentence Jones had been given. Allen felt the whole incident was a sure sign of
the police state's takeover of the judicial system and one more example of
the prejudice against blacks that was rampant in the country. Even Allen
was surprised by the level of corruption that the case revealed, from the
jury selection to hearsay evidence to the judge's final refusal of probation.

As Allen traveled around the country, he had the opportunity to stop at
the grave of Joseph McCarthy one snowy day in Appleton, Wisconsin, the
senator's home town. The night before he had given a reading in Appleton
with the Fugs and the next morning about seventy-five people, including Ed
Sanders and Tuli Kupferberg, had met him at St. Mary's Cemetery on the
edge of town. Jack Newfield, the *Village Voice* columnist, had suggested that
they try an exorcism to disperse the demons that Senator McCarthy had unleashed into America. The incantation might not have worked, but it did
provide good street theater. Then on February 29, he flew to Washington to
discuss the legalization of drugs with his own senator, Robert Kennedy, who
was a presidential candidate at the time. Although he had the sense that
Kennedy was sympathetic, it did not lead to action. Kennedy   Chicago to Salt Lake by Air, *CP*, p. 498
was too wise to risk losing the election by supporting more
lenient drug laws. Allen couldn't believe that there was absolutely no one in power who wanted to listen to his commonsense talk.

The Movement, a blanket name that covered all sorts of youth groups
and organizations in the late 1960s, had been planning mass demonstrations
for that summer's Democratic Convention in Chicago. When Lyndon Johnson decided not to run for re-election and Bobby Kennedy looked like a viable peace candidate, some movement leaders began to think that Chicago
protests might not be a good idea. With Kennedy's assassination in early
June things changed again, but the leadership continued to debate whether a
large demonstration was advisable. Allen wanted to see a protest aimed at

ending the Vietnam War, but he also wanted to be certain that it was peaceful and not an excuse for a government bloodbath.

Manhattan Thirties
Flash, *CP*, p. 501
While the planning for Chicago was going on that spring and early summer, Allen's brother, acting as his lawyer, received final permission from the owners to occupy the house in Cherry Valley while the papers for the farm's sale were being drawn up. Peter, Julius, Barbara Rubin, Gordon Ball, and Candy, who had all been camping on the property in the VW, were now able to move into the house and get down to serious work. For Allen, the first and most important issue was to get Peter out of the city and away from speed. Allen DeLoach,[60] a friend and a professor at SUNY Buffalo, reminded Allen that he couldn't force Peter to give up amphetamines, but Allen was certain that settling permanently on the farm might help wean him away from them. After his long reading tour, Allen finally arrived at his new farm at the beginning of May, expecting to enjoy a happy reunion. When Peter heard the car approach he picked up the machete he had been using in the fields and raced up the path toward Allen, swinging it menacingly over his head all the while shouting unintelligibly. Everyone was terrified except Allen, who calmly walked toward Peter and greeted him warmly. Within a few moments Peter quieted and put down the machete.

The farm was intended to be a utopian experiment for Allen, yet it provided him with a practical education as well. He was overwhelmed by the immediate problems of owning a seriously neglected property, but buoyed by the help that Barbara, Gordon, and Candy were providing and optimistic that Peter would adapt and focus on serious manual labor. They had the summer to prepare the house for the long winter, more than enough time if everyone worked together. Allen arrived tired and depressed and resolved that after the next reading tour he would forever stop giving public appearances. Unfortu-

A Prophecy, *CP*, p. 504
nately, one of the first improvements Allen made to the farm was to have a telephone installed. Many visitors thought it strange to have a telephone in a house with no electricity, but to Allen the phone was the more important utility. His lifestyle was to continue much as it had in the city with the aid of his phone link to the incessant demands of the world outside the farm.

Having a phone was not nearly as daunting as the problems caused by all the characters on the farm. Barbara Rubin still hoped to transform Allen into a married farmer with a brood of children, which was probably the last thing

---

[60] Allen DeLoach was the editor of *Intrepid* magazine from 1964 to 1980.

in the world he wanted. Barbara wanted to be a Jewish mother even more than she wanted to be Allen's wife, and she dominated the farm, expecting and receiving almost total acquiescence. Peter continued to have serious substance abuse and mental problems, and Allen noted much of his erratic behavior in his journal. Peter could often be found roaming the farm mooing like a cow or running naked through the woods. Poor Julius was completely at Peter's mercy and was probably terrified to be so isolated; Peter treated him as his personal whipping boy and no one felt they should intervene between the brothers. Gordon and Candy had so much work to do that they fell into bed exhausted each night. Allen faulted Barbara the most for inhibiting sexual activities on the farm, because Allen wished a free and open sex life for all of them. When it became obvious to Barbara that marriage with Allen was not in the cards, she focused on her spiritual interests, in the form of the pious Chassidic community in the next town, Sharon Springs. Eventually she moved there and changed her name to Bracha Levy. Before long she married a young rabbinical student in a traditional Orthodox ceremony on Long Island. She only returned once to see the farm which she had discovered for Allen. She divorced, later married a rabbi, and moved to a Chassidic commune in the south of France, where she had five children successively. She died a few weeks after giving birth to her fifth baby.

The problems brought by the farm's many visitors and guests only added to the challenges faced by the residents. One of the original reasons Allen gave for buying the farm was that it could serve as a retreat for Kerouac. Allen little understood his old friend, for Jack would never leave the security provided by his new wife, Stella, and his mother, Gabrielle. Instead, Corso, Huncke, and Bremser descended on Cherry Valley and brought along their own stash of drugs and alcohol, despite Allen's prohibitions on such things. There was no way Peter could be weaned from speed with all the other drug addicts in the house. Allen established firm rules about not allowing needle drugs on the farm, but for Huncke and Corso rules were meant to be broken, and they ignored his feeble attempts at regulation. Occasionally, Allen would convince himself that Peter had given up speed, and he wrote to his friends repeatedly that the problem was solved. Allen abstained from initiating any sex with Peter, hoping that it would take the pressure off their relationship.

Before long the farm grew to include dairy goats, a cow, a horse, chickens, ducks, pigeons, and an assortment of dogs and cats. There was a small barn for livestock, but each new animal increased the amount of work Gordon, as farm manager, had to do. Luckily, their friendly neighbor, Ed Urich, was willing to give them advice and help on practical matters. Urich had lived alone in Cherry Valley since the war, doing odd jobs for a living. The townspeople called him the hermit, since he was single, but he was more social than anyone. Their biggest project that summer was to clean out the well and figure out some way to get water into the house. That was a difficult task without electricity. They explored several ways to do it, and the expenses continued to mount. The house and property had cost nine thousand dollars, but Allen ended up putting at least that much into fixing it up over the next few years. The farmhouse itself was a hundred years old and in such bad shape that tearing it down and starting over would probably have been the more cost-efficient way to go; they hoped to salvage the house at minimal expense by doing most of the hard work themselves. The experience came in handy later when Allen decided to build on his California property. By then he knew it was simpler to build from scratch.

At this same time, Allen privately wrote his most sexually explicit poem to date, called "Please Master." It was a poem so "dirty" even he couldn't imagine ever being able to read it in public. The poem re-

Please Master, vealed his masochist side more openly than anything he had
CP, p. 502 written before and hinted at how he had managed to get himself into so many bad situations. Since Allen felt it couldn't be read in public, he read it in public. It was tolerated, if not adored, by an audience at his next San Francisco poetry reading. Allen believed that by graphically cataloging his own sexual peculiarities, things that others were ashamed to speak about, it would force people to talk and they would no longer be embarrassed by their individual sexual longings, whatever they were.

By June Allen had begun to meet with Abbie Hoffman, Jerry Rubin, and Paul Krassner, all members of a loosely organized group known as the Yippies (or Youth International Party), to discuss the upcoming Democratic National Convention. The organizers were already having problems with the city of Chicago, which had refused to grant them park permits for peace rallies and camping. The police and city leaders had adopted a "get-tough" attitude, and the "peace" marchers themselves were divided over whether confrontation would help or hurt their cause. The more radical groups thought that it was time to take violence into the street and confront the government by literally fighting against the war. Allen believed that the umbrella organization called the Yippies was in the hands of the wrong leaders. Although he liked Hoffman, he wasn't certain he could trust the peacefulness of people like Jerry Rubin, and he had real doubts about other activist organizations, such as the SDS, and some of the more militant Black Power organizations that also planned to march. Fearing that violence would only beget more violence, he wanted any demonstrations he lent his name to, to be peaceful.

That summer, before Allen went to Chicago, Louis and Edith met him in San Francisco and Ferlinghetti offered them the use of his cabin. They all loved the remote beach and green forests and it inspired both Allen and Louis to write several new poems. Allen confided to his father that his short bucolic poem "Bixby Canyon" was written while he was relaxing with a joint. A few days earlier at a reading, Allen had met a young poet named Andy Clausen who lived in Berkeley. After hearing some of Clausen's poems, Allen went to see him to talk to him about his work. He liked Clausen's young, exuberant, working man's poetry. It was the beginning of another important mentoring relationship, as Allen took Clausen under his wing while Andy continued the literary legacy begun by the Beat Generation.

Bixby Canyon, *CP*, p. 505

Back in New York City for a few weeks, Allen had the apartment to himself since everyone was up at Cherry Valley. He attended to his mail, had some dental work done, and wrote several poems. Then he took a short vacation in Mexico with his brother, Eugene, his sister-in-law, and their children via car all the way from New York. They caught up on family news and had a pleasant visit. It was fun for Allen to show his brother around his Mexico, until the Mexicans threatened Allen with expulsion for sporting a beard. The U.S. consul had to intervene on Allen's behalf. They climbed the Pyramid of the Moon, revisited Orizaba Street in Mexico City, and drove over some of the same roads he and Lucien had taken during his first trip two decades earlier. The scenery was as beautiful as ever. After the vacation, Allen stopped in California to pay his respects to Carolyn Cassady and to touch Neal's ashes on her mantel.

Crossing Nation, *CP*, p. 507

Smoke Rolling Down Street, *CP*, p. 509

Pertussin, *CP*, p. 509

Swirls of black dust on Avenue D, *CP*, p. 510

Violence, *CP*, p. 511

Past Silver Durango Over Mexic Sierra-Wrinkles, *CP*, p. 512

On Neal's Ashes, *CP*, p. 513

Then, following a brief stop back at the farm, Allen flew off to Chicago for the convention demonstrations. Although it was billed as a "Festival of Life," Allen felt that he was alone among the organizers in his commitment to nonviolence. He agreed that they should use guerrilla theater and street comedy to get their messages across, but he made them promise that no violence would be tolerated. That was his sole condition for cooperation, and Allen repeatedly stated that he didn't want to take part in anything that might lead to bloodshed. In Chicago a mood of confrontation was in the air. Most of the protests were to take place in Lincoln Park, even without permits, but all factions agreed that if the police decided to shut down the demonstration, everyone would leave the park peacefully. A week earlier, Allen had tried again unsuccessfully to get the Chicago authorities to grant permits for the peaceful use of the park. No one knew what would happen when thousands of demonstrators showed up. Allen trusted a few of the organizers because he'd worked with them before in Berkeley to diffuse the violence aimed at the Vietnam Day marchers by the Hells Angels. Some of the newer activists, whom he didn't know as well, seemed much more combative.

Going to Chicago, CP, p. 514

Officially, Allen had press credentials issued by *Esquire*. They had commissioned Allen, William Burroughs, Terry Southern, and Jean Genet to cover the convention for their magazine. Allen was thrilled to be able to spend some time with Genet. As it turned out, Genet had to sneak into the country from Canada because the U.S. government would not give him a visa, due to his French prison record. In the days leading up to the convention, the crowd of demonstrators grew to about ten thousand people, and a worried police force began to overreact with threats of violence and mass arrests. At the height of the protests, a virtual police riot ensued, earning more media coverage than the nomination of Hubert Humphrey, which went on simultaneously inside the heavily guarded auditorium.

On August 25, the Sunday afternoon before the convention's keynote speech, the police unexpectedly surrounded the park, armed with guns and clubs. Many people panicked, not knowing if the police would attack or not. At the time there was no communication at all between the police and the demonstrators. Since he was in the country illegally, Genet was lucky to sneak out quietly before the trouble started, but Allen stayed in the park to exercise passive resistance. Some of the Maoist leaders tried to provoke a confrontation, while Allen and other pacifists looked for ways to avoid conflict by leaving the park. As the police had unwisely decided to block all the exits, there was to be no escape.

Allen witnessed the problem as it developed and immediately sat down in the center of a large group of demonstrators and began chanting "OM" into a portable microphone. He intended to chant for about twenty minutes and calm himself and the crowd immediately around him. It seemed to work, so he continued chanting as the circle around him grew larger. Allen ended up chanting for seven and a half hours, until he lost his voice completely. During the process he became aware that his chanting was causing a physiological change in himself, an unmistakable electric sensation that crept over his body, like nothing he had experienced before. Allen's breathing became more regular and steady, as if he were breathing in the air of heaven and then circulating it back out into the universe. The Hindus call it *prana*, when you realize that the air inside you and the air outside you are one and the same life force. It was an enlightening experience for Allen, who until that moment had seen mantra only as a type of song. This experience altered that impression and he became aware of the very air itself as vital and evanescent. He now realized that it was possible to alter states of consciousness solely by chanting. In the past he'd had euphorias and ecstasies through the use of drugs, but this was the first time that his old fear of death had disappeared completely. Allen realized that he was in fact already dead and that the body was only a revolving mass of electricity.

On the political level, Allen was extremely disappointed by what happened in the streets of Chicago. As the week progressed the police brutality worsened and President Johnson called out the National Guard to restore order. It was the same week that the Soviets chose to invade Czechoslovakia with their own tanks. For five days Chicago was under siege, all of it beamed into living rooms across America. Allen was shocked by the violence and regretted that he had taken part and encouraged others to get involved. The demonstrations were poorly organized and the message that was sent across the country was not an affirmation of life, as the Yippies had promised. Much later, after the war had dragged on for several more years, Allen would shock many of his fellow protestors by summing up the antiwar movement as a failure. "More and more by hindsight, I think all of our activity in the late sixties may have prolonged the Vietnam war. As Jerry Rubin remarked about '68, he was so gleeful he had torpedoed the Democrats. Yet it may have been the refusal of the Left to vote for Humphrey that gave us Nixon. So that might be the karma of the Left, because of their anger, their excessive hatred of their fathers and the liberals, their pride, their vanity . . . our vanity, our pride, our excessive hatred. It may be that we have on our karma the continuation of the Vietnam war in its worst form with more killing than before. . . . What was the point of the Left? It was saying, 'End the war.' What was the action of the Left? It refused to support Humphrey because he wasn't 'pure' enough."

In 1976 Allen wrote to Charles Upton[61] addressing the same issue. By

Grant Park: August 28, 1968, *CP*, p. 515

---

[61] Charles Upton: Poet, author of *Panic Grass* (City Lights, 1968).

that time he had formulated his ideas more precisely and said that anger and pride had made him and others on the left blind to the fact that they had helped elect Nixon and thus prolong the war. Allen said he was reluctant to believe that it might have been as much his fault as anyone else's that the war went on as long as it did, but in the end he knew it was true. "We thought we were doing right but so does everybody," Allen commented honestly. He suggested that no one should believe that he owned the truth and demand his own way as he had done against Johnson and Humphrey. He urged Upton to remember that "any gesture taken in anxiety will spread anxiety in any situation; any gesture involving aggression will chain-reaction equal aggression one place or another." Allen remembered that the more he argued and shouted at his father about the war, the more Louis defended the government's position. Then one day by accident, Allen overheard his father taking Allen's side in an argument with strangers. The lesson he learned was to give adversaries enough space to alter their views by themselves.

When Allen returned to Cherry Valley in September, he immediately set up the attic as a meditation room, complete with altar shrine at one end. On a mirrored tray under the eaves he placed the large *vajrasattva* statue that he had bought in San Francisco's Chinatown that summer. Beside it he put some wooden beads that Phil Whalen had brought from Japan, his *dorje* (a thunderbolt), a *drilbu* (ritual bell), a wand, and a conch shell. He also placed on the shrine his own assortment of spiritual souvenirs: a statue of a Mexican god from Teotihuacán, a transparent Comanche stone, an iron incense plate from Cost-Plus, a wooden fish, a cactus skeleton, a fossil, candles, and a wooden spoon from Russia. On the wall he hung his favorite *thangka* (scroll painting) and a poster of the angel of the annunciation by Fra Angelico.

Now that he was out of the city much of the time, he worried about the manuscripts he had left behind in his apartment and in his father's house in Paterson. When Allen mentioned this to Lionel Trilling, he suggested that Allen store them in the Rare Book Department of the Columbia University Library. There the papers would be safe and also available to students who might want to look at them. Allen had always been a pack rat, and his archive had grown so large that it was beginning to take up too much of his own time to manage it. He had carefully saved everything of importance since he was a boy, and aside from his earlier donation of the *Kaddish* manuscript to the Living Theater auction, he had never parted with anything. He had even saved airplane ticket stubs, calendars, phone message books, and canceled checks. The Special Collections Department agreed to place dozens of boxes on deposit in the library's vault. Over the next few decades he made periodic additions, which grew to fill hundreds and hundreds of boxes. Allen didn't plan to sell them immediately, but wanted a safe place to store them for the short term. "I intend to sell them eventually when there is need for money for the poetic community or for myself in distress; at the moment & for the next few years there seems to be no need," he wrote to Charles Mixer, the librarian in charge of his collection.

Allen spent most of his time that fall on the farm. He learned quickly about cows, barns, goats, snow, wood fires, and organic gardening. They had still not figured out how to get the water from the well to the house, and that became a priority. They hoped to solve some of their other problems by installing a wind-charger, which would give them the power they needed without hooking up to the electric company's grid, which was beyond their financial means. Unfortunately, try as they did for years, the wind-charger never met their needs for electricity.

Around this time Allen embarked on a project that was to become as important to him as his own poetry. For many years he had been studying Blake's *Songs of Innocence and Experience*. Now, in light of what he had witnessed in Chicago, Blake's prophetic words seemed to have even more importance. Blake had first sung his poems to his friends, hence the title *Songs*, but the music had not been notated in Blake's day and was long ago forgotten. Allen decided to compose his own music to his favorite Blake poems. On the Chicago trip he wrote the first tune, to go with Blake's "The Grey Monk," whose verses seemed so prophetic to Allen at that moment. "But vain the Sword and vain the Bow, / They never can work War's overthrow. / The Hermit's prayer and the Widow's tear / Alone can free the World from fear." In the course of the next few weeks more than twenty additional songs followed. Allen did not attempt to recreate Blake's music, an impossible task, but instead wrote contemporary scores. He found an old A. B. Chase pedal-action stop organ and set it up in the living room of the farmhouse. He used that and his Indian harmonium to compose simple tunes, which he then recorded onto his tape recorder, since he did not know how to write music. Barry Miles came to visit from London and helped with the recording, and Allen felt he would have enough for a record in no time.

One of the visitors to the farm that November was Lawrence Ferlinghetti, who came for a brief stopover on his way to Italy. Allen, Gordon, and Julius jumped into the station wagon to go along for the ride when the time came for Peter to drive him back to the Albany airport. It was a rainy, chilly evening and after seeing Lawrence off, they all got back into the car for the sixty-mile drive home. As Peter pulled out of the blue-lit airport parking lot, he smashed into another car coming along the main road that he hadn't seen. It was a serious accident; both cars were badly damaged and their station wagon was a total loss. Allen, who was sitting in the middle of the front seat, hit the dashboard and suffered a fractured hip and four cracked ribs. No one else in either of the cars was injured except for minor cuts and bruises. As soon as the cars collided Allen felt the pain and knew he had been hurt. He wrote that his first thoughts were, "Ooh Jesus, how'd I get stuck in this body-stump again, and what kind of mortification got to pass to get out of this fix?" Allen was rushed to the Albany hospital and remained there for a few weeks. The doctors prescribed crutches for two months of convalescence at the farm. It was the first time Allen had ever broken a bone and for him it was a welcome sentence. He needed a forced slowdown and a respite from being the famous "Allen Ginsberg" for a while. Through the cold winter he stayed on East Hill and wrote poems and worked on his Blake project. It was a good excuse not to travel, to be lazy, and maybe to try to quit smoking once more. No one ever suggested that it was anything other than an accident even though Peter was strung out and acting increasingly crazy in many ways.

Car Crash, *CP*, p. 516

1969 ～

ALLEN'S IMMEDIATE PLANS for the early part of the year were changed by the car wreck. He was forced to stay put and forgo his travels until the first of February. His sentence was made easier for him by the heavy snow that surrounded the little farmhouse that January. Even in the winter the farm continued to attract Allen's friends, and friends of Allen's friends, some of whom couldn't resist bringing needle drugs with them to Cherry Valley in spite of Allen's wishes. He had to remind Huncke and his friend Louis Cartwright many times of his rule. "As you remember this place was set up as refuge from chemical city conditions," he would write, but only Allen seemed determined to keep the farm drug-free. He had to tell his guests, including Huncke and Corso, that they were not welcome at his farm unless they abided by his dictates on this particular subject. The reasons were twofold. First, Allen knew that the police were keeping an eye on him and would like nothing better than to bust him and his friends for drug possession. Second, Allen had seen that people like Peter had been changed dramatically by speed, and it was his primary concern to preserve the farm as a retreat where Peter could clean up. But Allen was slow to act when he discovered that his friends were smuggling in needle drugs, and eventually he himself had to conduct searches for the offensive drugs. Allen's loyalty to his friends made it difficult for him to follow through with his threats, and the drug use continued nearly unabated.

Aside from the serious issue of drug use, there was a nagging if less insidious problem with those guests who came to the farm expecting someone to

care for them. The farm was intended to be self-sufficient,
yet several visitors offered no help with the chores. The regular residents of the farm resented it when they were burdened with the extra work of cooking and cleaning while
some people lazed around doing nothing. They tried posting
lists of chores to elicit help with the work on the farm, but to
no avail. Some of the visitors were so inept at country ways
that they actually made more work for Gordon and Candy.
On Thanksgiving Candy had toiled in the kitchen preparing
the holiday meal for several people. In return she was treated
like a servant girl at the table, while people thanked Allen
profusely for the wonderful feast he had provided. She split
up with Gordon and left the farm during that winter, in part
because of the work she performed for which she got no
thanks.

Over Denver Again,
CP, p. 519
Imaginary Universes,
CP, p. 520
Rising over
night-blackened Detroit
Streets, CP, p. 521
To Poe: Over the Planet,
Air Albany–Baltimore,
CP, p. 522
Easter Sunday, CP,
p. 524
Falling Asleep in
America, CP, p. 525

One day at the beginning of April, Allen awoke to find the left side of his
face paralyzed. It was an utterly frightening situation, but his doctor quickly
diagnosed his problem as Bell's Palsy.[62] He assured Allen that it was only a
temporary condition, yet even the name made it worrisome. The effects of
the palsy were not as temporary as the doctor had predicted, and his left eye
and mouth drooped a bit for the rest of his life. Possibly the palsy had been
brought on by the medication he was taking for his leg, but the cause was
never made clear.

A few more of his engagements had to be canceled as a result of his illnesses, but he did keep his promise to visit the University of Arizona in late
April. While in Tucson, he used a cane to get around. There
Allen held a press conference at the Ruth Stephan Poetry
Center that was attended by reporters and students alike. It
was a typical question-and-answer session until Bob Thomas,
one of the reporters, entered into an argument with Allen on the subject of
homosexuality. Attempting to make his point, Allen called Thomas a "cocksucker," which further infuriated the man. As Allen left the press conference,
Thomas punched him in the mouth, cutting his lip and knocking him to the
ground. The altercation made it into several newspapers the following day, as
well as Time magazine, where Allen was described inaccurately as following

Northwest Passage,
CP, p. 526

---

[62] Bell's Palsy: A condition caused by trauma to the cranial nerve that results in weakened or paralyzed
facial muscles.

Thomas out of the room "shouting a string of obscenities at him." Once again, Allen was reminded of the power of words and the heated emotions they could raise. He regretted that he had opened his mouth so rudely, and resolved to do better in the future when faced with hostility.

Sonora Desert-Edge, *CP*, p. 530

By June, Allen felt much better and prepared to go into the studio to record his Blake songs. Allen and Miles rented studio time in New York City and asked several of their musician friends to back Allen up. Some, such as Don Cherry and Julius Watkins, did it for free, and others, like Elvin Jones, needed a larger fee for their time. Miles was able to interest his friends at MGM/Verve in releasing the record and they advanced Allen the ten thousand dollars he had already invested in studio time for the project. Allen was insistent that Peter take part in all the recordings even though his drug use made him more a problem than an asset. He felt that Peter's wide vocal range allowed him to reach the high notes and cover up some of Allen's own musical shortcomings. One of the young musicians who had first visited the farm that spring was Rosebud's seventeen-year-old younger sister, Denise Feliu. She was a guitarist and nearly lived for rock 'n' roll. During her short stay at the farm, she and Peter hit it off well. His appetite for sex, which had been diminished by all the speed, was reawakened by the young girl.

Reflections in Sleepy Eye, *CP*, p. 532

That summer the IRS pursued Allen for refusal to pay nearly fifteen hundred dollars in taxes, the result of the Vietnam War tax-resistance position that he had adopted in 1967. In July he wrote to Secretary of the Treasury David Kennedy, "I am obliged to inform you that I spent all of the modest amount of money I earned that last year in keeping alive and helping others maintain their lives. You should also know that I am physically, mentally and morally unable to earn moneys to pay for the Vietnam war. Basic, traditional ethics of my profession of poetry prohibit me from assigning money earned incidental to the publication of literary compositions pronouncing the inhumanity and ungodliness and un-American nature of this war toward funding the very same war." His statement of principle did not deter the IRS from trying to collect the money from Ginsberg one way or another.

Independence Day, *CP*, p. 534

One event stood out more than the others that summer at the Cherry Valley farm. On July 20, all the residents of the farmhouse crowded into Ed Urich's tiny one-room shack to watch the television he had hooked up to an old antenna and a series of car batteries. Walter Cronkite had broken into CBS's regular programming to report on man's first step onto the moon.

Along with everyone on earth, they watched Neil Armstrong take his walk on the surface of the moon and plant the American flag in the dust.

In a Moonlit Hermit's Cabin, *CP*, p. 535

It is hard to believe that Allen missed the Woodstock music festival in August, since it was held eighty miles from his Cherry Valley farm. He had been invited, but since he

Rain-wet asphalt heat, garbage curbed cans overflowing, *CP*, p. 537

had been traveling so much, he wanted to relax on the farm and catch up on work. All weekend people passed through Cherry Valley on their way to and from Woodstock, proclaiming it a glory to the planet. At the time, everyone on the farm had been involved with building a hydraulic ram house with an earthmover and shovels, so they couldn't get away. Huncke was living on the farm that summer, too, and even he helped as much as he was physically able. Peter continued to be a problem, fluctuating between drug-induced highs and lows.

In early September they made some repairs to the barn, which caused a lot of dissension among the group. Peter was treating Julius as his personal slave, and Allen tried to intercede on Julius's behalf, which only made Peter more obstinate and hostile. Sometimes Peter would make Julius work long into the evening, forcing Allen, Huncke, and the rest to delay their evening meal. Julius was wary of all of them and never knew whom to obey. Those arguments led Allen to the unhappy understanding that if he and Peter could not live in harmony, it was impossible for whole cultures, like Jews and Arabs, to live peacefully. Maybe America would never agree to less stringent drug laws or end the Vietnam War. It all seemed hopeless in light of their much less complicated yet equally insolvable domestic problems. Allen worried constantly that Peter's and Herbert's drug use would bring trouble to the farm. John Sinclair, poet and militant founder of the White Panther Party, had been sentenced in Detroit on July 28 to nine and a half to ten years for the possession of two joints. If the police raided the farm and discovered Huncke's stash of needle drugs there would be even greater punishment. Allen's journal from this period is filled with lists of worries, many more than even his usual litany of fears. "Will the Government trap me on the farm for tax refusals? Will my notebooks survive poesy reading tour? What can I say to thousands of students I'm trapped into chanting to, who want revolution? Tell them, [quoting Burroughs] 'The planet is finished?' Will Peter be happy with Julius on farm forever? Who'll care for East Hill's cows, goats and chickens, ducklings and horse, basement and

Death on All Fronts, *CP*, p. 538

roof if I go east to Brindiban or Peter takes off for Benares?" Allen worried that Barbara Rubin's Garden of Eden was turning into a hell on earth.

With these concerns on his mind, Allen had to go out and earn the money needed to support the people living on the farm; it was far from being self-sufficient. Everyone depended on his readings for the cash needed to operate and improve the place. He also had more benefit readings scheduled, with several approaching in Detroit in mid-October to support John Sinclair's defense.

Unexpectedly, on Tuesday, October 21, 1969, Jack Kerouac died in St. Petersburg, Florida. The call came in much the same way as it had for Neal's death a year earlier, out of the blue, without warning. Allen knew that Jack's drinking had gone out of control and that he was sick, but he had not guessed that the end would be so sudden. The day before, while watching television, Jack had vomited blood and was rushed to the hospital, where he died the following day of stomach hemorrhages caused by severe alcoholism.

Allen spent most of the day on the telephone making calls to such old friends as John Clellon Holmes, Lucien Carr, and Robert Creeley, and to his father. He called Stella, Jack's widow, in Florida, who told Allen that his last letter to Jack had "made him feel bad." Allen sat in the dark farmhouse that night, listening to the clock ticking, thinking of the death of the man who had been his closest friend twenty years earlier. He read and reread Jack's last article, which appeared in the October 22 issue of the *Washington Post*, "After Me, the Deluge," and realized once again that Jack had been right. "The meat suffering in the middle of existence was a sensitive pain greater than any political anger or hope," Allen thought. He realized that he, himself, was also in the process of dying. The only escape from life was death. He and Gregory, who happened to be at the farm when the call came, took a long walk in the woods through the autumn leaves, remembering their old friend and remarking as they looked up at the sky that Jack had lived long enough to see man walk on the moon. Then they stopped along the path to carve Jack's initials into the bark of an old tree. Everyone in the house was sad. Gregory burst into tears in the middle of the night and Allen couldn't stop sobbing. His thoughts and Jack's had been so much in tune when they were younger that Allen often considered them of one mind. "The days of my youth rise fresh in my mind," he noted in his bedside journal. The image of Jack watching Allen say farewell to the steps of the Union Theological Seminary dorm on the day they met twenty-five years earlier was as fresh as if it had happened yesterday.

Allen, Gregory, and Peter flew to New Haven, where Allen was scheduled to read, and then they all drove up to Lowell with John Clellon Holmes for the funeral. They saw Jack laid out in his coffin in the Archambault Funeral Home on Pawtucket Street. He was holding a rosary in his wrinkled hands and looked large-headed and grim-lipped, with a tiny bald spot on the top of his skull that Allen hadn't noticed before. The furrow on his brow was familiar to Allen, but his middle-aged heavy appearance reminded Allen more of Jack's father, Leo. To Allen, seeing the corpse was like beholding a Buddha in a *Parinirvana* pose who had been on earth only long enough to deliver a message and then left the shell of his body behind. Allen turned to Ann and Sam Charters, Jack's bibliographer and her husband, and said, "I have the feeling now that Jack has imagined us all."

Heavily committed to readings, Allen did not have much time to grieve his loss. He sat long enough to write down bits and pieces that he collected into a poem called "Memory Gardens." Amid the recollections of his old friend he questioned what he was doing on earth himself and wrote, "Well, while I'm here I'll/do the work—/and what's the Work?/To ease the pain of living./Everything else, drunken/dumbshow."

Memory Gardens, CP, p. 539

Flash Back, CP, p. 542

Graffiti 12th Cubicle Men's Room Syracuse Airport, CP, p. 543

With no chance to slow down now, Allen had to be on his way again. Every time Allen left the country during the Vietnam War era, he was under continual surveillance. In early November customs officers detained him while they diligently searched his suitcase, which contained nothing more dangerous than his clothes, a Tibetan seal, a position paper on narcotics prepared for the late senator Robert Kennedy, a springboard binder of typed poems, several large copybooks of original manuscripts, and the handwritten manuscript of his poem "These States." He had a clipping from the *New York Times* with him about several narcotics agents who had resigned because they were caught pushing dope, suspicions that Allen had claimed for years. And last but not least, he carried a few issues of Montreal's underground newspaper, *Logos,* one of which contained a short contribution by Allen. The customs inspectors couldn't decide whether *Logos* was pornographic or not, so they sealed it in his valise for closer inspection by the experts at New York's Kennedy Airport. By the late sixties, Allen's name appeared on all the government's lists of suspicious persons, and although he had no warrants for his arrest, the authorities stopped to search him at every opportunity. In this case *Logos* was merely another of the dozens of underground newspapers published by the counterculture. It was becoming a nuisance for Allen to travel out of the country because of bogus searches like this.

After Thoughts, CP, p. 544

In December Allen flew to Chicago to testify at the conspiracy trial of

Abbie Hoffman, Jerry Rubin, David Dellinger, and the others known collectively as the Chicago Seven. They were all charged with conspiracy to
incite a riot during the Democratic National Convention. The trial itself
was a microcosm of the clash in values between the youth movement and
the older establishment. Allen's appearance became famous in and of itself
when he angered the judge by chanting "Hari Krishna, Hari Krishna" on
the witness stand. Judge Julius Hoffman reminded him that the language
of the court was English, not Sanskrit, and his patience was tested further
when Allen began to chant "OM" as he had in Lincoln Park. The trial
evolved into a mixture of comedy and tragedy; even Allen couldn't resist
cursing the court with his hand gestures under the pretext of demonstrating *mudras*.

During the last week of 1969, Allen was scheduled to read with his father at the Marine Stadium in Miami as part of a benefit sponsored by *Planet
News*, yet another underground newspaper. Allen was looking forward to relaxing a few days afterward with Louis, because they had been quarreling
more than usual over their differences on the war in Vietnam and the militant group known as the Weathermen. Allen tried to convince his father that
the police were more of a problem in America than the Weathermen were.
In rebuttal Louis had told Allen that he hoped the police would "bloody their
asses." Allen was horrified and wanted to have a calmer discussion to reach
some kind of rapport with his dad. They planned to visit Haiti together
along with Edith right after the reading.

The city of Miami had been especially cautious about public performances ever since Jim Morrison's March 1 "alleged" public unveiling of his
private parts on stage during a performance at the Key Dinner Auditorium
in Coconut Grove. Extra security was assigned for Allen's and Louis' readings. As Allen read his poem "This Form of Life Needs Sex," the police scurried about, not certain how to handle such lines as "I will have to accept
women/if I want to continue the race,/kiss breasts, accept/strange hairy
lips behind/buttocks." After many conferences in the back of the auditorium, the police pulled the plug while Allen was reading his much less sexually offensive poem "Pentagon Exorcism." They turned on the house lights
and announced that the reading was over. When Allen asked them to at
least allow his father to give his half of the reading, his request was refused.
Louis considered Allen's reading offensive, too, but he would never have
expressed that opinion in public. He always cringed at Allen's use of words
like *cocksucker* in public. The disappointed audience filed out without any

disturbance. The next day Allen took the city to court for interrupting his reading, and although the judge failed to award Allen damages, he did side with Allen, concurring that the police had no right to stop his reading. The judge ordered the city to make the stadium available to him to complete his reading but restricted the sale of additional tickets. Allen felt vindicated and finished his reading a week later, after he and his family had returned from a few days on a Caribbean beach.

1970 ~

ON JANUARY 10, Charles Olson died at the age of sixty, continuing the long string of premature deaths among Allen's circle of friends. Along with fellow writers John Wieners, Ed Dorn, Harvey Brown, and Ed Sanders, Allen was asked to be a pallbearer at his funeral in Gloucester, a fishing town north of Boston. Olson was another of the older literary giants Allen had admired. As those poets died off, Allen was becoming the elder statesman of modern poetry. He didn't shy away from that mantle, but felt that his old mentors, Williams, Kerouac, and now Olson, were irreplaceable. Meeting Harvey Brown, the publisher of Frontier Press books, at this time proved to be serendipitous. Brown was in a position to give COP forty-five thousand dollars, and Allen distributed that money to Huncke, Ornette Coleman, Don Cherry, John Wieners, Ed Sanders, Gregory Corso, and a few others who found themselves in need. Some of the money also went to winterize the Cherry Valley farmhouse, so Allen was doubly thankful to have Brown's support. He wanted nothing more than to finish his current reading tour with enough money to enable him to retire from performing for a while. But his dreams of retirement didn't stop him from drawing plans for a small cabin to be built on his twenty-four acres of land in the Sierras, next to Gary Snyder's Kitkitdizee property. Although it had cost him only six thousand dollars a few years earlier, he had done nothing with the land. Now he visualized a small retreat, which he would call Bedrock Mortar.

G. S. Reading Poesy at Princeton, *CP*, p. 545

In the early part of 1970 Allen stayed on the road, earning money so that fellow poets like Ray Bremser could finish manuscripts for new books. On one of his trips Allen visited the Japanese poet Nanao Sakaki in Albuquerque. He had met Nanao through Gary Snyder in Japan in 1963, when he was on his way back from India. Allen liked Nanao and learned a good deal about Japanese poetics from him. They enjoyed inventing koans for one another. "Where is Ryoanji Garden?" they might ask. "I don't know." "That's a very good answer," was usually the reply.

During the first week of March, Allen rode with Eugene and his family to see a total solar eclipse in Tidewater Virginia. Since childhood, Eugene had been interested in astronomy and loved telescopes and everything involving outer space. By now Allen was so famous that he was recognized everywhere, and Eugene noticed that Allen was torn between wanting his privacy with his family and wanting to be noticed. It was only a short break in his schedule before he went on to other reading commitments around the country, winding up in San Francisco, where he would visit Corso, Snyder, and McClure. By early summer he hoped to be back on the farm at Cherry Valley in time to help with their extensive gardens. He was still obsessed with death and now, approaching forty-four, Allen felt he was legitimately old enough to think about his own old age and death. His recently diagnosed hiatus hernia,[63] not too painful but usually more common in people over sixty, and the broken bones from the car crash, coupled with the early deaths of Kerouac, Cassady, and Olson, gave him cause to ponder and to write melodramatically about "the fading of the play," as he put it.

Friday the Thirteenth, CP, p. 546

On May Day, Allen was invited to New Haven to speak at a rally in support of Bobby Seale and seven other Black Panthers who had been charged in the 1969 murder of Wayne Kimbo, a former Panther member and suspected FBI informant. The rally was large enough to shut down the Yale campus for the weekend and was even supported by the president of the college, who spoke that day, expressing his wishes that the trial would be moved out of New Haven to ensure a fair decision. As Dave Dellinger reported, the demonstration was peaceful, but later in the day, government Cointelpro agents spread the rumor that a demonstrator had been killed and tried to instigate violence against the police so that the police would be justified to react with violence against the marchers. As in Chicago, Allen took over the microphone onstage and chanted "OM" to the fifteen thousand or more

---

[63] Hiatus hernia: A problem occurring when the stomach moves up into the chest cavity through a hole in the diaphragm.

people in attendance, helping avert a riot. Jean Genet was also there, to give an unofficial commencement speech to the students. Later, Allen sent Genet's speech to Ferlinghetti and encouraged him to publish it. City Lights printed it as a pamphlet with an introduction by Allen, who described the event as he saw it from the podium.

That same day, Allen spoke with Al McCoy about a book McCoy was working on that was close to Allen's heart. It was to be called *The Politics of Heroin in Southeast Asia*, and it tracked the history of the government's involvement in illegal opium dealing around the world. Allen had always believed that the police and the government were involved more heavily in drug smuggling than they would admit. Along with McCoy he set about to prove his point. In what little free time he had, Ginsberg went to Washington and did research at the Institute for Policy Studies on the subject. He talked to several ex-CIA agents and helped uncover bits and pieces of a much larger picture of corruption and hypocrisy. At one point Allen challenged Richard Helms, then the director of the CIA, to a bet. Allen wagered that if he were correct and the CIA was deeply involved in drug smuggling and dope dealing, Helms would have to sit and meditate an hour a day for the rest of his life. If Ginsberg were wrong, Allen would give him his Tibetan *dorje*, a ritual thunderbolt implement. Allen spent years amassing files and researching the topic. The most frustrating part about it was that he was never able to convince the editors of his hometown newspaper, the *New York Times*, to take the story seriously. It seemed that they couldn't care less whether the CIA was dealing dope or not. In 1971 Allen had lunch with C. L. Sulzberger, who had been the chief foreign correspondent for the *Times*. He was a member of the Sulzberger family, which owned a large percentage of the newspaper, and it was his considered opinion that Allen was "full of beans." It would be nearly ten years before anyone on the *Times* staff admitted that Allen had been right, and no one ever gave an explanation of why they never bothered to investigate the serious charges that Allen and other members of the underground press had made.

At the end of April, President Nixon expanded the war and ordered the invasion of Cambodia. Demonstrators in cities and on campuses across the country sprang into action to protest. On May 4, protesters at Kent State University were fired on by the National Guard and four students were killed. In the wake of the Cambodian incursion and the Kent State killings, more than one hundred thousand people gathered in Washington on May 9 to voice their opposition to Nixon and to the war. That May more people protested against American policies than during any

other month in the nation's history. Allen went to Washington to sur-
round the White House before chanting "OM" with demonstrators in
front of the Washington Monument. He decided to spend
a few extra days in the capital to proceed with his own
CIA drug research. In the course of several years he collected enough information and pursued his investigations
in such a thorough and professional manner that it impressed even his
critics.

Anti-Vietnam War
Peace Mobilization,
CP, p. 549

Back in Cherry Valley Allen had settled down to work on his heroin traf-
ficking research and to catch up with the stack of unanswered mail that continued to grow on his desk. He enjoyed having the break from travel and
enough time to practice at the organ. He wanted to learn how to notate music, as he worked his way through more of Blake's songs. With Gordon's
help, the farm had become more functional, and the monthly expenses had
dropped to one thousand dollars from the two thousand dollars Allen had
been sinking into it. The wind-charger was set up on the platform next to the
ram house with batteries and a solid-state inverter, yet it still didn't work.
They hoped that come the winter, when the wind was stronger, it would be
able to generate some electricity.

Although often an unrewarding burden to Allen, occasionally the farm
was a welcome retreat from a world that seemed ever more gloomy. Leary
and Sinclair were both in jail, the war was raging on, and the evidence that
he was unearthing about his own government's involvement in drug pushing indicated a hopeless morass of hypocrisy. He took comfort in the farm,
and enjoyed the vast garden. The physical labor took his mind off other
things, but even on the farm there persisted the inescapable problems of Peter, drugs, and personal conflicts. Allen often wondered why he continued to
make these quixotic investments and what benefits came from them. They
plodded on, planting an orchard of fruit trees, as well as strawberries and asparagus beds on the hill above the house, as if they would stay there forever.

The daily domestic grind meant that Allen didn't get much time for his
own creative writing. It was clear, too, that his sexual relationship with Peter
had ended long ago. Allen might fantasize that there had been great moments, but those moments had usually come at times when Peter acquiesced
to Allen's relentless desires and not often through Peter's own initiative.
Now Peter was so involved with the farm, his girlfriends (currently Denise),
and drugs that there wasn't time for Allen. Allen knew better than to pressure Peter sexually; it only added to the strain on their already fragile relationship. Ray Bremser was a bad influence on Peter, too. Aside from drugs,

they both drank to excess and then became even more difficult to get along with. On top of all that Gordon and Bonnie Bremser, Ray's wife, were the only ones who did any productive work at all, now that Candy had left. Seeing them work so hard made Allen feel guilty, too, for they were almost like his employees. "They work for me, I capitalist, provide the cash," he wrote. It wasn't a happy time for him. He repeatedly got angry with Peter, who continued to abuse Julius. Allen didn't know what to do about any of the discord. He felt like the tyrannical head of a dysfunctional family.

In midsummer Corso showed up, and things that seemed as if they couldn't get any worse, did. Gregory loved to drink as much as Ray and Peter did. They smuggled beer in from town and drank it down by the new pond. Before long they became mean and nasty with each other and especially toward Allen. Bad days were usually followed by a peaceful day of hungover repentance, but the following day they'd get drunk on vodka and start all over again. One afternoon, an inebriated Corso picked a fight and left Gordon with a black eye, which in true Corso style, he tried to deny.

From time to time Peter tried to quit speed cold turkey, and these attempts always encouraged Allen. Peter's technique for kicking was to work as hard and as long as he could. The goal was to exhaust himself to the point where he wouldn't be able to think about amphetamines. Unfortunately, that method only made him more manic, and he never succeeded in quitting for long. To most people it was clear he needed professional help to overcome his addiction.

Life had become so complicated on the farm that Allen decided to simplify things. There were too many animals that required too much work and attention, so he got rid of the cow, horse, pig, and goats. There was a long list of things that needed attention, from adding barbed-wire fencing around the meadow to pruning the apple trees. And sometimes the improvements they made actually caused new problems. Peter had the idea to dig an outside entrance to the basement of the house, so they would have easier access to the cellar. After that it became impossible to store canned goods and food supplies in the basement, since now those supplies froze in the winter, instead of being insulated by the ground and foundation walls.

Through it all, East Hill farm saw a steady stream of visitors. Occasionally in the summer there were as many as a dozen guests staying on the farm at any given time. Miles's visits were always a welcome diversion for Allen because he could work on his recordings. The most serious handicap to working on those tapes was the farm's lack of electricity. With the batteries charged by the windmill, Miles could do a little work, but all too frequently

Maretta would use up all the power playing records on her phonograph, so progress was rather slow. In addition to his technical help with Allen's Blake songs, Miles indexed more than a hundred reels of taped readings Allen had accumulated over the past decade.

Claude Pelieu and Mary Beach, Allen's French translators, visited along with Charlie and Pam Plymell and their baby. They all loved the area and later moved to the region themselves; even Allen's brother, Eugene, bought a piece of property nearby, where he hoped to one day build a cabin. Allen was more often able to enlist help with his office work, typing, and letter writing than with the hard manual labor of the farm, which few of his friends seemed suited to. It was a vicious cycle—the more people who visited, the more people had to be fed and cleaned up after. Allen wrote to Ferlinghetti in desperation and told him he needed help in handling his literary affairs. It was becoming more difficult for Allen to keep up with the large volume of mail he received. His conscientious answers to each letter only encouraged more questions and requests. He often reminded Ferlinghetti that his one desire was to have his collected poetry published in hardcover by someone, as they had discussed for years, but he didn't want to make a move without his old publisher's agreement. Even though Grove Press was very interested in making a deal, no progress was ever made.

After Corso left the farm to teach in Buffalo, Allen had strong reservations about allowing him back again. He wrote to Gregory and suggested that he check himself into a hospital to kick his habit. Allen was fearful that Corso was on a self-destructive path just like Kerouac and that he would not live long if he did not get help. He told Gregory that his offer of loving and friendly care was not enough for Corso and that the hospital was the best route. As usual, Allen promised to help pay for his treatment if Gregory would enroll in a detox program. Corso wouldn't give up, though, and continued to ask Allen for money each week, promising that he would seek help soon. After a while, Allen lost his patience and told him, "You can get money the same way I can, sit down type your poems and work. I refuse to work for you anymore." Despite his tough stance, Allen could not put his foot down without offering something more, so he promised Gregory that if he sent his poems out to publishers, Allen would pay him fifty dollars for each rejection slip he received. As much as Allen wanted to be exacting, he was always a pushover.

Even though Allen experienced the problems of addiction at the farm, he was still interested in the effects of drugs on his own mind. He and Maretta shared a Mexican psilocybin mushroom (*Psilocybe Mexicana*) and en-

joyed a mild trip. He walked around for six hours over the hills and through
the woods seeing everything as if with new eyes. It reminded him of being in
a fantastic Tolkien landscape. It was his first such experience since his *Wales
Visitation* and he found it remarkably rewarding. Allen owned a beautifully
illustrated copy of R. Gordon Wasson's book *Soma: Divine
Mushroom of Immortality*, in which Wasson made the argu-   Ecologue, *CP*, p. 550
ment that the ancient drug *soma* referred to in sacred texts
for a thousand years was what is commonly called fly agaric (*Amanita mus-
caria*), which could be found in the area around Cherry Valley. Although they
collected several specimens of the white-spotted bright-red mushroom caps,
Allen wanted to wait until he found an expert more knowledgeable about
them before his own experimentation.

That fall, in need of money and secretly wanting to distance himself
from the farm and its problems, Allen left for an extended reading tour. He
went to Richmond and New Orleans on his way to the Caribbean for a series
of conferences with William Kunstler, the defense attorney for the Chicago
Seven. They spent time on several islands and Allen relaxed by snorkeling
and taking hikes to see thousand-year-old Arawak petroglyphs. On the plane
from Antigua to Bermuda he lost the manuscript for his next book, a springboard binder containing his last five years of poetry. After that setback, he returned to Cherry Valley in November and took a bus down to New York City
to hear Charles Reznikoff read his 1920s vignettes at St. Mark's Church. By
then Allen was trying to sit in *darshan* with every elder poet who had influenced his work while they were still alive.

One practical way that Allen found to calm himself was to sit each
morning for an hour and to breathe slowly through his whole body repeating the "Guru Om" mantra that he had practiced for years.
He was able to slowly relax as he thought about the multi-   Guru Om, *CP*, p. 561
tudinous mass of business he had to attend to. Ferlinghetti
had received an invitation for him and Allen to do a reading tour of Australia
the following May; it was just the kind of escape that Allen could look forward to. It would give him some distance from the farm for a month or so,
enable him to explore a part of the world he had not seen be-
fore, and earn some extra money to support the farm. He   "Have You Seen This
even considered extending his trip so that he could visit India   Movie?," *CP*, p. 563
again, or maybe Persia. He needed to be on his own and
cleanse his system.

November was a peaceful month on the farm. Denise, Peter's girlfriend,
exerted a calming effect on him, but unfortunately it didn't last for long.

Cherry Valley farm in winter ~

When Lafcadio came to visit, Peter made Laf get cleaned up so that he could get in bed with Allen for a welcome-home screw. When Lafcadio balked at the idea, Peter became furious and spent the night banging pots and pans in the kitchen shouting to himself. Allen wished he was back in the city for a dozen different reasons; he saw the "farm as vast creaky" and not fulfilling his needs. When Peter went back to the city for occasional visits, things were peaceful for a change, and Allen was able to work on his opium-trafficking research as much as he wanted to. Then, as if he didn't have enough to do, he started another investigation. He wanted to do a survey of the government's repression of the underground press for a PEN[64] report, another project that would take years to complete. He even found time to squeeze in a visit with Louis Zukofsky, another poet about his father's age. Allen sat at Zukofsky's parlor piano in Brooklyn Heights and played his Blake songs for him and listened to his advice about poetics.

It was also in November that Allen was publicly accused of being a member of the Communist Party by Donald Manes, a New York City politician.

---

[64] PEN: An international organization of concerned writers and editors who work together on political and social issues.

"I am not, as a matter of fact, a member of the Communist Party, nor am I dedicated to the overthrow of this or any government by violence. I must say that I see little difference between the armed and violent governments both communist and capitalist that I have observed." Allen's political positions took center stage so often that he had to remind himself that he was first and foremost a poet and that his fame stemmed from that.

By that time, even if the literary establishment disliked his politics or his poetry, it was difficult for them to discount Allen's influence and the significance of his work on the course of American literature. As a sign of that importance, he, along with Richard Howard, W. D. Snodgrass, and Carolyn Kizer, was asked to judge that year's National Book Award for poetry. Allen hoped that he might be able to help Snyder, McClure, Corso, or Lamantia achieve long-overdue recognition and a much-deserved award for their books. When the committee would not agree to any of Allen's candidates and gave the poetry award to Mona Van Duyn for her book *To See, To Take*, Allen was incredulous. He had nothing against Van Duyn or her poetry, but he could not believe that the judges considered this more creative or inspired than Corso's new book, *Elegiac Feelings American*. The rift between the judges caused a stir in the newspapers that was fueled by Allen's candid, usually critical comments, and Mona Van Duyn found herself drawn into the fray in defense of her own poetry.

By Christmastime, drugs had pushed Peter over the line once again. He raged at Maretta Greer, screaming that she was no saint and accusing her of laziness and indolence around the house. True, she was one of the less productive members of the household, but still it was a frightening thing to see Peter in one of his angry fits. Peter went back to the city during the holidays to get away from the farm and left Allen and Maretta alone to manage the remaining farm animals. Allen, who was beginning to enjoy being left alone for short periods of time on the quiet farm, worked and meditated peacefully over the holidays without having to worry about Peter.

1971 ~

AS THE NEW YEAR BEGAN, Allen had still not decided what to do with his land in the Sierras. Lew Welch offered to buy it from him, but Allen didn't want to sell. He had always hoped that someone like Welch or Whalen would live on his property for a few years, until he could retire there in his old age. He asked Snyder if he thought the property was large enough to split into thirds, giving Welch, Whalen, and himself equal shares. Gary replied that the land couldn't sustain three homes and the idea was scrapped. The point became moot in May 1971 when Welch hiked into the nearby woods with his rifle and was never heard from again.

Allen hadn't seen Bob Dylan for several years, so he looked forward to Barbara Rubin's wedding in late January, where Dylan was also to be a guest. Everyone enjoyed themselves at the reception, and even though the men and women were separated, as was the custom, the women couldn't resist peeking into the men's room to see Dylan. That evening helped Allen renew his friendship with the increasingly reclusive singer. Later that year, Dylan took jazz composer David Amram with him to hear Allen read at NYU. After the reading they all went over to Allen's apartment on Tenth Street and held an impromptu jam session. When Allen tried to record the session, Dylan asked him to turn off the machine. Although he didn't want to be recorded, he didn't mind helping Allen with the music for his new songs, an opportunity Allen couldn't refuse. One night a few months later they went to a recording studio together and spent six hours taping some of his Blake tunes, like "Nurse's Song" and "Spring." Allen improvised the words to a song about flying to Puerto Rico, with Dylan providing the music; Allen called it "Vomit Express." Dylan liked it and sweetly encouraged Allen to improvise more songs during his performances and run the risk of making a fool of himself onstage. It was the perfect suggestion for Allen.

Vomit Express, *FB*, p. 1

Going to San Diego, *FB*, p. 3

Jimmy Berman Rag, *FB*, p. 4

Many Loves, *FB*, p. 7

That winter Allen stayed in his quiet New York apartment for a few weeks and saw other old friends, including John Wieners. To Allen, John was now as nutty as a fruitcake, "but his texts delicious," he added. Miles was in from England and stayed at the Chelsea Hotel, where they worked late into the nights editing and indexing all the tapes from his poetry readings. Allen was generally pleased with the recordings, but complained that they were sometimes flawed by inferior equipment. In his earlier days he was sometimes drunk at readings, so those recordings were occasionally garbled. Although Fantasy Records backed out of producing the whole eighteen hours of the complete Ginsberg tapes, the best of the readings that were spliced together were used for commercial releases of his poetry in the decades to come.

Apart from editing his tapes with Miles, Allen's major projects continued to be the CIA dope-dealing research and the PEN underground press project. In March he returned to the Institute for Policy Studies in Washington to continue research on his opium-smuggling paper and while there, he read at the Corcoran Gallery with his father. In the audience was none other than Richard Helms, the director of the CIA. Talking to him after the reading, Allen tried to convince Helms of the truth behind the charges about government dope smuggling and tactfully omitted any reference to their earlier bet. But it was impossible for Allen to believe that the CIA director did not know that his agents were using drug deals to finance their activities. In Allen's mind, McCoy's book would set the record straight once and for all when it was released the following year.

That spring he began to view his Cherry Valley farm as an albatross around his neck that he regretted ever letting himself be talked into. Gordon Ball was growing tired of the farm, too, and was happy when Allen asked him to accompany him on a reading trip to Ohio, Wisconsin, Wyoming, and California. Allen's voice barely held out on the tour, becoming strained by the constant singing and chanting. Gordon acted as his road manager, making travel arrangements

Over Laramie, *CP*, p. 566

and helping with the luggage and musical instruments, so life on the road became a little easier for Allen. After the tour Gordon stayed on in California and the farm limped along without a manager.

After a reading at UC Davis in late April, Allen and Gordon visited Gary Snyder in the Sierras. As he sat on a rug on the wooden floor by the fire pit in the peaceful calm of Snyder's house, Allen realized that this was the kind of rural life he wanted. By building a cabin in the Sierras, he hoped to find the peace and quiet that had eluded him in Cherry Valley. They stayed for a week to enjoy the beautiful Japanese-style household that Snyder had built for himself with the help of a local crew of Zen woodsmen carpenters. Each morning Allen walked along the footpath to the cedar temple in the woods for an hour of meditation and talked to Gary about his plans to build a cabin of his own. He was so far behind in his writing projects that he was relieved when the trip to Australia with Ferlinghetti was postponed. He decided to stay in California to catch up on his paperwork. In May, while spending another week at Fer-

Bixby Canyon Ocean Path Word Breeze, *CP*, p. 567

linghetti's Big Sur cabin where he wrote his poem *Bixby Canyon Ocean Path Word Breeze*, Allen broke his little finger while skipping rocks in the ocean. It was a silly accident, but it meant that he could barely hold a pen to write. True to form, Allen managed to get a good deal of work done in spite of the inconvenience. He finished work on the twenty reel-to-reel compilations of his complete readings and was able to put one of his major projects to rest at last. It was

Hūm Bom!, *CP*, p. 576

sexually rewarding to be in California, too, where he said he could chase ass as much as he wanted and make out in the gay bars of San Francisco whenever the mood struck him. His celebrity status was making it much easier to meet men; finally, his fame was being put to good use, he thought.

On September 12, 1970, Timothy Leary had escaped from the California minimum security prison in San Luis Obispo where he had been serving a ten-year sentence and fled to Algeria. There he hid out with Eldridge Cleaver and the Black Panthers. After an argument with Cleaver, Leary had gone to Switzerland, where he was now fighting extradition. On July 8, Allen completed a *Declaration of Independence for Timothy Leary* with the help of the San Francisco Bay Area Prose Poets Phalanx, a group loosely organized to help Leary out of his legal troubles. Allen spent much time at the Fitz Hugh Ludlow Library on Columbus Avenue, near the City Lights bookstore, where Michael Horowitz, Robert Barker, and William Dailey had combined their large personal collections to form one enormous library of drug information. Anything that Allen wanted to know he could find there. It was from this private library that the efforts to secure Leary's pardon were being coordinated.

Since returning from India in 1963, Allen's spiritual life had stagnated. One evening that summer of 1971, Allen had the good fortune to spend a drunken night with Lama Chögyam Trungpa Rinpoche,[65] a master of the school of Tibetan Buddhism founded by Milarepa, a Tibetan saint and song-writer of the eleventh century. Allen saw in Trungpa a little bit of Jack Ker-ouac, especially in his drinking habits. Quite by accident Allen had bumped into Rinpoche one day in New York a year earlier. At the time, Allen was with his father, who was feeling a little faint, so Allen stole the taxi that Trungpa had flagged down for himself in front of a Manhattan theater. Allen recognized Trungpa, but didn't have the time to talk to him or explain why he was stealing his cab. Allen saluted him with a *namaste*,[66] recited the *Pad-masambhava* mantra, and then took his cab and dashed off with his ill father. Now he was glad to meet him in a more leisurely way and to apologize. It wasn't until years later that they realized Allen had actually met Trungpa even earlier while on his 1962–63 trip to India. Then Allen and Gary Snyder had visited the monastery where the young lama was training after his es-cape from Tibet.

Allen had never gone so far as to adopt his own meditation teacher, though he had thought about it for years. He had dabbled in Buddhism, but as with everything else, hadn't applied himself to the rigors of the discipline enough to become expert. During their initial discussions, Trungpa advised Allen to shave off his beard. He felt that Allen was too preoccupied with his own identity, symbolized by the wild beard that made him instantly recog-nizable. Without the beard, he said, Allen would be more anonymous and not be as focused on being "Allen Ginsberg." He also recommended that Allen ad lib and improvise more of his poetry in front of his audiences and not rely so much on reading, a suggestion similar to Dylan's advice on musical improvisation. "Why don't you do like the great poets do, like Milarepa? Trust your own mind," Trungpa advised.

Milarepa Taste, *CP*, p. 565

Allen was familiar with the general iconography of Buddhism and had

---

[65] Chögyam Trungpa Rinpoche (1940–87): Tibetan master of the Kagyüpa and Nyingmapa schools and founder of the Vajradhatu organization of Tibetan Buddhism.

[66] *Namaste*: A greeting made by pressing the two hands together near the breast and bowing the head gently.

read books by Evans-Wentz[67] and other Buddhist scholars. His interest went as far back as the books recommended to him by Raymond Weaver, one of his Columbia professors in the mid-1940s, and the books recommended by Kerouac. The major obstacles to Allen's studies had been his lack of a teacher and his reluctance to set aside time to sit and meditate every day. Trungpa's basic approach to meditation was to begin with *shamatha*, a Sanskrit word meaning the development of peaceful mindedness, to create a tranquillity of mind. Trungpa told him that the way to achieve tranquillity was to pay attention to the breath coming out of the nostrils and dissolving into space, which paralleled Allen's own experiences with breathing at the Chicago demonstration. Trungpa's repeated refrain, "If you don't sit, there is no point in my teaching you. It is as simple as that,"[68] served as Allen's call to daily practice.

While these new ideas about meditation were percolating in his head, something else came up. On September 1, Allen flew to Calcutta to witness the conditions in refugee camps there. Friends of Keith Richards of the Rolling Stones paid Allen's way so that he could report on the terrible tragedy of the millions of people fleeing the civil war in Bangladesh. It was a last-minute trip that he didn't have time for, but Allen was enthusiastic about helping in any way he could. In Calcutta it was the height of the monsoon season, and he found it more crowded than it had been ten years earlier. He bought a thirty-key harmonium that was smaller than his other one and would be easier to carry around on tour. Along with his friend and fellow poet John Giorno, who was also in India that year, Allen went back to Benares for a few days to visit his old haunts.

Both came back in time for the official visit to the Salt Lake refugee camps north of Calcutta. The camps consisted of thousands of makeshift tents and cardboard houses that stretched as far as the eye could see. The landscape was covered with people gathering in long lines for food and mothers holding sick babies and waiting for medicine. There were no sanitary facilities of any kind, and for mile after mile, the muddy roads were impassible and flooded knee deep from the rain. Seeing millions of hopeless human beings crowded into a tiny space in an already overpopulated country was heartbreaking. Allen began one of his greatest poems, *September on Jessore Road*, in an effort to describe the tragedy he witnessed during those

---

[67] W. Y. Evans-Wentz had helped introduce Tibetan Buddhism to the West through his translation of the *Tibetan Book of the Dead*.
[68] "View, Meditation and Action," *Vajradhatu Sun*, December 1979, p. 8.

weeks in India. The long poem paints a moving picture of the suffering caused by man's inhumanity to his fellow beings. It calls attention to the fact that the United States has resources enough to bomb Southeast Asia relentlessly, but can't help millions of starving refugees who want nothing more than a little rice to eat. "Where is America's Air Force of Light?/Bombing North Laos all day and all night?" he wrote.

September on Jessore Road, *CP*, p. 579

Once more he visited Calcutta's burning ghats to refresh his memories and bought a Shiva trident like the holy men carried to take home as a souvenir. He dropped in on old friends, like Sunil Gangopadhyay (Ganguli), who was now a successful writer working for a leading Bengali-language newspaper, and Jyoti Datta. They talked about old times, nostalgic for the College Street coffeehouse days of 1962.

As soon as he was back in the United States, Allen drove to Syracuse to visit John Lennon and Yoko Ono, who were performing there on October 9 as part of a long tour. They had asked him to drop in to see them in their hotel room, and Allen was eager to renew his relationship with one of his most famous friends. He read parts of *Jessore Road* to John, which brought tears to the musician's eyes. Then Allen brought out his new harmonium and finger cymbals and chanted "Om Ah Hum Vajra Guru Padma Siddhi Hum" to producer Phil Spector, while Lennon joined in on his guitar. Jonas Mekas was there, lucky to record them together when they played several mantras and a few of Allen's Blake songs. Always starstruck, Allen was elated to be in their company and he couldn't help but wish he were a rock star; in fact, most of his efforts during this period were in the form of songs, gathered together in his book *First Blues*.

4 AM Blues, *FB*, p. 9

New York Blues, *FB*, p. 11

NY Youth Call Annunciation, *FB*, p. 13

1972 ~

OVER THE HOLIDAYS, Allen paid a visit to his family in Paterson
and asked his niece and nephews to bring their musical instruments along
to help him rehearse. Allen liked to practice his music, and he was willing to
pick up accompanists wherever he could, whether it was Bob Dylan, John

Come Back Christmas,
FB, p. 17

Lennon, or his brother's teenage children. On January 5, he
performed at St. Mark's Church, in what turned out to be
more of a community sing-along than a poetry reading.
That evening he asked a variety of musicians to back him up
with guitars and an organ. He continued to record his new blues poetry
whenever he could and sank most of his extra cash into financing those productions. The Beatles' recording company, Apple, had surprised Allen by
asking him to prepare an entire album. He was determined to have enough

Macdougal Street Blues,
FB, p. 19

CIA Dope Calypso,
FB, p. 21

Troost Street Blues,
FB, p. 26

good material, and he asked Dylan to assist him as his musical consultant. While working on the Apple record, Allen's
spirits were higher than they had been in years. He dreamed
of becoming a rock 'n' roll star, although on a practical level
he realized he was far too interested in the words and knew
much too little about music. Stranger things had occurred,
though, and Allen was determined to improve his musical
talent as much as he could. Gary Getz brought his guitar from the *Catholic
Worker* farm in nearby Tivoli to Cherry Valley to help an optimistic Ginsberg compose more music that month. By January 20, the mixing for the

record was completed, and Allen wrote the liner notes and designed the jacket. Later in the year Dylan gave his permission to use his voice on the album gratis, but he also asked that his name not be used. With that marketing restriction Apple's interest in Allen's record waned and they never got around to releasing it.

Gordon Ball was still in California and had expressed an interest in doing something other than farming, so Allen suggested he assemble a collection of Allen's speeches for a book. He encouraged him to transcribe the tapes he had made on their tour across the country the previous year. If Gordon could get a book deal out of it, Allen said he would sit down with him to help him edit the pieces and fill in the blanks. Gordon could keep the royalties from the book and Allen would keep the copyright to the text in case he wanted to use it in the future. It was yet another example of Allen's generosity. That book was to become *Allen Verbatim* and would be published by McGraw-Hill in 1974 and receive a nomination for a Pulitzer Prize.

Put Down Yr Cigarette Rag, *FB*, p. 29, *CP*, p. 1028

At the end of February, Allen and Ferlinghetti, along with Lawrence's nine-year-old son, Lorenzo, finally flew off to Australia. They stopped for a day in Hawaii to talk with Michael Weiner, an ethnobotanist who was a trailblazer in the field of alternative medicine, and he and Allen compared notes on their shared interest in natural psychedelics. Then they flew to Fiji and stayed for a week to break up the long flight to Australia. They visited the Sigatoka coral beaches where they relaxed in the sun and snorkeled. They rode around the muddy island roads in native buses and swam in clear blue lagoons, saw fire walkers and stayed in nice hotels for a change before setting off again. Allen jotted down lyrics and tunes for new songs like "Siratoka [*sic*] Beach Croon" and "Bus Ride Ballad Road to Suva," many of which were published in *First Blues* by Anne Waldman's Full Court Press. During the course of his month away, he gave up smoking again and to reinforce it in his mind he composed "Put Down Yr Cigarette Rag," which became one of his most popular songs. He performed it hundreds of times, but each time he fell off the wagon and took up smoking again, he removed the song from his repertoire, not to be hypocritical.

Slack Key Guitar, *FB*, p. 32

Flying to Fiji, *FB*, p. 33

Postcard to D-, *FB*, p. 34

Reef Mantra, *FB*, p. 35

Siratoka Beach Croon, *FB*, p. 36

Bus Ride Ballad Road to Suva, *FB*, p. 38

When they landed in Australia, Allen was delighted to hear that Andrei Voznesensky was going to read in several of the venues with them.

He considered Voznesensky the one living genius in Russian poetry, and he tried to spend as much time with him as he could, both on- and off stage. An anti-Russian demonstration threatened to break up one of their readings, but Ferlinghetti told Voznesensky to let the protesters make noise, and after they quieted and were removed from the auditorium Andrei's reading continued. At a reading in Adelaide, Allen encountered some aborigines who used traditional song sticks to sing about their history and culture. They intrigued Allen, and the next evening at a gala reading in Adelaide's Town Hall, Allen began his usual mantra chanting, this time with dobro,[69] guitar, and sitar backup. Then he invited four aborigines up onto the stage. They were dressed in makeshift bathing suits, which revealed most of their bodies, which were painted with native designs. Officially the song men had not been asked to participate in the festival, and it created a controversy when Allen incorporated them into his reading, for in Australia the aborigines were treated as second-class citizens and were seldom issued such invitations. Allen was captivated by their tradition of oral poetry, with songs that told their story back to the very creation. They taught Allen how to keep time with song sticks as the audience clapped in unison. In turn Allen sang Blake to them and read several of his longer poems, including *Wales Visitation* and *September on Jessore Road*. They traded poems onstage for four hours, much to the delight of the crowd, if not the sponsors. Allen ended the evening by improvising some new verses using the native song sticks to keep rhythm. He loved his new friends, describing them in his letters as "big fat old baby eyed happy giggly men with painted bodies who dance like kangaroos." He was pleased, too, when the young twenty-year-old dobro player stayed overnight with him and taught him a little Yoga. Together they gave several more readings with the aborigines in parks and schools around town, then were off to Melbourne and Sydney.

When Allen was on the road he always tried to see and do everything that he could possibly fit into his itinerary. Naturally, he couldn't pass up the chance to see Ayers Rock, a thousand-foot-high sacred red rock sitting right in the middle of the flat plains of central Australia. In those days tourists were permitted to climb to the top of the rock, where Allen sat and meditated. He found that most of his thoughts were about his love for his father,

Ayers Rock / Uluru Song, *CP*, p. 587

Voznesensky's "Silent Tingling," *CP*, p. 588

---

[69] Dobro: A variety of resonator guitar.

who was very much on his mind at the time. He wrote a few postcards and composed "Ayers Rock/Uluru Song"[70] in the style of the aborigine song men. Before long he and Voznesensky were off to Arnhem Land in the north of Australia, where they did some joint readings and dropped some weak psilocybin mushrooms together.

On his way back to New York, Allen had scheduled a reading tour of the West Coast, which included a trip to Alaska in April. Then, once home, he saw a play based on his poem *Kaddish*, which had been onstage in New York since January. It received good reviews, even from the veteran critic Clive Barnes of the *New York Times*. Allen hadn't had much to do with the adaptation and even though he was a tough critic himself, he pronounced it "very solid."

On May 5, he flew back out to Denver to give a benefit reading with Gary Snyder, Robert Bly, and Chögyam Trungpa for Karma Dzong, Trungpa's new center for Shambhala training in Boulder. He and Trungpa continued to discuss Trungpa's newest idea, the founding of a Buddhist university in North America. At the time Trungpa toyed with the name Nalanda for the school, because it was to be modeled after an important learning center of that name that had thrived in India a thousand years earlier. After further consideration it was decided to call the school the Naropa Institute, which eventually became the first accredited Buddhist college in America. Trungpa's goal was not only to teach Buddhist doctrine but to combine it with courses in the arts and sciences as well. That was where Allen came in, and Trungpa explored the possibility of Allen's teaching poetics in the new school and establishing a curriculum.

On May 6, still in Denver, Allen took his *bodhisattva* vow (or *Pranidhana*) at Karma Dzong. The ceremony meant that Allen promised to seek buddhahood through the systematic practice of the fifty-eight rules set down in the *Bodhisattva-shila*. He was to follow the practices and renounce entry into nirvana until all beings were saved. Allen had found his path and his guru, or possibly his guru had found him. Allen knew instinctively that Chögyam Trungpa was exactly the right teacher for him. His Kagyüpa lineage of "crazy wisdom" was tailor-made for Allen, and it gave him the spiritual structure that he had long been searching for. Allen defined crazy wisdom to mean the same as "Mistake or Mishap lineage" where the student "learns from mistakes and alchemizes shit into roses."

---

[70] Uluru: The aboriginal name for Ayers Rock.

In the years that followed, Allen could never remember whether he or Trungpa created the phrase "First thought best thought." It was an aphorism that would stick in his mind for the rest of his life. They had been taking turns composing lines of verse for a chain poem, when Allen said, "The monk bent in his chair and laced his animal shoes." Trungpa questioned him about the phrase animal shoes, meaning leather, and they decided that it was essential because it was his original thought, the first thought. "First Thought Best Thought" became a favorite slogan for both of them, and Trungpa used it as the title of his own book of poetry. Allen developed this idea to refer to the primordial mind, the nonconceptualized sensation-contact with something that is not verbal, but comes out accidentally.

While in Denver Allen took the time to revisit Neal Cassady's old neighborhood on Larimer Street, but found the area so changed and so cleaned up that he couldn't locate the old places that he and Neal had frequented twenty years earlier. He remembered "fucking Neal in the mouth in the basement near the Capitol building on my lonely bed, 'I feel like a big woman whore' said he, after I leaned backward, my prick in between his lips, my ass sat on his breast, I leaned back and stretched in sexual thrill, opening my belly to heaven, the basement room's lightbulbed ceiling. A rare moment of joy and beauty in life. Who can tell at the time what's memorable?" he wrote in his journal.

On June 11, he wrote to Peter from Jackson Hole, Wyoming, to tell him that he had taken two tabs of strawberry LSD the day before and ridden a ski lift to the mountaintop to meditate. He stayed there all day, observing the fluffy clouds drifting over the snowy mountaintops of the Grand Tetons. He went to Butte, where he met a young man who reminded him a lot of Neal. The man worked as a laborer for the Anaconda Mining Company, whose Berkeley copper pit outside Butte was nearly a mile across and eighteen hundred feet deep. At 3:00 A.M. he gave Allen a joyride down into the giant strip mine in a one-hundred-ton "borrowed" dump truck.

Tear Gas Rag, FB, p. 43

From Butte, Allen drove down to Santa Fe with another friend, an ordained Buddhist nun named Tsultrim Allione. She had lived in Nepal and India, where she had volunteered to work with Mother Teresa, helping the poor of Calcutta. Tsultrim reminded Allen of Maretta Greer, only she was calm and helpful and sang beautifully, and, like Maretta, she helped Allen learn some new mantras. On their trip Allen finished reading Kerouac's masterpiece, *Visions of Cody*, and also reread *On the Road*. Viking Press had invited Allen to write an introduction to *Visions*, and he was delighted. He wanted to write a beautiful piece in homage to his great friend and fellow

writer. He and Tsultrim spent a week in Santa Fe with Nanao Sakaki, Bhagavan Das, Ram Dass, and Chögyam Trungpa, all visiting in the same house at
the same time. If there were ever a summit meeting of alternative spirituality in the early 1970s, this was it.

He returned to Cherry Valley that summer, where he described to Peter Trungpa's plans for the Naropa Institute. Peter was generally interested
in everything that interested Allen and had considered him his intellectual
guide since the day they met. Recently, Peter had been working compulsively in the garden for as many as sixteen hours a day, but without Gordon's commonsense guidance had planted a huge crop of inedible and
useless squash. During the first week of August, Allen was sent to the hospital in Cooperstown for a hernia operation. It left him with an ugly five-
inch-long scar but afforded him enough time to catch up on his most
recent pile of correspondence. As soon as he could get around again he
took part in several demonstrations against the Vietnam War, which continued to drag on.

Allen spent some productive days in Cherry Valley revising the manuscript of *The Fall of America*. Following Trungpa's suggestion, he tried to sit
and meditate an hour each day, fixing his mind on his out-breath into the immense universe and the in-breath into his interior immensity. He found that
meditation helped him remain calm and relaxed, but it was hard for him to
set aside an hour every day. He wanted to do it, but the pressures of an active
public life always got in his way.

Senator George McGovern was running for president against Richard
Nixon that year, and Allen did all he could to help elect McGovern. Peter,
Denise, and Allen spent the last of Allen's savings to fly to Miami Beach to
demonstrate at the Republican National Convention, where Nixon was officially nominated for a second term. They found Miami quiet compared to
the Chicago convention four years earlier. By now many
people in the country seemed to have given up hope that the   These States: to
Vietnam War would ever end. Allen continued to practice   Miami Presidential
peaceful civil disobedience and spent two nights in jail after   Convention, *CP*, p. 590
being tear-gased on the street for chanting "AH," his new
mantra. He had changed from "Ommm" to "Ahhh" at Trungpa's suggestion
because it was a more natural American exclamation. Traditionally "Ah" was
the seed syllable for pure speech and the literal appreciation of space—"Ah,"
like the blue color of the sky.

After the convention, Allen found himself in debt again. He had been
spending a good deal of his money on recording projects, none of which

had brought any financial returns to offset studio costs, Miles's wages, and other expenses. Out of the blue, however, *Newsday* commissioned him to write an article on the convention. This piece, titled "Ah Wake Up!," got them out of debt temporarily.

Allen committed himself to another long reading tour in the autumn to meet his financial obligations. He also volunteered to appear at a host of fund-raisers in support of McGovern. All that kept him busy traveling around the country through the end of the year. While read-

Blue Gossip, *FB*, p. 44   ing at Webster College in early November, Allen received word that Ezra Pound had died. Although he was aware of Pound's frail condition, he was still surprised and saddened when he heard the news.

That Christmas Allen stayed at Cherry Valley alone.

The House of the Rising   There were no more farm animals left to take care of, only a
Sun, *FB*, p. 47   few dogs for company, and Allen was able to enjoy the winter
Xmas Gift, *CP*, p. 595   solitude. He slept downstairs near the old stove and worked at his kitchen table to keep warm, while a foot of snow blanketed the ground outside. Allen meditated and spent time on long-overdue projects, including the introduction to a book of Ed Marshall's poetry. He had made no plans and did not have to budge from the house until late February. Peter was in New York City with Denise; she had organized a series of gigs for her all-girl rock band, The Stimulators, through the winter and needed to stay in town. In the bitterest cold Peter traversed the city wearing nothing but a T-shirt and shorts. Miraculously, he managed to remain healthy.

1973 ~

As January wore on, Allen's solitude on the farm was interrupted by a visit from Gregory Corso. By the time Gregory arrived, Allen was already sick and tired of having to take care of Peter and Denise's pack of dogs. He was continually annoyed that he had to disturb his "poetic beauty" to put on his jacket and go outside to feed and water them. He had always liked cats but was not fond of the dogs and he considered them a major nuisance. Now, with Corso there, he was spending all of his time taking care of others. On one particularly cold day he went out to the barn to feed the dogs, stomping madly as he walked. As he stepped off the porch, his feet went out from under him on the ice and he fell into the snow near the front door. He felt a sudden numbness in his leg and knew instantly that he had broken a bone. It reminded him of the sharp pain after the car crash at the airport. He called out to Gregory, who fortunately was sitting near the kitchen stove within earshot. Corso was able to drag him into the house, where he stayed on the kitchen floor wrapped in his blue Air Force jacket until the ambulance arrived. As he had suspected, Allen did have a broken bone, and remained at the hospital for several days. The doctors conducted a few tests, which revealed that he had high blood pressure as well as chronic hepatitis. They suggested that Allen cut down on salty foods, lose weight, and exercise. This was sound advice, but Allen always found a strict regimen difficult to follow for long.

Thoughts Sitting Breathing, *CP*, p. 597

"What would you do if you lost it?," *CP*, p. 600

Ginsberg after breaking leg in front of farmhouse ~

Eventually, Allen came to consider his broken leg a blessing. The pain and discomfort led to a slower pace and a more regular meditation practice, which relieved his fear of future pain. The more he meditated, the more he realized that it was time to lessen his attachment to his body. Above his bed he hung a Buddhist woodcut of two skeletons dancing in appreciation of their release from their bodies. His injury had been a severe fracture, the cast covering his leg from toe to hip, and it took a long time to heal. Chögyam Trungpa had already warned Allen to "prepare for death," and this incident reinforced his notion that the human body was nothing but "a meat house on loan for an all too brief period of time."

Who, *CP,* p. 603

Everybody Sing, *FB,* p. 49

Prayer Blues, *FB,* p. 51

Broken Bone Blues, *FB,* p. 57

He was bedridden on the farm for a month, and various friends stayed to nurse him. At one point John Giorno took over for a week and he and Allen enjoyed long quiet talks about poetics and Buddhist practice. By the end of February Allen was able to hop around on crutches, and Peter drove him to a few readings that were scheduled with his father. By March he was almost as active as ever, but still had to use crutches to get around. It wasn't until the end of June that he was able to put weight on his foot again and switch from crutches to a cane.

Yes and It's Hopeless, *CP,* p. 604

While he was laid up, Allen received a copy of Ann Charters's *Kerouac: A*

Biography, the first book-length biography of Jack. Before he saw the finished version, Allen had written a short blurb in praise of the book. He now read it quickly with what he called "increasing unease" due to what he considered a belittling of Kerouac's awareness, intentions, and accomplishments. He felt that Charters unfairly depicted Jack as shallow and immature, because she chose to paraphrase Kerouac instead of quoting his own words exactly. As it happened, Charters's publisher had not been able to get permission from Kerouac's widow to use direct quotations, and the editors rewrote all the quotations without asking Charters to correct the final text. For more than a month, Allen fretted about having endorsed what he saw as an effort that did not honor Jack as he deserved. Charters, a consummate scholar, was eventually able to get back in Allen's good graces by her continued efforts to promote the writing of Kerouac, but Allen resolved not to rush into contributing to anyone's books in the future.

When news of the Watergate scandal broke in May, Allen was on a West Coast reading trip to raise money for Timothy Leary's continuing defense. He compared the Watergate scandal to a woolen sweater—once one thread began to unravel, the whole cloth finally falls apart. Allen thought that Nixon's downfall would lead to a public realization that the country had been brainwashed by the Vietnam propaganda promulgated by the government. It was the same thing that the Pentagon Papers had already proved, but this time he was confident that all Americans would see the subterfuge and commerce behind the continued prosecution of the war. It reminded Allen of Wendell Phillips's statement, "Eternal vigilance is the price of liberty," a warning he felt was the watchword of the age. The general public, of course, just wanted to be rid of Nixon at that point and was not interested in digging much deeper.

> Under the world there's a lot of ass, a lot of cunt, *CP*, p. 606
>
> Returning to the Country for a Brief Visit, *CP*, p. 607

Despite the growing consensus that the Beat Generation had made a lasting impact on the course of American letters, individual members of the movement, including Allen, were still being treated with disdain by the "academy" of conservative writers and scholars. The academic recognition that he hoped for finally came to Allen in May, when he was nominated to the prestigious National Institute of Arts and Letters by his old friend Kenneth Rexroth; Muriel Rukeyser seconded. He was inducted into the distinguished fellowship at the following year's ceremony, wearing dungarees as any good iconoclast would. Soon after, though, he decided to wear a suit and tie on such occasions, after the example set by his new guru, Chögyam Trungpa. Allen realized that if he wanted people to listen to him and to take him seriously, he needed to project his authority through his attire and his professional image.

Allen saw his election to the institute as an opportunity to get inside the academy and work for change from within. Soon he was nominating his own candidates for membership and awards. It took him a few years to learn how to politick for votes but eventually he was able to change the makeup of the academy itself. In his first year he nominated Basil Bunting, Mao Tse Tung, John Lennon, and Nicanor Parra for awards, but picked up no support. After he learned how to lobby for his candidates, he was able to see William S. Burroughs and Gary Snyder become members, inclusions that never would have been conceivable without him. The institute drew the line at Corso, who would never become a member, although Allen continued to nominate him each year and referred to him on the ballots as the greatest poet of his generation, "the true *Poète Maudit.*"

Even with some academic acceptance, Allen continued to have political problems. On June 2, he was stopped at the Canadian border by a zealous immigration examiner in Vancouver, where he was scheduled to do a benefit reading for the Tibetan Yoga Center. The authorities asked him a series of inappropriate questions, such as "Have you ever committed a crime for which you've never been convicted?" and "Have you ever smoked cannabis or hashish?" Allen tried to ignore the questions but they persisted until he answered, "Not to my knowledge," to most of them. The examiner then showed him a copy of his 1966 Senate testimony about his drug experiences and would only grant him a three-day entry permit. He was able to appear for the reading, but then had to leave Canada immediately.

By summer Allen's leg had healed enough to enable him to travel widely once again, and he spent a couple of months in Europe. His largest reading was at a nightclub in Holland before a group of rock 'n' roll–hungry youths. He was hobbling around onstage with crutches and cane, but most of the pain was gone. In Amsterdam he stayed with his Dutch translator, Simon Vinkenoog, in his house overlooking the Amstel Canal near the Hall of Records. It was very comfortable for Allen; he liked Simon, whom he had known since his first trip to Amsterdam in 1957, and felt at home with his family. Word arrived that his aging father, Louis, had suffered a slight stroke, but he seemed to be improving, and Allen didn't think it was necessary to return to Paterson. At the end of June, Allen was scheduled to read in England for an international poetry festival in the company of W. H. Auden and Hugh MacDiarmid, Scotland's greatest living poet. England had changed dramatically in the six years since his 1967 visit at the height of the Beatles'

influence. Now he could feel the depression that accompanied a weak economy, and he noticed far less spirit in the audiences. Even the fashions had become more sedate, and Allen sensed less poetic vivacity than he had felt
before. A party was given one day in Allen's honor by
Bernard Stone at his Turret Bookshop on Kensington   Night Gleam, *CP*, p. 609
Church Walk. A hundred people came to see him, and Allen   On Reading Dylan's
stayed up all night talking to British writers and old friends   Writings, *FB*, p. 60
such as Harry Fainlight and Alex Trocchi.

Despite the subdued mood in England, he had a good time and
toured some of the countryside. Claude Pelieu and Mary Beach were
then living in Sussex County, and he took a trip to Scotland
with Scott Eden, a young poet, to visit Hugh MacDiarmid   What I'd Like to Do,
on the occasion of his eighty-first birthday. He toured   *CP*, p. 610
Northumbria with Basil Bunting and even saw Olga   On Illness, *CP*, p. 611
Rudge, Pound's companion, who was visiting England,
too. By the date of his departure, August 20, he was ready to return home
for a rest.

Abbie Hoffman was arrested in New York on August 28 in a Times
Square hotel after selling three pounds of low-grade cocaine to undercover
cops. Immediately, Allen and others were called upon to work in his defense.
Hoffman insisted that he had been set up by the police, and Allen wrote numerous letters appealing for common sense in his case. Two weeks later Abbie skipped bail and disappeared underground for the next seven years,
assuming a new identity in upstate New York. In the meantime, Allen's desk
was piled high with unanswered letters and unpaid bills. Peter had bought a
forty-horsepower tractor to help with some of the heavy
farmwork. Anne Waldman and Michael Brownstein had   News Bulletin,
spent the summer in residence there and although they did a   *CP*, p. 613
great deal of manual work, there were still additional expen-
ditures that Allen had to finance.

The only way Allen could secure any time to relax was to schedule it, so
shortly after arriving back in the States, he flew to Jackson Hole, Wyoming,
for a three-month retreat with Chögyam Trungpa. He arrived on September 15 with a group of about sixty other meditation students to stay in the
Crystal Springs Inn, which had been reserved through December 7. Allen
had prior engagements during that period, and had planned
to stay in Jackson Hole for all but twenty-two days. The   On Neruda's Death,
group started meditating at six-thirty each morning and af-   *CP*, p. 615
ter breakfast they sat again until noon. Lunch was followed

by more sitting, and they finished with a final hour each night. Allen was taught exactly how to sit and how to regulate his breathing; they did the ba-
sic *shamatha* sitting, the practice of attending to the breath as it moved into and out of the nostrils. The practice awak-ened Allen's awareness of the space around the room and around the planet. Although his broken leg still ached and it was uncomfortable for him to sit in one position for long, he did his best. He was delighted that Bhagavan Das was his roommate; he assured Allen that he had found his proper niche with Trungpa. The scheduling of retreats enabled Allen not only to advance his Buddhist practice, but also to recharge his sensibilities.

Mind Breaths,
CP, p. 617

The gossip Allen heard about Trungpa from friends who had traveled through India was that the lama was famous in the Tibetan community for being a good meditation teacher; he was well-trained in some of the highest traditional doctrines. Other lamas voiced concern over his heavy drinking and womanizing. Trungpa's lineage of Buddhism required no vow of sobriety or chastity, and this freedom from puritanical strictures was endearing to Allen. Trungpa's basic position was that there is no nirvana or wisdom, only disillusionment with fantasies and hopes that cover up suffering and boredom. He reminded Allen a great deal of Kerouac, who had long ago realized that the experience of suffering leads to compassion. Trungpa believed that through examining total boredom, everything would come into compassionate focus. Politically, Trungpa felt that hostile or aggressive action leads to more hostility and aggression, and those were the sources for society's woes. Allen already believed this, so teacher and student seemed to be in perfect harmony.

For once he was at peace with everything. The heavy Yoga practice and regulated meals were just what he needed physically, and the quiet solitude was what he needed spiritually. Trungpa gave a fantastic series of lectures that began with an overview of Tibetan Buddhist mindfulness exercises. Allen kept copious notes on his teachings for later reference. Peter came to visit for three days and sat ten hours each day; Allen viewed Peter's interest as a miracle and hoped that if he began a practice of sitting it would help him to conquer his addiction to drugs. Eventually Peter became an even more devoted follower of Trungpa's teachings than Allen, which blurred the lines of their relationship even more. From then on, Buddhism, not sexual attraction, was the one thing that they had in common. As once it had been easier to be with Peter if there was a girl in bed with them, now it would become Buddhist meditation that held them together.

Late in October, Allen left Jackson Hole to give a series of benefit readings with Chögyam Trungpa, Ram Dass, and Bhagavan Das to raise money
for the Buddhist community and for the Naropa Institute. At Trungpa's urging Allen improvised more than ever, usually using blues chords on his harmonium as accompaniment. Every night he made up spontaneous songs
and poems onstage. He tried to use whatever topic was buzzing around the
hall, be it politics, the *dharma*, or sex, his personal favorite. While on retreat,
he also had long discussions with Trungpa on how to organize the curriculum at the Naropa Institute. Trungpa asked Allen to personally set up the
poetry courses for a five-week summer program he was offering in 1974 in
cooperation with the University of Colorado in Boulder. Allen was happy
to volunteer to do this for his guru. He immediately enlisted help from
Anne Waldman and Diane di Prima. At one seminal school meeting, which
included luminaries like John Cage and Jackson MacLow, Trungpa turned
to Waldman and said, "It's a hundred year project at least." She and Allen
raced back to their apartment and starting making lists for the "academy of
the future." Waldman had learned organizing skills by being the editor of
several magazines and the director of the St. Mark's Poetry Project in New
York, and with her interest in Buddhism, Allen thought she would be the
perfect partner. Unfortunately, the position paid nothing and amounted to
charity work. Each instructor would receive two hundred dollars plus travel
and accommodations for five weeks of teaching what they decided to call
"spiritual poetics." Allen hoped they could entice Snyder, Whalen, and Mc-
Clure to teach as well, to give the whole Naropa program some weight in
the poetry world.

While on retreat Allen had time to write letters and work on manuscripts
when he was not sitting in the meditation hall. He began to make long-range
plans to turn over the Cherry Valley farm to Peter, so that Peter would feel he
had security there. Someone had told Allen that Peter's problems stemmed
from not having anything of his own; everything in his life, both tangible and
intangible, belonged to Allen. To help with Peter's own sense of identity,
Allen believed it would be best to separate their finances and possessions
more formally. He had bought the property mainly as a retreat for Peter and
Jack, so it rightly should belong to Peter. Allen also thought that he should
pay him a salary to be the farm manager, as he had Gordon, and he could use
that money in turn to buy the farm from Allen. By the time the retreat ended
Allen had also made a new will, leaving everything to Peter and Eugene.

The land in California was a different matter. Allen considered that spot
his retirement hermitage, and he asked Peter to help him build a house there

during the following summer. Peter agreed to help, but wanted Allen's promise that he could stay there, too, from time to time. Allen said that Peter would always be welcome, but believed that most of Peter's time in the future would be taken up with the Cherry Valley farm, especially if he owned it. All of these arrangements made Allen look toward the future with new eyes. He redesigned the house in the Sierras so that it would be large enough for both him and Peter and after retirement it would have room enough for an attendant to care for him in his dotage. He hoped that the project would not cost him more than five thousand dollars. If it did, he'd build it in stages, so that he could spend time there before the project was completed. The idea that Phil Whalen would live there for a while was squashed by Whalen's *roshi*,[71] who pronounced it impractical. One of Snyder's friends drew up the new plans for the cabin, and Allen set up a reading tour to raise the money he'd need to construct it.

While Allen was on retreat in Wyoming he heard that Auden had died on September 29. He clipped the photo of him from the obituary and placed it on the altar in the shrine room for forty-nine days of prayer and thought and good wishes, as prescribed by the *Tibetan Book of the Dead*. It was to sit next to a photo of Alan Watts, the author who had done so much to popularize Buddhism in the West with books like *The Way of Zen*, who died a few weeks after Auden. By the second week of December, Allen was back on the East Coast, heading for Cherry Valley.

Flying Elegy, *CP*, p. 620
Teton Village, *CP*, p. 620

---

[71] *Roshi*. A venerable master in Zen Buddhism.

1974 ~

THE FARM IN WINTER WAS BEAUTIFUL, even if it was harsh and stark at times. Allen continued to sit as frequently as he could, sometimes as much as eight hours a day. He sat on a *zafu* (prayer cushion) near the attic window and looked out over the snowy hilltops. The attic was a cozy place, insulated from the noise and clatter of the rest of the house. Allen's main problem was, as he put it, "the fucking karmic mail" that poured in relentlessly. There was more mail than Allen, with all his energy and best intentions, could possibly answer. On January 12, Allen went into the city to give a benefit reading at Columbia University with Trungpa. Trungpa continued to discuss with Allen his role in assembling a writing program for Naropa's first session that coming summer.

Stay Away From the White House, *FB*, p. 61

Sweet Boy, Gimme Yr Ass, *CP*, p. 621

Jaweh and Allah Battle, *CP*, p. 622

Manifesto, *CP*, p. 625

Allen was scheduled to go back on tour at the end of January, and after the retreat and his month on the farm he was well rested and in good health. Peter was on the farm, too, that winter, but not in as good shape. He had kept busy with a myriad of winter farm chores. He had stripped and bottled the basil leaves he had hung in the attic to dry, ending up with enough basil to last for a lifetime. On a whim, he decided to paint everything inside the farmhouse an impractical hospital white. Allen was happy, for he liked things bright and clean looking, but the problem was that Peter couldn't stop painting once he started, a side effect of his drug habit. Allen didn't seem to recognize how odd Peter's behavior was becoming and remarked in several letters how well Peter was doing. Maretta stopped in to visit for a few weeks, back from living on the streets of Rawalpindi and Islamabad in northern Pakistan, where she had contracted both scabies and scurvy while spending months in jail for vagrancy.

The best news of the season was that William Burroughs was returning to New York from London. There he had been continuing his psychic experiments that had begun with the cut-ups and the electronic sound splicing a decade ago in Tangier. Allen had recommended William for a job as the writer in residence for CCNY's spring semester, to begin in February. He was accepted and was to share a chair in the English Department for eight thousand dollars, which was considered a good salary for one term of teaching. When Burroughs arrived, he quickly found himself alone with a lot of office work. A year earlier Allen had met James Grauerholz, a young man visiting from the Midwest, who was now back in New York planning to live there permanently and in need of work. So Allen suggested that he call Burroughs and offer to help him with part-time secretarial work. William and James got along well, so well in fact that over the course of the following decades, James became his steady companion, secretary, and business manager.

Between the end of January and the middle of May, Allen made thirty-seven different reading stops around the country. The highlight was a week-long beat conference in North Dakota in honor of City Lights' achievements over their past twenty years in business. Besides Allen, other friends, such as Snyder, McClure, Rexroth, Ferlinghetti, Corso, Orlovsky, and Kenneth Patchen's widow, Miriam, flew in for the symposium. It was the first of many conferences that would look back on the Beat Generation with both nostalgia and appreciation for their contribution to literature. As time passed many of the beat writers would be offered prestigious faculty positions and even become members of the academy as Allen had, proof that the general perception of their writings had drastically changed.

2 AM Dirty Jersey Blues, *FB*, p. 66

Allen was so busy on the road that he asked Peter to deliver his acceptance speech for the National Book Award, which he had won that year for *The Fall of America*. His tour culminated in a reading with his father at the Zen Center in San Francisco on May 14. After that he headed to the High Sierras to build his cabin. The land first had to be cleared with mattock, branch saw, ax, and hoe. Allen contracted poison ivy all over his arms and was so exhausted that he literally collapsed into bed every night. He was too tired to even write many letters. Before long he realized that the house would cost much more than he had budgeted. He was determined to build it correctly, so that it would not become the sinkhole for money that Cherry Valley was. While in the mountains he tried to find an hour each day to meditate in the little Zen temple that Gary had built above his cabin.

Peter arrived at Bedrock Mortar some time after Allen. The name they had chosen for the cabin was inspired by the old Maidu Indian mortars hollowed into the bedrock outcroppings on the land. Along with some of Gary's friends, Allen and Peter dug the foundation for the cabin and made the concrete forms. They cut pine trees from their property to use as pillars and hauled them a hundred yards to the construction site. Each night they camped out under the stars in the middle of a beautiful circle of Ponderosa pines. Peter was in his element and labored all day long, naked most of the time. He astonished everyone with his strength and endurance, but there was also a concern that he might injure himself in his fever to work. Gary and his neighbors pitched in to help Allen like an old-fashioned barn raising, and Allen felt welcome in the community of the Buddhist carpenter hippies. To get the extra money he needed to finish the cabin, Allen sold the letters that Jack Kerouac had written to him to the rare book library at Columbia, where he expected all his papers would eventually wind up. In the meantime Allen learned how to wield an ax, hammer a nail, and push a wheelbarrow. Since there was no electricity on site, everything was done by hand. On the solstice, the whole group put on a play written by Michael McClure in the starlit meadow between Gary's house and Allen's site. Allen's broken leg should have healed by now, but it began to hurt from the exertion, so he went to a local acupuncturist for treatments to relieve the pain. He wrote to his father that building the house taught him something that most city dwellers, including himself, had forgotten. Food and shelter come from hard work, and he found it rewarding to create it with his own hands.

Allen was scheduled to give a benefit reading for Naropa in Boulder that July 30 and then stay to teach. Naropa's organizers had been hoping for a few hundred students but nearly two thousand turned up for that first summer session, which featured instructors like composer John Cage and social scientist Gregory Bateson in addition to all the poets Allen had gathered. It was an extremely stimulating time for Allen. He enjoyed meeting the Buddhist scholars and appreciated the total chaos that Trungpa seemed to delight in. Naropa was liberal enough to allow instructors to develop their own courses: Ram Dass gave lectures critical of Trungpa's approach to meditation instruction and Bhagavan Das taught his classes to improvise long chain

Allen, Peter, and friends working on
Bedrock Mortar, 1974 ~

poem songs. It was a fertile period for Allen, who came to believe that the college might develop into something extraordinary if given time. His courses on Blake and William Carlos Williams were heavily attended and gave him the chance to study their works in greater depth. He was also interested in the possibility of trying to combine Buddhist wisdom with Western teaching methods. On the first day of class he presented his students with the koan, "A goose is in a bottle, how do you get it out without breaking the bottle, or harming the goose?" On the final day of class he explained the koan to the still-puzzled students. Clapping his hands he said, "The Goose is now out of the bottle," perhaps meaning that a writer could do anything.

That summer, Chögyam Trungpa formally asked Allen to found a poetry school as a permanent part of Naropa. Trungpa's idea was to train students in the arts and sciences as well as meditation, and Allen concurred. In the beginning, Allen naïvely thought he might be able to work from a distance and spend a month or two a year in Boulder. In reality, directing the poetics department took up more of Allen's time over the next decade than anything else he ever did. It necessitated his move to Boulder for much of each year and left him with the practical headaches of maintaining his properties in California, Cherry Valley, and New York City.

While Allen was teaching in Colorado that first summer, Peter and Denise continued to work on Bedrock Mortar and made substantial progress. When Allen got back in mid-August, the roof of the cabin was about to be put on by the carpenters. He   Hardon Blues, *FB*, p. 67 hoped that the work on the body of the house would be completed within the month, and then the rest of the work could be done as time and money allowed. Allen sat and answered mail, while Peter rushed to finish the house before winter. While he was there, Allen completed the draft of the manuscript for *First Blues*, his earliest collection of songs.

It was pleasurable for Allen to work with his hands for a change; he became much more involved in the construction once the roof was on the house. He helped build a side porch of oak poles and learned the art of notching and sawing logs for lintels. Then he   Sad Dust Glories, learned how to cut tar paper for insulation. The roof was   *CP*, p. 626 covered with asphalt shingles and paneling was added to the inside walls. The setting for the cabin was idyllic, and Allen compared it, as he had once compared Cherry Valley, with the Forest of Arden, here surrounded by oak trees, tall Ponderosa pine, and manzanita bushes. The cabin measured ten by twenty feet and was divided into three tatami rooms for sitting and sleeping. Everyone worked together easily until the beginning of October, when it was time to close up and return to New York for the winter.

In 1973 Timothy Leary had been spirited out of Afghanistan illegally by U.S. government agents and returned to California to finish his prison sentence, now extended due to his escape. He was being held incommunicado and was shuttled between a series of twenty-nine jails over the following three years. No one was able to see him face-to-face. Leary's statements from jail seemed to contradict his earlier positions and indicated that he was preparing to turn state's evidence and rat on his friends. Allen did not understand what had happened with Leary, but he guessed that Leary had somehow been tricked or blackmailed by the police. Allen's first priority was to try to see Leary in person and find out whether he wanted people to continue working toward his release. Over the following months, Allen became more entangled in Leary's predicament, but he couldn't unravel it. While others became disgusted with Leary's apparent turnabout and abandoned him, Allen wanted to hear from Leary's own lips that he was rejecting their help.

Allen agreed to come to a meeting with other former friends of Leary's, such as Jerry Rubin, Ram Dass, and Leary's son, Jack, in Berkeley in September. It turned out that the event was sponsored by PILL (People Investigating Leary's Lies), an organization that surprised Allen by denouncing Leary. Even Timothy's own son was against him, and only Allen suggested that they should get to the bottom of the mystery first. "Is this a hotel room in Russia where we turn against our friends?" Allen asked. "None of you have ever believed a word the police have said to you, but now you want to believe them because it's easier than continuing to care about this man in prison." It soon became clear that it would require several lawyers to sort the affair out, which meant raising more money for the legal fees.

Since Allen couldn't communicate directly with Leary, he did not know if he was hearing Leary's true story or a "control agent's" version of the story. Allen was certain it was a sinister plot, quite possibly with Leary's own girlfriend, Joanna, working as a double agent. It was unclear exactly what was going on. Government infiltration of the counterculture was rampant during that period and allegiances were unclear. There had even been rumors in the Buddhist community that Trungpa was being funded by the CIA. It all sounded very Burroughsian to Allen, and on some level he enjoyed the intrigues.

The Dharma Festival in San Francisco that October drew some of Buddhism's biggest names. His Holiness, Gyalwa Karmapa, the spiritual head of the Kagyü sect and Trungpa's chief lama, arrived from Sikkim. He was the sixteenth embodiment of an unbroken line of *Vajrayana* teachers extending back nearly a thousand years. At the festival there were readings by a host of poets including McClure, Duncan, di Prima, Kyger, Meltzer, Waldman, and Allen. Whalen acted as the master of ceremonies for the reading. Kyger impressed Allen as never before with her poetry, and he began to take notice of her writing after that. He remarked that she had a superior style, better than he realized; it was the first time he ever saw her poetry working. Apart from the poetry, Allen was impressed by the enthusiasm surrounding the event, and he had the opportunity to engage in sex with some new young men. By now he was finding that his celebrity status drew fans who sometimes accepted Allen's affections and occasionally even initiated sex with him for a change, instead of the other way around. Allen felt as if he was coming into his own and hoped he might not have to work as hard to find sexual partners in the future.

One of Allen's greatest problems was his rather large ego, and he struggled with that self-indulgence continually. He recognized the fact that he thought very highly of himself, in fact he always had, as is apparent in some

of his boyhood journals. One of the things he hoped that his Buddhist studies would teach him was how to control his ego and cut through it. His desire to be known as the most brilliant man in America, or a
modern-day prophet, was still strong, but he believed that it   Ego Confession,
was an emotional roadblock that he needed to get past. He   CP, p. 631
composed his poem "Ego Confession" to address this, calling
it a great burlesque and a takeoff on himself. By becoming more aware of
his own nature, he was able to be less egocentric in many situations, but he
was never able to say he had lost his ego.

Floating high on the adrenaline of the Dharma Festival, Allen was not
prepared for what happened when he got back to New York City. Early on
the evening of November 2, he was grabbed by a bunch of tough street kids
outside his apartment. They dragged him into an abandoned basement in a
burned-out building on the next block and threatened, "Shut up or we'll kill
you." He knew they were serious, and he had the presence of mind to begin
chanting "Om ah hum" to calm himself as well as his attackers. They ripped
his watch from his wrist and took his wallet with seventy dollars cash, leaving him frightened but otherwise unharmed. They did not touch the book
bag he carried with what amounted to tens of thousands of dollars' worth of
poetry manuscripts inside. When Allen got home he wrote a poem, "Mug-
ging," subsequently published as a feature by the New York
Times, for which they paid him $250. With typical resiliency,   Mugging, CP, p. 633
Allen remarked that he had come away from the experience
with more than he started out with. It did make him realize that the neighborhood had grown too dangerous, and after ten years on East Tenth Street,
he and Peter resigned themselves to packing up and moving again.

That winter he threw himself into organizing the new poetics department at Naropa, which entailed writing letters and drawing up endless plans
and proposals. He hoped to keep the department modest in size at first and
gradually let the program grow over time. He was afraid of getting in over
his head because he knew that he and Anne Waldman, his codirector, could
only do so much with no budget or staff. By December they had received
commitments from Burroughs, Corso, Whalen, di Prima, Ted Berrigan, and
Ed Sanders to join them the following summer teaching at what they playfully named "The Jack Kerouac School of Disembodied Poetics." Since there
was no physical office or location for the department, they thought the word
disembodied was fitting. It also carried some of the "crazy wisdom" meaning
with it and honored other ancestors like Dante, Blake, and Sappho, too.
Waldman lobbied to name the school after Gertrude Stein, but Allen saw it

as one more opportunity to keep the name of his Jack alive. Since Anne and many of the writers of her own generation, such as Ted Berrigan and Clark Coolidge, saw Kerouac as a direct influence as well as being quintessentially American, it wasn't difficult for them to agree on the school's name. Kerouac's writings had mostly fallen out of print during the 1970s; his widow Stella Sampas had no interest in promoting Jack's work and did not act as an advocate for it. It fell on Allen's shoulders to continue to promote Kerouac's books, which he did for decades by reminding people at his readings and during interviews that Jack's writing deserved to be read. Allen said that "people have to remember that Kerouac opened up the true interior rumination and rhapsody of America." During the 1980s when a revival of interest in Beat Generation literature began, Allen continued to lobby for the reissue of all Jack's books, much as he had done in the 1950s when he was trying to get them published in the first place. Kerouac's re-emergence as one of the most important writers of midcentury America is due in large part to Ginsberg's remarkable loyalty and endless enthusiasm.

Who Runs America?,
CP, p. 636

Thoughts on a Breath,
CP, p. 637

We Rise on Sun Beams
and Fall in the Night,
CP, p. 640

Dope Fiend Blues,
FB, p. 68

After a peaceful interlude in the Sierras, Allen was on tour again, traveling from city to city to raise money to refill COP's bank account and to support his farm and his friends; now he also had to think about funding for the new Jack Kerouac School. He passed through New York at the end of the year, staying long enough to have Christmas Eve dinner with Burroughs, who by now had settled into city life. Allen was nostalgic for the old days, and visiting Burroughs always made him feel connected to his more carefree past. Allen said of that evening that he and William were "purified by looking in each other's eyes for half an hour's time trying to see each other."

1975 ~

Trungpa visited New York City during the early part of 1975, at which time Allen took instruction from him in Buddhist prostrations and attended several of his lectures on tantra. Although Allen had hoped to spend that winter in meditation practice, a good deal of his time was taken up with administrative preparations for Naropa. Following some dental work, which involved having two teeth extracted, he had a bout with the flu. After that, his old bronchitis problem recurred so violently that he spent a weekend in a hospital in Amherst while he was on a reading tour through Massachusetts. While in Boston Allen helped prepare affidavits for Leary's writ of habeas corpus, still trying to ascertain if his unusual silence was voluntary or under duress.

Allen, Peter, and Denise hadn't found a new apartment yet; they were looking for something farther west, closer to First Avenue, where it was considered a bit safer. During the winter Allen had need of a typist to help with his growing pile of office paperwork. Anne Waldman, then director of the St. Mark's Poetry Project, suggested that he hire Shelley Kraut, who was a young poet and artist and the secretary for the Poetry Project. He asked her to type up some legal papers having to do with the Leary case, and while talking to Shelley and her husband, Bob Rosenthal, he learned that their building at 437 East Twelfth Street near Avenue A was filled with poets. They also told Allen that two adjoining apartments were soon to be available in the building. Allen and Peter went to see the landlady the next day and charmed her into renting them the two apartments for the low rate of $160 a month. The apartments were laid out in such a way that the small rooms gave living and work space to Allen, and allowed Peter and Denise to have a separate room to themselves. They sanded and varnished the floors and made a small library by adding a wall to the one big room that had a bathtub. In March Allen moved all his books from the old apartment into his new space. His immediate housekeeping goal was to organize all the books and papers he had and to ship more boxes off to the Columbia library for safe-keeping so that he could find things when he needed them. Before he got much done he was off to Chicago for five readings with Bur-roughs. Allen found William a delightful reading compan-ion. Surprisingly, after thirty years of friendship, they had never formally read together. It was a relief for Allen to have someone dependable onstage with him after two decades of Corso's quixotic behavior and Peter's unpredictable shenani-gans. At least for a few nights Allen could relax onstage and enjoy each performance.

Written on Hotel Napkin: Chicago Futures, *CP*, p. 641

End Vietnam War, *FB*, p. 70

Guru Blues, *FB*, p. 72

In May, Allen made plans to teach a poetry seminar at Trungpa's new Padma Jong retreat center in northern California. He asked Marc Olmstead, a twenty-year-old man, to go along with him for three or four days while he taught. Marc, who was to act as Allen's secretary, was also being courted by Allen. This was Allen's opportunity to be intimate with someone, to keep his mind from wandering to thoughts of seducing other handsome male students, he said. Although Olmstead was straight, he was willing to go along with Allen's needs in exchange for the opportunity to learn what the older poet had to teach. It was a short-lived dream for Allen, because he wound up in the hospital instead. One day in April he awoke to find the left side of his face paralyzed; it was a recurrence of his Bell's Palsy. Allen learned that it was brought on by the antibiotic Keflex, which his doctor prescribed for him following a prostate biopsy. The drug may have caused a viral infection to the nerves of his head, which in turn led to the Bell's Palsy. The doctor assured Allen that it was only a temporary condition, but it was utterly frightening all the same. He stayed in the hospital for several weeks while the doctors tried to fur-ther diagnose his problem. The effects of the palsy were not as temporary as the doctor had predicted and, needless to say, the trip to Padma Jong and the rendezvous with Olmstead were canceled.

Hospital Window, *CP*, p. 642

Hadda Be Playing on the Jukebox, *CP*, p. 643

Allen had two country homes, but no time to enjoy either one. He hadn't been to Cherry Valley in almost a year, and he wrote to Snyder that he wouldn't make it out to the Sierras that summer either. He asked Gary to let one of his carpenter friends stay in his cabin in exchange for working on it. Allen at least hoped that he'd be feeling well enough to get to Boulder by June 9 when his courses were scheduled to begin.

That summer in Boulder was lovelier and livelier than Allen had expected. Even though he was recovering from his illness and complained of lethargy, he managed to do more work than ten people. Burroughs came to Naropa that year as a favor to Allen to teach a course and to learn something of Trungpa's teachings. He and Trungpa were not on the same wavelength, but Allen said they respected each other's opinions and were able to communicate best when they were both drunk. Buddhism did not appeal to William, as he was much too cynical and independent to put himself under the tutelage of a guru. Conversely, Allen was always willing to defer to a teacher or mentor who knew more about a topic than he did.

As usual, it was Corso who proved to be one of Allen's biggest challenges at Naropa that term. He did his best to disrupt everything that he was involved in. During one of Trungpa's talks to the entire community, or *sangha*, Gregory stood up in the audience and called him a "dumb asshole." The normally placid Trungpa became enraged, shouting, "Shut up! Shut up!" as his helpers escorted Corso out of the hall. Allen thought it was amazing that Trungpa and Corso were able to have tea together the next day and be charmingly sociable, but Gregory never failed to do outrageous things. He borrowed money from his students and was often too drunk to teach his classes. Allen naïvely believed that Gregory was off dope and merely taking an occasional Darvon in addition to drinking. Jocelyn Stern, Corso's French girlfriend, helped keep him occupied and out of trouble. That was the summer she became pregnant with Corso's son, Max. It was always difficult with Gregory around.

About the only fringe benefit Allen had from teaching at Naropa was an apartment the school provided for him. Louis and Edith visited with him there for a couple of weeks in the "poetry ghetto," as he liked to call their building. He

Sickness Blues, *CP*, p. 647

and most of the other visiting writers lived in the same place, making it an interesting literary community. What little salary he did receive he generously donated back to the school, so he had to rely on outside readings for money. He and Waldman had put together a spectacular roster of poets and each week brought someone new and interesting to teach in Boulder. Ed Sanders was there, and Whalen visited, too. Anne brought her friends Ted Berrigan and Dick Gallup out from New York and Jack Collom, a poet who lived in the area, taught classes and became another close friend of

Chögyam Trungpa ~

Allen's. W. S. Merwin and John Ashbery also gave readings to large audiences. Allen even invited Peter to teach "bucolic poesy" to students for a week at the end of the summer. Of Allen's immediate circle of friends, his only disappointment was that Gary Snyder wasn't able to come.

As it turned out, Allen was a wonderful teacher. Gregory taught his class for the first week while Allen was sick, but after that he took over teaching Percy Shelley, Andrew Marvell, and Christopher Smart to his students. When Allen discovered that half the class had never read anything besides Kerouac, Snyder, and *Howl* in school, he went back to the basics, introducing them to the five hundred years of poetry that led up to the Beat Generation. Allen also knew how to take advantage of talent where he found it. While his father was there, Allen enlisted him to teach a class on Keats, and on another day he had Merwin, Waldman, Corso, and himself each read and interpret Shelley's "Ode to the West Wind." Allen sped through the years, ending with William Carlos Williams and Kerouac. It was a tremendous undertaking and although hard work for the students, they had to admit they had learned something.

An unexpected bonus of teaching for Allen was that he met many young people on a more intimate level than he had at his poetry readings. Allen had always felt open to sex and free love wherever he found it, and was usually drawn to younger men, frequently younger straight men. He wasn't a pedophile who molested children, but he did like good-looking college boys and had no reservations about sleeping with them if the opportunity arose. He had found a justification for it in the example of the classical Greek teachers, who said that the best teaching was often done in bed. Allen felt that the taboo against sex between student and teacher was unnatural. In an interview he was quoted as saying that "a certain kind of genius among students is best brought out in bed: things having to do with tolerance, humor, grounding, humanization, recognition of the body, recognition of ordinary mind, recognition of impulse, recognition of diversity. Given some basic honesty, some vulnerability on the part of teacher and student then trust can arise."

Come All Ye Brave Boys, CP, p. 645

Allen had been further encouraged in this idea years earlier by Gavin Arthur in San Francisco. Arthur had told Allen that Walt Whitman had slept with Edward Carpenter and that when he had slept with Carpenter, Carpenter had described Whitman's sexual techniques to him. After Neal Cassady slept with both Arthur and Ginsberg, Allen felt that he had a direct link with Whitman. He recalled talking at great length with Arthur about the line of transmission from older men to younger, which to him was similar to the Buddhist transmissions of teachings from guru to pupil. Arthur, who was an old man at the time, felt it was a charming practice for older and younger people to be sexually intimate. Allen was more enthusiastic about it now that he was nearly fifty than he had been when he was twenty-five and an older Burroughs was trying to get him into bed. Nevertheless, he believed it was nothing to be defensive about, but rather something that should be encouraged. He felt it was completely healthy and rejected accusations that sex with younger men was a sick neurotic dependency. The important thing, he said, was to communicate with your partner regardless of age. Older people had ken, experience, history, memory, information, and also power and money, which are often unavailable to younger people. Younger people had intelligence, enthusiasm, sexuality, energy, vitality, an open mind, and athletic prowess. Allen felt that both parties could profit from such a relationship. On paper, at least, he stated that it was more than a sexual relationship; it was an exchange of strengths, an exchange of gifts, and an exchange of accomplishments. "When you sleep with somebody younger you do gain a little vitality of breadth and bounce," Allen admitted in one interview.

Professors' sleeping with their students was not something that was encouraged in most colleges, but as long as the students were not coerced, it was something that the Naropa administration chose to ignore. Trungpa and some of the other administrators did it, so why not the faculty? Allen couldn't see any downside to it; he could only see the positive effects. He was so open and candid about the topic that no one was surprised by his position, and he didn't have any backlash from either the students or the faculty. As Allen noted in a letter to Alan Ansen, "I seem to have had a sexual renaissance in last few years due to fame or money or magical authority as veteran spiritual beatnik. So have slept with half a hundred young boys, students, poets, rock-kids, I meet at poetry readings or Naropa. As a tantric institute sleeping with students is not discouraged. 'Attachments' and 'grasping' is considered bad form karmically tho. Common sense." Even though he made it sound idyllic to Ansen, years later when walking past the Varsity Townhouses in Boulder with his secretary, Allen pointed to his old apartment and sadly said, "I've had hundreds of lovers there and I can't remember one of their names."

When his father and stepmother came to Boulder in mid-July, Allen took a week off to travel with them to Santa Fe and to visit friends Ram Dass and a wealthy patron of Buddhist activities, David Padwa. Allen still suffered from a slight paralysis of his face, which was highly unusual for Bell's Palsy, a temporary condition. Now the lax eyelid muscles and drooping cheek were diagnosed as Raymond's Syndrome. As soon as he got back from Santa Fe, Allen started seeing a homeopathic doctor in Boulder, but found little relief. After Peter's course was finished they went to the Rocky Mountain Dharma Center high in the mountains near the Wyoming border for a retreat. Allen was thrilled that Peter was beginning to take an active inter-

Cabin in the Rockies,
CP, p. 653

est in Buddhism. While on retreat, Allen did a thousand prostrations a day, ten times more than his usual daily goal, but his ribs and muscles ached by the end of each day. After Peter left for New York, Allen stayed on by himself a few extra weeks to sit with Kobun Chino Roshi of the Zen Center in San Francisco, who taught him some slow Zen *kinhin* walking techniques that were not as taxing.

Following the retreat, Allen decided to put his files and correspondence in order once and for all and needed some help. James Grauerholz suggested a close friend of his, Richard Elovich, who was a student at NYU at the time. Allen hired Elovich to help him plow through the paperwork that covered his desk and ship new files to Columbia for his archive deposit. At Naropa he had found it useful to have student apprentices working with him, since it enabled him to get so much done. In return, his apprentice got a practical look at how a famous poet lived and worked. Allen was most generous with his time and often spent long hours helping his assistants with their own manuscripts, so it was a good trade.

One day in the mail Allen found an envelope of poems from a troubled, sexually confused seventeen-year-old by the name of Jonathan Robbins. He was writing in the tradition of nineteenth-century poets like Poe and Baudelaire, so much so that Allen wrote back to him, "Really yours, not stolen from history?" Allen took an instant liking to his work, and to the good-looking young man himself when they met later in the year. Robbins began to visit Ginsberg in New York, and the two discussed the course of modern poetry, with the older Ginsberg looking to the future and the younger Robbins fixed on the past. Generous with his time as always, Allen went over Jonathan's manuscripts, praising parts and making practical suggestions where he thought it would improve the poetry.

Gospel Noble Truths,
CP, p. 649

Even though Allen had scheduled a month's retreat for November at the Tail of the Tiger meditation center in Vermont, he canceled those plans when Bob Dylan asked him to join his Rolling Thunder tour. Allen jumped at the invitation. Of all Allen's famous friends, Dylan was by far his greatest hero. Their friendship fed into Allen's dream of being a rock star, and a few times on tour Dylan had asked Allen up onstage in front of thousands of screaming fans. Allen felt that Dylan "stood atop a column of air. His songs and his ideas rose up from within him and emerged uncluttered and pure, as if his mind, soul, body and talent were all one." Allen, Peter, and Denise had been recording with Dylan in a New York studio one night when Dylan asked Allen about working together on a project; he wanted to make a movie while on tour and thought Allen might be able to lend his expertise. Dylan's idea was to establish what he thought of as a "working rock family commune of the arts" and then allow them to improvise a film as they traveled. At one point early in the filming Allen asked Dylan what he expected him to do, but Dylan replied that he had no idea. He told Allen that he was the king and should go ahead and do whatever he wanted to do. He could offer him a platform but in the end it was up to Allen to wake up his sleeping countrymen in his own way. Allen was quoted as saying he couldn't tell whether Dylan was leading him to the top of a mountain or to hell, but it was exciting to be along for the ride.

Allen joined Rolling Thunder as they drove around Massachusetts performing everywhere from Plymouth Rock to Kerouac's hometown of Lowell. The tour convinced Allen of what he already knew, that a poet-troubadour

could reach more people than a poet. He witnessed with his own eyes the incredible power Dylan held over his audience. Backstage he asked Dylan what
was the force that drove him. Dylan surprised him by saying that at one time
he had done it for pleasure, to counteract all the pain he had witnessed, but he
found that the more pleasure he got, the more pain there was. Since that realization Dylan pursued his interests without seeking pleasure, which alleviated
the pain, so moderation was the key to it all. It may have been sound advice,
but Allen wasn't about to give up his own search for pleasure. He daydreamed

that he and Dylan should sleep together during the tour and

Rolling Thunder Stones, that their conversation as they awoke naked in bed would be
CP, p. 651 filmed. If he suggested the idea to Dylan, his answer is un-
recorded, but no such scene was encouraged.

The more Allen thought about Dylan, the more he realized that he
didn't really know him at all, and he commented that he thought it was
possibly because there was no "him" to know. He was beginning to think
that Dylan didn't have a self at all. Dylan asked if they could film a scene
in Lowell as a tribute to Kerouac. One afternoon he and Allen and a film
crew went to a Stations of the Cross that was outdoors along the Merri-
mack River. Jack had used the spot as an important backdrop in his novel
Doctor Sax. Above a grotto was a life-size statue of Christ on the cross,
which Dylan began talking to. He asked Christ how it felt to be up there,
which struck Allen as autobiographical, since many fans regarded Dylan
as being Christlike. To Allen it was Dylan's way of saying he did not want
to be crucified like Jesus. It seemed that the singer wanted to know why
Christ submitted to his crucifixion. Allen interpreted his comments as his
being a good Jew questioning why anyone would insist on being the Messiah against the advice of the rabbis.

They filmed at Kerouac's grave in the Edson Cemetery and read his epitaph aloud: "He honored the world." With the November leaves swirling
around them they sat and read poems from Jack's *Mexico City Blues* to one another. Dylan played Allen's harmonium while Allen improvised a ten-stanza
song about Jack looking down from the clouds. Then Dylan played some
blues chords on his own guitar, before walking down the long row of tomb-
stones in the bright sunlight. Peter and Denise were nearly as thrilled as
Allen to be traveling with Dylan as the tour moved through Massachusetts,
Vermont, and on to Niagara Falls. When Allen read part of the poem *Kaddish* in a resort hotel to a convention of what he called "*mahjong* playing
grandmothers," it was a surreal scene, with only Dylan and Peter paying any
attention to him. He was only background noise for the ladies' games.

Dylan's ability to enunciate each vowel and syllable in a rhythmic progression that epitomized all American poetics from Poe through Vachel Lindsay left an impression on Allen. Bob was able to sing intricately rhymed, irregular-lined narrative poems to a continuous downbeat with a relatively complex instrumentation. Allen felt Dylan was able to emphasize the words in a way that had not been done since the Greeks. Allen truly considered him a genius of poetry who in musical performance transcended everything Allen had seen before.

The Rolling Thunder tour traveled by bus and for the most part played small, intimate halls and auditoriums. Allen continued to improvise his assigned role in the movie as an alchemist king, with Peter yodeling incessantly in the background. The purported themes of the movie were redemption and community, which Allen expanded to mean the redemption of America. He tried to imagine a future where everyone came together in wholesome egoless cooperation, bringing out the best in the world. Larry Sloman, in his book about the Rolling Thunder Revue, *On the Road with Bob Dylan*, remarked that during the entire time Allen was on the tour he was not much more than a glorified groupie, watching every one of the performances from the wings and hoping, usually in vain, that Dylan would invite him onstage.

In December, Allen and Richard Elovich got down to the work of answering mail and reviewing manuscripts. Allen deceived himself into believing that Peter was over his speed-freak days and was settling down. Peter had been with Denise for six years now and had recently begun to study the banjo. Denise went with Peter to Cherry Valley for the Christmas holidays while Allen went on to Vermont to spend a week sitting in retreat with Trungpa. This time he took along his nephew Alan Brooks, who was becoming interested in Buddhism himself.

1 9 7 6 ~

ALLEN HAD ALWAYS BEEN willing to offer his opinion of other poets' writings, but now that he was a professor, his critiques flowed more naturally. Occasionally, he did not reserve his comments to his actual students.
Along with a letter, Ferlinghetti sent Allen a copy of a wonderful new poem
he had written entitled "The Old Italians Dying." In response Allen sent him
a list of suggestions for several cuts and revisions, as if he were his teacher.
Since Lawrence had not asked for editorial help, he was understandably irritated by Allen's chutzpah. With increasing frequency Allen found himself
unconsciously "correcting" other people's writing, usually to their delight
but sometimes not. Since he was recognized as one of the greatest poets in
America, many people wrote to him for advice and help with their own poetry, which he was happy to give. He did not know when to quit, though,
and sometimes insulted friends with unsolicited criticism.

Since his summers were now reserved for teaching at
Naropa, Allen made the most of the winters by giving readings to earn the money to cover his escalating expenses. He
also struggled with chronic ill health and by springtime was
battling another kidney stone attack. There was always something wrong;
that year he had minor surgery on a toe to get rid of a bone spur, then another hernia operation, which forced him to cancel a two-week break he
planned at Bedrock Mortar. During much of the 1970s he could barely keep
up with his reading schedule, which took him all over the United States and
to Europe as well. In January he flew to Brussels and then on to Paris,

Reading French Poetry,
CP, p. 654

where he had only a few spare hours to see Corso, who was living there with his girlfriend, Jocelyn.

Within the week Allen was back in Washington, D.C., to read with William Burroughs at the Corcoran Gallery on February 9. Burroughs had turned sixty-two on February 5, the same day that Ian Sommerville, his old boyfriend from Tangier days, had been killed in a car accident in England. Burroughs was shaken and sad, but the reading went on. That evening they attended a party thrown for Allen at Ira Lowe's house. Lowe was the Washington attorney who helped Allen gain release of the FBI files under the Freedom of Information Act. Allen needed more legal help with the Leary case and wanted to solicit Lowe's assistance for that as well. Although Leary had asked Allen to keep out of his affairs, Allen could not give up on a friend. He continued working with several lawyers and PEN to gain Leary's release from prison, until later that same year Leary was finally released by Governor Jerry Brown. Allen's father was in the last stages of his battle with cancer, and Allen wanted to spend time with him. Amid his rigorous reading schedule, Allen gave as much time to Louis as he could. Every time he visited him he'd make more notes for a long poem that developed into "Don't Grow Old."

That spring Allen returned to the recording studio to work on his *First Blues* album. John Hammond, Sr., the man who had discovered Billie Holiday and recorded Bob Dylan's first album for Columbia, was the producer. He had already approved the rough cuts that Allen had been making of his work, dirty songs and all. The next step was to make quality studio masters. A few years earlier, Allen had recorded many of his songs solo at the Chelsea Hotel using Harry Smith's Wollensack recorder. Now, in the studio, friends and musicians took turns working with Allen on various cuts. Arthur Russell, who at one time lived upstairs in Allen's apartment building, came to play cello, and David Mansfield, whom Allen knew from Dylan's Rolling Thunder tour, sat in on a few cuts. Allen described Mansfield as a "19-year-old Botticelli faced genius musician." On different songs Mansfield played piano, violin, guitar, and mandolin. When the recording came out it garnered lukewarm reviews even though it was undoubtedly one of the best albums ever produced by a poet. As a piece of music it fell short of catching the public's fancy and did not win a large audience. Allen was disappointed by the flat reception, but nothing would deter him from his quest to be a rock star.

In April, Allen went to Boulder to develop his curriculum and to apply for grants for the summer session of

Don't Grow Old, parts 1–2, CP, p. 659

Two Dreams, CP, p. 655

C'mon Jack, CP, p. 657

Naropa. While he was there, Allen taught a course on Blake as well as one on Charles Reznikoff's poetry, which he found moving in its sheer simplicity. Teaching often gave Allen the chance to reacquaint himself with poetry he otherwise might have forgotten. Each term he tried to expand his knowledge of the field, and he was not content to teach the same poets year after year. William Burroughs's son, Billy (now twenty-nine), was in Boulder at that time, and Allen asked him to teach his father's prose to the class for a small honorarium. The financial problems of Naropa were still acute. The school had no money, instructors earned only two hundred dollars a week for the summer classes, so having Allen draw on his friends was a great help to the school. Most of Allen's friends were willing to teach as a favor to him, or to follow their own Buddhist practice, or simply to relax with him for a week or two in Boulder. Occasionally Allen paid them out of his own pocket, if there was no other way.

After years of practice, Allen finally attained his first ten thousand prostrations while working with Gordon Ball on his next big literary project. Ball was editing Allen's journals from the early 1950s and early 1960s for his doctoral dissertation at the University of North Carolina. It was a lengthy project, but the resulting book, which was published by Grove Press in 1977, was an important piece of literary scholarship. Peter went to the farm in Cherry Valley alone that year and planted a whole forest of nut trees on the property. Although he worked hard, fueled by speed as usual, the trees he selected were not appropriate for the harsh winters and they died within the first few years. In his absence, Denise had gone to work for Allen part-time as another secretarial assistant and devoted the rest of her free time to her rock 'n' roll group.

One day while passing the Dakota apartments, Allen decided to stop and ask the doorman to ring John Lennon and Yoko Ono's bell. They invited him up to their home, where Lennon said he had retired temporarily from the Los Angeles music scene. They were staying in New York with their new baby to try, like Allen, to maintain a healthy lifestyle. John and Yoko had gone on a forty-day fast after the baby's birth in October 1975 and had been careful about their food ever since. Lennon preferred New York after all the cocaine madness around Hollywood. He told how one night as he listened to the radio he heard someone reading a long poem on the air. He thought maybe it was Dylan until the announcer said that it was Ginsberg reciting *Howl*. Lennon admitted that he had never understood the poem before and told Allen that usually he couldn't "get anything from print." Once he heard *Howl* read aloud he suddenly understood why Dylan dug it so much. For a decade Lennon had known Allen was famous, but had never understood his true importance until then. Immediately afterward Allen mailed John several cassettes of his readings of *Howl*, *Kaddish*, and Blake. Starstruck as always, Allen was proud that someone of Lennon's stature considered him a fellow artist worth listening to.

At one performance at Glassboro State College in New Jersey on May 4, Allen was accompanied by a young music student, a handsome guitar player by the name of Steven Taylor. He had a sweet voice and had more musical talent than Allen's previous accompanists. As luck would have it the two harmonized perfectly. Taylor was not happy with college, and although he was enrolled in music courses, he couldn't see himself being a choir director for the rest of his life, so he was looking for something else. Aside from being handsome, Steven was a genius at anticipating Allen's rhythm and cadence and added his own touches to help the musical presentation frame Allen's voice and words. After a single performance Allen recognized the young man's talent and hoped that they might be able to work together again in the future. Steven's family happened to live not far from Paterson, so a few weeks later he visited Allen and met Louis and Edith and they all went out to the International House of Pancakes. Allen invited Steven to come with him to watch him record in John Hammond's studio. Naturally, he was thrilled that one of America's most remarkable poets was taking an interest in him, and before long they started working together whenever Allen performed in the area.

Don't Grow Old, part 3, *CP*, p. 660

In June a large group of friends descended on Naropa to visit Allen. Burroughs, Brion Gysin, Grauerholz, Elovich, and Steven Lowe arrived en masse and filled his house. When Dylan's Rolling Thunder tour reached the Rockies, Allen took a few days off from classes to attend several more concerts. In Fort Collins, Dylan asked him to appear at intermission and Allen spoke before nearly twenty-seven thousand people in a giant college football stadium, the largest crowd he would ever address. He read his eight-line poem about seeing Cassady's remains, "On Neal's Ashes." Then, in Salt Lake City, Allen went onstage to read "The Holy Ghost on the Nod" to a crowd that numbered eleven thousand. It was thrilling but also humbling to be reminded that poetry could not reach nearly as many people as music could.

By June, Allen was in Paterson, as Louis was growing worse each day. Allen could not decide whether he should go to Boulder or stay with his father, and Whalen offered to substitute teach for him. Relying on the doctor's advice that

Don't Grow Old, part 4, *CP*, p. 661

Louis was stable enough for him to leave, Allen flew back to Boulder for the first term at Naropa and planned to play it by ear after that. At Allen's urging the doctors agreed to tell Louis that his cancer was terminal; he hadn't been made fully aware of the finality of his condition until then. It gave Louis some peace of mind, as he had feared that he was dying of a brain tumor. By spring the muscles in his thin arms had wasted away and he no longer had enough strength left to stand up in the bathtub. Peter, after his years as a hospital orderly, was the person Allen relied on to help physically with Louis. As Peter gently helped him out of bed one day Louis smiled at him and said, "Don't grow old." At one point Louis recited Wordsworth's "Intimations of Immortality" from memory and commented, "It's correct, but not true."

A primary worry was how to keep the Kerouac School afloat financially. Naropa only had a total of five hundred students that year, and the administration had cut the poetics department's already low budget again. Even with new austerity measures, it did not look as if they could make it. The time had come for drastic action, and for the first time in his life, Allen asked Dylan directly for money for Naropa. It was something he was loath to do, but for a cause this important to him and Trungpa, he made an exception. "Now you know we're not perfect and we're fools, but we been around long enough to have some common sense and sense of direction for teaching younger generations what we've learned." Naropa was then ninety thousand dollars in debt and Allen did all he could that summer to keep it going. Dylan did not respond to the letter, but the college managed to limp through another year. The only assets the Kerouac School had were the poets that Allen cajoled into coming. That summer Robert Duncan and Helen Adam kicked off the session. They were followed by Michael McClure, John Ashbery, and Dick Gallup. Later in the summer, Ted Berrigan and John Giorno would each teach a week, followed by Whalen, di Prima, and Creeley with his wife, Bobbie Louise Hawkins. Once again, it was an inspiring term, and Allen was happily sleeping with as many of his students as he could entice.

Pussy Blues, *CP*, p. 658

In Paterson, Louis suffered through most of June too weak to get out of bed and slowly faded away. On the night of July 7, Edith had her last conversation with him. "If I have cancer, I'd better ask Dr. Levy for some morphine" were his final words to her as he fell asleep curled up in the fetal position. When she awoke to check on him in the morning, she found that he had passed away quietly in his sleep. Allen was called in Boulder and flew home to be with his family right away. On the plane he composed his most moving song, "Father Death Blues," which ends poignantly, "Father Breath

once more farewell/Birth you gave was no thing ill/My heart is still, as time
will tell." Being back in Paterson at that painful moment, Allen sensed that
all his old connections to his childhood were gone; he felt
more alone than ever. To help Edith pay the funeral ex-   Father Death Blues,
penses, Allen sold another small batch of precious letters to *CP*, p. 663
the Columbia Library. After returning to Boulder he wrote   Don't Grow Old, parts
to Edith, "Hope you're enjoying your freedom. Why not?   6–7, *CP*, p. 664
You've worked for it and suffered for it, so now a little open
space is healthy." He tried to follow the spiritual example of Trungpa, who
had responded to the news of Louis' death by telling Allen, "I extend my
thought so that your father may dissolve into the *Dharmakaya*. Please let him
go and keep up your celebration," a quotation Allen would use many times
in the future to console his friends in times of grief and loss.

Even as Louis was dying in Paterson, Billy Burroughs, Jr., received a new
chance at life in Denver that summer in the form of a liver transplant. At a
young age he had become a heavy drinker and had overindulged in every
type of drug he could lay his hands on. The alcoholism had led to his vomiting blood, which was a clear sign of cirrhosis of the liver. That was followed
by liver cancer as his drinking continued unabated. Before his transplant operation, Trungpa had counseled Billy, "You will live or you will die, both are
good," which may have given him some solace. After his body healed from
the operation and accepted the new liver, it was crucial that he give up drinking completely, but Billy could not, or would not, stop. No sooner was he
home from the hospital than he was drinking again. Nothing could stop his
self-destructiveness. William stayed in Boulder that summer but wasn't emotionally equipped to give Billy much fatherly guidance or support, so his
days appeared to be numbered.

Allen was always enthusiastic about strong new poets when he found
them, and at the end of the summer, he received a manuscript of a poem
called *Factory* from a talented poet who went by the sole name Antler. Allen
cried and laughed out loud as he read the poem. He considered it "the most
enlightening and magnanimous American poem I've seen since *Howl* of my
own generation." Allen invited Antler to Naropa for the following summer
and offered to let him work as his teaching assistant. Michael Scholnick, an
able young poet from New York, had been Allen's assistant that year but was
handicapped by his inability to type well. Allen hoped that Antler was not
only a first-rate poet but maybe a competent typist, too.

During the summer Allen's relationship with Peter had stabilized. The
illness and death of Louis had drawn them closer together for a while. They

bickered constantly, but were seemingly resigned to staying together, even if it was only by force of habit. Allen rented another apartment next door to his own in New York as separate quarters for Peter and Denise. They had their own entrance and key, so Peter could truly live a life distinct from Allen, if that was what he wanted. In the fall they moved some furniture into the apartment and set up two households, side by side. The one point that they still shared was Buddhism. Peter's interest had grown stronger with time, and he accompanied Allen on many of his retreats. In October, after Allen took a brief trip to Berlin, they both went to northern Wisconsin with Trungpa and a hundred other meditation students for a retreat that lasted until early December. Trungpa had leased the large Kings Gateway Hotel in Land O'Lakes, which was empty for the season. Once more Allen welcomed the discipline of a healthy regimen. Everyone rose at 6:00 A.M. and meditated for an hour, then after breakfast the group did prostrations until lunchtime. Following a short break and more Yoga, the students assembled to hear Trungpa's lectures. Allen enjoyed the physical activity of Yoga and the retreat helped him to regain his physical and mental strength.

"Junk Mail," *CP*, p. 665

"Drive All Blames into One," *CP*, p. 669

"You Might Get in Trouble," *CP*, p. 668

Land O'Lakes, Wisc., *CP*, p. 669

Land O'Lakes, Wisconsin: Vajrayana Seminary, *CP*, p. 670

For Creeley's Ear, *CP*, p. 671

1977 ~

D URING HIS RETREAT Allen had corresponded with Jonathan Robbins, the young, eighteen-year-old poet he was smitten with at the time. Robbins was criticizing Ginsberg for being a poetry showman and not being
serious enough in his study of older texts. He challenged Allen to get serious
with the form of his own poetry and forget the world for a while. Allen decided to take him up on the suggestion and they arranged to spend two
weeks together in Baltimore at the beginning of January. Jonathan hoped to
convince Allen that Poe was every bit as interesting a poet as Blake and worth
equal study. Their goal was to read the complete works of Blake and Poe. In
the evenings they tried to read Milton's *Paradise Lost* aloud to each other, but
concentrated mostly on Blake. The two weeks were intended as a total immersion in poetry, much as the Buddhist retreats Allen attended were a total
immersion in meditation. It was rare that he had that much time free from
obligations, and since he had been trying to get Jonathan into
bed with him, Allen had an ulterior motive for the vacation.   Haunting Poe's
Each day they spent ten hours reading and studying the texts,   Baltimore, *CP*, p. 672
which led Allen to some inspired changes of thinking about
Blake's work. At long last he was able to comprehend Blake's incredibly complex system, which might never have happened without this concentrated
opportunity to read his work from beginning to end.

The trip inspired Allen to write a long Blakean poem of his own, *The Contest of Bards*, which Allen considered one of his better efforts. It featured two
characters, one a lecherous old bard and the other a young chaste messenger,

who challenged each other to a poetic/erotic contest. It was more than symbolic of the situation in Baltimore between Robbins and Allen's unsatisfied sexual desire. For his part, Jonathan wanted to show Allen the depth of Poe's poetry, so they visited Poe's grave and the little brick house where he stayed before his death on his final trip there. Jonathan counseled Allen to read and write poetry and to stop wasting his time and energy traveling around the world as a poetry luminary. The two went to the library several times to consult the beautiful Trianon Press facsimile editions of Blake with their spectacular colored engravings. Allen's song "The Rune" was composed as part of the longer *Contest* and after the trip he began to sing it at most of his readings. Although his critics didn't agree, Allen believed that this new long poem was very good and for a decade or more tried to convince his detractors. Probably because the trip itself was seminal to his Blake understanding, Allen felt that the poem he composed was revelatory.

Contest of Bards, CP, p. 673

Immediately after his Baltimore sabbatical, Allen returned to his grueling schedule of readings. More of his trips included benefits for Buddhist organizations and any time that he contracted for a paying gig, he would attempt to read for nonprofit groups in that area as well. He began all his readings with at least ten or fifteen minutes of meditation and then sang songs accompanying himself on the harmonium, sometimes with musicians to back him up. Usually the musicians were amateur and often there was little or no time for rehearsal, but Allen enjoyed seeing what might result from each musical collaboration, no matter how modest.

It was around that time that William Burroughs decided to settle permanently in New York City for the first time since the 1940s, and Allen visited him as often as he could when he was in town. John Giorno had told William about a vacant apartment in a former YMCA building at 222 Bowery, then New York's own version of Skid Row. Giorno had an apartment on the third floor and when the landlord showed William the vacant, windowless space that had been serving as a storage area, he rented it immediately. He felt the cavelike atmosphere was an appropriate home for an old junkie and having Giorno upstairs was icing on the cake. He loved the space; it was quiet, dark, and nearly airtight, and it lent itself to its nickname, "The Bunker." The new apartment became the scene for many fabulous literary gatherings and conversations over the coming years.

I Lay Love on My Knee, CP, p. 688

On February 23, Allen read his poetry at St. Mark's Church with Robert Lowell. By then Lowell was only a few days shy of his sixtieth birthday and had recently been released from a mental hospital. The reading was billed as the first time these two legends had shared the stage. They had met a few times before, but Lowell had always considered Allen a bit of a phony. Twenty years earlier Lowell had written that Allen and his friends were pathetic and doomed, calling their poetry "so-so," and his opinion was still pretty much the same. But to read with one of America's literary legends was another high point for Allen, as he had respected Lowell's work for decades. Unfortunately, Allen came down with the flu that night and didn't read at his best. Corso was there to liven things up, and he heckled Lowell unmercifully until he was silenced by the other members of the audience. Allen, who saw that Gregory was drunk as usual, suggested he leave. The evening was tiring for Lowell, and sadly he would be dead before the year was out.

In his role as codirector at the Kerouac School, Allen's work was more administrative than he would have liked. As the school grew larger, his responsibilities expanded and he had to spend more time there. That year he flew to Boulder for the spring term and taught during the summer program as well. He left Richard Elovich behind in New York to take care of business and hired Ted Berrigan to help shepherd Peter's first real collection of poems, *Clean Asshole Poems and Smiling Vegetable Songs,* into print for City Lights. Peter was no longer capable of doing the revisions that were needed and Ted was ideally suited for the job. He worked on Peter's poems carefully and discussed his choices and suggestions with both Peter and Allen. Peter had little interest in his book and went with Allen to Boulder for the spring semester. By May Allen felt that Peter was "doing fine, circulating around sociable sensible and working, taking care of himself." He still indulged in bouts with drugs and liquor, but was able to conceal their effects from Allen when he chose to. Allen turned a blind eye in order to deceive himself so he could leave Peter alone without guilt when it was time for his next reading tour.

One trademark of Allen's was that he always promoted his friends' poetry to publishers, and Peter's book was certainly published as a direct result of Allen's efforts. It is unlikely that without his urging Peter would ever have written a single poem; certainly no book would ever have been published. The same year Allen also tried to convince Ferlinghetti to publish books with three other young poets he had taken under his wing: Antler, Andy Clausen, and David Cope. Ferlinghetti thought that it would be financial suicide to publish three poetry books by unknown writers simultaneously and suggested that they be grouped together in a single volume. That compromise

Punk Rock Your My Big Crybaby, *CP*, p. 691

didn't please any of the three poets and the whole topic became an aggravation for City Lights. After endless negotiation, Antler's first book, *Factory*,
was published in 1980 as the thirty-eighth book in City Lights' prestigious
Pocket Poets Series. Allen helped Cope and Clausen find other publishers
and continued to promote all three poets for the next twenty years.

That summer's session at Naropa was yet another convocation of
Allen's close friends. Once again Corso taught a course and lived next door
to Allen in the Varsity Townhouse apartments, which took on the feel of a
dormitory. Allen liked the setup and left his door wide open so that everyone
would feel free to drop in at any time. When they did, they were certain to
find a pot of soup on the stove and plenty of poets to talk with. That year
Steve Silberman enrolled in the summer programs at Naropa with the hope
of becoming Allen's apprentice, secretly dreaming of becoming Allen's "soul-
mate." He was an English major from Oberlin College and had identified
with Allen's poetry even before Allen read at his college earlier in the year. It
seemed as if Allen slept with every other male student that

Love Replied, *CP*, p. 692

summer, but to Steve's disappointment, Allen didn't approach him. At the beginning of the term Allen had another
kidney stone attack and managed to get through it using Demerol to kill the
pain. All the discomfort was forgotten when Allen found his new heartthrob,
Bobby Meyers. Meyers was a cherubic-looking boy, tender toward Allen, and
he spent the whole summer studying with the fifty-one-year-old poet. At
seventeen, Meyers had already written a sheaf of poetry, but under close examination by Ginsberg, he became ashamed of every poem. Nevertheless, it
was inspiring to have Allen as a tutor, and he learned quite a bit about poetics. The following year Meyers spent another summer at Naropa as Allen's
teaching assistant, watching Allen become infatuated with some of the
young men in the next class of students.

One unfortunate incident came to threaten Naropa's very existence and
became an all-consuming scandal for many of Trungpa's followers, and
Allen was no exception. Although Allen wasn't directly involved, he was
swept up in the controversy that came as a result. It had begun years earlier
in 1975 at one of Chögyam Trungpa's Vajradhatu Seminary retreats in the
mountains at Snowmass near Aspen. The poet W. S. Merwin and his girlfriend, the poet Dana Naone, had been invited to attend the retreat. Probably because of Merwin's fame, they were given special dispensation to be
there even though they did not have the background teachings necessary for
full understanding. At Halloween Trungpa threw a party for all the participants and Merwin and Naone opted not to attend, possibly not aware that

their absence would be viewed as an insult to their host. Irritated, Trungpa sent his guards to strip the couple and bring them to the party naked, over their heated protests.

At the time, it was little noted, and neither Merwin nor Naone made a big issue of it. They did not subscribe to what had happened, but in the best Buddhist tradition, they had decided to let go of the affair without making a fuss. In the Buddhist community, though, gossip about the incident was rampant, and the story would not go away. It came to a head during the summer of 1977 when Ed Sanders taught a course in what he called "Investigative Poetics." His class surprised him by voting to investigate the Trungpa/Merwin affair, which Sanders, not being a Buddhist, was hearing about for the first time. His students checked out all the accusations and rumors and issued an "official" report as the class's final paper. Instead of putting an end to the debate, the report further polarized the Boulder community into camps for and against Trungpa's actions. A local magazine, the *Boulder Monthly*, ran an article written by Tom Clark called "When the Party's Over" in its March 1979 issue. Clark had become increasingly suspicious of Trungpa and his motives, and his critical story drew more unwanted attention to the school.

Since Allen had not been on the retreat, he felt it was none of his business, and he did his best to not take sides on the issue. Because he was devoted to Trungpa and Naropa, Allen wished the whole affair would blow over, yet the debate escalated with each new article. Unfortunately, in an interview with old friends Tom Clark and Ed Dorn, Allen spoke candidly about his personal views of the situation. Allen thought that he would have a chance to edit his comments before publication, but Clark was pressed by his deadline and deemed it fair to publish what Allen had said unedited. Allen had told him that he believed Merwin had reacted like a panicked boy, who needed compassion more than anything else, since his pride had been hurt. Merwin hadn't understood Buddhist devotion to teachers enough to have been permitted to go on this retreat in the first place. Basically, Allen believed that Trungpa showed solid human common sense and needed and deserved respect in this and every matter. He conceded that Trungpa was drunk that night and angry with Merwin, but that was as far as his criticism of his own guru would extend. Since Allen had not been at the event, he knew nothing about it firsthand, and all too soon he regretted saying anything about it at all. A week later, Allen received a copy of Clark's article and edited his own comments carefully. "I was more interested in talking to you and Ed as friend poets than publishing my thoughts, lest I escalate mis-understanding and continue foolish gossip trend," Allen wrote to Clark. When the magazine was published without Allen's changes, he felt that his comments appeared out of context. But the damage was done and Allen had to apologize to all concerned. He worried that more controversy would only hurt Naropa at a time when it was desperately trying to keep afloat financially. Both Sanders and Clark eventually published books on the subject, and the controversy continued to rage on for years, but somehow Naropa managed to survive. Through all those years Allen tried to keep out of this public fray and confided only to his journal. For the first time in his life, he felt he was a hypocrite, but he refused to be forced to make a choice or to question his allegiance to Trungpa. Inherently, he realized that if he couldn't maintain faith in his meditation teacher, he was "up shit's creek." It did bring up the whole issue of just how far "spiritual obedience" should go. True to his forgiving nature, even after all the trouble caused by Clark's and Dorn's comments, Allen continued to invite them to take part in the Naropa programs.

In spite of all the turmoil caused by the Poetry Wars, Naropa was still a vibrant place to be that summer. Allen taught a course on "The Literary History of the Beat Generation," which focused on the 1940s. In the following years he extended the scope of the course into the 1950s and 1960s, and eventually brought it up to the present. No other course at Naropa was as popular. Also that year Antler came for a visit, and Andy Clausen brought his wife and children. It was there that Clausen met Corso for the first time and realized how much they had in common as poets. To celebrate the end of the session, Peter and Allen gave a spirited reading backed by a motley orchestra composed of students from Allen's poetics classes. At the end of August, Allen and Peter took a ten-day retreat to the Libre Commune in Farisita, south of Pueblo, Colorado. On a peaceful mountaintop overlooking the Huerfano Valley, Allen was able to leave the Poetry Wars behind at last.

After a decade of talk no progress had yet been made on Allen's *Collected Poems*. City Lights was unable to reach an agreement with any of the publishers who offered to do a comprehensive hardback edition, and once again Allen begged Ferlinghetti to make a deal with a larger New York publisher. He repeated his promise to stick with City Lights as long as Lawrence was actively in charge; that was Allen's only condition for loyalty. "Since I'm staying faithfully with main poetry and other books with you as personal decentralized publishing project mutual work, and sacrificing maybe some money from Big City Big Time NY books, I hope you think it's fair of me to make provision that the condition be that we stick to it together." Allen continued to speak and to give readings at colleges, since his book royalties from City Lights were not enough to cover his ever-growing expenses. At that time Allen was even providing financial assistance to his nephew Lyle Brooks, whose college tuition was more than Eugene could afford.

By the time Allen returned to New York City in the fall, his secretary, Richard Elovich, had already departed for Europe with no plans to return any time soon. The enormous pile of office paperwork Allen found on his desk was overwhelming, and Ted Berrigan, who was still working on Peter's book, suggested that Allen hire Bob Rosenthal at least part-time. Rosenthal, whose wife, Shelley Kraut, had helped Allen type the Leary documents, was in need of a job. Bob and Shelley were both poets and had come to New York City from Chicago in large part because Berrigan was there. Shelley was about to have their first child, so the money Allen offered would go a long way to help pay their modest bills. Bob's first assignment was to pay Allen's electric bill. Allen couldn't get over how effortlessly Bob did the relatively simple task and exclaimed, "You're a genius!" As time went by, Bob's "temporary" status became permanent, and he proved to be a good match for Allen. As a poet he was familiar with many of the people in the literary community around the St. Mark's Poetry Project. He also knew how to keep Allen on track when it was time to work. Since there was no sexual relationship between them, work was completed without conflict or drama. Over the next twenty years Bob remained Allen's secretary, taking on more responsibilities and bringing stability to his business office. They set up a formal work space in one of the rooms in Allen's apartment, using a large piece of blue plywood placed on top of two file cabinets for a desk. Every day began with Bob stopping at the post office around the corner to collect the bundle of mail piled in Box 582. Once back at Allen's he would sort it, answer what he could, and put the rest aside for Allen's eventual attention.

With Rosenthal in the office, Allen was free to travel more than ever, secure in the knowledge that his affairs were under control back home. That fall his trips took him to Tulsa and Minneapolis, then San Francisco, where he stayed in North Beach with Shig as usual. He was looking forward to participating in an LSD conference slated for October in Santa Cruz, and to "prepare" for it, he took a small dose for the first time in years. While high he pondered whether the CIA had "by conscious plan or inadvertent Pandora's Box, let loose the whole LSD fad on the U.S. and the world?" At the conference he saw old drug comrades Timothy Leary, Ram Dass Alpert, and Ralph Metzner and talked for the first time with Dr. Albert Hofmann, the scientist who had accidentally discovered LSD's psychedelic properties in 1943. Allen

Bob Rosenthal and Allen Ginsberg ~

had many questions for Hofmann, who remained somewhat ambivalent about his discovery. Hofmann had always hoped that the drug would play a larger medicinal role, and he was dubious about the social significance placed on it by the hippie community. The title of his book, *LSD—My Problem Child,* suggested those doubts. Allen asked Hofmann why he didn't take LSD any longer, to which Hofmann replied that since he had already had the experience, there was no need to repeat it continually. Allen could not help but agree. In Santa Cruz he also had a chance to finally sit down with Leary to discuss his past years of prison and legal difficulties. Unfortunately, Allen was not able to get a clear picture of exactly what had happened to Leary or even what was currently going on in Leary's head.

After that conference, on a flight to Hawaii for an East-West Convergence conference, Allen decided to make a comparison between Himalayan-American *Vajrayana* practice and the LSD experience. His speech on that topic and the discussion afterward went well. On his way home he stopped over in Los Angeles long enough to work with Dylan on the final editing of the movie that had been made during the Rolling Thunder tour, now titled *Renaldo and Clara.* It was released in 1978 as a four-hour film, receiving mediocre reviews.

What's Dead?,
CP, p. 697

Also on the plane, Allen wrote a recommendation for a grant from the California Arts Council for Gregory Corso. It was only one of the hundreds he wrote during his life, but he felt that Corso deserved a grant more than anyone else he knew. He had always believed that Gregory was one of the most important, yet unheralded, poets in America. Often he would say that Corso was a better poet than himself, a compliment Gregory couldn't accept graciously. "By building me up, he was able to enhance his own reputation. He used his own false-modesty to bring more attention to himself," Gregory said. With his friend Peter Coyote on the California award committee, Allen thought there was a good chance Corso would win a grant. Writing from his own firsthand experience, Allen said that he had seen students at Naropa come alive in Corso's classes, and he viewed Gregory as the most inspiring of teachers. Even though Gregory was a troublemaker and a total iconoclast, Allen hoped that the arts council would put personality aside and give him a grant based solely on his wild, playful imagination, his serious verse, and his overall literary excellence. He called Gregory a poet's poet as well as a "seminal culture-generational inspirer whose written work has had enormous influence on later decades of poets." In the end, Gregory was given a very generous award.

Because he had so little free time, Allen began to write poetry during odd moments in the wee hours of the morning or when he was traveling on planes and trains. He continued to be prolific in spite of his hectic schedule, and new work filled his journals. By year's end, two important books were published. The first, *As Ever*, was a collection of the correspondence between Allen and Neal Cassady. Generous as ever, Allen agreed to give his share of the royalties to Carolyn Cassady, as long as he retained the copyright. Then on

Grim Skeleton, *CP*, p. 698

January 1, 1978, City Lights released his next book of poetry, *Mind Breaths, Poems 1972–77*. Allen's work was now in constant demand, and whatever he wrote could be published easily, a dramatic change from the early days. It was both a blessing and a curse, as he couldn't pay as much attention to the overall quality of what was being published as he once had. Two decades earlier he had been writing material that sat maturing in his notebook for years and was then carefully edited before publication. Now publishers' demand for his work was so great that there was little time between composition and publication. A good deal of unripened writing was rushed into print, especially in periodicals.

1978 ~

GINSBERG'S PROUDEST MOMENT in 1978 was the receipt of a short note from
C. L. Sulzberger of the *New York Times*. "I fear I owe you an apology," he
wrote. "I have been reading a succession of pieces about CIA involvement
in the dope trade in South East Asia and I remember when
you first suggested I look into this I thought you were full
of beans. Indeed you were right and I acknowledge the
fact." Allen felt vindicated and could not resist enlarging
on his statements, so he replied to Sulzberger that now "marijuana arrests
were being used consciously and widespread for suppression of dissenting
social and political opinion." Allen felt confident that the newspaper of
record would now have no choice but to report on the government's
hypocrisy and corruption. He even believed that Richard Helms would finally have to apologize to him and make good on their bet by meditating
each day. Sulzberger's note was among the letters that he read as he sat in
the attic of his rented house on Pine Street in Boulder. He used the quiet
attic as a meditation room each morning while everyone else was asleep,
but he tended to do more paperwork there than meditation. A mattress
was laid under the eaves on the green-carpeted floor as a getaway when
the house below was filled with young friends, as it often
was. Bobby Meyers was staying with him, too, helping him
type a syllabus of Blake's work for his next class, so there
were reasons to feel content.
    Other events that year were not as sweet. Billy Burroughs's new liver was

Ballade of Poisons,
CP, p. 700

Lack Love, *CP*, p. 701
Father Guru, *CP*, p. 702

already beginning to show signs of failure. He was living in Boulder and Allen contacted his doctor on March 5 to see what he could do. Not only was Billy drinking heavily, but he also was showing signs of nervous instability and extreme mood swings with suicidal depressions. Since nothing else was working, Allen hoped that a psychological intervention might make a difference, but unfortunately it was a busy time for Allen, and all he could do was consult with Billy's doctors and hire companions to stay with him.

In May, Allen stopped back in New York City to take part in the UN Mobilization for Survival antinuclear march before returning to Naropa. In Boulder he began to take an active role in the sit-ins that were being staged outside the gates of the Rocky Flats Nuclear Plant a few miles south of town. The government had long used the top secret factory to manufacture plutonium triggers for nuclear weapons, so symbolically it was a focal point. Now demonstrators were trying to get attention by blocking the railroad tracks in order to stop the trains that delivered the raw materials to the facility. The demonstrations were peaceful, but fifteen people including Allen, Peter, and activist Daniel Ellsberg were arrested as they sat to meditate on the tracks. The arrest prompted Allen to write his *Plutonian Ode*, a long poem on the basic element in the bomb, plutonium. At his trial, he read an early draft of it to the court. The guilty decision was successfully appealed, and all the charges against the demonstrators were dismissed. That protest led Allen to question himself and his tactics once again. He wondered to himself whether it was appropriate to use meditation for the purpose of a protest demonstration and speculated that it was probably a misuse of something originally intended to be independent of aggression.

Summers at Naropa were always full of hard, tedious work for Allen, but they also brought many of his friends to campus and he loved seeing them, hearing about their new work, and catching up on their gossip. Corso taught again that summer and brought along his new girlfriend, Lisa Brinker, and his young son, Max. Lisa had more or less adopted Max and was raising him in San Francisco. While many others viewed Corso as a nuisance, Allen saw him as one of the great treasures of the Kerouac School. He kept life interesting and his outrageous remarks never ceased to inspire Allen. He wrote, "Gregory next door in and out of alcoholic derangement from week to week, when sober he's charming." In mid-July, Gregory, drunk on Chinese beer, heckled Trungpa so much that Naropa's president,

Manhattan May Day Midnight, *CP*, p. 703

Nagasaki Days, *CP*, p. 707

Plutonian Ode, *CP*, p. 710

Billy McKeever, told him that if he disrupted any lecture again, he'd be kicked out permanently. Of course, threats had no impact on Gregory—in fact, it was the second time that month they had threatened him with the same expulsion.

In the fall, Allen was able to get back to Bedrock Mortar for a few weeks. In his absence most of the work on the cabin had been completed, and a sundeck was added to the west side of the structure. While driving up into the Sierras from San Francisco, Allen, Peter, Antler, and his companion, Jeff Poniewaz, had borrowed Ferlinghetti's VW and ruined both the car's transmission and its generator. Repairs put Allen further in debt, and he was forced to make a long reading trip all over the Northeast and Midwest to cover his obligations. Some financial relief now began to come from new sources. Ever since his induction into the American Academy and Institute of Arts and Letters he had begun to receive awards. On October 15, he was feted by the *New York Quarterly* at the ritzy Pierre Hotel with a National Poetry Day dinner in his honor. Earlier that same day he had given a reading at the much seedier West End Bar, where thirty-five years before he had first hung out with Lucien Carr and Edie Parker. Then quite unexpectedly Allen was asked to substitute for John Ashbery as a professor at Brooklyn College. Ashbery was a Distinguished Professor in their English Department and was taking off a semester to teach at the University of Cincinnati. The job offered good pay and Allen already had plenty of teaching experience from Naropa, and he could live at home for a term, so he was enthusiastic about the position.

After another long reading trip, Allen returned to New York in time for Peter's first and only book party, held on December 18. Allen had helped plan the celebration at the Gotham Book Mart, to which Peter contributed a hundred quarts of his own homemade Orlovsky apple juice from the Cherry Valley farm. A large crowd of Allen's friends turned out to toast Peter that evening, including Andrei Voznesensky and John Ashbery. *Clean Asshole Poems and Smiling Vegetable Songs* was a difficult book for City Lights to sell; the title alone made reviews in the establishment press practically impossible. Even Allen didn't have enough time to promote it, for right after the party, he packed again for the winter term at Naropa.

Old Pond, *CP*, p. 715

Blame the Thought, Cling to the Bummer, *CP*, p. 717

"Don't Grow Old," *CP*, p. 718

Love Returned, *CP*, p. 720

December 31, 1978, *CP*, p. 722

1979 ～

BY THE LATE SEVENTIES, Allen was teaching nine months every year at Naropa for no pay and no benefits. Since they were in Boulder so much of the time, he and Peter decided they needed more permanent quarters, so they rented a small brick semiattached house at 1439 Mapleton Avenue. The living-room windows faced south and bright sunlight cascaded in every afternoon. There were two bedrooms, a dining room, and a kitchen, all within an easy walk of the downtown pedestrian mall where Naropa's classes were held. That year Allen taught a course on William Blake that began with the Lambeth prophecies and continued through the "Four Zoas." His classes met in the Casey Jr. High School building around the corner from Naropa's main offices. In the winter Lafcadio came to visit them, as jittery and innocent as ever. His entire body was covered with a rash and as a result he scratched himself continually. Peter felt the hives were caused by too much sugar, and much to Lafcadio's displeasure, Peter eliminated all sugar from his diet. When Burroughs witnessed the incessant bickering that went on between the two brothers, he couldn't believe that anyone could get anything done amid the racket. Allen reminded him that he was quite used to it from his volatile childhood days with Naomi. Burroughs needed a quiet, undisturbed atmosphere in which to write, but Allen seemed to be able to thrive amid confusion and chaos.

By now, so much misinformation about the Beat Generation had been written that Allen was spending a good deal of his time trying to set the record straight. On January 15, he stayed up all night to write a long letter to

Diana Trilling explaining the details of his suspension from Columbia for writing "Fuck the Jews" on his dorm window. Diana was still trying to make the point that his actions were proof positive of his Jewish self-hatred; in fact, she found an anti-Semitic bias in all his work. Allen reminded her that he had also written "Butler Has No Balls" on the window and that it was only a boyhood prank intended to shame the lazy maid into cleaning the windows. "It is not your information or opinions I am contesting, correcting or challenging here: what I'm aiming at is decades old, an attitudinal vanity masked as moral responsibility, and inability to get basic facts straight disguised as superior sinceritas," he wrote to her. The two were never to see eye to eye on this or many other subjects.

Allen frequently interrupted his teaching at Naropa to go on quick poetry tours or, as on February 22, to receive an award. The New York–based National Arts Club's Gold Medal for Literature was presented to him in their elegant, hundred-year-old clubhouse on Gramercy Park that day. Allen, beard neatly trimmed and dressed in a tuxedo for the occasion, looked every bit the academic. Although his appearance was professorial, his opinions and statements were decidedly not in agreement with those of any academy. However, on this day, it was not Allen who shocked the audience the most, but rather the city's cultural affairs commissioner, Henry Geldzahler, who took the opportunity to disclose his homosexuality in public for the first time. During Allen's acceptance speech he stunned many of the gray-haired ladies in the gathering by sincerely thanking Geldzahler for putting "the stamp of the city's approval on cocksucking." For good measure, he read a few of his more sordid poems, without realizing that he had ruffled the feathers of quite a few of the club's members, who were unaware of the nature of his poetry on the topic.

Allen's stint as Ashbery's replacement at Brooklyn College began in mid-March, so he and Peter packed up to return to New York from Boulder. He was scheduled to teach in Brooklyn through the end of May, at which time he had to leave for a reading tour in Europe. This time he wasn't sorry to be leaving Boulder behind. The Naropa Poetry Wars had reached their zenith, and he had recently found himself screaming at Clark and Dorn several times over their continued publication of articles on the Trungpa/Merwin affair. At night he was kept awake by doubts—"Do I trust Trungpa or not?" Every morning he'd wake wondering how to extract himself from the whole mess.

To Allen, Trungpa was much wiser and more serious than Tom Clark and the other critics depicted him. As time went by, people like Dick Gallup and Michael Brownstein became uneasy about their affiliation with the Kerouac School; Ed Sanders had also grown suspicious. Al Santoli, one of the students in Sanders's class, was obsessed with his own idea of "Buddhist Fascism," and Jim Hartz, an ex-Buddhist seminarian, sent Allen a page of his poem *Plutonian Ode* that he had used to wipe up his own excrement. Merwin himself had bumped into Allen at a recent meeting of the American Academy and Institute of Arts and Letters and had remarked, "I don't trust you, Ginsberg!" By then Allen felt that Merwin lacked the humor needed to deal with Trungpa. He wrote in his journal that he thought about the whole affair every single day for two years and could never resolve his own feelings about it. He tried to determine if he was lying to himself to cover Trungpa's hierarchical secrecy, or if he was lying to Clark by not confronting him over his journalistic spitefulness and love for intrigue. This conflict and subsequent self-analysis served to inhibit Allen's own writing, the worst byproduct of the scandal for him personally. Allen's great genius was to write candidly whatever was on his mind, but he didn't want to write about this particular issue and fan the flames of controversy, so as a result he didn't write at all. Allen was also flat broke after teaching at Naropa for all these years. He hadn't been able to do as many paid outside readings because of his teaching schedule. At least at Brooklyn College he would earn a decent wage for his efforts. That spring Allen taught creative writing there two days a week to undergraduates and found it such hard work to critique all the student papers that he swore he'd never do it again.

Brooklyn College Brain, *CP*, p. 725

Early in April Roger Richards, the owner of a local bookstore and friend of many of the beat writers, including Allen, presented a two-night reading at the Village Gate nightclub on Bleecker Street. Ray Bremser and Herbert Huncke were both sober for a change and performed like elder statesmen of the group. Janine Pommy Vega, Allen, Peter, Carl Solomon, and Jack Micheline all read, too, and Ted Berrigan improvised clever introductions. For the first time, Allen read the completed *Plutonian Ode* in public and finished his set with some Blake songs.

A day or two later, Corso showed up in New York from San Francisco where he had gotten into trouble not only with the law, but with Ferlinghetti as well. Gregory had broken into the City Lights Bookstore late one night and rifled the cash register. The bookstore manager had been aware that cash had been disappearing, and he had changed the lock the day before the break-in. It seemed obvious that Gregory must have had a key to the store, and when he discovered that it didn't work anymore, he simply broke in to get at the money. Corso said he only stole from the till once and denied responsibility for all the other thefts. He said he believed that he was doing nothing more than taking an advance on his royalties that night. The string of lootings had put City Lights in a dangerous financial position, so it was a good time for Corso to leave town. It's remarkable that Allen believed Corso's side of the story so readily, since any time Gregory needed cash in New York he stole books from Allen's apartment and sold them to rare book dealers. Occasionally he confessed the thefts to Allen, who would then go to the dealers and buy back his own books. Allen was always patient with Gregory's larceny, but he did become upset when Corso took his most precious Blake books, which were difficult for Allen to replace.

Although Allen was now quite famous and constantly surrounded by adoring fans, he often felt alone. After twenty-five years together Peter had become more of a responsibility than a partner. Due to his active schedule Allen didn't have many day-to-day friends, and his office staff became his closest associates, almost a second family. On May 2, Allen attended a party for Andrei Voznesensky in a swanky apartment on Central Park West. When Corso arrived, his face had the pallor of a Bowery bum, according to James Jones's widow, Gloria. Before long Norman Mailer got into a heated argument with Corso when Gregory asked him for a handout. He told Gregory in no uncertain terms that he was an "asshole, a big clunk who was going to die soon." Gregory, drunker by the minute on all the free booze, toppled a lamp while talking to Harrison Salisbury and then fell over a book rack. Everyone begged Allen to take Gregory home, but Raymond Foye, a young friend, noted that once Gregory left, "the room emptied." Gregory, for all his bedevilment and abrasiveness, was always the life of any party.

At the end of his Brooklyn College term in May, Allen left New York with Peter and Steven Taylor. Taylor now traveled with Allen as his musical accompanist whenever they could financially swing it, and the two became close. Looking back on it, Steven said he always trusted Allen and thought of him in those days as a rather strange uncle. Together they made a whirlwind tour through Italy, reading in some youth clubs in Milan, a large outdoor square in Genoa, and venues in Spoleto and Rome. A routine developed where Peter handled the baggage, Steven handled the arrangements, and Allen handled himself. In every town they rushed around to see all the tourist spots during their free time. Allen enjoyed introducing Steven to architectural wonders like the Campidoglio, which had been designed by Michelangelo, and the ruins of the Coliseum not far away. It was fun for both of them, but exhausting as well, yet Allen didn't want his young friend to miss anything. In Paris they settled down for four consecutive nights to

Garden State, *CP*, p. 726

perform at the new Beaubourg Museum. From there Allen reported to his friends that Peter was a big hit with fans, who enjoyed his hog-calling yodels and banjo playing.

By the beginning of June they were on their way to stay in London with Miles for a few days before stopping in the industrial town of Manchester to perform at a Buddhist benefit. A side trip took them to Morecambe Bay to visit Steven Taylor's relatives on the coast of the Irish Sea. In Cambridge they teamed up with Anne Waldman and Kenneth Koch for a large reading and together visited Wordsworth's grave in St. Oswald's Churchyard in Grasmere. It was much too hurried, but Allen kept his Baedecker guide handy and missed little along the way. After stopping to pay his respects to an aging Basil Bunting and give one last reading, they flew to Rotterdam, where Allen wanted to go see a small version of one of his favorite Brueghel paintings, *The Tower of Babel*.

Allen flew back to Boulder on June 20, only to turn around again and zip back across the Atlantic on the twenty-ninth for three more days in Rome. Sponsors had pledged four thousand dollars to Naropa if Allen would read for an international poetry event at Rome's beach resort of Ostia. It was too large a sum of money to pass up, even if he and Peter were exhausted from all the travel. The Ostia reading proved to be almost more than they bargained for. Burroughs, Waldman, Corso, Berrigan, Giorno, Leroi Jones, Yevtushenko, Ferlinghetti, and di Prima were all there to read in front of a crowd estimated to be almost twenty thousand strong. Midway through Yevtushenko's reading, Italian anarchists stormed the stage with a large cauldron of soup "to feed the public," they said. Burroughs grabbed a chair, more than willing to fight off the hordes, but Peter was the acknowledged hero of the evening when he pushed his way onto the stage, wrested the microphone from the anarchists, and then personally cleared the platform. He called Allen back to the podium and asked him to chant "AH" for five minutes of meditation to calm the audience. Then Allen invoked to the crowd: "Anyone who wants a poetry reading sit down and shut up, anyone who doesn't make all the noise you want." All but twenty-five people sat down, which effectively isolated the troublemakers, who were then forced to be quiet by the rest of the audience. Yevtushenko returned to the stage and finished his reading.

Immediately after that festival, Allen and Peter returned to Boulder. Peter, whose relationship with Denise was nearing an end, started to see another woman, Beverly Isis. Beverly was a personable, outgoing woman, interested in both

Spring Fashions, *CP*, p. 727

Buddhism and poetry. She was a student in Allen's Blake course that summer and fell in love with the handsome Peter as soon as she saw him. She had an old VW bus that she had driven from New York to Boulder and from there she went on to California where she met up with Allen and Peter and drove them to Bedrock Mortar for a much-needed holiday. There was some tension with their neighbor, Gary Snyder, who demanded a more rigid adherence to rules than Allen was used to, and after a few days, they were glad to be on their way again. As Allen sat in the backseat riding out of the hills, he couldn't help slapping his legs like a little kid and chanting, "We're out from under Gary Snyder, we're out from under Gary Snyder."

Las Vegas: Verses Improvised for El Dorado H.S. Newspaper, *CP*, p. 728

Allen went on to do other readings in the West while Beverly and Peter returned to New York. The couple had hit it off from the start and soon were seeing a good deal of each other.

Allen stopped in New York that fall only long enough to go over paperwork with Rosenthal, who was settling in nicely as Allen's permanent secretary. By October Allen and Steven Taylor were back in Europe for another long three-month reading tour that began in England. On this trip Steven brought along his college girlfriend, Maria. Allen had long since accepted the fact that the young men he liked would always have their own girlfriends, so the arrangement was fine with him. It was rare that Allen was attracted to a gay man, which meant that even when a young man was willing to get in bed with Allen and make him happy, the relationship could not remain sexual for long. Inevitably, the man would realize he preferred sex with women, or Allen would find someone younger, sexier, and more inaccessible to lust after. This may have been his convenient way of avoiding a long-term relationship, which would involve a level of compromise that was impossible for him. Peter had not been strong-minded enough to break away from Allen when he was younger, as Allen's other straight partners had. He became enmeshed in an odd relationship in which he adopted the role of a somewhat slow-witted, loving, yet hostile brother to Allen.

Allen, Steven, and Maria stayed a few days in Miles's London apartment before Maria flew home. Allen and Steven kept themselves so busy that Allen later noted he didn't even have time to appreciate how much fun he was having. In retrospect, those days in London would prove to be the best for a long time to come. Allen had coffee with Seymour Wyse, Kerouac's old friend from Horace Mann prep school days, and once more got together with Simon Albury and Tom Maschler to discuss the long-delayed publication of his *Collected Poems*. The project was still on Allen's mind, but after years of contractual problems with City Lights, it looked as if it might never happen. Allen also wanted to introduce Steven to more of his favorite spots in England. An important site on the list was Felpham, where Blake had lived in a rose-covered cottage for three pivotal years of his life. Allen showed Steven the spot on which Blake had seen a little girl named Ololon descend from heaven into his garden. During the same vision, Blake had also witnessed John Milton confront Satan, the inspiration for Blake's poem *Milton*. It was highly similar to Allen's own encounter with Blake's voice in his East Harlem apartment.

To the Punks of Dawlish, *CP*, p. 729

After several weeks of travel in England, they went on to a week of readings in Holland and Belgium before heading to Italy, where they were to rendezvous with Orlovsky and Corso and tour with members of the Living Theater. Julian Beck and Judith Malina met them in Ravenna, where Allen took the time to investigate the celebrated Byzantine frescoes and mosaics. Then, on their way to Turin, Allen persuaded them to stop at the Bergamo basilica of Santa Maria Maggiore to see the masterpieces. He enjoyed touring with friends, and he found Steven an interested companion; besides being good company, he added a commonsense stability to the performances. Gregory was in rare form, "mostly sober," Allen said, while others might have said, "sometimes drunk." Allen saw him as less abrasive and somewhat more mature than usual, and for a while, Peter seemed to be stable, too.

The poets left the Living Theater troupe in Italy and went on to a four-city tour of Germany. Before going to their hotel room in Hamburg, one of their final stops on the tour, Peter decided to go to the red-light district to check out the prostitutes. The women sat on display in numbered windows, similar to Amsterdam's brothels, and Peter found a long-faced girl in pink underwear whom he liked. The cost was fifty marks for a half hour, so Allen and Steven waited for him in a bar down the street drinking a concoction of Coca-Cola mixed with corn liquor. Before long they noticed Peter outside on the street, vomiting. He said that he had been given some putrid hash to smoke and then the whores had stolen all his money and his watch. Allen was annoyed when he had to go back to the whorehouse and pay an additional fifty marks to retrieve Peter's watch. Peter was sick for a day or two and they never figured out what had really happened, but they suspected that Peter had hocked his watch to buy what turned out to be rancid drugs.

Some Love, *CP*, p. 730
Maybe Love, *CP*, p. 731
Ruhr-Gebiet, *CP*, p. 734
Love Forgiven, *CP*, p. 737
Tübingen-Hamburg Schlafwagen, *CP*, p. 736

By the time they returned to New York City in December, Peter seemed fine again, and quite a pleasant Christmas gift was waiting for them. Allen and Peter had each been awarded ten-thousand-dollar grants from the NEA. Bob Rosenthal had taken the initiative and sent in applications for them, since he knew that Ron Padgett, one of the poets connected with the St. Mark's Poetry Project, was on the NEA awards committee that year. Bob knew that Padgett respected Allen's poetry and would consider each of their applications fairly. The windfall was welcome news around the apartment, as once again Allen's funds had hit rock bottom. He also needed more money to distribute to his ever-growing list of friends in need. For a while Peter toyed with the idea of using his grant money to buy his own place in Cherry Valley from Charles Plymell. Allen's plans to transfer the farm to Peter now looked less likely, as Peter was becoming more strung out on drugs and less able to care for a farm. In the end Peter donated his entire ten thousand dollars to Chögyam Trungpa. The awards, especially the one to Peter, caused a good deal of negative press, and the NEA was roundly criticized as the National Endowment for Pornography when it was revealed that so much money had been given to a poet whose only published book was called *Clean Asshole Poems*.

The day after Christmas Allen woke up from a terrifying dream he was having about a mysterious and unknown woman. He wondered why he was haunted by women in his dreams and speculated that these dreams sprang from his abandonment of love with women and his clinging to love with men. He tortured himself with the identity of this nameless creature and pondered who it might be. He searched inside himself for an answer to these disturbing reveries. He wrote, "How did I, Allen Ginsberg get to be gay?/Who's this me, in love with boys since forty years?/What's the old secret of my feminine fears?/Why kiss men's smooth cheeks, while now my own beard is gray?/I wonder as you, and ask myself the same question."

1980 ~

AFTER THE NEW YEAR'S BREAK, Allen left New York to teach
in Boulder. He had recently been diagnosed with high blood pressure, which
he blamed on his anxiety over the endless Poetry Wars as well as his countless obligations. His doctor advised him once again to alter his diet, cut out
salt, rest more, and reduce his stress if he wanted to live a long, healthy life.
Allen simply could not follow that advice, as he proved within a few weeks
on a rigorous trip that took him to Philadelphia for a reading, then on to
Canada, a stop in New York overnight, back to Boston to perform at Passim's
in Harvard Square, then over to Amherst for a lecture before he flew out to
Boulder. While in Boston, he posed for his old friend Elsa Dorfman, who
used her new, giant 20×24 camera for a double portrait of Allen, clothed and
nude. In New York he did squeeze in an appointment with Dr. Ho, his
acupuncturist, who wisely recommended herbs and abdominal breathing exercises to lower his blood pressure. Those were both things Allen could do,
at least for a short period of time. Now he was always too busy "being Allen
Ginsberg" to slow down permanently.

The flap over the Trungpa/Merwin affair, now five years old, continued to
rage on. In March, Allen finally received a copy of the complete transcript of
the interview he had given years earlier to Clark and Dorn. He sat down with
the papers and filled forty-eight pages of his notebook with dense commentary, going over each point, most of it in defense of Trungpa's actions. Allen
could not understand why Clark was attacking Tibetan Buddhism when his
complaints seemed to be solely against Trungpa. "Isn't that 'throwing out the

baby with the bathwater'?" he wondered. He was devoting a great deal of his time and energy to keeping the Jack Kerouac School afloat and this continuing controversy had impaired the image of the college and made it difficult to get funding. Allen wished that he could simply tell everyone that this incident was between Merwin and Trungpa and should not be open to public discussion, unless one of them insisted on it. He wanted to remind everyone that the incident had not even happened at Naropa, but at a seminary in another town. All he wanted to do was teach poetics in a meditative environment. In his mind there was no relationship between that misadventure and the Jack Kerouac School. He had placed himself in the hands of Trungpa as his spiritual teacher and invested his unwavering faith in his own master's judgment. This conflict was a dilemma for Allen and one that he was never able to resolve to his own satisfaction. Practically speaking, it

Verses Written for Student Antidraft Registration Rally 1980, *CP*, p. 738

Homework, *CP*, p. 739

After Whitman & Reznikoff, *CP*, p. 740

Reflections at Lake Louise, *CP*, p. 741

boiled down to a question of faith, and Allen understood rationally that faith could not and should not be questioned.

In the spring, Allen visited another of Trungpa's seminaries. It was devoted to studying the three *yanas* or vehicles of Buddhism, *Hinayana*, *Mahayana*, and *Vajrayana*, and was held in a luxurious resort at Lake Louise in the Canadian Rockies. Anne Waldman was there with about three hundred others for the three-month intensive seminary. Due to his teaching schedule Allen could stay only for a week. He wanted a break from Naropa, but he also needed to talk to Trungpa personally about the negative publicity over the Merwin affair. As he talked to his guru, Allen sensed that he was more worried about the scandal than his teacher was. Even realizing that, the debacle continued to weigh on Allen's mind. He felt guilty that he had contributed to the scandal by talking too much and didn't quite know how to extricate himself from it. For years he had tried to remain neutral and to mediate problems, but he felt he had to eventually take a side in this conflict that was threatening to tear the Buddhist poetry community apart, a community he had worked tirelessly to unite. Over time the controversy more or less faded away, without a final resolution or closure. Those who trusted Trungpa continued to trust him and those who were suspicious of him and his motives remained so.

Red cheeked boyfriends, *CP*, p. 743

Fourth Floor, Dawn, Up All Night Writing Letters, *CP*, p. 744

In June Allen got away from Boulder to give a month of readings around New York and California. He was glad to escape to San Francisco where he could see his old friends and stay at Shig's, far removed from the Naropa mess. Allen was also quite happy to see more of Raymond Foye, his young, handsome literary friend of several years, who had worked on a variety of projects for City Lights ranging from Edgar Allan Poe and Bob Kaufman to Samuel Greenberg. Raymond took the opportunity to arrange a gig for Allen at a North Beach jazz club called the Keystone Korner.

During Naropa's summer term that year, Allen asked Eliot Katz, a poet and political activist he knew from New Jersey, to be his student intern. Eliot helped Allen with his voluminous paperwork, but also rekindled his interest in political issues and environmental causes beyond the Buddhist wars. When classes ended, Allen and Peter closed up their house and went directly to the Bisbee Poetry Festival in Arizona, where the title of Peter's book alone was enough to raise the hackles of several sensitive souls. McClure, Kyger, and Bobbie Louise Hawkins were also scheduled to appear, and they joined in support of Peter's poetry against his critics. After enduring a minor protest from civic-minded censors during the festival, they retreated to the calm of Drummond Hadley's ranch. Peter loved working on the ranch, and both Allen and Peter earned a reputation for being the most helpful guests that the Hadleys ever had. In the evenings they discussed farming, music, and poetry, and Allen showed Drum some tricks that Williams had taught him about finding the "hot language" of poetry. On that visit Allen read Drum's poetry and liked his long melodious vernacular lines so much that he compared them to those of Robert Service. He wrote to Ferlinghetti right away to suggest he publish a volume of Hadley's cowboy poems.

Porch Scribbles, CP, p. 843

Ode to Failure, CP, p. 745

After completing an American reading tour that fall, Allen took off with Peter and Steven for two months in Yugoslavia, the Balkans, and parts of German-speaking Europe. He had set up a busy conference and reading schedule that included some cities he had never visited before. In Dubrovnik the trio stayed in a hotel on a quiet square, enjoying mussels for dinner and the fresh fruit they bought from the local farmers' market for breakfast. Dubrovnik was an ancient walled city built of white marble, once the rival of Venice in beauty and importance. It proved to be a good place to recover from jet lag before pressing on to Belgrade, but it was so hot that Allen couldn't sleep. He kept getting up and rearranging his sheets, until an exhausted Steven Taylor told him to be quiet. At four-thirty in the morning Allen went down to the lobby of the hotel and composed the poem "Birdbrain!" in which he wrote the line, "Birdbrain wakes up in middle of night and arranges his sheets." The next evening at a concert he wrote the poem "Eroica" while listening to the strains of Beethoven's great symphony in the marble

Birdbrain!, CP, p. 746

Eroica, CP, p. 748

columned courtyard of the Rector's House. Before leaving town, Peter slipped and fell on the well-worn pavement that had been made smooth as glass by centuries of wear, fracturing his shoulder. Although his arm had to be put in a sling, it didn't slow him down much, and he was even able to play his banjo. In Belgrade they stayed in a posh apartment arranged for them by their hosts. It was near the Writer's Club where they took their meals late each night. They ate pork with oily, roasted peppers mashed to a paste, prosciut-tos and cheeses, exactly the kind of food Allen should have been avoiding. Peter and Steven found girlfriends easily, but Allen was not as successful finding young men, and spent much of his free time alone, exploring Belgrade's castles, forts, and monasteries.

"Defending the Faith," *CP*, p. 750

Their next major stop was Budapest, where Allen discovered that a rock 'n' roll group called Hobo had made a hit record from a translation of his early poem *The Shrouded Stranger*. Allen was surprised to find that Hungarian teenagers knew all the words to the poem by heart and found that as a result he was treated like a celebrity. They were put up by the local chapter of PEN in an expensive hotel for one week, but Peter and Steven were disappointed to find that it was against hotel policy to invite girls to their room. By the time they arrived in Vienna, Allen was feeling nauseated. He had overdone it with rich foods and sweets, and he decided to adjust his diet and eat healthy food for the balance of his trip, which in Eastern Europe would not be easy. They wandered from city to city through Austria and Switzerland enjoying the culture and scenery, even taking a tiny mountain train to the top of the Jungfrau on a foggy day when there was nothing to be seen but the clouds. They were well received at every poetry reading, and, as usual, Allen was in-terviewed continually by the press. Then, the sad and shocking news arrived from New York that John Lennon had been assassinated. "Just like Jesus!" Allen wrote to McClure. "Goodness and innocence is not its own protec-tion!" He and Lennon had been in touch from time to time and Allen had always hoped they'd record something to-gether, but that was not to be. In mid-December, Allen ar-rived back in the States, with a schedule filled with more readings in Texas and points southwest.

Capitol Air, *CP*, p. 751

While they were in Europe, *Straight Hearts' Delight*, the correspondence between Allen and Peter, was published by Gay Sunshine Press. The couple had been together for twenty-five years and this book served as their an-niversary observance. It encouraged the general public to believe that Allen and Peter were still romantically intimate, something that was far from the truth. Like the spouse of any celebrity, Peter bore the burden of being referred to as "Allen Ginsberg's partner." It was difficult for him to lead his own life and to have his own friends, since everything circled around Allen. Their prolonged reading trips together exacerbated the problem of his having his own separate identity, and Allen's insistence that Peter perform with him onstage made Peter feel that he had no choice. Peter's use of drugs and alcohol had never diminished, and his addictions worried Allen whenever he could bring himself to acknowledge them. Theirs was a complicated, codependent relationship, not fulfilling for either of them and difficult for even their best friends to fathom.

1981 ～

IN JANUARY PETER'S FATHER, Oleg, was admitted to a hospital in Astoria, Queens. When Peter and Allen visited his bedside they saw the frail old man with an oxygen tube in his nose and hardly recognized him. His illness was serious enough that Allen's brother, Eugene, was called to the hospital to help him make a last will and testament. Beverly Isis visited him in the hospital every few days and spent time with him until Peter was able to move him closer to home in Manhattan's Mt. Sinai Hospital. At eighty-one years of age, Oleg was nearing the end of his life. Despite the fact that he had barely seen his father over the years, Peter nursed him lovingly as he had other sick friends and relations.

Following months of nonstop travel Allen came down with a bad case of the flu and had to spend much of January in bed in New York. At his bedside he placed a table to serve as his Buddhist shrine and covered it with a finely embroidered silky blue cloth on which he laid his collection of ritual implements and meditation aids. His bedroom had just been freshly painted a bright white by Lucien Carr's son, Caleb Carr, who needed work. A decade later Caleb would write a best seller of his own entitled *The Alienist*. Allen recuperated in the captain's bed he had helped design, a flat platform with hidden compartments for his most precious tapes and a headboard to lean on when he read or wrote in his journal. A foam rubber mattress helped give support to his aching back. Since the doorbell didn't work, the key to his apartment was put in a sock that could be dropped from the front window when visitors arrived and shouted up for admittance. It was peaceful at home that winter. The bells of Mary Help of Christians Church rang out directly across the street from his windows and reverberated off his walls, but Allen didn't mind the interruption.

Since he had some free time while sick, Allen took advantage of the opportunity by jotting down his worries in his bedside notebook. He began with the big things. He feared the resurgence of capitalism and the hierarchy of the militaristic Buddhists and lamented the lack of progress toward building a better society during his lifetime. He noted his lack of income and the impermanence of his housing. His apartment building was currently up for sale and no one knew what the result would be. The Lower East Side in 1981 was not the best neighborhood in the city, but it was one of the few that had remained cheap enough for Allen to afford. The landlord had cut off the heat and hot water to the building and refused to make any repairs, hoping to force tenants out. Several times his ceilings had collapsed due to plumbing problems, and Allen had to pay for the repairs out of his own pocket. Since his apartment was rent controlled, he could not be evicted, and that was the only blessing. His real worry was that the landlord might abandon the building as so many others had in that part of town. It was common for landlords to walk away from their properties when the expenses of maintaining the rent-controlled apartments exceeded the income they collected. The neighborhood was heavily dotted with the burned-out shells of buildings and the vacant lots that resulted.

Allen was beginning to hope that new negotiations between City Lights, New Directions, and Knopf might lead to an eventual contract for his *Collected Poems*. That might even give him a little extra money to relieve his immediate financial woes, but those negotiations were dragging on, as had all the others. It didn't stop Allen from being generous with what little money he did have, though. In February he sent sixteen hundred dollars to Charlie Plymell to help with the expenses of printing Huncke's book *The Evening Sun Turned Crimson*. Allen's office expenses were increasing, too. Even though Bob Rosenthal was working full time now, he occasionally needed extra staff to help with Allen's many projects. The unanticipated result of having an office staff was that although it freed Allen to produce work, it also meant that more of his own attention had to be given to checking and revising that work. The cycle never stopped. The more help he could get to do his work, the more work he would create, and slowly, what Rosenthal liked to refer to as Allen's "cottage industry" was born. At some points he kept as many as five or six people on his payroll busy.

In spite of always being low on funds, Allen continued to welcome both friends and friends of friends into his apartment if they were visiting New

York and had need of a room. Usually Allen would provide food for them as well. He enjoyed seeing his old friends and meeting new people, but the constant stream of guests robbed him of his privacy. Many visitors remember staying in Allen's apartment without ever seeing him to thank in person. Next door to Allen, Peter and Denise had problems of their own. Peter flew into one of his violent rages and threw her sewing machine through a glass window and then proceeded to trash the apartment. Allen paid to have the damage repaired, but Denise had endured enough of Peter's savage behavior and left for good.

On March 3, before Allen returned to Naropa to teach for the spring term, Billy Burroughs, Jr., died, a victim of his continued alcohol abuse. He was cremated and his ashes were given to Allen, who placed them in the shrine room of the Karma Dzong meditation hall in Boulder. Later, he would get to the mountains to scatter them at the Rocky Mountain Dharma Center. By coincidence, that spring Allen was lodged in the Varsity Manor apartments where Burroughs had lived while teaching at Naropa in the late 1970s. His apartment was neat and cozy and faced onto a bright courtyard. Peter had gone to Cherry Valley alone for the spring to plant more trees and to work on the farmhouse. He planned to join Allen in June. Although Allen continued to lecture without a salary, at least Naropa paid for his room at the Varsity Manor, so he managed to make ends meet. In addition, Allen was personally providing the meager salaries of some of the writers he had invited to teach there, such as Tom Pickard from England. Allen only wished he could do more. Even though Naropa had weathered the Trungpa/Merwin storm, it was now under consideration for accreditation, and any signs of financial instability could jeopardize the whole thing. They hoped to become the first accredited Buddhist college in the country. In order to do that, they needed Allen and relied on his ability to draw world-class poets to their faculty for little or no cost.

Industrial Waves, *CP*, p. 845

By the early 1980s El Salvador had become a flashpoint for political trouble in Central America, and the U.S. government seemed to be up to its old tricks of backing the very tyrants they should be opposing. In Allen's opinion, American policy was forcing El Salvador into the position of accepting aid from Cuba. He saw this as a plot whereby America could then denounce El Salvador for accepting communist aid and intervene on the side of the right-wing death squads who opposed the communists. As he made his rounds to college campuses throughout the country, Allen took every opportunity to address the state of affairs in Central America. He was becoming weary of all sides in these conflicts as reflected in his song "Capitol Air."

"No hope Communism no hope Capitalism Yeah/Everybody's lying on both sides."

Health problems continued to plague Allen, too. Traveling as much as he did, it was impossible for him to maintain a proper diet. He couldn't keep his blood pressure down or stop smoking either. He wished he could sit in quiet meditation regularly, but with so many distractions it seemed that would never happen.

In the back of his mind Allen still dreamed of becoming a rock 'n' roll star. John Hammond wanted to put out the Ginsberg record album they had worked on sporadically since the mid-seventies. It had once been scuttled by corporate decision makers due to his openly gay references, but Hammond decided to produce it under his own label that fall. With Steven Taylor's help, Allen's songs had matured and the album promised to be more organized and cohesive than his previous efforts.

Early in June Allen was invited by the Clash, a popular punk rock group headed by a soulful musician named Joe Strummer, to watch their performance at Bond's, a large club in Times Square. When Allen was introduced to them backstage after the concert, Strummer asked him when he planned to run for president. "I'm not," Allen promised, "because my guru said if I was President I'd wind up in diamond hell." The Clash asked Allen to help them with the lyrics to a song they were composing, and Allen was only too happy to offer advice. At one of the Bond performances they asked him to come onstage, and Allen was thrilled to sing before a crowd of eight thousand rowdy, screaming fans. "I can die happy having satisfied my shop girl ambitions!" he wrote to Creeley about his rock 'n' roll success. Of course, his appetite for performing was only whetted by sharing the stage with his musical friends, not satisfied. He wished that he could command the same respect for his music as he did for his poetry.

None of these musical activities brought in any money for Allen, and the last of his bank account was wiped out when he spent fifteen hundred dollars on a used Volvo station wagon for Peter. Even though the beats were becoming a hot commodity again during the early 1980s, Allen was reluctant to cash in on the revival. When the director of the movie *Heart Beat* asked Allen to look over the script for the film, instead of asking to be paid, Allen ordered them to remove his name completely. They complied by changing the name of the character who was supposed to be Allen to "Ira Stryker" and went ahead with the project. It turned out to be an awkward movie at best. It was based on part of Carolyn Cassady's memoir of the same name and featured good actors like Sissy Spacek, Nick Nolte, and

John Heard in the leading roles, but it was not an accurate depiction of Allen or his friends.

Even though he didn't want to profit by his "Beat Generation" persona, Allen was learning how to make good use of his membership in the American Academy and Institute of Arts and Letters. For the sixth consecutive year he nominated Burroughs for membership. By that time, he knew how to gain loyalty from the other academy members by seconding their nominees, and this meant that they would be more likely to support his nominees. Finally he was able to put together enough votes to have Burroughs elected.

That summer, an eighteen-year-old student named Brian Jackson arrived at Naropa from the Midwest. He had first met Allen the previous fall when Ginsberg and Burroughs read together at the University of Kansas. Allen had taken the time to talk to Brian after the reading and had given him a list of books to read, encouraging him to come to Boulder the following summer. When he arrived, Allen made him his teaching assistant, and they spent most of the summer together, first in the Varsity Townhouses and then later at Allen's new rental house at 2141 Bluff Street.

Those Two, *CP*, p. 849

Homage Vajracarya, *CP*, p. 850

In the summer of 1981, City Lights published Allen's PEN report on FBI harassment of the underground press during the 1960s and 1970s as part of a book they called *The Campaign Against the Underground Press: Un-american Activities.* Allen's essay was titled "Smoking Typewriters," and it was the most important political paper he had worked on since he had helped research America's involvement in the Southeast Asian opium trade a decade earlier. Allen knew that government agents had infiltrated the underground press and helped destroy it from both within and without, but the government's conspiracy was far more organized that even he had imagined. By the 1980s, though, no one was shocked to hear about dirty tricks from their own government; in fact, after Watergate, a cynical public grew to expect governmental foul play.

Allen's Buddhist practice provided the only solace for him. He tried to commit himself to a daily meditation practice and was ashamed that he hadn't made sitting his first priority. He resolved to be more conscientious in the future. If his students were able to sit several hours a day, he should be able to match their self-discipline.

Why I Meditate, *CP*, p. 851

He had all the excuses—the demands of conducting classes, answering mail, reading newspapers, doing readings, and giving interviews. Even though he realized he was out of control and was spending all his energy on his own "insatiable thirst" for fame, he couldn't stop himself.

In August, Peter and Allen filled their Volvo with Brian Jackson, his girl-friend, and several other students and drove up to Mt. Evans in the Rockies for an overnight camping trip. Allen brought some mescaline with him, the first he had taken since 1958. Back then, the experience had frightened him out of his wits during a Greenwich Village cab ride with Gregory and Peter. Now, twenty-three years later, the experience gave him more reasons to ex-amine himself and his motives. It made him aware that he had grown old in the interim, and he should be preparing himself for death instead of regaling people about psychedelic experiences he had long since discontinued. He saw himself as "a big slob fraud." On the mountain under a mescaline high, he could feel the earth revolving under the sky, see the rock cliffs moving and vibrating, and see the trees shimmering in the bright sunlight more clearly than ever before. He became cognizant of his own ambitions and his vast ego was spread out before him. He even experienced a few paranoid mo-ments that reminded him of his mother. It helped him to realize that he was obsessed with achieving sainthood and to see that Kerouac had been right all along, that he was nothing but "a hairy loss." Allen wrote in his journal, "The uncertainty of any situation I'm in—or the empty basis of it—becomes more glaring. Teaching: I'm not a scholar and feel as if I'm filling up time with unworthy students too few, with merely repetitive general recollection of ideas I once had thought. Meditating: I'm lazy, hesitant and far behind in prostrations." He was almost as hard on himself as his critics were. As a younger man he had been able to take his time and do what he pleased be-cause there were no pressures being placed on him by others. Now, everyone wanted a piece of him, wanted at least a conversation or a nod from him, wanted him to read their poetry, wanted him to "discover" them and ac-knowledge them in some way. Allen tried to do as much for each person as he could, but it was too much. Once when he was being interviewed by stu-dents for their school newspaper, Allen appeared to be tiring after several hours of steady questions. His assistant asked him if he wanted to take a break and rest, but Allen earnestly replied, "I can't take a break from my life."

Over the years Allen developed an entire philosophy about giving inter-views. He began to see it as another way of teaching. He spoke to all people as if they were future Buddhas, honestly and openly, heart to heart. He treated the interview as an art form for transmitting knowledge from one generation to another as the Japanese *roshis* do. In fact, Ginsberg's conversa-tional ability was perhaps his most remarkable quality, aside from his literary talent. He was a receptive listener as well as an astute speaker. He was sym-pathetic and sensitive to every person he spoke with, and he was able to tune out the rest of the world and focus on what was transpiring between him and his conversant. Everyone wanted to talk with Allen, and he was somehow able to connect with them for only a moment after a reading or at a party and have a meaningful interchange that they remembered for the rest of their lives. He had a gift for listening to what people were saying in a manner quite uncommon in other celebrities. In each encounter, a person had the feeling that he was truly talking to only him, and, in fact, he was. He believed that if he were candid and honest, any bad karma coming out of an interview or a conversation would be the responsibility of the other person and not his own. For that reason he never said anything he did not mean and always tried to speak as candidly as possible with each person. He became fond of the quotation "Candor ends paranoia."

As a guest at an International Poetry Festival in Mexico City in August, Allen stayed at a luxurious hotel called the Chapultepec Presidente, with distinguished colleagues like W. S. Merwin, Jorge Luis Borges, Andrei Voznesensky, and Günter Grass. It would have been inconvenient to stay miles away in the run-down hotels he had preferred on his earlier trips to Mexico, but surrounded by such opulence in a land of poverty made Allen feel hypocritical. He was especially glad to have the chance to talk to Merwin and Dana Naone privately at the hotel. Allen apologized again for speaking with Tom Clark about what he believed was their own private business, and he came away feeling that they had resolved their differences.

In September, Allen returned to Italy for another series of readings. This time he stayed in Rome to sightsee and to revisit some of his favorite spots. He saw Keats's house again and sat on the Spanish Steps where he had been arrested in 1967 and bailed out by his father. This time, instead of chasing good-looking boys, he overindulged on ice cream at the Piazza Navona. In Florence, he and Nanda Pivano recited his poetry before thousands of people gathered in the Piazza della Signoria, under the watchful eyes of Michelangelo's nude, teenaged *David*. Then he sang "Father Death Blues" and "Birdbrain!" while Nanda did her best to keep up with the Italian translations.

Most of the fees he collected for these appearances went directly into the COP account. As a rule of thumb Allen tried to live on his royalties and donated his personal appearance fees to either COP or Naropa, but occasionally he had to supplement the modest amounts he received from City Lights with other money. He also continued his practice of giving free benefit readings, especially for Buddhist groups, in the towns where he had paying gigs. When he had the idea of hosting a twenty-fifth-anniversary conference in honor of Kerouac's *On the Road* the next summer, Allen knew

he would have to come up with serious money, for Naropa had no funds to spare. His dream was to organize a suitably large and impressive conference and invite everyone who had known Kerouac to participate, but that would require tens of thousands of dollars. He was determined not to give up his vision, so he sent out the invitations and decided to worry about finding the money to finance it later. The conference would also help dramatically with Naropa's accreditation process and, he hoped, put the Poetry Wars behind them once and for all. From that moment until the conference was over, most of Allen's time and all his money was Love Comes, *CP*, p. 852
spent preparing for it. At the same time as all that planning Old Love Story, *CP*,
was going on, Rosenthal was assembling *Plutonian Ode and* p. 856
Other Poems, Allen's next City Lights book. Airplane Blues, *CP*,
p. 859

Before the *On the Road* reunion took place, an invitation arrived from Columbia University asking Allen to read *Howl* at the McMillin Theater to commemorate the twenty-fifth anniversary of its creation and publication. Allen was delighted to return to his alma mater one more time to read, and it was all the more special because the auditorium was to be the same one where he had read poetry on February 5, 1959, with Gregory and Peter. About that long-ago night, Diana Trilling had written her article in which she began, "I took one look at the crowd Do the Meditation
and was certain that it would smell bad." On this evening in Rock, *CP*, p. 863
1981, Allen returned as a conquering hero.

1982 ~

AFTER GIVING A FEW readings around Atlanta in January, Allen flew to Managua, Nicaragua. Following the 1979 fall of Anastasio Somoza, that country had been governed by a junta headed by Daniel Ortega, the leader of the Sandinista National Liberation Front (FSLN). President Carter had supported the efforts to keep Nicaragua neutral, but with the election of Ronald Reagan, the United States had decided to back the contra terrorists who were trying to overthrow the junta. Reagan favored an embargo against Nicaragua and secretly approved funding for the mining of Nicaragua's harbors, an act of war in itself. It had quickly become another political tinderbox. As usual Allen wanted to find out firsthand what the real situation was, and if necessary call attention to the wrong-headed thinking of the Reagan administration. Nicaragua was especially interesting to Allen because Ortega was not only a soldier but a poet as well, and the country's minister of culture was none other than his old friend Ernesto Cardenal, a great poet in his own right.

When Allen arrived in Managua, he found the streets filled with uniformed soldiers preparing for a U.S.-backed military invasion. Ortega himself greeted Allen at the airport along with Yevgeny Yevtushenko, who had timed his visit to coincide with Allen's. While at the airport Allen took Ortega aside and asked him which of his texts might be too controversial to read in Nicaragua. He wanted to warn Ortega that in the past he'd been expelled from both Cuba and Czechoslovakia for speaking his mind. Ortega told Allen that he hoped he wouldn't focus too much on the internal problems of Nicaragua, because all their efforts now had to be devoted toward

the threat of an American invasion. He asked Allen to focus on his early poems and the *Fall of America*, which he felt talked more about the ills of impe-
rialism, and requested that he not bring up gay rights or freedom of the press
as major issues on this visit. There would be time for those things later, he
said.

Yevtushenko, Cardenal, and Ginsberg agreed that the best thing they
could do would be to sit down together and write a manifesto asking for
nonintervention in Nicaragua by the superpowers. Why not let the
Nicaraguans solve their own problems without making it into another bat-
tleground of U.S./USSR interests? They called their statement the "Declaration of Three," and it was carried as front-page news by the Managuan
press and even made it into the *Nation* and the *Washington Tribune* back in
the States. In spite of the political and military turmoil in
Nicaragua, Allen enjoyed his visit. The landscape was lush   The Little Fish Devours
and tropical, like Florida in many ways, except for the   the Big Fish, *CP*, p. 865
bombed-out buildings. Everyone he met seemed to be a
poet, and literacy was one of the highest priorities with the new government. The delegation visited the huge freshwater Lago de Nicaragua,
fringed by tiny islands and stone-walled cottages. They gave several readings to audiences that consisted mostly of interested soldiers. Allen did not
enjoy finding himself in an armed society, but he felt that their government had good intentions overall. He objected to the junta's closure of opposition newspapers and its suppression of freedom of speech, but
remembering the lessons he had learned in Havana and Prague he kept his
opinions to himself. His impression was that the U.S. government's military threats and economic blockade were acting as a self-fulfilling
prophecy for a certain Iron Curtain takeover just as they had in El Salvador. Preparing for an attack had forced Nicaragua to use its meager resources to fund the military, and they had to look for help from Russia or
Cuba. Back at home, Allen tried to spread the word that Nicaragua wanted
to remain neutral, but the Reagan administration policy was pushing
Nicaragua to the left, it was as simple as that.

In Los Angeles on his way back home, Allen met Steven Taylor long
enough to visit Dylan's recording studio, and they taped two new songs with
Dylan playing bass. John Hammond wanted to wrap up the
record soon, and Allen was optimistic enough about it that   Happening Now?, *CP*,
he began to plan a publicity tour for the release. Back East at   p. 868
the end of March, he blocked out time for a three-week retreat with Trungpa
in Bedford Springs, Pennsylvania, before he left to drive to Naropa for classes.

In the middle of his retreat he had another severe kidney stone attack, but with medication he was able to complete his stay.

When he got to Boulder, he settled in to the serious work of preparing for the Kerouac conference. Peter had been unbalanced for several weeks, and it was then that Allen first heard that Peter had given his ten-thousand-dollar NEA grant to Trungpa in a fit of either mania or devotion. Allen was pleased that Peter was so generous but sorry that he had given it all away, as they might have made better use of some of the money, especially with the upcoming *On the Road* conference. On the last day of April, a group of Dutch poets came through town publicizing a new anthology of their poetry. They read at Naropa and the great Dutch artist Karel Appel, who was along for the ride, collaborated with Allen on some paintings advertising the upcoming conference. To Allen's surprise nearly everyone that he had invited to the conference accepted. Burroughs, Corso, Orlovsky, Creeley, Ferlinghetti, McClure, di Prima, Kesey, Berrigan, Carl Solomon, Ray Bremser, Jack Micheline, Robert Frank, Herbert Huncke, David Amram, Abbie Hoffman, Timothy Leary, Jan Kerouac, and many others wrote to say they would be there. It promised to be a glorious event; now all Allen had to do was find enough money to pay for their travel and expenses.

Negotiations with both New Directions and Grove Press had broken off, and Ferlinghetti was now talking with Knopf and Dial about the publication of Ginsberg's *Collected Poems*. Even Allen was giving up hope. The release of the Hammond record was postponed a few months, too, so everything seemed to be on hold except the conference. Plans for that were going along smoothly, probably because it was completely under Allen's control. As he had hoped, the event was snowballing into a giant reunion of Kerouac's friends, and as more people signed up to participate, more people wanted to attend. Robert Frank found a backer to advance him enough money to shoot a black-and-white documentary film on the conference, which thrilled Allen. In addition to having Frank attend, now Allen would have a permanent record of the event. Allen's only regrets were that Gary Snyder could not be there and that Voznesensky could not get a visa. Although it wasn't intended to be a nostalgia trip, that was what it became. Allen was satisfied even with that, because it gave the younger generation a chance to see all the remaining beats in one place and offered the possibility of a transmission of spirit from old to young, the valuable act of *darshan*.

Many of the writers stayed at the peaceful Columbine Lodge in the 1898 Chautauqua camp on the hill above Boulder, where the front porch of the

A Public Poetry, *CP*, p. 869

"What You Up To?," *CP*, p. 870

Maturity, *CP*, p. 872

lodge became the de facto center of the ten-day conference. John Clellon Holmes correctly summed it up as "a festival of old friendships that had turned into a celebration of the value of camaraderie itself." What was the Beat Generation anyway if not Ginsberg's friends? By the middle of August when the conference ended, Allen felt proud that he had managed to pull off an extraordinary event. Even Corso rose to the occasion and read a new long poem called "The Day After Humankind." It was as good as anything he'd done since "Bomb."

As soon as the festival was over, Allen, Peter, and Gregory got into the Volvo and drove to Santa Fe. Allen wanted to participate in an antinuclear rally there with Ram Dass, and Peter and Gregory wanted time to relax. From Santa Fe they took a series of buses and trains through northern Mexico on an extended getaway together. It was a part of the world that Allen had always loved; the scenery was incomparable and the relaxed pace was just what they all needed. On board the train from Chihuahua to the town of Los Mochis on the West Coast, they passed through a dramatic lightning storm with a sky filled with flashes, veins, bolts, and glimmers over the Sierra Madre mountains. They enjoyed the spur-of-the-moment trip, as they had as young men, but the trip didn't improve Allen's health. The spicy Mexican food aggravated his already elevated blood pressure, which his doctor was unsuccessfully trying to lower with medication.

"Throw Out the Yellow Journalists of Bad Grammar & Terrible Manner," *CP*, p. 873

Going to the World of the Dead, *CP*, p. 875

After their trip, amid the many projects on his desk, Allen found a note from Jerry Aronson asking for permission to make a feature-length documentary about his life. Allen had bumped into Aronson at the *On the Road* conference, and they had spoken briefly about the film. Although flattered by the offer, he was so busy that he hoped the film would not take up too much of his own time. He well knew that other people's projects always turned into extra work for him, no matter what assurances were made in the beginning. It took ten years to complete, but in 1993 the film *The Life and Times of Allen Ginsberg* premiered, and of course Allen had ended up investing considerable time in it. More honors awaited Allen. The *Los Angeles Times* Book Award was to be given to him in November for his *Plutonian Ode* and the thousand-dollar prize money was used to lessen the debt left after the *On the Road* conference. When he wrote to Whalen with the good news he couldn't help but tack on a list of his chronic complaints. "I have hi blood pressure, a half-thumbnail-sized kidney stone hovering around the urethra corner waiting to drop into my bladder, a backache, and complete aversion to paperwork,

Irritable Vegetable, *CP*, p. 877

letters, business, teaching schedules, in fact the whole prison of my life to date." He also told Whalen that he would need to change his whole routine soon or face the consequences.

Somehow Allen knew he'd have to break away from Naropa, where he had been for nearly ten years, so he scheduled a meeting with Trungpa to ask him for permission to retire. Trungpa, appreciative of Allen's help over the past decade, approved, but asked that Allen stay on for two more years and leave after the 1983 term. Allen was only too happy to agree; having a retirement date was consolation enough. It wasn't merely the rigors of teaching that aggravated him. His life had become too expensive, trying to maintain apartments in New York and Boulder as well as the Bedrock Mortar and Cherry Valley houses. At least closing the house in Boulder would help him economize. In the future he wanted to attend more of Trungpa's retreats and find private time to meditate, read, and write. "Fat chance," he added to Whalen, realistically. Almost immediately he began to pack his wardrobe, which had been purchased mostly from the Salvation Army store in Boulder. He had a handsome brown cashmere overcoat that cost him thirty-five dollars and a virtually indestructible Brooks Brothers suit that he bought there for a couple of dollars. Everything had to be sent back to New York, including dozens of boxes of books and manuscripts that had piled up in Boulder.

Back in New York, Peter's father was hospitalized again
Thoughts Sitting   in serious condition, so Peter flew from Boulder to be with
Breathing II, *CP*, p. 878   him at the end. Allen encouraged him to go, since he regretted not being with his own father at his death. A few days later, eighty-four-year-old Oleg died on November 13 in Cabrini Hospital, literally around the corner from where Peter had been born. Apart from his old clothes, the only possession that Oleg had to leave to Peter was a machete. Allen couldn't return for the funeral but he did stop to spend a few days with Peter a month later on his way to another reading tour in Europe. They talked it over and decided that Peter would fly over at the beginning of the year to join Allen and Steven Taylor. It was destined to be the last reading trip Peter would make with Allen.

Allen kicked off his trip on December 8 with a reading in Paris as part of UNESCO's "War on War" international poetry festival attended by Ferlinghetti and Voznesensky. Afterward Allen traveled around France and Italy and did a few readings while managing to squeeze in some sightseeing, too. Taylor went off to visit his brother, who was then stationed with the U.S. Army near Nuremberg while Allen went by himself to the town of

Charleville near the Belgian border. Poet Arthur Rimbaud had lived there when he was sixteen and an academic conference was being held in his honor. A friendly teacher and her mother lived in Rimbaud's old house, and they invited Allen to stay with them while he took part in the event. "How sad his dark old wooden steep stairway," Allen noted. One night when Allen woke up at 4:00 A.M., he saw a spectral figure standing by his door. It would have been the first ghost he had ever seen, had he not realized that it was only the TV set glowing eerily in the dark. The next day he went to the countryside to visit the actual barn in which Rimbaud had written his *Season in Hell*. An eccentric couple had converted it into a little museum, and Allen found the collection interesting and quirky. The conference itself was not stimulating and he sat through several incomprehensible lectures in French.

When Steven joined him in Amsterdam they stayed with Simon and Barbara Vinkenoog and their four children and waited for Peter's arrival from New York. Allen enjoyed living with the Vinkenoog family and saw Simon as a kindred spirit, a masterful translator of his poetry. That year the family shared their traditional Christmas dinner with Allen and surprised him the night afterward with a special Japanese meal, ideal for Allen's new diet. While in town Allen toured Rembrandt's house, the Van Gogh Museum, and stopped to see every Vermeer.

1 9 8 3 ~

ALLEN HAD COME to Amsterdam to record Steven Taylor's orchestration of *September on Jessore Road*, gracefully set to music for a string quartet. Years earlier John Lennon had suggested that Allen record the poem with strings, but until Allen met Steven, he had no one to work out the complicated musical arrangements. Allen, Steven, Simon Vinkenoog, and Benn Posset were all equally enthusiastic about the project and hoped it would bring a new audience to one of Allen's greatest but less known poems. On January 3 they worked late into the night at the recording studio before returning to Vinkenoog's. Peter, who had just arrived, was acting even stranger than usual. He had stayed behind at Vinkenoog's home that evening and when they came into the house around 1:00 A.M., he was still awake, cleaning the already immaculate house. He wheezed and sniffed and cursed Ronald Reagan under his breath, repeating words in some kind of insane mantra. He stayed up all night, trancelike, cleaning and recleaning the sink, fat-bellied and naked except for his bikini briefs. By morning he was hoarse, red-faced, sweating, and laughing like a madman. Even Allen had to admit that he was in a less than perfect mental state. At first Allen tried to attribute his strange behavior to an excess of coffee or vodka or cigarettes. Then onstage at a reading later that week, when it was Peter's turn, he stalled in his delivery of a poem. He sipped more vodka, laughed to himself, and then began to hit himself on the head violently between each line of his poem "America, Give a Shit!" He barely whispered his next few poems

What the Sea Throws Up at Vlissingen, *CP*, p. 880

in front of the audience of two hundred people. Allen did not dwell on it because Peter had acted irrationally in the past and always had his highs and
lows. Usually it did not last that long, and Allen was unsure how to handle
it anyway, or even if he should "handle" it.

This time Peter's behavior was magnified since he was in a foreign country, staying in someone else's house with a family of several children. Out in
the meadows of Cherry Valley, Peter could roam naked through the snow-
drifts without attracting attention, but in the middle of Amsterdam, letting
nature take its own course was impossible. Peter stayed up all the next night
playing his banjo as loudly as he could and then didn't sleep at all the following day either, sewing things that didn't need to be mended. It was obvious,
even to Allen, that Peter was on something. During the day Peter went out
for long walks in the Dutch winter wearing only shorts, no shirt or shoes,
and stuck gummed reinforcements to his forehead, ears, and chest as orna-
ment. Steven had to go out to find him on the streets and lead him back
home. Peter was not nearly as hostile toward Steven as he was to Allen,
whom he began addressing in a loud voice as "Mr. Ginsberg, sir." On several
occasions over the next few days, Peter threatened to kill himself and knives
had to be taken away from him by force. As usual, Allen was extremely patient with this unhinged behavior and continued to include Peter in the readings, as if nothing were wrong. Then Peter began to make his translator
repeat each and every word in Dutch, one word at a time. Allen seemed to
be trying to make himself believe it was Peter's unique way of composing a
new poem. For whatever reason, he could not see, or did not want to believe, that Peter was in serious trouble and needed help.

The time came when the Vinkenoogs felt that a doctor had to be called,
with or without Allen's consent. Benn Posset summoned a physician in
town he knew, and when the doctor arrived Peter greeted him, "Hello,
would you like to fuck my wife?" As soon as the doctor pulled out an
ominous-looking hypodermic needle, though, Peter snapped out of it and
avoided the sedative. At one point after the doctor left, Peter drew Allen
into a slapping match, as if he were a little child. His strange behavior continued until finally, while Peter was playing the same short riff over and
over again robotically on his banjo, Allen approached him. Peter snapped
and shouted, "Fuck you, don't talk to me, don't even speak, leave me
alone." It was only then that Allen realized their last thread of communication had been broken. It reminded him of the day when he realized he
could no longer break through to Naomi in her crazy world. Allen, Steven,
and their hosts sat down and calmly discussed the situation as a group.

Steven Taylor, Ginsberg, and Orlovsky, European tour, 1983 ~

Steven did not want Peter to continue the tour in his current condition, and Simon wholeheartedly agreed. It was all too disruptive. Allen couldn't help but recognize the same traits in Peter's actions toward him that he had seen forty years earlier in Naomi's behavior toward Louis. He had to stop pretending and appreciate what might be in store for both of them. "What if we grow old and I'm sick in bed and need to get up to phone or pee or in pain, what if he gets into this manic depressive state?" he asked himself. It proved to be an uncannily accurate premonition.

Deep down Allen knew that Peter's acute behavior had not just started in Amsterdam, but had been going on for a long time. Allen had been unwilling to see it. The previous winter at the seminary in Bedford Springs, Peter had wakened in the middle of the night, left Allen behind, and driven hundreds of miles to the Cherry Valley farm. The Clausen family, who were then the farm's caretakers, were frightened to death by his nocturnal visit to the remote farmhouse. On that occasion, Peter had gone into a catatonic trance for several days before snapping out of it. Allen remembered that Peter had once confided in him that Richard Helms of the CIA had followed him home in his car and the only way Peter was able to ward off an attack was to sing all night long in a high falsetto voice. At the time his comments had not registered as being all that odd to Allen. On other occasions, Peter had threatened to cut off his hand or put out his eye whenever he had been

Peter, Lafcadio, Kate, and Marie Orlovsky ~

angry with Allen. To get under Allen's skin, Peter would buy ten-pound sacks of birdseed and coax pigeons inside the apartment. He started by attracting them into his own room, but before long he was making trails of birdseed into the rest of the apartment so that the birds walked around at will, much to Allen's annoyance.

Along with these hindsight realizations came Allen's usual self-recrimination. Allen knew that he had been playing a paternal role with Peter for many years, often overdominating, always ordering him around, commenting on his behavior, criticizing his readings, generally interfering in every move he made. It was the same way Peter treated his own brothers, and it was no wonder that he rebelled, or maybe he was simply fulfilling his genetic fate. Up until that time, drugs had always masked what might have been the signs of Peter's own mental problems. At any one time, it was difficult for anyone to know if he was crazy, high, just drunk, or a combination.

From Amsterdam they all moved on to some readings in Aarhus, Denmark, where they stayed with friends of Rosebud and Denise. While there Peter got worse and smashed his prized banjo, going completely berserk on several occasions, walking naked in the midwinter snow. To Steven's dismay, Allen continued to permit Peter to tour with them, although admittedly they couldn't have forced him to go home anyway. The option of canceling the tour and taking him home never was mentioned. All Allen could do was sit and meditate when the situation became too intense; otherwise, he was at a complete loss as to what to do. They visited Stockholm and Helsinki and stayed with Ann and Sam Charters in their home, where a near-perfect reading of *Howl* was recorded professionally. It was while staying with the Charterses that Peter contracted the flu and miraculously became calm for the rest of the trip. In the aftermath of the illness, Allen was convinced Peter was "okay" again. Allen was once again eager to put Peter's problems aside, be they chemical or mental, so that he would not have to acknowledge them or take action.

Amid this emotional angst on the trip, Steven's own self-doubts had surfaced. He was still quite young and did not know what he wanted to do with his life. On a train one day, Steven had lamented to Allen, "I'll always be poor." Allen comforted him and encouraged him to always do his own art anyway, even if it did not lead to financial security, and "if worst comes to worst, I'll take care of you." Steven was genuinely touched and meekly asked, "You will?" Allen felt his heart melt, and yet when he wrote about this moment in his journal, he could not ignore his sexual attraction for Taylor. While comforting the confused young man struggling with his own uncertainties, Allen recorded that it had given him a hard-on. Even in a moment of peaceful intimacy between them, Allen could not escape his own libido. It was reminiscent of the day when Corso, beaten up in a barroom brawl, was consoled by Allen and taken to his bed.

As Allen was packing in Helsinki for their move to Oslo, he received a call from Bob Rosenthal with news that a contract had been signed with Knopf for his *Collected Poems*. Allen was ecstatic; his decades of waiting were over. Perhaps this book would rectify his dire financial situation once and for all. Unfortunately, the announcement was premature and this book contract, like all the others before, was not to be.

With Peter's problems solved, at least to Allen's satisfaction, he resolved to focus more on his own health problems. Although he had not been to bed with anyone since leaving America in December, he discovered a hard, knot-like growth at the base of his penis, which ached slightly when he had an erection. A Danish doctor diagnosed it as Peyronie's disease, a condition common in older men, brought on by a trauma or bump to the penis. The treatment prescribed was simply to take aspirin and allow it to heal itself, unless the pain worsened, in which case surgery would be required. Such an operation would probably end Allen's ability to have erections, so he did not want to risk that, unless there was no other choice. He invented his own theory that it had been caused by energetic lovemaking with Alene Lee back in 1953. There was no evidence to suggest that the condition could lie dormant for thirty years, but it was a story Allen swore by. "She bent my dick," he told as many friends as would listen. Alene had been very much in love with Allen back then, although Kerouac's novel *The Subterraneans* doesn't allude to that at all.

In Berlin at the beginning of February, Allen received his advance copies of Hammond's *First Blues* double album. He had never been so happy with a project. He loved everything about the album, including the cover photo taken by Robert Frank. Robert had stopped doing black-and-white photography, but as a special favor to Allen he had made an exception. A week later they were all back from Europe after what had been an exhausting and emotionally draining trip. Allen's travels were not over, because he had scheduled readings at the Folger Library in Washington as well as Yale and Harvard, but he was relieved to be back and not to have to worry about Peter's becoming deranged while they were abroad.

That winter, Brian Jackson was living in the apartment that Denise had vacated next door to Allen. Brian had gone back to school at NYU and Allen had generously offered him the use of the apartment, since it was empty at the time. One day, Allen's cousin, Mindy Gorlin, came to visit Allen for a few days and bumped into Brian. They struck up a conversation and before long had fallen in love, and she moved in with Brian. For several months a minor soap opera was played out among the three, complicated even more by the arrival of Gregory Corso, who also used a spare room in Brian and Mindy's apartment. Allen had hoped that Jackson, now twenty years old, would settle down and apply himself to his studies and became jealous when Mindy began to take up all of Brian's time. Brian was young and realized that sleeping with Mindy was more to his liking than being chased by Allen, so they found another place to live, explaining to Allen that he was going "through changes." It was typical of many of the young men Allen fell in love with, but what hurt him most in this case was that the woman who stole him away was his own cousin. Feeling sorry for himself, Allen wrote in his journal about how the patterns of his life had been established early and repeated often. He asked himself if he had been bribing younger men to be with him by the promise of companionship with a famous poet. He remembered that it was much the same as when he was a boy in Paterson. His brother had accused him of buying his companions' friendship by purchasing baby chickens to play with or by stealing tiles from his neighbor's garage roof, both done to become popular with the boys. He wondered to what lengths he might go as an adult to find a companion.

In May, Allen resumed teaching at Naropa. The school had moved to larger quarters in a former grammar school on Arapahoe Avenue. It was a more dignified and traditional campus than the downtown mall had been. That spring Allen still was not feeling very well and suffered

I Am Not, *CP*, p. 881

I'm a Prisoner of Allen Ginsberg, *CP*, p. 882

from adverse reactions to various experimental high-blood-pressure medicines he had been trying. On some days when his brain was quite foggy and he felt dizzy due to the medication, he found it beneficial to lie down and nap every few hours. At the same time he began to see an acupuncturist for what he characterized as a "geneto-urinary kidney liver bladder pecker discomfort and malfunction." That summer he would be fifty-seven years old, and he no longer had his former energy. He was getting old.

In June he took a month's retreat with Peter at the Rocky Mountain Dharma Center. They camped out together in a big green tent on the edge of an alpine field filled with yellow daisies and buttercups. Through practice Allen had become strong enough to do as many as six or

221 Syllables at Rocky Mountain Dharma Center, *CP*, p. 883

seven hours of prostrations each day with a little *shamatha* practice thrown in for good measure. In the tent each night, he had time to relax as he skimmed through a new Kerouac biography.

Following that summer session at Naropa where he hosted Diane di Prima and her partner, Sheppard Powell, Allen flew to Orono, Maine, with Jonathan Robbins, to take part in a William Carlos Williams festival with Robert Creeley. He also hoped to be able to spend an afternoon with the photographer Berenice Abbott, who was in Maine at the time. Allen was just then beginning to rediscover the treasure trove of old photographs that he had stored away in his archive. For several years his archivist had been sorting box after box of Allen's papers in the Columbia library and so far he had uncovered a half dozen boxes of vintage photos. He had been nagging Allen to identify the people in the pictures for the sake of future research, knowing that only Allen would be able to recognize many of his subjects. As Allen looked closely at the images he had taken of Kerouac, Burroughs, Cassady, and the others, he realized that he possessed an intuitive photographer's eye. The realization inspired him to pick up his camera again after a two-decade hiatus. That diversion led to his renewed friendship with Robert Frank, and later to the publication of several books of photography and dozens of gallery and museum exhibitions. Thus began yet another career for Allen, and before long it replaced the Cherry Valley farm as the number-one drain on his bank account.

Hank O'Neal, who had worked with John Hammond on Allen's recent double album, was also a photographer and a close friend of Berenice Abbott's, and it was he who had arranged an introduction. Hank invited both Allen and Jonathan, Allen's companion on the Maine trip, to visit her in her "fey little house in the woods." Her reminiscences of old friends like Hart Crane and Marsden Hartley fascinated Allen. When the subject finally turned to photography, she told Allen that he should buy an old-fashioned 8 × 10 camera so that he could get both panorama and tiny details in a single shot. She confessed that a large-format camera like that had been her key to success.

From then on, hardly a day went by when Allen didn't take a photo or two. He found that he did not need to buy a large camera for panoramas, because he rarely took pictures of landscapes. In fact, he focused his lens exclusively on his friends, usually taking portraits of them as they sat across the table talking with him. He treated their lives as transitory, just as he did his own, and the camera helped preserve those fleeting moments of intimacy. Since Allen was acutely aware that he was here only temporarily, his eye reflected life as a melancholy, sweet, sorrowful, and sometimes joyful series of images. The process of taking portraits of friends became something sacred to him. Soon he consulted with his friend Robert Frank and asked him for additional pointers about taking pictures. Frank introduced Allen to his printmakers, Brian Graham and Sid Kaplan, who began making museum-quality enlargements of Allen's old snapshots and printed his new portraits expertly. As Allen began to get more involved in photography, he grew to depend on Frank's opinion of what was good and what was not. Every now and then he would carry a box of enlargements to Frank's for his critique.

What set Allen's photos apart were his incisive captions. Early on Hank O'Neal had told Allen that he had taped one-paragraph comments by Abbott onto each of her photos. He felt the comments provided interesting background information about each photograph. At Raymond Foye's suggestion, Allen took that idea one step further and began to write his captions in ink on the photo paper just below the image itself. Foye had been impressed with Elsa Dorfman's short captions in her book of photos and essays called *Elsa's Housebook*. As time went by, Allen's captions grew longer and were revised every time he signed another copy of the same image. They expanded until his penetrating captions became small essays in themselves. Some captions were revised and enlarged dozens of times over the years, as in his famous picture of Kerouac on the fire escape. When they became so large, Sid Kaplan was forced to print the image smaller and smaller to accommodate the larger margin Allen needed for his ever-lengthening captions.

It certainly was not the right time for Allen to adopt a new habit as expensive as photography, for he was sixty-six hundred dollars in debt from his unprofitable recording ventures. At the end of the year he was due to retire from Naropa, and he resolved to change his life. He decided to find a literary agent and consolidate all his publishing under one roof. Allen was bitterly disappointed to learn that "Ferlinghetti confounded the Knopf contract," as he put it, but it was not the first time his *Collected Poems* had been thwarted. His old friends Miles and Victor Bockris made Allen consider the advantages of hiring a literary agent. At the time, Miles was visiting from England and had proposed to do the first full-length biography of Ginsberg. Miles had for his agent his old friend Andrew Wylie, who had given up being a poet, writer, and cabdriver to become a literary agent. He started business with the philosopher I. F. Stone as his first client and was interested in expanding his roster to include Allen. Wylie had managed to land a lucrative contract from Simon and Schuster with a one-hundred-thousand-dollar advance for Miles's biography, more money than Allen had made from any of his books at City Lights. Having an agent to represent his interests was tempting for Allen, who felt he was getting too old to earn a living by giving readings.

Wylie, a genuinely literate agent, was happy to have Ginsberg as a client, for he had always admired his writing. Andrew had known Allen from Andrew's own work with Giuseppo Ungaretti in the late 1960s and through their mutual friend, Elsa Dorfman. By late September, Allen had informed Ferlinghetti that he had hired Wylie to work as his agent "to reconstruct my publishing life and get a NY publisher for *Collected Poems*, essays, interviews, mid-1950s journals . . . After 27 years of publishing I'd like to make a living from writing, even if it is mostly poetry," he said in a formal letter to his old friend and publisher. During negotiations Allen went out of his way to protect City Lights and make certain that no matter what happened, they would always be able to continue printing the small black-and-white volumes of *Howl* and *Kaddish* on which their publishing business depended.

Almost immediately Wylie landed a great contract for the publication of Allen's *Collected Poems* with Harper and Row. The agreement he negotiated with them was a six-book package that included Allen's next two books of poetry, an annotated edition of *Howl*, and his journals from the mid-fifties. With an advance of a little more than twenty-five thousand dollars per book, it was still quite a bit less than Miles's advance for the biography, but it allowed Allen to repay his immediate debts and have a small nest egg left over,

Fighting Phantoms
Fighting Phantoms,
CP, p. 884

with the promise of more money in the future. Allen became one of the cornerstones for Wylie's agency and shortly
afterward, William Burroughs joined his stable, too.

One day in October after Allen had reread all of Poe's
poetry, he dozed off and was visited by his mother in a
dream. The dream was so vivid that when he awoke, he was
sure that it had truly happened and he scribbled it down in
his bedside journal in detail, later to be shaped into the poem
"White Shroud." After writing *Kaddish* Allen believed that he
had exorcised Naomi's ghost once and for all, but she came
back to him countless times during his life, and those dreams inspired some
of his greatest work.

Now that Trungpa had released him from his obligation to Naropa, Allen
spent time re-examining himself and his goals. On Thanksgiving he took
stock of his sexual life and wrote, "Looks like I'll masturbate as main erotic
completion till my deathbed." All his life he had looked for lovers, and although he'd found temporary partners, he had found "none at liberty for a
lifetime," he wrote, not mentioning Peter. He always believed that "by age
forty or certainly sixty," this part of his life would be well settled and he would
have a love partner. Now came the realization that he'd never find one person
to share his life with, and the finality of that statement surprised him. He regretted that he had hung on to his naïve sexual fantasies in that regard for as
long as he had. Perhaps he exercised his own common sense to acknowledge
the fact that the young boys he repeatedly fell in love with always grew older,
just like Peter, Neal, and all the others, and were always basically heterosexual, too. Not much to build a long-term relationship on. He knew that at
some point long ago he had given up his dream of being forever romantically
in love with Peter, but he was not aware of exactly when it had happened.
Now he had settled into a relationship with Peter that was based on a different
kind of love and companionship. Due to Allen's steadfast loyalty, it would be
impossible to end their relationship, even if Peter had wished it.

Arguments, *CP*, p. 885

Sunday Prayer, *CP*, p. 886

Brown Rice Quatrains, *CP*, p. 887

They're All Phantoms of My Imagining, *CP*, p. 888

White Shroud, *CP*, p. 889

1984 ~

ALLEN WELCOMED IN the new year by singing "Do the Meditation Rock" with Peter and Steven for video artist Nam June Paik's public television special, "Good Morning, Mr. Orwell." It was broadcast via a new technology featuring an international satellite hook-up performance with John Cage, Merce Cunningham, and Laurie Anderson performing simultaneously in different locations around the globe. Allen spent the rest of New Year's Day composing a letter to Ferlinghetti meant to reassure him that Wylie would find a way for all parties to be happy with the new Harper and Row contract. Allen wanted to make it clear to his old publisher that although he intended to go ahead with the long-hoped-for publication of his *Collected Poems*, he would also do everything in his power to support City Lights. Ferlinghetti's biggest concern was that losing Allen would permanently damage the publishing company. As it turned out, the City Lights editions of Allen's poems continued to sell more copies each year, despite the new Harper and Row editions.

By New Year's Peter also had a new girlfriend living with him. Juanita Lieberman, an attractive New York girl, had been a student of Peter's at Naropa the year before. She had fallen in love with Peter the first time she ever saw him as a sixteen-year-old high school student in 1978. One day Juanita had gone to see Allen and Peter read and decided then and there that she was in love with him. At the time he was ruggedly handsome and seemed like he would be fun to know. She wasn't aware of the complicated relationship between Allen and Peter but she knew that Peter was the man she wanted to spend her life with. Later, as a student at Colby College, she decided to go to Naropa in the summer of 1982 to attend the *On the Road* conference, hoping she'd meet Peter. It wasn't difficult for her to strike up a conversation with him, for he was equally attracted to her. While they were talking Allen came up to them and told Juanita to stop in to see them in New York if she ever needed a job. For the rest of the conference, Peter and Juanita spent a good deal of time together and agreed to reunite back in New York City. She was merely twenty years old, and it was a romantic adventure for her. She moved into Peter's room beside the kitchen on East Twelfth Street, and when the apartment next door became vacant, they set up housekeeping on their own there. Allen made a note in his journal one day, when he overheard Juanita asking Peter why he always depended on Allen for his opinion. She suggested he rely on his own thoughts about things. If Juanita could coax Peter away from his dependency on Allen it seemed like a good thing. In a way Allen hoped that this might open up new space for them both. Allen was able to get along with Juanita and secretly hoped that she would have a positive effect on Peter.

Rescuing Peter from his absorption in Allen's life sounded like a good idea, but the web was too tightly wrapped around them. The lease to Peter's apartment was in Allen's name, the money for Peter's expenses came from Allen's pocket, Peter's friends were really Allen's friends, and even when Juanita got a job to help support them, it was as Allen's assistant. It was difficult to make a division between what was Allen's and what was Peter's when their lives had been so entwined for more than thirty years. Complicating matters further was the fact that deep in his heart, Allen still wasn't sure he wanted to give Peter up.

Most of the time, Allen was too busy to expend energy working on intimate relationships anyway. He was producing enough work to keep a whole team of assistants busy. In addition to his poetry, photography, music, teaching, interviews, and creating and transcribing journals and tapes, his correspondence occupied more time than any other single activity. He frequently wrote long letters replying to strangers who had written to ask him a favor. Typically, his reply began with an explanation of how overworked he was. He would emphasize the fact that he did not have time to answer fan mail and instead he needed to devote his time to his own work. Then he would add a few paragraphs describing in detail ex- Empire Air, *CP*, p. 893 actly what he had to do in the near future. That built up his resentment for being bothered in the first place and he would complain, "I can't correspond like this. It literally takes time from my own poetry writing

and editing. Would you ask Mr. Van Gogh to please stop painting his sunflowers to explain just how he paints his sunflowers, so you can be a 'mystic'
like him?" He felt the need to respond to each and every letter that was written to him, and he couldn't resist the opportunity to communicate with anyone who took the time to write him.

On February 5, William Burroughs was in New York from Kansas,
where he had moved with James Grauerholz. He was celebrating his seventi-
eth birthday at a party given in his honor at a New Wave nightclub. Everyone from Sting to Kurt Vonnegut turned out to share in that milestone
occasion. While William was in town, Allen had dinner with him, joined by
Miles and Grauerholz, and they reminisced about the old days. Allen told
them he had "retired" from Naropa after ten years of teaching and now he
would only volunteer to help run the summer poetry program (a full-time
job in itself). Burroughs expressed his continued skepticism about Buddhism, for he was not convinced that the Buddhists had discovered any secrets that couldn't be found without them.

With Juanita's arrival as Peter's permanent girlfriend and their move to
the apartment next door, Allen and Bob Rosenthal decided to rearrange the
apartment. They had six small rooms to work with, so they moved the office
from the room next to Allen's bedroom and set it up in the room that had
once been Peter's bedroom on the other side of the kitchen. The new layout
gave Allen more privacy and separation from the office activity, since Rosenthal and at least one part-time typist were there every day. All afternoon
there was constant activity and the telephones rang incessantly. Allen needed
a place for quiet time when he wanted it, and yet he was close enough to
hear what he wanted to hear. They set up a stereo, a television, and a futon
for guests in what had been the office, and his large closet was converted into
a "library" where he stored thousands of rare volumes of poetry. Even with
the expanded space, there were dozens of boxes of books that wouldn't fit
onto the shelves, so more things were sent to Columbia for safekeeping.
They set up the big plywood desk in the office, where he and Bob worked
side by side, reviewing manuscripts and proofs and corresponding with the
world. He put his father's tiny wooden desk in his bedroom for his own private use. Along one wall of the office they stacked seven large file cabinets,
which held much of his correspondence and files of clippings about drugs
and political corruption. A little closet-sized room off the kitchen became
his long-term guest room with just enough space to fit a small bed beside an
old upright piano. There was no room for anything else except some miscellaneous files and tape recordings of readings and interviews.

The real hub of the household was the large kitchen, the central gathering place for everything that went on in Allen's life. Bob Dylan, Paul McCartney, Arthur Miller, and many other well-known figures sat at Allen's kitchen table at one time or another. Every day Allen scrubbed the table and used it to display his most recent books or his newest photographs. Then he would prepare soup for his guests or wash dishes and talk with friends over a mug of tea. It all fit perfectly with Allen's personality, for he acted like a stereotypical Jewish mother whenever he had people in. As his health became more of an issue, his cooking became more wholesome, and various combinations of rice and seaweed dishes were tried. Some of these concoctions were delicious, while others were virtually unpalatable, but Allen never felt the need to resort to a cookbook.

Allen saw Berenice Abbott again in March at the Armstrong Gallery and asked if he could take her picture. Gruffly, she told him to move back, that he was too close. When Allen asked why, she said, "get a little distance [about six feet instead of four], otherwise one eye is bigger than the other or the brow too big or one cheekbone smaller." Allen loved these practical tips and always learned from them. Robert Frank once told him to always include the subject's hands in the frame when he took a photograph because it made a portrait more interesting. It was a good tip and he followed it assiduously. In several of Allen's photographs his subjects can be seen holding up their hands as if on display, in reaction to Allen's saying, "Get your hands in the picture." It was also Robert who told Allen that a Leica camera with a Zeiss lens was good, not because of the camera body, but because of the high-quality lens, and he helped him buy one at a local camera shop.

During the 1980s, Allen became more politically lethargic than he had been in the sixties and seventies. "Perhaps I'm the next generation of CIA slave," he thought. He was still riddled with doubts about whether protesting against the Vietnam War had made things better or if the antiwar movement had actually prolonged the war by making it impossible for the American government to change its position. The immediate result of the U.S. evacuation from South Vietnam was that the North Vietnamese came down to destroy the South's infrastructure and impose an anti-Buddhist tyranny. As the U.S. hawks had predicted, Cambodia was invaded by the Maoists, the populace was tortured, and genocide was conducted by the French-trained Khmer Rouge. Allen felt that he had lost the confidence he needed to speak out against U.S. policy in the future, if the time should come again.

Allen had been writing poetry for thirty-five years in the belief that "only art could serve mankind, only art could justify the sufferings and thoughts of a lifetime. Not business, not comforts of the body, not construction of skyscrapers, not physical architecture—but only creations of the spectral mind transmitted generation after generation, century after century to ennoble the efforts of the human body." Now he pondered in his notebook, "My ambition was childish, to save or awaken mankind. This grew more possible as I realized the vanity of my motives, in the limitation of my high school perspective—despair at attaining what I most desire liberated me to appreciate my own imagination. What was it I did desire, how large was my heart, anyone's heart, how vast was my mind, everyone's mind? . . . I always depended on others for opinion, judgment, insight, clarification, reassurance. That made me open to other people's opinions, despite my own prejudices." Allen fretted endlessly about the choices he had made in his life. He worried that he had contributed to millions of deaths in Cambodia. He wondered if it was worthwhile to spend his life writing poetry. Should he point out that when anyone used the pencils on his desk, they should resharpen them before returning them to the drawer? It was all becoming equally worrisome to Allen.

Concerning literary matters, he had fewer reasons to worry, and Allen was pleased with the agreement that Wylie had worked out between Harper and Row and City Lights. For the first time he was to have complete control over all aspects of his books, even to the point of approving the cover design. He would earn an advance for each book whether it sold well or not, which was a welcome change after waiting for months after publication for his royalties from City Lights' sales. At first Allen considered asking Willem de Kooning to create a cover for his *Collected Poems*, but upon further reflection he asked his old filmmaker friend, Harry Smith, to design a cover logo that he could use on the entire series of Harper and Row books. Allen wanted to use the design of three fish that share a common head, the image that he had discovered in Bodh Gaya, India. Harry was exactly the kind of meticulous draftsman who could make it into an attractive logo. He could also make good use of the design money, as he was another of the penniless artists Allen was supporting through grants from COP.

By May, Allen had finished collating the texts and written nearly seventy-five pages of notes for the *Collected Poems*. He worked quickly because he was eager to see it all between the covers of one hardback book. He finished his work just as he was about to depart for another European tour with Steven; Peter was left behind this time. Steven had told Allen in no uncertain terms that he didn't want to travel with him again if Peter was going to go along. Their last trip had been too unpleasant and tense and neither Allen nor Steven had the strength to put up with Peter's antics again. The shock of hearing Steven put it into words made Allen feel as if he had been punched in the stomach, though. After their transatlantic flight, Allen was more exhausted than ever, and it took him a full three days to recover from jet lag, which was unusual for him. The Dutch poets who had stayed with Allen in Boulder invited them to tour the Netherlands, so Allen settled down for a week in the lowlands. In Ghent he spent a few sunny days visiting the museums to see their notable Van Eyck collections. He also went to several castles and took long, pleasant walks through the ancient town. At their largest reading in Brussels, a crowd of nearly six thousand people turned out to hear him.

On May 20 Allen flew directly from Europe to New Smyrna Beach, Florida, to teach for three weeks in collaboration with Robert Frank and the jazz drummer Elvin Jones at the Florida Atlantic Center for Arts. Allen was putting more creative energy into his photography, and he welcomed the chance to spend so much time with Robert. He hoped to pick up as many pointers as he could from the master himself, for it was always Allen's habit to learn from people more expert than himself. That was true when Kerouac first taught him about Buddhism, when Dylan taught him music chords, and when Trungpa taught him meditation. After his teaching was over in Florida he asked Raymond Foye, now living in New York, to help him sort all the photographs and negatives that had been found in the Columbia archives. Foye was a student of photography and had contacts in the art world. He thought that Allen's best work would enlarge well, and he blew some of the images up to show Allen. The results were spectacular and Raymond felt that he could find a gallery to show Allen's work. Before that could happen negatives would have to be sorted, identified, printed, and captioned; it took time and a good deal of money to do it all. Allen continued to religiously snap pictures whenever he was with his friends, and since they felt relaxed around him, it made for candid and intimate portraits. As more of his early pictures were enlarged and reprinted Foye recognized Allen's ability to select and frame great shots. The consistent theme that carried from his 1940s and 1950s pictures to those of 1984 was his celebration of the dignity of his friends. His talent was that he saw them as individual humans, not as models for posed pictures.

During the summer Peter continued to drink heavily and act out in an erratic fashion. Allen said that Juanita looked pale and nervous, worn out from her anxiety over Peter. After going to a Buddhist conference in Nova Scotia, Peter told her that he wanted to buy a house in Halifax and move permanently out of the country. He continued to pressure Juanita to have children with him, but even though she was still madly in love with him, she knew she wasn't ready for that commitment, yet. One day when Peter was out of their apartment, Juanita showed Allen his stash of liquor bottles and told him that Peter's drinking had been worsening each day. The alcohol combined with drugs and Peter's bipolar problems made him nearly impossible to live with. On one occasion he had drunkenly pulled out his father's machete and threatened Juanita with it because she wouldn't go meditate with him at the local Dharmadhatu Center. Allen had halfheartedly been trying to extricate himself from the situation, since doctors counseled him to keep a distance, but obviously he was a big part of the problem. Now he didn't know what to do. He was even getting mixed signals from Juanita. On the one hand, she wanted Allen to intervene to solve Peter's alcohol and drug problems, and on the other hand, she forbade Peter to even enter Allen's apartment, trying to keep a healthy distance between them. Without saying so, Allen wished that Juanita would manage the situation entirely by herself, for his usual method of dealing with Peter was to do nothing and allow things to resolve themselves.

Surprise Mind, *CP*, p. 895

In spite of his great success with the contract and work on the *Collected Poems* and his new career as a photographer, Allen was plagued by nagging self-doubt. On a short retreat to Karmê Chöling, Trungpa's meditation center in Vermont, Allen composed a poem listing all of his shortcomings. It wasn't much of a poem, but it reveals his state of mind. "Poet, but sick of writing about myself/Homosexual, role-model noted for stable relationship, but separated out from companion and now worried about lack love who's going to take care of me in deathbed senility/Buddhist agitator, but bad meditator with hi blood pressure/Scholar but hardly read books no patience anymore/Peacenik protester but coward and bored with confrontation/Left Wing but suspicious of communism and revolutions including American Revolution/Anti-Bourgeois but want a house and garden and car/Musician, but haven't written new songs for years/Democrat but following guru leader/Anarchist individualist but involved in *sangha*/Every political cause I tried went sour: / Communist-Socialist sympathies 1937 Spain, later disillusioned by reports of Red double-dealing/Vietnam idealization disillusioned by loss of civil liberties/Cuba kicked out/The Shah's overthrow led to more repression in Iran." He left the poem unfinished, but clearly Allen was more obsessed with his mistakes than his successes.

Student Love, *CP*, p. 896

Back at Naropa during the summer session, Allen managed to pick up his spirits by spending time with friends like Philip Whalen, Drummond Hadley,

Diane di Prima, and Amiri Baraka (né Leroi Jones), all of whom came to teach. For the purpose of doing research on his biography, Miles rented an apartment in New York and conducted several long interviews with Allen and other contacts. Always willing to cooperate, Allen opened his files to Miles and facilitated his work as much as he could. From then on, Allen relied on Miles to answer his biographical questions when he couldn't remember something. Gordon Ball came to Boulder to continue work on the *Journals Mid-Fifties* project and Allen received the final galleys of his *Collected Poems*, which he proofread carefully and returned to Harper and Row by the middle of summer. With the completion of that giant project he felt a weight lifted from his shoulders. Unfortunately, his overall health was not good, and he continued to see Dr. Ho, his acupuncturist, who was treating his liver. Holistic medicine seemed to suit Allen best and he tried combining Tibetan and Chinese medical practices with the inexpensive herbs that his acupuncturist prescribed.

In My Kitchen in New York, *CP*, p. 898

It's All So Brief, *CP*, p. 899

In 1982 Allen had been a member of a delegation of noted American writers who hosted some writers from the Peking Writers' Union of the People's Republic of China at a UCLA conference. The Americans, including Kurt Vonnegut, Arthur Miller, Susan Sontag, and Gary Snyder, were now planning an exchange visit to China in October 1984. Allen, who had never been to China, wanted to make this trip if he could. More than anything he loved being a tourist and seeing new places. Not satisfied with the prearranged itinerary of the delegation, he wanted to extend the trip, and he asked his Chinese hosts to arrange a few extra months of teaching for him at some Chinese universities. Generously, they were able to put together a program that would enable him to stay through the end of the year.

On October 14 Allen left for China after one last reading at Berkeley. On his flight were several of the other delegates, including Gary Snyder and his wife, Masa, Francine du Plessix Gray, and Harrison Salisbury. When they landed he was pleasantly surprised to find China "clean and safe and vast and comfortable," as he wrote to his stepmother, Edith. He compared it to a "clean crowded India." He found the conference itself quite boring, like so many literary conferences, but it was meeting the people that made travel exciting for Allen. He loved being able to explore the markets and crowded streets outside the controlled environment of the Writer's Union functions. It was nice to have Gary Snyder and his wife along, too, as they were able to translate signs and explain the fine points of the culture to Allen. He didn't mention it in his letters to his stepmother, but he was surprised to find that gay liberation was completely

Improvisation in
Beijing, *CP*, p. 937 unknown in China and unexplainable to the people he met there. It was as if they did not realize that homosexuality existed on the planet, and the people he talked to certainly denied that it existed in China.

Traveling as a group, the American delegates went to many of the most famous tourist destinations, the Chinese acrobat theater, the Imperial Palace, and a section of the Great Wall. Nearly four hundred students showed up for each of their readings at the Institute of Foreign Languages, where Allen found that many of the students knew about Kerouac and the Beat Generation, but few of their works were available in Chinese translation. They were cognizant of Allen's earlier poems, like *Howl*, but the students were completely unaware of what, if anything, he had been doing since then. The relatively large turnouts might encourage the publication of more of his poetry, Allen hoped, but he felt that most of his gay references would be lost on the Chinese students. What would a line like "America, I'm putting my queer shoulder to the wheel" mean in China anyway, he wondered?

After a week in Beijing, the group went to the neighboring city of Xian to view the twenty-two-hundred-year-old life-sized clay warriors from the tomb of China's first emperor, Qin, before moving on to Shanghai. Some of the giant Buddhist temples in that city had been torn down during the Cultural Revolution, and they were glad to see they had been rebuilt. They went to visit the nearby Tang Gardens in Suchou and Gary was delighted to be able to visit Han Shan's[72] Cold Mountain with the delegation. Snyder wrote an excellent poem about Han Shan's bell resounding across the ocean all the way to California. All the new small-scale free enterprise ventures that were being introduced into China impressed the Americans. It seemed that everyone Allen spoke with agreed that the Cultural Revolution of 1968–78 had been a big mistake and a nightmare for millions of people, but now they were looking forward to greater freedom in a new era, while keeping their commitment to a socialized economic system. It was all so interesting that Allen was sorry his health was poor for the whole trip. From the time he landed in China he had been coping with a chest cold. He even stopped smoking again to relieve his coughing, but with all the smoke and pollution in the air nothing seemed to help.

On November 6 the official delegation prepared to leave China, and Allen went to the station with Gary and Masa to see them off on their train to Hong Kong. The next day he flew alone to Chungking, where he boarded

---

[72] Han Shan: Anonymous ninth-century Chinese hermit/poet who called himself Cold Mountain (Han-shan).

Ginsberg on the Yangtze River ~

a riverboat to Wuhan for the famous three-day trip down the Yangtze, passing through the beautiful Three Gorges on the way. The lazy steamer made
its way slowly through the steep mountain gorges and took hairpin river
bends. Even here the air was thick with mist and soft coal smoke, so thick
that Allen noted that all of China seemed to be covered in an eternal smog.
He was escorted everywhere by kindly Chinese bureaucrats who took him
to the proper tourist hotels and ordered his meals for him. He found himself
envying a pair of bearded hippies he met who were traveling on their own in
fourth class and eating nothing but tangerines and bananas. He missed the
old days when he could travel anonymously without a chaperon.

From Wuhan Allen flew back to Beijing and taught there for a few days
before moving around to various universities over the next month and a half.
Most of his time in Baoding was spent in bed, now that his bad cold had
developed into bronchitis. In his classes at the university he found that his
students were all "virginal innocent frightened eager boys and girls," encouraged to study English by the new modernization and Westernization policies
of the same government that had previously forbidden it. Baoding was a

provincial working-class town and represented the real China to Allen, far from the tourist circuit. There he continued his crash course on Chinese sex-uality and was shocked to learn that premarital relations were against the law. Although he was tempted to ask ques-tions and make controversial public statements about homo-sexuality, he remembered his experiences in Cuba and Czechoslovakia and kept silent on these topics in public.

I Love Old Whitman So, *CP*, p. 900

Written in My Dream by W. C. Williams, *CP*, p. 901

One Morning I Took a Walk in China, *CP*, p. 903

Visiting Father & Friends, *CP*, p. 940

On December 2, Allen took the overnight sleeper to Shanghai only to arrive there sick and miserable. He spent most of his first week in bed nursing his worsening bronchi-tis. He was glad to be pampered; they gave him a nice big room with overstuffed armchairs and a warm space heater, which was a most welcome luxury. When he began to feel better he went out on the narrow, crowded city streets to explore the shops and markets. His teaching duties were light, but he enjoyed meeting the students and was careful not to cross the line of Chinese propriety when he spoke about sex or politics. He realized that an individual would talk frankly with him one to one, but three was a crowd. Allen believed that the populace feared that they might be turned in to the secret police if their true thoughts were overheard. On December 10, Allen took the train to Nanking to see the Ming tombs and was happy to find that a handful of Zen monks were still al-lowed to practice there. In each town Allen heard horror stories about the Cultural Revolution during which all the intellectuals were rounded up and sent to the work camps and farms to clean latrines and plant rice.

Reading Bai Juyi, *CP*, p. 905

Black Shroud, *CP*, p. 911

World Karma, *CP*, p. 913

By the time Allen returned home to New York at the end of that year, there had been major developments in his life. The long-awaited publication of his *Collected Poems 1947–1980* was now a fact and an 837-page book waited for him on his office desk. He found it extremely handsome in its bright-red dust jacket with Harry Smith's design on the cover. It had been extensively footnoted by Allen and his office staff, so that it would be a useful reference tool. Allen was as proud of this book as he had been when he received his first copy of *Howl and Other Poems* nearly thirty years earlier. Reviews generally praised the book, but many also pointed out that not all of his poems were up to the standards set by *Howl* and *Kaddish*. Never willing to praise Allen in the first place, the *New York Times* said that "the strong poems are few, and that between them are pages of dull poetry." Since they had never bothered to review the earlier poems, which they now referred to as "undeniable successes" and "brilliant," it was hard to understand how they could criticize his life's work as not measuring up to those masterpieces. Many other reviewers were more laudatory. Harper and Row had set up a publicity tour with interviews and book signings around the country that would keep him busy for several months.

The satisfaction of seeing the *Collected Poems* in print was counterbalanced by more sobering events. While Allen had been in China, Peter had become more deranged than ever before. Through the autumn he had continued to take drugs and drink heavily, sake when he could get it, but anything would do as long as it got him high. No one was sure what else he might have been taking—it might have been crack because his rages were frightening and he had become uncontrollable. His behavior reached a breaking point the day he entered Allen's office brandishing his father's machete. He threatened to hurt himself, and when he failed to get much of a reaction to that, he threatened to hurt Rosenthal's two young boys. Worried just how far Peter might go, Bob talked to Juanita, who couldn't reason with Peter either. Someone got the machete away from Peter, but before long he was back in Allen's apartment nude with a pair of scissors. He proceeded to hack off all his hair, then pulled the blade of the scissors across his arms and drew blood in several places. Bob and Juanita could think of no way to quiet him, so in desperation, the police were called. Just that week the police had been involved in a highly publicized case where they had shot a hysterical old woman wielding a butcher knife, so they arrived in full battle gear. Their new strategy was to subdue any crazy person with overwhelming force in order to avoid injury to either party. The minute Peter saw the police, he barricaded himself inside his apartment and refused to come out. Under the ruse of bringing him more sake, the police finally forced open the door and strapped him to a hospital chair while a dozen officers held him down. He was carried away, screaming, to Bellevue's mental ward.

Allen, in China, was informed about what was going on, but it would have been difficult for him to cut short his trip and return home. He thought that since he was a large part of Peter's problem, it might be best if he weren't there anyway. Peter was held for observation and assigned to a psychiatrist, who began a series of therapy sessions with him. It wasn't the last time that Peter would be hauled off to Bellevue over the next few years, and in fact this became a too-often-repeated occurrence. The psychiatrist offered therapy to Juanita and Allen, too, which Allen thoroughly loved. He always enjoyed going to counselors and psychiatrists to talk with professionals about his own emotional circumstances. Peter was prescribed medications to calm him, with varying degrees of success, over the following years. Later the doctors recommended a permanent separation between Peter and Allen, and Peter found accommodations in a series of halfway houses where his medications could be monitored.

1985 ～

JUANITA WAS DEVASTATED by what had happened and she wept continually. She had hoped that in Allen's absence things with Peter would improve, but just the opposite had transpired. No matter how much she was in love with Peter, living on this kind of Prophecy, *CP*, p. 915 tightrope wasn't sustainable. Allen didn't know what to do about Peter either. After two weeks in Bellevue the doctors were obliged to release him, and he halfheartedly promised to start going to AA or some other support program for addicts. Allen wanted to go to the AA meetings given for people like him who were termed "enablers" and hoped he could learn how to better handle these situations. He did not like the advice of "tough love" advocates who told him to give Peter an ultimatum and then cut him loose if he didn't respond to his demands. Allen was reminded again of his mother when she was alone in the mental institution and he had signed the papers for her lobotomy. He was the one person who should have stood by her. Now he couldn't bear to cut Peter out of his life after their years together, even if it was for Peter's own good. He loved him just as much as ever and was loath to sever their ties.

Allen put an optimistic spin on the resolution of the problem when he wrote to Brion Gysin and told him that the situation with Peter had been "a mess, but nice to clean up once for all." The subtle aspect that the doctors did not fully understand was that Allen was stimulated by the madness in people around him, and in many ways he thrived on it. Allen also believed that when a crisis occurred and things hit rock bottom they were bound to get better since they couldn't get worse. Unfortunately, by this time his commitments were so great that he could not take time off for his personal life, so he was not available to solve problems as they came up. He was forced into choosing between being the famous "Allen Ginsberg" and being Peter's partner. His ego wouldn't let him stop being a celebrity.

Raymond Foye, now acting as Allen's photographic agent, had lined up two prestigious galleries to exhibit Allen's pictures. The first was the Holly Solomon Gallery, an important avant-garde venue in New York. Working with Holly Solomon herself, Allen and Raymond assembled his first one-man exhibition, which opened in her gallery shortly after Allen returned from China at the beginning of January. On opening night, although Peter was not there, many of Allen's other old friends were, most of them the subjects of the photographs themselves. Carl Solomon, Henry Geldzahler, Helen Adam, and his brother, Eugene, mingled with new friends like artists Francesco Clemente, David Hockney, and Nikos Calas. Allen presided at a table signing copies of *Collected Poems* underneath the graffiti he had scrawled with a Magic Marker on the gallery's wall announcing the exhibit's title as "Hideous Human Angels." Later that year the Middendorf Gallery in Washington presented many of the same photos in an exhibition called "Memory Gardens." Along with a modest number of sales, both shows garnered nice reviews, calling attention to Allen's skill at showing "photography at its most personal." Allen's career as a photographer was under way, and Raymond worked hard to line up more shows and print more pictures.

In the meantime, Allen's new literary agent had helped make a significant impact on his financial situation. Even with the added expense of photographic supplies, he had a predictable income now and did not need to wait for his next gig to balance his checkbook. As a result, he started to cut back on the number of readings he scheduled. His financial worries were not completely over, however. Peter, Allen, and Bob Rosenthal visited a lawyer together on January 15 to discuss the landlord's eviction notice that had been served while Allen was away in China. Peter's head was still showing the signs of the rough shaving he had given himself a month earlier. Allen remarked on how old and heavy he looked with his distended pot belly, much like his father, Oleg. Although Peter was powerfully built, he somehow looked much more fragile now. Juanita had not allowed Allen to see or speak with Peter since Allen's return, so he was shocked by this dramatic change in his appearance. Keeping the rent-controlled, $260-per-month apartment was the one thing that made Allen's lifestyle affordable, so they decided to fight the eviction at any cost. The battle over the lease went on for years, during which time they kept their apartments on East Twelfth Street, hoping the court would rule in their favor.

Not long after their visit to the lawyer, Allen discovered Peter in his underwear drunk and wandering in the hallway carrying a tire iron, with blood on his hands and cheeks. At first Allen thought Peter might have hurt Juanita, but the blood turned out to be Peter's own. He was moaning incoherently about finding a Tibetan wife and having children. Allen brought Peter into his apartment to dress his wounds, where Peter viciously smashed a mirror with the tire iron. This precipitated a scuffle, and Peter wrestled Allen to the ground, breaking Allen's glasses and upsetting the furniture. When Rosenthal heard the commotion, he came out of the office armed with a hammer, ready to help Allen if the fight got too far out of control, but Peter bolted for the door and ran downstairs. When he had recovered enough to think straight, Allen asked Bob to call the police to take Peter to Bellevue again. As they waited for the cops to arrive, Allen sat in his kitchen in disbelief that Peter had actually hit him. During their fight Peter told Allen that he had only studied Buddhism because Allen ordered him to do it, and that crushed Allen's spirit even more than the physical violence. When the police came they put Peter in handcuffs and asked him a lot of questions, but Peter's answers were all gibberish. They draped Allen's winter coat over Peter's bare shoulders and took him to the hospital, where he had to sober up before being admitted to the psychiatric ward. Allen, always documenting his life in one way or another, snapped photos of Peter handcuffed in his kitchen chair with the police in the background. When he rode with Peter to the hospital he noted that Peter's only sane comment was, "I wish I were out there walking in the snow." Allen sat in the waiting room at Bellevue for a few hours, until the staff told him to go home and come back tomorrow after Peter was admitted.

When Allen got back to the building he discovered that Peter had not limited his destruction that day to their own apartments. He had also broken into a newly renovated apartment downstairs and wrecked it completely, smashing the toilet bowl with the tire iron, knocking the sink from the wall, dragging giant plastic bags full of garbage in from the street and dumping them out on the floor. There was ten thousand dollars' worth of damage done, and the landlord, who wanted them out of the building anyway, pressed criminal charges, later dropped due to Peter's mental condition. Juanita tried to remain faithful and supportive of Peter through these crises, but when she discovered that Peter was seeing other girlfriends, such as Beverly Isis, it was the last straw, and she realized that it was time to say goodbye.

Peter being taken to Bellevue, 1985 ~

Allen negotiated with the Buddhist *sangha* at Karmê Chöling to take Peter in, under the conditions that he would take Antabuse[73] for a month and continue to see a psychiatrist. After a few weeks, he stopped meditating and became hyperactive once again, manically cleaning the kitchen and washing the floors over and over again. He was able to hold it together for a couple more months mainly by dividing his time between Vermont and New York City.

Memory Cousins, *CP*, p. 916

During all this turmoil, Allen had managed to pick up another permanent houseguest, Harry Smith. Harry was broke and alcoholic himself, and stayed with Allen because he had nowhere else to go. While lodging with Allen "for just a few days" Harry had been hit by a car, fracturing his knee and relegating him to crutches. Asking the feeble old man to leave would have been unkind, even though Harry was cantankerous and nearly impossible to live with. He was a genius when it came to anthropology, ethnographic music, and filmmaking, but also a true curmudgeon and as irritable as anyone Allen knew. He ensconced himself in the tiny guest room next to the kitchen, where he made paintings with his own shit and saved his urine, à la Howard Hughes, in old milk

---

[73] Antabuse: Disulfiram, used to treat alcoholism, has the effect of making the patient sick if he drinks while on the medication.

The photo is marked along its right edge: PHOTO COURTESY OF ALLEN GINSBERG TRUST

containers that accumulated on the floor. Rosenthal's job was becoming something more than the secretarial position he had signed on for almost a decade earlier; now he was the housemother and caretaker for a group of increasingly eccentric people. The only way to accomplish any work and keep from going crazy himself was to move the office from Allen's apartment, so Bob began looking for outside space.

Moral Majority, *CP*, p. 917
The Guest, *CP*, p. 918
After Antipater, *CP*, p. 921

In late March, Dylan made a rare visit to Allen in the middle of the night. They discussed possible titles for Dylan's next album, and Allen showed him some of the photographs he'd been taking, including photos of Harry Smith and nude pictures of a handsome young man, Patrick Warner. Dylan was curious to know if Patrick was Allen's new boyfriend, but Allen sadly answered, "No, just a friend." Dylan was impressed with Allen's talent as a photographer and was anxious to meet Harry Smith, who had put together the influential *Anthology of American Folk Music* for Folkways in 1952, a seminal project that had sparked Dylan's initial interest in folk music. Since Harry was in the next room, Allen asked him to come out and meet Dylan, but an unimpressed Smith slammed the door in his face.

As usual, Allen's time was booked solid. After spending a week teaching at Naropa in April, he flew to England on a publicity tour for the British edition of *Collected Poems*. His journals from China were transcribed and appeared as a syndicated article in many newspapers around the country, and he continued to

Jumping the Gun on the Sun, *CP*, p. 922

be interviewed widely. By the Memorial Day weekend, he had made the decision to close the Cherry Valley farmhouse for good. Peter was in no shape to run the farm, and Allen realized he had never had much interest in it anyway. To him it had always been a white elephant that siphoned off too much of his earnings and never provided the bucolic sanctuary that he had hoped for. Peter and a few others from Karmê Chöling drove over to the farm and took the old pump organ back to Vermont with them, and Allen stayed there for his last time over the holiday with a small group of friends who helped him secure the house. They packed up everything that they wanted to keep and tried to leave the house clean and uncluttered for some unknown future occupant. It was a pleasant, nostalgic weekend for Allen and he spent time reminiscing about the past eighteen years since he'd first come to Cherry Valley with Barbara Rubin. "We've grown older here, from middle age to our fifties, he's 52 and I'm 58, we're breaking up!" Allen wrote that night in his journal, thinking of Peter. Allen called their relationship "a mythic comradeship that had disappeared like a rainbow." Everyone, from Juanita,

Rosenthal, and Trungpa to the psychiatrists, had told Allen to let Peter go, for Peter's own good. Now Allen wrote, "He's a stranger with drunken humor I don't know or understand after 32 years of identity!" Spitefully, Peter had asked for his old harmonium back or two thousand dollars in cash. It was the same harmonium that Allen had been using in performance for the past decade, ever since he had lost his own on a New York subway. He wanted to buy it from Peter, but he had promised the doctors not to give him any more money, so Allen was faced with another dilemma. He made a deal with Peter to trade the harmonium, in exchange for which Allen would take care of the debt Peter owed to the landlord for trashing the ground-floor apartment. From then on Peter was supposed to assume his own responsibilities about money, a job, and an apartment, and he would be free to live his own life. Even Trungpa advised Allen to stay away and only "be there for emergencies, let him free, don't hold on."

Cadillac Squawk, *CP*, p. 925

Just as he had once been plagued by second thoughts about his actions during the Trungpa/Merwin affair, Allen was now haunted by guilt about what he might have done wrong in his relationship with Peter. He speculated that he had dominated Peter with his own strong will, with money, with cars, with households, with readings. Possibly he had further controlled Peter by urging him to write poetry and by introducing him to Buddhist meditation. He realized that Peter had been living in his shadow for nearly thirty years, something that had never occurred to him before. Of all the friends they shared, only Robert Frank and Lucien Carr seemed to like Peter for himself. Fifteen years earlier Peter had cried in the snow at Cherry Valley, "Everything is yours, I don't own anything," but Allen had never listened to what he was saying. On his fifty-ninth birthday, Allen woke up and made a list of the greatest mistakes in life, and his failed relationship with Peter was at the top of the list.

As Peter tried to regain a balance in his life, Allen was overburdened with work. He zigzagged across the country reading, teaching, interviewing, and photographing on a punishing schedule. Harry Smith stayed in the tiny guest room with no intention of leaving Allen's apartment for any reason. During the summer Harry began building a domed city in Allen's kitchen made of eggshells glued to toilet paper tubes, which he later smashed to pieces in a drunken temper tantrum. One day Allen sadly looked into the bathroom mirror and saw "an older sloppy hair professorial looking fatso with a pot belly bulging over his pajamas." He was completely alone now, even with Harry Smith sleeping only a few feet away in the next room. He saw the piles of unedited prose, the letters, journals, essays, and interviews

waiting to be worked on, as a giant karmic trap, an albatross around his neck
that he would never be rid of. But unlike his youthful depressions, this one
found him with no time to spare wallowing in self-pity.

After his usual summer teaching stint at Naropa, Allen
went on a three-week retreat to the Rocky Mountain
Dharma Center. He decided to postpone some of the long-
term projects he'd been working on, such as his 1940s journals and a book of collected essays. He continued to work on the *Annotated
Howl* and his *White Shroud* poems for Harper and Row and curtailed his correspondence as much as he could. Of all his current projects, he enjoyed the
nostalgic work on the *Annotated Howl* the most. He liked refreshing his
memory on the genesis of *Howl* and wrote to everyone mentioned or alluded to in the text. He wrote to Michael McClure, "I have the odd occasion
to do my own exposition or annotation of *Howl,* and on the chance that it
may be useful to someone as an aesthetic demonstration, social history or
idiosyncratic composition method, I'm working with Miles to do a thorough
job. Not many poets have had the opportunity to 'rewrite history' their way,
so I'd like to do it meticulously." For Allen, it was the closest he would ever
come to writing his own autobiography.

On a trip to the West Coast at summer's end, Allen took part in a panel
discussion at the First Unitarian Church in San Francisco on the topic of
sexuality and spirituality with his friend Tsultrim Allione. She introduced
Allen to a friend of hers by the name of Susan Rashkis. Susan was thirty-
two and a Jewish student of the *dharma* like Allen. That evening at a dinner
party in Berkeley, Allen and Susan hit it off immediately and had a nice
long conversation, during which Allen proposed the idea of marrying her
and having children. Trungpa had recently suggested that Allen have a family, and as usual, Allen was willing to follow any suggestion that his teacher
made. Nearly sixty, he had no idea what raising a family meant, but he and
Peter had frequently talked about it. Allen always thought it would be Peter
who would father the child, but now with Peter out of the picture, Allen
began to give fatherhood halfhearted consideration. A few weeks later he
wrote to Rashkis, "That was such a nice conversation we had in Berkeley I
went away light hearted, tho I had no real idea if the notion of marriage—
to anyone—was workable or actually desirable. Still it was a relief from the
claustrophobia of my mental situation." It wasn't much more than a fleeting dream, however, and although he and Rashkis maintained a cordial correspondence and visited each other occasionally, nothing much came of
the idea.

Things I Don't
Know, *CP,* p. 926

In November, Allen got the chance to visit Russia once again, this time as a member of a large delegation of American writers. Harrison Salisbury and Susan Sontag, who had been on the trip to China the previous year, went, as well as William Gaddis and Louis Auchincloss. They visited Vilnius and Minsk together by train, and Allen spent a good deal of time on the trip talking and sightseeing with Arthur Miller and his wife, Inge. The two writers shared the same political views and stirred up a small controversy by questioning Russia's imprisonment of some distinguished writer/activists. At one of the conference meetings, Allen brought up the topic of gay liberation, a forbidden topic in the Soviet Union, but no problems arose because of it. Just as he had in China, Allen asked to stay longer in Russia to teach after the delegation left, but at the last minute he was thwarted by bureaucratic red tape. Even with Yevtushenko's help he was only able to have his visa extended for an additional two weeks for travel as a tourist. During those two weeks he visited Tbilisi, where he met a Soviet victim of blacklisting, the film director Sergei Parajanov. He had spent several years in a Russian prison and now lived in a big house full of young bohemian artists, where he made collages and clothing from whatever materials he could find. As a gift he gave Allen a wild handmade formal suit he had embroidered himself. As Allen stepped onto the plane to leave the USSR for the last time, he noted that things hadn't changed much in twenty years.

1986 ～

AT THE END OF JANUARY, Allen returned to Nicaragua at the invitation of Ernesto Cardenal. Patrick Warner went along with him as his guest, taking photographs and recording the readings on his tape recorder. Allen was interested in Patrick, but since the young man was not interested in leaving Massachusetts for New York, nothing much came from the relationship except occasional visits. They stayed for ten days to participate in the Ruben Dario Poetry Festival, but Allen was curious to see how the revolution had progressed since his visit there in 1982. It seemed to him that both sides in the civil war were equally right and wrong. The insurgent army of contras that the U.S. government had been supporting was composed mostly of ex–National Guard Samocistas, little more than wild mercenaries, who were cruel and bloodthirsty. On the other side, the Sandinistas had become more repressive and their military forces brutally squashed any dissent. The opposition press consisted of one newspaper, and Allen suspected that they were being funded by the CIA. Overall, Allen found Nicaragua's progress disappointing. It looked as if the United States had managed to bring out the worst in both sides. A group of students from Naropa also went with Allen to get a firsthand look at the situation and to hear the poetry of José Coronel Urtecho, Jorge Luis Borges, and Ernesto Cardenal. Back home again, Allen met with Arthur Miller and Günter Grass to draft a statement for the PEN Center asking that America put a

You Don't Know It, *CP*, p. 942

On the Conduct of the World Seeking Beauty Against Government, *CP*, p. 946

Hard Labor, *CP*, p. 947

Velocity of Money, *CP*, p. 948

stop to funding the rebel forces and end U.S. military intervention in Nicaragua's internal affairs.

Late that winter, a young poet named Chris Ide contacted Allen. Ide admired the beats and identified strongly with them as a group. In addition, he developed an affinity with Arthur Rimbaud, which was reflected not only in his poetry, but in his lifestyle, too. He carried a copy of Rimbaud's *A Season in Hell* with him and inhaled stories about the suffering artist. Allen met Ide in Detroit on one of his reading tours, and the two began corresponding and exchanging poems. Allen was impressed with his poetry and quickly came to regard Ide as one of the younger geniuses that he was so pleased to discover. Once again Allen approached Ferlinghetti to advocate for Ide's work and tried unsuccessfully to interest him in publishing it. That summer Ide went to Boulder and hung out with Allen around Naropa much of the time and became acquainted with many of Allen's friends.

Sphincter, CP, p. 949

During the spring and early summer Allen spent a good deal of time working with Gordon Ball and Miles on their various Ginsberg projects. Allen compromised a bit by beginning to give readings in order to pay others to work on his projects. He tired himself out through his constant work to refill the COP checking account. That May he was at least cheered by the news that Naropa had finally been granted formal intercollegiate accreditation.

Spot Anger, CP, p. 950
London Dream Doors, CP, p. 951

In June a dinner party was thrown for Allen at an East Village Ukrainian restaurant in celebration of his sixtieth birthday. He was surrounded by many of his friends and family in a circle of good fellowship. The painter Francesco Clemente, whom Allen knew through Raymond Foye, was at the dinner and sketched Allen on the white tablecloth. Andrew Wylie couldn't resist taking this memento with him, much to the dismay of the waiters. He had it framed and hung it on the wall of his office. More than a hundred of Allen's friends, from Burroughs to Yevtushenko, had sent tributes and greetings from around the world, and all the good wishes were presented to him that evening in a Festschrift, appropriately titled *Best Minds*.

Cosmopolitan Greetings, CP, p. 953
Fifth Internationale, CP, p. 956

His most important trip of the year was in late August to Struga, Yugoslavia, to accept a lifetime achievement award called the Golden Wreath. Allen and Steven Taylor flew to Budapest, where they stayed with Allen's translator and friend István Eörsi. Steven went off to explore on his own with plans to meet Allen in Struga in time for the reading. That gave Allen a week to relax in Budapest in a wonderful room with twenty-foot-high windows opening out on to a view of the Danube. From his room he could see the old bridges and turreted castles along the river. He spent some of his time cutting a record with the Hobo Blues Band, who had been making Allen's poetry famous throughout Hungary. One evening they joined Allen in a combination poetry reading and rock concert in a huge outdoor amphitheater in Budapest, and for once Allen felt like a rock star, albeit a Hungarian one.

The Struga committee presented Allen with a solid gold laurel wreath, crafted by a team of goldsmiths. Allen was proud of it but also saw it as a completely useless toy and did not know exactly what to do with it or how to display it once he got it home. Onstage, in their beautiful cathedral before an image of a black Madonna, he performed *September on Jessore Road* and recited "White Shroud" backed up by Steven Taylor and the Pro Arte string quartet. As an honored guest of the Croatian Writers Union, he was able to stay in the upscale Intercontinental Hotel during his visit. From there he decided to make a tour of Eastern Europe and gave a literary lecture and reading with Taylor in Zagreb. Then, in Belgrade, the USIA hosted him for a reading and chauffeured him around town in a limousine. From there the pair rode to Krakow by train for two performances in a theater and spent a week in Warsaw, returning home in September.

Europe, Who Knows?, *CP*, p. 958

Allen needed to get back to New York in order to teach that fall at Brooklyn College. The college had recently appointed Allen a Distinguished Professor in the English Department, giving him the chair John Ashbery had vacated after he received a lucrative MacArthur Grant. It put Allen on the fast track for faculty tenure. The first course he taught to his graduate students was called Twentieth Century Expansive Heroic Verse.

Graphic Winces, *CP*, p. 959

As Allen began his new teaching career in Brooklyn, Peter was sent to Bellevue once more for an episode of deranged behavior. This time he was on the verge of having the DTs before the emergency-room staff could stabilize him. Allen's own health had not improved in the past few years either and he was being treated by a specialist for heart disease. His doctor explained to him that he had a temporary stress arrhythmia, which could go away if he stopped traveling and got plenty of rest. He also suffered from what they termed "reactive hyperglycemia" and was put on a strict diet to control that problem. He had to say farewell to matzoh ball soup, bread, rice, candy, honey, pasta, and potatoes, all of which he loved and would dearly miss. Allen was determined to make the most of his new diet and appreciate what he was allowed to have, instead of fretting about what he could not have. Following a short retreat at Karmê Chöling that winter, he also vowed to resume meditating every day.

1987 ~

ALONG WITH ALLEN'S APPOINTMENT at Brooklyn College came the security of health insurance and a pension plan. With these benefits and the publishing money that Wylie was bringing in, Allen felt financially secure for the first time in his life. However, when he received his initial paycheck from the college he was shocked to see that half of his salary went to cover federal, state, and city taxes, social security, insurance, union dues, and god knew what else. He had not received a regular paycheck since he stopped working in market research thirty-five years earlier, so the amount of his deductions surprised him. Along with his new, quieter life he decided to fix up his apartment again, and he hired Steven Taylor to paint the walls and sand and polyurethane the wooden floors.

Now that he was in a stable academic position, Allen could apply for foundation grants and invite his friends to read at Brooklyn College. With the help of the Wolfe Institute, Allen was able to provide the poets a reasonable stipend, so he began to produce an important series of readings at the college that continued over the next decade. At one time or another he asked virtually every writer he knew to read at the college. That first year he started with Creeley, Huncke, Burroughs, Whalen, Bremser, Solomon, Orlovsky, and McClure. It was great fun, but it turned out to be time consuming for his office staff, since they had to make the travel arrangements and see to the needs of each of the speakers. Allen even designed the fliers that announced the readings and stayed involved in every detail no matter how small. Student interns usually helped to lighten his load, but more work was generated with each new idea he had.

That winter Allen continued to see his psychiatrist once a week. He struggled with the difficult task of keeping distance between Peter and himself. Peter was supposed to be on his own, yet was still in the apartment next door. He had repeated manic episodes and was sent to rehab periodically. Photography came to be the only thing that Allen did for pure pleasure. He took pictures and made enlargements at every opportunity and his newfound extra money was eaten up by the costs of film processing.

Imitation of K.S., *CP*, p. 960

Allen decided to take his stepmother, Edith, and Harry Smith with him on a short reading tour to the Mississippi River delta that spring. It gave Harry the chance to revisit the blues country, where many of the recordings he had collected for the *Anthology of American Folk Music* had first been made. By a stroke of luck, Mary Beach and Claude Pelieu, Allen's early French translators,

I Went to the Movie of Life, *CP*, p. 961

had offered to take Harry off Allen's hands as soon as he got back from the South. Mary and Claude lived in the country upstate near Cooperstown, and they believed it would be fun to have Harry live with them for a while. Once Harry settled in they quickly realized that they had bitten off more than they could chew, but Allen was not about to invite him back. He liked Harry, but never wanted to live with him again. Mary and Claude took care of him for a while, until Allen was able to get him appointed to the faculty at Naropa, where Harry stayed for the next few years.

At 8:05 on the evening of April 4, Chögyam Trungpa Rinpoche died in the Halifax Infirmary, entering into *Parinirvana*. He was forty-eight years old. His passing was attributed to diabetes and high blood pressure, both aggravated by his heavy drinking. Although Trungpa had suffered a heart attack several months earlier, Allen had not been expecting his death. He received the news over the phone from John Muglietea quietly and went next door to tell Peter, who was not home at the time. Saddened, Allen walked over to the Dharmadhatu Center and sat in meditation, thinking about his guru and friend. When he got home, Peter was there and had already learned the news that their teacher was dead. That night Allen dreamed that Trungpa visited him one last time and in the dream told him, "No, he [Allen] wasn't ok and [he] should meditate and practice again."

In the summer a new young friend Allen had made in
Boulder came to visit him in New York. He was friendly and   When the Light
handsome and reminded some people of the way Neal Cas-   Appears, *CP*, p. 965
sady had looked in his youth. Peter Hale had first seen Allen
when the poet read at his Boulder high school several years earlier. As he
grew older, he saw Allen from time to time around town. Hale's friends, who
knew of Allen's reputation for chasing young boys, advised Hale not to let his
guard down or Allen would have him in bed in a flash. Hale was more interested in meeting William Burroughs than he was in Ginsberg, but circumstances led him to always miss Burroughs and instead he bumped into Allen
much more frequently. Since Hale was gay and had been warned about Allen,
he was surprised that Allen did not pressure him for sex, but seemed genuinely interested in him as a person. Allen wanted to know all about Peter and
his experiences growing up in Boulder. Chris Ide was one of Hale's close
friends, so there were many things that the two had in common. In the end
Allen invited Hale to visit him in the city, a visit that accidentally coincided
with Trungpa's cremation.

Trungpa's body had been flown from Canada to Vermont, where Allen
drove with Peter, Beverly, and Peter Hale for the public cremation on May 26.
Trungpa's closest followers had prepared his body in the traditional Tibetan
way, bathing it in saffron water and dressing it in a ceremonial brocade robe.
The body had been placed on a throne, and Trungpa's followers were invited
to witness his *samadhi*, which lasted for three days following his death. Once
at Karmê Chöling the corpse was preserved in the shrine room for several
weeks until it was carried to the meadow and placed on a twenty-two-foot-
high pyre or *purkhang*. One by one each of his students placed a white scarf,
called a *kata*, on the pyre, before it was set on fire in front of the crowd of
nearly two thousand people. As the body burned a rainbow
appeared around the sun and a cloud, shaped like a dragon,   On Cremation of
floated across the sky. These heavenly phenomena marked   Chögyam Trungpa,
the departure of an exceptional teacher, and many students,   Vidyadhara, *CP*, p. 966
including Allen, interpreted them as auspicious signs.

The following day they all drove home in the old blue Volvo. After his
eighteen-month battle with alcohol and drugs, punctuated by many trips
back to Bellevue's mental ward, Peter seemed to have calmed down to a degree. Allen felt that Peter had stabilized enough to allow him to return to
Boulder that summer to resume teaching. True to form, Peter wasn't recovered, and only Allen seemed unaware of it. When Peter had money, he spent

it on liquor and drugs, or sometimes he went on mad spending sprees, buying expensive cameras and tape recorders that he would never learn to use. One evening in Boulder, Peter got into a wild fistfight with an equally drunk R. D. Laing, the well-known British psychiatrist who was then also teaching at Naropa. Peter socked Laing in the mouth and then bit him so hard that the wound swelled up a bright blue color. In the scuffle Allen hurt his shin trying to break them up. When the police arrived, they pushed Peter, who toppled into Allen, knocking him to the pavement. As a result, Allen wound up with an injured knee and a fractured pinky finger. During the fracas Peter had overturned all the furniture and thrown juice bottles against the wall and made such a mess that Allen and a Naropa friend, Jacqueline Gens, spent the next day cleaning. He tried to make Peter feel remorseful by telling him that some of the books he had damaged were rare editions by Louis Zukofsky, but Peter was beyond feeling guilty. Even the irreplaceable harmonium had been hit by flying milk and apple juice. Unrealistically, Allen expected Peter to repent and to atone for his outbreaks, but after thirty years of substance abuse this was an impossible dream. Peter was no longer in control of himself.

Everyone at Naropa blamed Allen for "enabling" Peter once more and reminded him of the doctor's advice that they should not live together or even be in touch regularly. This reactivated Allen's psychological trauma at having to abandon Peter as he believed he had abandoned his mother. The summer continued much the same, with Peter undergoing various crises and exhibiting varying degrees of madness. Allen had thought that if he "hired" Peter to help with Allen's work, it would make Peter feel that he was earning his own keep, but the effect was just the opposite. Allen eventually came to admit that he was blind to what was happening when it came to Peter. He loved him very much, but began to see that he was dependent on Peter for a sense of continuity in his otherwise irregular life. He could not come to the realization that Peter was totally dependent on him for everything in his life.

Nanao, *CP*, p. 968

One day Allen spoke with Marianne Faithfull, the well-known singer and an old friend. She had recently been released from the Hazelden Foundation in Minneapolis, one of the pioneer hospitals that treated patients for alcoholism and drug addiction. She counseled Allen, "You've got to continue to love the person but reject the behavior which is part of a sickness, like cancer or any physical illness, with no 'moral' judgment involved." It was good advice. Allen was still seeing his own psychiatrist regularly, ever since Peter's first Bellevue hospitalization, and he was going through a protracted psychotherapy program. He loved it. He was beginning to understand the dynamics behind the early stress he'd had with his own parents. It would take longer before he'd get to the problems with Peter, but in the meantime, he and Beverly Isis went to Hazelden for a weeklong intensive therapy program addressing the issues of alcoholism and codependency. Peter, who was supposed to go along with them, backed out at the last minute, but Allen and Beverly found the program fascinating and focused on the tenet that codependency was based on low self-esteem and illusions of worthlessness. Although Allen knew he had a giant ego, he wondered if low self-esteem could be a large part of this dynamic that he had overlooked.

Personals Ad, *CP*, p. 969

Proclamation, *CP*, p. 970

After the tussle between Peter and Laing, Allen's knee did not heal well, and he underwent arthroscopic surgery in November. They removed the torn ligament and he recovered quickly from that. At the same time, Allen met a thirty-year-old musical genius named Hal Willner, the music coordinator for *Saturday Night Live*. Willner had developed the art of mixing records to perfection, and his compilations were both creative and inspired. He and Allen worked on a twenty-four-track computerized recording of Allen's spoken poetry mixed with lively jazz melodies. In the end he produced an innovative recording, especially good for a poet. They called it *The Lion for Real*, and it surpassed any recording Allen had made since *First Blues*.

During the winter Burroughs came to New York to promote his newest novel, *The Western Lands*. By then he was living permanently in Lawrence, Kansas, where he had moved years earlier with James Grauerholz. Allen was always happy to see Burroughs and catch up on all the news, which was now largely focused on their health. The trip coincided with the opening of an exhibition of sixty of Burroughs's "shotgun" paintings at the trendy Larry Gagosian

To Jacob Rabinowitz, *CP*, p. 971

gallery. Now both Allen and William had become recognized as talented visual artists.

With Harry's room empty, Julius came to stay at Allen's Twelfth Street apartment for a month and was more talkative than Allen could ever remember. He was living in a halfway house upstate, but Peter wanted to move him to an adult home nearer to the city, so he could visit him regularly. In truth, after years of deteriorating mental health, Peter was in need of nearly as much help and supervision as Julius.

1 9 8 8 ∿

ON JANUARY 5 Allen left on a three-week teaching assignment with Robert Frank at the Camera Obscura School of Art in Tel Aviv. It was a perfect time to be with Robert, for Allen was in the process of selecting the photographs that would be used in his first large collection of photography, slated for publication by the prestigious Twelvetrees Press. Allen planned to include 108 photos because that was a sacred number on the Indian subcontinent and the number of beads on the Chinese Buddhist *mala* (rosary). Robert's opinions and suggestions were always important to Allen, and he was happy when Robert confirmed that the photogravure process Twelvetrees was planning to use was the best method for reproducing work like his. In Israel, Allen and his translator Natan Zach gave several readings at universities in Tel Aviv, Haifa, and Jerusalem. Steven Taylor flew over to provide music for the performances, and they had a good time sightseeing in Jerusalem, staying in a room that overlooked Gehenna, a ravine outside the walls, and synonymous with Hell. Most important to Allen, it was the legendary home of Moloch, whom he had evoked in *Howl*. They visited the Wailing Wall, where Allen found himself weeping as he thought of the thousands of years of sorrows associated with that sacred place, ever since God first commanded Abraham to sacrifice his son, Isaac, on the same spot. The tense political situation in Israel was palpable everywhere. Allen visited the Knesset to talk with Palestinian moderates Mubarak Awad and Hanna Senoria and then addressed a huge throng at a Peace Now Rally.

Late one night Allen disappeared and didn't come back to his room. He remained missing for a few days, and Steven debated whether to call the police and report his disappearance. Since Allen had made it a point to suggest they meet in Tel Aviv if they were separated, Steven decided to go there to wait for him. It turned out that Allen had snuck into Palestinian territory and spent several days there with some of the boys who made a living by collecting spent Israeli ammunition for scrap metal. Allen found it ironic when they showed him fragments of bombs made in the United States by the Bethlehem Steel company. Just when Steven was going to notify the authorities, Allen appeared again, safe and sound after his adventure.

Although Allen was sympathetic with many of the Israeli concerns, he believed that both sides were so entrenched in their own positions that peace could not be achieved as long as hard-liners were in control. When he got back to New York, Allen organized a PEN Center protest campaign against Israel's censorship of Palestinian writers. Near the end of his trip he'd come down with severe bronchitis again. Gary Snyder had been suggesting that they take a trip to Tibet together, and although Allen wanted to go more than anything else, he doubted that he would be up to such a trip physically for a long time.

Other problems besides health kept Allen close to home, too. His landlord continued the eviction proceedings against him, and they dragged on slowly through the courts. The uncertainty of whether Allen and Peter would be able to stay weighed on Allen's mind. He thought of buying a place where he would not be subject to a landlord's whims, but the Lower East Side was becoming fashionable and real estate prices were skyrocketing. The landlord was intent on booting them from their apartment, since other apartments in the same building were now being rented for more than a thousand dollars a month. Allen looked at an apartment for sale near Avenue B and Second Street, in a run-down area that was not yet gentrified. It was being offered at three hundred thousand dollars, more money than Allen could ever dream of raising. Even if he could afford it, the building was dilapidated and would need years of work and plenty of money to restore it. His only course of action was to continue to work with his lawyers to block an eviction from East Twelfth Street.

Although Wylie's book contracts and Allen's teaching at Brooklyn College had eased his financial worries, he still poured all his own money back into helping others. Grants for the reading series he had established fell short of the funds he needed, so he ended up financing about a quarter of the expenses from his own pocket. It was his choice and he didn't complain, but it stretched his finances even thinner.

Grandma Earth's Song,
CP, p. 972

At that time new FCC rules started to be implemented to keep "indecent" material from the airwaves. There had been few censorship battles in the country since the court's decisions in favor of *Howl* and *Naked Lunch*. But now, with the rise of the right-wing "Moral Majority" led by the Heritage Foundation and politicians like Senators Jesse Helms and Newt Gingrich, the government began a new crackdown on what they perceived as filth. Allen began to devote time to fighting these measures, which, in effect, banned his poetry. Conservatives had discovered that the way to circumvent the previous court rulings was to make the radio and television stations censor themselves. The FCC wasn't interested in passing any statutes against "pornography" that could be fought in court, they merely threatened to revoke licenses. Each radio station was left to make decisions based on economics, and most decided not to risk an expensive court battle by airing "borderline" material, such as Allen's poetry. His work, which the courts had ruled not obscene and which was once read on the air, was beginning to be censored by the stations themselves, for fear of losing their licenses. For example, while Allen was in Israel teaching, the Pacifica Radio Network had canceled its broadcast of *Howl* on a nationwide program about censorship called "Open Ears/Open Minds." The network had been threatened a few months earlier when it broadcast a play dealing with homosexuality, and it literally could not afford to take a chance with Allen's work. Even though his poetry could be published, it could not be read over the public airwaves without censorship between the hours of 6:00 A.M. and midnight.

In 1988 a federal appeals court ruled that the FCC had gone too far in its November 1987 ruling to restrict adult programming to the midnight to 6:00 A.M. slot and overturned the daytime ban. In retaliation Senator Jesse Helms introduced a new law to ban the broadcast of all "indecent" speech, twenty-four hours a day. At that time rock 'n' roll recordings were also being self-rated according to their content, and songs such as "Makin' Bacon" and albums by the Dead Kennedys were under attack. To Allen it was as if America was slipping back to the repression of the 1950s once again. He began to do all that he could to bring the rather complicated issue to the public's attention, and he spoke about censorship at every opportunity and in every interview.

Salutations to Fernando
Pessoa, *CP*, p. 975
May Days 1988, *CP*,
p. 978

After his courses at Brooklyn College were over in May, Allen went to California on a reading tour. He teamed up with Gary Snyder and Michael McClure to help Nanao Sakaki raise money for the protection of Japan's last living coral reef. It was good to have an environmental cause that he could sink his teeth into again and great to get back to Bedrock Mortar to see his old friends and sleep in his cabin. True to form, though, Allen soon had to be off to new commitments. Robert Wilson had developed a staged version of Allen's *Cosmopolitan Greetings,* and he wanted Allen to be in Hamburg for the premiere in June. Wilson had created an elaborate production incorporating elements of opera, jazz, parody, pantomime, ballet, and modern dance. After receiving good reviews abroad, the program was booked into the Brooklyn Academy of Music for the next season.

In June Allen also went to Lowell to help unveil a memorial park dedicated to Jack Kerouac. Jack's hometown had erected marble steles on which were inscribed excerpts from his books. The overall effect was quite dramatic. Many old friends gathered in the little park to honor Kerouac at the ceremony, while the local newspaper debated whether it was proper to glorify a man who was known to many as the town drunk. Allen saw people like Edie Kerouac and Henri Cru and gave a reading with Ferlinghetti to a standing-room-only crowd.

Summer classes at Naropa were pretty much the same as they had been for the past decade. Allen asked Chris Ide, his young poet "discovery," to teach his class for a week. Because most of his students were older and more experienced than he was, Chris felt uncomfortable as "Professor Ide." As a result, he partied even more than usual, missed his classes, and generally bungled his teaching opportunity. He lacked self-confidence even though Allen invariably encouraged him and even brought him onstage to read his work. As was his habit, Allen would then stand in the back of the room and proceed to shout things like, "We can't hear you, speak up!" meaning to be helpful, but it only served to unnerve the young man. Ide was abusing drugs regularly and often stole prescription medicine from the bathroom cabinets of friends, even Allen. Naïvely, Allen never believed that Ide would lie to him, so he suspected that Peter Hale was the one emptying his pain pill bottles. Over the next few years Allen tried to help Ide get into rehabilitation and paid for a methadone treatment program, but Ide also abused that. In 1994 he died of a heroin overdose alone after sleeping on park benches, dirty and homeless in his final years. Corso told Allen, "Look who their role models are: Huncke, Burroughs, Kerouac," leaving out his own name, of course.

Although most of the time it was Allen who pursued younger men, occasionally the tables were turned. One seventeen-year-old gay high school student from Atlanta, Mark Ewert, flew to Boulder with the single purpose of sleeping with Allen. Ewert was cute and sufficiently interested in literature for Allen to be attracted to him. At Naropa's orientation party that summer, Mark introduced himself to Allen, offering to make breakfast, lunch, or dinner for him. When Allen asked him if he could cook, Mark had to sheepishly admit that he couldn't. His lack of culinary skills did not hamper their relationship, and for the rest of the summer, Allen and Mark spent a good deal of their time with each other. In the end Allen introduced Mark to a wide range of literature and art and acted like a kindly old professor with a bright student.

Once back from teaching, Allen immersed himself in more activity in New York City. His apartment was only two blocks from Tompkins Square Park, where, over the weekend of August 6, a confrontation took place. Squatters, who had taken over and were living in the park, were being forcibly evicted by an enormous police battalion. That led to skirmishes outside the park for several nights between the police and those who were opposed to the eviction. Allen was a witness and made friends with many of the combatants, documenting the scene with his ever-present camera. He believed that the police had overreacted to the violent protests and had escalated the riot through their own zealous actions. It was reminiscent of Chicago, but on a much smaller scale. Eventually the squatters were forced out, and the park was completely refurbished.

Nanao Sakaki's fight to save the Japanese coral reef continued well into the year, and in October Allen took a flight to Japan to do a series of benefit readings for the cause. The trip was planned to coincide with the opening of an exhibit of his photography at the Watari Gallery in Tokyo. More tired than usual, Allen needed to conserve his strength on this trip and asked the gallery owner not to schedule many interviews for him; he wanted his stay to be low key. His blood pressure had shot up again, and he began to feel that he was getting too old for too much more adventure or publicity. Nanao took him to a remote area in the mountains outside Matsumoto for a few days to hike quietly and meet some of his ecologically minded friends who lived on farms and communes there. In spite of his need for rest, Allen was eager to see everything that he could and to meet all of Nanao's friends.

The same week that Allen finished his third year of psychotherapy, he suffered a gall bladder attack. It was removed at Lenox Hill Hospital in December, and his recovery was slower than expected. Mark Ewert flew to New York to stay with him for a week while he was recovering. Allen had been a workaholic for so long that he had no idea how to slow down, but in the end physical weakness kept him at home. One important exception that year was the Lincoln Center premiere of *Wichita Vortex Sutra,* his collabora-

*Gehlek Rinpoche wears
Allen's Uncle Sam hat ~*

tion with Philip Glass. Allen enjoyed his artistic partnership with Glass, and was also interested to learn more from Glass, a fellow Buddhist, about Glass's own meditation teacher, Gehlek Rinpoche. Now that Trungpa was dead, Allen was without a teacher, and he was interested in Gehlek's approach, which was much different from Trungpa's. Glass was a member of Gehlek's Jewel Heart *sangha* and introduced Allen to his teacher. It was uncommon for a practitioner of the Kagyüpa school of "Crazy Wisdom" like Allen to transfer his allegiance to the Gelugpa "School of the Virtuous" that Gehlek followed, but Allen was more interested in the personality of his gurus than in the methodology they taught. He found that he liked the friendly Gehlek and his cheerful Jewel Heart students.

1 9 8 9 ∿

A LLEN'S GALL BLADDER SURGERY gave him the excuse he needed to cancel what was sure to be a strenuous trip to Bhopal, India, that he had been planning with Lucien Carr, still a close friend after forty-five years. He had also been expected while there to spend time with some Indian writers who had come to New York for an earlier Festival of Indian Poetry reading. With his health in the balance, Allen bowed out of the trip and asked Bob Rosenthal to take his place beside Anne Waldman. The whole program had been suggested by Allen, and the Indians stuck with it even though Allen was unable to go. While Bob was in India that winter, Allen continued to write letters, prepare manuscripts, and do more work than he probably should have. Miles gave him a copy of the manuscript of the biography he had been writing, which was due to be published by Simon and Schuster later in the year. He took the time to go through certain sections meticulously, noting all the problems he spotted, and consulted Jacqueline Gens about many of the Buddhist references. He made over three thousand suggestions, which were both welcome and problematic for the author. Allen was most bothered by Miles's treatment of Tibetan Buddhism and the Chinese takeover of Tibet. Miles put the Maoists in a positive light and was not sympathetic enough about the expulsion of the Tibetans from their own homeland for Allen's taste. "His view of Maoism in Tibet then colors his view of Trungpa and my relation to him and the Merwin scene," Allen wrote. He feared that his sympathy and liking for Trungpa made him hypersensitive to Miles's "animosity," but he could not resist trying to convince

Miles to alter the tone of his book. The biography "lies like a tombstone on my soul," Allen wrote a month later. He knew this book would create problems within the Buddhist community when it was published, but he agonized about what control he should exercise over a book that was not his, even though it was written by one of his friends.

During this period Allen started to use the term "Negative Capability" more and more when referring to his ability to hold two opposing opinions in his mind. Keats had spoken of this seeming contradiction as a virtue, especially when it was applied to writers. In 1817 he wrote, "I mean negative capability, that is, when a man is capable of being in uncertainties, mysteries, doubts, without any irritable reaching after fact and reason." He seemed to suggest that a poet should be able to accept the presence of various viewpoints in his work and write effectively about things he might not agree with. Allen knew that Whitman took it a step further by saying, "Do I contradict myself? Very well then I contradict myself, I am large, I contain multitudes." Although it is a quality a person might not want to see in his doctor, it worked well for poetry, allowing for unusual juxtapositions of ideas and fostering discussions about new ideas within a work of art. Allen became fond of quoting both Keats and Whitman on the subject. It helped him to understand how he was able to respect Trungpa without needing to agree with his every action. It also provided Allen a way out when he wanted to keep faith in his friends. He knew now that he didn't have to understand everything completely.

On March 27, Allen was granted a court order of protection against Peter Orlovsky. For weeks Peter had been in his apartment next to Allen's drinking heavily and raving madly. He banged on the wall that separated his room from Allen's and cursed loudly through the door whenever Allen tried to talk calmly with him. Beverly Isis had been working with public assistance social workers to find professional help for Peter at the suggestion of his psychiatrist, Dr. Fortner, but without much success. It was a sad time for Allen. In addition to problems with Peter, Gregory had been calling and haranguing Allen about money; he always needed more. In spite of the fact that Allen had set Harry Smith up with a teaching position at Naropa, he was still paying all of Harry's expenses, too, and he had found out that Harry had been using the money for liquor instead of paying his rent. Allen hired a Naropa student, Rani Singh, to act as Harry's caretaker in Boulder and sent the checks for rent and food directly to her. Unfortunately, the Buddhist community suffered another scandal when it was discovered that Ösel Tenzing (né Robert Rich), Chögyam Trungpa's regent, had been having sex with some of his students, even though he was well aware that he was HIV positive. Amid these depressing events, Allen worked on his photography book, making slow progress. He was still selecting and captioning the photos he wanted to include and writing bios of his subjects, but he could never find enough time to finish the job.

In the late spring, Ginsberg talked to Alene Lee and happened to mention that he and Bob were looking for affordable office space outside his apartment. The problems with Peter and other houseguests were incentive enough to put some distance between work and home, but the move might also give Allen a boundary for separating his private and public time. He needed space where he could escape from work, but that was impossible with the business office only a few feet away. Alene and her daughter, Crystal, ran a typing and secretarial service and had extra office space, so they were happy to sublet two rooms to Allen. The office was conveniently located a few blocks away on the corner of Second Avenue and Fourteenth Street. At first the apartment seemed quiet without the constant ringing of the telephone, and Allen was happy to have more privacy. He could easily walk to the office, and he got into the habit of going there late each afternoon and working into the wee hours of the morning. Jacqueline Gens had been helping to organize Allen's photography business on visits, but now she moved to New York and began to work full time on the project. At the time, Rosenthal was involved in his own homesteading project and needed the extra help with Allen's paperwork, and Allen liked having someone around with a deeper knowledge of Buddhism than his own.

Now that the office had moved out of his apartment, Allen had more room for guests. When Jack Shuai, a young man Allen had met in China five years earlier, wrote and asked if he would sponsor him to attend college in the United States that fall, Allen invited him to stay at his place. "The CUNY scholarship here is still open," Allen wrote, encouraging Shuai to apply for something Allen had told him about. Shuai was an eager student, athletic, filled with energy and ideas. He was interested in American culture, especially the more liberal attitude toward sex. He wasn't gay, but he was interested in learning everything about all forms of sex, and Allen was happy to teach him what he knew on the subject. With Allen's recommendation, Shuai won the scholarship and once in New York became another of Allen's long-term guests. At least Shuai cooked and cleaned up after himself, unlike most of Allen's other visitors. By the time Shuai arrived from Chungking, Allen had received tenure at Brooklyn College and felt he had security at last, for as long as he wanted to keep working.

When Miles's biography was published that September, Allen began receiving complaints about it from his Buddhist friends almost immediately.

Administrators at Naropa felt that the book's anti-Tibetan stance would adversely affect their ability to raise money for the school. Allen was troubled by Miles's chapters on his expulsion from Havana and Prague, since Miles was more sympathetic to the Marxists than he was to Allen and considered Allen's political viewpoints at the time to have been naïve. On a personal note, Allen had been insulted to read in the manuscript that Miles thought that his poetry had declined after he became involved with Trungpa in 1973. Allen told him in no uncertain terms that he thought *Plutonian Ode*, "Father Death Blues," "Capitol Air," and "White Shroud" were all exceptional poems. He was relieved to see that Miles had removed some of the more offensive criticism about the negative influence of his teacher.

Having his business office out of his home and Shuai as a productive new resident seemed to be good medicine for Allen. His spirits picked up, and he began to enjoy sexual relationships again. He went to readings, parties, and classes more joyfully than he had in years. Peter remained his one major problem, though. His abuse of alcohol and drugs followed a predictable cycle. At the beginning of each month when he received his VA check, he bought whatever liquor or drugs he wanted and proceeded to raise hell. By the end of the month when his money ran out, he became calm and quiet, only to repeat the same pattern the following month. Allen restrained himself from interfering, but that was difficult since they shared a common wall. His own health had not improved as much as he had hoped, and he was confined in bed with stomach problems several more times before the end of the year.

That fall Patrick Warner came to New York to visit, which always cheered Allen, but his stay was brief and only a temporary relief to Allen's loneliness. His love life was even bumpier and more erratic than before. He was happy one week and sad, jealous, and lonely the next, with various young men passing through his apartment for an evening or at best a few days at a time.

In November Allen was greatly encouraged by the news that the Berlin Wall had been torn down and that the end of the Cold War seemed near. He wrote to many of his friends in East Europe and promised to visit them in the spring. Optimistically he began to think that with the help of a new democratic government in Czechoslovakia led by Vaclav Havel, himself a writer, he might retrieve the notebook that the secret police had taken from him in 1965. It was not to be, but at least the new government made attempts to find it. They did discover a typescript of a Czech translation of excerpts from the notebook, so Allen was able to fill in some of the gaps in his Iron Curtain journals.

1 9 9 0 ～

W ith the promise of new freedom in Eastern Europe, it was even more discouraging for Allen to have to wage another battle against censorship in his own country. In March he wrote to the American Academy and Institute of Arts and Letters to enlist their support in his fight to stop the FCC from banning his poetry over the public airwaves. In spite of the cost, legal briefs had been filed by Pacifica Network on behalf of National Public Radio and the PEN American Center, and Allen hoped that some of the members of the academy would write letters of support, but it proved to be a slow, uphill battle. The climate in the country under President Reagan had become more conservative, and many believed that people like Allen should be censored "to protect the children."

Numbers in U.S. File Cabinet, *CP*, p. 981

At the end of April, Allen flew to a now democratic Prague, meeting Anne Waldman, Nanao Sakaki, and Andy Clausen there. They were all quite interested in the political changes that were under way in Eastern Europe. At one point Allen was shown secret cubbyholes where people, afraid of police arrest, had hidden well-worn copies of his poetry. They gave a poetry reading one night in a large nightclub where Czech president Vaclav Havel sat in the front row, listening to their poetry and drinking beer. Even the new mayor of Prague, Jaroslav Koran, was a poet of stature and had once translated some of Gary Snyder's poetry. He arranged to escort Allen to the main square where fifty thousand students were about to crown a new King of May. The lord mayor introduced Allen as "the longest reigning King of May in history," since they had not been allowed to crown a king after his 1965 visit twenty-five years earlier. He placed a gold paper crown on Allen's head, and Allen read a poem he had written for the occasion, "Return of Kral Majales." Then he passed the crown on to the student who'd been elected that year as his successor.

Return of Kral Majales, *CP*, p. 983

Back in New York, Jack Shuai had removed himself from Allen's sexual life completely, realizing that he did, in fact, prefer women, but he continued to live in the tiny room off the kitchen as Allen's informal housekeeper in exchange for his room and board. His English had improved so much that he was able to hold down several jobs teaching while he continued to work toward his doctorate in English literature from CUNY. In fact, he had more jobs and earned more money than he was permitted under the terms of his scholarship, so at least one of Allen's dependents was prospering. After a brief stopover home, Allen left again for a longer trip to Europe in the summer. He visited London in June on a publicity tour for his new *Lion for Real* album, and with Steven Taylor as his companion, he enjoyed playing the role of tourist again. From England he flew to Turkey where he met up with Philip Glass and Elise and Stanley Grinstein. The Grinsteins were wealthy friends who had offered to pay for Allen's hotel and dinner bills, since they wanted to stay in first-class hotels, well beyond Allen's means. Allen enjoyed Philip's company and was in the process of developing a strong friendship with him based in large part on their shared interest in Buddhism. They spent time talking about Gehlek Rinpoche, who was now beginning to give Allen meditation advice in the void created by Trungpa's death. Twice a year after that Allen went with Philip Glass to Gehlek's retreats, usually as Philip's roommate, "so we can cook up more mischief," Allen liked to say, although the mischief was pretty harmless and mostly of a musical variety. Glass put several more of Allen's poems to music, such as "The Weight of the World Is Love," "Iron Horse," and "The Cremation of Chögyam Trungpa." They made a good creative team and frequently performed together at Buddhist benefits, Glass on piano with Allen reciting. Allen thought the works Glass composed for his poetry were heartfelt and exuberant, but more important, he felt comfortable with him.

As they cruised along the Aegean coast he and Philip visited many of the Greek and Roman ruins, the temples to Diana and Aphrodite and the Temple of the Pythian Oracle at Didyma. Allen's guidebook informed him that there were many more ancient Greek sites preserved in Turkey than in Greece, and the two enjoyed talking about Homer, Herodotus, and Heraclitus. After steeping themselves in ancient culture, they went on to Rome and Spoleto where *Hydrogen Jukebox* was being performed.

Elephant in the
Meditation Hall, *CP*,
p. 984

That summer Alene Lee lost the lease to the office space she was sharing with Allen, so the business office had to move. This time they found quarters on the fourteenth floor of a building overlooking Union Square. They rented one long room with large windows along two walls and closets and a sink at one end, room enough for Allen and three or four people to work at the same time. By now Allen generated enough work to employ Bob and Jacqueline plus a bookkeeper, a secretarial assistant for Bob, and an assistant for Allen's growing photography hobby/business. His bibliographer and a person who catalogued his tape recordings frequently worked in the same space. By now several computers were being used to handle much of the work. Not being mechanical, Allen never learned how to use a computer and had trouble mastering even an electric typewriter. He loved his bright, sunny new office, only a fifteen-minute walk from his apartment, and he would often work late at night captioning photographs and answering his voluminous mail.

One of the more sensitive issues that was frequently discussed in the office was Allen's membership in NAMBLA, the North American Man Boy Love Association. In 1989 Allen had given a benefit reading for that organization at their convention and was one of the few members who allowed his real name to be used in their publications; everyone else preferred anonymity. The idea of an organization that promoted pedophilia was outrageous, even in liberal gay circles, and Allen came under fire from nearly everyone for his support of NAMBLA. He was adamant in his conviction that this was merely another freedom of speech issue. To him, NAMBLA members should be free to speak their minds, like other fringe groups such as the American Nazi Party or the Flat World Society. Allen did love handsome young men, but he wasn't sexually interested in prepubescent boys as many of the other NAMBLA members were. He told the *New York Times,* "I myself don't like underage boys." However, he felt that a person's age was not the issue, rather whether the young men were old enough to know what they felt.

Allen himself never considered physically forcing anyone into anything. He didn't hang around schoolyards waiting for preteens to get out of class, but he sympathized with the men who did, and thought that it was healthy and even helpful for them to be permitted to talk about their sexual feelings frankly and openly. He found it an American homophobic double standard that older men who chased after teenage "lolitas" were snickered at for being silly, but if the same man chased after a high school football hero he was considered a criminal and needed to be removed from society forever. Rosenthal had two young boys and there was never any fear of Allen's molesting them, but there was plenty of incredulity about his belonging to a group like NAMBLA. "How could you join a group of perverts like that?" was a question often asked. Allen was intractable on the subject. Deep down he enjoyed stirring up controversy, and he took every opportunity to tweak a hypocritical society's nose. More disturbing was Allen's comment that he wished he had been taken advantage of by an older man when he was a shy young boy himself. He felt that it might have forced his awareness of his own homosexuality earlier. It was difficult to believe he imagined that being molested would have brought him any good, but he sincerely felt that it would have been helpful to have recognized his sexual identity earlier than he did.

Allen spent the last two weeks of August at a Poetry Congress in Korea. He had agreed to go there only because he had never visited that country before, but the conference turned out to be a colossal waste of his time. He reported it as the equivalent of a meeting with a million Poetry Society of America–type ladies who wrote boring poetry and tittered nervously when he made any candid statements at all. He did his best to call attention to the fact that some Korean poets had been jailed for political reasons, and he read with a group of political dissidents himself. When he had originally been invited to the conference and realized that it was funded by the Korean government, he had faxed them that he would be happy to attend but only with the understanding that he would be free to criticize their government for putting their writers in prison. The official hosts were embarrassed, but there were no incidents. Voznesensky was there, as was the exiled Chinese poet Bei Dao, whom Allen knew, and they had a good time poking around the country together after the conference.

Later in August, Peter found himself in dire straits yet again. He suffered a number of severe episodes and had wrecked his own apartment one more time. It was the same pattern as before, drinking and smoking crack until his money ran out and then suffering through withdrawal until his next VA check came at the first of the month. By September Peter was back in Bellevue, being held for one month this time until he agreed to enter a VA hospital for detox. During one of his more manic periods, Robert Frank had filmed him for an hour as he roamed the subways and streets. When Allen saw it, he thought it "hilarious and tragic both at once." After all these years he still could not believe that Peter needed professional help and medical supervision. With every day that Peter was calm Allen would think, "Well, Peter's okay now, it will all be better." He traveled so much that he missed some of Peter's most demented behavior, but there wasn't much he could have done at that point to help Peter any-

Poem in the Form of a Snake That Bites Its Tail, *CP*, p. 986

way. After several delays, including one postponement in November due to the death of Peter's mother, Kate, Peter went upstate to a rehab center near Elmira. It was a strictly voluntary halfway house, where he could get psychiatric help and perhaps even find a job. To Allen he seemed better immediately. "He's more back to sanity now," he wrote to Corso.

In the meantime, Eliot Katz, Allen's poet friend from Rutgers, had introduced Allen to David Greenberg, another young student from New Jersey. He was an interesting nineteen-year-old poet with a good imagination, and Allen took a liking to him at once. Allen showed him some poetic tricks about how to "tailor" a manuscript, for Allen disliked the word *revise*. Then before long Allen was off to Paris on yet another reading tour.

1991 ～

ON NEW YEAR'S DAY, Allen went to the hospital to visit Alene Lee, who was dying of cancer. He said that the room seemed calm and extremely peaceful, which Allen believed meant that Alene was prepared for death to take her. He had discussed the human mind during its final hours of life with Gehlek Rinpoche, and Gehlek had reminded him that the key was concentration. Rinpoche counseled Allen that when his time came, he should not look back, for it would be too late anyway. He should concentrate as befit the level of Buddhist practice he had attained by that time and meditate on the idea of compassion for all sentient beings. Practicing those thoughts so that he could use them during his final moments became one of Allen's goals. Gehlek further suggested that Allen cultivate feelings of sympathy and emptiness to ensure his own easy passage, advice that helped Allen prepare for his own death.

On January 17, shortly after his last visit with Alene, the U.S. government launched Operation Desert Storm against Iraq in retaliation for Saddam Hussein's invasion of Kuwait. Small demonstrations against the war broke out in many cities, and Allen took part in a few of the marches. He felt a dread in the pit of his stomach over yet another senseless war, realizing it was the "Fall of America" all over again. By the time President Bush ordered a cease-fire in February, Harry Smith had returned to town to receive a Grammy Award at Radio City Music Hall for his overall contribution to music through his work on the *Anthology of American Folk Music.* Allen was happy to see his old friend receive official recognition at last, but he also made sure Harry had a place to

Mistaken Introductions, *CP*, p. 994

stay and a return ticket. There was no way he would ever let him live in his apartment again.

Peter, now in a rehabilitation program upstate at the Bath VA hospital, had been clean and straight for nearly six months. As a side effect of his medication, he had gained a considerable amount of weight; it also fogged his mind and made him sleep a good deal of the time. When he was awake he had barely enough energy to keep up with current political affairs, still his one consuming passion. He spent his few waking hours glued to the TV or reading newspaper accounts of the war. Against the doctor's advice, Allen went up to see him for four days, and they talked about what Peter should do when he was released. Allen was relieved when he saw Peter sober and somewhat lucid for a change, even if he was heavily medicated. Once more he felt that all their troubles were behind them. Now with Peter on lithium, Allen optimistically believed that he would be fine and less subject to violent manias and depressions. Like many patients, though, Peter felt the medications were worse than the addictions and couldn't wait to be off them.

Another thing that cheered Allen at the end of March that year was Twelvetrees' release of his picture book, called simply *Photographs*. It had taken him years to put together but now when he saw the large photo book laid out on his kitchen table he was as proud of it as anything he had ever done. It was a wonderful collection of pictures of all his friends going back as far as 1944, and the book convincingly showcased his considerable talents as a photographer. During the selection process, Allen had to be reminded by his staff that he had not picked any pictures of women to include in the volume, something that he had not noticed until it was pointed out. He decided to include a picture of Juanita Lieberman and one he had taken of his grandmother in 1953, when she sat at the Seder table in their Paterson home. A print of that later picture of Buba was purchased by Peter Galassi, the chief curator of photography for the Metropolitan Museum of Art. He said it was a wonderful example of a picture that worked beautifully as a whole, even though everything about it was wrong individually.

Allen's office staff teased him for omitting images of women, an oversight that Allen made unconsciously and repeatedly. His lack of awareness of women was something that even he counted among his own shortcomings. In a 1982 interview he responded candidly to the question of whether he hated women or not by saying, "Every so often I don't know if it's true or not." Once at a conference he was asked why there weren't many women beat writers, to which Allen replied, "Is it our fault that there weren't any women of genius in the group?" As usual, he tried to be honest and candid, but he couldn't see that he had always been receptive and encouraging to male poets he met, and generally uninterested in the women writers. If he had taken the same amount of time to look at the early work of Joanne Kyger, Hettie Jones, or even Elise Cowen, he would have seen their genius, too.

During the month of May, Allen spent a week in Lawrence, Kansas, visiting with William Burroughs in his little house. William, now seventy-seven, was on a walker recovering from triple bypass surgery, and they both had a great time gossiping. Burroughs had been writing quite a bit and spent the rest of his time creating artworks. He made paintings and sculptures using found materials, sometimes shooting holes in them with shotguns and splattering them with paint to add a random touch. There had already been numerous gallery exhibitions of his work, and he and Allen collaborated on a few paintings during that week. Allen's contributions always tended to be realistic and figurative, while William was much freer, more abstract and expressionistic.

Supplication for the Rebirth of the Vidyadhara Chögyam Trungpa, Rinpoche, *CP*, p. 1008

In June, Peter left the VA hospital and moved back into his apartment for a short time. He and Allen had discussed his accommodations and had decided that he should find an apartment of his own somewhere or move into a room at the Chelsea Hotel. He seemed in fine mental shape to Allen, but after nine months of drug therapy and inactivity, he was sporting a forty-four-inch waist. Twice a week he was supposed to attend support group meetings at the local VA hospital to continue his substance abuse therapy.

Ironically, as Peter was preparing to move out, their decade-long legal battle with the landlord was resolved. The court decided in their favor and directed the landlord to give Allen a lease with Peter's name on it, too. Allen had to pay the landlord twenty-eight thousand dollars in back rent, which he had not been putting aside in escrow as he should have been, and that wiped out his bank account. In fact he had to borrow the last thirty-five hundred dollars from Eugene to settle the case, but he felt that it was well worth it to have his rent-controlled apartment with no strings attached. He could now stay there forever, and it gave him a sense of much-needed security, since that June he would be turning sixty-five and would officially become a senior citizen. Happily he applied for his senior discount bus and subway pass.

On June 11, while a million people crowded into the streets of lower Manhattan to cheer for the victors of Operation Desert Storm, Allen walked through the crowds disappointed that America never seemed to learn its lesson. One hundred thousand Iraqis had died, and Allen wondered how many more would have to die so that America could celebrate the next time. He wrote a poem called "After the Big Parade" as soon as he returned to the apartment and sadly asked, "Have they forgotten the Corridors of Death that gave such victory?"

After the Big Parade,
CP, p. 1009

That summer Allen dedicated most of his time to his classes at Naropa, teaching with Andy Clausen and Gary Snyder. It was Snyder's first summer at Naropa, so for Allen it was a watershed. It meant that every poet he cared about had now taught at the Kerouac School. At the same time he was concerned about his high blood pressure, which was now complicated by diabetes, and he tried to adhere to a strict macrobiotic diet while in Boulder. Despite his valiant efforts, the temptations were everywhere, and it was difficult to eat the right foods, especially on reading tours.

Despite their myriad problems, Allen and Peter went on retreat together after the summer session ended. They even shared the same tent once more at the Rocky Mountain Dharma Center, completely contrary to all the professional advice from doctors and social workers. Though it was only late summer, the nights were already cold and they slept under warm comforters and sleeping bags. Rain and hail kept them awake several nights during their stay, and they enjoyed eating strict vegetarian meals. Allen had trouble catching his breath, and his overall energy level was low at the seventy-five-hundred-foot altitude, but after a few weeks he was able to acclimate and became stronger. Over the period of the month-long retreat, Allen built up the number of prostrations he could do each day. Peter seemed more stable, and Allen was convinced that everything was perfectly all right now.

Allen got little peace, however. He discovered that Harry Smith had run up an enormous tab at the Chelsea Hotel, and Allen felt obligated to help him with that debt. Harry also owed more than five thousand dollars in back rent to his landlord in Boulder, which Allen was trying to gradually pay off. He finally had to tell Harry that he couldn't afford to support him any longer. Allen's continual worry was that as he got older, more and more of his friends would become financially dependent on him. He was the principal supporter of Peter, Harry Smith, Herbert Huncke, Gregory Corso, and several other friends, too, not to mention Jack Shuai and Allen's office staff, who were dependent on him for their paychecks. If something happened to his income or if he could no longer venture out on reading trips, he didn't know how he would take care of them all. Occasionally to lighten the mood Rosenthal would have a little fun distributing Allen's charity checks. He knew that Gregory and Herbert did not get along and bickered continually. Each of them would prefer to pick up his checks privately, but Bob found it irresistible to schedule both of them to come to the office at the same time and to make them wait together while he printed out their checks. They had spent decades competing for Allen's financial support and were jealous of what he gave the other person. Like two spoiled children, they even refused to speak to each other directly, instead asking Bob to tell the other one this or that. When they got their money they went their separate ways, but it was devilish fun to annoy them. On extremely rare days Bob would try to get Harry Smith in the office at the same time to pick up his check, and Harry had a way of chafing everyone. Huncke summed it up at Harry Smith's memorial service when he said, "I didn't like Harry very much, but I didn't want to see him dead either."

Peter's rehabilitation was short-lived once he moved out of the apartment and was on his own. He stopped taking his lithium, since it made him feel bloated and lethargic, and before long he was drinking and using coke again, winding up back at Bellevue in November. With Peter gone, Jack Shuai moved out of his tiny room beside Allen's kitchen and into

the three-room apartment next door, which had been Peter's. Now that Shuai had a steady girlfriend, the couple wanted to have their own place. Jack continued to help Allen with the housekeeping and cooking in exchange for free rent. Financially, Jack was doing pretty well, teaching several college English courses and saving his earnings by living with Allen. Allen regarded him as a cheerful Chinese boy, affectionately taking care of his aging uncle Allen.

The Modern Language Association held its annual convention in San Francisco in December and honored Allen with a special session on *Kaddish*. Allen rarely read the entire poem anymore because he didn't want it to become routine or stale, but for this occasion he made an exception. Helen Vendler and Gordon Ball, now a

Ph.D., chaired the well-attended gathering. By Christmastime, Allen found himself back in the hospital in Cooperstown, diagnosed with congestive heart failure. As he lay in bed he realized that he could not continue doing all the things that he had been pushing himself to do. He asked Rosenthal to cut back on his engagements and to schedule larger blocks of time for rest. Resting to Allen didn't mean that he was inactive, though. Even in the hospital he continued to write, correspond, and call his friends. He usually did more writing when he was sick in bed than he did at other times. His notebook was always on the nightstand, and each time he woke up he'd turn on the light and jot down his dreams or whatever was on his mind.

1 9 9 2 ～

W I T H   T H E   D I A G N O S I S of heart disease made, Allen hoped that his
doctors could provide him some relief, but his chronic medical problems
wouldn't go away. On a trip to Europe in January he wrote a note to Rosenthal updating him: "Persistent night cramps left lower leg, occasional slight
cramps jaw daytime. I'd discontinued Dr. Tallury's[74] Slow-K[75] (potassium) on
phone advice of Dr. Tallury and writ and phone advice of Cooperstown Bassett [Hospital] Dr. Bauer[76] because of increase in Vasotec[77] from 20 mg to 30
mg daily. I guess to compensate for Lasix[78] 40 mg daily generally." It wasn't
clear exactly what was wrong with him, but the doctors tried several adjust-
ments to his medications in the hope that they'd hit on the right combination. Allen had enough energy to perform, but after a reading he would need
to go back to bed to recover his strength. He was unable to make his normal
rounds to all the various museums and sites that he loved. His bronchitis recurred while he was on tour in Amsterdam, but he pushed on through
France and Italy as scheduled.

Lunchtime, *CP*, p. 1016   In mid-February Peter was released from Bellevue into
the care of a supervised halfway house in Brooklyn. The

---

[74] Dr. Viswanathan Tallury: Ginsberg's cardiologist at the time.
[75] Slow-K: A pill to replace potassium lost due to the use of diuretics.
[76] Dr. Michael Bauer: The pulmonologist Ginsberg had been seeing at the Mary Imogene Bassett Hospital.
[77] Vasotec: A medicine for the treatment of high blood pressure.
[78] Lasix: Commonly called "water pill," used to reduce fluid retention in the body.

structured schedule of enforced rehabilitation worked for other addicts, and the doctors hoped it would help Peter as well. As Allen sat at home worrying about him, Bob Dylan called to ask Allen to take his picture. He had seen the portraits in Allen's Twelvetrees book and was impressed with their quality. Flattered, Allen picked up his Rolleiflex camera and the two went to Tompkins Square Park for some outdoor shots, but as soon as he began taking Dylan's picture some of the park derelicts spotted them. The bums assumed that Allen was surreptitiously taking their photos and began pelting them with bottles. They had no idea who Dylan and Ginsberg were and chased them out of the park. In the quieter East River Park Allen was able to finish the photo shoot. "Fame is a curse, without redeeming value," Dylan told Allen. In some ways Allen had the best of both worlds. Although many people recognized him and knew who he was, he could also be anonymous and blend into the streetscape. Dylan, on the other hand, needed guards for his home and couldn't go anywhere in public alone. Even though Allen was aware that the price of fame was a forfeit of privacy, he would have traded places with Dylan   After Lalon, *CP*, p. 1018 in an instant.

In spite of Allen's chronic heart problems, he went to Los Angeles to sing and perform onstage when Glass's *Hydrogen Jukebox* opened there. He stayed up late each night on tour trying to answer all the mail that continually piled up. The doctors warned him that water was accumulating around his lungs and putting a strain on his heart. They told him that a combination of too little sleep and too much salty food was aggravating his condition and would lead to worse problems. In spite of the warning, he went to Holland with Anne Waldman for readings at the Paradiso Club as a favor to the organizer, Benn Posset. Then he spent two weeks on retreat with Gehlek Rinpoche at his Jewel Heart Center in Amsterdam. For a while, he felt rested and went on to perform in opera houses in Turin and Modena with Philip Glass.

Peter seemed to be doing well in the Brooklyn halfway house, but Allen asked for permission to take him out long enough to visit Dr. Oscar Janiger, Allen's cousin, who lived in Santa Monica. Janiger was an expert on the psychological and physical effects of drugs in all their forms, both prescription and recreational, and Allen trusted his judgment. Allen wanted to get Oscar's opinion on all the medication that Peter was being given, because Peter continued to complain about their side effects and wanted to get off them all as soon as possible. Janiger felt that he might not be manic depressive at all, but just improperly medicated. Once he examined Peter, however, he did not recommend any changes and agreed that the medication being prescribed was appropriate for Peter's condition.

In an effort to simplify his life, Allen sold Bedrock Mortar to Gary Snyder around that time and put the proceeds from the sale into an account for Peter. Though he had often dreamed of retiring to the Sierras, Allen had rarely used the cabin since he built it. He realized as he grew older that he would not be able to manage the rugged outdoor life in the mountains. Gary would be able to make better use of the land since it abutted his own property. On the way home, Allen stopped off in Kansas, eager to see Burroughs once again. The two went through a Native American sweat lodge purification ceremony that lasted all afternoon and evening. They even took in the new film *Naked Lunch* by David Cronenberg, which was both horrific and funny. It was no longer Burroughs's novel, but a cut-up of all his works, presented as a collage. Still, they both enjoyed seeing it.

That August Allen went to see Philip Glass in his summer house on a sea cliff in Nova Scotia. After a short visit he went to the nearby Gampo Abbey Buddhist monastery at the tip of Cape Breton Island for another retreat. The monastery overlooked the Atlantic Ocean, and Allen could see whales playing and diving for food from the window of his room. The Buddhists had taken over an old wooden hotel building dramatically situated seventy feet above the sea. It was an ideal location for meditation, with a panoramic view of the ocean. Peter asked to be released from the halfway house in order to accompany Allen on this retreat. He was portly now, but subdued, still taking his medications regularly.

While on retreat Allen had time to read Jean Genet's *Prisoner of Love* and some articles about his late guru, Chögyam Trungpa. In one article, Trungpa described the world as a charnel ground. Everything dies and out of it flowers grow, animals feed, and new things arise, he wrote. Since everything is in flux, he suggested that the individual would be well served to observe this and to appreciate the place where he found himself at any given moment, because tomorrow it would all be different. As with most of Trungpa's comments, Allen thought it a wise observation. He realized that he hadn't observed or written about his own neighborhood in the East Village in a long time. As soon as he was back home, he made it a point to go for a long walk, carefully observing everything that was happening around him.

Marginal notes:

Get It?, *CP*, p. 1023
Research, *CP*, p. 1025

Violent Collaborations, *CP*, p. 1032

Calm Panic Campaign Promise, *CP*, p. 1034

Now and Forever, *CP*, p. 1035

Who Eats Who?, *CP*, p. 1036

He sat down in his bedroom at his father's little desk and wrote "The Charnel Ground," one of his important later poems.

He had barely finished writing the poem when a welcome visitor arrived in town from London. Peter Hale had been working in a pub there for the summer, following his graduation from the University of Colorado, and he came back to the States without any idea what he'd do next. He asked Allen if he needed any help around the office. Allen was only too happy to hire his beautiful young friend, but Rosenthal was not as sure. Every time that he had hired someone who was even remotely involved sexually with Allen, it turned out badly. Bob felt that one of the main reasons he and Allen worked so well together was that he was straight, married with two children, and had never been on Allen's sexual radar screen. There was no sticky layer of sexual history between them. Jacqueline, by now an integral part of Allen's office staff, vouched for Hale, and reluctantly Bob agreed to add him to the payroll. Hale's first job was to work with Allen's ever-growing photography business, and in the course of time, he proved himself a conscientious worker. His responsibilities grew as did Bob's confidence in his abilities, and before long the two had become close friends. Hale settled in to stay in New York and work for Allen permanently when Jacqueline left in late 1994.

> The Charnel Ground, *CP*, p. 1037
>
> Everyday, *CP*, p. 1041

Still trying to figure out various ways to lessen the financial burden of helping his impoverished friends, Allen asked a wealthy Japanese artist, Hiro Yamagata, if he would provide rent money for Corso. Hiro had always admired Corso's poetry and agreed to give Gregory a generous monthly stipend that enabled him to live in relative comfort for the rest of his life. Peter Orlovsky's problems could not be solved as easily. Once back from their retreat, he stopped taking his medication again and immediately wound up back in Bellevue after a binge on coke and alcohol. He went through many cycles from melancholia to mania to depression in the course of a month, and it was difficult to know what he was on at any given time. Allen hired some of the young men who hung around his apartment to transcribe Peter's journals and letters. He hoped that Peter would regain enough interest in his writing to complete an "Orlovsky Reader," which Ferlinghetti had offered to publish. Allen's codependency on Peter's sufferings would not allow him to break from the cycle himself. Everything that Allen tried to do for Peter enraged Peter further, but underneath all the madness and drugs Allen believed that Peter still loved him.

> Fun House Antique Store, *CP*, p. 1042
>
> News Stays News, *CP*, p. 1044

> Autumn Leaves, *CP*, p. 1045

As time passed, Allen forgot his own resolve to slow down and began to do more traveling, more reading, and more photography. He appeared on the Charlie Rose television program and Garrison Keillor's radio show. He was awarded the Chevalier de l'Ordre des Artes et des Lettres by Jacques Lang, the French minister of culture in Paris, and was elected a Fellow of the American Academy of Arts and Sciences in Boston. Even though he knew that he should be conserving his energy, his life remained one continual series of readings, hotel rooms, and airplane flights. His calendar and telephone address books became his most important documents, and he panicked whenever he mislaid them. Late that year a second biography about him, Michael Schumacher's *Dharma Lion*, was published by St. Martin's Press to good reviews. Allen liked Schumacher's handling of the Trungpa affair and his deft evaluation of Allen's poetics better than Miles's version. Since Allen took no issue with Schumacher's handling of the political and personal issues, he did not become obsessed with the matter.

In the Benjo, *CP*, p. 1046

1993 ~

A S H E G R E W O L D E R , Allen's health problems took up a greater part of his time. By following a proper diet he was able to quit taking the insulin the doctors had been prescribing for his diabetes, and he felt much better physically. He lost weight and resigned himself to following a healthy diet for the rest of his life, which for Allen, a man who enjoyed most foods, was difficult to stick with.

New Democracy Wish List, *CP*, p. 1063

His old friend Carl Solomon had been diagnosed with lung cancer early in January. Carl was told that he wouldn't live for more than a year, but he died much sooner, on February 28, days before his sixty-fifth birthday. Earlier Allen had lost friends through tragic accidents and addictions, but now he was beginning to lose comrades to illness and old age. These losses gave him further reason to focus on his own mortality.

He continued to include Peter in his life, despite Peter's problems. One night in February, Peter went with Allen to dinner at the posh La Cote Basque restaurant, as the guests of Lita Hornick. She was a wealthy patron of the arts who had funded many projects through her Kulchur Foundation. She was also the editor of *Kulchur Magazine* and the producer of a well-respected series of readings by contemporary poets at the Museum of Modern Art. For this particular dinner Peter dressed himself in a policeman's uniform that he had found somewhere and caused several minor disturbances at their table in the elegant dining room. Lita, in her wheelchair, politely got through the difficult evening with grace, but asked Allen not to bring Peter again. Peter's caseworker continued to strongly urge Allen to keep his distance from Peter, and Allen claimed that he was trying. An incurable optimist, Allen always expected that Peter would be "all right" soon again, and he didn't want to lose touch with him as he waited for that magical day. On February 24 Allen wrote a letter to Peter asking him to make a budget showing how much money he would need from Allen for his expenses each month. Allen had decided to continue supporting Peter financially, this time in exchange for Peter's promise not to drink anymore. That letter was never sent, because Peter was back in Bellevue before the ink was dry. Upon his release, his caseworker found him a room at the Stratford Arms, a single-resident occupancy hotel on the Upper West Side for people on welfare and in need of supervision. Peter was still sneaking out to drink, but after his long manic period he seemed quieter, now plagued by a profound depression.

Allen's bronchitis returned with renewed force and although he kept his appointments to read at colleges from Idaho to Massachusetts, he suffered for it. The macrobiotic diet helped him slim down to 150 pounds

Peace in Bosnia-
Herzegovina, *CP*, p. 1066

from his high of 167, but he was painfully short of breath every time he climbed the stairs to his apartment. He wrote a short ironic haiku mentioning it in a whimsical way: "Put on my tie in a taxi, short of breath, rushing to meditate."

During the summer, Rosenthal, Hale, and Gens all worked full time in the Ginsberg office on Union Square, with part-time help from a photography assistant, Althea Crawford, and a bookkeeper, Kay Spurlock. Several other people worked on special projects, so on some days it was a full house. In spite of his chronic fatigue, Allen was able to create more work than they could all handle. He was teaching most of the year at Brooklyn College and spending his summers at Naropa. That fall he decided to take a six-month sabbatical from his teaching responsibilities, but to him that meant working even harder on his other projects.

In September he left on an extended reading tour of a dozen European countries, beginning first in Austria. There a group of poets had set up a writing school in Vienna, which they called the Schule Für Dichtung, modeled along the lines of the Naropa Institute. Allen and Anne Waldman adopted the new school as a pet project and helped establish it by giving readings and teaching poetics there from time to time. Allen's primary concern was that the school should also have a meditation component, like Naropa. He told the school's leaders, Ide Hintze, Christian Loidl, and Christine Huber, that without the meditation program, the school would be no different than other writing programs around the world. Vienna was such an

elegant and beautiful city that it was always a pleasure to visit the school.
The mayor of Vienna welcomed them and gave Allen orchestra seats to see
Mozart's *Abduction from the Seraglio*. Once again Allen paid a special visit to
the museum to see Brueghel's *Tower of Babel*, still one of his
all-time favorite paintings.

After the Party, *CP*,
p. 1068

On this trip, as always, Allen exhausted himself, but this
time he was not able to bounce back with a few days' rest. He started to
leave notes requesting that he not be wakened in the mornings. This was unusual for him, as normally he didn't want to miss a thing. Accompanied by
his friend and translator István Eörsi, he took a train from Budapest to Yugoslavia and then on to Germany for several more appearances. While he
was in Europe, Allen's stepmother, Edith, eighty-seven at the time, was admitted to the hospital to receive a pacemaker. He worried about her and
kept in touch daily as she made a remarkably speedy recovery from the surgery. On and on he went, through Poland and England, arriving in Ireland in
October for his first-ever visit there. Bono, the tremendously popular lead
singer of the rock band U2, came to hear him read to a capacity audience of
eight hundred people. After the performance Bono came backstage and
asked Allen if he'd like to perform "Hum Bom!" and "Put Down Yr Cigarette Rag" for a television special he was organizing to be broadcast
throughout Europe and America. Allen was thrilled to be involved with
Bono, who was one of the most intelligent and socially committed of the
new generation of rock stars. For the occasion, Allen wore his new Irish
tweed suit, which he had received in payment for a reading. It was the first
new suit he had owned in decades; everything else in his wardrobe came
from the secondhand shops that he loved so much.

Since it was his first visit to Ireland, Allen had a long itinerary of places
he wanted to see. At the top of this list was County Sligo where William Butler Yeats, his father's favorite poet, had lived. He wanted to stop at the Drumcliffe cemetery to see Yeats's grave and visit the ancient stone tower that
figures prominently in his poem "The Tower." "Under bare Ben Bulben's
head/In Drumcliffe churchyard Yeats is laid" begins the poet's self-written
epitaph, which ends with the famous phrase, "Horseman, pass by!" While
traveling Allen continued to see doctors for checkups and to get his prescriptions refilled. They couldn't offer him more than cough syrup and antibiotics
for his bronchitis, but those helped get him through the most difficult days
on tour. He didn't want to disappoint his audiences by canceling scheduled
appearances, so he was soon off to Norway and then back to Germany. By
that time his bronchitis seemed to have improved, but after reading two

nights in a row in Munich to large crowds, he began to cough

After Olav H. Hauge,
CP, p. 1069
These knowing age,
CP, p. 1070
uncontrollably and was prescribed a stronger antibiotic. Instead of sightseeing, he was forced to spend his free time resting. In Olomouc, in the newly created Czech Republic, he went to the hospital for an EEG and sonogram tests. The doctors there felt that his severe bronchitis was traceable to liver and heart problems, not isolated to his lungs alone. They prescribed extra vitamins and supplementary potassium, before sending him on his way to Poland and Spain.

In Barcelona his oldest friend, Lucien Carr, joined him for a few days of vacation, and they traveled to Madrid where Allen gave huge readings to audiences of hundreds of young fans. Lucien had retired from his job with UPI and welcomed the vacation, but unfortunately both he and Allen came down with the flu. As Ginsberg left for his next stop, Carr returned home, exhausted. Allen had purposely scheduled readings in Athens so that he could visit another old friend, Alan Ansen. Ansen had moved there decades earlier and lived on a quiet street in a nice three-room apartment, which he shared with thousands of books stacked floor to ceiling on industrial steel shelving. Like Ginsberg, Ansen was in declining health, and now he was to the point of being housebound. He had an arthritic hip, which kept him confined to a wheelchair. That was fine with him, he said; all he wanted was to stay home and read his books. With a good-looking young man to do the shopping and the laundry, he was quite content. He and Allen spent a few days discussing Greek prosody and reminiscing about the

C'mon Pigs of Western
Civilization Eat More
Grease, CP, p. 1071
boys they had known and loved. Allen was able to walk around the Plaka at night and up to the Acropolis one afternoon. It was a warm, sunny day in December and the Parthenon was stunning against the bright blue sky.

A few days before Christmas, Allen flew into Tangier on a four-day stopover. He had not been back to Morocco since he left via ferry in 1961 to meet Peter in Israel and continue together to India. This time, he checked in to the Hotel Minzah, the best hotel in town, far beyond his financial means in 1961. After dropping his bag in his room, he went out for a long walk around the town. Tangier hadn't changed much in terms of architecture, but the pace of life was much faster and the traffic more congested than he remembered. He thought about Peter most of the day and remembered fondly all the places they had been together. His first stop was the Villa Muniria, still in business after thirty years. Inside, he broke down in tears on the stairway to their old verandah room, as he recalled how innocently happy they had been. He didn't recollect that this period had been hell for Peter because of Burroughs's hostile jealousy. "What happened to our lives together and can't we ever return to each other?" he sadly wrote in a letter to Peter. He knew it was impossible to go back to his lighthearted youth except in his memory, but he indulged himself in nostalgia for the next few days. Their room in the Muniria seemed smaller than he recalled, the garden smaller, too, but the big palm tree under which he had taken pictures of their whole group was still there. Allen splurged and rented his old room for the day, even though he had a room at the Minzah. He sat on the bed and dreamed of his more carefree youth with Peter. He remembered Peter and Kerouac horsing around on the beach in the bright sunlight. He had snapped their pictures during those happy days, their whole lives ahead of them. It was like a miracle to come back and walk the same streets again.

At dusk he went to the *medina* to sit in the Petit Socco for a glass of mint tea. Now cars clogged the market square instead of donkeys, and a nasty old Arab who recognized that Allen was Jewish told him he should die. The following day he visited Paul Bowles, about to turn eighty-three. Paul was confined to his bed with a bad leg, but they sat and enjoyed a long literary conversation and promised to talk each day that Allen was there. This last stop was restorative for Allen. It was a luxury for him to take the time to remember the old days and to cry about the past. It was good therapy and he was refreshed when he left Tangier.

1994 ～

THE DAY AFTER HE RETURNED TO NEW YORK, Allen flew to Ann Arbor for a weeklong *Vajrayogini* retreat at Jewel Heart with Gehlek Rinpoche. Then, at last, he returned home to East Twelfth Street. No matter how often he promised, it was impossible for Allen to leave Peter alone. Once more Peter had left the halfway house and was living in the East Village in cheap flophouse hotels. He had moved all his manuscripts and possessions into a storage locker and wanted to live a nomadic urban life for a while. He longed to escape the watchful eyes of the social workers, and by the time Allen got back, he was staying in places where other near-destitute street people lived on a few dollars a day. Allen took Peter to dinner and found him sober. That convinced Allen that Peter was rehabilitated at least, and he wondered immediately if he shouldn't give him some money to tide him over.

Here We Go 'Round the Mulberry Bush, *CP*, p. 1073

That term Allen taught "The History of the Beat Generation" and two other courses at Brooklyn College, but before long he was overtaxing himself again. Allen was a marvelous teacher who demanded a great deal from his students. He never made a distinction between literature classes and writing classes, but always discussed them together, feeling they were inseparable. He had learned to pick out gems of language and rhythm from Kerouac and Burroughs, and he encouraged his students to read the classics. More than anything, Allen tried to pass on what he had learned from his own mentors. Professor Ginsberg assigned readings and work for his classes, trying to give

them a deeper perception of the world. He carefully read and graded all
their papers himself, to encourage them. He willingly made himself available to any student who wanted extra help. With three
classes, there were too many students to accommodate,
since he gave individual attention to each one. In addition to
his classes, he also continued to host the poetry reading pro-

Tuesday Morn, *CP*,
p. 1074

gram that brought in writers from around the country every week. At the
end of each term he threw a big party for his classes at his apartment, which
was something that he and his students always looked for-
ward to. He couldn't give any of this up, but it was much too

God, *CP*, p. 1076

rigorous for him after his four-month "sabbatical" in Europe.

Although he now considered himself a student of Gehlek Rinpoche,
Allen remained equally devoted to Trungpa's heritage and to the Naropa
Institute in particular. One day the Gap clothing chain asked Allen to endorse their khaki pants for an advertising campaign, which also featured
the images of Kerouac and Marlon Brando. Allen had always turned down
commercial endorsements, but this time it struck him as the perfect opportunity to help the always financially strapped Kerouac School. He decided to ask for an exorbitant amount of money, twenty thousand dollars,
for the use of his picture. He felt they would never pay that amount, but if
they did, all the money would go to Naropa. Much to his surprise, the
Gap took him up on his offer and before he knew it, ads were appearing
showing him wearing khaki pants, as he sat cross-legged on the floor in
front of his bedroom shrine. He insisted that they run a disclaimer with
the ad, stating that the proceeds would go solely toward funding Naropa,
but a swell of criticism arose. Most of those who complained about Ginsberg "selling out" did not bother to read the disclaimer in their rush to
criticize. The controversy fell into the category of "you can't win." Allen
couldn't understand why people believed it was wrong for him to make
money from his work or to accept a fee for his time. He lived in near
poverty because of his generosity, both to friends and to the causes he believed in. The Gap ad wasn't a selling out, but an extension of his generosity. No other hero of the counterculture was held to such strict standards.
Dylan, Mick Jagger, and all of the remaining Beatles lived in fabulous luxury compared to Allen, and still they had the respect of their fans. The
money helped the Kerouac School limp through another summer, so
Allen felt it was worth the controversy. Later Allen allowed Microsoft to
use his image for double what the Gap had paid. That money also went directly to Naropa, but by then the criticism had evaporated.

Ah War, *CP*, p. 1077

Excrement, *CP*, p. 1078

New Stanzas for *Amazing Grace*, *CP*, p. 1080

City Lights City, *CP*, p. 1081

That spring, from May 17 to 22, New York University put together a conference on the beats, calling it "The Beat Generation: Legacy and Celebration." It marked one of the first times that a major institution recognized the importance of the writers of his circle, and for the first time it brought together all the scholars and academicians who had studied and taught the beats with the writers themselves. It was the largest such gathering since Naropa's twenty-fifth anniversary of *On the Road* and many of the older writers saw each other for the last time. Since it was in Allen's "hometown," he felt responsible and worked with cochair Ann Charters to make everyone feel welcome. The high point of the week was the Town Hall readings by Ginsberg, Ferlinghetti, Corso, Amram, McClure, and others.

Allen's own Buddhist practice suffered as a result of his compulsive work habits. He was so busy that most of his days went by without time to meditate. For that reason he looked forward to the Buddhist retreats as an enforced way to catch up on his practice. He especially liked Gehlek and trusted in him and his teachings. His advice to Allen was to keep in the public eye, to keep writing and giving readings because it gave lucidity and joy to the world. The advice supported Allen's own need to satisfy his ego by performing onstage.

Allen's long-awaited boxed set of four CDs was issued that year under the title *Holy Soul Jelly Roll*. It was a compilation of all the music Allen had composed over the thirty years since he had returned from India and begun chanting the Hari Krishna mantra at each of his readings. The cuts went back even further to a capella songs that he had taped as early as 1953. Those songs were followed by the collaborations he did with Bob Dylan, Elvin Jones, and Don Cherry and on through his work with the cellist Arthur Russell. Hal Willner produced the recordings and the set was received with high critical praise. Reviewers noted that it was an "astounding aural compendium" and that Allen gave an "inspired performance." All his old tapes had been floating around for years unused in his archive, so Allen was happy to have what he called his "treasures in eternity" available for public consumption.

Naropa celebrated its twentieth anniversary that July, and Allen flew out to take part in the celebrations. The whole month was devoted to visits from great poets such as di Prima, Snyder, Creeley, Ferlinghetti, Baraka, and Kenneth Koch, who each stayed in residence for at least a week at the Kerouac School. The first week of July was a tribute to Allen himself, during which time the new college library was officially dedicated as the "Allen Ginsberg Library." Dignitaries spoke and a choir of yellow-hatted Buddhist monks delivered their spellbinding deep bass chants. Each day panels were held that focused on Allen, his life and work. In the evenings the poets read to packed audiences in the auditorium. As a special favor, Ken Kesey drove down from Oregon and put on his newest play, *Twister*, late one night at the Boulder Theater. He used racial stereotypes in a way that proved offensive to some in the crowd, and many found it extremely long and disappointing overall. Allen, who had a small cameo in the play, rushed to the defense of his old friend. Kesey triumphed in the end by bravely reading his children's book, *Little Tricker the Squirrel Meets Big Double the Bear*, the following evening in front of a packed house full of people who had threatened to walk out in protest if he dared go onstage. Everyone sat enthralled, as Kesey mesmerized a crowd of one thousand people with his rendition of a story about a bear. It was a classic display of Kesey's courage. The enrollment that summer was larger than ever, encouraging proof that the school was on firm footing at last. Sadly, Peter couldn't be with him that summer as he had been admitted to the mental ward of St. Luke's Hospital.

In the late summer it came as something of a surprise to everyone when Stanford University negotiated the purchase of Ginsberg's enormous archive. Collecting manuscripts, correspondence, and books to document his world and the Beat Generation had been Allen's lifelong pursuit. His archive included everything from the original manuscript of *Howl* to his most recent journals and letters. Allen had hoped that someday Columbia University would acquire the collection, since the beats were born on the campus, but their budget and the library director's lack of enthusiasm for Allen's work prevented them from making an offer for his papers.

In the end, Allen's deteriorating health was the real motivation for the sale. Although he had a lease on his rent-controlled apartment, where he knew he could live forever, he found it increasingly difficult to climb the stairs to his fourth-floor walk-up. The older he became, the more he had to stop to catch his breath on each landing. His solution was to buy something either on the first floor or in a building equipped with an elevator, but by the mid-1990s, the East Village was the hottest real estate district in New York and rents were skyrocketing. Allen's only asset was his archive, which had once been appraised for well over five million dollars. Such a figure wasn't possible to realize unless the collection was broken up into smaller sections, which Allen did not want to even consider. It was then that Stanford negotiated with Allen's archivist, myself, and offered one million dollars for everything. That was more money than he ever dreamed of having and enough for him to buy a modest apartment. An agreement was reached and I packed up hundreds of boxes of material and shipped them to California. Everyone agreed not to disclose the sale price, but true to form, Allen could not be anything but candid and volunteered the information to the first reporter who asked him. When the *San Jose Mercury News* heard about the sale and the price Stanford paid, they had a field day. Allen was still a controversial figure, so his critics opined that no university should pay that kind of money to Allen Ginsberg. Letters were written condemning the library for buying the papers of a "known pedophile" like Ginsberg, a member of NAMBLA, not to mention his being a communist and a dirty-mouthed beatnik. One college paper led with the headline, "Pro-Pedophile Poet Paid $1M by Stanford." None of the newspapers bothered to research what the actual value of the purchase was, or what was included in the sale. On the other side of the aisle, Allen was also criticized and taken to task by the liberal press for selling out, as he had been for the Gap ad.

After expenses and taxes Allen had just enough money left to buy and renovate a loft in an elevator building on East Thirteenth Street, around the corner from his old apartment. Although he found the loft through a newspaper ad, it was a coincidence that the building was owned by another friend, the painter Larry Rivers, who was selling a few of the lofts in his building. Allen signed the contract, and he and Bob began to draw up plans with an architect to convert the open space into an apartment with space set aside for an office. The loft would be wheelchair accessible and convenient for any future health contingency. Bob felt that with Allen's declining health, it was a good time to reintegrate the office into his living quarters, making it convenient for someone to always be close at hand.

At the end of the year Allen spent a few weeks in Paris as the guest of *Nouvel Observateur* with George Condo, a painter who had become fond of Allen. Condo did a few portraits of Ginsberg while he was there, one of which was later used on the cover of Ginsberg's *Selected Poems*. Allen's friend and assistant Peter Hale went along for company and to help Allen with practical matters like carrying luggage and arranging tickets. It made travel easier for Allen, whose heart, per his doctor's diagnosis, was now functioning at only 70 percent of capacity.

1995 ~

EVEN AFTER YEARS OF SEPARATION, Peter Orlovsky was never far from Allen's thoughts. In January, Allen wrote to Snyder, "Orlovsky now 6 months clean, at present at Spring Lake Ranch in Vermont, I'll visit him this weekend, after 3 months in rehab in New Jersey. So there's some hope after 10 years, maybe he hit bottom after all." Even though he continued to be concerned about Peter, Allen's own health was not improving. He became short of breath more easily and felt less energetic with each passing day. He was looking forward to moving into his new apartment, but the space needed to be completely renovated before it would be ready to occupy. In February he went to Stanford to visit the new home of his archive and gave a reading there. The library staff was amazed by the warm reception Allen received from their students. The large auditorium was jammed, and Allen made room enough onstage to squeeze in a few dozen more listeners. As soon as he got back to New York, though, he had to rest and recuperate and he canceled book tours to Boston, Denver, and San Francisco. These cancellations were out of character for Allen and an indication of just how tired he felt. He slowed down, but went to Nebraska and Ohio for Buddhist benefits with Philip Glass. He doubted that he would be strong enough by the summer to go with Gehlek Rinpoche on a proposed trip to Tibet, but he hoped to make the journey. It was the one important place on earth he had never been able to visit. Gehlek's plans fell through, but Allen wouldn't have been strong enough to make the trip anyway.

Newt Gingrich Declares War on "McGovernik Counterculture," *CP*, p. 1082

The Ballad of the Skeletons, *CP*, p. 1091

Even in bad health, Allen had great determination. In April he mounted a campaign against the diminishment of funding for the NEA in the wake of a controversial Robert Mapplethorpe photography exhibition, which had been partly funded by NEA money. Politicians like Newt Gingrich and Jesse Helms had declared war on the counterculture, and Allen felt it was the intention of the right to control people's minds, as Stalin or the televangelists did. He was prepared to take on a new fight.

His spring itinerary called for an April trip to Ireland and Wales where he spent a few leisurely days in Galway with Bono. The two found that they had a mutual interest in Oscar Wilde's work and spent a good deal of time discussing political issues like unrest in Central America and the practices of the World Bank. Bono liked Allen and later said that Allen "didn't like art in a box, he liked art to stray out of its boundaries into real life." In Dublin Ginsberg visited Joycean sights and gave three readings before stopping at Dylan Thomas's hometown of Swansea, Wales. There he visited Thomas's old house and saw his writing desk in a tiny shack that overlooked the bay. By the time he got back to New York his new loft had been gutted and the renovations of the large open space were well under way.

Allen's newest discovery that summer was Geoffrey Manaugh, a seventeen-year-old poet who had approached Allen at a reading and handed him a copy of a self-published chapbook of his poetry called *Mystic's Fists*. Allen told the boy that he was very busy and probably wouldn't be able to respond to the poems, let alone write an introduction for them, which was what Manaugh had hoped for. That night Allen stayed up late reading the poems and declared them extraordinary, even reading a few in front of an audience at Naropa the next day. Immediately, he wrote to Manaugh asking to see more poems, and before long Allen was writing to Ferlinghetti to propose Manaugh for a book. The promising poet was bowled over by Allen's generous spirit and his attempts on his behalf to find a publisher, even if no book came as a result.

Every time his phone rang it seemed to be with an offer of a new project. Colin Still, a British filmmaker, asked Allen to sit for a series of interviews for a new Ginsberg film biography he was making for the BBC, and Allen agreed. At the start of June, he was asked to do a week of readings at the Knitting Factory, an avant-garde music club in Tribeca. Allen thought it would be great to take advantage of the opportunity to read straight through the entire manuscript for his *Selected Poems*, from beginning to end. Before the reading he asked a few friends to read his *Collected Poems* and point out the work they thought worthy of being included in a shorter selected edition. He collated all their lists, added some more of his own, and came up with a four-hundred-page collection. That list became the basic structure for the Knitting Factory readings. He divided the poems into ten segments and, for two shows a night, five nights in a row, Allen read chronologically through his entire body of work. It was a monumental series of readings, possibly unequalled in the field of poetry. Unfortunately the publicity was not well organized and no one had explained the concept to the press, so many fans thought he was going to read the same work at every performance each night. Since they only thought they needed to come once, many waited until later in the week, so the audience the first two nights was sparse when he read his masterpieces *Howl* and *Kaddish*. By the time the news spread about what he was doing, larger crowds showed up for every performance. He moved chronologically through his more recent work and on the final nights there were sell-out crowds standing to hear him read. Steven Taylor accompanied him on a selection of his greatest musical hits to begin and end each set of poetry. It was rewarding for everyone, especially Allen, who was able to see which poems worked well before an audience and which should not be included in a "greatest hits" compilation. Naturally, he was quite exhausted by the end of the week.

The intensity of those readings helped lead to a painful following week spent in bed with a pulmonary embolism. The embolism caused knifelike pains in the right side of his chest and a blood clot detached from his right heart valve. Had it been the left side of his heart, the doctors told him, it would have been much more dangerous. Allen recovered in time to help New York University celebrate Kerouac's life with a special conference in early June called "The Writings of Jack Kerouac." One panel Allen was on was interrupted by a few people who wanted to discuss Jan Kerouac's lawsuit against the heirs of the Kerouac estate. Allen defused the situation by asking the audience what they wanted to talk about, and they overwhelmingly voted to hear the scheduled speakers, much to the disappointment of the protesters. At the closing extravaganza at Town Hall on June 6, a group of poets calling themselves "The Unbearables" formed a small picket line in front of the theater. They were protesting Ginsberg's "selling out," and they argued that the conference's relatively high registration price of $120 was unfair. They singled out Ginsberg, since he had just sold his archive to Stanford, and they harped on the Gap ad, since they had not read or understood his disclaimer. The irony of their protest is that one of the leaders of The Unbearables was about to sell his own archive to NYU's Fales Library and pocket the money for himself. However, it made good media theater, which was what the unbearable poets craved most.

With a full schedule, Allen flew off to Venice to exhibit 108 of his photographs during the Biennale. Hiro Yamagata, whose wildly painted limousines were on exhibit there, had arranged for a gallery to display Allen's pictures at the same time. A beautiful book of photographs of Yamagata's and Ginsberg's work was published for the occasion. After a busy few days in Venice, Allen was exhausted and went off with Francesco Clemente and his family to their home in Amalfi. By now Clemente had been a friend of Allen's for more than a decade and had sketched his portrait several times. He realized Allen needed a quiet rest, and Amalfi was just the right place for that. To Allen, Clemente was an aristocrat who lived the kind of genteel artist's life that Allen knew nothing about. Francesco and his wife Alba's house looked out over the seaside village to the church steeple on the other side of the valley, a fairy tale setting. There were 180 steps from the house down to the beach, where Allen could relax with no one to bother him. Alba had been born in this house, and they returned each summer to sit under the lemon trees in the terraced gardens and renew themselves far away from the supercharged New York art world. Allen hoped that complete rest and convalescence would restore him as well. While he was in Amalfi, he received word through Bob that Edith had made another trip to the hospital. Worried, he wrote to her to hang on so she could enjoy the special room he was planning for her in his new loft. He wanted her to move in with him now that she was getting older, so she could share in the pleasure of an elevator and the convenience of city living. Her health improved and she was home before Allen returned from his trip.

For a whole week, Allen relaxed in Amalfi, puttering around on the Clementes' boat and sitting in the sun on the sandy beach. It was a rare treat for him to take so much time off doing nothing, and the rest did him a world of good. Clemente was mounting a large exhibition in a chateau in France's Loire Valley, and Allen left with him to see the installation process before he returned to New York on June 28.

Pastel Sentences (Selections), CP, p. 1083

He arrived home to find that Peter was staying in the Hazelden Fellowship Halfway House on Stuyvesant Square, a few blocks away. It was then that he realized that when he moved out of his East Twelfth Street apartment in the fall, he would lose the prized rent-controlled apartment forever. Since Peter was currently in a rehab program, Allen speculated that he would soon be fine and able to live on his own again. He felt that he could easily turn the old apartment over to Peter, since his name was on the lease, too. Immediately, his staff and his friends counseled Allen against this unrealistic plan. Since the psychiatrists and social workers had told Allen repeatedly that he should let Peter be independent and live his own life, a move like that would only draw Peter back into Allen's world again. Peter, for his part, wanted to escape from the supervision of the halfway house program at any cost. He wanted no one to have control over his life, and he would agree to anything if it meant he would be able to live independently. Naturally, he promised Allen that he would stay straight and clean. So plans were made that Peter would move into the old apartment as soon as Allen's new loft was ready. Allen would help by paying for a live-in companion to chaperone Peter and take care of his medications and day-to-day needs.

Work on the new loft proceeded slowly. It was a large, twenty-one-hundred-square-foot space that had been used for years by artists as raw work space and was not designed for residential use. A lot of demolition had to be done before the new bathrooms, kitchen, and partition walls could be built. Allen's idea was to keep one big room that could be divided into smaller units by a series of sliding doors and panels. There would be more space for guests and large groups of meditators could sit in front of his Buddhist shrine. Even before the work of demolition began, Allen hosted a catered dinner there for the benefit of Gehlek Rinpoche's Jewel Heart *sangha*, at which he and Philip Glass performed for a group of friends and supporters seated at rented tables. True to form, Allen was more enamored of the young waiters who had been sent by the caterer to serve the meal than by his official guests. The loft was bright and airy, with windows on three sides, looking out on the steeple of the church next door. Allen wouldn't miss the early morning bells he'd grown accustomed to on East Twelfth Street. Surprisingly, he became enthusiastic about the design phase of the project. It was his idea to turn an old elevator shaft into a walk-in closet, and he requested that small windows be placed in the wall by the elevator, so that he could see who was in the hallway. He even placed one window in the bathroom wall so he could look out onto First Avenue as he sat on the toilet. It was obvious that he was enjoying himself and happily anticipating settling into his new   Nazi Capish, *CP*, p. 1087 quarters.

In mid-October Allen flew to London to read once more at the Albert Hall, this time with Anne Waldman, Tom Pickard, and a group of other poets. At the end of the evening the audience of two thousand was taken by surprise when Paul McCartney joined Allen onstage to perform a rendition of Allen's "The Ballad of the Skeletons." Paul and Allen had become close friends since Lennon's death, and Allen had often made weekend visits to McCartney's home, where he and Linda McCartney swapped tips about photography. Before the Albert Hall concert, Allen had asked Paul if he

could recommend a young musician to back him up during the perform-
ance, and Paul replied that he would like to volunteer, since he admired the
Skeletons poem. Allen rehearsed a few times with him, and Paul even filmed
Allen reading the poem on his own super-eight-millimeter
Is About, *CP*, p. 1089   movie camera. Performing with Paul, Allen felt once again
his old desire to be a rock 'n' roll star.

By now both the Beat Generation and Allen Ginsberg had become the
subject for many retrospectives and conferences. Beat courses were popular
on college campuses, and the number of dissertations about Beat Generation writers grew every year. In the early days the beats had not even been
considered literate by the academy, and now countless Ph.D. theses were being written about them and their influence on the course of American literature and culture. Ginsberg welcomed these retrospectives in order to
convey his messages about resistance to censorship and the importance of
meditation to the next generation. He certainly didn't mind the fact that
dozens of young students would line up to talk to him after a reading. Always looking to shock people, he candidly told one college magazine interviewer that one of the main reasons he liked teaching was that it gave him
the chance to meet a lot of good-looking young men.

The Beat Generation became an even hotter commodity by the end of the
year when the Whitney Museum unveiled its giant exhibition "Beat Culture
and the New America: 1950–1965." This exhibition established the legitimacy
of the movement as both a literary revolution and a fertile period for the visual
arts. Allen loaned them anything they wanted for the exhibition out of his own
collection and sent lists of suggested artists and writers they should consider for
inclusion. Lisa Phillips, the curator for the show, singled Allen out in her ac-
knowledgments because of the help he gave her in developing the exhibit. The
show opened to record crowds in New York until February 4,
"You know what I'm   1996, when it moved on to the Walker Art Center in Min-
saying?," *CP*, p. 1096   neapolis, and then finally to the M. H. de Young Memorial Museum in San Francisco, where it also set attendance records.

1 9 9 6 ～

AT THE BEGINNING OF 1 9 9 6 Allen found himself in a Boston hospital for a short stay while he took another battery of tests. His heart specialist practiced in Boston and wanted to get to the bottom of Allen's many health problems. After the results were in, his diagnosis remained congestive heart failure, so Allen resolved to rest as much as he could during the coming year. Once more he asked Rosenthal to cut back his reading schedule and to program more time for rest after every appearance. Of course, Allen himself could not refuse when someone asked him to read, and he continued, over Rosenthal's protests, to fill in blank days on his calendar with new engagements. Later that January he performed at one of his regular venues, McCabe's Guitar Shop in Santa Monica. While there he worked on six poster-size lithographs of his drawings that Stanley Grinstein's Gemini G.E.L. artist's workshop planned to publish in a limited edition. Now he could expand his resume to include graphic artist in addition to poet and photographer.

Bowel Song, *CP*, p. 1097

Popular Tunes, *CP*, p. 1098

Besides poetry, music remained the one constant in Allen's life. French television had sent a team of people to set up a recording session with Ornette Coleman, Ginsberg, Corso, and Huncke in Coleman's Harlem studio. In the limousine that the producers had sent to collect the poets, Allen began to scold Huncke. Herbert had not applied his recent social security checks to his large unpaid bill from the Chelsea Hotel as they had agreed he would, spending the money on drugs instead. Allen was upset, since he had been supplementing Huncke's income out of his own pocket. It embarrassed Herbert to be chastised this way in front of strangers, and for once he spoke up bravely in his own defense, saying, "Allen, I will not have you talk that way to me in front of these people." Allen shut up. Once at the recording studio, they got down to serious work, recording several poems with Ornette responding on the saxophone.

It didn't seem that Allen was even trying to slow down as he appeared in Princeton, New York, Paris, Prague, Italy, France, and the Czech Republic, all within the space of a few months. Traveling with Peter Hale had worked out so well on his last trip that Allen invited him on tour again. By this time Hale knew the guitar well enough to accompany Allen in place of Steven Taylor, who had gone back to graduate school at Brown University to get his degree in ethnomusicology, specializing in the punk underground of the East Village. Allen also took along Geoffrey Manaugh, the young poet he had met in 1994; it was Geoff's first European trip. In Paris they were the guests at an enormous book fair, and Allen was greeted by President Jacques Chirac himself. Then they flew to Prague, where Allen asked Manaugh to read a few of his poems at his reading. Allen volunteered to share some of his fee with the young writer. Having only read onstage once or twice before in his life, Manaugh suffered from stage fright and was glad when he finished his poems. Manaugh spent most of his time exploring the nightlife with younger friends he made along the way, and Allen couldn't keep up with him. He wished Geoff had stayed by his side more, but he enjoyed showing him the sights when he could. Traveling with two handsome young men made Allen happy regardless. One night at a dinner another young man came up to Allen, wanting to speak with him about the cosmology he saw in Allen's poetry, but all Allen wanted to know was whether the young man had ever slept with another man. Dejected, the boy walked away after a while, shattered by his hero's singlemindedness. It seemed that Allen regarded sex as the only important experience worth talking about, and many of the people he met were disappointed. In Milan, after meeting with Nanda Pivano, Allen went on a minor shopping spree and splurged on a one-hundred-dollar Borsolino hat that made him look distinguished with his white beard and black cashmere scarf.

Five A.M., *CP*, p. 1100

Work on the loft continued while he was away, and Allen remained actively involved once he got back. Although Bob took care of the day-to-day details, Allen enjoyed shopping for the bathroom tiles and made suggestions for heated towel racks, a bidet, and an electric pants presser. In early August, after his courses ended at Naropa, he stopped in Lawrence to see

Power, *CP*, p. 1101

Anger, *CP*, p. 1102

Multiple Identity
Questionnaire, *CP*,
p. 1103

Burroughs, who was recovering from a minor stroke. Together they received the news that Herbert Huncke had passed away in New York's Beth Israel Hospital on August 8. Allen got back in time to view his old friend's body once more and to say goodbye at the funeral home before the cremation. He noted that after all the years and all the drugs, Huncke's corpse looked distinguished, with its thin, calm face, dark hair, and mustache.

By late summer, the renovations to his loft were nearing completion, and Allen began to move his furniture, books, and clothes to the new place. Peter was equally eager to move into East Twelfth Street as soon as Allen was out, so Allen left much of the furniture there for Peter. To relax, Allen went shopping. For the first time in his life he owned his own apartment, and he decided to have fun decorating it. In his wallet he kept a list of all the Salvation Army and Goodwill stores in Manhattan, and whenever he found himself near one of them, he went furniture shopping, invariably buying something. One day a white leather sofa was delivered, the next day a kitchen table, then lamps and an odd fixture with lights and mirrors that appeared to have been used as a liquor cabinet. Allen intended to use it for his stereo equipment. Nothing cost more than a few dollars, but his love of shopping was a side of Allen that no one had seen before. By the end of September, although the contractors were still at work on the space, Allen moved in. "I'm happy for the transitory moment," he wrote to Pivano.

Don't Get Angry with Me, CP, p. 1104

His video of "The Ballad of the Skeletons" with music by McCartney and Glass was released that September and received significant air time on MTV. The video's director, Gus Van Sant, had made an interesting film of Allen singing his song in an old Uncle Sam hat, belting out the lyrics like an old-time blues singer. Van Sant and Allen had lectured together at Princeton on one occasion. When Allen saw that Van Sant played the guitar, he asked him to accompany him onstage, so Gus was familiar with Allen's work firsthand. The new, professionally made music video format gave Allen a hint of what direction his songs and music might take in the future. To Allen, his dreams of becoming a rock 'n' roll star finally appeared to be a possibility.

Swan Songs in the Present, CP, p. 1105

In November, San Francisco's de Young Museum unveiled the West Coast version of the beat exhibition that had

Gone Gone Gone, CP, p. 1106

been on display the previous year at the Whitney Museum. The organizers invited Allen to fly out for their opening-night gala. It was another great event, at which Allen and Ferlinghetti read a bit of their work, and then everyone went out to a Chinese dinner with Dennis Hopper and other old friends from earlier beat days. To coincide with the beat show, Allen's photography was hung at the Koch Gallery down the street from the site of the Foster's cafeteria where Allen and Peter had pledged their undying love in 1955. As a condition for that gallery show, Allen made them promise to also mount an exhibition of Robert LaVigne's paintings. Robert was a difficult artist to work with and that bit of generosity cost Allen much extra work, coaxing and helping Robert to prepare his paintings for the show. Even with Allen's help, Robert was not able to assemble his pieces in time for the gallery's deadline.

After the openings, he flew off to other commitments, only to return to California again in December for a benefit at the Cow Palace. There he and his friend Mark Ewert (who was dressed as a high school "drag queen from Hell" that night) were backstage when they met Beck, a young rock star, who was also performing in front of the fourteen thousand in attendance. Allen and Beck hit it off, and the younger musician offered to perform with Allen at some future time, but for now Allen needed to slow down again on another retreat. At year's end he wrote to István Eörsi, "I leave tomorrow for ten day Buddhist retreat with Gehlek Rinpoche in Michigan, then January 8th to Boston, enter hospital for hernia operation and heart observation. I retire from Brooklyn College this May 1997 and be able to travel abroad more freely if health permits. Congestive heart failure comes and goes."

1997 ~

BETWEEN JANUARY AND MARCH, Allen made a few trips back and forth between his specialist in Boston and his apartment in New York, but his medical condition did not improve. By March he had canceled several more readings and was considering dropping his plans for an upcoming trip to Italy in April altogether. He hated to cancel, so he waited with hopes that he would feel better soon. For the first time in nearly a decade, he asked Peter Orlovsky to go with him and spend some time in Milan with Nanda Pivano. Allen thought he might be able to do it if he combined his need for rest with the trip and asked his Italian friend Luca Formenton, "Do you know of any inexpensive accommodation I can make for convalescence for a week or so? I can pay moderate rent." The doctor suggested that he spend at least another month in bed before making such an exhausting trip, but Allen continued to wait before canceling the trip, all the while watching his diet and monitoring his heart closely. It gave him a lot of free time to write, but most of what he came up with was nothing more than short ditties to familiar old tunes.

Virtual Impunity Blues, *CP*, p. 1119

Richard III, *CP*, p. 1129

Death & Fame, *CP*, p. 1130

Sexual Abuse, *CP*, p. 1133

Variations on Ma Rainey's See See Rider, *CP*, p. 1144

A fellow named Steven, *CP*, p. 1135

Half Asleep, *CP*, p. 1136

Objective Subject, *CP*, p. 1137

When Rosenthal got to the new loft on March 21, Allen was in great discomfort. He had scheduled an appointment to see his heart specialist in Boston the following week, but as Allen was in a great deal of pain, Bob decided to take immediate action. He called Joel Gaidemak, Allen's cousin who was also a medical doctor, for his opinion. After hearing the symptoms, Joel recommended getting Allen to a hospital as soon as possible. It was two short blocks to Beth Israel Hospital's emergency room, but Allen wasn't strong enough to walk that far, so they borrowed a wheelchair from the neighborhood drugstore and pushed him. After a brief wait Allen was admitted for observation and further testing. Even in the emergency room he could not escape his fame, as a young doctor handed him a poem he had written and asked for Allen's comments. As he had for his entire life, Allen looked it over and gave him a few pointers. They assigned him a private room in the Tenensky Pavilion, which had a view of his new loft down the street. That night in bed with a shaking hand, Allen wrote lines expanding his poem "American Sentences": "See the vast void infinite, look out the window into the blue sky," lines reminiscent of his Harlem epiphany fifty years earlier. He also wrote sadly, "That's why I feel alone. That's how I know I'm going to die." For several days he stayed in his hospital bed writing short poems and little scatological verses while the doctors continued to run tests on him. He had several visitors and still managed to complete a good deal of work. Peter Hale dropped in from the office every few hours to bring his mail and pick up his handwritten work for typing.

American Sentences 1995–1997, *CP*, p. 1141

By March 27 the doctors had made no headway in pinpointing the source of Allen's pain and decided to conduct more extensive testing, including a liver biopsy. On the morning of March 30, the results of the biopsy came back and Dr. Chain walked into Allen's room to give him the news. "How does it look?" asked Allen. "Not very good," was the doctor's reply. "Cancer?" Allen asked weakly, but he already knew the answer. The doctor said that they had found many cancer nodules in the liver and that it was too advanced for treatment. They were uncertain, but they thought he might have six months or perhaps as much as a year left to live, but Allen doubted their optimism.

Starry Rhymes, *CP*, p. 1150

Thirty State Bummers, *CP*, p. 1151

Bop Sh'bam, *CP*, p. 1158

Dream, *CP*, p. 1159

Rosenthal, Hale, and I were just sitting down at that time to eat lunch in the new kitchen of the loft to celebrate the unpacking of the last box of books. They were now all neatly arranged on the shelves in Allen's loft. We had ordered steamed bass, one of Allen's favorites, from the Chinese restaurant on the corner. It had taken months to unpack and organize everything, and the bookshelves had been the last things to be set in place. No sooner had we begun to eat than the phone rang. Bob answered it and went pale. Allen told him that he had terminal liver cancer. Allen seemed to accept the news calmly most of the day except for a few tears he shed when Orlovsky came to the hospital in the afternoon.

The fatal news set off another flurry of activity for Allen and the office staff. He wanted to call everyone he knew and tell them about his disease. Anne Waldman was in town from Boulder and dropped by the hospital to see Allen, learning about the diagnosis firsthand. He received calls and visits from many of his New York friends. In the wee hours of the morning he wrote "Things I'll Not Do (Nostalgias)," which was destined to be his last complete poem. As the title indicated, it was a list of the things he would not be able to enjoy again. He listed many of the faraway places he would not visit and also the more mundane activities, like climbing "E. 12th Street's stairway 3 flights again." As he had for most of his life, he captured exactly what thoughts were passing through his mind at that particular moment in time. It was a remarkable record made by someone who knew he did not have long to live.

Things I'll Not Do (Nostalgias), *CP*, p. 1160

As soon as he could, Allen talked to Gehlek Rinpoche and asked his advice. "Rest these next weeks in shape to practice short form *Vajrayogini*. Now's the time to focus on *Vajrayogini* practice to go to pureland, or *Dakini* land," his teacher told him. It was exactly the advice that Allen wanted to hear; his Buddhist practice had been leading up to this moment for the past twenty years, and he was eager to see it through as peacefully as he could.

The next day Allen asked the oncologist whether there had been warning signs that the doctors might have missed, since his specialists had focused so much on his heart instead of his liver. The doctor assured him that it would not have made a difference even if his cancer had been diagnosed earlier. Probably the hepatitis C that he had picked up in South America in 1960 had developed into cirrhosis of the liver and then progressed steadily to liver cancer. With hepatitis Allen would not have been a candidate for a liver transplant, and even with early detection, there would have been no course of treatment available to him in those days. It was consoling for Allen to know that even if something had been overlooked, it hadn't shortened his life.

On Monday, March 31, Allen continued to make dozens of phone calls to his friends. He wrote lists of things to do and kept Peter Hale running back and forth between the hospital and the office, where Bob was working to have the bedroom in Allen's loft quickly converted into a sickroom. He rented a hospital bed, a wheelchair, and other medical equipment Allen might need and talked at length with the doctors and nurses about hospice care. Allen intended to come home to die. He did not want to live out his days in a hospital and decided that he didn't want his life extended by any extraordinary means either. He had made his statement simply enough years earlier when he wrote, "Die when you die," and he wanted to follow his own advice now. His only wish was to be kept pain-free with whatever drugs they might be able to offer him, and beyond that he was prepared to let go. Realistically, it still seemed that he might have as many as six good months left. Allen asked Bob to begin making plans to install a state-of-the-art recording studio in the apartment so that when friends like Bob Dylan or Paul McCartney came to visit, they would have professional equipment to record on. There was even talk of doing an *MTV Unplugged* program from the loft. Before Allen was even discharged, Bob had ordered a good piano to be delivered, so that Philip Glass could play when he dropped in. All the unframed paintings that had been given to Allen by his many artist friends were taken from storage and brought to a framer, so that Allen could enjoy them during his final months. There was room on his walls at last to display most of the artwork he had collected over the past fifty years.

One afternoon before he left the hospital he drafted a letter to President Clinton and asked Hale to type it. The short letter told the president, "I have untreatable liver cancer and have 2–5 months to live. If you have some sort of award or medal for service in art or poetry, please send one along unless it's politically inadvisable or inexpedient. I don't want to bait the right wing for you. Maybe Gingrich might or might not mind. But don't take chances please, you've enough on hand." After a lifetime of enjoying such great success and worldwide fame in writing poetry it was bittersweet that Allen felt he needed a final pat on the back from someone like the president. That night in the hospital bathroom, Allen looked in the mirror and said out loud, "Stop scheming Ginsberg," thinking of that letter. However, when the draft was typed the next day, he signed it and had it mailed to the White House anyway. His own line, "Don't follow my path to extinction," had never been more appropriate.

In addition to contacting his friends, Allen worked feverishly revising the manuscripts of all the poems he had intended to assemble for his next book. "Death and Fame" was the name of one of the poems he had been working on for the last month. He had begun it long before he knew he was terminally ill, and he continued to refine the lines. He tried to think up a good title for the book, and for a while he considered *Sleeping with my Skeleton* as a possibility. In the end, *Death and Fame* seemed most appropriate. Peter Orlovsky came to visit each day and sat quietly with Allen in his hospital room for a few hours. For the past months he had been living in their old apartment on East Twelfth Street with a hired caretaker who, unbeknownst to Allen, had his own substance abuse problems. Peter was glad to be out of the halfway house, but without proper supervision he was not making progress. His social caseworker stopped in to visit him a few times a week, but the caseworker and other professionals felt that he had inadequate support, considering the severity of Peter's problems. Allen had never recognized the enormity of those problems, and now with his own death imminent, he couldn't focus on that. He only remembered how gently Peter had helped him take care of Louis when he was sick and how Peter had tended Oleg, his father, as he lay dying. Looking for compassionate care from his old love, he asked Peter if he would move into the loft on East Thirteenth Street to care for him when he was released from the hospital. Peter agreed to do all he could.

On Wednesday, April 2, Allen was discharged from Beth Israel and returned home to his new loft prepared to get down to serious work. When he entered the apartment he was delighted to find that all the boxes had been unpacked. He walked from item to item looking at everything and commenting on the history of each of his possessions and its significance to him. His shrine was set up at one end of the large open space and there, in the open arms of Buddha, he placed a little picture he'd clipped from the newspaper of a handsome young boxer. When Bob expressed his sorrow that Allen would not have time to enjoy his new loft, Allen disagreed and said that in fact he would enjoy every minute of it. All day long he stayed on the phone with friends and talked well into the evening in spite of Bob's suggestion to rest. After dinner, Robert Frank came to visit, and Allen snapped his picture standing next to a bearded, potbellied Peter. When Robert left, Peter went out with him.

Allen continued making phone calls to say goodbye to his friends and was determined to call nearly everyone in his address book. Some of the calls were sad and interrupted by tears and others were joyous and optimistic. He invited many of his friends to come over and see him one last time to say farewell in person. As morbid as it may sound, it was the kind of melodramatic event that Allen enjoyed. He spent all evening on the phone and then wrote in his journal until dawn. In the morning when the office staff arrived, Allen was still

Robert Frank and Peter Orlovsky,
Allen's last photo, 1997 ~

awake. He had worked all night, not unusual for him by any means, but certainly against the good advice of the doctor to conserve his strength and rest. He made breakfast for himself, then put on his pajamas and went to bed. During the day, everyone looked in on him from time to time but he slept peacefully. Once in the late afternoon he received a phone call from Italy. It was Nanda Pivano and her estranged husband, Ettore Sottsass, who both wanted to bid him *adieu*. While on the phone Allen began to vomit and was helped to the bathroom by Hale. On his way back to bed, he seemed embarrassed and said, "Gee, I never did that before." He fell asleep quickly and slept soundly for the rest of the day. Since Allen was so exhausted after staying up all night, Bob did not wake him when he left that evening. Peter Orlovsky was there, and if anything should happen, he had instructions to call Bob at once.

The next morning, Friday, April 4, both Rosenthal and I arrived earlier than usual, worried about Allen and hoping that he was feeling more refreshed after a good night's sleep. As soon as Bob arrived, he got into an argument with Peter Orlovsky. Peter had not stayed there all night but had gone out and purchased a stolen bicycle on the street for three hundred dollars. The bike now stood in the hallway blocking the entry to the loft. Peter left again and Bob decided to speak with Allen about the inadvisability of having Peter as his sole night nurse. When we went into his bedroom to see if Allen was awake, we found him breathing in a distressed manner, and try as we might we could not rouse him from his sleep. Something was clearly wrong. Bob called the hospice doctor, who immediately came to the apartment and dispatched a nurse to the bedside. Allen had suffered a massive stroke during the night and had fallen into a coma. The doctor advised Bob to call Allen's family, as it was apparent that the end was near. Peter returned and said that Allen had been asleep when he went out the night before, so he wasn't certain if he had woken up later or not. Eugene and Edith promised to drive in as fast as they could. Gehlek Rinpoche was notified and made plans to fly in from Ann Arbor to be with Allen at the end. As the news spread, many friends began to arrive at the loft. Allen had already made a long calling list of the people he would like to have notified at the end of his life. We informed those people that Allen was slipping away. The doctor thought he was close to death, and Allen's cousin, Dr. Joel Gaidemak, confirmed that Allen would not last more than a day or two.

In the evening about a dozen of his close friends and old lovers decided to sleep overnight in the loft on the sofas and floor. Joel and Bob took Allen's platform bed next to him in case he woke up during the night, and the hospice nurse remained at his side attending quietly to Allen's needs. Around two-thirty in the morning on April 5, 1997, Allen's labored breathing worsened and awoke everyone. Joel examined him and said that the end had come, and before long Allen stopped breathing. Ten years and a day after the death of his first Buddhist teacher, Chögyam Trungpa, Allen himself slipped away from his own world of suffering. Gehlek Rinpoche had given Peter Hale something to touch to Allen's lips to symbolize his last earthly meal; his body convulsed and he was dead. It had been a calm, peaceful death and it was hard not to recall his parting words to Michael McClure a few days earlier, "Fare thee well, old baby, fare thee well."

During the twenty-four hours that followed, Gehlek Rinpoche presided over the ritual of seeing Allen out of this world. He and several senior Tibetan Buddhist practitioners chanted for hours on end. Gehlek explained that they were repeating the lessons that Allen already knew and going over new lessons that he would need to know in his future state. After nearly eighteen hours Gehlek sensed that Allen's spirit had left his body. During that time his corpse had been left untouched in his bed, as was Tibetan custom. Friends and family came to his bedside to see the body and to pay their final respects. Gregory Corso, Roy Lichtenstein, Patti Smith, and a host of younger admirers stopped in; Larry Rivers came down from his apartment in his pajamas and played his saxophone for Allen. Jonas Mekas brought his camera and filmed some of this last homage from Allen's friends. The final irony came when the *New York Times* carried a long front-page obituary. It was bigger and more positive coverage than they had ever given Allen during his lifetime. In death Allen Ginsberg had become a safe topic.

In the days that followed Ginsberg's death, the world press took notice of the passing of a remarkable poet. A funeral service for Ginsberg's family and a few close friends was held the following day at Gehlek Rinpoche's Jewel Heart Center in New York, and that was followed on Monday by a larger ceremony for several hundred at Chögyam Trungpa's Shambhala Center. Gregory Corso, Lou Reed, and Kurt Vonnegut came to pay their respects and the Hebrew *kaddish* was recited as part of the formal Buddhist service.

Before these ceremonies the body had been cremated, and later, Allen's ashes were divided. Some of the ashes were interred next to his father in a small cemetery outside Newark. A portion of ashes was presented to Gehlek Rinpoche to scatter at his Jewel Heart Center in Michigan, where Allen had often gone for retreats, and a third portion was given to Trungpa's followers in Boulder to be placed on a *stupa* at the Rocky Mountain Dharma Center.

A year later, after several smaller services around the world, it seemed that the time was right to have a large public memorial service for Ginsberg in New York City. Bob Rosenthal made arrangements with the Cathedral of St. John the Divine near the Columbia University campus to host the event. St. John's was the largest church in the city and could seat upward of three thousand people. Like Westminster Abbey, it also had a poet's corner to commemorate writers and had a long history of activism and community outreach. It seemed like the appropriate venue for one last farewell gathering. A dozen of Allen's friends were asked to participate, and entertainers like Patti Smith, Natalie Merchant, and Philip Glass were only a few of the celebrities that performed that night.

The date for the memorial was set months in advance, but as the day approached, it became clear that an unforeseen scheduling conflict had occurred. May 14, the night set for the memorial, was also to be the night for the airing of the final episode of *Seinfeld*, a tremendously popular television program. Aside from the fact that a record number of people would be staying home to watch the program, it also turned out that much of the media's attention was going to focus on Tom's Restaurant, the actual coffee shop that had been used as the backdrop in many of the Seinfeld episodes. Tom's was less than a block from St. John's Cathedral, and the police had cordoned off many of the streets in each direction in anticipation of the crowds that were expected to be at Tom's watching the celebrities arrive for the cast party.

As if that wasn't enough, that morning the *New York Times* had printed the incorrect day for Allen's memorial. As the hour approached to open the church doors, it appeared as if the organizers would be lucky to fill a few hundred of the three thousand seats in the enormous church. When the doors were unlocked, a few people began to trickle into the hall, but the crowd grew steadily until every seat was filled and another thousand stood in the aisles. Once again Ginsberg had triumphed against the odds. It was an appropriate farewell to one of the century's greatest poets.

ACKNOWLEDGMENTS ~

Quentin Crisp once wrote me a note and ended it by saying, "I am well-wishing to the verge of idiocy." I owe such a great debt to so many people that I fear I'm in danger of succumbing to the same fate. Taking that risk, I would like to thank all of Allen's friends, both present and past, whom I came to know. I was lucky enough to work with Allen for nearly twenty years, and during that period his friends answered my endless questions with patience and candor. Above all I want to express my gratitude to Allen himself, who never was anything but gener- ous and kind to me. If this volume leads people to a greater understanding of and interest in his poetry, I believe he would forgive its flaws.

As the years passed I was delighted to make friends with the people who worked for Allen in his East Village cottage industry. Bob Rosenthal became one of my dearest friends and is yet another debt I owe to Allen. For the past decade he and Peter Hale, the heart of Allen's office, have shared lunch with me, and without their support and inspiration this book would not have been possible. Over the years Dave Breithaupt, Althea Crawford, Jacqueline Gens, Helena Hughes, Juanita Lieberman, Gina Pellicano, Victoria Smart, Kay Spurlock, and Vicki Stanbury have freely assisted in my various Ginsberg projects. I'm pleased that other close friends of Allen's have also become my friends. A special appreciation to them, Gordon Ball, Peter Orlovsky, and Steven Taylor.

So many people were generous enough to write or speak with me in the twenty-five years that this book was taking shape that I hope the reader will indulge me while I thank them individually. Sam Abrams, Kathy Acker, Helen Adam, Edward Albee, Simon Albury, Daisy Alden, Michael Aldrich, Don Allen, Tsultrim Allione, David Amram, Alan Ansen, Antler, Karl Appel, Al Aronowitz, Jerry Aronson, Lou Asekoff, John Ashbery, Richard Avedon, Amiri Baraka, Mary Beach, Julian Beck, Lois Beckwith, Jack Beeson, Bill Berkson, Daniel Berrigan, Ted Berrigan, Paul Bertram, Bhagavan Das, Robert Bly, Victor Bockris, Steven Bornstein, Christian Bourgois, Paul Bowles, Stan Brakhage, Ray Bremser, Lisa Brinker, Anne Brooks, Connie Brooks, Eugene Brooks, James Broughton, Andreas Brown, Eric Brown, William S. Buckley, William S. Burroughs, John Cage, Ernesto Cardenal, Lucien Carr, Luke

Carroll, Hayden Carruth, David Carter, Carolyn Cassady, John Allen Cassady, LuAnne Cassady, Ann Charters, Sam Charters, Neeli Cherkovski, John Ciardi, Tom Clark, Andy Clausen, Francesco Clemente, Andrei Codrescu, Ira Cohen, Jim Cohn, Harold Collen, George Condo, Kirby Congdon, David Cope, Gregory Corso, Malcolm Cowley, Robert Creeley, Kankabati Datta, Fielding Dawson, Allen DeLoach, Diane di Prima, Elsa Dorfman, George Dowden, Robert Duncan, Charlotte Durgin, Richard Eberhart, Kate Edgar, Helen Elliott, Daniel Ellsberg, Richard Elovich, Paul Engle, István Eörsi, Mark Ewert, Larry Fagin, Marianne Faithfull, Carlo Feltrinelli, Chris Felver, Lawrence Ferlinghetti, Lorenzo Ferlinghetti, Leslie Fiedler, Eric Fischl, Charles Henri Ford, Luca Formenton, Raymond Foye, Robert Frank, Brenda Frazer, Len Freedman, Ed Friedman, Chris Funkhauser, Cliff Fyman, Gary Gach, Joel Gaidemak, Sunil Gangopadhyay (Ganguli), Edith Ginsberg, John Giorno, Philip Glass, Ed Gold, Herbert Gold, Brad Gooch, Mindy Gorlin, Brian Graham, James Grauerholz, David Greenberg, Stanley Grinstein, Thom Gunn, Brion Gysin, Drummond Hadley, John Hammond, Bobbie Louise Hawkins, Philip Hicks, Terri Hinte, Hilary Holladay, John Hollander, Anselm Hollo, John Clellon Holmes, Lita Hornick, Michael Horowitz, Andrew Hoyem, Herbert Huncke, Lewis Hyde, Beverly Isis, Brian Jackson, Oscar Janiger, Ted Joans, Joyce Johnson, Gloria Jones, Hettie Jones, Sid Kaplan, Eliot Katz, Larry Keenan, John Kennedy, Jr., Bill Keogan, Ken Kesey, Galway Kinnell, Carolyn Kizer, Kenneth Koch, Allan Kornblum, Paul Krassner, Shelley Kraut, Stanley Kunitz, William Kunstler, Joanne Kyger, Philip Lamantia, James Laughlin, Robert LaVigne, Timothy Leary, Jean-Jacques Lebel, Alene Lee, Sam Leff, Elbert Lenrow, Yves LePellec, Denise Levertov, Hannah Litzky, Paula Litzky, Ira Lowe, Leila Hadley Luce, C. Townsend Luddington, Lewis MacAdams, Amy and Michael McClure, Kaye McDonough, Billy MacKay, David McReynolds, Norman Mailer, Gerard Malanga, Judith Malina, Sheila Maltz, Geoffrey Manaugh, Greil Marcus, John Martin, Sherri Martinelli, Taylor Mead, Jonas Mekas, Mellon, David Meltzer, Robert Meyers, Barry Miles, Arthur Miller, Shiv Mirabito, John Montgomery, Tim Moran, Ted Morgan, John Morthland, Eric Mottram, Shig Murao, Eileen Myles, Harold Norse, Marc Olmstead, Hank O'Neal, Yoko Ono, Julius Orlovsky, Lafcadio Orlovsky, Ron Padgett, Helen Parker, Thomas Parkinson, Claude Pelieu, Marjorie Perloff, Charles Peters, Nancy J. Peters, Rosebud Pettet, Simon Pettet, Tom Pickard, Fernanda Pivano, Jeff Poniewaz, Benn Posset, Sheppard Powell, Jerry Poynton, Carl Rakosi, Ram Dass, Lee Ranaldo, Margaret Randall, Susan Rashkis, Jonah Raskin, Irvyne Richards, Larry Rivers, Jonathan Robbins, David Rome, Stephen Ronan, Ned Rorem, Barney Rosset, Paul Roth, Charles Rothschild, Malay Roy Choudhury, Jerry Rubin, Oliver Sacks, Nanao Sakaki, John Sampas, Ed Sanders, Jason Schinder, Michael Schumacher, James Schuyler, Bob Sharrard, Jack Shuai, Steve Silberman, Harvey Silverglate, Herschel Silverman, Vojo Sindolic, Rani Singh, Harry Smith, Patti Smith, John Snow, Gary Snyder, Carl Solomon, Susan Sontag, Nile Southern, Stephen Spender, Colin Still, Robert Sutherland-Cohen, Warren Tallman, Virgil Thomson, Allen Tobias, Happy Traum, Diana Trilling, Chögyam Trungpa, John Tytell, John Updike, Janine Pommy Vega, Helen Vendler, Simon Vinkenoog, Kurt Vonnegut, Andrei Voznesensky, Anne Waldman, Barry Wallenstein, Patrick Warner, Shizuko Watari, Steve Watson, Helen Weaver, Regina Weinreich, Philip Whalen, Edward D. White, Ron Whitehead, George Whitman, Les Whitten, Ted and Joan Wilentz, Jonathan Williams, Hal Willner, Bob Wilson, Robert Anton Wilson, Andrew Wylie, Hiro Yamagata, Yevgeny Yevtushenko, Yu Suwa, and John Zervos.

A host of institutions have provided informational support. In particular Stanford University Library, where Ginsberg's archive is carefully preserved, and Columbia University Library, which took such good care of it for twenty-five years. The University of California at Berkeley has helped via its tremendous collections. In addition, research help was provided by the University of Arizona, University of California at Berkeley, University of California at Davis, University of California at San Diego, UCLA, Yale, University of Connecticut, University of Delaware, Georgetown University, Southern Illinois University, University of Chicago, Northwestern University, University of Illinois, Indiana University, Ball State University, University of Iowa, University of Kansas, University of Louisville, Louisiana State University, University of Maryland, Boston University, Harvard University, University of Michigan, Washington University, Dartmouth, Princeton, University of New Mexico, SUNY Buffalo, American Academy and Institute of Arts and Letters, Columbia University, New York Public Library, NYU, SUNY Stony Brook, Syracuse University, University of North Carolina, Duke University, Ohio State University, Kent State University, University of Pennsylvania, Brown University, University of Texas, University of Virginia, Simon Fraser University, and the British Library.

For help with the manuscript and publication of this book, I am in the debt of fellow bibliographer Jack Hagstrom and fellow librarian Bill Gargan. Paul Slovak and the staff at Viking—David Martin, Sharon Gonzalez, Carla Bolte, and Katy Riegel—and copy editor Sean Devlin have seen the work through the long process from original idea to finished product. Sterling Lord, my agent, had the faith in me that set the project in motion, and to him I owe much more than a commission.

An additional thank-you for lending their photographs to this book to Gordon Ball, John Cohen, Larry Keenan, Jr., Saul Shapiro, and most of all the Allen Ginsberg Trust.

Finally, without the love and support of Judy Matz, this book would never have been written; to her I owe my eternal gratitude.

SOURCES AND NOTES ~

The research for this book went hand-in-hand with work on a two-volume bibliography on the writings of Allen Ginsberg. Instead of repeating those 961 pages here, I refer researchers to *The Works of Allen Ginsberg, 1941–1994: A Descriptive Bibliography,* by Bill Morgan (Westport: Greenwood Press, 1995), and *The Response to Allen Ginsberg, 1926–1994: A Bibliography of Secondary Sources,* by Bill Morgan (Westport: Greenwood Press, 1996). Those lists are definitive and are the source of my knowledge on the subject of Allen Ginsberg. What follows here is merely a selected tip of the iceberg. The bulk of the resources examined may be found with the Ginsberg Archive in the Special Collections Department of the Stanford University Libraries.

Abbreviations Used:
AA: Alan Ansen
AC: Ann Charters
AG: Allen Ginsberg
AW: Anne Waldman
BM: Barry Miles
BR: Bob Rosenthal
CB: Connie Brooks
CC: Carolyn Cassady
DA: Don Allen
EB: Eugene Brooks (Ginsberg)
EG: Edith Ginsberg
ES: Ed Sanders
GB: Gordon Ball
GC: Gregory Corso
GS: Gary Snyder
HH: Herbert Huncke

JCH: John Clellon Holmes
JG: Joel Gaidemak
JK: Jack Kerouac
JL: James Laughlin
JW: Jonathan Williams
LC: Lucien Carr
LF: Lawrence Ferlinghetti
LG: Louis Ginsberg
LJ: Leroi Jones
LT: Lionel Trilling
MM: Michael McClure
MS: Michael Schumacher
NC: Neal Cassady
PH: Peter Hale
PL: Paula Litzky
PO: Peter Orlovsky
RC: Robert Creeley
RD: Robert Duncan
RL: Robert LaVigne
ST: Steven Taylor
TW: Ted Wilentz
WSB: William S. Burroughs

Foreword

Ginsberg's thoughts on Whitman come from a variety of sources and interviews. Two essays in particular were important: "On Walt Whitman, Composed on the Tongue" and "Whitman's Influence: A Mountain Too Vast To Be Seen," both of which are found in AG's *Deliberate Prose*.

Introduction

"Saturday Night Encounter" by David McReynolds and "That Little Queer" by Norman Mailer, in *Best Minds*. Author's interviews and correspondence with Lawrence Ferlinghetti, Nancy Peters, and Bob Rosenthal. AG's letter to Bill Clinton can be found in AG's papers at Stanford.

1895–1926
BEFORE THE BEGINNING: PARENTS

Interviews with AG, EB, EG, LG, CB, JG, Eliot Katz, PL, BM, BR, and MS. Interviews and correspondence with Honey Litzky and Harold Collen. Both BM's and MS's earlier biographies have done an excellent job of tracing AG's family tree. AG also gives bits and pieces of his family's history in letters, journal entries, and interviews throughout his life and in his *Family Business*, the letters between AG and LG, edited by MS. LG's poetry and EB's comments are from LG's *Collected Poems*.

1 9 2 6
B I R T H

Newark and New York newspapers were consulted for birth announcements and current news of the day.

1 9 3 0 – 3 3
B O Y H O O D :   F A I R   S T R E E T

Interviews and correspondence with AG, EB, LG. AG journals and psychiatric hospital reports. EG quoted in Jerry Aronson's film, *The Life and Times of Allen Ginsberg.*

1 9 3 3 – 3 7
1 5 5   H A L E D O N   A V E N U E

Interviews and correspondence with AG, EB, JG, LG, BR, ES. AG journals. Much of the early history can also be found in "Paterson's Principal Poet" by EB, which serves as the introduction to LG's *Collected Poems.*

1 9 3 7 – 4 0

Interviews and correspondence with AG, EB, JG, EG, LG, and PL. AG journals and school papers and report cards.

1 9 4 0 – 4 3
G R A H A M   A V E N U E

Interviews and correspondence with AG. AG's letters to Warren Barbour, EB, Gordon Canfield, Charles McNary, the *New York Times,* and Ben Soffer. AG journals, school papers, and publications. Comments about school are also found in "A Visionary Afternoon in High School" published in *Teachers Make a Difference.*

1 9 4 3
C O L U M B I A   U N I V E R S I T Y

Interviews and correspondence with AG, WSB, LC, and James Grauerholz. AG's letters to EB and Paul Roth. Letters to AG from EB, LG, William Hance, and Paul Roth. AG journals, school papers, publications, transcripts, and report cards. Kammerer information from obituaries. Ted Morgan's *Literary Outlaw* provided a wealth of information about WSB.

1 9 4 4

Interviews and correspondence with AG, WSB, LC, Ed Gold, James Grauerholz, Tim Moran, John Sampas, and Diana Trilling. AG's letters to EB, LG, and JK. Letters to AG from EB, LG, JK, and Nicholas McKnight. AG journals, school papers, publications, and transcripts. Unpublished manuscript of Edie Kerouac Parker's memoir, *You'll Be Okay,* and her "Fond Memories of Allen" in *Best Minds* courtesy of Tim Moran. Details about Kammerer's death were taken in part from newspaper accounts.

1 9 4 5

Interviews and correspondence with AG, James Grauerholz, HH, and Tim Moran. AG's letters to EB, LG, JK, Diana Trilling, and LT. Letters to AG from EB, LG, and JK. AG journals, school papers, publications, transcripts, and psychiatric hospital reports.

1 9 4 6

Interviews and correspondence with AG, James Grauerholz, and HH. AG's letters to Paul Bertram, EB, WSB, Harold Collen, LG, JK, Gene Pippin, and LT. Letters to AG from EB, WSB, LG, JK, Nicholas McKnight, LT, and Hans Wassing. AG journals, school papers, publications, and transcripts.

1 9 4 7

Interviews and correspondence with AG, CC, James Grauerholz, and HH. AG's letters to Paul Bertram, EB, WSB, NC, LG, JK, and Wilhelm Reich. Letters to AG from EB, WSB, NC, LG, JK, Nicholas McKnight, and Harry Worthing. AG journals, school papers, publications, and transcripts. Information about NC from his own memoir, *The First Third*, *As Ever*, and other biographies. CC's *Off the Road* speaks of this period, as does HH's *The Evening Sky Turned Crimson*.

1 9 4 8

Interviews and correspondence with AG. AG's letters to Paul Bertram, EB, WSB, NC, LG, JK, Jethro Robinson, LT, and Mark Van Doren. Letters to AG from EB, WSB, NC, LG, and JK. AG journals, school papers, publications, and transcripts.

1 9 4 9

Interviews and correspondence with AG, AA, Harold Collen, HH, Helen Parker, Jerry Poynton, and Carl Solomon. AG's letters to EB, WSB, NC, LG, JCH, JK, Ilo Orleans, Mr. Smith, John and Mary Snow, LT, and Mark Van Doren. Letters to AG from WSB, NC, LG, and JK. Letter from LG to LT. AG journals and hospital reports. Information about AG's arrest is from newspaper accounts and police reports. Information about Carl Solomon is found in AG's *Howl: Annotated Edition*.

1 9 5 0

Interviews and correspondence with AG, AA, C. T. Luddington, Helen Parker, and Carl Solomon. AG's letters to Paul Bertram, EB, WSB, NC, LG, James Grady, JCH, JK, Helen

Parker, Ezra Pound, Margie Slater, John and Mary Snow, Mark Van Doren, and William Carlos Williams. Letters to AG from NC, LG, JK, and Ezra Pound. NC letters to Diana Hansen. AG journals and hospital reports.

1951

Interviews and correspondence with AG, James Grauerholz, and Carl Solomon. AG's letters to WSB, NC, JCH, JK, Ezra Pound, and Mark Van Doren. Letters to AG from JK and NC. AG journals.

1952

Interviews and correspondence with AG, AA, GC, Helen Elliott, HH, and Jerry Poynton. AG's letters to WSB, CC, NC, Charles Henri Ford, JCH, JK, Ezra Pound, and Karl Shapiro. Letters to AG from LG, NC, and JK. AG journals.

1953

Interviews and correspondence with AG, AA, GC, Jacqueline Gens, Alene Lee, and BR. AG's letters to WSB, CC, NC, Dwight Eisenhower, Gabrielle Kerouac, JK, and LT. Letters to AG from NC, LG, and JK. AG journals. Information about Gore Vidal's night with JK is from Vidal's *Two Sisters*.

1954

Interviews and correspondence with AG, PO, LC, CC, Philip Hicks, RL, and MM. AG's letters to EB, WSB, LC, CC, NC, RD, LG, JCH, JK, RL, Ernest Von Harz, and Louis Zukofsky. Letters to AG from LG, NC, and JK. AG journals. Information about Sheila Williams's sad life is described in some detail in A. J. Albany's memoir, *Low Down*.

1955

Interviews and correspondence with AG, PO, Philip Hicks, RL, and MM. AG's letters to EB, WSB, LC, NC, LG, JCH, JK, RL, Sterling Lord, John Allen Ryan, and JW. Letters to AG from LG, NC, JK, and Marianne Moore. AG journals. Information about the death of Natalie Jackson from newspaper accounts.

1956

Interviews and correspondence with AG, PO, AA, Helen Elliott, LF, MM, and Helen Weaver. AG's letters to EB, LC, NC, RC, e.e. cummings, RD, Richard Eberhart, LF, Buba Ginsberg, LG, JCH, JK, Carolyn Kizer, JL, RL, Denise Levertov, Honey Litzky, PO, John Allen Ryan, GS, LT, and JW. Letters to AG from NC, e.e. cummings, LF, LG, JK, and John Allen Ryan. PO letter to Kate Orlovsky. AG journals.

1957

Interviews and correspondence with AG, PO, AA, LF, Joyce Johnson, BM, and Barney Rosset. AG's letters to Donald Allen, Paul Blackburn, EB, NC, GC, RC, Caresse Crosby, e.e. cummings, Richard Eberhart, LF, LG, Jack Hirschman, JCH, JK, RL, Denise Levertov, Ron Loewinsohn, Frank Miller, Charles Olson, PO, Barney Rosset, GS, Eugene Walter, John Wieners, and JW. Letters to AG from NC, LF, LG, JK, and John Wieners. AG journals.

1958

Interviews and correspondence with AG, PO, AA, Fielding Dawson, LF, Hettie Jones, RL, Elbert Lenrow, and Herschel Silverman. AG's letters to Daisy Aldan, DA, EB, WSB, LC, NC, Cid Corman, GC, RC, LF, LG, John Hollander, LJ, JK, Galway Kinnell, Bill Kinter, JL, RL, Elbert Lenrow, Denise Levertov, Honey Litzky, Ron Loewinsohn, MM, Robert MacGregor, Charles Olson, PO, Herschel Silverman, GS, John Wieners, and JW. Letters to AG from NC, LF, LG, and JK. AG journals.

1959

Interviews and correspondence with AG, PO, Al Aronowitz, AC, GC, Elsa Dorfman, LF, MM, and TW. AG's letters to Daisy Aldan, Fernando Alegria, DA, EB, Paul Carroll, CC, John Ciardi, GC, RC, e.e. cummings, RD, Richard Eberhart, Clayton Eshleman, Elaine Feinstein, LF, LG, Jack Hirschman, JCH, LJ, JK, Bill Kinter, Philip Lamantia, JL, RL, Ron Loewinsohn, Robert Lowell, Willard Maas, Clarence Major, Ed Marshall, *New York Times*, Charles Olson, PO, Miles Payne, Jerome Rothenberg, Herschel Silverman, *Time* magazine, LT, and John Wieners. Letters to AG from NC, LF, LG, JK, and RL. AG journals. Norman Podhoretz's comments are from his article "The Know-Nothing Bohemians," *Partisan Review*, vol. 25, no. 2 (Spring 1958), pp. 305–18.

1960

Interviews and correspondence with AG, PO, Elsa Dorfman, LF, Barney Rosset, Janine Pommy Vega, and TW. AG's letters to Daisy Aldan, DA, EB, WSB, LC, NC, GC, RC, Elsa Dorfman, Clayton Eshleman, LF, LG, Jack Hirschman, David Ignatow, LJ, JK, Joanne Kyger, Philip Lamantia, JL, Honey Litzky, Jackson MacLow, Willard Maas, PO, David Posner, GS, LT, Jon Webb, and JW. Letters to AG from NC, LF, LG, and JK. AG journals.

1961

Interviews and correspondence with AG, PO, Julian Beck, LF, John Kennedy, Jr., Timothy Leary, Judith Malina, Janine Pommy Vega, and TW. AG's letters to DA, A. Alvarez, Paul Blackburn, Paul Bowles, LC, NC, GC, Diane di Prima, Elsa Dorfman, RD, LF, John Fles, LG, Mr. Greenburger, James Jones, LJ, JK, Bill Kinter, Joanne Kyger, Philip Lamantia, JL, Denise Levertov, Honey Litzky, Kenny Love, Robert Lowell, MM, Willard Maas, Charles Olson, Lafcadio Orlovsky, PO, Nanda Pivano, David Posner, David Randall, Tom Raworth, Barney Rosset, GS, Henry Wenning, TW, and JW. Letters to AG from LF, LG, and JK. AG journals and PO journals.

1 9 6 2

Interviews and correspondence with AG, PO, LF, Sunil Ganguli, Joanne Kyger, Malay Roy Choudhury, GS, and TW. AG's letters to AA, Jane and Paul Bowles, EB, LC, NC, GC, RC, Elsa Dorfman, LF, LG, Michael Grinberg, *Harvard Crimson*, JCH, David Ignatow, LJ, John Kelley, JK, JL, Clarence Major, PO, Margaret Randall, Barney Rosset, Bertrand Russell, GS, Jon Webb, and Henry Wenning. Letters to AG from LF, LG, JK, Irving Rosenthal, and Bertrand Russell. AG journals and PO journals.

1 9 6 3

Interviews and correspondence with AG, PO, Lois Beckwith, LC, LF, Sunil Ganguli, Drummond Hadley, Joanne Kyger, MM, Malay Roy Choudhury, GS, and TW. AG's letters to AA, Paul Bowles, EB, Don Carpenter, LC, NC, GC, RC, Bonnie Crown, LF, LG, Geoffrey Hazard, Arno Hormia, Hettie Jones, LJ, JK, Philip Lamantia, MM, Charles Olson, PO, Nanda Pivano, *Poetry* magazine, Henry Rago, Ron Rice, Barney Rosset, Al Sally, Judith Schmidt, K. Shivaraj, GS, Warren Tallman, Barry Wallenstein, John Wieners, and TW. Letters to AG from LF, LG, and JK. AG journals and PO journals.

1 9 6 4

Interviews and correspondence with AG, PO, Diane di Prima, LF, ES, Herschel Silverman, and TW. AG's letters to DA, John Ashbery, Author's League Fund, Edwin Benjamin, Harold Birns, EB, William Cahn, Carnegie Fund for Authors, NC, Edward Cavanaugh, GC, Edward Costikyan, RC, Czechoslovakian Embassy, Joseph DiCarlo, Paul Engle, LF, Felicia Geffin, LG, Miguel Grinberg, Robert Kelly, JK, Francis Knight, Richard Kuh, Stanley Kunitz, Philip Lamantia, MM, Robert Morgenthau, Charles Olson, PO, Nanda Pivano, Henry Rago, A. S. Raman, Malay Roy Choudhury, Stephen Ruddy, *San Francisco Chronicle*, Herschel Silverman, GS, LT, YMHA, Robert Wagner, Chad Walsh, *Wichita Beacon*, Flossie Williams, and Mel Wolf. Letters to AG from LF, LG, and JK. AG journals.

1 9 6 5

Interviews and correspondence with AG, PO, John Ashbery, Ted Berrigan, Stephen Bornstein, CC, LF, Anselm Hollo, BM, Rosebud Pettet, ES, GS, and AW. AG's letters to DA, EB, WSB, CC, NC, GC, RC, LF, LG, HH, LJ, JK, Philip Lamantia, Denise Levertov, MM, Robert McNamara, Charles Olson, PO, Nicanor Parra, Barney Rosset, Jerome Rothenberg, ES, GS, Giuseppe Ungaretti, Max Weiss, TW, and Flossie Williams. Letters to AG from LF, LG, and JK. AG journals.

1 9 6 6

Interviews and correspondence with AG, PO, Stephen Bornstein, Diane di Prima, LF, EG, Timothy Leary, and ES. AG's letters to DA, Mr. Bean, Carol Berge, A. C. Bhaktivedanta, Paul Blackburn, EB, John Buckner, NC, Dan Cassidy, Leo Cherne, John Christian, GC, RC, RD, Bob Dylan, LF, LG, Bob Hawley, Jack Hirschman, JCH, Jacob Javits, Robert Kennedy, JK,

Michael Kirchberger, Jim Koller, Philip Lamantia, Keith Lampe, *Life*, Walter Lowenfels, MM, Howard McCord, Monarch Notes, Harold Norse, Charles Olson, PO, *Paris Review*, Henry Rago, Sir Roeder, Barney Rosset, Jerome Rothenberg, James Rundle, ES, Mr. Schiller, GS, Warren Tallman, Teresa Truszkowska, Andrei Voznesensky, Carl Weissner, John Wieners, TW, and JW. Letters to AG from LF, LG, and JK. AG journals.

1 9 6 7

Interviews and correspondence with AG , GB, LF, MM, and GS. AG's letters to EB, NC, GC, RC, Allen DeLoach, Paul Engle, LF, LG, David Glanz, A. N. Harradance, Richard Helms, Fred Jordan, Mrs. LaSalle, JL, Timothy Leary, Denise Levertov, MM, Gerard Malanga, Ralph Maud, Shig Murao, *New York Times*, S. P. Orlando, PO, Charles Osborne, Ezra Pound, Tom Raworth, John Roche, Edouard Roditi, Olga Rudge, Herschel Silverman, GS, Carl Solomon, C. L. Sulzberger, Warren Tallman, Jim Thurber, Helen Weaver, and TW. Letters to AG from GB, LF, and LG. AG journals.

1 9 6 8

Interviews and correspondence with AG, GB, Andy Clausen, LF, BM, Charles Rothschild, Jerry Rubin, GS, and Philip Whalen. AG's letters to Michael Aldrich, Baker Mfg., Gustav Bernau, EB, AC, GC, Allen DeLoach, Diane di Prima, LF, Felicia Geffin, Arthur Gelb, LG, Mark Green, Barry Hall, Edward Hamilton, Jan Herman, Jack Hirschman, Mr. Joelson, Fred Jordan, JK, Jacob Kisner, JL, Elbert Lenrow, Gerard Malanga, Charles Mixer, Shig Murao, Charles Olson, PO, *Playboy*, Charles Plymell, Annette Rosenshine, GS, Arthur Sulzberger, William Targ, LT, AW, and Bob Wilson. Letters to AG from LF and LG. AG journals.

1 9 6 9

Interviews and correspondence with AG, GB, AC, and LF. AG's letters to DA, GB, Shelley Braverman, EB, Andreas Brown, Harvey Brown, Lee Crabtree, GC, RC, LF, Stanley Flieschman, Felicia Geffin, LG, Jan Herman, HH, Robert Kempner, David Kennedy, JK, Joanne Kyger, JL, Living Theater, John Martin, Ralph Maud, Patrick Moynihan, PO, Charles Plymell, Ben Riker, Herschel Silverman, GS, Jim Sosiensky, Mike Standard, LT, AW, Helen Weaver, Jon Webb, Howard Wheeler, Mark Wilson, and Saul Zaentz. Letters to AG from LF and LG. AG journals.

1 9 7 0

Interviews and correspondence with AG, PO, GB, Mary Beach, LF, and Claude Pelieu. AG's letters to DA, President Babbidge, GB, Lester Bangs, Mary Beach, Paul Blackburn, EB, Andreas Brown, Harvey Brown, Gordon Cairnie, CC, Andy Clausen, GC, Allen DeLoach, Juan de Onis, George Dowden, LF, Hamilton Fish, Gary Getz, LG, Jan Herman, Michael Horowitz, IRS, Stanley Karnow, Ed Koch, JL, RL, Gary Lawless, Timothy Leary, Gerard Malanga, Donald Manness, John Martin, Ralph Maud, Ken Mikolowski, Geoffrey Miller, *Nickel Review*, PO, Bern Porter,

Jerome Rothenberg, Ted Sartwell, GS, C. L. Sulzberger, Vincent Tortora, AW, Helen Weaver, Joel Weishaus, Carl Weissner, and Flossie Williams. Letters to AG from LF and LG. AG journals.

1971

Interviews and correspondence with AG, PO, David Amram, GB, LF, Michael Horowitz, and BR. AG's letters to Richard Baker, GB, Mary Beach, Paul Blackburn, EB, Andreas Brown, AC, GC, Alan Cranston, RC, Allen DeLoach, Jerome Dolittle, Joyce Elkin, LF, LG, Brad Gooch, Maretta Greer, Richard Helms, Jerome Jaffe, Fred Jordan, Elbert Lenrow, Flora Lewis, MM, David Meltzer, Ken Mikolowski, National Book Award Committee, Harold Norse, PO, Claude Pelieu, PEN Club, Marc Raskin, GS, C. L. Sulzberger, Lewis Warsh, Eli Wilentz, and JW. Letters to AG from LF and LG. AG journals.

1972

Interviews and correspondence with AG, PO, Tsultrim Allione, GB, AC, Diane di Prima, LF, Lorenzo Ferlinghetti, and AW. AG's letters to DA, GB, Djuna Barnes, Mary Beach, Steve Berg, EB, Harvey Brown, Douglas Calhoun, Joseph Chaikin, AC, Andy Clausen, GC, RD, Larry Fagin, LF, John Fisher, LG, Jerome Jaffe, John Lennon, Ron Loewinsohn, Gerard Malanga, Herbert Martin, Paul Metcalf, Norman Moser, Marc Olmstead, Yoko Ono, PO, Claude Pelieu, Stephen Savage, Harry Smith, GS, C. L. Sulzberger, Carl Waldman, Marc Weber, JW, Bob Wilson, Nancy Wilson, and Ian Young. Letters to AG from LF and LG. AG journals.

1973

Interviews and correspondence with AG, PO, Tsultrim Allione, GB, AC, Diane di Prima, LF, and AW. AG's letters to DA, AA, GB, Mary Beach, Daniel Blum, EB, Andreas Brown, Harvey Brown, AC, GC, RC, Larry Fagin, LF, LG, Richard Helms, Mr. Heymann, Michael Horowitz, David Ignatow, JL, Gerald Lefcourt, Tom Lysaght, MM, Jay McHale, David McReynolds, Gerard Malanga, Robert Milewski, PO, Claude Pelieu, Anthony Raymond, Alan Reutzler, Seldon Rodman, Barney Rosset, Jerome Rothenberg, Herschel Silverman, GS, Carl Solomon, C. L. Sulzberger, Warren Tallman, AW, Philip Whalen, JW, Bob Wilson, and Alan Ziegler. Letters to AG from LF and LG. AG journals.

1974

Interviews and correspondence with AG, PO, LF, Joanne Kyger, Marc Olmstead, GS, and AW. AG's letters to Arche Anderson, Al Aronowitz, GB, EB, Andreas Brown, Harvey Brown, WSB, GC, RC, Ms. Curtis, John Doyle, Gerald Epstein, Larry Fagin, LF, LG, Paul Halvonik, William Hitchcock, Michael Horowitz, Peter Koch, Timothy Leary, Jean Jacques Lebel, Gerard Malanga, Naropa Institute, Harold Norse, Marc Olmstead, PO, Tom Pickard, Dan Propper, Steven Rodefer, GS, Janine Pommy Vega, AW, Jan Wenner, and Bob Wilson. Letters to AG from LF and LG. AG journals.

1 9 7 5

Interviews and correspondence with AG, GC, Richard Elovich, LF, Shelley Kraut, Marc Olmstead, Jonathan Robbins, BR, Harvey Silverglate, and AW. AG's letters to AA, GB, Bill Berkson, EB, WSB, Marshall Clements, GC, RD, Richard Eberhart, Larry Fagin, LF, LG, Doris Grumbach, Hugh Hefner, Stanley Kunitz, JL, Joanna Leary, Larry Mermelstein, Marc Olmstead, PO, Jerome Rothenberg, GS, AW, and Bob Wilson. Letters to AG from LF and LG. AG journals.

1 9 7 6

Interviews and correspondence with AG, Antler, GB, LF, Ira Lowe, Marc Olmstead, BR, and ST. AG's letters to Sam Abrams, Paul Ackerman, Antler, GB, Ron Benham, Bill Berkson, Polly Bolling, EB, WSB, David Cope, GC, Tim Craven, Bill Deemer, Bob Dylan, Richard Elovich, Ernest Estere, LF, Isabella Gardner, Barry Gifford, EG, LG, Fred Jordan, Robert Kelly, JL, Timothy Leary, Elbert Lenrow, Robert Lowell, David McReynolds, Jonas Mekas, BM, Shig Murao, Naropa, Harold Norse, Marc Olmstead, PO, Nancy Peters, GS, Carl Springer, Charles Upton, AW, Marilyn Webb, Allen Young, and Alan Ziegler. Letters to AG from LF and LG. AG journals.

1 9 7 7

Interviews and correspondence with AG, Antler, Ted Berrigan, Andy Clausen, David Cope, GC, Richard Elovich, LF, John Giorno, James Grauerholz, Jonathan Robbins, BR, ES, Steve Silberman, and ST. AG's letters to AA, GB, EB, William Buckley, Basil Bunting, WSB, Hugh Carey, LC, David Cope, GC, Peter Coyote, RC, Allen DeLoach, Kenward Elmslie, LF, EG, David Gitin, Jim Koller, JL, Marc Olmstead, PO, Nancy Peters, David Rome, Herschel Silverman, GS, Diana Trilling, AW, Andy Warhol, Joy Walsh, and Reed Whittemore. AG journals.

1 9 7 8

Interviews and correspondence with AG, PO, John Ashbery, Lisa Brinker, LC, Daniel Ellsberg, LF, BR, and AW. AG's letters to Fernando Alegria, Harold Anderson, EB, Charles Bukowski, LC, AC, David Chura, Dennis Cooper, David Cope, GC, RC, Richard Eberhart, LF, Raymond Foye, Barry Gifford, EG, Grady Hogue, James Hunt, Philip Lamantia, Margaret Mills, Mary Ann Montgomery, Marc Olmstead, PO, Joseph Papp, Nancy Peters, Bern Porter, Bob Sharrard, GS, Dr. Starzell, C. L. Sulzberger, Diana Trilling, Joy Walsh, Helen Weaver, and Eric Yoors. Letters to AG from C. L. Sulzberger. AG journals.

1 9 7 9

Interviews and correspondence with AG, PO, GC, Diane di Prima, LF, Raymond Foye, Beverly Isis, Brian Jackson, Gloria Jones, BM, Irvyne Richards, BR, ST, and AW. AG's letters to GB, Steve Berg, EB, Mr. Bunthaft, WSB, Bob Callahan, LC, Jimmy Carter, Tom Clark, Andy Clausen, GC, RC, Allen DeLoach, Robert Dole, Ed Dorn, Richard Eberhart, LF, Raymond Foye, EG, Denise Levertov, David McReynolds, W. S. Merwin, PO, Nancy Peters, Tom Pickard, Marzenna Raczkowski, Michael Redmond, Shambhala Press, GS, Sun & Moon Press, Warren Tallman, Diana Trilling, AW, Philip Whalen, and Jolen Yamrus. AG journals.

1 9 8 0

Interviews and correspondence with AG, PO, Elsa Dorfman, LF, Drummond Hadley, Eliot Katz, Joanne Kyger, MM, BR, and ST. AG's letters to AA, Antler, GB, EB, WSB, LC, AC, David Cope, GC, RC, Willem de Kooning, Ed Dorn, LF, Raymond Foye, EG, James Grauerholz, JCH, Elbert Lenrow, MM, David McReynolds, Marisol, Ken Mikolowski, Robert Morgenthau, Marc Olmstead, PO, Tom Pickard, ES, Herschel Silverman, GS, John Updike, AW, and Philip Whalen. AG journals.

1 9 8 1

Interviews and correspondence with AG, PO, EB, LF, Beverly Isis, Brian Jackson, Eliot Katz, Hank O'Neal, BR, ST, and AW. AG's letters to John Ashbery, Steven Berg, Kay Boyle, EB, William F. Buckley, WSB, Clive Bush, LC, AC, David Cope, GC, RC, RD, Kenward Elmslie, István Eörsi, LF, Raymond Foye, EG, John Hammond, Brian Jackson, Eliot Katz, Aaron Latham, Denise Levertov, MM, W. S. Merwin, Margaret Mills, Marc Olmstead, Hank O'Neal, PO, Nancy Peters, Michael Rectenwald, BR, GS, ST, Time-Life, AW, Frances Waldman, Joy Walsh, Jerry Wexler, Reed Whittemore, and JW. AG journals.

1 9 8 2

Interviews and correspondence with AG, PO, Jerry Aronson, BR, ST, and AW. AG's letters to John Ashbery, GB, Manuel Ballagas, Paul Bowles, EB, WSB, LC, AC, David Cope, GC, RC, Ernest Dube, RD, István Eörsi, LF, EG, James Grauerholz, Harley, Brian Jackson, Eliot Katz, Philip Lamantia, MacArthur Foundation, MM, Hank O'Neal, PO, Tom Pickard, Benn Posset, Al Poulin, Joel Redon, Tom Rogers, BR, Ellen Silverman, GS, Philip Whalen, Helen Weaver, and Yevgeny Yevtushenko. AG journals.

1 9 8 3

Interviews and correspondence with AG, PO, Victor Bockris, AC, Sam Charters, Andy Clausen, Diane di Prima, Elsa Dorfman, LF, Raymond Foye, Mindy Gorlin, Brian Jackson, Alene Lee, BM, Hank O'Neal, Jonathan Robbins, BR, ST, AW, and Andrew Wylie. AG's letters to Eric Anderson, GB, Denny Blouin, EB, Matthew J. Bruccoli, WSB, Ernesto Cardenal, LC, AC, David Cope, RC, RD, István Eörsi, LF, EG, Brion Gysin, John Hammond, Brian Jackson, MM, David McReynolds, W. S. Merwin, Margaret Mills, Dave Moore, Gerard Nicosia, Marc Olmstead, Hank O'Neal, PO, Tom Pickard, Paul Rifkin, BR, Charlie Rothschild, GS, AW, Joy Walsh, Philip Whalen, and Yevgeny Yevtushenko. AG journals.

1 9 8 4

Interviews and correspondence with AG, PO, LF, Raymond Foye, James Grauerholz, Beverly Isis, Sid Kaplan, Juanita Lieberman, BM, BR, Harry Smith, and ST. AG's letters to Berenice Abbott, John Ashbery, GB, Paul Bowles, EB, WSB, LC, David Cope, Ed Dorn, RD, István Eörsi, LF, Raymond Foye, EG, Brion Gysin, Mark Kemachter, Philip Lamantia, MM, John Martin, Hank O'Neal, PO, Tom Pickard, Nancy Peters, Rosebud Pettet, Simon Pettet, BR, ES, GS, ST, AW, Patrick Warner, Helen Weaver, and Yevgeny Yevtushenko. AG journals.

1 9 8 5

Interviews and correspondence with AG, PO, Tsultrim Allione, LF, Raymond Foye, Beverly Isis, Juanita Lieberman, BM, Susan Rashkis, BR, Harry Smith, and ST. AG's letters to GB, Holly Blivias, Pat Boone, EB, LC, Jim Cohn, RC, Alfonse D'Amato, LF, Jim Freeman, EG, Brion Gysin, David Ignatow, Brian Jackson, Eliot Katz, Philip Lamantia, JL, MM, BM, Margaret Mills, Patrick Moynihan, PO, Susan Rashkis, BR, Peter Siegenthaler, Herschel Silverman, Jeffrey Smalldon, GS, John Tytell, AW, Patrick Warner, Helen Weaver, Yevgeny Yevtushenko, and Wenjin Zhang. AG journals.

1 9 8 6

Interviews and correspondence with AG, PO, GB, István Eörsi, LF, PH, BM, Susan Rashkis, BR, Harry Smith, ST, and Patrick Warner. AG's letters to GB, David Breithaupt, EB, William F. Buckley, LC, Jim Cohn, David Cope, John Dengs, István Eörsi, Clayton Eshleman, LF, EG, Bruce Hays, Brian Jackson, Fred Jordan, Michael Kurtz, JL, Denise Levertov, MM, Margaret Mills, PO, Nancy Peters, Norman Podhoretz, BR, Bob Sharrard, Peter Siegenthaler, Herschel Silverman, GS, Joffre Stewart, Diana Trilling, AW, Patrick Warner, and Philip Whalen. AG journals.

1 9 8 7

Interviews and correspondence with AG, PO, LF, Jacqueline Gens, PH, Beverly Isis, Susan Rashkis, BR, Harry Smith, ST, and Hal Willner. AG's letters to AA, GB, David Breithaupt, David Cope, RD, LF, Chris Funkhauser, EG, Ingram Merrill Foundation, Brian Jackson, Carolyn Mason, MM, PO, James Perizzo, Susan Rashkis, Rene Ricard, Steven Rodefer, BR, GS, Frances Steloff, Sun & Moon Press, AW, Patrick Warner, Philip Whalen, and Yevgeny Yevtushenko. AG journals.

1 9 8 8

Interviews and correspondence with AG, PO, LF, PH, BR, and ST. AG's letters to EB, LC, David Cope, RC, Alfonse D'Amato, István Eörsi, LF, Charles Fort, Raymond Foye, EG, Mr. Goodman, Mikhail Gorbachev, Brian Jackson, Eliot Katz, Jim Kupicz-Menendez, Joanne Kyger, JL, MM, Margaret Mills, Susan Rashkis, David Rome, BR, Herschel Silverman, Vojo Sindolic, Harry Smith, GS, Hidetoshi Tomiyama, Jean Claude van Italie, AW, Patrick Warner, Mrs. Watari, and George Will. AG journals.

1 9 8 9

Interviews and correspondence with AG, PO, LC, LF, Jacqueline Gens, PH, Beverly Isis, BM, Susan Rashkis, BR, Jack Shuai, Rani Singh, Harry Smith, ST, AW, and Patrick Warner. AG's letters to Al Aronowitz, GB, AC, Andy Clausen, Jim Cohn, RC, Diane di Prima, István Eörsi, LF, Thom Gunn, Jesse Helms, Terrell Hunter, Brian Jackson, Eliot Katz, Mr. Kondriake, Bernadette Mayer, BM, Marc Olmstead, Michael Oreskes, William Packard, Susan Rashkis,

David Rome, Jack Shuai, Herschel Silverman, GS, Warren Tallman, Joseph B. Treaster, John Tytell, Helen Weaver, Bob Wilson, and Andrew Wylie. AG journals.

1 9 9 0

Interviews and correspondence with AG, PO, Andy Clausen, Jacqueline Gens, PH, Eliot Katz, BR, Jack Shuai, ST, and AW. AG's letters to Mmoja Ajabu, Peggy Biderman, EB, LC, AC, Andy Clausen, David Cope, GC, RC, Virginia Dajani, Jyoti Datta, Diane di Prima, István Eörsi, Raymond Foye, EG, Vaclav Havel, Michael Kohler, Joanne Kyger, Yves LePellec, J. D. McClatchy, MM, Edwin Miller, PO, Al Poulin, Bob Rixon, David Rome, Thomas J. Rozycki, Richard Sacher, Jacek Sceradzan, Herschel Silverman, Ralph Sipper, GS, AW, Helen Weaver, and Bob Wilson. AG journals.

1 9 9 1

Interviews and correspondence with AG, LF, Jacqueline Gens, PH, BR, and ST. AG's letters to GB, LC, AC, Jim Cohn, GC, Cynthia Edelberg, Mark Ewert, LF, James Florio, Raymond Foye, Chris Funkhauser, EG, Mr. Heuke, JL, Jean Jacques Lebel, MM, BM, PO, Mr. Petrovich, Herschel Silverman, Ralph Sipper, Harry Smith, GS, and Charles Upton. AG journals.

1 9 9 2

Interviews and correspondence with AG, PO, LF, Jacqueline Gens, PH, BR, and MS. AG's letters to Al Aronowitz, GB, Paul Bowles, EB, Kim Caputo, LC, Lois Catala, AC, Bernard Crystal, Richard Felger, Raymond Foye, EG, JL, Roy Lichtenstein, Alice Notley, Edie Kerouac Parker, BR, Nanao Sakaki, Herschel Silverman, Karen Smith, GS, and AW. AG journals.

1 9 9 3

Interviews and correspondence with AG, PO, AA, LC, LF, Jacqueline Gens, PH, and BR. AG's letters to Mike Alpert, Karl Appel, GB, Peter Biler, Nina Bouis, Douglas Brinkley, EB, WSB, LC, AC, Jim Cohn, Harold Collen, GC, RC, Ken Dimaggio, Bob Dylan, István Eörsi, Fred Feressa, LF, Ignacio Fernandez, Raymond Foye, Jacqueline Gens, EG, John Giorno, Barry Goldwater, Eliot Katz, Michael Kellner, Michael Kohler, Slavomira Kubickova, Philip Lamantia, Jean Jacques Lebel, Mr. Levchev, Ken Mikolowski, BM, Marc Olmstead, PO, Fernanda Pivano, Sally Riley, Mr. Rizzo, David Rome, BR, Charles Rothschild, St. Martin's Press, Herschel Silverman, GS, Carl Solomon, Viktor Sosnora, Karl Springer, Maria Straz-Kanska, Antonio Tapies, Andrea Tart, John Tytell, AW, Peter Werhle, and Ron Whitehead. AG journals.

1 9 9 4

Interviews and correspondence with AG, PO, Tsultrim Allione, LF, Raymond Foye, Jacqueline Gens, PH, Beverly Isis, Juanita Lieberman, BM, Susan Rashkis, BR, Jack Shuai, Harry Smith, ST, and Hal Willner. AG's letters to Karl Appel, Alan Barysk, Paul Bowles, RC, LF, Jacqueline

Gens, EG, PH, James Healy, Michael Kohler, Kush, Honey Litzky, Ken Mikolowski, Marc Olmstead, Hank O'Neal, Marie Orlovsky, BR, ES, GS, Helen Weaver, Ron Whitehead, and Hal Willner. AG journals.

1 9 9 5

Interviews and correspondence with AG, PO, LF, PH, Geoffrey Manaugh, and BR. AG's letters to Bill Belmont, EB, Andy Clausen, Randy Cunningham, LF, Luca Formenton, EG, MM, Susan Rashkis, Herschel Silverman, GS, AW, and Patrick Warner. Bono quoted from Jerry Aronson's film, *The Life and Times of Allen Ginsberg*. AG journals.

1 9 9 6

Interviews and correspondence with AG, PO, Mark Ewert, LF, James Grauerholz, PH, Geoffrey Manaugh, and BR. AG's letters to GB, EB, LC, Sam Charters, Andy Clausen, István Eörsi, Luca Formenton, EG, Eliot Katz, RL, Nanda Pivano, Susan Rashkis, Herschel Silverman, David Trinidad, and Janine Pommy Vega. AG journals.

1 9 9 7

Interviews and correspondence with AG, PO, Elsa Dorfman, LF, JG, PH, MM, BR, ST, and AW. AG's letters to Bill Clinton, Luca Formenton, and Bob Wilson. AG journals.

SELECTED BIBLIOGRAPHY ~

In addition to Allen's own works and interviews with him since 1980, many of the biographies of his friends and contemporaries served as resources and models for this book. Some of those books are listed below, but all of them are described in my two published bibliographies on Allen Ginsberg. To conserve space, periodical references are not included here but are found in the comprehensive bibliographies.

Albany, A. J. *Low Down: Junk, Jazz, and Other Fairy Tales from Childhood*. New York: Bloomsbury, 2003.

Allen, Donald M. *The New American Poetry: 1945–1960*. New York: Grove, 1960.

Amburn, Ellis. *Subterranean Kerouac*. New York: St. Martin's, 1998.

Amram, David. *Offbeat: Collaborating with Kerouac*. New York: Thunder's Mouth, 2002.

Ansen, Alan. *Contact Highs*. Elmwood Park, Ill.: Dalkey Archive Press, 1989.

———. *William Burroughs*. Sudbury, Mass.: Water Row Press, 1986.

Ball, Gordon. *'66 Frames*. Minneapolis: Coffee House Press, 1999.

Beatitude Anthology. San Francisco: City Lights, 1960.

Bockris, Victor. *With William Burroughs: A Report from the Bunker*. New York: Seaver Books, 1981.

Booker, Bob, and George Foster. *Pardon Me, Sir, But Is My Eye Hurting Your Elbow?* New York: Bernard Geis, 1968.

Boon, Marcus. *The Road of Excess: A History of Writers on Drugs*. Cambridge: Harvard University Press, 2002.

Bowles, Paul. *Without Stopping*. New York: Putnam's, 1972.

Breslin, James E. B., ed. *Something to Say: William Carlos Williams on Younger Poets*. New York: New Directions, 1985.

Brooks, Eugene. *Rites of Passage*. Privately printed, 1973.

Burger-Utzer, Brigitta, and Stefan Grissemann, eds. *Frank Films: The film and video work of Robert Frank*. New York: Scalo, 2003.

Burroughs, William S. *Junkie.* New York: Ace, 1953.

———. *Junky.* New York: Penguin, 1977.

———. *The Letters of William S. Burroughs, 1945–1959.* New York: Viking, 1993.

———. *Letters to Allen Ginsberg, 1953–1957.* New York: Full Court Press, 1982.

———. *Naked Lunch.* Paris: Olympia, 1959.

———. *Naked Lunch.* New York: Grove, 1966.

———. *Queer.* New York: Viking Penguin, 1985.

———. *The Soft Machine, Nova Express, The Wild Boys.* New York: Grove, 1980.

Burroughs, William S., and Allen Ginsberg. *The Yage Letters.* San Francisco: City Lights, 1963.

Carolan, Trevor. *Giving Up Poetry: With Allen Ginsberg at Hollyhock.* Banff: Banff Centre, 2001.

Cassady, Carolyn. *Heart Beat.* Berkeley: Creative Arts, 1976.

———. *Off the Road: My Years with Cassady, Kerouac, and Ginsberg.* New York: William Morrow, 1990.

Cassady, Neal. *Collected Letters, 1944–1967.* New York: Penguin, 2004.

———. *The First Third.* San Francisco: City Lights, 1971.

Caveney, Graham. *Screaming with Joy: The Life of Allen Ginsberg.* New York: Bloomsbury, 1999.

Chapman, Harold. *The Beat Hotel.* Montpellier, France: Gris Banal, 1984.

Charters, Ann. *Beats and Company.* Garden City, N.Y.: Doubleday, 1986.

———. *Kerouac: A biography.* San Francisco: Straight Arrow, 1973.

———. *Scenes Along the Road.* New York: Portents/Gotham Book Mart, 1970.

Cherkovski, Neeli. *Ferlinghetti: A Biography.* Garden City, N.Y.: Doubleday, 1979.

———. *Whitman's Wild Children.* Venice, Calif.: Lapis Press, 1988.

Clark, Tom. *The Great Naropa Poetry Wars.* Santa Barbara: Cadmus, 1980.

———. *Jack Kerouac.* New York: Harcourt Brace Jovanovich, 1984.

———. *Robert Creeley and the Genius of the American Common Place.* New York: New Directions, 1993.

Clavir, Judy, and John Spitzer, eds. *The Conspiracy Trial.* Indianapolis: Bobbs-Merrill, 1970.

Codrescu, Andrei. *The Disappearance of the Outside.* Reading, Mass.: Addison-Wesley, 1990.

Corso, Gregory. *An Accidental Autobiography.* New York: New Directions, 2003.

———. *Gasoline.* San Francisco: City Lights, 1958.

Creeley, Robert. *Contexts of Poetry.* Bolinas: Four Seasons Foundation, 1973.

di Prima, Diane. *Memoirs of a Beatnik.* New York: Olympia, 1969.

———. *Recollections of My Life as a Woman.* New York: Viking, 2001.

Dorfman, Elsa. *Elsa's Housebook.* Boston: Godine, 1974.

Dowden, George. *Allen Ginsberg: The Man/The Poet on Entering Earth Decade his Seventh.* Montreal: Alpha Beat Press, 1990.

Edwards, Susan. *The Wild West Wind: Remembering Allen Ginsberg.* Boulder, Ol.: Baksun, 1999.

Ehrlich, J. W., ed. *Howl of the Censor.* San Carlos: Nourse, 1961.

Ellingham, Lewis, and Kevin Killian. *Poet Be Like God.* Hanover: University Press of New England, 1998.

Faas, Ekbert. *Robert Creeley: A Biography.* Hanover, N.H.: University Press of New England, 2001.

Felver, Christopher. *The Late Great Allen Ginsberg.* New York: Thunder's Mouth, 2002.

Ferlinghetti, Lawrence, and Nancy J. Peters. *Literary San Francisco.* San Francisco: City Lights/Harper Row, 1980.

Fields, Rick. *How the Swans Came to the Lake*. Boulder, Colo.: Shambhala, 1981.

French, Warren. *The San Francisco Poetry Renaissance, 1955–1960*. Boston: Twayne, 1991.

Genet, Jean. *May Day Speech*. San Francisco: City Lights, 1970.

Gifford, Barry, and Lawrence Lee. *Jack's Book: An Oral Biography of Jack Kerouac*. New York: St. Martin's, 1978.

Ginsberg, Allen. *Allen Ginsberg: Photographs*. Altadena, Calif.: Twelvetrees, 1991.

———. *Allen Verbatim*. New York: McGraw-Hill, 1974.

———. *Chicago Trial Testimony*. San Francisco: City Lights, 1975.

———. *Collected Poems: 1947–1997*. New York: HarperCollins, 2006.

———. *Composed on the Tongue*. Bolinas: Grey Fox, 1980.

———. *Cosmopolitan Greetings*. New York: HarperCollins, 1994.

———. *Death and Fame*. New York: HarperCollins, 1999.

———. *Deliberate Prose: Selected Essays, 1952–1995*. New York: HarperCollins, 2000.

———. *Empty Mirror*. New York: Totem/Corinth, 1961.

———. *The Fall of America*. San Francisco: City Lights, 1972.

———. *First Blues*. New York: Full Court Press, 1975.

———. *The Gates of Wrath*. Bolinas: Grey Fox, 1972.

———. *Howl and Other Poems*. San Francisco: City Lights, 1956.

———. *Howl: Annotated Edition*. New York: Harper & Row, 1986.

———. *Indian Journals*. San Francisco: Dave Haselwood/City Lights, 1970.

———. *Journals Early Fifties Early Sixties*. New York: Grove, 1977.

———. *Journals Mid-Fifties*. New York: HarperCollins, 1994.

———. *Kaddish and Other Poems*. San Francisco: City Lights, 1961.

———. *Mind Breaths*. San Francisco: City Lights, 1978.

———. *Planet News 1961–1967*. San Francisco: City Lights, 1968.

———. *Plutonian Ode: Poems 1977–1980*. San Francisco: City Lights, 1982.

———. *Reality Sandwiches 1953–60*. San Francisco: City Lights, 1963.

———. *Spontaneous Mind*. New York: HarperCollins, 2001.

———. *The Visions of the Great Rememberer*. Amherst: Mulch, 1974.

———. *White Shroud Poems*. New York: Harper & Row, 1986.

Ginsberg, Allen, and Louis Ginsberg, *Family Business*. Schumacher, Michael, ed. New York: Bloomsbury, 2001.

Ginsberg, Allen, and Neal Cassady. *As Ever*. Berkeley: Creative Arts Book Co., 1977.

Ginsberg, Allen, and Peter Orlovsky. *Straight Hearts' Delight*. San Francisco: Gay Sunshine, 1980.

Ginsberg, Louis. *The Attic of the Past*. Boston: Small, Maynard and Co., 1920.

———. *Collected Poems*. Orono, Maine: Northern Lights, 1992.

———. *The Everlasting Minute and Other Lyrics*. New York: Liveright, 1937.

———. *Morning in Spring and Other Poems*. New York: Morrow, 1970.

Gooch, Brad. *City Poet: The Life and Times of Frank O'Hara*. New York: Knopf, 1993.

Green, Michelle. *The Dream at the End of the World*. New York: HarperCollins, 1991.

Gwynne, James B., ed., *Amiri Baraka: The Kaleidoscopic Torch*. New York: Steppingstones Press, 1985.

Halper, Jon, ed. *Gary Snyder: Dimensions of a Life*. San Francisco: Sierra Club Books, 1991.

Hamalian, Linda. *A Life of Kenneth Rexroth*. New York: Norton, 1990.

Hayagriva Dasa. *The Hare Krishna Explosion*. Singapore: Palace Press, 1985.

Heymann, C. David. *Ezra Pound: The Last Rower.* New York: Viking, 1976.

Hindus, Milton, ed. *Charles Reznikoff: Man and Poet.* Orono, Maine: National Poetry Foundation, 1984.

Hofmann, Albert. *LSD: My Problem Child.* New York: McGraw-Hill, 1980.

Holmes, John Clellon. *Go.* New York: Scribner's, 1952.

———. *Nothing More to Declare.* New York: Dutton, 1967.

Huncke, Herbert. *The Evening Sun Turned Crimson.* Cherry Valley, N.Y.: Cherry Valley Editions, 1980.

———. *Guilty of Everything.* New York: Paragon House, 1990.

———. *The Herbert Huncke Reader.* New York: Morrow, 1997.

Hyde, Lewis, ed. *On the Poetry of Allen Ginsberg.* Ann Arbor: University of Michigan Press, 1984.

Johnson, Joyce. *Minor Characters.* Boston: Houghton Mifflin, 1983.

Johnson, Ronna C., and Nancy M. Grace, eds. *Girls Who Wore Black: Women Writing the Beat Generation.* New Brunswick, N.J.: Rutgers, 2002.

Jones, Hettie. *How I Became Hettie Jones.* New York: Dutton, 1990.

Kashner, Sam. *When I Was Cool.* New York: HarperCollins, 2004.

Kerouac, Jack. *Big Sur.* New York: Farrar, Straus and Cudahy, 1962.

———. *Desolation Angels.* New York: Coward-McCann, 1965.

———. *The Dharma Bums.* New York: Viking, 1958.

———. *Doctor Sax.* New York: Grove Press, 1959.

———. *Lonesome Traveler.* New York: McGraw-Hill, 1960.

———. *Mexico City Blues.* New York: Grove, 1959.

———. *On the Road.* New York: Viking, 1957.

———. *The Scripture of the Golden Eternity.* New York: Totem/Corinth, 1960.

———. *Selected Letters, 1940–1956.* New York: Viking, 1995.

———. *Selected Letters, 1957–1969.* New York: Viking, 1999.

———. *The Subterraneans.* New York: Grove, 1958.

———. *The Town and the City.* New York: Harcourt Brace, 1950.

———. *Visions of Cody.* New York: McGraw-Hill, 1973.

———. *Windblown World.* New York: Viking, 2004.

———. Albert Saijo, and Lew Welch. *Trip Trap.* Bolinas: Grey Fox, 1973.

Knight, Arthur, and Kit Knight, eds. *The Beat Vision: A Primary Sourcebook.* New York: Paragon House, 1987.

———. *Kerouac and the Beats: A Primary Sourcebook.* New York: Paragon House, 1988.

Knight, Brenda. *Women of the Beat Generation.* Berkeley: Conari, 1996.

Korzybski, Alfred. *Science and Sanity.* Lakeville, Conn.: International Non-Aristotelian Library, 1941.

Kramer, Jane. *Allen Ginsberg in America.* New York: Random House, 1969.

Kyger, Joanne. *Japan and Indian Journals, 1960–1964.* Bolinas: Tombouctou, 1981.

Landesman, Jay. *Rebel Without Applause.* New York: Paragon House, 1987.

Lawlor, William T., ed. *Beat Culture: Icons, Lifestyles, and Impact.* Santa Barbara: ABC CLIO, 2005.

Leary, Timothy. *Flashbacks.* Los Angeles: Tarcher, 1983.

———. *High Priest.* New York: World, 1968.

Lee, Martin A, and Bruce Shlain. *Acid Dreams.* New York: Grove, 1985.

Lieberman, Elias. *Poems for Enjoyment*. New York: Harper and Brothers, 1931.

Loewinsohn, Ron. *Watermelons*. New York: Totem, 1959.

Luthin, Reinhard. *The Real Abraham Lincoln*. Englewood Cliffs, N.J.: Prentice-Hall, 1960.

McClure, Michael. *Lighting the Corners*. Albuquerque: American Poetry Book, 1993.

———. *Scratching the Beat Surface*. San Francisco: North Point, 1982.

McCoy, Alfred W. *The Politics of Heroin in Southeast Asia*. New York: Harper & Row, 1972.

McDarrah, Fred W. *Kerouac & Friends*. New York: William Morrow, 1985.

McNally, Dennis. *Desolate Angel: Jack Kerouac, the Beat Generation, and America*. New York: McGraw-Hill, 1979.

Maher, Paul. *Empty Phantoms: Interviews and Encounters with Jack Kerouac*. New York: Thunder's Mouth, 2005.

Maschler, Tom. *Publisher*. London: Picador, 2005.

Meltzer, David. *The San Francisco Poets*. New York: Ballantine, 1971.

———, ed. *San Francisco Beat*. San Francisco: City Lights, 2001.

Merrill, Thomas F. *Allen Ginsberg*. New York: Twayne, 1969.

Midal, Fabrice. *Chögyam Trungpa: His Life and Vision*. Boston: Shambhala, 2004.

Miles, Barry. *The Beat Hotel*. New York: Grove, 2000.

———. *Ginsberg, A Biography*. New York: Simon and Schuster, 1989.

———. *Two Lectures on the Work of Allen Ginsberg*. Turret Papers, 1992.

———. *William Burroughs: El Hombre Invisible: A Portrait*. London: Virgin, 1992.

Morgan, Bill. *The Beat Generation in New York*. San Francisco: City Lights, 1997.

———. *The Beat Generation in San Francisco*. San Francisco: City Lights, 2003.

———, ed. *Kanreki*. New York: Lospecchio, 1986.

———. *The Response to Allen Ginsberg, 1926–1994*. Westport, Conn.: Greenwood Press, 1996.

———. *The Works of Allen Ginsberg, 1941–1994*. Westport, Conn.: Greenwood Press, 1995.

Morgan, Bill, and Bob Rosenthal, eds. *Best Minds: A Tribute to Allen Ginsberg*. New York: Lospecchio Press, 1986.

Morgan, Ted. *Literary Outlaw: The Life and Times of William S. Burroughs*. New York: Henry Holt, 1988.

Mottram, Eric. *Allen Ginsberg in the Sixties*. Brighton, England: Unicorn, 1972.

Nicosia, Gerald. *Memory Babe*. New York: Grove, 1983.

Ossman, David. *The Sullen Art*. New York: Corinth, 1963.

Parkinson, Thomas, ed. *A Casebook on the Beat*. New York: Crowell, 1961.

Peabody, Richard, ed. *A Different Beat*. London: Serpent's Tail, 1997.

Phillips, Lisa, ed. *Beat Culture and the New America: 1950–1965*. New York: Whitney Museum / Flammarion, 1995.

Plymell, Charles. *The Harder They Come*. Santa Barbara: Am Here Books, 1985.

Podhoretz, Norman. *Ex-Friends*. New York: Free Press, 1999.

Portuges, Paul. *The Visionary Poetics of Allen Ginsberg*. Santa Barbara: Ross-Erikson, 1978.

Rips, Geoffrey, ed. *The Campaign Against the Underground Press*. San Francisco: City Lights, 1981.

Roy, Gregor. *Beat Literature*. New York: Monarch, 1966.

Sanders, Ed. *The Party: A Chronological Perspective on a Confrontation at a Buddhist Seminary*. Woodstock, N.Y.: Poetry, Crime & Culture Press, 1977.

———. *The Poetry and Life of Allen Ginsberg*. Woodstock, N.Y.: Overlook Press, 2000.

Saroyan, Aram. *Genesis Angels*. New York: William Morrow, 1979.

Sawyer-Laucanno, Christopher. *The Continual Pilgrimage*. New York: Grove, 1992.

Schumacher, Michael. *Dharma Lion: A Critical Biography of Allen Ginsberg.* New York: St. Martin's Press, 1992.

Selerie, Gavin, ed. *The Riverside Interviews: 1, Allen Ginsberg.* London: Binnacle Press, 1980.

Sheridan, Sue, ed. *Teachers Make a Difference.* Houston: Harris County Dept. of Ed., 1987.

Silesky, Barry. *Ferlinghetti: The Artist in His Time.* New York: Warner, 1990.

Silverman, Herschel. *High on the Beats.* Brooklyn: Pinched Nerves Press, 1992.

Sloman, Larry. *On the Road with Bob Dylan.* New York: Bantam, 1978.

Smith, Larry. *Lawrence Ferlinghetti: Poet-at-Large.* Carbondale: Southern Illinois University Press, 1983.

Snyder, Gary. *Passage Through India.* San Francisco: Grey Fox, 1983.

Solomon, Carl. *Emergency Messages.* New York: Paragon House, 1989.

Spengler, Oswald. *The Decline of the West.* New York: Knopf, 1927.

Stephenson, Gregory. *The Daybreak Boys.* Carbondale: Southern Illinois University Press, 1990.

———. *Exiled Angel: A Study of the Work of Gregory Corso.* London: Hearing Eye, 1989.

Suiter, John. *Poets on the Peaks.* Washington: Counterpoint, 2002.

Sukenick, Ronald. *Down and In.* New York: Beech Tree Books/William Morrow, 1987.

Taylor, Steven. *False Prophet: Field Notes from the Punk Underground.* Middletown, Conn.: Wesleyan University Press, 2003.

Terrell, Carroll F., ed. *William Carlos Williams: Man and Poet.* Orono, Maine: National Poetry Foundation, 1983.

Theado, Matt, ed. *The Beats: A Literary Reference.* New York: Carroll & Graf, 2001.

Turner, Steve. *Jack Kerouac: Angelheaded Hipster.* New York: Viking, 1996.

Tytell, John. *Ezra Pound: The Solitary Volcano.* New York: Anchor/Doubleday, 1987.

———. *The Living Theatre: Art, Exile and Outrage.* New York: Grove, 1995.

———. *Naked Angels: The Lives and Literature of the Beat Generation.* New York: McGraw-Hill, 1976.

———. *Paradise Outlaws: Remembering the Beats.* New York: Morrow, 1999.

Untermeyer, Louis, ed. *Modern American and British Poetry.* New York: Harcourt Brace, 1923.

Van Buskirk, Alden. *Lami.* San Francisco: Auerhahn, 1965.

Vidal, Gore. *Two Sisters.* Boston: Little Brown, 1970.

Waldman, Anne, and Marilyn Webb, eds. *Talking Poetics from Naropa Institute,* 2 volumes. Boulder, Colo.: Shambhala, 1979.

Weinberg, Jeffrey H., ed. *Writers Outside the Margin.* Sudbury, Mass.: Water Row, 1986.

Weinreich, Regina. *The Spontaneous Poetics of Jack Kerouac.* Carbondale: Southern Illinois University Press, 1987.

White, Edmund. *Genet: A Biography.* New York: Knopf, 1993.

Whitmer, Peter O. *Aquarius Revisited.* New York: Macmillan, 1987.

Williams, Paul. *Bob Dylan Performing Artist.* Novato, Calif.: Underwood-Miller, 1992.

Williams, William Carlos. *Paterson, Book 4.* New York: New Directions, 1951.

———. *Paterson, Book 5.* New York: New Directions, 1958.

Young, Allen. *Allen Ginsberg: Gay Sunshine Interview.* Bolinas: Grey Fox, 1974.

INDEX ～

Page numbers in *italics* refer to photographs.